D1191565

# Uniting Psychology and Biology

# Uniting Psychology and Biology

## *Integrative Perspectives on Human Development*

Edited by
Nancy L. Segal
Glenn E. Weisfeld
Carol C. Weisfeld

AMERICAN PSYCHOLOGICAL ASSOCIATION
WASHINGTON, DC

Published by
American Psychological Association
750 First Street, NE
Washington, DC 20002

Copies may be ordered from
APA Order Department
P.O. Box 92984
Washington, DC 20090-2984

In the UK and Europe, copies may be ordered from
American Psychological Association
3 Henrietta Street
Covent Garden, London
WC2E 8LU England

Typeset in Minion by WorldComp, Sterling, VA
Printer: United Book Press, Baltimore, MD
Cover Designer: Minker Design, Bethesda, MD
Editor/Project Manager: Debbie K. Hardin, Reston, VA

**Library of Congress Cataloging-in-Publication Data**

Uniting psychology and biology : integrative perspectives on human development / edited by Nancy L. Segal, Glenn E. Weisfeld, and Carol C. Weisfeld.

p. cm.

Includes bibliographic references and indexes.

ISBN 1-55798-428-X (alk. paper)

1. Developmental psychology. 2. Developmental psychobiology. I. Segal, Nancy L., 1951– . II. Weisfeld, Glenn, 1943– III. Weisfeld, Carol Cronin, 1946–

BF713.U55 1997 97-10903
150—dc21 CIP

**British Library Catologuing-in-Publication Data**

A CIP record is available from the British Library

*Printed in the United States of America*
*First Edition*

*For our families.*

# APA Science Volumes

*Best Methods for the Analysis of Change: Recent Advances, Unanswered Questions, Future Directions*

*Cardiovascular Reactivity to Psychological Stress and Disease*

*The Challenge in Mathematics and Science Education: Psychology's Response*

*Changing Employment Relations: Behavioral and Social Perspectives*

*Cognition: Conceptual and Methodological Issues*

*Cognitive Bases of Musical Communication*

*Conceptualization and Measurement of Organism–Environment Interaction*

*Converging Operations in the Study of Visual Selective Attention*

*Creative Thought: An Investigation of Conceptual Structures and Processes*

*Developmental Psychoacoustics*

*Diversity in Work Teams: Research Paradigms for a Changing Workplace*

*Emotion and Culture: Empirical Studies of Mutual Influence*

*Emotion, Disclosure, and Health*

*Evolving Explanations of Development: Ecological Approaches to Organism–Environment Systems*

*Examining Lives in Context: Perspectives on the Ecology of Human Development*

*Hostility, Coping, and Health*

*Measuring Patient Changes in Mood, Anxiety, and Personality Disorders: Toward a Core Battery*

*Organ Donation and Transplantation: Psychological and Behavioral Factors*

*The Perception of Structure*

*Perspectives on Socially Shared Cognition*

*Psychological Testing of Hispanics*

*Psychology of Women's Health: Progress and Challenges in Research and Application*

*Researching Community Psychology: Issues of Theory and Methods*

*Sleep and Cognition*

*Sleep Onset: Normal and Abnormal Processes*

*Stereotype Accuracy: Toward Appreciating Group Differences*

*Stereotyped Movements: Brain and Behavior Relationships*

*Studying Lives Through Time: Personality and Development*

*The Suggestibility of Children's Recollections: Implications for Eyewitness Testimony*

*Taste, Experience, and Feeding: Development and Learning*

*Temperament: Individual Differences at the Interface of Biology and Behavior*

*Through the Looking Glass: Issues of Psychological Well-Being in Captive Nonhuman Primates*

*Uniting Psychology and Biology: Integrative Perspectives on Human Development*

APA expects to publish volumes on the following conference topics:

Attribution Processes, Person Perception, and Social Interaction: The Legacy of Ned Jones

Children Exposed to Family Violence

Computational Modeling of Behavior Processes in Organizations

Experimental Psychopathology and Pathogenesis of Schizophrenia

Global Prospects for Education: Development, Culture, and Schooling

Intelligence on the Rise: Secular Changes in IQ and Related Measures

Marital and Family Therapy Outcome and Process Research

Models of Gender and Gender Differences: Then and Now

Occasion Setting: Theory and Data

Psychology Beyond the Threshold: Conference on General and Applied Experimental Psychology and a Festschrift of William N. Dember

Psychosocial Interventions for Cancer

As part of its continuing and expanding commitment to enhance the dissemination of scientific psychological knowledge, the Science Directorate of the APA established a Scientific Conferences Program. A series of volumes resulting from these conferences is produced jointly by the Science Directorate and the Office of Communications. A call for proposals is issued twice annually by the Scientific Directorate, which, collaboratively with the APA Board of Scientific Affairs, evaluates the proposals and selects several conferences for funding. This important effort has resulted in an exceptional series of meetings and scholarly volumes, each of which has contributed to the dissemination of research and dialogue in these topical areas.

The APA Science Directorate's conferences funding program has supported 47 conferences since its inception in 1988. To date, 33 volumes resulting from conferences have been published.

| | |
|---|---|
| William C. Howell, PhD<br>Executive Director | Virginia E. Holt<br>Assistant Executive Director |

# Contents

# Contributors

**J. Michael Bailey,** Department of Psychology, Northwestern University

**Jerome H. Barkow,** Department of Sociology and Social Anthropology, Dalhousie University, Halifax, Canada

**Gregory Carey,** Department of Psychology and Institute for Behavioral Genetics, University of Colorado, Boulder

**Lisa M. Diamond,** Department of Human Development, Cornell University

**Irenäus Eibl-Eibesfeldt,** Humanethologie id Max-Planck-Gesellschaft, Andrechs, Germany

**Paul Ekman,** Department of Psychiatry, Langley Porter Psychiatric Institute, University of California, San Francisco

**Daniel G. Freedman,** Department of Psychology, University of Chicago

**H. Hill Goldsmith,** Department of Psychology, University of Wisconsin, Madison

**Irving I. Gottesman,** Department of Psychology, University of Virginia

**Kristen Hawkes,** Department of Anthropology, University of Utah

**Nicholas G. Blurton Jones,** Departments of Anthropology, Education, and Psychiatry, University of California, Los Angeles

**Roger J. R. Levesque,** Department of Criminal Justice, Indiana University

**Robert A. LeVine,** Graduate School of Education, Harvard University

**Lewis P. Lipsitt,** Department of Psychology, Brown University

**Robert S. Marvin,** Department of Pediatrics, University of Virginia

**James F. O'Connell,** Department of Anthropology, University of Utah

**Ritch C. Savin-Williams,** Department of Human Development, Cornell University

**Wolfgang M. Schleidt,** Department of Human Biology, University of Vienna, Austria

**John Paul Scott,** Center for Research on Social Behavior, Bowling Green State University

**Nancy L. Segal,** Department of Psychology, California State University, Fullerton

**Robert L. Trivers,** Department of Anthropology, Rutgers University

**Susan L. Trumbetta,** School of Medicine, Department of Psychiatry, Dartmouth University

**Carol C. Weisfeld,** Department of Psychology, University of Detroit Mercy

**Glenn E. Weisfeld,** Department of Psychology, Wayne State University

**Peter H. Wolff,** Department of Psychiatry, Children's Hospital of Boston

# Foreword

Irenäus Eibl-Eibesfeldt

Today we are well aware that our behavior is shaped to a remarkable extent by our evolutionary history. The basic emotions and motivations and many motor patterns, including most of our facial expressions, were formed by our phylogeny. Our sensory apparatus is in many ways "biased" by phylogenetic adaptations; even our ways of thinking and talking are to a significant extent grounded and channeled by our evolutionary history. The range of modifiability is set within genetically influenced limits. It is also a generally accepted fact that evolutionary history unifies all the sciences dealing with our species, including the humanities. Whatever we do—whether we pray or not, follow a particular custom, or obey a particular ideology—an activity finally manifests itself as an investment of at least time, which enters into the final cost–benefit calculation and ultimately becomes measured by selection against the yardstick of inclusive fitness. Yet, this was far from being the accepted view at the time Daniel G. Freedman started his pioneering efforts to explore human behavior using an evolutionary approach. In some areas of the humanities and social sciences it was even considered an unacceptable way of thinking, which is all the more reason to appreciate and admire those pioneers whose search for truth led them to swim against the fashionable current.

Dr. Freedman started his investigations in human ethology with a study of the smiling response and the fear of strangers in infants (1964, 1974). His approach was characterized by detailed description and documentation by film. Among other things, he observed that children born blind respond to their mothers' voices by "looking" at the source of the sound, thus behaving as if they were seeing their mothers. The nystagmus of the blind is thereby arrested. This is evidence for a centrally programmed fixation process, the function of which seems to be to enhance maternal attachment. Mothers respond with delight to eye contact with their babies. They interpret it as a sign of personal attachment, which simultaneously rewards the mother and confers a selective advantage on such infant behavior.

The film documentation and publication of these exciting findings came out in 1964. This study was followed by others on human infancy (Freedman, 1974) and social hierarchy (Freedman, 1975). All these papers combined the evolutionary approach with consideration of cultural factors in what was, considering the latest theories, prescient recognition of the fact that nature and nurture interact in many ways. This interactive approach, characteristic of Dr. Freedman, is reflected in the subtitle of his book, *Human Sociobiology: A Holistic Approach* (1979). Traditional ethology based on thorough observation, documentation, and experimentation is here combined with modern model building based on sociobiological cost–benefit algorithms. These approaches are combined to powerful effect by Dr. Freedman. He has contributed enormously to the development of behavioral genetics, human ethology, and evolutionary psychology, and we owe him much.

This book is an expression of our gratitude.

## REFERENCES

Freedman, D. G. (1964). Smiling in blind infants and the issue of innate versus acquired. *Journal of Child Psychology and Psychiatry, 5,* 171–184.

Freedman, D. G. (1974). *Human infancy: An evolutionary perspective.* Hillsdale, NJ: Erlbaum.

Freedman, D. G. (1975). The development of social hierarchies. In L. Levi (Ed.), *Society, stress, and disease, Vol. 2: Childhood and adolescence* (pp. 36–42). New York: Oxford University Press.

Freedman, D. G. (1979). *Human sociobiology. A holistic approach.* New York: The Free Press.

# Preface

Nancy L. Segal, Glenn E. Weisfeld, and Carol C. Weisfeld

Intellectual respect, pride, and the pleasure of friendship have guided our efforts in crafting this volume. Our intention is to honor Daniel G. Freedman's unique contributions to the study of human behavior and to reflect on his special approach to scholarship.

This book aims to convey the sense of excitement that has accompanied the transformations that psychology, as an academic discipline, has undergone in recent years. There has been a proliferation of research activities directed toward elucidating biological and evolutionary influences on behavior and their interactions with environmental variables. These activities are traceable, in part, to recent discoveries in human genetics, renewed interest in naturalistic studies, and increased respect for the evolved bases of behavior. These important efforts have enhanced appreciation for the different levels of analysis (i.e., proximal and distal) required for full understanding of human psychological development. These events are also responsible for the newly focused attention to issues and problems located at the juncture of behavioral genetics, human ethology, and evolutionary psychology. A fresh approach to old issues (e.g., gender differences in cognition and variations in human social organiza-

We are grateful to the American Psychological Association Science Directorate for the generous support that made the Festschrift possible. Dr. Richard P. Saller, dean of the Social Sciences Division at the University of Chicago, was enormously supportive of our efforts. We wish to thank Professor Richard A. Shweder and Betty Cawelti (secretary) in the Committee on Human Development, at the University of Chicago, and Professor Daniel W. Kee, chair, Department of Psychology, California State University, Fullerton, for assistance and encouragement on behalf of Dr. Freedman and the conference. Marilee Bagshaw, Frances Sanchez, and Kay Karlson, at California State University, Fullerton, provided clerical assistance during the final stages of manuscript preparation. Countless other students and staff members, at the University of Chicago and at California State University, Fullerton, devoted many hours toward the success of this project. Mary Lynn Skutley and Andrea Phillippi, APA Books, offered invaluable guidance throughout the preparation of this book.

tion and affiliation) is evident in view of these multiple perspectives. New areas of commonality are being defined by researchers who previously conducted parallel investigations without the benefits of interaction and exchange. The papers that resulted from the October 1995 Festschrift for Dr. Freedman have brought these important perspectives and accomplishments to the fore. We encourage researchers and students to rethink current psychological problems and issues in light of this new material.

Psychology departments stand to benefit considerably from welcoming scholars with Dr. Freedman's brand of interdisciplinary virtuosity. Contributions from faculty members with specializations in biology, anthropology, sociology, and evolutionary history, as well as those with training in more traditional areas of human development, are needed if psychology programs are to remain dynamic, integrated, and current. Many students today are learning about genetic influences on shyness, evolved sex differences in mate selection, and the evolutionary basis of moral behavior from popular books and magazines, yet they cannot find courses that cover these topics. We trust that the present collection will inspire university administrators and department chairs to resolve this situation.

## OUR MENTOR

We were very fortunate to have had Dr. Freedman as our mentor in graduate school. Dr. Freedman was a dedicated teacher. He cared about us as students, sympathized with us, and also demanded our best efforts. Dr. Freedman's treatment of us was informal—he invited us to socialize with him, his family, and esteemed campus visitors alike. Much of what we learned took place outside the classroom and library, even beyond field research settings. When E. O. Wilson's ground-breaking book, *Sociobiology: The New Synthesis*, was published in 1975, Dr. Freedman organized a weekly discussion group for his graduate students. His classes were often informal, even a trifle unplanned! However, their very spontaneity carried the lesson that behavior is something that is easy to talk about and that scientific ideas can arise in unexpected ways.

We were aware that Dr. Freedman encountered a great deal of ideological opposition, mainly from people who misconstrued what evolutionists were saying. He did not avoid these debates and, in fact, seemed to take a certain pleasure in being an iconoclast. He handled opposition with dignity, and accorded his opponents the respect they sometimes denied him.

# Tribute to Dan

**Daniel G. Freedman** is a distinguished psychologist whose contributions to child development, behavioral genetics, human ethology, and evolutionary psychology continue to inspire numerous colleagues and students, both in the United States and abroad. Dr. Freedman was, in the words of a colleague, "ahead of his time in research and thinking about genes and behavior." Indeed, his articles and books anticipated the current climate

Photo courtesy of Carol C. Weisfeld.

of scholarly activity in the behavioral sciences. Dr. Freedman recognized that biological and evolutionary viewpoints were required for full understanding of the complex diversity of human behavior. These multiple perspectives are now being increasingly embraced by researchers in psychology and related fields.

Dr. Freedman received a BA degree in psychology from the University of California, Berkeley (1949), an MA degree in psychology from the University of Colorado, Boulder (1953), and a PhD degree in psychology from Brandeis University, Waltham, Massachusetts (1957). He held a U.S. Public Health Service Postdoctoral Fellowship at the Langley Porter Neuropsychiatric Institute, San Francisco (1957–1959), where he later directed a longitudinal study of infant twins (1960–1963). He received a National Institute of Health Special Fellowship for study at the Institute for Medical Genetics, Uppsala, Sweden (1963–1964). On returning to the United States, Dr. Freedman joined the University of Chicago, Committee on Human Development, as an assistant professor of biology (1964–1968). He then co-led (with Gregory Bateson) an observational study of cultures around the world with the International School of America (1971–1972) before rejoining the University of Chicago as a professor of psychology (1977–present). He has held visiting professorships and scholarships at the University of Denver (1966), the Australian National University, Canberra (1979), the Hebrew University of Jerusalem (1986), and the Institute for Juvenile Research, Chicago (1989). He was also associated with the Center for Family Studies at Northwestern University, Chicago (1985–1986). Most recently, he was a visiting scholar at Nankai University, Tianjin, China (1995), in the department of sociology.

Those of us who have worked closely with Dr. Freedman know that his goals concerning publication are very particular: "I would rather wait until I have something important to say" was the way he put it at the Festschrift in his honor at the University of Chicago in October 1995. Nonetheless, Dr. Freedman is the author or editor of three books and more than 50 scholarly articles. He is a filmmaker as well; he produced six documentaries on the behavior of puppies of various breeds and infants and children from various cultures.

Dr. Freedman is currently professor emeritus of psychology at the University of Chicago. Present research interests include cross-cultural variations in mother–infant interaction and internal working models of attachment. He is pursuing these interests from his new residence in New Mexico. His hope is to return to China to study the effects of the one-child-per-family policy on parenting and personality development.

SECTION I

# Introduction

# 1

# Pursuing the Big Picture

Nancy L. Segal, Glenn E. Weisfeld,
and Carol C. Weisfeld

This volume was inspired by the insights and discoveries of a distinguished psychologist. As a young investigator in the 1950s and 1960s, Daniel G. Freedman argued that the application of biological and evolutionary viewpoints was required for full understanding of the complexities and vagaries of human behavioral development. He upheld this view despite challenges from some psychologists who dismissed such theorizing as uninformative, irrelevant, or pessimistic with respect to understanding contemporary human development (see Scarr, 1995a; Smith, 1987, for extended discussion). His human ethological analyses were pioneering and encouraged appreciation for naturalistic studies concerned with the evolved bases of behavior. A species-wide comparative view of human behavior also helped set the stage for current interest in cross-cultural research.

There has been a recent "rediscovery" and growing respect for many of the concepts and themes that are clearly articulated in Dr. Freedman's early work. The contents of this book reflect this emerging reorientation within psychology and related fields. Principles, techniques, and interpretations from behavioral genetics, human ethology, evolutionary psychology, and cross-cultural analyses are uniquely interwoven. This collection is intended to continue his efforts toward increased acknowledgment of contributions to be made to psychological inquiry from these multiple perspectives.

Two of Dr. Freedman's classic studies, which continue to be cited in developmental psychology textbooks and in studies of infant development, mark the critical beginnings of a research program devoted to elucidating developmental processes and outcomes. The first study, published in 1958, examined interactions between genetic background, or *genotype*, and rearing practices among four different breeds of dog. The critical role of the genotype as a factor affecting the observed behavioral outcome, or *phenotype*, was a revelation to the young clinical psychologist whose orientation was primarily environmental. This intellectual epiphany launched a career focused on uniting the fields of psychology and biology. Questions of *biological function* (promotion of survival and reproduction) became paramount. In other words, how and why does a particular behavior affect the fitness of individuals in a given environment? What does evidence of genetic influence, or lack of genetic influence, imply with respect to the evolved bases of behavior? Research on the functional significance of the infant smile, fear of strangers, and fear of bearded male faces followed. This work led naturally to incorporating concepts from behavioral genetics, ethology, evolutionary psychology, and cross-cultural research into his studies. Most significant, Dr. Freedman recognized the interconnectedness among these areas and the fact that each alone provides only part of a bigger picture.

In another classic study, Freedman and Keller (1963) compared similarity in mental and motor abilities between identical, or *monozygotic* (MZ), twins and fraternal, or *dizygotic* (DZ), twins during the first year of life. The finding of greater resemblance between MZ twins, especially in motor behaviors, was consistent with a contribution from genetic factors.

These two early studies inspired many other investigators to consider more seriously the interplay of genetic and environmental factors underlying individual differences in behavior in humans and nonhumans.

These initial efforts launched a resume rich with theoretical and empirical analyses that examined behavior through new lenses. This work included studies of children's dominance hierarchies and gender differences in play behaviors. At the same time, Dr. Freedman's notions of psychological and biological connectedness were still evolving, and he subjected them to periodic reappraisal in several theoretical papers.

Throughout the years, Dr. Freedman's essential and unique contribution to psychology has been a commitment to a holistic view of *nature and nurture.* As Martin Daly and Margo Wilson put it, "The nature–nurture debate has been pronounced dead many times, but it won't stay buried" (1983, p. 249). More recently, other investigators have proposed new formulations relevant to the commitment to holism seen in Dr. Freedman's work. Thomas J. Bouchard, Jr., and colleagues, for example (Bouchard, Lykken, McGue, Segal, & Tellegen, 1990), recast *nature versus nurture* as *nature via nurture,* reflecting the conviction that the genome guides the individual to select particular environments during the course of development. This is a very effective way to view relationships between genes and culture, mind and body, and past and present environments, as Dr. Freedman has explained.

It is encouraging that some researchers are reconsidering the contributions made possible by interpreting behavioral data with reference to biological and evolutionary viewpoints. Interdisciplinary efforts promise to add richness and texture to what we can know about human development. However, there is still a long way to go, and it is our hope that this volume will make the case for the undecided.

## CHRONOLOGY OF COLLEAGUES

The organization of this volume was surprisingly simple given that contributors fell naturally into the various content sections. Their intellectual niches have variously overlapped with Dr. Freedman's outlook and interests at different stages in his career. In the mid-1950s, John Paul Scott chaired Dr. Freedman's doctoral work on behavioral differences among four dog breeds when he was a fellow at the Jackson Laboratories, in Bar Harbor, Maine. Dr. Freedman's friendship with Paul Ekman began in the late 1950s when both were associated with the Langley Porter Neuropsychiatric Institute, in San Francisco. Irving I. Gottesman met Dr. Freedman in 1960 at an early Behavioral Genetics meeting, hosted by the late Steven G. Vandenberg, then director of the behavioral section of the Louisville Twin Study. An early 1960s International Ethological Congress, held in The Netherlands, led to a meeting with Nicholas G. Blurton Jones; colleagues had encouraged them to meet given their mutual interests in biology and human development.

Associations with Peter H. Wolff during the 1960s and with Lewis P. Lipsitt during the early 1970s evolved out of common interests in human infancy and participation in professional meetings. International conferences on ethology in the 1960s facilitated a professional link with Wolfgang M. Schleidt who, according to Dr. Freedman, was a favorite student of Konrad Lorenz. In 1978, both attended the annual meeting of the American Association for the Advancement of Science, in Washington, D.C., where they witnessed the water dousing of E. O. Wilson, author of *Sociobiology: The New Synthesis*, by a group calling themselves the International Committee Against Racism (INCAR; also see Wilson, 1994). Their mutual outrage at this loathsome act bound them together as colleagues and friends.

Robert A. LeVine and Dr. Freedman held appointments as faculty members at the University of Chicago in the 1960s and 1970s, during which time Dr. Freedman served as an advisor on infancy for LeVine's human development project conducted in Nigeria. The excitement surrounding sociobiology in the mid-1970s and a meeting called by Irven DeVore in Cambridge, Massachusetts, were responsible for Dr. Freedman meeting with Robert L. Trivers, then a graduate student at Harvard University.

Seven of the twenty-four contributors to this book were graduate students who worked with Dr. Freedman at the University of Chicago between 1970 and 1990. Their thesis topics, listed below, reflect the intellectual breadth and creative approaches to understanding human development that Dr. Freedman brought to his role as mentor. These individuals include Jerome H. Barkow (*Hausa and Maguzawa: Processes of Group*

*Differentiation in a Rural Area in North Central State, Nigeria*, 1970), Robert S. Marvin (*Attachment, Exploratory and Communicative Behavior of Two-Year-Old, Three-Year-Old and Four-Year-Old Children*, 1972), Ritch C. Savin-Williams (*Dominance–Submission Behaviors and Hierarchies in Young Adolescents at a Summer Camp: Predictors, Styles, and Sex Differences*, 1977), Glenn E. Weisfeld (*Determinants and Behavioral Correlates of Dominance in Adolescent Boys*, 1978), Carol C. Weisfeld (*Boys and Girls in Competition: The Context and Communication of Female Inhibition*, 1980), Nancy L. Segal (*Cooperation, Competition and Altruism Within Twin Sets: A Reappraisal*, 1982), and Roger J. R. Levesque (*Adolescents in Love: An Exploration of Adolescent Love Experiences Across and Within Five Socio-Cultural Groups*, 1990).

Several contributors to this volume became acquainted with Dr. Freedman's work either through his writings or through his associations with their own colleagues. They include J. Michael Bailey, Gregory Carey, Lisa M. Diamond, H. Hill Goldsmith, Kristen Hawkes, James F. O'Connell, and Susan L. Trumbetta.

## ACROSS THE GENERATIONS

Embedded within the fabric of scholarly contributions are revealing insights into the developmental dynamics of teaching and research. One finds, for example, that similar behavioral phenomena are of interest to succeeding generations of the same intellectual "family." The following events exemplify this process. Harry Harlow directed Abraham Maslow's study of primate dominance at the Wisconsin Regional Primate Center in Madison, Wisconsin. Maslow, in turn, directed Dr. Freedman's study of dominant (and self-actualized) women in Massachusetts. Dr. Freedman then directed several studies of dominance in children around the world, conducted by his own students, Don Omark, Murray Edelman, Ritch Savin-Williams, Carol Weisfeld, Glenn Weisfeld, and others. At present, Glenn Weisfeld is continuing this work in Beijing, China, in collaboration with Qi Dong. Dr. Freedman's interests and influence now affect younger scholars via his former graduate students, who supervise dissertations on attachment, social relations, human emotions, gender differences, and related topics.

Dr. Freedman's work has also affected the research and thinking of contemporary scholars with whom his relationship has been less direct. For example, Plomin and Rowe (1979) launched a discussion of relationships among natural selection, individual differences, and behavioral genetics with reference to Dr. Freedman's studies of infant social behavior. Silverman (1987) reasoned that Dr. Freedman's findings of group differences in maternal style, which corresponded to differences in infant temperament, might hold clues about how inborn temperamental dispositions are affected by the environment to exert their influences on personality. Archer credited Dr. Freedman (1964, 1965) with demonstrating an innate basis to smiling. Dr. Freedman, wrote Archer, "noted in passing that the universal presence of smiling in different cultures" was consistent with this view (1992, p. 179). Later cross-cultural work by Eibl-Eibesfeldt and by Ekman in the 1960s and 1970s supported the universality of facial expressions and motor patterns, including the smile. Kagan, Arcus, and Snidman (1994) built on Dr. Freedman's findings of genetically based behavioral differences between Caucasian and Asian newborns (Freedman & Freedman, 1969) in a recent study of Irish and Chinese infants. Dr. Freedman's observational studies of dominance hierarchies have also inspired a book (1997) to be edited by Leon Sloman and Paul Gilbert, which views depression as a variant of subordination behavior.

Dr. Freedman's research interests have now refocused on cross-cultural differences in mother–infant attachment in evolutionary perspective. His recent visit to the laboratory of Professor Guoan Yue, at Nankai University, in Tianjin, China, will help shape the research activities of Chinese students working in that area. Factors influencing mother–infant interaction should be of considerable importance in China, given that social policy mandates one-child families in that nation.

Common to these scenarios is the fact that a similar problem is under consideration, but each new generation addresses it in a different way, by asking slightly different questions, applying new methodologies, or examining a different gender or stage of the life cycle. Their cumulative efforts illuminate areas that had been previously obscured, thereby highlighting the finest qualities of the teaching process.

## QUESTIONS AND CONTROVERSIES

Just as some issues and findings endure and develop, they can fuel conflicts and controversies over their veracity and implications. There is no question that Dr. Freedman's efforts have helped to move psychology toward greater integration as a field. Many more colleagues are now receptive to the pervasive effects of biological influences on human behavior—the growing body of relevant data, especially from behavioral genetic sources, cannot be easily dismissed. At the same time, there is considerable resistance to research that demonstrates genetic effects on human behavioral variation or that attempts to understand human nature in light of evolutionary principles. It is our position that this resistance reflects misconception of what genetic influence means and what evolutionary analyses may suggest.

As will be discussed in the introduction to section II, genetic influence does not mean that behavior is intractable. Behavior is, after all, a product of genes expressed in an environment. Environmental factors can modify behavioral outcomes, an effect that is apparent in the use of drug treatments to control mental disorder and language classes to improve the skills of learning-disabled students. It is also instructive to remind ourselves that the only source of difference between genetically identical twins is environmental, and even identical twins do not show perfect resemblance in any measured trait. However, some behaviors may be more or less resistant to the effects of available interventions. That some behaviors are harder to change than others is not news to anyone, although the basis for differences in malleability has sometimes been a source of contention. For example, recent twin research on the basis of human happiness finds that each individual's characteristic level, or "set point," is genetically influenced, whereas fluctuation around that point may be associated with chance events (Lykken & Tellegen, 1996). Lykken and Tellegen's suggestion that the failure of isolated joyful experiences to permanently elevate happiness is more comprehensible in light of these data.

We need not wander farther than our own doorsteps to know that siblings show considerable variation in intellectual skills and personality traits. Paradoxically, the "same" family environment may be quite different for different children in the same family. In fact, one of the most important behavioral genetic findings in recent years is that *nonshared* environmental events (i.e., events that individuals experience apart from family members and that are associated with differences among them) have greater influence on most behaviors than shared experiences (Plomin & Daniels, 1987). Siblings may, thus, respond differently to the opportunities and facilities available to them as a partial result of differences in genetically based interests and abilities. Objectively similar treatment by parents does not strongly predict similar developmental outcomes. Individual differences, whether within or between families, are just that—there is nothing inherent in them that warrants value judgements. In the wise words of Theodosius Dobzhansky, "differences are not deficits."

Some have asserted that behavioral–genetic investigations of human behavior are unproductive given the inseparability of genes and environments (Gottlieb, 1995; Lamb, 1994; Oyama, 1989; also see Rowe, 1994; commentaries by Burgess & Molenaar, 1995; Scarr, 1995b; and Turkheimer, Goldsmith, & Gottesman, 1995, in response to Gottleib, 1995). It has also been argued that behavioral–genetic research may lead to misuse and discrimination within and between groups (Baumrind, 1993; Jackson, 1993; also see reply by Scarr, 1993). Again, it is helpful to return to the words of Dobzhansky and to assert that efforts that may assist understanding of the human condition are worth doing. Fear of misuse by a misguided minority should not hinder progress, but should strengthen resolve to ensure appropriate and respectful interpretation. The history of psychology includes many examples of how findings of genetic influence have been truly beneficial. For example, studies on the origins of autism have removed misplaced blame on parental rearing practices and focused attention on characteristics of the child.

Objections to evolutionary interpretations of human behavior by developmental psychologists are ably summarized by Smith (1987). Many of these same objections still echo through the literature, despite nearly a decade of subsequent investigation; see, for example, a compelling review by Kenrick (1995). Perhaps most disturbing to some researchers is that evolutionary research on human behavior will perpetuate the *naturalistic fallacy*, the notion that what is natural for the species is necessarily good, thus generating complacency toward, for example, human aggression. As Smith (1987) explained, evolutionary researchers *do not* dismiss or condone such behaviors. Instead, as with other phenotypes, they try to understand the presence of these behaviors in light of our evolved history—that is, if and how they may have affected human survival and reproduction in the past. Understanding the factors that influence such behaviors may suggest methods for their control.

Evolutionary arguments are not incompatible with social explanations, but they can lend another level of analysis to psychological investigations. For example social-learning theory may explain how children learn to be aggressive, yet at the same time, males may be more evolutionarily predisposed toward the acquisition of such behavior (Smith, 1987).

Dr. Freedman's commitment to a holistic view of human development was a driving force throughout his career. It facilitated his pursuit of the "big picture."

## THEMES AND ORGANIZATION OF THE VOLUME

The present volume is multifaceted and integrative with respect to theory, content area, and methodology. This is a natural outcome of the diverse perspectives and issues that occupied Dr. Freedman throughout his career and continue to engage his colleagues and students. This ripple effect is apparent in the separate contributions, each of which extends a theme, a thread, or a thought raised by Dr. Freedman in chapters 2 and 3. All chapters stand alone, yet each is part of the grander scheme that he called for so often in his writings and lectures.

Content sections were generated by four organizing disciplines: behavioral genetics, human ethology, evolutionary psychology, and culture, all areas in which Dr. Freedman made significant contributions. In particular, his efforts brought points of commonality among these disciplines into sharper focus, and it is this legacy that serves as the central unifying theme of the volume. Its interdisciplinary flavor is reflected by the representation of several individuals in more than one content section and by multiple cross-referencing by contributors.

The sequence of the eight content sections mirrors the scholarly path taken by Dr. Freedman, with some exceptions. Chapters 2 and 3 represent the anchor points of his academic career. He first reflects on the influences that shaped his thinking as a young student before confronting various current issues and problems. From the outset, the editors felt it was important to provide a clear sense of Dr. Freedman, both as an individual and as a scholar, to enable full appreciation of his resounding influence on the chapters that follow; these beginning chapters accomplish this goal.

Chapter 4 begins with a question: Are genetically based individual differences compatible with species-wide adaptations? In this chapter, J. Michael Bailey explores the interrelatedness of behavioral genetics, human ethology, evolutionary psychology, and culture. It follows Dr. Freedman's chapters because it pursues discussion of some critical issues raised by Dr. Freedman and other contributors, such as the meaning and measurement of *heritability* (the proportion of behavioral variation associated with genetic factors), and the nature and implications of gender differences in behavior.

The ordering of themes represented by Sections II through V generally reflects their entry in the timetable of Dr. Freedman's career. Section II (Genetic Bases of Behavior: Contributions to Psychological Research) documents critical insights into human and nonhuman behavior that have been provided by behavioral–genetic research. In chapter 5, Irving I. Gottesman, H. Hill Goldsmith, and Gregory Carey offer a developmental–genetic analysis of aggression with reference to twin studies of criminality, juvenile delinquency, antisocial traits, and personality characteristics. John Paul Scott in chapter 6 examines variations in social interactional outcomes and processes as a function of the genotype of the organism. Specific examples of how twin research designs may be creatively applied in behavioral genetic, ethological, and evolutionary analyses are provided by Nancy L. Segal in chapter 7.

Clarifying the processes underlying development was central to Dr. Freedman's research programs. Section III (Biological Approaches to Developmental Issues: Rethinking the Data) brings together new perspectives on phenotypes of current interest. In chapter 8, Robert S. Marvin examines mother–infant attachment and interaction in normal and motor-impaired infants in an ethologically based analysis. Ritch C. Savin-Williams and Lisa M. Diamond compare current viewpoints on the origins of sexual orientation and present new data on attitudes concerning the nature and implications of developmental studies on sexuality in chapter 9. The nature and bases of two complex phenotypes, the alcohol flushing response and blushing, with reference to within- and between-group differences, are considered by Peter H. Wolff in chapter 10.

Dr. Freedman's research projects often took him to different countries and cultures. He frequently emphasized the importance of reconciling laboratory findings with a naturalistic approach. Section IV (Naturalistic Studies of Behavior: How Does a Cross-Cultural Approach Inform Ongoing Research?) reminds us of the human universals and cross-cultural differences in behavior that emerge when we step outside familiar territory. In chapter 11, Nicholas G. Blurton Jones presents a unique analysis of the function of gathering behavior among Hadza children in Africa, with reference to gender differences and the significance of this behavior in other contexts. Paul Ekman in chapter 12 elucidates the variety of messages that facial expressions convey. He attempts to remedy recent confusion over whether facial expressions provide information about emotion or are better considered signals about intentions or motivations. In chapter 13, Robert A. LeVine examines the issue of whether social interaction in infancy constitutes enculturation of the child, and presents new data from African, German, Japanese, and American studies. Carol C. Weisfeld discusses factors related to marital satisfaction, based on surveys of couples in England, Turkey, and the United States, in chapter 14.

The current climate of research activity in evolutionary psychology was anticipated by Dr. Freedman in his seminal books, *Human Infancy: An Evolutionary Perspective* (1972) and *Human Sociobiology: A Holistic Approach* (1979). Section V (Evolutionary Analyses: New Issues and Continuing Controversies) introduces critical reappraisal of some common human problems in light of evolutionary theorizing. In chapter 15, Robert L. Trivers examines intrapsychic conflict with respect to new information on genomic imprinting (the differential expression of some alleles in offspring depending on whether inheritance of these alleles was from the mother or father) and its implications for genetic relatedness. Jerome H. Barkow in chapter 16 compares diverse approaches to the meaning, assessment, and fostering of human happiness, and suggests that ancestral human environments may offer clues for alleviating distress. The application of ethological and evolutionary perspectives to the problem of identifying the basic human emotions, with special reference to pride and shame, is considered by Glenn E. Weisfeld in chapter 17.

The use of film as a technique in observational studies of human and animal behavior was a truly exceptional aspect of Dr. Freedman's work. More than most other investigators, he capitalized on the power of this method for capturing and portraying the subtleties and intricacies of playfulness and aggressivity in canines, the smile of a blind infant, and the social sensitivities of young children. A special section devoted to the use of film is included at this point in the volume to illustrate a unique data collection procedure for examining hypotheses and questions generated by the preceding discussions. In the introduction to section VI (Film Retrospective: The Method and the Medium), Dr. Freedman addresses the multiple roles served by film in the study of behavior that include teaching, documenting, and entertaining. Eibl-Eibesfeldt (see the Foreword to this volume) wrote that "motion picture film has become the ethologist's most important means of documentation," because only film includes all elements of behavior, including what the observer's bias would have omitted (Eibl-Eibesfeldt, 1970, p. 12). Dr. Freedman's films, in both edited and analyzed versions, have served these purposes well and will continue to do so in the years to come. For many students who have worked with him, it was in the process of filming, watching, coding, and analyzing frames of film that most of what was understood about behavior came to light. Excerpts from several film analyses supplement Dr. Freedman's insightful overview of this area. This is followed by detailed commentaries in chapter 18 by John Paul Scott, who supervised Dr. Freedman's research on puppies, and in chapter 19 by Lewis P. Lipsitt, with whom Dr. Freedman has a shared interest in newborn behavior.

Section VII (Behavior Genetics, Human Ethology, Evolutionary Psychology, and Culture: Looking to the Future) brings the fields of behavioral genetics, human ethology, evolutionary psychology and culture into the present and beyond. In chapters 20 to 22, Susan L. Trumbetta and Irving I. Gottesman, Wolfgang M. Schleidt, and Roger J. R. Levesque, who represent these disciplines, examine issues in marital status, mating behavior, and family violence from the purview of their areas of expertise. Future research directions and goals are outlined. A synthesis of these discussions and an attempt at resolution of controversies is presented by Dr. Freedman in the section conclusion.

Section VIII (Final Overview: Uniting Psychology and Biology), the final part of the volume, describes the potential contributions of modern Darwinism to the discipline of psychology. This section is presented by the three editors, all of whom owe a great deal to their teacher for pointing them in the direction of the big picture.

## REFERENCES

Archer, J. (1992). *Ethology and human development.* Hemel Hempstead, UK: Harvester Wheatsheaf.

Barkow, J. H. (1970). Hausa and Maguzawa: Processes of group differentiation in a rural area in North Central State, Nigeria. *Dissertation Abstracts, ADD-1971,* 203.

Baumrind, D. (1993). The average expectable environment is not good enough: A response to Scarr. *Child Development, 64,* 1299–1317.

Bouchard, T. J., Jr., Lykken, D. T., McGue, M., Segal, N. L., & Tellegen, A. (1990). Sources of human psychological differences: The Minnesota Study of Twins Reared Apart. *Science, 250,* 223–228.

Burgess, R. L., & Molenaar, P. C. M. (1995). Commentary. *Human Development, 38*, 159–164.

Daly, M., & Wilson, M. (1983). *Sex, evolution, and behavior.* Boston: Willard Grant Press.

Eibl-Eibesfeldt, I. (1970). *Ethology: The biology of behavior.* New York: Holt, Rinehart & Winston.

Freedman, D. G. (1958). Constitutional and environmental interactions in rearing of four breeds of dogs. *Science, 127*, 585–586.

Freedman, D. G. (1964). Smiling in blind infants and the issue of innate versus acquired. *Journal of Child Psychology and Psychiatry, 5*, 171–189.

Freedman, D. G. (1965). Hereditary control of early social behavior. In B. M. Foss (Ed.), *Determinants of infant behavior: Vol. III* (pp. 149–159). London: Methuen.

Freedman, D. G. (1974). *Human infancy: An evolutionary perspective.* Hillsdale, NJ: Erlbaum.

Freedman, D. G. (1979). *Human sociobiology: A holistic approach.* New York: Free Press.

Freedman, D. G., & Freedman, N. C. (1969). Behavioral differences between Chinese–American and European–American newborns. *Nature, 224*, 1227.

Freedman, D. G., & Keller, B. (1963). Inheritance of behavior in infants. *Science, 140*, 196–198.

Gottlieb, G. (1995). Some conceptual deficiencies in "developmental" behavior genetics. *Human Development, 38*, 131–141.

Jackson, J. F. (1993). Human behavioral genetics, Scarr's theory, and her views on interventions: A critical review and commentary on their implications for African American children. *Child Development, 64*, 1318–1332.

Kagan J., Arcus, S., & Snidman, N. (1994). The idea of temperament: Where do we go from here? In R. Plomin & G. E. McClearn (Eds.), *Nature, nurture and psychology* (pp. 197–210). Washington, DC: American Psychological Association.

Kenrick, D. T. (1995). Evolutionary theory versus the confederacy of dunces. *Psychological Inquiry, 6*, 56–62.

Lamb, M. E. (1994). Heredity, environment, and the question "why?" *Behavioral and Brain Sciences, 17*, 751.

Levesque, R. J. R. (1990). *Adolescents in love: An exploration of adolescent love experiences across and within five socio-cultural groups.* Unpublished doctoral dissertation, University of Chicago.

Lykken, D., & Tellegen, A. (1996). Happiness is a stochastic phenomenon. *Psychological Science, 7,* 186–189.

Marvin, R. S. (1972). Attachment, exploratory, and communicative behavior of two-year-old, three-year-old, and four-year-old children. *Dissertation Abstracts, ADD-1972.*

Oyama, S. (1989). Ontogeny and the central dogma: Do we need the concept of genetic programming in order to have an evolutionary perspective? In M. R. Gunnar & E. Thelen (Eds.), *Systems and development* (pp. 1–34). Hillsdale, NJ: Erlbaum.

Plomin, R., & Daniels, D. (1987). Why are children in the same family so different from one another? *Behavioral and Brain Sciences, 10,* 1–16.

Plomin, R., & Rowe, D. C. (1979). Genetic and environmental etiology of social behavior in infancy. *Developmental Psychology, 21,* 391–402.

Rowe, D. C. (1994). *The limits of family influence: Genes, experience, and behavior.* New York: Guilford Press.

Savin-Williams, R. C. (1977). Dominance-submission behaviors and hierarchies in young adolescents at a summer camp: Predictors, styles, and sex differences. *Dissertation Abstracts International, 38-08B,* 3948.

Scarr, S. (1993). Biological and cultural diversity: The legacy of Darwin for development. *Child Development, 64,* 1333–1353.

Scarr, S. (1995a). Psychology will be truly evolutionary when behavior genetics is included. *Psychological Inquiry, 6,* 68–71.

Scarr, S. (1995b). Commentary. *Human Development, 38,* 154–158.

Segal, N. L. (1982). Cooperation, competition, and altruism within twin sets: A reappaisal. *Dissertation Abstracts International, 43-06B,* 2034.

Silverman, I. (1987). Race, race differences, and race relations: Perspectives from psychology and sociobiology. In C. Crawford, M. Smith, & D. Krebs (Eds.), *Sociobiology and psychology: Ideas, issues and applications* (pp. 205–221). Hillsdale, NJ: Erlbaum.

Sloman, L., & Gilbert, P. (Eds.). (1997). *Successful defeat: What Darwin didn't tell us.* Manuscript in preparation.

Smith, M. S. (1987). Evolution and developmental psychology: Toward a sociobiology of human development. In C. Crawford, M. Smith, & D. Krebs (Eds.),

*Sociobiology and psychology: Ideas, issues and applications* (pp. 225–252). Hillsdale, NJ: Erlbaum.

Turkheimer, E., Goldsmith, H. H., & Gottesman, I. I. (1995). Commentary. *Human Development, 38*, 42–53.

Weisfeld, C. C. (1980). Boys and girls in competition: The context and communication of female inhibition. *Dissertation Abstracts International, 41-01B*, 417.

Weisfeld, G. E. (1978). Determinants and behavioral correlates of dominance in adolescent boys. *Dissertation Abstracts International, 39-05B*, 2566.

Wilson, E. O. (1994). *Naturalist.* New York: Warner Books.

2

# My Three Mentors

Daniel G. Freedman

I have had very pleasurable feelings writing this chapter. It is an opportunity to pay homage to the three persons who most influenced my academic career: Abe Maslow, Kurt Goldstein, and Gregory Bateson. Each was for me a person to worship, as well as a friend, although I did not hob-nob with Goldstein (already in his latter years) as I did with the other two. Perhaps only in America can a student "hob-nob" with the illustrious and consider such worshiped ones friends.

Although each was a committed scientist, all three were spiritual gurus as well as academic guides. That came as much from me as from them; I was of a cohort that sought the spiritual in science, and the commitment of each to his science was so total it bordered on the sacred. Unlike Sir John Eccles, who led two lives (that of an academic and that of a deeply committed Catholic), my gurus were atheists who sought the sacred in their work.

As for my own spiritual growth, in recent years I have found more attractive horizons outside academia, largely in East Indian concepts of nonduality, and of course I am not alone in that. Both Maslow and Bateson were both attracted in this direction, but both had made an earlier commitment to science. Maslow, in his later years, was to reap the frustration of a half-hearted spiritual commitment by taking for himself the thankless and lonely role of psychologist as prophet, whereas Bateson sought valiantly to cyberneticize God's territory and to render the sacred scientific. He, too, became "prophetic" in his later years, warning that the world's inhabitants will either adopt a wiser epistemology or descend deeper into the wilderness. Neither man went softly into the night.

By contrast, Goldstein saw himself as a teacher, not as a prophet, perhaps because he was naturally less lofty and, as he said of himself, a "concrete" thinker. He was the most obviously spiritual and probably the most optimistic of the three. In any case I loved each of them, and writing this chapter has been deeply moving.

## ABRAHAM MASLOW

I first met Abe Maslow when I was an undergraduate at the University of California in Berkeley, in the summer of 1948. He had been on leave from Brooklyn College because of an illness and was helping to run a family cooperage (barrel-making and repairing) business near the Bay area. Later, when I knew him better, he complained of rumors of his nervous breakdown—that he was spending the time in California recovering—when in fact he had enjoyed a fine and relaxing 2 years, largely devoted to the family business. However, after reading his biography (Hoffman, 1988) my impression was that this illness was indeed as psychological as it was physical and that it may have been his "dark night of the soul" insofar as it preceded the enormously productive period that followed. I feel fortunate to have met him at this juncture, because he was fully energized and bursting with ideas.

For me, Maslow was a heroic figure—one for modern sensibilities. He was tall, elegantly intelligent, aloof, but friendly. When spoken to, he had a distracted way of softly whistling while looking off, obviously reformulating things in that very active theorist's brain. Although refined and in some ways elitist, he preferred to be called Abe rather than Professor Maslow. He swore, although with the words perfectly pronounced, gossiped about colleagues, but rarely with malice, and he blushed often and easily—which gave him a charming, boyish aspect. Although his Berkeley lectures appeared to be off the cuff, Abe had all the material organized in his mind. Later, when working with him on a paper, I was awed at his ability to compose fully literate pages of text in a simple conversational first draft. (I thought this talent worked against him when his diaries, which were no more than disparate conversations with himself, were published posthumously simply because they read so well.)

Abe was formidably intelligent, and as a graduate student of Thorndike at Columbia, he had broken the ceiling on Thorndike's IQ test, at about the 190 level. He told me that after Thorndike saw these results he was given carte blanche and was thereafter free to pursue whatever he wished. For Abe, IQ was an essential trait, and in his assessment of people it was prominent. We were once together at a lecture given by Margaret Mead, whom he knew, and he lamented that her enormous intelligence was not being applied to deeper issues. He considered intelligence an essential part of a person's being, like good looks or good health, and he encouraged his students to get tested so that they might better know themselves. In his letters of recommendation for me, for example, he included a rather accurate estimate of my IQ, which usually served to depress me, for one is never sufficiently endowed. My vision about this was Maslow sitting high on Mt. Olympus gazing down at lesser images of himself—again, the elitist motif.

In his Berkeley summer school lectures Maslow made frequent reference to the heroism and courage of certain self-actualized individuals in both literature and life. Most memorable for me was Abe's choice of the architect hero of *The Fountainhead* by Ayn Rand as a fictional example of someone who was self-actualized. The hero, Howard Rourke, was depicted as a somewhat icy, social isolate, who demonstrated deep moral courage by blowing up a new housing project because the builders had misused his architectural plans. Clearly, Ayn Rand's point was that by changing the structural beauty of the original plans, the project was doomed to become an ugly slum—for beauty is necessary to bring out the beauty in people, whereas architectural ugliness will induce squalor and meanness.

Needless to say, the blowing-up of a new housing project, for any reason, might not play well everywhere, and there were some heated discussions in and out of class. For Abe, however, Rourke demonstrated the traits he extolled: courage in the face of the larger, often corrupt "system."

Another of the examples of a self-actualized person was Albert Einstein. Abe was particularly impressed with the report that on hearing that his wife had died, Einstein was in a conventional sense unmoved, saying only, "Let's get her buried." The point was, I believe, that Einstein's purview included life and death as integral parts of the universe, and that this realization separated him from most of us and placed him among a small group of *self-actualizers.* Nowadays, with the general influence of Eastern thought in the West, the word *enlightened* might more readily be used.

For Maslow, the self-actualized wore convention as a cloak, to be removed at will; thus, they sometimes appeared insensitive to the more conventional. It now seems to me that they were, in part, incarnations of mythic American film heros such as John Wayne and Gary Cooper (who, in fact, played the role of Howard Rourke in the filmed "Fountainhead"), men who "stood tall" for what they knew to be right, thus exemplifying a particularly potent American—if not universal—archetype. Some of us loved Maslow for breaking away from the rigors of statistical sampling, which had bored us to tears, and for talking about things that were intrinsically interesting—courage, heroism, beauty, wisdom, maturity, unconventionality, and human peak experiences. Abe emboldened me to denigrate the compulsive, number-ridden, experimental psychologists, who could choke on their meaningless data!

Needless to say, there was a good deal of controversy in the class, and some of the critics tried to be vicious. Maslow, however, held his own, as when one over-intellectualized student spoke of Professor Maslow's having said this and that, and didn't Professor Maslow realize, and so forth—to which Maslow replied by asking why he was being addressed as if he were a streetcar. There were no notes and no formal lectures, but subject matter was wide ranging, tilted toward the wisdom of Gestalt psychology and dynamic psychiatry and away from the narrowness of hard science and learning theory. There was Clark Hull's (e.g., Hull, 1930) laboratory-based scientized treatment of memory contrasted with Bartlett's (1932) cross-cultural, naturalistic approach, and it became a somewhat good-natured morality play in which scientism and reductionism were depicted as dehumanism, always contrasted with dynamic psychology (psychoanalysis), Gestalt psychology, and naturalistic, anthropological observations. Ruth Benedict's *Patterns of Culture* (1934) exemplified the latter approach, and it was Maslow who first made me aware of it—and a wonderful new world of literature. It was one of those courses in which books, referred to here and there in the lectures, provided me with reading for the next decade.

Maslow evinced deep appreciation of psychoanalysis, even as I too was drawn to it, and in general the tilt to our inclinations ran parallel. We were both put off by reductionism (American learning theory), both thrilled by genius and heroism in the arts and sciences, both inclined to find truth in literature as well as science, both biological in orientation and believers in the power of instinct (and the unconscious), and both respectful of Eastern thought. I had found an intellectual and ethnic soulmate, and I was thrilled and awed; he was the genius professor for whom I had been searching. And generous and loving teacher that he was, he was to be my guide for years to come.

I had been in the Navy at the end of the war in 1945, and I was in school courtesy of the GI Bill. I had had classes with a number of other "star" psychologists in my 3 years at Berkeley, but Maslow was my sort, and I apparently his. Because I was in my last year as an undergraduate when he came into my life, I proposed—and he accepted—that I go back East and work with him on his research, take graduate courses at the New School for Social Research, and enter a personal psychoanalysis. I find it touching in retrospect—but found it embarrassing at the time—that my parents, thankful that a professor of such stature had undertaken my guidance, sent Abe a crate of California grapefruit in token of their appreciation.

To pay for my existence and my analysis I sought a job as an attendant at Brooklyn's King's County Hospital, hoping to join the psychiatric facility there, for I had been similarly employed in psychiatric facilities in

California. I found temporary quarters in Brooklyn, but King's County was a nightmare largely because I was never transferred to psychiatry. My main memory is of warm, foul-smelling bedpans. I left when I was hired as an attendant at the famous Bellevue Psychiatric Pavilion, the facility serving New York City—where I worked for some 3 years in the most satisfying job I had ever had. I had minimal responsibility and the stimulation of daily contact with various forms of insanity. Like Tennessee Williams, I felt—at the time—most at home with madness.

This brings up the issue of my own psychoanalysis and Maslow's hand in it. Although he gave me some names of potential analysts, his main contribution was a bit of advice that I have since passed on to others. "Since there is plenty of crap that, as a matter of course, will come up in the analysis, don't go to someone whose own personality will become an issue. Choose someone whose lap you want to sit on and whose cheeks you want to pinch." That is to say, it is not "transference" if you find your analyst a sonofabitch and he more or less is one. Thus encouraged to follow my own intuition, I found a person who was a fine, warm, deeply moral human being, Paul Zimring, toward whom I always felt a strong affection—and who helped me emerge from my sea of anxiety. I did not know it at the time, but Zimring came from the same politically left background in which I had grown up, and it is clear that we were attuned at several levels I was not aware of at the time.

My work with Abe consisted of interviewing women Abe knew and whom he considered both dominant and self-actualizing. It later became clear that this work was directly descended from his dissertation at the University of Wisconsin (loosely supervised by Harry Harlow, who was only 3 years older than Abe) on dominance in a group of monkeys at the Madison Zoo. Abe was Harlow's first graduate student, and they apparently got on very well. In this work, which resulted in some very original papers (see, e.g., Maslow, 1936), Abe became infatuated with traits related to dominance, and this led eventually to his self-actualizing studies.

I must note that he had found dominant young men not nearly as interesting as dominant young women, and I now believe that there are valid reasons for this. My guess is that there is a higher correlation between female dominance and creative intelligence and that dominant young men tend to be athletes rather than potentially creative scientists or artists. This intuition derives from my own work on dominance hierarchies among children (Freedman, 1980), and I have only now become aware that this work probably had its secret inception with my experiences as Maslow's apprentice.

In general, the potential self-actualizers that I met were highly intelligent people who were rather more striking than average. Only one woman interviewee still stands out in my memory, the wife of Werner Munsterburg, a psychoanalytic anthropologist. She had been a student with Maslow at Brooklyn College, and she struck me as enormously self-confident and strong, despite marriage to an obviously dominant male. She was tall, dark, vivacious, bemused at having been chosen as a possible self-actualizer, and very lucid in everything she said. At the Maslow home in Brooklyn, I ran into another memorable "case" Abe had designated as self-actualized, an uncle of Abe's. Abe was a full-time psychologist and his daily experiences provided his "laboratory" data. I remember this old-country Russian–Jewish gentleman as warm, deeply philosophic, humorous, and a socialist. He endeared himself to me for all time when he compared me with Tolstoy after I had captured a beetle and released it outside the front door.

Somewhat later, while in the master's program at City College of New York, I took a course from the man who had coined the term *self-actualization,* Kurt Goldstein. Only then did I realize that self-actualization was originally meant to describe a universal process of unfolding, that it was a verb and not an achieved state—a process, not a package. Goldstein, when he found I worked with Maslow, asked in good-natured wonderment, "What is Maslow trying to do?" He was truly befuddled with Maslow's positing of a self-actualized end state. Although I found Goldstein's own position entirely convincing, the fact is that Maslow's concretization and idealization of the concept is what led to its ready use among the young people of my day, myself included. It became a heroic state toward which one might strive, similar to the equally elusive notion of *enlightenment.* I must emphasize that, despite the differences in emphasis in their definitions of self-actualization, Maslow felt deeply beholden to Goldstein, and both he and I agreed that in Holism (as expressed in *The Organism*; 1939), Goldstein had his hand on the truth—or, at least, on a larger portion of truth than anyone else.

(When in China in February 1995, as a guest lecturer at Nankai University in Tianjin, I was astounded and pleased to learn that Maslow was perhaps the most popular psychologist in all of China. My host said, "Today, more young people know Maslow than know Marx." A translation of *Motivation and Personality* had been published in 1987, prior to the demonstrations at Tiananmen Square, and it became clear that *self-actualization* involved a set of ideas the Chinese were hungering for. As one student put it: "In China we have lived by orders from above—and it is time to express our own needs." Another student, who had been a leader of the democracy movement in Harbin, said that reading Maslow made him feel better than he is, optimistic for the future, and empowered. A professor of social psychology told me that students are demanding to be "taught Maslow" and that he generally obliges, despite some misgivings about the theory. Thus Abe has assumed heroic proportions, and one young woman at my lecture resisted my Goldsteinian version of self-actualization and insisted that Abe himself must have been self-actualized, in the Maslovian sense—that is, she felt he had achieved an exalted state of being. Ironically, in this country hip college students are talking of Buddhist spirituality and enlightenment; there are posters of the Dalai Lama in dormitories; and Maslow is a vaguely familiar name out of the recent past. One naturally wonders if our next intellectual export to China will be an Americanized version of Tibetan spirituality.)

I had enrolled in the City College of New York's master's program with Maslow's help and advice and found a star-studded faculty there, many of whom had fled Nazi persecution: In addition to Goldstein's class, I took courses with René Spitz, Katherine Wolf, Ernst Kris, David Beres, Ruth Munroe, Florence Halpern, Gardner Murphy, and Lois Barclay Murphy. I did a term paper for Lois Murphy's class on child development using data that Maslow supplied on his own daughters, Ann and Ellen.

He had made notes on their development starting immediately after birth, and we were both impressed with the continuity, over time, in their personalities and temperaments. In addition, I administered some simple figure-drawing tests and wrote the paper. Lois Murphy was totally taken by the portrayals, which I disguised as children of a University of Chicago professor. It turned out that she was the child of a rather famous University of Chicago professor (of religion), and as she read the paper she experienced a deep kinship with the girls. That academic exercise led to several lifelong friendships for which I am most grateful: a relationship with Lois and Gardner Murphy (after I received my doctorate, Gardner offered me a position at the Menninger Clinic where he had become the director of research); and relationships with Ann and especially Ellen Maslow, with whom I remain in touch to this day. I eventually learned, via feedback from my own children, that kids probably prefer not serving as guinea pigs for their psychologist parents.

After the master's program at City College I attempted to enter New York University for the PhD, but, as I am fond of saying, failed my Rorschach test. This was part of the entrance requirement, and I believe my proclivity for seeing whole responses on each card—making a Gestalt even where none seems warranted—was something of a warning to Florence Halpern, the talented clinician who was doing the screening. This tendency has been both a blessing (I am constantly looking for the big picture) and a problem (insufficient attention to the detail demanded by, say, grant reviewers). One can perhaps see how someone with such a tendency would take to Abe Maslow and vice versa.

In 1953, after spending almost 2 years earning yet another master's degree at the University of Colorado, where Maslow had assisted my admission with a wonderful letter of recommendation, I applied and was admitted to the newly formed psychology department at Brandeis University, where Maslow was the founding chair. I had not liked the "dustbowl empiricism" of the University of Colorado, where no one admitted to having an unconscious, and I had made no close attachments there with any of the faculty. I was joyous at the prospect of again working with my old mentor and guide and can still recall the feeling of elation as the airplane came down in the Boston area. It was my first trip to New England, which was surprisingly lush and green, and I felt very, very lucky.

Maslow had envisioned a psychology department for Brandeis modeled on the ideas of Carl Rogers, where an elite group of graduate students would be permitted total freedom to pursue their own interests (even as Thorndike had done for him). This sense of freedom was exhilarating, and the initial dissertations, my own included, were considerably more creative than average. However, the ideal eroded, and the Brandeis University psychology department soon resembled any other, with required courses and examinations. It should also be said that, ironically, although Abe's international reputation soared, his local effect on graduate students had waned, and the excitement I had experienced at Berkeley was rarely seen. There was instead a disturbing cynicism among the students that I can recall but still cannot explain. The academic highlights in those years (1953–1955) were Kurt Goldstein's seminars. Abe had arranged for Goldstein, who had so influenced him, to be flown to Boston from New York City each week, and for many of us it was like taking a course with an archetype (that of "the wise old man"). Abe's demise as a teacher is covered rather well in Hoffman's (1988) biography.

My stay at Brandeis lasted only 2 years: I had become involved in a pilot project in which we reared and studied a litter of puppies born to the campus mascot, work later recounted in Freedman (1967). Maslow suggested I present the results of the study at the Jackson Laboratories in Bar Harbor, Maine, where I found an enthusiastic audience. The chief of the behavioral division, Dr. John Paul Scott, asked me to do my dissertation there using their large population of dogs—under the joint sponsorship of the Jackson Laboratories and Brandeis University. I gladly accepted and, as it turned out, my professional career was thereby launched (see Scott, chapter 6, this volume).

I have, in fact, swerved little from the path set on at Bar Harbor, a career culminating recently (October 1995) in a Festschrift for me at the University of Chicago. My Bar Harbor mentor, Paul Scott, at 87 years of age, was at the Festschrift, and Abe Maslow's spirit was there as well. He was present in me and in my students, whether they knew it or not. When my former student, Donald Omark, said to me, "Your ideas will always be with me," he might as well have been addressing Abe Maslow. I have had other important teachers, but Maslow came into my life at a critical time, and he became part of me. And now that spirit has been passed on to another generation of teachers, and to their students. Teaching, when the timing is right, can be a wonderfully touching business, and then it may permanently affect one's heart and mind.

## KURT GOLDSTEIN

The most salient of my teachers was Kurt Goldstein. His book, *The Organism* (1939) became my bible: I often had it with me, and it appeared to radiate truth. As mentioned previously, I came on Goldstein through Abe Maslow, for whom he was also a major influence. When I enrolled in Goldstein's course at the City College of New York in 1950, he was in his 70s. Vigorous, totally dedicated, and enthusiastic about his message of "holism," he made each class a celebration—a privilege we 60 or so students shared.

What did Goldstein mean by *holism?* He had been a neurologist at the hospital in Frankfurt that treated the brain-injured in World War I, and later chief of a similar hospital in Berlin. He had become impressed with self-correcting forces of the brain following brain injury, and with observations that neural reorganization and the return of lost function were the rule, rather than the exception. (These near mystical experiences with the inner potential for growth and repair also became the basis for the collateral concept of self-actualization.)

The idea expressed by holism grew out of the Gestalt movement in German psychology from whence came the motto, "The whole is greater than the sum of the parts." This movement had been born in reaction to the deterministic theories prevalent at the turn of the century: For example, Goldstein recounted some of the early neural deterministic beliefs of Sherrington, in which he had hoped that a neural theory of complex behavior might be constructed with simple reflexes as its building blocks (Sherrington, 1911). Nowadays, even physics no longer ties its future to discoveries of more basic particles but views the "whole" as consisting of interacting and interdependent forces (cf. Bohm, 1980). In biology, however, the determinist–holist feud is still alive, as between those who think in terms of "selfish genes" versus the newly revived group selectionists (e.g., Wilson & Sober, 1994).

Many of the brain injuries of Goldstein's patients resulted in unusual behavior, and most of the symptoms were explained by Goldstein in terms of concrete versus abstract behaviors. I recall the example of one patient who could not willfully initiate sexual activity with his wife, but if she placed his penis in her, the automated part of sex would take over. According to Goldstein the inability to summon up conscious desire was due to impairment of the "abstract attitude," but the "concrete" functions were still intact. Goldstein saw these functions as complementary and refused to make a higher–lower distinction between abstract and concrete, citing himself as an example of a very concrete thinker. This illustrates a most charming aspect of the man—his refusal to judgmentally hierarchize into higher and lower, better or worse; hence, his bafflement at Maslow's hierarchy of needs.

Another concept of Goldstein's was the *catastrophic reaction.* The brain-injured were constantly on the verge of having their apperceived world fall apart, or of experiencing a catastrophic reaction, because of their impaired abstraction. As a result, they led extraordinarily restricted and controlled lives, and in the safety of hospital conditions often did quite well. Their lockers were exceptionally neat—for any disorganization could bring about anxiety. Detecting this need for neatness and order became part of Goldstein's diagnostic procedure, as in the Goldstein–Scheerer tests (1941). For Goldstein, human-ness itself was closely associated with the abstract attitude, and he was fiercely opposed to the then common operation of lobotomy, meant to make tractable violent schizophrenic patients. Goldstein held that the surgery had rendered these patients brain-injured and had permanently robbed them of the human gift of abstraction.

Goldstein was not a name dropper, but Albert Einstein was a friend, and Goldstein told the class of Einstein's query about whether animal intelligence differs from human intelligence as a matter of degree or kind. The message to us was that even the great Einstein did not understand the distinction between abstract and concrete behavior and that Goldstein had to explain it to him. For Goldstein, the abstract attitude involved anticipation of the future, cognizance of the past, and the ability to act "as if" something were true. I have always found this definition helpful, particularly when responding to someone asking Einstein's question.

Inasmuch as I had started classes and was simultaneously searching for an analyst, I seriously considered going to Goldstein as a patient. My sense was, however, that theory was too dominant in his being, concrete though he felt he was, and that my innards might be a secondary consideration. In addition, he was not an "analyst" and did not have his patients lie down, and I was geared for the free-association route. He certainly fit the bill otherwise (loving, generous, caring, emotionally present). In retrospect, and having engaged in face-to-face psychotherapy as both therapist and patient, I believe Goldstein would have been a fine therapist for me, although as I have said, I will always be grateful to the analyst I chose.

I have been disappointed that Goldstein never received the general acclaim he deserved, but also heartened that certain perceptive students, when introduced to his William James lectures (1951) for example, are struck by the depth and modernity of his thought. His was a message of abiding faith—perhaps not in a biblical God, but certainly in an inner force for healing.

I myself tend to thank natural selection for the self-actualizing processes, but the fact is that Goldstein, like his teacher Jacob von Uexküll, was very suspicious of Darwinism! Both asked, how can such beauty of design be achieved by chance? I have always found this questioning to be charming, and loved Goldstein for his deeply felt naivetes. However, it is well known that his friend Einstein also had trouble with the image of God rolling dice, but in his case, somehow, the term "naive" does not seem appropriate. Another, less momentous naivete arose later, in 1954, when Goldstein taught at Brandeis. He thought it improper for Riegelman to run as a Republican candidate for Mayor of New York City, for it seemed to him morally amiss for a Jew to vote Republican—let alone run as a Republican. I am sure my father would have agreed.

When at City College, I once confronted Goldstein with an experiment done by the famous neurobiologist, Paul Weiss, who had claimed it as evidence against holism (Weiss, 1947). Weiss had surgically removed the hind limbs of a salamander and then reattached them front to back. When confronted by a fire source, the rearranged animal scooted into it and, of course, died. Goldstein's response was immediate. Weiss, he said, had so drastically changed the nature of the salamander that death was its only alternative. Self-actualization, he added, sometimes requires death. In retrospect, I wish I had gone on to discuss the further implications of his view of self-actualization, for they were here bordering on the mystic, but I was not then prepared to do so.

Because I am tracing intellectual ancestry, I will note that I was pleased when I learned that Goldstein and another important influence on my work, Konrad Lorenz, were both close students of Jacob von Uexküll, the great naturalist (see Schiller, 1957) who is considered the grandfather of ethology. Like Goldstein, von Uexküll preferred a sacred explanation of Nature's wonders rather than a Darwinian one, whereas Lorenz, of course, took the Darwinian route. Goldstein spoke of another interesting connection one day when I mentioned that I was taking a course with Wolfgang Köhler at the New School for Social Research: Köhler, the great Gestalt psychologist who had discovered "insight" learning in chimpanzees, had done so in a laboratory run by Goldstein's father-in-law on Tenerife Island, off the African coast, where all were interned during World War I. Although such connections feel mysteriously synchronous, they are also simply an accounting of intellectual genealogies.

Although I did not know Goldstein as intimately as I knew Maslow, he became the major theoretical force in my thinking, teaching, and research. The essentially aesthetic idea that a scientist, like an architect, needs to start with an image of "the whole," even while working on the details, has been more than useful—it has become a way of being. It gave me the courage to follow hunches that seemed to fit the bigger picture, and, practically speaking, it helped form the methodology of my dissertation at the Jackson Laboratory at Bar Harbor, Maine. I have always tried, in my own teaching, to pass that message on, including its respect for creative intuition, but I must say that students most often found this unfolding process a dangerous path. Somewhat like Goldstein's patients, they often opted for the safety of an assigned topic. Clearly, creativity requires a strong dash of courage, and that, Goldstein would have agreed, is an essentially unteachable organismic property.

## GREGORY BATESON

I was a senior at the University of California at Berkeley when I first encountered Gregory Bateson in 1949. Bateson was a guest lecturer in a general course in cultural anthropology. He showed the class an anticommunist film, *Hitlerjunge Quex,* made by the Nazis in 1933, which he had analyzed while working for the Office of Strategic Services as part of the war effort. I thought his analysis was brilliant. I came to the podium afterward with a question that, for me, was uppermost in my mind because of Maslow, whose course I had taken the previous summer: What is the healthiest culture thus far studied by anthropologists, and what were its characteristics? Margaret Mead had asked a similar question in her *Competition and Cooperation* (1937), where she concluded that the Eskimo had the most balanced combination of traits in the title.

Bateson, however, had a different sort of answer. "The Balinese," he said, "are schizoid enough for me." I thought it a marvelous and eye-opening response, reflecting both who Bateson was (remote, dreamy, deeply aesthetic, always checking with how he really felt about things before answering) and the essential relativity of the question. It was, in retrospect, a "Goldsteinian" rather than "Maslovian" response in that self-actualization was an individual matter and in its spirit beyond human judgment. (The exquisite beauty of the Balinese and Bali was to be revealed to me directly in 1972 when I visited the island with Bateson.)

Many years were to pass before I would meet Bateson again. I had completed my dissertation at Bar Harbor and had received a postdoctoral fellowship to work at Mt. Zion Hospital and the Langley Porter Neuropsychiatric Institute in San Francisco, California. It was 1958, and I was invited to present my research to Palo Alto's Mental Research Institute (MRI), where Bateson (along with Don Jackson, Paul Watzlawick, Virginia Satir, and John Weakland) were studying the families of schizophrenics. I presented a film of my findings with four breeds of dogs, raised in two very different ways, and Bateson was clearly impressed with the wonderful complexity of the findings.

The study of the dogs was a compelling demonstration of what Gardner and Lois Murphy had earlier noted to me: that heredity and environment were inextricably bound and that untangling them might well result in the loss of the phenomena themselves. (I was later to hear D. T. Suzuki, the Zen scholar, say the same thing when addressing the 1968 International Congress of Neuropsychiatry in Japan: "You have taken heredity and environment apart; now you are stuck with the impossible task of putting them together again.") In retrospect, I believe Bateson, the Murphys, Suzuki, and I shared the notion that the beautiful mysteries of life must be preserved and saved from scientific dissection. I would, of course, add Goldstein and Maslow to this list of like minds. Later I was to learn that the entire Bateson family—all scientists and naturalists—revered the poet Blake, who said, "a tear is an intellectual thing" and admonished that we not be lulled into "Newton's sleep" (Lipset, 1980).

Over the 4 years that I was in the Bay Area (1958 to 1962) I met with Bateson a number of times and found him to be a guru to the younger psychiatrists in the area. Hosting such groups seemed to constitute his social life, until he settled on a social worker attendee, Lois (Cammack), who became his wife. By 1961, the Scottish Rite money that had helped support his research at the Palo Alto VA Hospital had been terminated, as one reviewing physician gossiped to me, because of Bateson's "arrogance" in his renewal applications—by which he seemed to mean the dearth of hypotheses, lists of future studies, and accounts of accomplishments. This particular official seemed angry, perhaps in order to gear up for the cutting off of a man so respected in the field. My sense was that in American science, as in business, one must yield tangible products, preferably on time, and that talk about ideas not tied to any specific intentions was viewed as snobbish elitism.

Bateson was already widely known for his notion that schizophrenogenic parents place their children in "double binds" (Bateson, 1972) and, as a consequence, he had become a major figure in psychiatry. He, and the previously mentioned group at MRI, had started investigating family dynamics by actually watching and filming families interact. I have never forgotten a film Gregory showed of his neighbor's family deciding on a vacation alongside comparable footage of a schizophrenic's family. The latter group seemed incapable of resolving the question because of their unspoken agendas. By contrast, the neighbors were clear and ultimately decisive. Crucially for me, Bateson pointed out that the neighbors were in the process of divorce but that the family members of the schizophrenic were so totally enmeshed that separations of any sort were unthinkable and certainly unworkable.[1]

Bateson had become the major theorist of the then fledgling family therapy movement by introducing cybernetic thinking (systems theory). This allowed psychotherapists to break away from the psychoanalytic model of individual treatment and to deal with the family "system" as the unit to be treated. All this notwithstanding, he decided to turn his back on research into schizophrenia (after some 12 years) and, accustomed to the itinerant life, decided to study communication among dolphins in the Virgin Islands with John Lilly, who had extended the invitation. Things had taken a strong turn to the applied and the manipulative as Don Jackson took over MRI and Bateson, who just wanted to understand *(verstehen)*, had an aversion to engineered change, where the fallout was totally unpredictable.

Later, during a visit I made to my in-laws in Hawaii, Bateson told me

[1] The double-bind theory of schizophrenia—i.e., the view that schizophrenia is caused by particular pattens of pathogenic communication within families, has been virtually abandoned. More recent data from twin and adoption studies demonstrate that living with a schizophrenic family member is unable to explain familial resemblance for this disorder. Current thinking is that social–interactional features of the family may contribute to the onset of schizophrenia, but only in interaction with a predisposed genotype (Gottesman, 1991).—Eds.

that working for Lilly had not been ideal and that life in the Virgin Islands was oppressive because of black on white racism. Although he was on an NIMH Career Development Award, funds to run the facility had run out, and when a similar position was offered to him at Sea Life Park in Honolulu, he accepted. His job was to acquire an understanding of dolphin communication, and he was deadly earnest about this charge, approaching it from all angles. I recall a large human pinna he had constructed in order to better listen to dolphin whistling; the model was five times the normal because sound travels five times faster under water (Lipset, 1980). I learned for the first time that the ear's folds break up sound waves so that even a single ear can determine direction. I myself was then deeply into the adaptive nature of human structures (e.g., fingernails, beards, rumps, later discussed in my book, *Human Sociobiology*, 1979), and came away very impressed. Although Bateson lamented over what he felt was a lack of progress, the questions asked were basic, as usual: "Dan, what are these creatures really about?"

I recall petting one dolphin in a holding tank at Sea Life Park. Feeling its positive response, I told Bateson that were I working with dolphins I would personalize my research, becoming as intimate as possible with them—much as I had done with the puppies in my dissertation. However, this sort of thing was a younger person's game, particularly with a seagoing mammal, and Gregory was rather more theoretical and cognitive. Like myself, he was prejudiced against the Skinnerian reward learning used at Sea Life Park, but some major surprises came out of it. Perhaps the most interesting finding was made by the co-owner of the Park, Karen Pryor, when she discovered that one can induce dolphins to produce wildly novel behavior by rewarding them for doing something they had not before done. This observation served to bring out unsuspected creativity, and it was a grand example of deutero-learning—Bateson's idea of learning how to learn.

Gregory had a lovely home in Hawaii, and its centerpiece was a great oaken table he had had sent from the family home in England. After dinner we sat around it, amused by a pet gibbon Gregory had purchased from a sailor, talking, and especially listening. I was totally enamored with this mind that leapt from Blake to Collingwood, extolled the virtues of Lamarck, and dared to criticize Darwin for setting science back 100 years. During this visit—I with my young family and Gregory recently married—we became more intimate, and it was not long afterward that I received a call from him, inviting my whole family to join him and his wife and daughter on a world trip with some 25 students, mostly undergraduates from Harvard University.

The compatibility I had with Gregory arose, I think, from my own critical, somewhat rebellious attitude toward prevailing views in the social sciences, my unswerving holism, as well as my relative youth and ingenuousness. We were also both keen observers; he had been committed to filmed observation, even as I was at the time. He was totally accepting of each and every query I ever made, even if it seemed to come out of the blue. No question or comment was undeserving of consideration, particularly if it arose spontaneously. Bateson, in fact, seemed to operate at a cirrus level, and although he had pet formulations, they seemed never to intrude into the flow of the conversation. It felt as if he had "democratic genes," and I never felt put down—nor even in danger of it. The ideas themselves were the thing.

With peers it may have been different. Gregory knew very much about many things, and Lipset quoted Eric Erikson as having felt "very inferior to . . . Gregory" (1980, p. 172n). After all, how does a committed psychoanalyst handle a remark such as " . . . psychoanalysis is a monument to the value and importance of loose thinking" (Lipset, 1980, pp. 171–172). I saw him operate at one major conference in Berkeley at which he typically stood at the back, and from that vantage point offered the most cogent and provocative remarks of the afternoon. Thinking was his game, and he was among the best at it. When I mentioned to my neighbor in Hyde Park, Alex Morin, editor of Aldine Press (a major publisher of anthropological texts) that I was soon to leave on a years journey around the world with Gregory Bateson, he remarked, "A year! A week with Gregory Bateson is like a year with anyone else."

Shortly before the trip, at a memorial meeting honoring the psychiatrist Lawrence K. Frank with whom Gregory and Margaret Mead had lived on their return from Bali, I heard Catherine Bateson (their daughter) tell the following: On Cape Cod one summer she had cut her foot walking barefoot. Finding herself halfway between Larry Frank's place and the cottage that Gregory was occupying, she opted to head for the Frank house. "While Daddy would know the details of the injury, would treat it properly and be able to describe the healing process, Uncle Larry would kiss it." I repeat it here for, like a dream, it condenses so much.

The trip, sponsored by the International School of America, started in Hawaii, moved then to Japan, Hong Kong, Bali, Ceylon, India, and ended in Kenya, with some 4 to 6 weeks in each place. It lasted a full academic year, starting in the fall of 1972 and going through June 1973. The students stayed with native families in each place, and our two families stayed in separate accommodations. Bateson and I tried to engage in lecturing, but that gave way to allowing the students to simply experience each culture and family, easily a full-time occupation. A final report was expected from each student. My guess is that everyone was affected by Bateson for the rest of his or her life. David Lipset, now a cultural anthropologist, became his biographer (Lipset, 1980); Rodney Donaldson edited a volume of his papers (Bateson, 1991); and the others (including myself) have remained under his spell in various ways.

It was a year of living in a fish-bowl, and our largenesses and smallnesses were eventually displayed. Having myself grown up in a volatile family, I was deeply impressed that Gregory was a gentleman and a democrat under almost all circumstances. In only two instances do I remember him pulling rank, and both were with my 7-year-old son, also named Gregory (after my mother's brother, a "renegade" Trotskyite who had been executed by Stalin). The first instance was when Bateson caught my son and 5-year-old Nora, his daughter, naked in a bath house at our Hong Kong hotel. To our amusement, he was especially shocked at the boy's hubris. The second instance was in Ceylon during a Bateson lecture to the assembled students, when Gregory became annoyed with young Greg's behavior and ordered him from the room. Young Greg felt this was an injustice and refused to leave, much to my secret delight, for I too felt he had been picked on. The elder Gregory grew red, not knowing how to handle this insubordination. The day was saved by young Greg's favorite student, Dan Wolfe, who gently suggested he leave—and that he, Dan, would follow.

Gregory rarely wore socks and he had a rumpled look. His shirt was frequently hanging out of his pants, often with the underwear top showing; all this on a 6'5" frame that could draw awesome attention. Although the badly tucked clothes may have been an affectation, it also signified that there were important things in the world, and how one dressed was not one of them. Once, when in Hong Kong with our group of students and disgusted by the mercantilism of the place, I said in exasperation, "This is not a place for getting new ideas, it's a place for getting new suits." He loved the assessment, and was happy that we both felt the same about this disappointing stop.

Gregory rarely spoke from notes. I recall a lecture at the Langley Porter Institute's Wednesday-noon lecture series, in which he used himself as an example of the communication issues he was trying to deal with. "If I sit thusly, on the table, you will have a different set than if I'm at the podium." I was always semi-embarrassed for him, wondering if he was going to pull it off. Of course he usually did, but his goal was not a brilliant finished product, which I always strove for in my own lecturing. Instead, Gregory seemed to feel that groping for the right idea and the right way to say it was the point of the lecture. I witnessed this again when I was his host at the University of Chicago, just before the trip. Many attended the lecture, but few were edified. They knew that they were having a peek at the thought processes of a brilliant man but wished he had offered some memorable formulations or crystallized ideas. Of course, he had many in his lifetime, presented brilliantly in his written work, but lectures were for developing them, not delivering them.

This practice was taken as teasing by some, as an affectation exploiting the fact that unfinished thoughts are more titillating. I think it was a matter of veracity. In person, and as a lecturer, Gregory felt he must transmit where his head was, and he was certainly not an entertainer. He might offer a joke or two, but it was the ideas and their development that held the center. Further, the lesson was deutero: "I'm teaching that thinking is OK, and that expressing unfinished ideas is OK."

I refresh myself with Bateson's corpus of ideas from time to time. On this occasion, I have reread his Korzybski lecture (1972), perhaps his most summative single piece, and I am again in his thrall, struck by the Jeremiac stance and the beautiful use of his previous ideas. Korzybski had said, and Bateson often repeated, that the map is not the territory. This generally means that theories can get you into trouble if they claim to be the territory, and that the territory is badly represented in some theories (shall we say Descartes's dualism?).

Bateson often quoted St. Paul (Galatians 6:7), "God is not mocked." In the present context this means, for me, that the territory itself is holy, is God's own, and that maps, probably all maps, are some kind of mockery. I said as much in my book *Human Sociobiology* (1979) when I called sociobiology a "game," albeit a powerfully predictive one. This recalls yet another favorite quote of Gregory's, one by Pascal, "The heart has its reasons, of which reason knows nothing." Again, in the present context, the heart is God's territory, reason the map.

Another thrust of the Korzybski lecture was the "immanence of mind." Gregory emphasized that the mind is not bound to the body and instead is immanent in our tools and in that which engages us, whether consciously or not. When immanent minds meet, then, a new epistemology is born—one based on union, rather than ego-centeredness and ethnocentrism. This constituted his message to the future: Change your epistemology to conform with God's (read cybernetic) territory, or remain lost in this present wilderness. Indeed, persuading, even goading, toward a new, appropriate epistemology for humankind, seemed Gregory's role toward the end. I often confront my own amoral Darwinism, as it is tragically confirmed time and again, say in Bosnia or Rwanda, with the hope for such a new day, but I daresay I have never been optimistic about "minds," controlled as they are by those damned hormones. But Gregory's was a deeply moral position and, in general, God was never far from his thoughts, atheistic cyberneticist though he was.

Whitehead and Russell's (1910–1913) *logical typing* was a frequently occurring concept in Bateson's thinking, and I have found it an enlightening, elusive, and heady idea. I wrote a small piece appropriating logical typing as its centerpiece (see appendix of Freedman & Gorman, 1993). I developed a hierarchical, yet circular, schema as my response to a coteaching quarter with Professor Richard Shweder at the University of Chicago, and it was meant to inform Rick and the class that one could be a committed geneticist, evolutionary biologist, family therapist, and anthropologist all at the same time. It helped organize a great deal of material for me, from DNA, through individual, family, ethnic, and species levels, to a sense of God. In this schema, I was pleased to include another Bateson favorite, Jung's concept of pleroma, a mystic place in which all distinctions disappear (described in the "Seven Sermons to the Dead," now an appendix to Jung's [1965] biography). Given my uncertain attraction to logical typing, I was perversely pleased to read in Lipset (1980) that it was both an attraction and a cause of endless, sometimes rancorous, debate at MRI in the early 1960s.

Another legacy from Bateson has been family therapy itself. A nearly unknown mode of treatment before the 1960s, the field was launched by Bateson's research on schizophrenia and his take on systems theory. My own professional interest in the field dates to the break-up of my marriage in 1984; I started training as a family therapist the following year. I began practicing family therapy in 1986 and have also been teaching a course by that title for almost 10 years. In it I have tried to maintain a spirit of inquiry, but I can understand why Bateson left the field, given the competition of schools stressing this or that technique. The spirit of high-level inquiry is almost gone, particularly in an era of the quick fix, managed care, and competition for patients. For example, I lost a very close friend, a family therapist, because following his presentation to my class (which was something of an advertisement for himself), I felt compelled to ask about the honesty of an enterprise in which only successes are reported. In clinical lingo, this created a narcissistic wound, and he hasn't spoken with me since.

I knew Bateson before the era of sociobiology and the selfish gene, circa 1975, but I think I can guess his reaction. Genes are quanta, and biological information consists of patterns. To the extent that genes form patterns, the information becomes phenotypic—or conversely, as expressed by Lewontin (1974), the gene ripped from its genome becomes meaningless. In speaking, then, of "differences that make a difference," as Bateson did, genes per se are not news of a difference but rather their patterned effects, complex though that news must be. Genomic selection, then, must be via patterns, and the idea of selfishly endowed single genes would have been for Bateson a gross example of Whitehead's misplaced concreteness.

I seem always to have been a nondualist and therefore have gravitated to mentors who themselves were of that mind. Gregory certainly reinforced this sense, and in this spirit I dedicated to him a piece I wrote called, "The Social and the Biological: A Necessary Unity" (Freedman, 1980), which paraphrased his book's title, *Mind and nature: A necessary unity* (1979). It is probably at this near spiritual level that he has meant most to me. Appreciation of beauty, too, played a strong role in our commonality. I never heard him say, "truth is beauty and beauty is truth," but when we arrived in Bali and I was overcome and cried over the sheer beauty of the place, he understood completely. After all, a tear is an intellectual thing.

Some final words. I consider Bateson's sort of attainment as of another order than my own, and he has been larger than life for me—not only in retrospect, but also when we were together. He had the intelligence, the class, the family, and the education, all wrapped in three generations of Cambridge, perhaps the greatest university tradition the world has yet known. One has but to read the Bateson family letters to one another (Lipset, 1980) to see the ease with language, the high standards of honesty and articulateness, that would naturally awe someone with my background, a son of Yiddish-speaking small-town, middle-European immigrants.

However, when we were together, I simply felt I was with someone I enjoyed. I once met with Gregory and a former MRI colleague of his at Fisherman's Wharf in San Francisco, and the contrast between the two was instructive. The colleague was discussing how popular he had become, going around the country with a message of "what's new." For him, it was a sufficient level of abstraction to point out that in our culture people are continuously hungry for "what's new" and would pay to hear it. Gregory listened politely, but his mind was elsewhere. After the colleague left, we relaxed, and let our hearts and minds play over more congenial material. Perhaps we were alike in that we were both trying to describe God and that the everyday ways of the world were distractions, however necessary.

In this sense, I was perhaps as prepared for searching out the sacred as was Bateson, for my father's father had been a denizen of the synagogue of his small Polish village, searching for God day and night while his wife eked out a living. My own dad, a communist who "rejected" the Bible, was also a dreamer and a romantic Yiddish writer, and lack of success in the marketplace was for him a badge of honor. Via Lipset (1980) I understood the commonalities in our heritages: The Batesons were fierce atheists who found their way to God via William Blake, the great atheist theist. Blake was father William's and Gregory's favorite poet who, like them, sought the Real God in nature's ways. Further, William was always suspicious of his profession, science, because it did not touch the heart of the matter—for the heart was a matter for poets and, in his estimation, "true" genius.

This, perhaps, gets at Gregory's disposition to leave things partially unsaid. The Jews, after all, institutionalized that theme with G____, the matter being too great for designation. (The Navajos leave their rugs imperfect out of a similar sense of deity.) It is true that Gregory sometimes smiled knowingly, as if he had perceived some ultimate truth, but much of the time he was indeed in a quandary, and he is best described as oscillating between the two states. I loved him for it and have always been grateful for the truth it spoke.

## REFERENCES

Bartlett, F. C. (1932). *Remembering. A study in experimental and social psychology.* Cambridge: Cambridge University Press.

Bateson, G. (1972). *Form, substance, and difference.* In *Steps to an ecology of mind.* New York: Ballantine.

Bateson, G. (1979). *Mind and nature: A necessary unity.* New York: Dutton.

Bateson, G. (1991). *A sacred unity.* New York: Harper-Collins.

Benedict, R. (1934). *Patterns of culture.* Boston: Houghton-Mifflin.

Bohm, D. (1980). *Wholeness and the implicate order.* London: Ark.

Freedman, D. G. (1967, November). The origins of social behavior. *Science Journal,* 66–73.

Freedman, D. G. (1979). *Human sociobiology: A holistic approach.* New York: Free Press.

Freedman, D. G. (1980). The social and the biological: A necessary unity. *Zygon, 15,* 117–132.

Freedman, D. G., & Gorman, J. (1993). Attachment and the transmission of culture—An evolutionary perspective. *Journal of Social and Evolutionary Systems, 16,* 297–329.

Goldstein, K. (1939). *The organism.* New York: American Book.

Goldstein, K. (1951). *Human nature in the light of psychopathology.* Cambridge, MA: Harvard University Press.

Goldstein, K., & Scheerer, M. (1941). Abstract and concrete behavior—An experimental study with special tests. *Psychological Monographs,* Whole no. 39.

Gottesman, I. I. (1991). *Schizophrenia genesis: The origins of madness.* New York: W. H. Freeman.

Hoffman, E. (1988). *The right to be human: A biography of Abraham Maslow.* New York: St. Martin's Press.

Hull, C. L. (1930). Simple trial-and-error learning: A study in psychological theory. *Psychological Review, 37,* 241–256.

Jung, C. G. (1916). Seven sermons to the dead. Reprinted in C. G. Jung (1965), *Memories, dreams, and reflections* (pp. 378–390). New York: Vintage Books.

Lewontin, R. (1974). *The genetic basis of evolutionary change.* New York: Columbia University Press.

Lipset, D. (1980). *Gregory Bateson: The legacy of a scientist.* Englewood Cliffs, NJ: Prentice-Hall.

Maslow, A. H. (1936). The role of dominance in the social and sensual behavior of infra human primates. IV. The determination of hierarchy in pairs and groups. *Journal of Genetic Psychology, 49,* 161–198.

Mead, M. (1937). *Cooperation and competition among primitive peoples.* Revised edition, 1961. Boston: Beacon.

Sherrington, C. S. (1911). *The integrative action of the nervous system.* New Haven, CT: Yale University Press.

Schiller, C. H. (1997). *Instinctive behavior.* New York: International Universities Press.

Weiss, P. (1947). The problem of specificity in growth and development. *Yale Journal of Biology and Medicine, 19,* 235–278.

Whitehead, A. N., & Russell, B. (1910–1913). *Principia mathematica* (Vol. 1–3). Cambridge: Cambridge University.

Wilson, D. S., & Sober, E. (1994). Reintroducing group selection to the human behavioral sciences. *Behavioral and Brain Sciences, 17,* 585–654.

3

# Is Nonduality Possible in the Social and Biological Sciences? Small Essays on Holism and Related Issues

Daniel G. Freedman

*Look around you, and if you are not there as a separate person, you are experiencing nonduality.*

**H. W. L. Poonjaji on the Internet (1996)**

I have long been interested in the classic dichotomies: mind–body, heredity–environment, innate–acquired, culture–biology, atomism–holism and its various incarnations—individual versus group selection.

In each case my intuition led me to think about and wrestle with a nondichotomous position. This, in turn, has led me to Eastern Advaitist thought in which nonduality is acknowledged as a proper solution to the conundrums such divisions inevitably entail (Klein, 1984; Loy, 1988). In general, theoretical biologists do not employ such solutions, and, in fact, without dichotomies they would be largely out of work (see Sober, 1984).

The reductionism–holism debate, for one, is alive and well, and translates in recent times to the reductionism of such stellar biologists as

Williams (1966), Dawkins (1982), and Smith (1988) versus the holism of the new science of "complexity" (Waldrop, 1992). In this particular duality, I am renewed in my respect for holistic intuition, so creatively exhibited by Kauffman (1995, and see later discussion), in contrast to the brilliant but problematic reductionism of the sociobiology movement. This is not to say that that movement has not been extraordinarily productive, and I commented on this irony in 1979 in *Human Sociobiology*, which I subtitled "A holistic approach"—so that I could have my cake and eat it, too.

One of the major sins of reductionism was to relegate group selection to a minor, almost nonexistent role in natural selection by falsely invoking Occam's razor—and thereby misleading an entire generation of biologists (see Wilson & Sober, 1994). Mathematics, the "deciding" science, was used to prove a position based on the biased initial assumptions so pursuasively expressed by Williams (1966). I am compelled to add that, as a psychologist who had been steeped in holism and Gestalt thinking, Williams's reductive move had sounded familiar, so that despite being a stranger to the byways of biological research, I had intuitively rejected his derision of group selection.

A few words on the mind–body problem. In the 1950s, when I was a graduate student at the New School in New York, I attended a course on the mind–body problem offered by Wolfgang Köhler. He proposed *psychophysical isomorphism* as a solution (echoed by David Hull, 1984), the idea that neurology and mind are joined in some algorithmic way. This was his attempt to maintain, yet overcome, the classic fission. As a deeply committed scientist, Köhler pursued the idea with a series of interesting, but weakly supportive, experiments. My sense, even then, was that the problem would not be resolved by experiment, but that it would require some new mind set. Nor is this conclusion affected by Crick's (1994) sophisticated attempt to join up-to-date neural anatomy of the brain with "consciousness."

The following comments, then, are in this vein. They are attempts to examine familiar issues in a nondualistic way, using my strong suit, intuition, as well as the concepts of my mentors, particularly those of

Gregory Bateson. To begin with, I look back at my career and how it interfaces with this interest in nonduality.

## THE IDEOGRAPHIC AND THE AESTHETIC, THE CULTURAL AND THE BIOLOGICAL: LOOKING BACK ON A CAREER

My initial academic interests were clinical, and as an undergraduate at UC Berkeley and a graduate student at the City College of New York and the New School for Social Research, I favored courses with psychodynamic content. Thus, my introduction to behavior genetics was somewhat accidental. Under the influence of Konrad Lorenz, with his emphasis on naturalistic observation, and inspired as well by David Levy's psychodynamic hypothesis concerning psychopathy (Levy, 1943), my colleague, Norbett Mintz, and I had conducted some preliminary studies with puppies on the campus of Brandeis University (Freedman, 1967). It was a special pleasure for me to work with puppies, because I had completed a master's thesis at the University of Colorado with rats in which the animals were more or less tools for assessing theory, and I had felt little or no affection for the creatures. I can, in fact, imagine studies in which that could change—in other words, naturalistic studies of rodents in the wild where the excitement of discovery attends one's daily observations.

In our preliminary studies we exploited the sociality of the puppies by varying their early life experiences with humans in a number of ways. One of these ways involved rejecting their social advances, and I felt very bad over what I had agreed to do. I began to realize that if the "whole person" participates in a study, the investigator's own emotions become part of the findings. In the main study, conducted later at Bar Harbor, I had contracted to act in authoritarian fashion with one group of pups and as an indulgent parent with their littermates, behaviors that were actually two salient aspects of myself. As I think back, I am sure that the authenticity of my behavior played an important part in obtaining the clear-cut findings reported in my thesis (Freedman, 1957).

I must mention here that Lorenz, because of his general influence, became an important source of permission to do such personal and naturalistic work, and I feel deeply grateful for his humanization of animal study. At a more personal level, Dr. John Paul Scott, chair of behavioral research at Bar Harbor, was totally accepting of my joining the experimental and the natural, and he became a lifelong source of encouragement (see Scott, chapter 6, this volume).

The fact that the pups sorted themselves out according to breed was totally unexpected by me. I still recall my initial play with the indulged, when the pups were a beguiling 3 weeks of age: the eager interactions of the beagles; the already fierce little wire-haired terriers; the shy, dainty Shetland sheep dogs; and the aloof basenjis. Although this opened many intellectual pathways, I have remained committed to working in real relationship with my research participants, no matter the theoretical point. I am sure that the pleasure viewers experience over the films of this study (Freedman, 1962) is a result largely to the realness of the trainer–puppy encounters. It is no accident that my wife and collaborator, Jane Gorman, has also been disposed to doing studies based on real relationships, in the field of social work (Gorman, 1995).

The next major study was of a relatively small group of infant identical and fraternal twins ($N = 21$ pairs), again kept small so that I might know them all very well. Even so, the 21 pairs had to be divided between an assistant, Barbara Keller, and myself, so that we might do justice to these 42 developing lives. I have felt hurt on those few occasions when colleagues, from their perspective of studies of hundreds of twins, have derided the small *N*. To this day I seem incapable of conducting a study in which I cannot directly experience the participants in the study. We made a film of the twin study, which harkened back to my training at City College of New York with Katherine Wolf (Spitz & Wolf, 1946) in that it focused on two of Spitz's three *organizers*—the development of the smile and of the fear of strangers (he considered these milestones the behavioral equivalents of embryological organizers). It included footage of the development of the smile in Tony, my first child, and in a blind infant, and it also anticipated Carolyn Goren's thesis (discussed later).

The twin method evolved into further creative variations among my students: Marilyn DeBoer (1983) studied developing sex differences in infant boy–girl twins, and Nancy Segal (1988), in her well known work, studied competition and cooperation within monozygotic and dizygotic pairs. Nancy's most recent creative leap is her ongoing study of unrelated sibling pairs of the same age raised together (Segal, 1997, and this volume).

I continued my interest in ideographic research and filmed records while pursuing an NIMH postdoctoral fellowship at the Institute for Human Genetics in Uppsala, Sweden, in 1962–1963. In addition to taking courses, I filmed the development of two infants, one with Down's syndrome and the other blind from birth. Aside from being impressed with how loving both mothers were, I found that the Down's child progressed "normally" except that development was in slow motion. Everything was delayed, so that, for example, the social smile appeared at 5 months instead of at 3.

Yvonne, the blind child, was most interesting. Her nystagmus stopped when she smiled and "turned her eyes to" her mother's voice, or when her eyes shifted in the direction of a bell or a waft of fanned air. Also, at 3 months, I saw her "examining" her hands at length, as if she had sight. It suggested that this common developmental event, in which seeing 3-month-olds demonstrate a fascination with their hands, is largely maturational—perhaps a mechanism that ensures eye–hand coordination (reported in Freedman, 1964).

After the year in Sweden, where my second child, Gregory Anders, was born, we came to the University of Chicago where interactions with a wonderful group of students began and continue to this day. Somehow, the Committee on Human Development has always drawn spectacular people, although we faculty did not necessarily appreciate it at the time. Among the undergraduates who worked closely with me, and with whom I have stayed in contact, are Natalie Gans, Helmuth Hirsch (now a professor at SUNY Albany), Sharon Kayser, and Samir Ali. Some of the graduate students are contributors to this volume, but I want to mention a few who are not. Carolyn Goren, now PhD, MD, arrived with major research experience, and she proceeded to read all my reprints on infant behavior. She then designed a reasonably foolproof study to determine if there is an unlearned preference for simulated *moving* human faces in day-old newborns (inactive faces had yielded equivocal results), and that was, in fact, what she found (reported in Freedman, 1974). Later in medical school she repeated the study with infants 24 minutes or younger, and again the neonates preferred facial outlines over competing stimuli. Although the study was reported in a major journal, *Pediatrics* (Goren, Sarty, & Wu, 1975), it was obviously ahead of its time and was essentially ignored for one and a half decades. However, it has been recently replicated (twice) and featured in Johnson and Morton's *Biology and Cognitive Development* (1991), a book that is part of the "new" cognitive psychology (discussed later). This and many other studies by University of Chicago students, some "merely" term papers, were integrated into my book, *Human Sociobiology* (Freedman, 1979).

Other students whose PhD theses were highly original and anticipated later research developments were the gender and dominance–hierarchy studies of Omark and Edelman (1976), and a study by Joan Kuchner (1973) comparing Chinese and Caucasian mother–infant interactions over the first year of life. Dr. Kuchner, who has not yet published her findings, is still a unique reference in the field, and I have continually referred to her work (e.g., Freedman, 1979; Freedman & Gorman, 1993).

Soon after coming to Chicago, my first wife Nina, who was extraordinarily attuned to neonates, and I began our studies of ethnic differences in newborns. Using an examination schedule developed with T. Berry Brazelton (Brazelton & Freedman, 1971), we would spend an average of 45 minutes with each baby, recording both its behaviors and our subjective responses, sometimes filming the procedure. This was, in essence, our continuation of the puppy study, and we sought an answer to the question, "Are there human behavioral differences associated with inbreeding that are apparent at birth?"

The first study, comparing Chinese and Caucasian babies born in the Kaiser Hospital, San Francisco—over the same 2-month period, with the same doctors and procedures—provided clear-cut results: The Chinese newborns were less excitable, were easier to pacify when crying, habituated more readily to a penlight repeatedly shone on the eyes, tended not to swipe at a cloth placed over the nose, and were less bothered and less likely to cry when placed face-down in the bassinet (Freedman & Freedman, 1969). The results were disconcerting for many, because it was (and still is) a common misconception that significant group differences do not exist so early in life. A film, *Cross-Cultural Differences in Newborn Behavior* (Freedman, 1980), featured differences between Navajo and Caucasian newborns that were much like the Chinese–Caucasian comparisons. The film has proven very convincing and has demonstrated, again, the importance of collecting data that are simple, readily observable, and intuitively important.

At about this juncture (1972) my family and I went on an around-the-world trip with some 30 students, with Gregory Bateson as leader and myself as co-leader. The trip was an opportunity to continue research on newborns, and we obtained further data in Japan, Bali, Australia (Aboriginals), India, and Africa (Kenya). We also gathered considerable cross-cultural data on gender differences via children's drawings and videotapes of play (Freedman, 1976, 1979). Incidentally, while at Kobe Maternity Hospital, in Japan, I learned that Peter Wolff (see chapter 10, this volume) had been in residence the previous year, and it was evident that his forceful presence was still felt by the pediatric staff.

This trip changed the course of many lives, including my own. I returned with the romantic sense that I must henceforth obtain phenomenally authentic cross-cultural data and I, as a consequence, became a serious filmmaker. The results were two totally atheoretical films, *Navajo Childhood*, made with John W. Callaghan, who had been a student on the world trip; and *The Children of Edward River*, made in Aboriginal Queensland with my niece, Julie Singer Fleming. Both films were shot with a loving camera, and in *Edward River* the influence of Sergei Eisenstein's Mexican footage is perhaps visible as the camera lingers on Aboriginal children's faces. A third film on Hopi childhood was nipped short when I was asked to leave First Mesa where I thought I had been welcomed. This event led to considerable soul-searching about my true motivation for doing films—what part love and what part egocentric need for prestige?

After he spent a year in film school, Jack Callaghan, now chief of adult mental health in the state of New Mexico, and I cotaught a seminar on anthropological filmmaking, but the festering hurt of the experience on First Mesa and the difficulties of funding anthropological films brought this phase of my career to a halt. It had also become clear that my professional concerns and serious filmmaking were incompatible and, with the two films only partially completed, I somewhat reluctantly returned to the job of gathering data and writing. In addition to the ethical turmoil I experienced over filming native peoples, it is only now clear that I was conducting a war within myself, pitting the aesthetic and personal against the scientific and theoretic.

In the past dozen years I have attempted to wed these two forces in two ways. First, I returned to my clinical roots, and after training at Chicago's Institute of Family Therapy, I started a small, deeply satisfying private practice. Second, my students and I began comparative behavioral studies of mothers and toddlers of various ethnic groups. I must mention Dr. Sheila Smith, at present a director of the Fund for Child Development, as my first collaborator in this work (Smith & Freedman, 1982), conducted in Chicago's Chinatown. We made videotapes of mothers with their toddlers, in their homes, in "standard" situations (e.g., mother helping the child with a shape-sorter task).

Lonna Brooks (1990) followed Smith's work with a study of Korean 5-year-olds and 6-year-olds adopted into U.S. Caucasian families as young infants. Mothers and children were compared with both Korean and Caucasian biological dyads, and Brooks developed an excellent case for inborn temperamental differences between Asian and Caucasian populations. Her plan is to continue such studies using ethnic differences as a tool for the study of temperament. If these studies are funded, they may yield the most powerful data yet accumulated in the area of temperament.

In later studies, we subjected the videotapes of mothers and toddlers to Q-sort analysis with a 100-item sort we developed. The Q-sort's purpose was to provide a means of statistical assessment of qualitative events, and although our use of it is unique, certainly unlike anything its inventor foresaw (Stephenson, 1953), I think this marriage of the aesthetic and scientific has been reasonably successful. I owe great thanks to Professor Everett Waters for providing the software for scoring and assessing the sorts and for his general encouragement.

Over the years, I have personally gathered videotaped data on mothers and toddlers in Northern and Southern Italy (aided by Fausto and Antonella Massimini), and from Israeli kibbutzim, Arab villages, and White families with adopted Korean children in the United States. Students have gathered comparable tapes in Korea, India, China, and Iceland, and among Chinese, Japanese, Bengalis, and Koreans living in the United States. It has all been Q-sorted and coded by a number of undergraduate assistants who were generally more computer literate than I.

More recently, we have started to administer the clinically sensitive Adult Attachment Interview (George, Kaplan, & Main, 1985) to the mothers. Studies using the AAI include the theses of Olafsdottir (1991), Kim (1994), and Mitra (1994), and a manuscript in progress (Park, Yue, & Freedman). Aside from the interesting study by Messinger comparing autonomous behavior in Japanese and Caucasian-American 2-year-olds (Messinger, 1987; Messinger & Freedman, 1993), these data have yet to be organized for publication, but Vala Olafsdottir and I are working on a paper focusing on the very striking results from Iceland. The detachment between mothers and toddlers, sometimes painful to watch, are echoed in Icelandic mothers' memories of their own childhoods and, incidentally, in the work of one of Iceland's greatest modern writers, H. K. Laxness (1957).

At present, I am retired from the University of Chicago and living in a wonderful adobe home in rural New Mexico, where meditation and thinking about nonduality seem quite natural. As I enter the seventh decade of life my thoughts quite naturally have turned to the eternal—the big picture—and it has perhaps become too easy to set aside the writing of grant requests and the other workaday tasks of an academic. The practical effects are most evident in my teaching, which is far more heart-centered than in the past, and I give and receive love as never before. Some further thoughts along this line are presented in the last section of this chapter.

## ESSAYS

### Evolutionary Biology

E. O. Wilson's (1975) *Sociobiology* was a great landmark work that was important because of its encyclopedic breadth and theoretical force. It has helped change the face of biopsychology, lending it the theory that was to replace the innate–learned simplicity of ethology (see later discussion). The new theory was based in the vision that competing, replicating genes were the basis of life, and that organisms, however complex, were merely vehicles for genes.

It seems apparent now, but did not then because of the excitement attending its introduction, that sociobiological theory is inflated to the extent that it conceives of itself as having a lock on the basic units of life. That was the essence of Wilson's Herculean claim that the social sciences would eventually become biologized. I initially went along with this self-proclaimed leadership, proving my fickle allegiance to holism. Second and third thoughts have brought me back to the mountain, where one can at least glimpse the whole—seen as a nested hierarchy in the appendix to Freedman and Gorman (1993). Science can hope to avoid self-delusion only by keeping in mind the Korzybski injunction: The map is not the territory (theory is not sacred)!

Evolutionary psychology (Barkow, Cosmides, & Tooby, 1992) is the newest product of sociobiology and asks, "Has natural selection shaped how humans reason?" It is a welcome demonstration that psychology and evolutionary biology are, in fact, not separable disciplines, and to that extent it is changing the face of cognitive psychology. Like Jerry Fodor (1983), Cosmides and Tooby (1992) think in terms of inherited modules that guide our social intercourse, but *modules* suggest fixed neural networks in the brain. Goldstein would have doubted, or at least tempered, such a proposition, given his data on brain reorganization in response to injury (Goldstein, 1939). However, progress involves one step at a time, and this biological move into psychology is definitely progress.

## Ecology and Group Selection

D. S. Wilson (1980), who helped resuscitate group selection for younger biologists, is a key player in this field, as is my colleague at the University of Chicago, Michael Wade (1982). I know it has been frustrating for them and their students not to get the recognition they have long deserved. The theoretical centrality of genes (replicators) and individuals as their "vehicles" (Dawkins, 1982) is so predominant in biology that group selectionists, despite having logic and common sense on their side, have been kept peripheral. I believe the Wilson and Sober (1994) article, aimed directly at the behavioral sciences, is of sufficient scope to help change this climate.

Wilson and Sober do an excellent job of restating the issues in terms of Dawkins's own vehicle metaphor. If the organism is a vehicle for genes, the gene is a vehicle for base pairs, and the social group a vehicle for individuals. However, for Wilson and Sober this nested hierarchy ends at the point at which competition between vehicles can no longer occur, and so, unlike myself (see appendix to Freedman & Gorman, 1979), they dismiss the Gaia hypothesis because evolution of a homeostatic planet (Gaia), in standard Darwinism, would require interplanetary competition.

That seems a rather rigid adherence to the claim that nothing new emerges save through competition (something Sober has elsewhere denied; see Sober, 1984), and it appears in the Wilson and Sober (1994) article that they chose to steer clear of emergence. However, there is no evidence that homeostasis in organisms, to take one example, came about through competition between organisms, and it may well be an instance of Kauffman's (1995) organization "for free" (see later discussion). Atomic organization (nuclei surrounded by electrons) and the appearance of sexuality may also qualify as emergent organizations, for I know of no reasonable causal models. Both George Williams (1975) and John Maynard Smith (1975), ardent reductionists though they are, agree that there is no satisfactory reconstruction of the origins of sexuality or of meiosis.

## Self-Organizing Systems

There is something aesthetically pleasing about the organization "for free" that Stuart Kauffman both posits and documents (1995). It is in the tradition of Harold Urey who, in assessing research into the origin of life, proposed that, given the earth's circumstances, life was not a longshot but inevitable (see Miller & Orgel, 1974). The idea is that "cause" can be an unpredictable set of circumstances, as when hydrogen and oxygen join into water. In a similar way, points of equilibrium or organization in developing complex systems can occur with the sudden unique and unpredictable interplay of parts, particularly when the mix is on the verge of chaos. This sounds much the same as the *emergence* that reductive learning theorists rejected philosophically as a "doctrine of despair." I thus see in psychology's Gestalt versus learning theory debates of the 1930s and 1940s a preview of what is today happening in biology on a grander scale.

Kauffman, however, is not polemical and does not contrast "organization for free" with reductive Darwinism—but he does call himself an "unrepentent holist," and Darwinism, as currently defined, relies rather exclusively on causal explanation at the level of genes or individuals (1995). It must, then, be very disconcerting for a convinced sociobiological reductionist to try to amalgamate Kauffman's considerable data into the reductive world view, and I know of no one who has formally accepted the challenge.

I believe more sins have been committed in turning from emergence than in its acceptance. For example, in trying to avoid the accusation of *vitalism*—the notion that there is a special life force—Lorenz began to analyze behavioral "mechanisms" into chains of "intercalated" links of learned versus innate behaviors (Freedman, 1982; Lorenz, 1965). Although such analyses were amazingly fruitful with insects, fish, and birds, they were essentially useless with mammals for which learning is involved in every phase of behavior. My own contribution to the 1964 meeting of the International Ethological Congress in Zurich was meant to save the day by introducing the nondual term *evolved behavior* to replace both *innate* and *acquired*, because "evolved" was not opposed to "learned," which logically had also evolved (reproduced in Freedman, 1979, pp. 141–143). That particular congress was not ready to hear such a proposal, but after many years of thinking about it, my good friend and colleague, Erich Klinghammer, eventually informed me that I was "right." I must admit that after having experienced considerable ill will in Zurich, the positive feedback from a committed ethologist made me feel good.

## GENETICS: FROM SINGLE NOTES TO MELODIES, AND FROM DICHOTOMY TO COMPLEXITY

In recent years the evidence for genetic influences on behavior, both normal and abnormal, has become overwhelming (e.g., *Nature Genetics*, 1996). The future of experimentation seems exceptionally exciting: Genes can be excised from one species and implanted in another; parts of chromosomes can be excised, inverted, transplanted, and the organism can be studied for phenotypic effects. However, genetic *patterns* will probably become objects of inquiry as more sophisticated techniques are developed, for we know that is how the great majority of genes are phenotypically expressed (Lewontin, 1974). If the genes are notes, we will soon be seeking the melodies, harmonies, and rhythms that they, as an assemblage, form (e.g., Lykken, McGue, & Tellegen, 1992).

As far as I know, all models of heritability artfully separate heredity and environment and, thus, at its very core the field is based on a problematic duality. Although dualities indeed generate considerable literature, because there are contradictions at every step, they eventually fail, as in the innate–acquired "opposition." I once wrote a piece on the well-known logical slipperiness of the 60–40 solution to heredity and environment. The point was that in one setting 60% of the variation of a hypothetical trait may be hereditary and 40% may be environmental, whereas in another setting 40% of the variation may be hereditary and 60% environmental (reprinted in Freedman, 1979).

I thus have been very fond of the Scarr and McCartney (1983) proposal that genotypes seek out their own environments and that by implication there is recurring feedback between genotype and environment. This is not merely "interaction" between two separable elements—it is the acknowledgment that a cybersystem exists with so-called parts that are dynamic and evanescent, and that do not really exist as entities. If behavior genetics is to thrive, feedback dynamics of this complex order must be modeled and, indeed, a growing number of behavior geneticists and developmental psychologists are addressing this issue (e.g., Bronfenbrenner & Ceci, 1993; Goldsmith, 1993).

## BEHAVIOR GENETICS AND RACE

When the field of behavior genetics deals with race it is largely around the issue of the heritability of intelligence. I recently attended a public lecture by Mark Feldman, of Stanford University, called "The Bell Curse." The title told it all. It was a scientific rave against estimates of heritability at the $h = 0.70$ level, as advocated, in this instance, by Thomas Bouchard and colleagues (Bouchard, Lykken, McGue, Segal, & Tellegen, 1990). This was clearly a political lecture the point of which was that good (liberal) thinkers advocated 0.3 and bad (conservative) thinkers 0.7. When an audience member noted that even 0.3 is potentially meaningful, Feldman, essentially negating his entire lecture, said the numbers were not important. Although the numbers clearly show that biology has a major impact on intelligence, I tend to agree with his final position in which he seemed to be trying to escape the duality. Only if one gets beyond the numbers war are fruitful and creative discussions possible, for the nastiness about who has the right number resembles a domestic squabble in which both sides feel hurt, unheard, and defensive.[1]

Lewontin (1972) "solved" the race issue by declaring the word *race* scientifically unusable because there are no genetically delineable races, a position more recently espoused in Cavalli-Sforza, Menozzi, and Piazza (1994). These are attempts by well-meaning biologists to combat racism, but, phenomenally, "race" is an everyday reality. A notorious researcher in this area is J. Philippe Rushton, often persona non grata at meetings because of his politically incorrect message: Compared to Caucasian and Asian individuals, individuals of African descent are on average more sexually active, stronger and quicker, more volatile, smaller-skulled, less capable in abstract intellectual skills, and more likely to get in trouble with the law—not just in the United States and England but worldwide (Rushton, 1995). Insofar as they are gathered from a wide variety of sources, the data Rushton has assembled are not readily dismissible, although many have tried. Barash's (1995) review of Rushton (1995), for example, was so emotionally charged and vicious that it was best seen as an act of exorcism for the reviewer.

My major problem with Rushton's book, as it was with Jensen's (1969) monograph, is not with the assemblages of data but with the emotionally distant nature of the scientific presentations. In this arena, especially, cold science will not do, *for only with love and warmth will the proper things be looked at, the proper things said, and a sympathetic picture of the study participants emerge.* An example of what I mean are the studies of the Yanomamo Indians by Napoleon Chagnon (1972, 1988). The Yanomamo, as a group, were often mean and nasty, but Chagnon's commitment, respect, and affection always shines through. (It is ironic to note that

[1] *Heritability* refers to the proportion of observed phenotypic variation in a population that is associated with genetic factors. The wide range in heritability estimates reported for IQ can be explained by several factors, such as the method of estimation and the age of the sample. Direct estimates of heritability, which are based on biological relatives reared apart (e.g., monozygotic twins separated at birth), tend to exceed indirect estimates of heritability, which are based on the difference between two correlations (e.g., biological versus nonbiological parent–child pairs). Until recently, the vast majority of IQ analyses have been based on children. Recent studies indicate that estimates of genetic influence on individual differences in intelligence increase from childhood to adulthood; see McGue, Bouchard, Iacono, & Lykken (1993) and references therein. Extended discussion of this issue is available in Plomin (1990).—Eds.

because of his sociobiological orientation, he has been forced to defend himself against charges of racism; see Chagnon, 1989). Lorenz has said, and I agree, that affectionate regard should be an integral part of the scientific method, whether working with animals or humans. I might add that, if at all possible, this should hold even when working with other people's data.

At the level of logic, the counter-argument to Rushton's collection of data usually takes the form, "You cannot transfer data gathered from individuals to groups, for groups have distinct histories (e.g., oppression and no tradition of schooling), and this could bring the group average down without affecting heritability." Although that is a position similar to the one I take regarding the psychologizing of culture (next section), when it comes to biology and culture I tend to think in terms of people fashioning their own environments (their own cultures, if you will), which of course renders the heritability model, and the separation of heredity from environment, problematic. That is, if low intelligence affects crime statistics, and if a familial history of crime affects offspring intelligence, where does environment leave off and heredity start? Further, as already mentioned, the concept of heredity–environment "interaction" is here barely helpful.

One intellectual solution to judgments about biological determinism is to admit the problems with present models of heritability and, as suggested earlier, focus on the construction of models that take account of the obvious fact that genotypes affect their own environments. It is, of course, hard to imagine that such a model would serve to lessen the severity of interracial judgments, because it can be taken to imply that ghetto inhabitants are responsible, in a biological sense, for the ghetto, and that superior ability seeks out good schools and subsequent wealth.

Thus, behavior genetics is not a tool for fighting prejudice and neither fosters nor ameliorates it. Prejudice is a way of hierarchizing groups, and as Sumner (1906) suggested, the syndrome is largely "built-in," so that we need little teaching to develop the sense that our own group is the better one (see the last section). For this reason, I have generally eschewed classroom discussions of race unless all the participants first dig down and find the part of themselves that is racist. Only then is there the possibility of learning something about ourselves and about racism.

## PSYCHOLOGY'S FUNCTIONAL BLINDNESS TO CULTURE: THE CASE OF ATTACHMENT THEORY

High on the list of "patterns that make a difference" (Bateson, 1972) is culture, but the majority of psychologists and evolutionary psychologists do not take its effects seriously. They necessarily give it lip service but act as if the phenomena they are working with (e.g., attachment, altruism) have dimensions apart from culture and, thus, can be universalized at the individual level, independently of culture. That's like trying to understand the function of a liver while giving lip service to the organism—it has recognizable dimensions, but it is nigh impossible to assess function once it has been removed.

Let us consider attachment theory and work in that area as a case in point. The central concept of the internal working model (IWM) conveys the idea that early social experiences frequently act as models or guides for subsequent social encounters in one's life. It is as if expectancies or forecasts are set up via the child's unique and generally unconscious interpretations of its first (and most salient) social experiences. As a result we organize our lives so that familiar outcomes generally occur again and again, whether painful, joyous, or in between. The evolutionary mechanism seems akin to that in animal imprinting, a built-in need to learn the details of the early caretaking environment so that social and sexual relationships are appropriately negotiated within that generation.

What we humans learn within our families of origin about how people relate is rarely straightforward, and frequently pain and anxiety enhance the process. Much of this learning is, thus, what Bateson termed "deutero" learning—learning about how to learn, and this would appear to be the basis of our IWMs. Such deutero learning must also be reflective of the family's many-layered surroundings—in other words, the culture in all its aspects.

At this theoretical level there is probably little to argue with. However, the attachment literature merely flirts with cross-cultural context (as in the cross-cultural selections in the edited monograph of Bretherton & Waters, 1985), and it has only minimally gone beyond reporting the relative frequencies of the three types of attachment (along with recently added subtypes). Thus, the logical problem with attachment research, done cross-culturally, is that the studies are largely centered on individual differences, without seriously shifting to the next higher level of organization (culture) even when the data cry out for such refocusing (LeVine & Miller, 1990). Growing up, for example, German or as an Israeli kibbutznik are obviously very different experiences, but attachment research has thus far not centered on such comparative realities.

Freedman and Gorman (1993) presented a systems view of attachment, which is quite simple: One's IWM is set early by a combination of genetic predispositions and by one's unique experience within the family, itself operating within a social–cultural context. In our Chinese data, for example, obtained from mothers who had been young children during the Cultural Revolution, it was clear that the entire cohort had been variously affected by the disruptions of that era, and that birth order, temperament, parental character, and other individual factors interacted in complex ways with the political events of the time. It was further evident that, as a cultural group, these Chinese mothers were very different from our U.S. mothers, and that what their own children were experiencing (and the IWMs they were acquiring) were, in very important ways, culturally filtered. Say, then, that this population can be apportioned into the standard categories of attachment (there is no reason to believe it cannot), an exclusive focus on these individual differences would downplay, if not eliminate, the culturally mediated information. Stated another way, individual differences and culture are not *two things* but are rather *two aspects of one thing.*

As for the classification system itself, securely attached children, like self-actualized persons, seem to represent idealized categories. Sroufe and Fleeson (1986) reported that securely attached kids are a pleasure to be with and that teachers love them because they are dependable, easy-going, and helpful to others. I am told (S. Hans, 1995, personal communication) that ghetto schools probably have fewer such children. If so, attention would naturally shift to the societal level from the level of individual differences, perhaps with the question, "What does population *A* have that population *B* does not have?" To my mind, only if the individual level can shed light on such a primary question does the investigation of attachment classifications of ghetto families become sensible.

The message is by now familiar: To be alert to the right questions requires wide-ranging vision, and a minimal requirement seems to be nonallegiance to any one academic discipline or level of organization.

## LIBIDO, PERSONAL WHOLENESS, AND SCIENCE

What motivates an anthropologist? I loved driving on Nigerian back roads with Bob LeVine in 1969 (see chapter 13, this volume). I recall with particular pleasure flirtations along the road (where participants are safe from consequences), as remarkably beautiful young women, working in the fields or carrying packs on their heads, waved and smiled as we slowly and appreciatively passed. What better way to lose your heart to a place than through such passing sensuality? Many of my fondest travel memories are of flirtatious exchanges: Quebec, China, Japan, Italy, Africa all evoke memories made sweeter by flirtation. The French were on to something when they made it an integral part of their lives, and perhaps flirting prepared me for the generalized love I feel for most living creatures, in these my later, more Whitmanesque years.

Is there more to this? I once wrote the start of a paper ("Towards Libidinized Research"), the theme of which was that sensuality ought to be considered part of good research design. My own love for puppies and babies was the primary ingredient in my early studies—and the actual research was devised after heart and reason were rejoined. When I think of the average dissertation in my department, wider displays of investigator sensuality would have helped enliven a very dour intellectual climate. Head and heart were rarely joined at the University of Chicago, and students learned to rely on the former and to keep the latter under wraps, however respectfully.

Some of my saddest experiences at the university were with some potentially creative students who lacked the courage to "follow their bliss," despite encouragement to do so. They instead followed a professor's program and spent their considerable energies on minor issues. They were probably never to know the thrill of truly original exploration, for it is rare for students to change their scripts after graduation. As Abraham Maslow often intoned, if you do not do what you are capable of, you can only become cynical.

In some way this is tied to issues of honesty in doing research as well as engaging in clinical work. I stopped my early clinical career when I was compelled to act more "together" than I felt, and I resumed it, many years later, when I was closer to being myself in the session. It obviously takes some of us time and much introspective work to feel whole, and my dissatisfaction with presenting a partial self to a client felt much like my dissatisfaction with dichotomous theory. At some deep level both seem lacking and dishonest.

## FAMILY THERAPY AND SYSTEMS THEORY

Holism and systems theory are, logically, closely related. Holism enjoins us to take an imagined look at the whole while working on the parts—in order not to lose sight of a part's role in the functionally whole *organism.* Systems theory appears to go further by specifying how a part relates to other parts in the *system* (von Bertalanffy, 1981). In Goldstein's notion of holism the system in question was the organism, whereas for Bateson (1972) the holistic vision was extended to societies, ecology—or to any context the mind might devise, including the mystic.

*Cybernetics* introduced feedback into systems theory. Because the term comes from engineering (Wiener, 1948), it is concerned with the mathematical details of closed systems and, as in anti-aircraft gunnery, there is a practical aspect to how it deals with feedback. This lent Bateson's transfer of cybernetics to family organization a sense that one could engineer change in families—a belief most notably explored by Don Jackson and the short-term therapy group at the Palo Alto Mental Research Institute (e.g., Haley, 1963). If the family is indeed a cybernetic system, can we not reengineer how the parts participate in the whole?

The trouble is that families are less like closed anti-aircraft systems and more like relatively open ecosystems. Every family member is intertwined with one another even as each seeks his or her own way, and it all happens within a cultural and sociopolitical setting. It would, thus, take someone with enormous hubris (or unusual creativity—e.g., Madanes, 1995) to try to reengineer such an intricately organized system. When a strategy goes well, it is a time for celebration, but I should like to see a collection of failed maneuverings to counterbalance the more frequently reported heart-warming successes, for the failures might well be more instructive.

To elaborate, family therapy is often unknowingly contending with larger biosocial systems. For example, the monogamous family, which family therapists are more or less committed to preserve, is—from an evolutionary perspective—a temporary conjugal alliance, now weakly propped by cultural and religious convention (e.g., Symons, 1979). The current pattern in the United States of male remarriage, in which a mother and her children are left on their own, is (among other things) a consequence of our economic largesse. Or, consider that at the level of individual differences, temperament and "internal working models" acquired early in life have a biosocial fixity that affects all family systems (Freedman & Gorman, 1993).

It may be because of this complexity of relationships between systems (geopolitical, socioeconomic, biosocial, familial) that there is a fairly constant eye out for what is new in treatment, because present methods are never sufficient. At the 1996 meetings of the American Family Therapy Association it was the relatively new narrative approach that received the biggest play: Respectfully listen to people's stories and thereby help them to respect their own individuality.

I am no longer practicing, but my own approach, although not antithetical to narrative, has been most like the one suggested by Carl

Whitaker (e.g., Whitaker & Malone, 1981): Good therapy depends on a therapist who is growing as much as the patients, and when he or she stops growing (when it becomes a craft), therapy ceases. In other words, therapy has to constantly remain an adventure for everyone concerned.

Given the complexity of systems acting on and within the family, hitting the right therapeutic notes would involve both wide-ranging knowledge and an active, trustworthy intuition. Regarding this balance, I am reminded of Pascal's (1670/1941) warning against an imbalance between logic and intuition. Watch out, he said, for mathematicians who have no intuition and who "wish to treat matters of intuition mathematically," and for intuitive persons who ignore the "first principles" of logic.

Along with Whitaker, I believe that a therapist who has worked on himself or herself a great deal—say through therapy and self reflection, and thereby honed a relatively accurate intuition—is in a good position to come up with correct therapeutic action, whatever it may be. Whitaker's position was that even a bad hunch sprung from the therapist's unconscious gets people into those levels of existence in which they need to be. I like to think that the remarks of Jean Klein (1984), the Advaitist philosopher, offer a parallel idea when he said (to paraphrase), "It is not in words but in a deeply respectful space of silence that creative interaction occurs."

It is ironic that Bateson was himself never interested in "curing," and perhaps even looked down on such hubris. But he always maintained an attitide of "respectful understanding" with his patients and families, the element Frieda Fromm-Reichmann (1960) considered most basic to psychotherapy. Along with Whitaker, who bragged that he was crazy, Bateson was even more authentically as much patient as therapist, and I cannot imagine a patient of his having the sense of being scrutinized or used. We are all in this together was his message—as indeed we are.

## NATURE–NURTURE

If we look back at Darwin's (1872) *Expression of Emotion in Man and Animals* we see that we have actually learned a great deal about social organization in animals since that time. Modern thinking about primate behavior, for example, takes the hierarchized social group as a unit and sees such units as interacting on a regular basis with neighboring troops. Darwin knew none of this. Nor did he know of wolf-pack behavior nor of how wild cats behaved. The new knowledge of primate intra- and intertroop behavior has given human ethnocentrism a phyletic footing, and when a modern animal behaviorist sees ethnic cleansing in Bosnia and Rwanda, he or she realizes that there is a strong biological element at work and that "pseudo-speciation" (Lorenz's term) of the other group is the rule rather than the exception.

The academic left's response to such biologizing has been to call it "marketplace science" (e.g., Sahlins, 1976), but it seems clear enough by now that all extant economic systems have exhibited Sumner's self-serving, ethnocentric traits (Sumner, 1906), and that, once again, the duality of biology versus culture just does not work. Dividing the human world into nature and nurture makes analysis possible, but it is an analysis that is always problematic because of the artificially separated parts. It recalls the Zen scholar D. T. Suzuki's admonition to psychiatry, "You have taken heredity and environment apart, and now you are stuck with putting them together again." To me this division clearly entails a problem in logic, yet such analyses are the rule (K. Bailey, 1996; Boyd & Richerson, 1985; Dawkins, 1976; Durham, 1978; Ruse, 1979).[2]

I take it that LeVine and Campbell (1972) would now give a biological interpretation greater centrality than when their studies of ethnocentrism first appeared. I am not so sure about Bateson. According to Haley (see Lipset, 1980), he was deeply biased against power as an innate motive, and so preferred to speak of a wrong-headed epistemology—which of course would be located in the mind. In the Korzybski lecture, Bateson

[2]The inseparability of nature and nurture in fashioning behavioral phenotypes of *individuals* is acknowledged by behavioral genetic researchers. However, statistical separation of these effects enables estimates of the extent to which they may influence observed behavioral variation at the *population level.* Such analyses may, thus, serve as an early step toward elucidating the specific mechanisms underlying individual differences in behavior. If, for example, a given behavior showed little genetic variation, attention could be appropriately directed toward identifying trait-relevant environmental influences on its development. Extended discussion of this issue is presented in Plomin (1986, 1988) and in Plomin, DeFries, and McClearn (1990).—Eds.

(1972) admitted working on the extension of his own boundaries, and he perhaps saw power and egocenteredness as facultative traits—and that the pertinent hormones could be neutralized by improving one's epistemology. Dualities are attractive because they provide a platform on which to take a stand. They imply that we can do something to improve our lot (nurture), or they can reinforce a "superior," cynical stance (nature), or for the more sensitive, they permit us to vacillate between the two.

Part of the problem addressed is precisely sociobiology's marriage to duality. What originally seemed like a solution—that nature leads and nurture follows—was pleasing to those of us impatient with the hegemony of learning theory. But the focus is back on the split so that Dawkins (1976/1991), for example, divided replication in two, genes for our bodies, memes for our cultural memories, and as already mentioned, this has been taken up by many others in ours and adjacent fields. [Kauffman (1995) is the first, I believe, to use the idea of memes in a meaningful way: His far-ranging search for autocatalytic self-organization has taken him from the biotic soup of 2 billion years ago, to the formation of cells, through embryogenesis, to immune and economic systems. Thus, for him "memes" are not in dualistic contrast with genes but rather are a potential tool for analyzing cultures for creative successions between chaos and organization.]

In general, when it comes to altruism versus selfishness, the sociobiological point is that altruism is most easily directed to kin, ergo it is a selfish altruism. Any further altruism involves expectation of reciprocation (Trivers, 1971), with the implication that this is either not biological or less biological, as in game theory (see later discussion).

Perhaps ironically, a nondual view would hold that we are *evolutionarily* of two minds. We favor our own but try, nevertheless, to be fair because of an equally innate inner goddess of love who may be compromised but not defeated by our selfish intentions. Such a view rejects, if only on logical grounds, the dualistic idea that biological selfishness is basic, whereas the job of culture, with its legal systems, is to restrain evil and make us better than we really are. Freud, Spencer, and Darwin all entered a similar duality in their respective discussions of self-interest versus cooperation when each concluded that self-interest is biologically more basic than cooperation.

This was the point that aroused Kropotkin to write the articles that became *Mutual Aid* (1914), which he intended as an addendum to Darwinism rather than as an argument against it. Kropotkin has, however, been effectively ignored—because to individually oriented biologists, cooperation appears antithetical to the survival of the fittest, unless it is self-seeking, as in game theory (Axelrod & Hamilton, 1981). In a similar sense, Allee's work (1938), which points to the phyletic history of cooperation, is not currently "important." Let me, then, note that Nancy Segal's (1988) studies of cooperation and competition between identical and fraternal twins indeed indicated that kinship genetics played a strong role: Identical twins were sometimes more competitive than cooperative with one another, yet they were better able to "inhibit selfishness" than were fraternal pairs (see chapter 7, this volume). The general results, however, bear out Kropotkin and Allee in that cooperative effort came easily, and self-centeredness and cooperation were most often simultaneously present. From a phenomenological view, all this is obvious, and the current biological irrelevance of cooperation seems a case of theory determining perception.

## AN EVOLUTIONARY VIEW OF SUFFERING AND CONCLUDING WORDS ON NONDUALISM

I recently had a clarifying vision of our globe, with its different time zones and daylight hours, different cultures and languages, different modes of child-rearing, various hostilities, goodnesses, talents, and so forth. Within each setting, I saw individual lives being played out, each with its own complement of suffering and happiness, no matter the social class. Unlike the compassionate Buddha, who vowed not to rest until all who suffer might find peace, I am more inclined to see suffering as universal and as always awaiting a chance to reappear, in all cultures and economic systems.

Strange to say, this point of view has been handled at a scientific level in the work of James Neel. He and his group (e.g., Neel & Ward, 1970) have gathered evidence among South and Central American Indian tribes that a process of *lineal fissioning* (splitting along lines of kinship) is responsible for tribal proliferation. Based on Chagnon's (e.g., 1979) observations among the Yanomamo of Venezuela as a basis for interpretation of data from some 12 tribal groups, it would appear that when tribes reach a population of about 350 individuals, there is an increasing likelihood of competing kinship factions—which, in turn, often induces the weaker faction to leave the village. They either join with another village or else found a new one, with their former second cousins (the average level of kinship in a village) now the enemy. It is presumed that this process repeats generation after generation, and as it proceeds, dialect distinctions turn into language distinctions. Also, judging by blood group differentiation among villages, Neel estimated that rates of evolution are 100 times those found in other mammals. Neel felt that this may indeed have been a basic process of human dispersal, one that eventually propelled our species into every available niche on earth.

I have used this example many times (most recently in Freedman & Gorman, 1993) because it seems to account for much about the human species. It tells us that both kinship cohesion and intergroup aggression are basic to human dispersal and intergroup relationships, and it seems clear that exactly those factors enter into almost all tribal altercations, most recently Bosnia and Rwanda. I have tried to apply the Neel–Chagnon model, in a nonmathematical way, to the Australian Aboriginal situation, and I believe it best accounts for the (precontact) existence of some 650 tribes in firmly held territories, spread over the entire continent in a matter of just 2200 years (Freedman, 1986). Australia provides an exceptional laboratory, having been largely isolated for more than 40,000 years, and it would be of great scientific value for someone gifted in mathematics to reconstruct the human occupation using several models to see which best accounts for the timing and tribal dispersal so painstakingly documented by Tindale (1974).

Chagnon's data (1972, 1979, 1988), in particular, offer several biobehavioral staples: At the intragroup level, he has demonstrated allegiance to close kin, male dominance–submission hierarchies, and polygamy—with the most feared, dangerous males possessing more wives and leaving more offspring. The intergroup level features ethnocentrism, anger with "previous" relatives, warfare, murder, exogamy (including the stealing of wives), and temporary intergroup alliances to make war on common enemies—a list of behaviors made-to-order for sociobiology.

I think it is clear, at this historical juncture, that sociobiology provides a more realistic model of group relations and human nature than, say, that espoused in the Union of Soviet Socialist Republics, based as it was on a dream of human brotherhood that turned into an autocratic nightmare. I came from a left-wing family that believed in that dream and then watched it disintegrate. However, unhappy with the cynicism that sociobiology seems to encourage (everything is basically selfish), I have found in Eastern nondualism (say, Advaita Hinduism as exemplified by the *Bhagavad Gita*) the coherence of good and evil sporting a single face. The death camps of Hitler and the love-ins at Esalen are both features of my species, and although I personally cannot forgive the former and can barely participate in the latter, I can (on occasion) envision a state of being in which there are no distinctions of love and hate, good and evil, as in Jung's *pleroma* (a sacred, mystic realm, beyond distinctions, enveloping and interspersed with the one we inhabit as creatures; Jung, 1916). I have heard Jacques Derrida's brilliant deconstruction of linguistic distinctions, boundaries, and categories and thought to myself, only in pleroma, or nonduality, is this savage critique undisturbing (see Loy, 1988).

Bateson was deeply attracted to Jung's magical little paper, but what he called *immanent mind* (as opposed to *transcendent mind*) is as far as Bateson went with mysticism. By holding that the mind is immanent in all things, mind becomes our sacred organ, our way to God. Transcendence was the church's way, immanence the direct (gnostic) way of experiencing the sacred, as when tearfully touched by the beauty of ordinary things—a bird, a hill, a cloud. Bateson tended not to use the word *love*, but perhaps feeling perpetual love is the way to perpetual immanence. This suggests a definition of interpersonal "enlightenment" as *perpetually experiencing love—even when angry or annoyed* (something my cat helped clarify). I have teased my children that the mistakes I made with them—for example, getting so angry as to lose sight of love—helped me to properly raise my pets. However, getting older, a lowered testosterone level, and spiritual healing have doubtless helped me get beyond my Yanomamo self.

A final word and a confession of the obvious: Writing this chapter has been very helpful. I see more clearly my tendency to take a biological stance in the nature–nurture debate, as well as my militant pro-holism/anti-reductionism stance, despite the fact that I have long taught and defended the sociobiological vision. This militance, along with a need to invent enemies, is a longstanding fault, and it is at some level clear to me that nonduality does not concern itself with the distinctions I have upheld. Yet, as an argumentative and often times angry scientist, bent on asserting what I considered superior logic, I had in the past known no other way.

Nonduality cannot be reached through argument. The only way I know to see or experience it is through intuition accompanying meditative practice. That is, it is finally seeing something that is already there. For many, including myself, such practice has been a natural continuation of psychotherapy, in which one also seeks wholeness by working on the self, and it is as if dualism is an epistemological neurosis. Some day I hope to spell this out, but for now I will assert that a mind/heart located in nonduality is wondrous, loving, and infinite. I experience this from time to time and, naturally, hope to experience it more often, perhaps even as a steady state.

With regard, then, to the question in the title, the answer requires that investigators first shed dualism, say through meditative practice, and then, if they are indeed still investigators, let their science follow. My guess is that studies based in nonduality will be several cuts above what we are averaging today because, no matter the intellectual content, they will not be self-aggrandizing and will be based in deep affection for the individuals being studied and the subject matter. I recognize that these are dismissible, "new age" remarks, but as I see it, the alternative is a curse: to continue choosing sides and to reexperience these divisions forever.

## REFERENCES

Allee, W. C. (1938). *The social life of animals.* New York: Norton.

Axelrod, R., & Hamilton, W. D. (1981). The evolution of cooperation. *Science, 211,* 1390–1396.

Bailey, K. (1996, February). Mismatch theory. *ASCAP Newsletter,* University of Texas Medical Branch, Galveston.

Bateson, G. (1972). *Steps to an ecology of mind.* New York: Ballantine.

Barash, D. (1995). Review of Rushton, J. P. Race, evolution and behavior. *Animal Behavior, 49,* 1131–1133.

Barkow, J., Cosmides, L., & Tooby, J. (1992). *The adapted mind: Evolutionary psychology and the generation of culture.* New York: Oxford University Press.

von Bertalanffy, L. (1981). *A systems view of man.* Boulder, CO: Westview.

Bouchard, T. J., Jr., Lykken, D. T., McGue, M., Segal, N. L., & Tellegen, A. (1990). Sources of human psychological differences: The Minnesota study of twins reared apart. *Science, 250,* 223–228.

Boyd, R., & Richerson, P. J. (1985). *Culture and the evolutionary process.* Chicago: University of Chicago Press.

Brazelton, T. B., & Freedman, D. G. (1971). The Cambridge Neonatal Scales. In G. B. A. Stoelinga & J. A. Van der Werff ten Bosch (Eds.), *Normal and abnormal development of brain and behavior* (pp. 104–132). Leiden, Netherlands: Leiden University.

Bretherton, I., & Waters, E. (Eds.). (1985). Growing points in attachment theory and research. *Monographs of the Society for Research in Child Development, 50*(1/2, serial no. 209).

Bronfenbrenner, U., & Ceci, S. (1993). Heredity, environment, and the question "how?"—A first approximation. In R. Plomin & G. E. McLearn (Eds.), *Nature, nurture and psychology* (pp. 59–76), Washington, DC: American Psychological Association.

Brooks, L. K. (1990). *Temperament in 5 and 6 year-old Anglo-American, Korean-American, and adopted Korean children.* Unpublished doctoral dissertation, University of Chicago.

Cavalli-Sforza, L. L., Menozzi, P., & Piazza, A. (1994). *The history and geography of human genes.* Princeton, NJ: Princeton University.

Chagnon, N. A. (1972). *Studying the Yanomamo.* New York: Holt, Rinehart & Winston.

Chagnon, N. A. (1979). Mate competition, favoring close kin, and village fissioning among the Yanomamo Indians. In N. Chagnon & W. Irons (Eds.), *Evolutionary biology and human social behavior* (pp. 86–132). North Scituate, MA: Duxbury.

Chagnon, N. A. (1988). Life histories, blood revenge, and warfare in a tribal population. *Science, 239*, 985–992.

Chagnon, N. (1989). Yanomamo survival (Letter). *Science, 243*, 1141.

Cosmides, L., & Tooby, J. (1992). Cognitive adaptations for social exchange. In J. H. Barkow, L. Cosmides, & J. Tooby (Eds.), *The adapted mind: Evolutionary psychology and the generation of culture* (pp. 163–228). Oxford: Oxford University Press.

Crick, F. (1994). *The astonishing hypothesis; the secret search for the soul.* New York: Scribner

Darwin, C. (1872/1965). *Expression of emotions in man and animals.* Chicago: University of Chicago Press.

Dawkins, R. (1976/1991). *The selfish gene.* New York: Oxford University.

Dawkins, R. (1982). Replicators and vehicles. In King's College Sociobiology Group (Eds.), *Current problems in sociobiology* (pp. 45–64). Cambridge: Cambridge University Press.

DeBoer, M. M. (1983). *Sex differences in the bahavior of infant boy–girl twins.* Unpublished doctoral dissertation, University of Chicago.

Durham, W. H. (1978). Toward a co-evolutionary theory of human biology and culture. In A. C. Kaplan (Ed.), *The sociobiology debate* (pp. 428–448). New York: Harper.

Fodor, J. (1983). *The modularity of mind.* Cambridge, MA: MIT.

Freedman, D. G. (1957), *Constitutional and environmental interactions in rearing four breeds of dogs.* Unpublished doctoral dissertation, Brandeis University, Waltham, MA.

Freedman, D. G. (1962). *Constitutional and environmental interactions in rearing four breeds of dogs* [Film]. (Available from Pennsylvania State University Audio-Visual Services, University Park, PA, PCR-2124K)

Freedman, D. G. (1964). Smiling in blind infants and the issue of innate vs. acquired. *Journal of Child Psychology and Psychiatry, 5*, 171–189.

Freedman, D. G. (1967, November). The origins of social behavior. *Science Journal,* 66–73.

Freedman, D. G. (1974). *Human infancy; An evolutionary perspective.* Hillsdale, NJ: Erlbaum.

Freedman, D. G. (1976). Infancy, culture, and biology. In L. P. Lipsitt (Ed.), *Developmental psychobiology: The significance of infancy.* Hillsdale, NJ: Erlbaum.

Freedman, D. G. (1979). *Human socobiology: A holistic approach.* New York: Free Press.

Freedman, D. G. (1980). *Cross-cultural differences in newborn behavior* [Film]. (Available from Pennsylvania State University Audio-Visual Services, University Park, PA, PCR-22605)

Freedman, D. G. (1982). Review of K. Lorenz' "Foundations of ethology." *Ethology and Sociobiology, 3,* 151.

Freedman, D. G. (1986). The biology of behavior, with inquiries into the inheritance of temperament, stone-age art, and the peopling of Australia. In *Variability and Behavioral Evolution. Quaderno N. 259,* 237–261. Academia Nazionale Dei Linzei, Rome.

Freedman, D. G., & Freedman, N. C. (1969). Behavioral differences between Chinese-American and European-American newborns. *Nature, 224,* 1227.

Freedman, D. G., & Gorman, J. (1993). Attachment and the transmission of culture—An evolutionary perspective. *Journal of Social and Evolutionary Systems, 19,* 297–329.

Fromm-Reichmann, F. (1960). *Psychoanalysis and psychotherapy.* Chicago: University of Chicago.

George, C., Kaplan, N., & Main, M. (1985). *The Berkeley Adult Attachment Interview.* Unpublished protocol, Department of Psychology, University of California, Berkeley.

Goldsmith, H. H. (1993). Nature–nurture issues in the behavioral genetics context: Overcoming barriers to communication. In R. Plomin & G. E. McLearn (Eds.), *Nature, nurture, and psychology* (pp. 325–339). Washington, DC: American Psychological Association.

Goren, C. G., Sarty, M., & Wu, P. (1975). Visual following and pattern discrimination of face-like stimuli by newborn infants. *Pediatrics, 56,* 544–549.

Gorman, J. (1995). Being and doing; Practicing a secret profession. *Reflections, 1,* 35–40.

Goldstein, K. (1939). *The organism.* New York: American Book.

Haley, J. (1963). *Strategies of psychotherapy.* New York: Grune & Stratton.

Hull, D. L. (1984). Informal aspects of theory reduction. In E. Sober (Ed.), *Conceptual issues in evolutionary biology* (pp. 462–476). Cambridge, MA: MIT.

Jensen, A. R. (1969). How much can we boost I.Q. and scholastic achievement? *Harvard Educational Review, 39,* 1–123.

Johnson, M. H., & Morton, J. (1991). *Biology and cognitive development.* Oxford: Blackwell.

Jung, C. G. (1916). Seven sermons to the dead. Reprinted as an appendix in C. G. Jung, 1965, *Memories, dreams, and reflections* (pp. 378–390). New York: Vintage Books.

Kauffman, S. (1995). *At home in the universe.* New York: Oxford University.

Kim, L. (1994). *Attachment in two generations of Korean-Americans.* Unpublished master's thesis, University of Chicago.

Klein, J. (1984). *The case of being.* Durham, NC: Acorn Press.

Kropotkin, P. (1914/1955). *Mutual aid.* Boston: Extending Horizons.

Kuchner, J. (1973). *Chinese and Caucasian mother–infant interaction in the first year.* Unpublished doctoral dissertation, University of Chicago.

Laxness, H. K. (1957). *Brekkukotsannall.* Reykjavik: Helgafell.

LeVine, R. A., & Campbell, D. T. (1972). *Ethnocentrism: Theories of conflict, ethnic attitudes, and group behavior.* New York: Wiley.

LeVine, R. A., & Miller, P. M. (1990). Commentary. *Human Development, 33,* 73–80.

Levy, D. (1943). *Maternal overprotection.* New York: Columbia University.

Lewontin, R. C. (1972). The apportionment of human diversity. *Evolutionary Biology, 6,* 381–398.

Lewontin, R. C. (1974). *The genetic basis of evolutionary change.* New York: Columbia.

Lewontin, R. C., Rose, S., & Kamin, L. J. (1972). *Not in our genes.* New York: Pantheon.

Lipset, D. (1980). *Gregory Bateson: The legacy of a scientist.* Englewood Cliffs, NJ: Prentice-Hall.

Lorenz, K. (1965). *Evolution and modification of behavior.* Chicago: University of Chicago Press.

Loy, D. (1988). *Nonduality.* Princeton, NJ: Princeton University Press.

Lykken, D. T., McGue, M., & Tellegen, A. (1992). Emergensis: Genetic traits that may not run in families. *American Psychologist, 47,* 1565–1577.

Madanes, C. (1995). *The violence of men.* Palo Alto, CA: Jossey-Bass.

McGue, M., Bouchard, T. J., Jr., Iacono, W. G., & Lykken, D. T. (1993). Behavioral genetics of cognitive ability: A life-span perspective. In R. Plomin & G. E. McClearn (Eds.), *Nature, nurture and psychology* (pp. 59–76). Washington, DC: American Psychological Association.

Messinger, D. (1987). *Differences in child autonomy in the task-oriented interactions of 12 Japanese and 12 American 2-year-olds and their mothers.* Unpublished master's thesis, University of Chicago.

Messinger, D., & Freedman, D. G. (1992). Autonomy and interdependence in Japanese and American mother–toddler dyads. *Early Development and Parenting, 1,* 33–38.

Miller, S. L., & Orgel, L. E. (1974). *The origins of life on earth.* Englewood Cliffs, NJ: Prentice-Hall.

Mitra, P. (1994). *Attachment in two generations of Bengali-Americans.* Unpublished master's thesis, University of Chicago.

*Nature Genetics.* (1996, January). Vol. 12.

Neel, J. V., & Ward, J. H. (1970). Village and tribal genetic distances among American Indians, the possible implications for human evolution. *Proceedings of the American Academy of Sciences, 65,* 323–330.

Olafsdottir, V. (1991). *Mother-child relations in Iceland.* Unpublished master's thesis, University of Chicago.

Omark, D., & Edelman, M. (1976). The development of attention-structure in young children. In M. R. A. Chance & R. R. Larsen (Eds.), *The social structure of attention.* London: Wiley.

Park, L., Yue, G., & Freedman, D. G. (1995). *Mother-child relationship and transmission of culture in urban China.* Unpublished manuscript.

Pascal, B. (1941). *Pensées.* New York: Modern Library

Plomin, R. (1986). *Development, genetics, and psychology.* Hillsdale, NJ: Erlbaum.

Plomin, R. (1988). Reply to Sysan Oyama's Review of *Development, genetics, and psychology. Developmental Psychology, 21,* 107–112.

Plomin, R. (1990). *Nature and nurture: An introduction to human behavioral genetics.* Pacific Grove, CA: Brooks/Cole.

Plomin, R., DeFries, J. C., & McClearn, G. E. (1990). *Behavioral genetics: A primer* (2nd ed.). New York: W. H. Freeman.

Ruse, M. (1979). *Sociobiology: Sense or nonsense.* London: Reidel.

Rushton, J. P. (1995). *Race, evolution, and behavior.* New Brunswick, NJ: Transaction.

Sahlins, M. (1976). *The use and abuse of biology.* Ann Arbor: University of Michigan Press.

Scarr, S., & McCartney, K. (1983). How people make their own environments: A theory about genotype–environment effects. *Child Development, 54,* 424–435.

Segal, N. L. (1988). Cooperation, competition and altruism in human twinships. In K. B. MacDonald (Ed.), *Sociobiological perspectives on húman development* (pp. 168–206). New York: Springer.

Segal, N. L. (1997). Same-aged unrelated siblings; a unique test of within-family environmental influences on I.Q. similarities. *Journal of Educational Psychology, 89,* 381–390.

Smith, J. M. (1975). *The theory of evolution* (3rd ed.). New York: Penguin.

Smith, J. M. (1988). Evolutionary progress and levels of selection. In M. H. Nitecki (Ed.), *Evolutionary progress.* Chicago: University of Chicago.

Smith, S., & Freedman, D. G. (1982). *Mother-toddler interaction and maternal perception of child temperament in two ethnic groups: Chinese-American and European-American.* Unpublished paper presented to biannual meetings of the Society for Research in Child Development, Detroit, MI.

Sober, E. (1984). Holism, individualism, and the units of selection. In E. Sober (Ed.), *Conceptual issues in evolutionary biology* (pp. 184–209). Cambridge, MA: MIT.

Spitz, R., & Wolf, K. M. (1946). The smiling response. *Genetic Psychology Monographs, 34,* 57–125.

Sroufe, L. A., & Fleeson, J. (1986). Attachment and the construction of relationships. In W. W. Hartup & Z. Rubin (Eds.), *The nature and development of relationships.* Hillsdale, NJ: Erlbaum.

Stephenson, W. (1953). *The study of behavior.* Chicago: University of Chicago.

Sumner, W. G. (1906). *Folkways.* Boston: Ginn.

Symons, D. (1979). *The evolution of human sexuality.* New York: Oxford University Press.

Tindale, N. B. (1974). *The aboriginal tribes of Australia.* Berkeley: University of California Press.

Trivers, R. (1971). The evolution of reciprocal altruism. *Quarterly Review of Biology, 46,* 35–39, 45–47.

Wade, M. J. (1982). Group selection: Migrations and differentiation of small populations. *Evolution, 96,* 945–961.

Waldrop, M. M. (1992). *Complexity: The emerging science at the edge of order and chaos.* New York: Simon & Schuster.

Whitaker, C., & Malone, T. (1981). *The roots of psychotherapy.* New York: Brunner-Mazel.

Wiener, N. (1948). *Cybernetics.* New York: Wiley.

Williams, G. C. (1966). *Adaptation and natural selection.* Princeton, NJ: Princeton University Press.

Williams, G. C. (1975). *Sex and evolution.* Princeton, NJ: Princeton University Press.

Wilson, D. S. (1980). *The natural selection of populations and communities.* Menlo Park, CA: Benjamin-Cummings.

Wilson, D. S., & Sober, E. (1994). Reintroducing group selection to the human behavioral sciences. *Behavioral and Brain Sciences, 17,* 585–654.

Wilson, E. O. (1975). *Sociobiology: The new synthesis.* Cambridge, MA: Harvard University Press.

4

# Are Genetically Based Individual Differences Compatible With Species-Wide Adaptations?

J. Michael Bailey

In my graduate psychopathology class at the University of Texas in 1982, we read Dr. Freedman's classic 1958 study of different dog breeds' reactions to different training styles. Although the study had been published 25 years earlier, it was still a highlight, a vivid demonstration of the interaction between genes and environments.

Contemporary evolutionary psychological theories typically attempt to explain human universals (e.g., why the genders differ on a particular trait across cultures). Thus, the fact that there is often substantial genetic variability for the trait presents a problem to evolutionary accounts. In this chapter, I attempt to clarify the tension between evolutionary behavioral science and behavioral genetics, and to delineate how each discipline might contribute to the other.

Evolutionary psychology and behavior genetics are both exciting, vibrant disciplines, and on the surface, they appear to have much to contribute to each other. The modern synthesis forever linked evolutionary theory and quantitative genetics. Evolutionary psychology is a special case of the former; behavior genetics of the latter. Both evolutionary psychologists and behavior geneticists oppose the cultural hegemonists who believe that besides the basics of sexual intercourse, eating, and defecation, everything is learned by a blank-slated mind from agents of socialization. Evolutionary theories presuppose the existence of historical additive genetic variation for characteristics the evolution of which one wishes to explain, and it is the job of behavior geneticists to demonstrate the contemporary presence or absence of such variation.

It is somewhat surprising, then, that there is very little overlap between the two disciplines. I know few behavior geneticists who have ever attempted to integrate an evolutionary approach into their empirical work. Nor have many articles in evolutionary-oriented journals examined twins, or computed heritabilities or for that matter environmentality estimates. In a recent search of the Medline database, I counted the number of articles referenced during the past decade by each of the following keywords—*evolution, genetics, behavior,* and *human*—and by that combination of keywords together. Although each word was referenced by several thousand articles, only one article in the database referenced all four (Carey, 1991), and it was a highly theoretical (i.e., nonempirical) paper.

To be sure, there are several relevant articles not referenced by the database. Several such papers can be found in a 1990 issue of the *Journal of Personality* edited by David Buss, which should be required reading for anyone interested in the topic of evolutionary psychology and individual differences. Still another paper came from Nancy Segal (1993), former student of Daniel Freedman. Dr. Freedman is one of a very few individuals who has made important contributions to both behavior genetics (Freedman, 1967) and evolutionary psychology (Freedman 1971, 1979). Nevertheless, these are exceptions to a rule that at first consideration is quite puzzling.

A deeper consideration of evolutionary psychology and behavior genetics reveals good reasons why it has been difficult to integrate the two, both conceptually and empirically. These reasons make up a major focus of this chapter. First, however, I will briefly review findings from contemporary behavior genetics.

## BEHAVIOR GENETICS

Behavioral genetic methods include family, twin, and adoption methods, and generally aim to elucidate the determinants of behavioral variation. Thus, for example, similarity of monozygotic (MZ) twins reared apart must be attributable to shared genes. Similarity of adoptive siblings reared together must be due to shared environment. Some other designs require more than one type of relative, which differ in exactly one (typically, genetic or shared environmental) respect.

### Heritability

One major focus (though certainly not the only one) of behaviorial genetic studies has been the computation of heritabilities—that is, the extent to which behavioral trait variation is caused by genetic variation. Heritabilities range from 0 (no genetic influence) to 1 (completely genetic), and there have by now been hundreds of studies investigating heritabilities for scores of traits. (For a review, see Rose, 1995.) One conclusion from these studies is both general and unassailable. Virtually all *variable* traits that behavior geneticists have studied appear to be at least somewhat heritable. To get more specific, most studies find evidence for moderate heritabilities.

I used not to believe this. For example, my favorite counter-example used to be social and political attitudes. It seemed reasonable to me that families should inculcate these values in their children. And indeed most studies have found evidence for familial environmental effects for such attitudes. However, during the past few years, there have been two careful studies finding moderate heritabilities for such attitudes as well (Martin et al., 1986; Tesser, 1993). Another counterexample I used was alcoholism in women. More than one empirical study found low to zero heritabilities. However, Kendler et al. (Kendler, Heath, Neale, Kessler, & Eaves, 1992) published an article using the large Virginia twin registry suggesting that alcoholism is as heritable in women as in men. This is an instructive example; perhaps most of the studies finding heritability values near zero have had small samples and heritability values with large standard errors.

I can think of no variable trait that has consistently been found to be nonheritable. Among the traits the moderate heritabilities of which have been established beyond reasonable doubt are intelligence (Herrnstein & Murray, 1994), schizophrenia (Gottesman, 1991), manic depression (Tsuang & Faraone, 1990), extraversion and neuroticism (Eaves, Eysenck, & Martin, 1989; Loehlin, 1992). Though less well established, heritability findings have also been reported for religiosity (Waller, Kojetin, Bouchard, Lykken, & Tellegen, 1990), time spent watching television (Plomin, Corley, DeFries, & Fulker, 1990), and divorce (McGue & Lykken, 1992). The general finding of widespread genetic variation is quite consistent with the animal literature, in which virtually every attempt to select for a given trait has been successful.

Waller and Shaver (1994) found that individual differences in romantic love styles are a result almost exclusively to nongenetic influences. This finding is of interest, although further research in this area is warranted. The point is that after behavior genetics has demonstrated repeatedly (some would say ad nauseam) that heritability substantially exceeds zero for most everything, the null hypothesis that heritability equals zero is no longer a very interesting one. The null hypothesis that I have informally adopted is that heritability is equal to .4 plus or minus .2. (I have tried without success to publicize this general finding as "Bailey's Law.")

Findings of significant heritabilities are no longer surprising, not only because they are so common. Most traits that are studied by behavior geneticists are quite complex, undoubtedly multifactorially determined, and so it is not surprising that genes matter as well. Take the recent finding by the Minnesota group that divorce is heritable at about 50% (McGue & Lykken, 1992). Divorce surely is related to a number of interesting factors such as one's judgment, impulsivity, and conventionality, among many others. Each of the traits I mentioned has been previously demonstrated to be heritable as well. The fact that divorce is heritable appears to be neither very surprising nor very interesting. A more interesting observation, it seems, was the widespread amazement that greeted this finding. In the lay press, this can probably be explained by the general public's inability to believe in the fact of determinism. *(Determinism,* as used in this context, implies that all events, including those that are psychological or behavioral, are completely determined by causal antecedents, which might be either genetic or environmental in nature.)

### Genotype–Phenotype Pathway

It is likely that psychologists think that behavior geneticists are saying something more interesting than we really can say. There is a widespread mistaken tendency for people to infer from heritability findings that there is a rather straightforward genotype-to-phenotype pathway. But those of us who do heritability studies cannot really hope to discover much about genotype-to-phenotype pathways. For example, I have offered imperfect evidence that sexual orientation is somewhat heritable in men and women (Bailey & Pillard, 1991; Bailey, Pillard, & Agyei, 1993; and by the way, sexual orientation is one trait for which I retain the traditional null hypothesis of heritability equals zero). But even given the validity of my heritability inference, there is a large number of possible genotype-to-phenotype pathways that might obtain. The pathway I find most promising is relatively direct: that "gay genes" affect the sexual differentiation of the hypothalamus, leading to a homosexual orientation (LeVay, 1991).

To see this, compare two other possible genotype-to-phenotype pathways. A second possible route would have relevant genes influencing an attribute of a male child, say feminine beauty, which then might elicit differential treatment from others, such as feminine socialization from the parents, leading to a homosexual orientation. This theory would even be agreeable to some psychoanalysts. Although I do not believe that theory, findings that sexual orientation is heritable are by themselves no less consistent with it than with the one I prefer. The third causal model might be called the Social Constructionist Genetic Theory of Sexual Orientation. According to this theory genes affect some aspect of personality, such as nonconformity or independence, which lead some to reject the patriarchal, heterosexist status quo and adopt a homosexual identity. Again, I do not believe it, but we cannot decide among these three theories using heritability evidence.

In other words, quantitative behavior genetic explanations are not very good ones. To say that IQ is 60% heritable means that genetic differences explain 60% of the variance in IQ scores. A value of .60 sounds quite impressive; however, this does not tell us much about the development of IQ. Many of my behavior genetics colleagues still pay lip service to the desirability of using our techniques to elucidate developmental mechanisms, and a few of them have even managed to do so in a limited way. But I am pessimistic that quantitative behavior genetics as it is now practiced can deliver.

In contrast, the molecular revolution has provided techniques that hold great promise in elaborating the developmental process. Techniques such as linkage analysis have made it possible to discover major genes affecting traits. If genes for a given trait can be discovered, then it will be possible to find what the genes code for, how they affect the trait of interest. Unfortunately, there is ample reason to doubt that behavior genetics will soon benefit from the molecular revolution. Genetic variation in behavior appears to be primarily polygenic (Plomin, 1990), and polygenes will be quite difficult to find for the near future.

Before I conclude my whirlwind summary of behavior genetics, I want to consider the question of just how trustworthy behavior genetics findings are. Because behavior genetics has had many critics, there have been many methodological criticisms, and together they might leave the impression that findings are all noise and no signal. (For a review of some of these criticisms, see Block & Dworkin, 1976, or Plomin, DeFries, & McClearn, 1989.)

## A Methodological Example: Equal Environments

I shall briefly discuss one example of how behavior geneticists have attempted to deal with methodological criticisms. Perhaps the most common criticism I have encountered in my own work concerns the equal environments assumption. The classical twin study, which is the most common kind of study done by contemporary human behavior geneticists, uses monozygotic and dizygotic twins reared together to study heritability. If monozygotic (or MZ) twins are more similar than dizygotic (DZ) twins for a given trait, this pattern is assumed to reflect the closer genetic similarity of the former, and the trait is concluded to be at least somewhat heritable. This inference requires the assumption that the trait-relevant environment is no more similar for monozygotic than for dizygotic twins, which is the equal environments assumption. Critics frequently object that MZ twins are reared more similarly—dressed alike, given the same toys—and that this, rather than heredity, could account for their high degree of phenotypic similarity. However, there is a relevant literature that argues against this interpretation of MZ twin similarity (for a review, see Plomin, DeFries, & McClearn, 1989). In brief, not all parents of identical twins try to treat them identically. And for those traits studied so far, twins whose parents have the "identical treatment philosophy" do not turn out any more similarly than twins whose parents have the "encourage individuality philosophy." Not uncommonly, parents mislabel identical twins as fraternal twins or vice versa. In these cases, the degree of similarity reflects their real zygosity rather than their presumed zygosity. Furthermore, what data we have suggest that for IQ and personality MZ twins reared apart correlate about as highly as MZ twins reared together (Bouchard, Lykken, McGue, Segal, & Tellegen, 1990). It is quite possible that the "equal environments assumption" may be false for some traits not yet investigated, and it is certainly worthy of further attention. But it seems unreasonable to me to dismiss heritability studies using twins based on an unsupported assertion that the equal environments assumption is false.

## CAN BEHAVIOR GENETICS CONTRIBUTE TO EVOLUTIONARY PSYCHOLOGY?

In his book *Vaulting Ambition: Sociobiology and the Quest for Human Nature* (1985), Phillip Kitcher attempted to dismantle what he called "Wilson's ladder," the basic arguments he alleged to comprise human sociobiology. One of the rungs of the ladder he criticized was the assumption by sociobiologists that historical genetic variation existed for the characteristics the evolution of which they wished to explain. If my basic review of behavior genetics is correct, then that particular rung is sturdy indeed. Furthermore, if genetic variation in psychological traits is rampant, it is difficult to imagine that all such variation has remained immune to evolutionary selection pressures. That is, contemporary behavior genetics findings have established the a priori likelihood that at least some mental adaptations exist.

However, scientists have not yet accomplished a more meaningful integration of the two disciplines, and there are good reasons why this is so. Behavior geneticists and evolutionists have major focuses that are independent of each other. Evolutionists are concerned with the origins of species-typical behavior—that is, behavior that has evolved to be more or less uniform throughout the species because it is so important. Selection usually reduces genetic variation. In contrast, behavior geneticists are concerned with individual differences within a species—in other words, behavior that has remained variable, perhaps precisely because it was not important enough to be fixed by selection. High heritabilities excite behavior geneticists because they signify the importance of biological processes that concern them. High heritabilities worry evolutionists, who must explain how genetic variance persists despite the selection they believe has occurred. Behavior geneticists are concerned with variances, whereas evolutionists are concerned with means.

## Are Genetic Differences Strategic?

The evolutionist can account for contemporary genetic variation in several ways, most of which are uninteresting—to the behaviorally oriented evolutionist, at least. (For a discussion of some of these, see Bailey, in press.) One possibility is that the trait of interest is uncorrelated with any life history traits that might conceivably be related to fitness. Perhaps, for example, introverts have just as many sex partners as extroverts, at about the same ages, and merely attend fewer parties. If so, and if they are just as good at rearing children successfully, and so on, the evolutionist is unlikely to care much about extroversion and will be unconcerned that extroversion is moderately heritable. In this case, genes for extroversion would be "genetic junk." If one were to accept this model, one would have to conclude that just about every trait behavior geneticists have studied are half full of genetic junk and, thus, selectively neutral.

In fact, we know little about the sex lives of introverts and extroverts, though the topic is worth exploring. But some other traits that have been studied appear both to be highly heritable and to have reproductive consequences. For example, evolutionists have made a persuasive case that men are more interested than women in emotionally uncommitted sex, and indeed, there is a large gender difference on this trait (Bailey, Gaulin, Agyei, & Gladue, 1994; Oliver & Hyde, 1993).

However, there is also considerable overlap between the genders on this trait (Bailey et al., 1994), and existing evidence suggests that much of the within-gender variation is heritable, especially for women. Gangestad and Simpson (1990) examined a scale (Zeta) that has been closely linked to their sociosexuality scale, a measure of tendency to engage in casual sex. They found very high heritability for women. Recently, we have examined the heritability of a related scale using the Australian Twin Registry (Bailey & Martin, 1996) and found heritabilities of approximately .20 for men and .60 for women.

Although it may be the case that highly sociosexual people leave about the same number of descendants as do more sexually conservative people, they almost certainly go about reproduction in a markedly different fashion. To consider a more extreme example, the mean number of offspring of men must equal that for women, yet no one would argue that sex is a reproductively neutral trait and the sex determination gene genetic junk. Maleness and femaleness are frequency-dependent reproductive strategies. And indeed, Gangestad and Simpson (1990) speculated that high versus low sociosexuality may be alternative frequency-dependent strategies, at least for women. This is the most interesting potential explanation of genetic variance for behavior—that some of it represents alternative genetic strategies with important life history differences.

The major problem with an ambitious version of this general approach, as noted by Tooby and Cosmides (1990), is that the genetic recombination that accompanies sexual reproduction precludes the building and maintenance of genetic architectures that could code for complex strategies. For example, imagine what it would entail to argue that "Fortune 500 Executive" and "Confidence Man" represented different genetically predisposed reproductive strategies. It would not be so difficult to make a strategic interpretation of the two phenotypes. It is not unlikely that frequency dependence obtains between the two groups. It would certainly be the case that the characteristics that allow one to become a Confidence Man or a Fortune 500 Executive would be about as heritable as any other behaviors. Case histories of MZ twins reared apart reveal concordance for many complex behaviors and traits (see, for example, Newman, Freeman, & Holzinger, 1937). The problem is that the relevant genotypes would almost certainly involve hundreds, if not thousands, of loci, which would differ between the two strategies. Assuming anything approaching random breeding, in each generation, the optimal genotypes would be broken up. The Fortune 500 genotype crossed with another would not yield anything approaching itself. If the Fortune 500 genotype were the single optimum across the population, then we would all get there eventually, through the gradual elimination of alleles that coded for other phenotypes. But in the ambitious frequency-dependence case, remember, we are assuming that there is at least one alternative phenotype that will be selectively maintained. I agree with Tooby and Cosmides's (1990) conclusion that sexual recombination precludes the selection of multiple optima in multivariate genetic space within a single more or less randomly interbreeding population.

## Contingent Genetic Variation

There are, however, less ambitious theories that could account for less remarkable amounts of coordinated genetic variation, and I am less pessimistic about these. For example, pleiotropy seems to be the rule rather than the exception: Most genes have multiple effects. If so, it seems plausible, even likely, that the most competitive alleles will be those that have multiple sympathetic effects. By this picture, genes that make one large and strong might well be expected to make one more aggressive as well. Tight genetic linkage—say, between strength genes and aggressiveness genes—could also allow for adaptive covariation. Linkage would have to be tight enough so that weak, aggressive offspring, who would be at a disadvantage, would be relatively rare. Neither pleiotropy nor linkage would be expected to generate large genetic correlations. It would be too much to expect that all strength genes are tightly linked with all aggression genes. I would expect coordinated genetic variation to be dimensional, rather than typological, and to show a rather modest degree of coordination. Behavior geneticists might conceivably contribute to the demonstration of such coordinated variation via the analysis of genetic correlations, which is certainly one of the things we do. However, it is difficult to conceive of a systematic theory-driven research program targeted at the kind of coordinated genetic variation just mentioned.

Tooby and Cosmides (1990) have argued that the most impressive examples of adaptive individual differences will be triggered by environmental or uncoordinated genetic variation. Beautiful women may have very different reproductive strategies than other women. So may impulsive men with relatively poor economic prospects. But the idea is that we all have a developmental program that says something like, "If at a certain age you get certain signals that you are a beautiful woman, then adopt strategy X." There is less of a problem explaining the evolution of such contingent strategies. To the extent that they exist, then sociobiology is largely, as Crawford and Anderson (1989) called it, an environmentalist discipline. Paradoxically, it is the evolutionist taking an *environmentalist* approach to individual differences who has the greatest need to know about behavior genetics. The rest of the world may yawn, but environmentalists ignore behavior genetics at their peril.

The reason for this is that correlations between putative environmental influences and phenotypes of interest may be entirely genetic. Thus, for decades we believed that parents' economic success and education were the primary determinants of their children's IQs. It now looks as if much, if not all, of the correlation between parents' sociocultural characteristics and children's IQs is genetically mediated (Herrnstein & Murray, 1994). Phenotypic correlations cannot be assumed to reflect environmental causation unless other possibilities have been excluded. I can think of several phenotypic correlations that are taken for granted in the social sciences as reflecting environmental causation that might conceivably reflect genetic covariation instead: For example, there is a correlation between parenting behavior and the quality of attachment between parent and child (Isabella & Belsky, 1991). This could conceivably be a result of genes shared by both some mothers and their children, causing both apparently ineffective parenting and insecure attachment behavior. The correlation between early sexual abuse and adult psychopathology could conceivably reflect the possibility that psychopathological parents both molest their children and pass their psychopathological genes on to their children.

Draper and Belsky have reviewed several interesting correlations between psychosexual development and characteristics of the family, such as an absent father or parental conflict (Belsky, Steinberg, & Draper, 1991). One of the most interesting findings was a relationship between parental conflict and pubertal timing, with girls from families of divorce maturing somewhat early. With the heritability of divorce approximately .50, it will be important to demonstrate that early maturity and propensity to divorce are not merely different manifestations of the same genes. (To their credit, Belsky et al. acknowledged the need for strong inference about the nature of the association.) For example, one must demonstrate that within families, those sisters who had reached puberty at the time of parental divorce were older at menarche than their sisters who were prepubescent at the time of the divorce. I am not arguing that these correlations are primarily genetically, rather than environmentally, mediated. I am only saying that we do not know until we have excluded one or the other possibility.

Environmentalist intuitions have had a spotty record in the social sciences. We were mostly wrong about the family as the primary creator of individual differences, for example. Behavior genetics studies have shown repeatedly, if not invariably, that environmental effects largely operate within families, to make siblings different from each other—or, for that matter, to make MZ reared-together twins different from each other (Rowe, 1994). Thus, it is important to be particularly careful before accepting the conclusion that a familial correlation is a result of the familial environment.

## INDIVIDUAL DIFFERENCES AS A WINDOW ON DEVELOPMENT

Evolutionists have an interest in understanding developmental mechanisms (Kitcher, 1990). For example, the claim that a psychological sex difference is an adaptation entails the implicit claim that evolution has shaped the brains of men and women to be different, and that the sex difference is not merely a result of arbitrary socialization differences. The study of individual differences, and their covariation, can sometimes be useful in elucidating development.

For example, consider human sexual orientation. Sexual orientation is one of the largest psychological sex differences. The vast majority of men prefer female partners, and an even higher percentage of women prefer male partners. In this sense, gay men are quite feminine and lesbians masculine. Sexual orientation is closely associated with some other sex differences, such as childhood play patterns (Bailey & Zucker, 1995). As children, and on average, gay men were more feminine and lesbians more masculine than their heterosexual same-sex counterparts.

However, we have shown that in some other respects, homosexual individuals are gender-typical (Bailey et al., 1994). We administered questionnaire measures of mating preferences to heterosexual and homosexual participants. In both "Interest in Casual Sex" and "Importance of Partner's Sexual Attractiveness," gay men were quite similar to heterosexual men, obtaining much higher scores than both heterosexual and lesbian women. These findings constrain explanations of the heterosexual sex difference. For example, the fact that they suggest that women's lower interest in sexual variety is not caused by fear of male violence (i.e., because sexual involvement with unfamiliar men could be especially risky). If it were, lesbians should be more open to multiple partners compared to heterosexual women. The findings for "Importance of Partner's Sexual Attractiveness" are inconsistent with an explanation involving the culture's emphasis of female beauty. Gay men are just as focused as heterosexual men on their partners' looks. Although these findings cannot provide unambiguous support for any particular explanation, evolutionary or otherwise, they usefully narrow the range of candidate explanations. I note, however, that these findings concern individual differences and not behavior genetics per se.

## GROUP DIFFERENCES

I turn now to differences between populations. The argument against complex genetically based strategic individual differences assumed one population of interbreeding individuals. The story is quite different with populations that are reproductively separated, especially those in radically different environments. Differences between populations in the intensity of directional selection for a trait is a highly effective mechanism in producing genetic differences between populations. Tiny differences in selection intensity can lead to large differences in a number of generations modest in evolutionary time. In their classic work "Race Differences in Intelligence," Loehlin, Lindzey, and Spuhler (1975) showed that a one-standard-deviation difference in IQ could be induced between two populations in approximately 500 generations, assuming moderate heritability and seemingly trivial differences in selection intensity.

The different ethnic groups are similar in their basic morphologies; yet, there are recognizable physical differences between them that are surely genetic. I can think of no reason why we should not expect the same to be true of genetically influenced behavioral traits. I think it is exceedingly likely that some ethnic groups will differ from each other on some behavioral traits for genetic reasons. I find it nearly impossible to imagine that only trivial mean differences exist between, say, the Inuit and the Zulu in all of their evolved (and, hence, genetically based) behavior. The problem, of course, is to determine which behaviors. (Freedman has also contributed to this general area; see Freedman, 1979.)

Behavior genetics has had some experience with group differences. Arguably, contemporary behavior genetics was born with Arthur Jensen's article, "How Far Can We Boost IQ and Scholastic Achievement?" (1969), in which he argued that the one-standard deviation Black–White IQ difference is substantially genetic in origin. Much behavior genetics research in the 1970s was organized around this controversy. The fact is that we do not yet know whether any or all of the Black–White IQ difference is genetic. I cannot possibly review here the kinds of studies that have been done, the findings supporting either side of the issue, or the intricate methodological arguments. Basically, most available evidence has manifold interpretations. The studies that were potentially definitive—particularly cross-fostering studies of Black children adopted by White families and studies examining the association between racial admixture and IQ—turned out to be anything but definitive (Loehlin, Lindzey, & Spuhler, 1981; Scarr, 1981).

The reason why we cannot answer the question is not because we have never tried, though it is true that we have virtually stopped trying now. It is because such questions are extraordinarily difficult to answer. This is because the two variables that compete to account for the difference are strongly correlated. Across people the hypothetical cultural factors that might be causing the difference are very much confounded with the hypothetical genetic factors. It is true that we have made some headway in narrowing the range of acceptable explanations. The Black–White IQ difference cannot be accounted for by differences in education, socioeconomic status, or test bias (Herrnstein & Murray, 1994). However, there is an inexhaustible supply of alternative environmental explanations to replace each environmental candidate that has been eliminated.

Current efforts to explore potential genetic differences between ethnic groups come primarily from the evolutionary perspective: Phil Rushton's interesting work in the context of r-K theory and differences among the three major racial groups (Rushton, 1995). The general possibility of evolved racial differences in reproductive strategy is certainly plausible, and an evolutionary perspective could be an asset to the more atheoretical empirical approaches that have predominated in behavior genetics. Surely it is a good thing to widen the focus to behaviors other than IQ, as Rushton has done. It is possible that this general kind of work could increase our understanding of the origins of important behavioral differences between ethnic groups and, more important, enhance our understanding about the evolution of human behavior. At the same time, it is important to be extremely cautious in evaluating hypotheses concerning race differences, because of the sensitivity of the topic.

## SPECIAL STUDY PARTICIPANTS

The final potential contribution of behavior genetics to evolutionary psychology that I shall mention concerns study participants. In order to disentangle genes and environment, behavior geneticists have been forced to find people with rather unusual and exotic patterns of genetic and environmental relatedness. For example, MZ twins are genetic clones. In contrast, adoptive siblings are siblings in environment only. Evolutionists are interested in a number of phenomena that could benefit from using these kinds of participants, including altruism and incest avoidance.

For example, surely the most dramatic case of incest was reported by Bouchard's group in a study of homosexuality in MZ twins reared apart (Eckert, Bouchard, Bohlen, & Heston, 1986). One pair of separated male MZ twins met in a gay bar and subsequently became lovers. In another pair concordant for bisexuality, one of the twins admitted to sexual attraction for the other. MZ twins reared apart are the opposite end of a spectrum from unrelated children of the kibbutz reared together, and they seem to have opposite outcomes as well. We may be programmed to mate with those who look and act like us, provided that we did not grow up with them. The phenomenon of biological relatives separated at birth who, at adult reunion, become sexually attracted to each other is common enough that an article about it was commissioned by a national adoption newsletter.

MZ twins seem to be interesting study participants with whom to examine the degree to which altruism toward kin depends on phenotypic similarity rather than other factors such as being reared together or the knowledge of putative kinship. Adoptive siblings would also be interesting in this regard. In a fascinating study, Segal demonstrated dramatic differences in patterns of cooperation and competition between MZ and DZ twins (for a review of this and other studies, see Segal, 1993, and chapter 7, this volume).

## CONCLUSIONS

This chapter has attempted to clarify the different foci of evolutionary psychology, which address questions such as, "Why do males and females differ in their interest in casual sex?" and behavioral genetics, which addresses questions such as, "Why do women vary in their interest in casual sex?" Furthermore, because nearly all trait variation has a substantial genetic component, I have tried to explore ways in which genetic variation can persist despite selection pressures that should reduce it. Daniel Freedman is one of a very few scientists who has made important contributions to both evolutionary psychology and behavioral genetics.

Behavior genetics and evolutionary psychology have had limited influence on each other. This is partly because of serious difficulties in accounting for the persistence of genetic variation despite selection pressures—at least doing so in an interesting, empirically fruitful manner. One of the most legitimate areas for integration, racial and ethnic differences, has been neglected by most investigators, probably because it is so controversial. To the extent that evolutionary theories posit contingent relations between environmental signals and developmental outcomes, behavior genetics methods will be necessary to ensure that such relations are not genetically mediated. Finally, evolutionary psychologists should examine how they might fruitfully employ unusual participants, such as twins and adoptees, that have long been employed in behavior genetic studies.

## REFERENCES

Bailey, J. M. (in press). Can behavior genetics contribute to evolutionary behavioral science? In C. Crawford & D. Krebs (Eds.), *Evolution and human behavior: Ideas, issues, and applications.* Hillsdale, NJ: Erlbaum.

Bailey, J. M., Gaulin, S., Agyei, Y., & Gladue, B. A. (1994). Effects of gender and sexual orientation on evolutionarily relevant aspects of human mating psychology. *Journal of Personality and Social Psychology, 66,* 1081–1093.

Bailey, J. M., & Martin, N. G. (1996). [Australian Twin Registry study of sexuality]. Unpublished raw data.

Bailey, J. M., & Pillard, R. C. (1991). A genetic study of male sexual orientation. *Archives of General Psychiatry, 48,* 1089–1096.

Bailey, J. M., Pillard, R. C., & Agyei, Y. (1993). Heritable factors influence sexual orientation in women. *Archives of General Psychiatry, 50,* 217–223.

Bailey, J. M., & Zucker, K. J. (1995). Childhood sex-typed behavior and sexual orientation: A conceptual analysis and quantitative review. *Developmental Psychology, 31,* 43–55.

Belsky, J., Steinberg, L., & Draper, P. (1991). Childhood experience, interpersonal development, and reproductive strategy: An evolutionary theory of socialization. *Child Development, 62,* 647–670.

Block, N. J., & Dworkin, G. (1976). *The IQ controversy.* New York: Pantheon.

Bouchard, T. J., Jr., Lykken, D. T., McGue, M., Segal, N. L., & Tellegen, A. (1990). Sources of human psychological differences: The Minnesota Study of Twins Reared Apart. *Science, 250,* 223–228.

Buss, D. M. (1990). Biological foundations of personality: Evolution, behavioral genetics, and psychophysiology. *Journal of Personality, 58* (Special Issue), 1–345.

Carey, G. (1991). Evolution and path models in human behavioral genetics. *Behavior Genetics, 21,* 433–444.

Crawford, C. B., & Anderson, J. L. (1989). Sociobiology: An environmentalist discipline? *American Psychologist, 44,* 1449–1459.

Eaves, L. J., Eysenck, H. J., & Martin, N. G. (1989). *Genes, culture and personality.* London: Academic Press.

Eckert, E. D., Bouchard, T. J., Bohlen, J., & Heston, L. L. (1986). Homosexuality in monozygotic twins reared apart. *British Journal of Psychiatry, 148,* 421–425.

Freedman, D. G. (1967). The origins of social behaviour. *Science Journal, 3,* 69–73.

Freedman, D. G. (1979). Biological and cultural differences in early child development. *Annual Review of Anthropology, 8,* 579–600.

Freedman, D. G. (1971). An evolutionary approach to research on the life cycle. *Human Development, 14,* 87–99.

Gangestad, S. W., & Simpson, J. A. (1990). Toward an evolutionary history of female sociosexual variation. *Journal of Personality, 58,* 69–96.

Gottesman, I. I. (1991). *Schizophrenia genesis.* San Francisco: Freeman.

Herrnstein, R. J., & Murray, C. (1994). *The bell curve: Intelligence and class structure in American life.* New York: Free Press.

Isabella, R. A., & Belsky, J. (1991). Interactional synchrony and the origins of infant–mother attachment: A replication study. *Child Development, 62,* 373–384.

Jensen, A. R. (1969). How much can we boost IQ and scholastic achievement? *Harvard Educational Review, 39,* 1–123.

Kendler, K. S., Heath, A. C., Neale, M. C., Kessler, R. C., & Eaves, L. J. (1992). A population-based twin study of alcoholism in women. *Journal of the American Medical Association, 268,* 1877–1882.

Kitcher, P. (1985). *Vaulting ambition: Sociobiology and the quest for human nature.* Cambridge, MA: MIT Press.

Kitcher, P. (1990). Developmental decomposition and the future of human behavioral ecology. *Philosophy of Science, 57,* 96–117.

LeVay, S. (1991). A difference in hypothalmic structure between heterosexual and homosexual men. *Science, 253,* 1034–1037.

Loehlin, J. C. (1992). *Genes and environment in personality development.* Newbury Park, CA: Sage.

Loehlin, J. C., Lindzey, G., & Spuhler, J. N. (1975). *Race differences in intelligence.* San Francisco: Freeman.

Martin, N. G., Eaves, L. J., Heath, A. C., Jardine, R., Feingold, L. M., & Eysenck, H. J. (1986). Transmission of social attitudes. *Proceedings of the National Academy of Sciences, USA, 83,* 4364–4368.

McGue, M., & Lykken, D. T. (1992). Genetic influence on risk of divorce. *Psychological Science, 3,* 368–373.

Newman, H. H., Freeman, F. N., & Holzinger, K. J. (1937). *Twins: A study of heredity and environment.* Chicago: University of Chicago Press.

Oliver, M. B., & Hyde, J. S. (1993). Gender differences in sexuality: A meta-analysis. *Psychological Bulletin, 114,* 29–51.

Plomin, R. (1990). The role of inheritance in behavior. *Science, 248,* 183–188.

Plomin, R., Corley, R., DeFries, J. C., & Fulker, D. W. (1990). Individual differences in television viewing in early childhood: Nature as well as nurture. *Psychological Science, 1,* 371–377.

Plomin, R., DeFries, J. C., & McClearn, G. E. (1989). *Behavioral genetics: A primer.* New York: W. H. Freeman.

Rose, R. J. (1995). Genes and human behavior. *Annual Review of Psychology, 46,* 625–654.

Rowe, D. C. (1994). *The limits of family influence: Genes, experience, and behavior.* New York: Guilford Press.

Rushton, J. P. (1995). *Race, evolution, and behavior: A life history perspective.* New Brunswick, NJ: Transaction Publishers.

Scarr, S. (1981). *Race, social class, and individual differences in IQ.* Hillsdale, NJ: Erlbaum.

Segal, N. L. (1993). Twin, sibling, and adoption methods: Tests of evolutionary hypotheses. *American Psychologist, 48,* 943–956.

Tesser, A. (1993). The importance of heritability in psychological research: The case of attitudes. *Psychological Review, 100,* 129–142.

Tooby, J., & Cosmides, L. (1990). On the universality of human nature and the uniqueness of the individual: The role of genetics and adaptation. *Journal of Personality, 58,* 17–67.

Tsuang, M. T., & Faraone, S. V. (1990). *The genetics of mood disorders.* Baltimore: Johns Hopkins University Press.

Waller, N. G., Kojetin, B. A., Bouchard, T. J., Lykken, D. T., & Tellegen, A. (1990). Genetic and environmental influences on religious interests, attitudes, and values: A study of twins reared apart and together. *Psychological Science, 1,* 138–142.

Waller, N. G., & Shaver, P. R. (1994). The importance of nongenetic influences on romantic love styles: A twin-family study. *Psychological Science, 5,* 268–274.

SECTION II

# Genetic Bases of Behavior: Contributions to Psychological Research

# Genetic Bases of Behavior: Contributions to Psychological Research

Nancy L. Segal

Behavior genetics is the study of genetic and environmental factors associated with behavioral differences among individuals. According to quantitative genetic theory, the magnitude of resemblance between relatives for continuous traits (i.e., traits influenced by multiple genes) should vary as a function of their genetic relatedness. If, for example, genetic factors influence the expression of a given trait, full siblings would be expected to display greater resemblance than half-siblings who, in turn, should be more alike than adoptive siblings. Continuous traits are also influenced by environmental factors. Biological relatives who share a common environment may show similarities or differences associated with either genetic or environmental factors; indeed, these effects are confounded in intact biological families. (However, the genetic transmission of single gene traits—e.g., color-blindness, which is carried on the X chromosome—may be more traceable across generations.) If family members fail to show resemblance for a given trait, this indicates that neither common genetic, nor common environmental, factors significantly influence the expression of that trait.

The most informative research designs for disentangling influences associated with nature and nurture are twin and adoption studies. The logic of the twin method, as defined by Sir Francis Galton in the late 1870s, is really quite simple: "It is, that their history affords means of distinguishing between the effects of tendencies received at birth, and of those that were imposed by the circumstances of their after lives; in other words, between the effects of nature and nurture" (Galton, 1875, p. 391). In other words, increased resemblance between genetically identical (monozygotic, or MZ) twins, relative to genetically nonidentical (dizygotic, or DZ) twins suggests genetic influence on the trait of interest. The biology of twinning was not well understood in Galton's time, yet he correctly reasoned that meaningful interpretations of his findings were possible only with reference to a critical distinction between twin types.

Adoption studies compare the magnitude of resemblance between biological relatives raised apart or between unrelated individuals raised together. Resemblance between biological relatives raised apart is associated with shared genes, in the absence of correlated, trait-relevant rearing environments. Resemblance between unrelated individuals living together is associated with shared environmental influences. Most adoption research has focused on IQ resemblance between pairs of adopted-away children and their biological parents, adoptive parents and children, and adoptive siblings.

Human behavioral genetic research was conducted very early in the twentieth century but remained outside the mainstream of the behavioral sciences until the 1980s. It has now achieved new respectability as an area of study, owing to advances in molecular genetic analysis, growing disenchantment with environmental perspectives on behavior, and increased sophistication in behavioral–genetic methodology. However, human behavioral genetics is not without controversy. The notion that genetic influence implies fixity of behavior remains pervasive despite efforts to clarify this misconception. The best example to the contrary is that of PKU, or phenylketonuria, a metabolic disorder associated with mental retardation. Administration of a phenylalanine-free diet early in life can offset the adverse effects of this genetic condition. In addition, tendencies by some investigators to apply value judgments to individual differences in behavior has also provoked criticism.

Nonhuman behavioral genetic analyses offer considerable experimental control over genetic and environmental factors underlying behavior. One approach to accomplishing this task is the establishment of inbred animal strains in which all members are genetically identical. A second approach includes selection studies in which the selected lines differ in genes relevant to the behavior of interest. The environment may be selectively modified to identify gene x environment interactions. It is also possible to create uniform environmental settings in order to highlight genetic effects. The relatively brief life spans of some nonhuman organisms enable study of genetic transmission across multiple generations.

Behavioral genetics is a discipline in which Dr. Freedman made significant contributions early in his career, both in nonhuman and human areas. His 1957 doctoral thesis demonstrated that different dog breeds respond differently to varying treatment regimens (also see Freedman, 1958). Findings from this classic study exemplify research concerned with gene x environment interactions. This work was supervised by John Paul Scott. In 1963, Dr. Freedman and Barbara Keller published a longitudinal study of infant MZ and DZ twins, which showed significant genetic influence across measures of social and motor behavior. Most noteworthy about this study was that raters evaluated each twin separately by means of filmed segments, thus avoiding biased judgments. Both of these studies are given additional treatment in sections I and VI. Most important, the necessity of a closer association between behavioral genetics and evolutionary psychology emerged from this work to become a prominent theme in Dr. Freedman's publications. Specifically, it was noted that evolutionary psychology might offer insights into why analyses of behavior in different domains may yield differential heritabilities.

The contributors to this section have applied their unique perspectives and expertise toward comprehending the role of genetic analysis in psychological research. Irving I. Gottesman and colleagues have considered developmental–genetic aspects of aggression with reference to twin data on activity and anger in infants, and on antisocial traits, personality characteristics and criminal acts in older individuals. They remind us that the enormous variability and complexity of aggressive behavior precludes easy understanding of etiology or simple formulation of policy implications. John Paul Scott has reviewed research concerned with the genetic analysis of social behavior in animals and humans. The greater part of his career has been devoted to documenting and comprehending variations in social responses associated with gene x environment interactions. His chapter summarizes his seminal work on genetic influences on species differences in social behavior and organization, and suggests goals and directions for controlling violence in human societies. Nancy L. Segal has extended the theme of increased collaboration between behavioral genetics and evolutionary psychology, introduced by J. Michael Bailey. Specifically, a series of novel twin designs that can address evolutionary-based hypotheses and predictions are described. Data from a new behavioral–genetic design, which uses unrelated siblings of the same age, are summarized.

Discussion of the chapters from this section is provided by Robert L. Trivers. Given his background in evolutionary biology and behavior, his perspective helps to draw behavioral genetics and evolutionary psychology closer together.

## REFERENCES

Freedman, D. G. (1957). *The effects of indulgent and disciplinary rearing in four breeds of dogs.* Unpublished doctoral dissertation, Brandeis University, Waltham, MA.

Freedman, D. G. (1958). Constitutional and environmental interactions in rearing of four dog breeds. *Science, 127*, 585–586.

Freedman, D. G., & Keller, B. (1963). Inheritance of behavior in infants. *Science, 140*, 196–198.

Galton, F. (1875). The history of twins as a criterion of the relative powers of nature and nurture. *Journal of the Anthropological Institute, 5*, 391–406.

# 5

# A Developmental *and* a Genetic Perspective on Aggression

Irving I. Gottesman, H. Hill Goldsmith, and Gregory Carey

Freedman's prescient research on individual differences in the temperament of the dog breeds available at Bar Harbor in the 1950s, followed shortly by his parallel work on individual differences in the temperament of infants with different ethnic and genetic backgrounds, informs the present chapter on aggression in humans across the life span. All three efforts seek the facts without a priori prejudices about what the answer "ought to be" to satisfy the expectations of society and its self-appointed watchdogs. The interface between psychology and genetics, and that between genetics and culture, has always been controversial; Dr. Freedman has shown us that controversy may lead to important insights about our species.

It was wise of the editors of this book to organize the various perspectives on human development that have illuminated and have been illuminated by the career contributions of Dr. Freedman (1965, 1974, 1979) under four separate rubrics—genetic, ethological, cultural, and evolution-

---

In addition to new material presented in this chapter, we have taken the liberty of drawing on our recent work that presents some of the results and ideas here at greater length and in more detail (cf. Carey, 1994; Goldsmith & Gottesman, 1996; Gottesman & Goldsmith, 1994).

ary. Such a stratagem eliminates much of the tension and sometimes rancor that goes with a logical, but often controversial, rubric known as "psychobiology" (Hamilton, 1964; Trivers, 1985; Wilson, 1975; Wilson & Daly, 1996) That particular term *might* encompass all the contributions to this volume, but the term itself is too easily encumbered with surplus meanings that lead to many behavioral geneticists, including ourselves, distancing themselves from being too closely identified with such a "field" or its close relative "evolutionary psychology" (Buss, 1995; Segal, 1993). We prefer to reserve the right to differ among ourselves as well as with other observers in regard to whether the relations among these perspectives are either necessary or sufficient for various research programs into human development, thus reserving our options to engage in cooperative play, parallel play, or isolated play with respect to each of the perspectives identified (cf. Segal, chapter 7, this volume).

## ORGANIZING CONCEPTS AND CONSTRUCTS

In both the popular and scientific lexicons, genes are implicated in the language we use to discuss the origins of individual differences in the liability to developing behavioral disorders or trait "scores." We speak of the *genesis* of problems; we believe that *diatheses* interact with stressors and view genetic factors as key elements of the diatheses; we speak of genetic *liability* predisposing some individuals to develop a disorder. We prefer the term *ontogenesis* to imply a dynamic view of development and the term *epigenesis* to escalate the needed complexity of that term to allow for simultaneous and alternating reciprocal changes in both effective genotypes and behavioral phenotypes. Genes have only a probabilistic effect on the development of behavior, both normal and disordered. However, the degree of probability ranges widely according to the genotype and the phenotype under analysis. The unfortunate individual who inherits a particular pair of recessive genes on chromosome pair 12 will definitely exhibit the symptoms of phenylketonuria early in life. Only one copy of a stretch of a particular dominant mutant gene on chromosome 4 will also guarantee the development of Huntington Disease, although the affected person will live for 40 or 50 years before frank signs of the illness appear. Thus, the probability of a particular gene leading to a *mendelizing* disorder can be 100%.

However, for disorders such as schizophrenia, we can conclude from studies of identical twins that an individual with an "average" genotype for schizophrenia (average for schizophrenics, not for the general population) has only, roughly, a 50% chance of eventually developing enough symptoms to be diagnosed as schizophrenic. Thus, for complex, nonmendelizing genetically influenced disorders (cf. King, Rotter, & Motulsky, 1992) such as schizophrenia, the path from genotype to behavioral manifestation is indeed probabilistic. The chances of developing schizophrenia range from 0% to 55% (Gottesman, 1991) depending on ill-understood processes involving interactions, thresholds, and biopsychosocial contingencies.

Thinking about genetic risk factors for more universal behavioral patterns, such as aggressiveness or antisocial behavior, becomes even more complex. And the complexity is compounded from a developmental perspective. In this chapter, we treat the controversial (Carey & Gottesman, 1996; Ciba Foundation, 1996; Reiss & Roth, 1993) issue of genetic aspects of aggression and antisocial behavioral patterns and attempt to explain some of the complexities involved within the framework provided by the other chapters in this book. The reader's receptivity to the notion that genetic and/or biological factors of various kinds must be given their due as credible risk factors for various pathological outcomes in adolescence and adulthood involving antisocial behaviors will probably depend on exposure to purveyors of such ideas in the past. Even enlightened advocates for giving genes a chance to explain some of the variance observed within a population must acknowledge the misguided, naive, and sometimes inhuman efforts to misapply biological concepts (Gottesman & Bertelsen, 1996; Proctor, 1988) in order to guarantee "law and order." Attitudes toward the explanatory power of possible genetic factors for such traits as lust and anger, aggression, disruptive behaviors, delinquency, criminality, and antisocial personality have varied greatly over the past five centuries, depending on which discipline chose to appoint itself as caretaker of the public order. The pendulum swung far to the sociopolitical right with such naive early studies of "crime families" as the Jukes and the Kallikaks at the beginning of this century (see Reilly, 1991, for more history). Such misguided efforts have led to the ridicule of genetic and biological constructs up to the present day. The pendulum has swung back toward the middle in recent years, to a multifactorial and probabilistic framework (Carey, 1994; Carey & Gottesman, 1996; Goldsmith & Gottesman, 1996). Researchers are aware of the many steps in gene-to-behavior pathways that give such global variables as individual differences in liability to antisocial behaviors, socioecological differences [nutrition, poverty, gun control (or *un*-control) laws, racism in criminal justice systems], and parenting differences (abuse, divorce, discipline) a chance to improve or to worsen the fit of explanations for a general causal model.

## EPIDEMIOLOGY AND AGGRESSION

A brief survey of some demographic and psychiatric epidemiological facts will reveal that antisocial behaviors are too important to be left in the hands of any one discipline's professionals, such as criminologists, sociologists, behavioral geneticists, lawyers, or neuroscientists. In a report (1996) sponsored by the National Institute of Justice—"Victim Costs and Consequences: A New Look"—annual crime costs that take into account running the justice system, pain, suffering, and reduction in the quality of life, child abuse, and domestic violence reach the amazing figure of almost $500 billion. Contrast that with the 1995 Defense Department budget of half that amount! Even if the number is inflated by a factor of five, prevention based on scientific facts appears to be an excellent alternative. United States Bureau of the Census (1991) statistics tell us that 23.5 million households were "touched by crime" in 1 year (1989) as victims; 11.3 million citizens were arrested (1989; 82% males and 15.5% under age 18); and 3.7 million adults were under correctional supervision.

We are concerned with a much broader phenotype as an indicator of aggression and antisocial behaviors than those adjudicated by the criminal justice system. Epidemiological studies of structured-interview determined rates of *DSM-III-R* antisocial personality (ASP) in the massive sample of 19,182 adults (93% in households, 7% in institutions) in the Epidemiologic Catchment Area (ECA) study were reported by Robins and Regier (1991) and their colleagues. It contains a gold mine of information for the developmental psychopathologist.

ASP—by the conventions of *DSM-III-R*—requires a diagnosis of conduct disorder (CD) as a "gateway" diagnosis before age 15, by meeting any 3 of 12 criteria, as well as 4 of 10 adult problem areas. The childhood problems emphasize aggression with 6 of the 12, encompassing fighting, weapon use, cruelty to humans or animals, forced sex, and mugging/armed robbery. Many problems exist about the taxonomy and nosology of disruptive behaviors (cf. Achenbach, 1993; Caron & Rutter, 1991; Lilienfeld & Waldman, 1990) and we shall return to these important problems of defining a useful phenotype for behavioral genetic analyses shortly. All of the research participants in the ECA were age 18 or older so that diagnoses of conduct disorder, and therefore of ASP, are necessarily retrospective. The best estimate for the lifetime prevalence (now or ever) of ASP was obtained by adding in extra questions about illegal activities, for the St. Louis sample, that were not allowed in the other four sites, yielding 7.3% in males and 1.0% in females (rates that are 53% higher by using such information). Such rates, when projected against the adult population of the United States, give minimal estimates of the proportion of the adult population that engage in, or have engaged in, nontrivial and syndromic antisocial behaviors of 8.87 million males and 1.27 million females. There were no differences in the rates between Blacks and Whites. The structure of the data gathered for ASP diagnoses (Robins, Tipp, & Przybeck, 1991) permit many additional analyses to inform the developmentalist interested in the "architecture" of aggression. The average age of the first symptom reported for satisfying the CD step was between the 8th and 9th birthday; of all males who ever had an ASP diagnosis, 53% reported no symptoms within the past 1 year, as did 50% of the females, a quite unexpected result that supports phenotypic plasticity for antisocial behaviors and embarrasses would-be "genetic determinists." Almost all of the ASPs apparently were in "remission" after they reached age 45; even then, the mean duration from first to last symptom in the "career" of the ASP was 19 years.

## MULTIPLE ROUTES TO AGGRESSION

Antisocial or aggressive behavior can have many developmental roots, each of the roots having its own set of genetic and environmental underpinnings. Among the dispositional roots might be such features as a robust constitution, a typically high energy level, a tendency to be a sensation seeker, low anxiety under conditions that typically evoke inhibition, testosterone levels and serotonin receptor densities, and other such tendencies or predispositions.

Each of these tendencies can have multiple—and divergent—outcomes. For example, the energetic mesomorph who is unafraid to enter dark alleys might be a successful mugger or a decorated police officer, depending on neighborhood heroes/heroines in childhood, attitudinal, cultural, and other chance factors that are easily imagined.

The behavior–genetic principles embodied in these two complications are (a) genetic heterogeneity and (b) pleiotropy. A behavioral pattern can have different genetic roots in different individuals (and no genetic roots at all in some—phenocopies), and a single genotype can have different behavioral manifestations in different individuals. When genetic heterogeneity and pleiotropy are the rule rather than the exception, as they surely must be for antisocial behavior, the genetic analysis of behavior becomes a daunting task.

The concept of proximal versus distal causes is also pertinent. Notions such as "genes for crime" are nonsense, but the following kind of notion appears to be reasonable: There may be *partially* genetically influenced *predispositions* for basic behavioral tendencies, such as impulsivity or novelty-seeking, that under certain experiential contexts make the *probability* of committing certain crimes higher than for individuals who possess lesser degrees of such behavioral tendencies. The most proximal causal factor in the spiral of influences leading to commission of a sanctioned act is the situation surrounding the act. The next most proximal cause is perhaps the reinforcement histories and coercive cycles emphasized by social learning theorists. But more distal factors concern who enters into these cycles and what helps maintain them. Genes might influence these more distal factors probabilistically.

Even the conditional statements that we have just made do not always apply. Some aggressive acts are influenced by genes common to all members of our species; these would include actions required to survive or to guarantee survival of kin or others under extreme conditions. In addition, there are surely some individuals with no genetic risk factors at all who commit crimes of all sorts. Crimes such as civil disobedience and reactions to spousal abuse come to mind.

It should not even be necessary to say that when the *norm* in a community is for an adolescent to join a gang, genetic factors become trivially important in predicting who will get into trouble; the very high base rates alone will frustrate genetic analyses. Neither should it be necessary to say that the behavior–genetic considerations we are using apply to *individual* variability rather than intergroup differences. But in these times of high tensions among ethnic groups worldwide, both of these obvious qualifications need to be stated explicitly.

What evidence is required to support the important role for genetic influences? One line of evidence is statistical and comes from the realm of genetic epidemiology (Plomin, Owen, & McGuffin, 1994). Documentation of the heritability of face-valid relevant behaviors, followed by the demonstration that they predict antisocial behaviors, forms the foundation for our arguments. Documentation that antisocial patterns of behavior are themselves heritable advances our case; however, we are acutely aware that the "phenotypes" provided by the legal systems of all countries are very imperfect ones to subject to genetic analyses, reflecting the whimsies, passions, and prejudices of the times. Another line of evidence is biological, involving both neurochemistry (e.g., Virkkunen, Goldman, & Linnoila, 1996) and the identification of specific stretches of DNA (such as Exon III in the D4DR locus) linked or associated with antisocial behavioral traits, indicators, or patterns (Cloninger, Adolfsson, & Svrakic, 1996; Goldman,

Lappalainen, & Ozaki, 1996). Space does not permit the pursuit of this evolving research area, but we must caution that isolated instances of reported linkage must be viewed with caution, and, if valid, may not generalize beyond the single pedigree in which they have been reported (Brunner, 1996; Vanyukov, Moss, Yu, & Deka, 1995).

## GENETICS AS A RISK FACTOR THROUGHOUT THE LIFE SPAN

One major fallacy that characterizes social scientists' views of genetic risk factors is that they think of genetics as a static rather than as a dynamic influence on development. This basic fallacy is manifest in several ways. For instance, we often read that genetic factors influencing some feature of aggressive or antisocial behaviors are already in place at the time of birth (a recent CNN show was titled, to our dismay as participants, "Born Bad"). Of course, millions of copies of all genes are already in place at birth and there's one copy at conception, but the genetic factors that influence antisocial behavior are perhaps no more "in place" at birth than are one's parents or social class. Genes and parenting are like switches, and they must be turned on to have effects. Another aspect of the basic fallacy is that we tend to think of genetic factors as processes that act early in life with subsequent changes a result of experience. The behavior–genetic data indicate otherwise. Consider some results from twin studies of temperament in infancy and in toddlers, as shown in Table 1 that may be related, later in life, to aggressive behaviors. It could be that the genes that operate during the neonatal period are invariant in the species. Analyses of older infants and young children in the Louisville Twin Study (Matheny, 1989) and in other studies suggest moderate heritability of the dimensions of activity and negative affectivity that are not heritable in the neonatal period (Riese, 1990) for the same twins.

Several interpretations of the difference between the neonatal and late infancy findings are possible, but the findings demonstrate that genetic *effects* are not a "given" at the beginning of life. Granted, genes can act to create some structures, such as receptors for transmitters in a particular

**Table 1**

**Twin Similarity for Normal Variation in Temperament Dimensions Possibly Relevant to Later Aggression[a]**

| Questionnaire Scales | Identical *R* | Same-sex Fraternal *R* | Opposite-sex Fraternal *R* | Pooled Fraternal *R* |
|---|---|---|---|---|
| Twin Similarity for Selected Scales of Rothbart's Infant Behavior Questionnaire[b] | | | | |
| Activity level | .55 | .37 | .33 | .35 |
| Distress to limitations | .65 | .39 | .12 | .25 |
| Twin Similarity for Selected Scales of Goldsmith's Toddler Behavior Assessment Questionnaire[c] | | | | |
| Activity level | .72 | .51 | .14 | .40 |
| Anger proneness | .72 | .49 | .55 | .53 |

*Source:* Adapted from Goldsmith & Gottesman, 1996, with permission of Oxford University Press.
[a]The correlations are adjusted for the effects of age within each of the two groups defined by assessment with the IBQ and TBAQ. Such adjustments typically showed minor differences from the raw correlations.
[b]The number of twin pairs in each group was as follows: identical ($n$ = 80), same-sex fraternal ($n$ = 65), opposite-sex fraternal ($n$ = 66), pooled fraternal ($n$ = 131).
[c]The number of twin pairs in each group was as follows: identical ($n$ = 88), same-sex fraternal ($n$ = 62), opposite-sex fraternal ($n$ = 34), pooled fraternal ($n$ = 96).

tissue, early in life, and the functioning of these structures can later be involved in behavioral dispositions such as poor impulse control in emotionally laden situations. However, gene action at any point in the life span can modify a physical structure or set in motion a physiological process that affects behavioral dispositions. It is clear that heritability established at one developmental period does not necessarily generalize to earlier or later periods.

Findings of moderate genetic influence are common, as shown by data in Table 1 on temperament reported by parents (Goldsmith, 1993, 1996), pooled from three small studies for the two scales of Rothbart's (1981) Infant Behavior Questionnaire (IBQ). These two scales, Activity Level and Distress to Limitations, seem most closely related to undercontrolled behavior. Greater identical than fraternal co-twin similarity for these scales is apparent. Other twin studies tend to support moderate heritability for parental report temperament questionnaire scales for toddlers in the bottom of Table 1, using the Toddler Behavior Assessment Questionnaire (TBAQ) for traits likely to be similar to those measured in infancy. Laboratory measures of overt behavior support the indirect measures. Consider infant fearfulness: Goldsmith and Campos (1986) showed a similar moderate genetic effect on the tendency to express fearful facial and vocal affect during the standardized approach of a stranger as well as on the well-known visual cliff experiment. Data from other studies on infants and on childhood are reviewed elsewhere (Goldsmith & Gottesman, 1996).

Our developing knowledge of gene regulation suggests a couple of caveats about twin studies. Positive evidence of heritability does not necessarily imply that gene action underlies the physiology directly relevant to a temperamental behavioral pattern (Goldsmith, 1988; Tooby & Cosmides, 1990). Direct evidence for this must await molecular genetic studies of temperament. A second caveat is that, although identical twins have identical *structural* genotypes (with the exception of somatic mutations), the active set of genes can differ. That is, identical twins can have different *functional* genotypes in a few cases (Gottesman & Bertelsen, 1989). The point is made well by the five known cases of identical female twins (and one case of identical female triplets) who are *discordant* for X chromosome traits (red–green color blindness, Duchenne muscular dystrophy, and Fragile X), due to the normal twin having most of the mutation-bearing X chromosomes inactivated and the affected co-twin having the opposite pattern (Jorgensen et al., 1992).

## REACTION RANGES AND SURFACES FOR AGGRESSION

As long as we do not take them too literally, a few heuristic concepts can help us grasp some of the complexities of development while we await explication at the molecular level. The concept that we want to emphasize is the "norm of reaction," which was introduced into genetics by Dobzhansky (and predecessors) and into psychology by Gottesman (1963a) as the "reaction range of behavior." One virtue of the reaction range idea is that it can be given quantitative meaning, and another is that it can relegate the deterministic, categorical nature versus nurture controversy to being the twentieth-century equivalent of the medieval controversy over the number of angels that could fit on the head of a pin (cf. Scarr, 1993). For instance, the largest differences observed between identical co-twins with varying experiences would be a lower bound estimate of the phenotypic plasticity for a given genotype. Figure 1 shows an evolution of this heuristic concept—the "reaction surface" of a behavioral trait (Gottesman & Goldsmith, 1994; Turkheimer, Goldsmith, & Gottesman, 1995; Turkheimer & Gottesman, 1991).

The conjectured reaction surfaces in Figure 1, at two stages of development such as childhood and adolescence, show degree of risk for antisocial behaviors on the vertical axis, with an arbitrary scale. The other two axes are the relevant genotypes and environments. The diagram does not embody assumptions about the frequency distributions of either genotypes or environments. The shape of the surface suggests nonlinear effects, which are meant to hint at the complexity of underlying processes (Turkheimer & Gottesman, 1996). The left side of the environmental axis would represent experiences conducive to the development of antisocial behavior; these experiences are designated "hazardous" in the figure. The right side of the environmental axis is labeled "protective." The shape of the surface implies that very hazardous environments—perhaps approached in some inner-city areas—result in antisocial behavior with very high probability in most young males, regardless of genotype. Also, the low level (with resistant genotypes) and gradual rise (with increasing genetic susceptibility) of antisocial behavior in protective environments (seen along the "front" edge of the surface) suggests that the predisposing effects of susceptible genotypes can be countered by experience. The effect of genotype is apparent at all levels of environment, but there is a multiplicative effect when both genotype and environment are high. This interaction can be discerned in the steeper slope of the surface as the environment becomes more hazardous and the genotype becomes more susceptible. Of course, the shape of the reaction surface is simply illustrative, supported by some data but

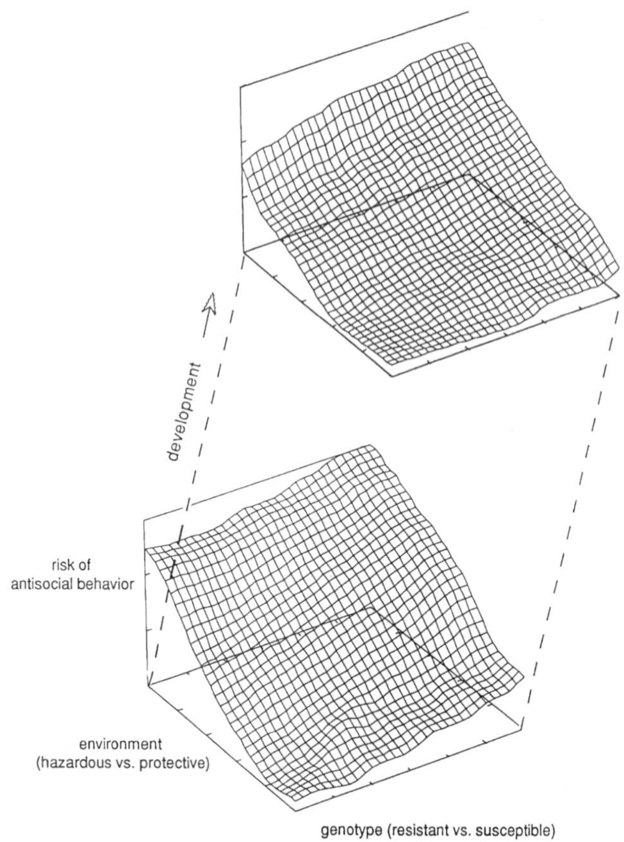


**Figure 1**

Hypothetical Reaction Surfaces for Aggressive/Antisocial Behaviors at Two Times in Development (adapted from Goldsmith & Gottesman, 1996; Turkheimer, Goldsmith, & Gottesman, 1995; Turkheimer & Gottesman, 1991). Copyright © I. I. Gottesman. Used by permission.

largely hypothetical. Even a diagram as complex as Figure 1 is inadequate to portray all the processes involved. One inadequacy of the diagram is the incomplete representation of individual development. Individual possibilities are represented in the sense that there is a wide—but variable—range of phenotypic outcomes for each genotype (Gottesman, 1974). One inadequacy of this schema is that the evidence strongly suggests heterogeneity in the causes of antisocial behavior, and the single axis for

**Table 2**

**Candidates for Components of the Reaction Range: Behavioral Tendencies Reflective of Genotype and Social Processes Reflective of Environment**

| Behavioral Tendencies That Might Be Genetically Influenced | Social Processes That Might Facilitate Development of Various Forms of Undercontrolled Behavioral Patterns |
|---|---|
| Impulse control | Processes that retard moral development |
| Need for stimulation | Processes that hinder perspective-taking and empathy |
| Activity level | Processes that lead to over-attribution of hostility |
| Anxiety proneness | Escalating cycles of coercive family interaction |
| Frustration tolerance | Peer group processes |

*Source:* Goldsmith & Gottesman (1996). Reproduced with the permission of Oxford University.

genotype does not capture this notion of heterogeneity. The same is true for environmental causes of antisocial behavior. We can be more concrete by hypothesizing what the relevant genotype might be for, say, frustration tolerance or delay of gratification, and the relevant environment for, say, processes that lead to over-attribution of hostility to others—a kind of paranoid ethnocentrism. When we begin to specify the processes more concretely, we see immediately that a multivariate family of reaction surfaces that incorporate genetically independent, risk-increasing traits and potentially independent environmental risk factors is needed. Table 2 outlines some specific traits and social processes that are implicated in the genesis of antisocial behavior. How these traits and social processes interact developmentally is a task for the next stage of developmental behavioral genetic research.

We could expand the conceptualization by adding putative biological markers of genotypes related to antisocial behavior. An overview of the field (Reiss & Roth, 1993) suggests some candidates: steroid hormones (testosterone and glucocorticoids) and their receptors; some functions of the neurotransmitters dopamine, norepinephrine, serotonin, acetylcholine, GABA, and various neuropeptides; and neurophysiological measures such as measures of EEG abnormalities and limbic system dysfunction (Raine, 1993). The genetic aspects of these and other candidates should be studied with the tools of behavioral genetics in both probands and their relatives and in the general population across the life span.

It is likely that insofar as genetic risk factors may be important, they are most relevant to a subset of individuals manifesting chronic antisocial behaviors with nonacute onsets. That such a subgroup exists has been repeatedly shown in the literature (cf. Farrington, Loeber, & Van Kammen, 1990). In both of the Philadelphia cohorts studied by Wolfgang and colleagues (Tracy, Wolfgang, & Figlio, 1990), chronic recidivists stood out from the crowd as did the fact that 46% of delinquents stopped after their first offense and a further 35% desisted after a second offense. In the 1945 birth cohort, 6% overall and 18% of the broad category of delinquents perpetrated 61% of the UCR Index crimes (71% of homicides, 73% of rapes, 82% of robberies, and 69% of aggravated assaults). In the 1958 birth cohort of boys, 8% were qualified as chronic recidivists, again defined as five or more offenses before their 18th birthday. By race, the chronic recidivists comprised 3% of White and 11% of Black youths, and together they perpetrated 68% of the index crimes. Two caveats are required at this point: The race difference mentioned is merely descriptive and cannot be taken as an indicator of the relevance of any kind of genetic explanation; and questions about genetic between-group differences in this area cannot be answered with available methods. Violence per se is an area of inquiry that is separable to a large degree from the broader concern with antisocial behaviors, especially if divided into acute and chronic violence; it is only the latter aspect that interests us here (cf. Carey, 1994; Reiss & Roth, 1993).

## SOME GENETIC CONSIDERATIONS IN JUVENILE AND ADULT ANTISOCIAL BEHAVIORS

The stage has now been set for an abridged review of evidence that bears on the question of the degree to which the observed familiarity of adolescent and adult antisocial behaviors merits a partial genetic explanation. We will divide the evidence into traits assessed with psychometric devices such as personality questionnaires with twins, and then look at violations of the law. We will concentrate on those scales that are associated with valid indicators of aggression such as the Pd scale of the Minnesota Multiphasic Personality Inventory (MMPI) and the Aggression scale of the Multidimensional Personality Questionnaire (MPQ). The Pd scale of the MMPI comprises items that reliably distinguish psychopaths from various comparison groups. The Aggression scale of the MPQ comprises rationally selected and factor-analytically verified items concerning physical acts of aggression, retaliation, and vengefulness. We will also consider evidence from twin studies of antisocial personality, criminality, and of adjudicated delinquency. Table 3 shows the correlational patterns for MMPI Pd and MPQ Aggression in various samples of identical or monozygotic (MZ) and fraternal or dizygotic (DZ) twins reared together and apart, together with recent findings that dimensionalized antisocial personality traits (ASP) assessed from a structured interview with very large samples of twin veterans from the Vietnam-era twin register (Lyons et al., 1995).

The consistent, replicable results should convince even the skeptical that the psychometric indicators of behavioral traits related to antisocial behavior are familial and that the familiarity is under important genetic influence. Various estimates of the heritability derived from doubling the difference between MZ and DZ correlations or from MZA (monozygotic twins reared apart) correlations alone are substantial. The McGue, Bacon, and Lykken study (1993) of normal twins at both ages 20 and 30, reported in the second part of Table 3, adds the information that the level of MPQ aggression decreases with maturity, the genetic effect on individual differences decreases with maturity, but the heritability values are substantial at both ages (> .60).

Additional twin studies using different instruments, as well as an array of adoption studies that are quite compatible with the twin studies and also serve to defend such studies from the criticism that twins are different from singletons or that the similarities observed for twins derive simply from their sharing of experiences, are presented elsewhere (Carey, 1994; Coccaro, Bergeman, & McClearn, 1993; Goldsmith & Gottesman, 1996; Slutske et al., in press).

With the foregoing as a bridge to the clinically relevant evidence that

## Table 3

**Quantitative Genetic Evidence for Self-Reported Antisocial Traits: Twins Reared Together and Apart**

Studies of Twins on a Single Occasion

| Study | Measure | MZR | DZR | *N*(MZ pairs, DZ pairs) |
|---|---|---|---|---|
| Gottesman (1963b), Minnesota | MMPI Pd | .57 | .18 | 34, 34 |
| Gottesman (1965), Boston | MMPI Pd | .46 | .25 | 80, 68 |
| Rose (1988),[a] Indiana | MMPI Pd | .47 | .23 | 228, 182 |
| DiLalla, Carey, Gottesman, & Bouchard (1996), Minnesota | | | | |
| • reared apart | MMPI Pd | .62 | .14 | 65, 54 |
| McCartney, Harris, & Bernieri (1990); (meta-analysis) | 8 aggression scales | .49 | .28 | |
| Tellegen et al. (1988), Minnesota | | | | |
| • reared apart | MPQ Aggression | .46 | .06 | 44, 27 |
| • reared together | MPQ Aggression | .43 | .14 | 217, 114 |
| Lyons et al. (1995), United States | ASP Traits-Adult | .47 | .27 | 1788, 1438 |
| | ASP Traits-Juvenile | .39 | .33 | 1788, 1438 |

The McGue et al. (1993) Longitudinal Twin Analysis of MPQ Personality Traits Conceptually Related to Antisocial Behavior

| | Aggression | MPQ Traits Control | Alienation |
|---|---|---|---|
| MZ Twin *R* at age 20 | .61 | .53 | .54 |
| DZ Twin *R* at age 20 | -.09 | .01 | .39 |
| MZ Twin *R* at age 30 | .58 | .44 | .41 |
| DZ Twin *R* at age 30 | -.14 | .19 | .30 |
| Stability from age 20 to 30 | .54 | .55 | .40 |
| MZ Cross-twin, cross-time *R* | .43 | .45 | .27 |
| DZ Cross-twin, cross-time *R* | -.11 | .01 | .06 |

*Source:* Adapted from Goldsmith & Gottesman (1996), with permission from Oxford University.
[a]These MMPI Pd data were provided by personal communication from R. J. Rose (June 1991), based on the same sample and assessment procedure described in Rose (1988).

**Table 4**

**Qualitative Genetic Evidence for Antisocial Behaviors: Twin Concordance[a]**

| Twin Studies of Adjudicated Juvenile Delinquency: Four Studies Pooled From North America, Japan, and England | |
|---|---|
| Total *n* of pairs | Pairwise Concordance Rate |
| 55 identical | 90.9% (se = 3.9%) |
| 30 fraternal | 73.3% (se = 8.1%) |
| **Twin Studies of Adult Criminality: Seven Studies Pooled From Germany, North America, Japan, Norway, and Denmark** | |
| Total *n* of pairs | Pairwise Concordance Rate |
| 229 identical | 51.5% (se = 3.3%) |
| 316 fraternal | 23.1% (se = 2.4%) |

*Source:* Adapted from Goldsmith & Gottesman (1996), with permission from Oxford University Press.
[a] Data from male twins only; se = standard error.

implicates genetic factors in the liability to developing antisocial behaviors, we can examine the twin studies of so called "juvenile delinquency" that have been conducted with varying degrees of sophistication (Walters, 1992; Walters & White, 1989) since 1941 in North America, Japan, and England, concentrating on males only. Table 4 shows little to support a genetic orientation to the results of the four available studies on adjudicated delinquency: The pairwise concordance rates for MZ and DZ twins are both very high and resemble the results obtained from studying such infectious diseases as measles or mumps. Consider also that the base rates of delinquency, variously defined, are 33% or so (in Philadelphia) and in some neighborhoods are close to 100% (Reiss & Roth, 1993). Rowe (1983) conducted a twin study with normal adolescent twins who were asked to self-report antisocial acts. This methodology clearly addresses a somewhat different question from the studies in Table 4 that began with delinquent probands. Both identical and fraternal twins showed substantial similarity, with reasonable evidence for both additive genetic and shared environmental factors. Twins in this study reported that they engaged jointly in

**Table 5**

**Details of Concordance Rates and Correlations for Registered Felonies in Christiansen's Twin Sample From the Danish Twin Register**

| | Pairing | Number of twins | Probandwise rates | | Tetrachoric |
|---|---|---|---|---|---|
| Zygosity | Proband–co-twin | Pairs | Freq./*N* | Percentage | Correlation |
| MZ | Male-male | 365 | 50/98 | 51.0 | .74 ± .07 |
| MZ | Female-female | 347 | 6/18 | 33.3 | .74 ± .12 |
| DZ | Male-male | 700 | 52/172 | 30.2 | .47 ± .06 |
| DZ | Female-male | 2073 | 7/30 | 23.3 | .23 ± .10 |
| DZ | Male-female | 2073 | 7/198 | 3.5 | .23 ± .10 |
| DZ | Female-female | 690 | 4/30 | 13.3 | .46 ± .11 |

NOTE: Adapted from Cloninger & Gottesman (1987). Used with permission from Cambridge University Press.

antisocial acts, a phenomenon that is perhaps biasing in some analyses (see Carey, 1992, and Rowe, 1994, for a detailed treatment of this issue).

Quite a contrasting picture from the delinquency data is obtained from the pooled studies of criminality, largely felony offenses, from seven studies conducted in North America, Germany, Japan, Norway, and Denmark since 1931, again concentrating on males only (female twin felons are rare; cf. Gottesman, Carey, & Hanson, 1983). Such differences in concordance rates as shown in Table 4, when contrasted with base rates of 10% or so in the general adult male population, generate heritabilities of the liability to the antisocial behaviors embodied in the penal codes of these countries that are quite close to those generated by the personality trait scores for the MMPI Pd and MPQ Aggression scales.

Details of the largest twin study of criminality in the literature, initiated by K. O. Christiansen in Denmark, are provided in Table 5 for both genders and for all three kinds of twin pairs. The more appropriate proband-wise rates can be reported (McGue, 1992) as well as the tetrachoric correlation coefficients of liability (Cloninger & Gottesman, 1987); the liability to felony offending in these Danish twins born around the turn of the century and followed to 1980 through various national registers is equally heritable in the two genders, about .54, with substantial shared environmental influences, $c^2 = .20$ (cf. Baker, Mack, Moffitt, & Mednick, 1989, for an elegant analysis of this issue in Danish adoptees). In this country with very few crimes of violence compared with the United States, we could calculate the heritability separately for recidivist property crime only versus violent crimes against persons: The former was .76 and the latter was .50, a nonsignificant difference that is nevertheless in the expected direction for environmentally triggered assaults (Carey, 1994).

## IMPLICATIONS FOR INTERDISCIPLINARY (FREEDMANIAN) HUMAN DEVELOPMENTALISTS

The general implications of the concepts and data that we have presented can be stated simply: The evidence for genetic influences on antisocial behavior is strong enough to convince developmentalists that they should make room for genetic concepts not only in their broad theorizing but also in their research programs. Surely, the twin fallacies of thinking of genetic effects as deterministic and as only being an "early" influence on behavior should be put to rest. And the concept of "genetic risk" should be appreciated as much broader than "family history." However, the complexity of behavioral transitions, the ubiquity of genetic heterogeneity, and the difficulty of specifying the processes whereby genotypes and experiences covary and interact demand that behavioral geneticists be modest in stating the implications of their findings and circumspect in drawing implications for development more generally, let alone for social policy making. The danger for public policy is not in the data—they are just the way things happen to turn out. Genes do imply biology, but genetic influences do not imply that medicine or surgery are the remedies. The challenge of valid genetic findings in this domain is to understand how the interdigitated scores of natural genetic and of natural environmental variation produce different symphonies. The challenge of today's bioethics for behavioral traits is to keep the "natural" in genetic variation and not to permit it to become defined by transient social or political whims.

# REFERENCES

Achenbach, T. M. (1993). Taxonomy and comorbidity of conduct problems: Evidence from empirically based approaches. *Development and Psychopathology, 5*, 51–64.

Baker, L. A., Mack, W., Moffitt, T. E., & Mednick, S. A. (1989). Sex differences in property crime in a Danish adoption cohort. *Behavior Genetics, 19*, 355–370.

Brunner, H. G. (1996). MAOA deficiency and abnormal behaviour: Perspectives on an association. In Ciba Foundation Symposium, *Genetics of Criminal and Antisocial Behaviour.* Chichester, UK: J. Wiley & Sons.

Buss, D. M. (1995). Evolutionary psychology: A new paradigm for psychological science. *Psychological Inquiry, 6*, 1–30.

Carey, G. (1992). Twin imitation for antisocial behavior: Implications for genetic and family environment research. *Journal of Abnormal Psychology, 101*, 18–25.

Carey, G. (1994). Genetics and violence. In A. J. Reiss, K. A. Miczek, & J. A. Roth (Eds.), *Understanding and Preventing Violence. Vol. 2 Biobehavioral Influences* (pp. 21–58). Washington DC: National Academy Press.

Carey, G., & Gottesman, I. I. (1996). Genetic strategies for exploring aggression: Substance vs. sound bytes. *Politics and the Life Sciences, 15*, 88–90.

Caron, C., & Rutter, M. (1991). Comorbidity in child psychopathology: Concepts, issues and research strategies. *Journal of Child Psychology and Psychiatry, 32*, 1063–1080.

Ciba Foundation Symposium 194. (1996). *Genetics of Criminal and Antisocial Behaviour.* Chichester, UK: J. Wiley & Sons.

Cloninger, C. R., Adolfsson, R., & Svrakic, N. M. (1996). Mapping genes for human personality. *Nature-Genetics, 12*, 3–4.

Cloninger, C. R., & Gottesman, I. I. (1987). Genetic and environmental factors in antisocial behavior disorders. In S. A. Mednick, T. E. Moffitt, & S. A. Stack (Eds.), *The causes of crime: New biological approaches* (pp. 92–109). New York: Cambridge University Press.

Coccaro, E. F., Bergeman, C. S., & McClearn, G. E. (1993). Heritability of irritable impulsiveness: A study of twins reared together and apart. *Psychiatry Research, 48*, 229–242.

DiLalla, D. L., Carey, G., Gottesman, I. I., & Bouchard, T. J. (1996). Heritability of MMPI indicators of personality psychopathology via MMPI in twins reared apart. *Journal of Abnormal Psychology, 105*, 491–499.

Farrington, D., Loeber, R., & Van Kammen, W. B. (1990). Long-term criminal outcomes of hyperactivity-impulsivity-attention deficit and conduct problems in childhood. In L. N. Robins & M. Rutter (Eds.), *Straight and devious pathways from childhood to adulthood* (pp. 62–81). New York: Cambridge University Press.

Freedman, D. G. (1965). An ethological approach to the genetical study of human behavior. In S. G. Vandenberg (Ed.), *Methods and goals in human behavior genetics.* New York: Academic Press.

Freedman, D. G. (1974). *Human infancy: An evolutionary perspective.* New York: Wiley.

Freedman, D. G. (1979), *Human sociobiology.* New York: Free Press.

Ghodsian-Carpey, J., & Baker, L. A. (1987). Genetic and environmental influences on aggression in 4- to 7-year-old twins. *Aggresssive Behavior, 13,* 173–186.

Goldman, D., Lappalainen, & Ozaki, N. (1996). Direct analysis of candidate genes in impulsive behaviours. In Ciba Foundation Symposium, *Genetics of Criminal and Antisocial Behaviour* (pp. 139–152). Chichester, UK: John Wiley & Sons.

Goldsmith, H. H. (1988). Human developmental behavioral genetics: Mapping the effects of genes and environments. *Annals of Child Development, 5,* 187–227.

Goldsmith, H. H. (1993). Temperament: Variability in developing emotion systems. In M. Lewis & J. M. Haviland (Eds.), *Handbook of emotion.* New York: Guilford Press.

Goldsmith, H. H. (1996). Studying temperament via construction of the Toddler Behavior Assessment Questionnaire. *Child Development, 67,* 218–235.

Goldsmith, H. H., & Campos, J. J. (1986). Fundamental issues in the study of early temperament: The Denver Twin Temperament Study. In M. E. Lamb, A. L. Brown, & B. Rogoff (Eds.), *Advances in developmental psychology* (Vol. 4, pp. 231–283). Hillsdale, NJ: Erlbaum.

Goldsmith, H. H., & Gottesman, I. I. (1996). Heritable variability and variable heritability in developmental psychopathology. In M. F. Lenzenweger & J. J. Haugaard (Eds.), *Frontiers of developmental psychopathology* (pp. 5–43). New York: Oxford University Press.

Gottesman, I. I. (1963a). Genetic aspects of intelligent behavior. In N. Ellis (Ed.), *The handbook of mental deficiency.* New York: McGraw-Hill.

Gottesman, I. I. (1963b). Heritability of personality: A demonstration. *Psychological Monographs, 77,* 1–21.

Gottesman, I. I. (1965). Personality and natural selection. In S. G. Vandenberg (Ed.), *Methods and Goals in Human Behavior Genetics.* New York: Academic Press.

Gottesman, I. I. (1974). Developmental genetics and ontogenetic psychology: Overdue detente and propositions from a matchmaker. In A. D. Pick (Ed.), *Minnesota symposia on child psychology* (pp. 55–80). Minneapolis: University of Minnesota Press.

Gottesman, I. I. (1991). *Schizophrenia genesis: The origins of madness.* New York: Freeman.

Gottesman, I. I., & Bertelsen, A. (1989). Confirming unexpressed genotypes for schizophrenia: Risks in the offspring of Fischer's Danish identical and fraternal discordant twins. *Archives of General Psychiatry, 46*, 867–872.

Gottesman, I. I., & Bertelsen, A. (1996). The legacy of German psychiatric genetics: Hindsight is always 20/20. *American Journal of Medical Genetics (Neuropsychiatric Genetics), 67*, 317–322.

Gottesman, I. I., Carey, G., & Hanson, D. R. (1983). Pearls and perils in epigenetic psychopathology. In S. B. Guze, E. J. Earls, & J. E. Barrett (Eds.), *Childhood psychopathology and development* (pp. 286–299). New York: Raven Press.

Gottesman, I. I., & Goldsmith, H. H. (1994). Developmental psychopathology of antisocial behavior: Inserting genes into its ontogenesis and epigenesis. In C. A. Nelson (Ed.), *Threats to optimal development: Integrating biological, psychological, and social risk factors* (pp. 69–104). Hillsdale, NJ: Erlbaum.

Hamilton, W. D. (1964). The genetical evolution of social behavior. *Journal of Theoretical Biology, 7*, 1–16.

Jorgensen, A. L., Philip, J., Raskind, W. H., Matsushita, M., Christensen, B., Dreyer, V., & Motulsky, A. G. (1992). Different patterns of X inactivation in MZ twins discordant for red–green color-vision deficiency. *American Journal of Human Genetics, 51*, 291–298.

King, R. A., Rotter, J. I., & Motulsky, A. G. (Eds.). (1992). *The genetics of common diseases.* London: Oxford University Press.

Lilienfeld, S. O., & Waldman, I. D. (1990). The relation between childhood attention-deficit hyperactivity disorder and adult antisocial behavior reexamined: The problem of heterogeneity. *Clinical Psychology Review, 10*, 699–725.

Lyons, M. J., True, W., Eisen, S., Goldberg, J., Meyer, J., Faraone, S. V., Eaves, L., & Tsuang, M. T. (1995). Differential heritability of adult and juvenile antisocial traits. *Archives of General Psychiatry, 52*, 906–915.

McCartney, K., Harris, M. J., & Bernieri, F. (1990). Growing up and growing apart: A developmental meta-analysis of twin studies. *Psychological Bulletin, 107*, 226–237.

Matheny, A. P. (1989). Children's behavioral inhibition over age and across situations: Genetic similarity for a trait during change. *Journal of Personality, 57,* 215–226.

McGue, M. (1992). When assessing twin concordance, use the probandwise not the pairwise rate. *Schizophrenia Bulletin, 18,* 171–176.

McGue, M., Bacon, S., & Lykken, D. T. (1993). Personality stability and change in early childhood: A behavioral genetic analysis. *Developmental Psychology, 29,* 96–109.

Plomin, R., Owen, M. J., & McGuffin, P. (1994). The genetic basis of complex human behaviors. *Science, 264,* 1733–1739.

Proctor, R. N. (1988). *Racial hygiene: Medicine under the Nazis.* Cambridge, MA: Harvard University Press.

Raine, A. (1993). *The psychopathology of crime.* New York: Academic Press.

Reilly, P. R. (1991). *The surgical solution.* Baltimore: Johns Hopkins University Press.

Reiss, A. J., & Roth, J. A. (1993). *Understanding and preventing violence.* Washington, DC: National Academy Press.

Riese, M. L. (1990). Neonatal temperament in monozygotic and dizygotic twin pairs. *Child Development, 61,* 1230–1237.

Robins, L. N., & Regier, D. A. (1991). *Psychiatric disorders in America.* New York: Free Press.

Robins, L. N., Tipp, J., & Przybeck, T. (1991). Antisocial personality. In L. N. Robins & D. A. Regier (Eds.), *Psychiatric disorders in America* (pp. 258–290). New York: Free Press.

Rose, R. J. (1988). Genetic and environmental variance in content dimensions of the MMPI. *Journal of Personality and Social Psychology, 55,* 302–311.

Rothbart, M. K. (1981). Measurement of temperament in infancy. *Child Development, 52,* 569–578.

Rowe, D. (1983). Biometrical genetic models of self-reported delinquent behavior: A twin study. *Behavior Genetics, 13,* 473–489.

Rowe, D. (1994). *The limits of family influence.* New York: Guilford Press.

Scarr, S. (1993). Biological and cultural diversity: The legacy of Darwin for development. *Child Development, 64,* 1333–1353.

Segal, N. L. (1993). Twin, sibling and adoption methods: Tests of evolutionary hypotheses. *American Psychologist, 48,* 943–956.

Slutske, W. S., Heath, A. C., Dinwiddie, S. H., Madden, P. A. F., Bucholz, K. K., Dunne, M. P., Statham, D. J., & Martin, N. G. (in press). Genetic and environmental influences in the etiology of conduct disorder: A study of 2682 adult twin pairs. *Journal of Abnormal Psychology.*

Tellegen, A., Lykken, D. T., Bouchard, T. J., Jr., Wilcox, K. J., Segal, N. L., & Rich, S. (1988). Personality similarity in twins reared apart and together. *Journal of Personality and Social Psychology, 54,* 1031–1039.

Tooby, J., & Cosmides, L. (1990). On the universality of human nature and the uniqueness of the individual: The role of genetics and adaptation. *Journal of Personality, 58,* 17–68.

Tracy, P. E., Wolfgang, M. E., & Figlio, R. M. (1990). *Delinquency careers in two birth cohorts.* New York: Plenum Press.

Trivers, R. (1985). *Social Evolution.* Menlo Park, CA: Benjamin/Cummings.

Turkheimer, E., Goldsmith, H. H., & Gottesman, I. I. (1995). Commentary—Some conceptual deficiencies in "developmental" behavior genetics. *Human Development, 38,* 142–153.

Turkheimer, E., & Gottesman, I. I. (1991). Individual differences and the canalization of behavior. *Developmental Psychology, 27,* 18–22.

Turkheimer, E., & Gottesman, I. I. (1996). Simulating the dynamics of genes and environment in development. *Development and Psychopathology, 8,* 667–677.

U. S. Bureau of Census (1991). *Statistical abstract of the United States: 1991* (111th ed.). Washington, DC: Author.

Vanyukov, M. M., Moss, H. H., Yu, L. M., & Deka, R. (1995). A dinucleotide repeat polymorphism at the gene for monoamine oxidase A and measures of aggressiveness. *Psychiatry Research, 59,* 35–41.

Virkkunen, M., Goldman, D., & Linnoila, M. (1996). Serotonin in alcoholic violent offenders. In Ciba Foundation Symposium, *Genetics of criminal and antisocial behaviour.* Chichester, UK: John Wiley & Sons.

Walters, G. D. (1992). A meta-analysis of the gene–crime relationship. *Criminology, 30,* 595–613.

Walters, G. D., & White, T. W. (1989). Heredity and crime: Bad genes or bad research? *Criminology, 27,* 455–485.

Wilson, E. O. (1975). *Sociobiology.* Cambridge, MA: Harvard University Press.

Wilson, M. I., & Daly, M. (1996). Male sexual proprietariness and violence against wives. *Current Directions in Psychological Science, 5,* 2–7.

# 6

# Genetic Analysis of Social Behavior

John Paul Scott

In 1945, Dr. Clarence Cook Little, director of the Jackson Laboratory, at Bar Harbor, Maine, was awarded a generous grant from the Rockefeller Foundation to support research on the genetic basis of behavior using domestic dogs as subjects. Dr. Little's first task was to locate a capable research staff to work on the project. He did not have far to look, because I was, at that time, the only trained geneticist in the country who had done research on behavior.

I accepted the job, provided I could freely set the direction of the research I chose to do by placing emphasis on genetics and social behavior. I would also be able to choose my associates and subordinates, which meant both staff members and research assistants.

One of these assistants was Daniel G. Freedman, who at the time was working with Abraham Maslow at Brandeis University. I offered Dan a research assistantship with the understanding that he would, as the main part of his dissertation research, conduct research on the developing behavior of puppies in our laboratory. As I have found with other graduate assistants, Dan affected my research as much as I directed his.

Observational and cross-breeding studies of pure-bred dog populations led to several major discoveries in which Freedman (1958) played an important role. (*Cross-breeding* involves matings between members of different animal breeds to create hybrids.) This procedure permits analyses of the effects of the genotype of an organism on behavioral processes and outcomes.

I shall describe two major lines of research, which span a 20-year period. The first area involves the discovery of a major social phenomenon, the critical period for social attachment (see, for example, Freedman, King, & Elliot, 1961; Scott, 1958). The second area concerns gender and breed differences in agonistic behavior (see Scott, 1992a). In this work, behavioral tests were always repeated at different ages. It was assumed that most of the important behavioral changes would appear during the first year of life, because most dogs, but not all, become sexually mature by 1 year. In this way it became possible to study the emergence of genetically influenced behavior. The most important finding to emerge from the research program was that *behavior is never inherited as such, but it is developed under the influence of genetic and physiological processes interacting with environmental stimuli.* (Also see chapter 5 in this volume for a related discussion by Gottesman and colleagues.)

## BEHAVIORAL GENETIC ANALYSIS

In the 1930s there was little scientific literature on the area that later became known as behavior genetics. Initial study of this subject, therefore, began with an intriguing observation in one of the stocks of drosophila maintained in the laboratory of Professor Sewell Wright at the University of Chicago. Specifically, it appeared that the drosophila carrying the *bw* gene (the primary effect of which was to produce brown pigment in a normally red eye) also showed heightened responsivity to strong light.

Extensive breeding experiments, including backcrossing, demonstrated that the response to light was not produced by the *bw* gene but by some other(s), the locus of which was unknown. (A *backcross* involves matings between members from the first generation, $F_1$, and members from the parental line. Such procedures are conducted with experimental animals to determine patterns of genetic transmission.) It is interesting to note that another eye-color gene, that for white-eye, did produce an effect on the fruit fly's response to light (Scott, 1943). However, this finding was not related to social behavior, nor are fruit flies closely related to humans, in whose social behavior I was primarily interested. Therefore, research efforts shifted to the agonistic behavior of inbred strains of house mice, which offered a more appropriate tool for genetic analysis. I found that there was indeed genetic variation among the inbred strains, leading to an extensive research program on social fighting in *Mus musculus,* the common house mouse.

## GENETICS OF SOCIAL BEHAVIOR

The opportunity to study the genetics of social behavior in the domestic dog followed shortly thereafter (Scott & Fuller, 1965). Social–genetic theory is concerned with the effects of the genotypes of individuals on social interaction (Fuller & Hahn, 1976; Hahn, 1990). Dyadic relationships are useful for experimental and theoretical treatments of behavior in this domain because of their simplicity and because they possess the general features of a social system (Scott, 1983).

The majority of developmental social–genetic research has utilized nonhuman rather than human research participants because of the increased control over matings and living arrangements afforded to investigators. Increased cooperation has been observed between genetically homogeneous partners relative to genetically heterogeneous partners, using dogs representing various breeds (Scott, 1977). Higher levels of exploratory and agonistic behaviors have been observed in groups of mixed-strain than same-strain mice (Hughes, 1989). The contribution of early social experience with genetically similar and dissimilar organisms to later social interactions is also of interest (Scott, 1977; see chapter 7 in which Segal illustrates the application of a developmental social–genetic perspective in an analysis of cooperation using monozygotic and dizygotic twins).

## Social Attachment

The first research project was called the "Wild Dog Experiment" (Freedman, King, & Elliot, 1961). In this study, puppies were reared apart from humans for the first 3 months of their lives. It was found that there was a critical period of social attachment, extending from approximately 4 to 10 weeks of age, with a peak occurring at approximately 8 weeks. This is a beautiful example of the interaction between genetic and environmental factors.

This work led to additional experimentation on the processes of attachment in dogs. It turned out that the process of site attachment (i.e., attachment to places) was much longer than the process of social attachment, ending at 5 or 6 months of age. A dog restricted to a kennel beyond 6 months developed the "kennel-dog syndrome." These animals simply did not become attached to an adoptive home, no matter how expert and kind the new owners were. Furthermore, they might become either aggressive or fearful toward humans, and no amount of tender care and contact would alleviate this behavior. This observation suggested that a similar phenomenon might exist in humans, which might contribute to fearful and aggressive behavior toward strangers, a topic considered in the next section.

## Agonistic Behavior

One of the developmental processes studied most thoroughly was that of *agonistic behavior*, or physical conflict between conspecifics. In dogs any form of conflict is absent at birth and first appears in immature puppies at approximately 2 weeks.

A reliable stimulus for arousing conflict between two puppies is a fresh bone. As such, puppies were tested for bone dominance every other week from 5 to 15 weeks of age and finally at 1 year.

As anticipated, breed differences in vocal signals, degrees of violence, and stability of dominance relationships were observed. The greatest differences among the samples of five breeds were between the beagles and wire-haired fox terriers. The former have been selected for pack hunting (usually rabbits) like other hound breeds. One apparent characteristic of the beagle breed is that fighting, either between puppies or between adults, is largely a matter of threats and vocalizations. Such animals, even if strange to each other, can work together in a pack with a minimum of fighting. Another observed characteristic was that in a maze-learning situation, the beagles were slow habit formers. A beagle that ran down a field in the same way day after day would not catch many rabbits. This was the *only* cognitive trait in which a pronounced breed difference was detected.

Terrier breeds, in contrast, have been selected as attack dogs. Fox terriers were chosen for their readiness to enter a cornered fox's burrow and attack it. Fox terriers are relatively insensitive to pain, and in their conflicts as puppies they frequently engage in serious fights involving group attacks on an individual. In one such case, the result was serious injury and death. It was found that the largest litter of terriers that could be reared together successfully was three. One terrier puppy can stand off two attackers, but not three, as might occur in a litter of four.

One of the most interesting set of genetic findings involved gender differences in behavior. Between male puppies, the contest for the bone would eventually erupt into an actual fight, in which each puppy attempted to grasp the other by the back of the neck and force it to the ground. The winner of the contest became dominant, a position enforced by threats on subsequent occasions. This same behavior would occur in male–female dyads, and because males are, on average, larger and heavier than females, the males usually won. However, within female pairs, dominance became established by threats and vocalizations in the absence of physical conflict. A small barking female might become dominant over a much larger but placid one.

Incidentally, such behavior is characteristic of canine mothers and their offspring. At the time of weaning, a mother may respond to a puppy's attempt at nursing with a ferocious growl. The puppy responds by rolling over on its back and screaming, even though the mother has not physically harmed it. In extended research experience with dogs, a mother was observed biting her puppies on only a single occasion. These bites inflicted serious injuries, and it was obvious that the offspring of such a mother would have a poor chance of survival. Any genetic tendency in this direction would be rapidly bred out of a population.

In summary, male and female dogs show differences in the expression of agonistic behavior. In the context of female–offspring interactions, such behavior has an obviously adaptive function, leading to improved chances for the survival of offspring. Whether comparable gender differences occur among humans remains an open question. Statistics for violent crimes reveal major gender differences in frequency of commission of aggressive behaviors, regardless of culture (Scott, 1994). This point will be discussed in greater detail later.

One of the most novel findings was that genetically influenced variation in behavior did not fall into normal curves. Furthermore, the combined effects of genes did not appear to be additive in nature. In the analyses, the data were forced into normal distributions by arbitrarily grouping different sections of a scale into what they would have been in a normally distributed set of data (stanines). The important point is that genes rarely combine in an additive fashion, but rather are expressed in interactive ways that can only be described physiologically.

## IMPLICATIONS FOR HUMAN BEHAVIOR

How does the foregoing relate to problems of human violence? In the first place, the issues just considered are unrelated to warfare, which is a peculiarly human phenomenon. At most, generalizations from one species to another provide grounds for hypotheses that can be tested in the human species. Dogs are not small humans with four legs, fur coats, and a tail. Even after 9000 years or more of selection for human–dog interaction, dogs remain dogs, with the same basic patterns of social behavior as wolves.

What dogs do share with humans is a critical period for social attachment, a finding confirmed by repeated observation and experimentation. Even here there are differences. The critical period for social attachment in puppies begins at approximately 4 weeks of age, reaches a maximum at approximately 8 weeks, and declines rather rapidly during the next 4 weeks. In contrast, in humans this process begins at approximately 2 months and reaches maximum speed during the next 4 months. A decline begins at approximately 6 months, but never entirely disappears. Furthermore, unlike puppies, human babies develop their primary social attachments while still incapable of independent locomotion, which means that the most likely object of primary social attachment is the mother or other adult caretaker. Puppies, in contrast, become attached not only to the mother but to other litter mates. (Possible exceptions at the human level concern social attachment processes between twins; see Vandell, Owen, Wilson, & Henderson, 1988.)

Other developmental processes may differ across the two species. For example, the dog achieves adult physical development very quickly, a process that is completed at about 1 year of age. A human may not achieve comparable maturity until after the age of 10 years at the earliest. There are, of course, many other differences in the process of sexual reproduction in the two species. In fact, there is no perfect animal model for human reproduction.

## THE BEHAVIORAL BASES OF SOCIAL ORGANIZATION

Every animal species has characteristic patterns of adaptive behavior. Adaptation requires differential responses to variation in the environment. One aspect of the environment is the presence of conspecifics. Responses to conspecifics establish behavioral patterns that are the bases of social organization. Historically, biologists and psychologists called such patterns *instincts,* defined as rigidly organized patterns of behavior (Slater, 1985). Unfortunately, such a concept leads nowhere with respect to the development of theories, particularly theories related to genetics, which is the science of variation. In my own work I have surveyed the animal kingdom and described and classified the types of behavior that lead to social organization.

## Animal Aggregations

The term *animal aggregations* was first used by the ecologist W. C. Allee (1931), a professor at the University of Chicago. He reported a general tendency for animals to mass together under unfavorable conditions, such as the presence of predators, thus bettering their chances for survival. However, this behavior does not necessarily lead to enduring associations and more elaborate social interactions, although it might possibly be the evolutionary origin of them.

## Sexual Behavior and Sexual Reproduction

Sexual reproduction is almost universal in the animal kingdom, providing the basis for genetic variation that is essential for evolutionary change. However, sexual behavior is common only in land-living animals that cannot otherwise bring their eggs and sperm together for the process of fertilization.

In most species, sexual behavior is reduced to the minimum association required for fertilization. It is only among certain mammals that its function is extended to social cohesion. Among wolves, females come into estrus gradually, being attractive to males for approximately a month, thereby facilitating close contact between males and females. Among anthropoid apes sexual behavior is extended for relatively long periods on either side of the precise time of ovulation. The human species carries this tendency to the maximum extent. Humans are one of the world's sexiest creatures, with the possible exception of the bonobo chimpanzees described by DeWaal (1995). With regard to social organization, the result in humans is sometimes a polygynous group, usually reduced to a monogamous pair in modern industrial societies, but only rarely a polyandrous group.

## Caregiving, or Epimeletic, Behavior

Reproduction is not solely a matter of fertilization. One sort of behavior that increases the survival rate of offspring is the feeding and care of the young. Among the lower invertebrates the tube-worm *Neanthes*, a marine annelid worm, is of interest. Each male builds a U-shaped tube in which he fans the sea water so that oxygen is continuously available. A female may enter, mate, and lay eggs. The male then ejects her, and remains in the tube fanning the eggs until they hatch and the young worms eventually leave. The male does not, however, feed the young. This example emphasizes the fact that caregiving behavior is not an exclusively female behavior. This is particularly true of birds. For example, mourning doves mate in pairs. The female lays two eggs, after which the male and female alternately provide care on a 6-hour schedule. Both parents feed the young with crop milk. Exclusively female care occurs even in some mammals, such as mountain sheep. In addition, care may be extended to unrelated young, as happens in many bird species (Barash, 1982) and even among humans, as in the case of adoption (Golombok, Cook, Bish, & Murray, 1995).

The importance of caregiving behavior as an emotional and motivational basis of social organization is not sufficiently recognized. This may be particularly true in Western cultures that emphasize individuality. The significance of caregiving behavior is also overlooked by many evolutionists. The explanation for the importance of parental care is simple enough: Mated pairs can compete over the survival rate of their offspring, even if there is no contact between pairs. Competition does not require direct physical harm inflicted on another individual, only that there be differential survival (Scott, 1989).

## Agonistic Behavior or Social Conflict

Conflict underlies one of the most important practical problems of human societies. It is a problem to which I have devoted a great deal of research (Scott, 1992b), beginning with early studies on fighting mice (Scott, 1943). This is also an area to which Daniel Freedman and his associates have directed considerable attention with respect to humans (Omark, Strayer, & Freedman, 1980). A summary of key findings is presented:

1. Agonistic behavior can lead to social organization. However, this phenomenon is common only among vertebrate animals, most likely because vertebrates possess superior eyesight that enables them to easily

distinguish individuals and react to them differentially. Distinguishing among individuals is prerequisite for social organization. Historically, the first discoveries of social organization were reported among birds, such as in Schjelderup-Ebbe's (1922) report of the pecking order in chickens and Howard's (1920) book, *Territory in Bird Life.* In the case of chickens, the result is a flock organized as a set of dominance–subordination relationships that determine the distribution of food, whereas conflict for the possession of living space may result in the formation of breeding territories. However, as was demonstrated by our studies of house mice, not every species forms effective dominance–subordination relationships, and these nocturnal animals show only a very loose territorial organization.

A number of investigators have reported that American children and adolescents are capable of forming dominance–subordination relationships (Omark, Strayer, & Freedman, 1980; Savin-Williams, 1987; Weisfeld, Weisfeld, & Callaghan, 1982). Parents may become dominant over children from their earliest years and may maintain this position indefinitely (Stephens, 1963). Territoriality is another feature of human social organization that exists at all levels from individuals to nations. Such organization is complicated by human language, a phenomenon that has only rudimentary counterparts in other species.

2. Destructive agonistic behavior is often a result of social disorganization. This can be experimentally demonstrated in nonhuman animal populations and is a well-documented occurrence in human populations (Daly & Wilson, 1988). Violent human criminals are most commonly males between 16 to 25 years of age, tend to come from broken homes or disorganized families, and are typically unemployed. Promoting stable social organization is, therefore, one of the most important and effective methods for controlling destructive individual violence.
3. Destructive violence can result from social organizations designed for this purpose. This is particularly true of human warfare but also can occur in the case of gangs (Thrasher, 1927). The destruc-

tive potential of human agonistic behavior is magnified by the use of tools invented for the purpose of killing. An unarmed human has very little biological potential for killing (e.g., humans lack claws and have small teeth). Historically, wars have usually been won by superior arms or tools (Darlington, 1969). Humans have the capacity to become either extremely destructive or extraordinarily peaceful. Historically, we can point to the example of the Norse Vikings, who were the terror of Western Europe in the eighth and ninth centuries. Today, their Scandinavian descendants live in some of the most well ordered and peaceful communities in the world (Moen, 1989).

The foregoing suggests that scientists today possess the scientific information required to organize a peaceful and productive world. Research should, therefore, be directed toward the problem of encouraging people to use these resources (Scott, 1992b), rather than following the well-worn road to destruction. Objective appraisal of agonistic behavior in the United States suggests that we may apply our knowledge most effectively toward the betterment of major social institutions. These institutions are human creations, each based on a code of behavior that is, in turn, based on language.

The oldest of these institutions is the family. As is now known from comparative anthropology, the nuclear family is not the basic unit of organization; rather, it is the ultimate stage of reduction of family organization. In almost all tribal societies, the extended family prevails, consisting of three generations who live in close proximity and cooperate in many ways (Stephens, 1963). In fact, from archeological evidence and from what is known about tribal human societies, even larger aggregations probably typified the primitive stage of human organization. Prehistorical societies most likely consisted of groups of 25 to 50 individuals, including both males and females from infancy to old age. Within the group, as well as in extant tribal societies, social functions are organized by specifying which males and females may mate, and who takes care of whom. Agonistic behavior is regulated in various ways, depending on the culture.

In the United States, the presently dominant social institution is not the family but economic institutions. In the particular form of economic organization seen in the United States, the code of behavior is based on individualism. Individualism assumes that every person should compete to gather as much wealth as possible, whether or not this interferes with other institutions. For example, even if an individual follows his or her own fortunes, the smallest unit of family organization remains the nuclear family. Even that may be breaking down into single-parent families, with the functions of child care and rearing becoming increasingly institutionalized.

Examined historically, the United States began an attempt to militarily conquer and economically exploit an area of the world that was less advanced in both respects. The early explorers of North America were looking for the wealth of the Indies. For whatever reason, the part of North America that became the United States was sparsely inhabited, mostly by Amerindian tribal societies that were easily overcome. The result of conquest was the virtual destruction of much of the social organization of these societies. These societies were replaced by immigrants from Western Europe who pose another case of social disorganization. Hundreds and even thousands of unrelated individuals were thrown together without previous organization. Thus, the United States was founded on violence and social disorganization, and we have not yet recovered from these historical effects, which have in many ways been incorporated into our institutions.

## WHAT CAN SCIENCE DO?

The careers of persons such as Daniel Freedman and myself were founded on the hope that if we could gather enough scientific information we could solve, or at last alleviate, some of the social problems just outlined. The answers as we found them are not simple. Understanding will not automatically produce solutions. If I were to begin my career today I would address efforts not to the discovery of basic causes but rather to the development of a science of social engineering, a form of "how to do it" science.

# REFERENCES

Allee, W. C. (1931). *Animal aggregations.* Chicago: University of Chicago Press.

Barash, D. P. (1982). *Sociobiology and behavior* (2nd ed.). New York: Elsevier.

Daly, M., & Wilson, M. (1988). *Homicide.* Hawthorne, NY: Aldine de Gruyter.

Darlington, C. D. (1969). *The evolution of man and society.* New York: Simon & Schuster.

DeWaal, F. B. M. (1995). Bonobo sex and society. *Scientific American, 1,* 82–88.

Freedman, D. G. (1958). Constitutional and environmental interactions in rearing of four dog breeds. *Science, 127,* 585–586.

Freedman, D. G., King, J. A., & Elliot, O. (1961). Critical period in the social development of dogs. *Science, 133,* 1016–1017.

Fuller, J. L., & Hahn, M. E. (1976). Issues in the genetics of social behavior. *Behavior Genetics, 6,* 391–406.

Golombok, S., Cook, R., Bish, A., & Murray, C. (1995). Families created by the new reproductive technologies: Quality of parenting and social and emotional development of the children. *Child Development, 66,* 285–298.

Hahn, M. E. (1990). Approaches to the study of genetic influence on developing social behaviors. In M. E. Hahn, J. K. Hewitt, N. D. Henderson, & R. H. Benno (Eds.), *Developmental behavior genetics: Neural, biometrical and evolutionary approaches* (pp. 60–80). New York: Oxford University Press.

Howard, E. (1920). *Territory in bird life.* London: John Murray.

Hughes, A. L. (1989). Interaction between strains in the social relations of inbred mice. *Behavior Genetics, 19,* 685–699.

Moen, P. (1989). *Working parents: Transformations in gender roles and public policies in Sweden.* Madison: University of Wisconsin Press.

Omark, D. R., Strayer, F. F., & Freedman, D. G. (Eds.). (1980). *Dominance relations: An ethological view of human conflict and social interaction.* New York: Garland.

Savin-Williams, R. (1987). *Adolescence: An ethological perspective.* New York: Springer.

Schjelderup-Ebbe, T. (1922). Beitrage zur Sozial-psychologies des Haushuhns. *Zeitschrift für Psychologie, 88,* 225–252.

Scott, J. P. (1943). Effects of single genes in the social behavior of inbred strains of mice. *American Naturalist, 77,* 184–190.

Scott, J. P. (1958). Critical periods in the development of social behavior of puppies. *Psychosomatic Medicine, 20,* 42–54.

Scott, J. P. (1977). Social genetics. *Behavior Genetics, 7*, 327–346.

Scott, J. P. (1983). Genetics of social behavior in nonhuman animals. In J. Fuller & E. C. Simmel (Eds.), *Behavior genetics: Principles and applications* (pp. 363–371). Hillsdale, NJ: Erlbaum.

Scott, J. P. (1989). *The evolution of social systems.* New York: Gordon & Breach.

Scott, J. P. (1992a). Aggression in canine females. In K. Bjorkqvist & C. P. Niemela (Eds.), *Of mice and women: Aspects of female aggression* (pp. 307–316). New York: Academic Press.

Scott, J. P. (1992b). Aggression: Functions and control in social systems. *Aggressive Behavior, 18*, 1–20.

Scott, J. P. (1994). Introduction: Sex differences in aggression. *Aggressive Behavior, 20*, 167–171.

Scott, J. P., & Fuller, J. L. (1965). *Genetics and the social behavior of the dog.* Chicago: University of Chicago Press.

Slater, P. J. B. (1985). *An introduction to ethology.* Cambridge: Cambridge University Press.

Stephens, W. N. (1963). *The family in cross-cultural perspective.* New York: Holt, Rinehart & Winston.

Thrasher, F. M. (1927). *The gang: A study of 1,313 gangs in Chicago.* Chicago: University of Chicago Press.

Vandell, D. L., Owen, M. T., Wilson, K. S., & Henderson, V. K. (1988). Social development in infant twins: Peer and mother–child relationships. *Child Development, 59*, 168–177.

Weisfeld, C. C., Weisfeld, G. E., & Callaghan, J. W. (1982). Female inhibition in mixed-sex competition among young adolescents. *Ethology and Sociobiology, 3*, 29–42.

7

# Twin Research Perspective on Human Development

Nancy L. Segal

Dan Freedman was one of the first investigators to articulate the meaningful relationships between behavior genetics and evolutionary psychology. His insights moved twin methods beyond their traditional application in studies of nature and nurture to a means for considering how relative genetic relatedness may influence human social behavior and organization. The studies described in this chapter flow naturally from that perspective. Potential contributions from additional novel extensions of twin and adoption designs are also examined.

## OVERVIEW

We seem to be rediscovering the twin method all the time. This is not surprising—the classic twin method and variations of that method offer simple and elegant ways of examining genetic and environmental influences underlying human behavioral variation. Monozygotic (MZ, or identical) twins share all their genes, whereas dizygotic (DZ, or fraternal) twins share half their genes, on average, by descent. Greater resemblance between MZ twins, relative to DZ twins, suggests genetic influence underlying variation in a trait of interest. It appears, however, that researchers have not taken full advantage of these methods for examining genetic and evolutionary-based hypotheses concerning human social behaviors. Application of twin research designs from a human ethological perspective have also been rare.

Twin studies have, however, proliferated in selected areas of the behavioral and medical sciences. Some outstanding empirical and theoretical developments are briefly summarized: (a) Intriguing new perspectives for interpreting behavioral similarity between opposite-sex co-twins have been applied. Possible masculinization of female fetuses as a result of prenatal exposure to male hormones may explain the resemblance of these co-twins in IQ, sensation-seeking, and spontaneous otoacoustic emissions (McFadden, 1993; Miller, 1994; Resnick, Gottesman, & McGue, 1993). (b) A new series of twin studies on attachment behavior (Finkel, Wille, & Matheny, 1993) and reanalysis of existing studies with reference to twin type have taken place (Ricciuti, 1993). Evidence of genetic influence on security of attachment has been found. Genetic variation in Ainsworth's Strange Situation classifications may be related to variation in emotional expressiveness and regulation. (c) There has been an important reappraisal of MZ and DZ twinning rates. A recent analysis, based on twin births in Minnesota between 1971 and 1984, reported a decline in the DZ twinning rate and a slight increase in the MZ twinning rate. Volunteer twin samples, which typically include two thirds MZ twins, may be more representative than previously suspected (Hur, McGue, & Iacono, 1995). However, current reproductive technologies, which tend to produce DZ twins, may be contributing to an increase in the rate of DZ twinning (see Luke, Bigger, Leurgans, & Sietsema, 1996; Martin, 1996). (d) Molecular genetic analyses of the timing of X chromosome inactivation have been assisted by twin studies (Trejo et al., 1994). Preliminary evidence suggests that dichorionic (relatively early splitting) MZ female twins show greater differences in X chromosome inactivation patterns than monochorionic (relatively late splitting) MZ female twins. X-inactivation may, thus, occur prior to, or following, the twinning event. There has, in addition, been marked progress in the refinement of data-analytic techniques, especially procedures that combine twins with members of biological and adoptive families (Neale & Cardon, 1992).

These various topics have received considerable attention in the psychological and medical literature. The purpose of this chapter is to outline other novel directions in which twin research might proceed, such as studying twins as couples and studying twins' processes of cooperation and bereavement. These suggestions are illustrated with new data from recent and ongoing research efforts. New applications of existing twin methods and new research designs, involving unrelated siblings of the same age, are also explored.

## TWINS AS COUPLES: A FRESH APPROACH TO SOCIAL RELATIONS

Studies that employ *twins as couples*, rather than as individuals in a pair, enable tests of hypotheses and predictions relevant to relative genetic relatedness and social affiliation. As indicated previously, traditional twin analyses compare the separate behaviors of MZ and DZ co-twins with respect to similarity, to determine if genetic relatedness is associated with phenotypic resemblance. However, by studying twins as couples, attention is shifted to the social–interactional outcomes and processes associated with dyads composed of genetically identical and nonidentical genotypes. The concept of the twin pair as a "couple" is not new (see Zazzo, 1960). Freedman has drawn intriguing parallels between identical twinship and inbred groups: "If greater inbreeding leads to greater altruism, what are the recognition mechanisms within the inbred group? . . . Perhaps, to the extent that the fine tuning is alike in sender and receiver, two may feel as one, and the two can consequently sacrifice for one another. . . . Is this, in fact, the way it works with twins?" (1979, p. 128). However, the application of the twins as couples design in human ethological and evolutionary research is novel.

Psychological twin studies have generally reported greater social closeness between MZ than DZ twins, despite differences in the theoretical perspectives and methodologies of the research (Segal, 1988). Greater cooperation within MZ twinships, relative to DZ twinships, is anticipated by the work of Hamilton (1964) and others on the evolution of altruism. Specifically, MZ–DZ differences in cooperation would be consistent with the view that benefits are more likely to be directed toward closely related kin than to more distantly related kin, as a mechanism for influencing representation of one's genes in future generations. Dawkins (1982/1992) emphasized that this would be the case in a relative, rather than in an absolute, sense: *Inclusive fitness* is a function of one's "own reproductive success plus his *effects* on the reproductive success of his relatives, each one weighed by the appropriate coefficient of relatedness" (p. 186). The effects of performing one action, as compared with an alternative action, are what modify the inclusive fitness of an individual.

Considerable debate has surrounded the nature of mechanisms enabling distinctions between kin and non-kin and among kin within a given category of relationship. Included among the proposed mechanisms are phenotypic matching, recognition alleles, spatial distribution, and familiarity (see Segal, 1993, for a review). Phenotypic matching has received considerable recent attention. It has been proposed that information is learned about one's own phenotypic characteristics or the phenotypic characteristics of relatives, eventuating in a "learned standard of appearance" (Trivers, 1985). This information is used to assess the similarity of the phenotype of an unfamiliar individual. Information about relatedness may be provided by the degree of perceived similarity between the new phenotype and standard.

It is conceivable that the close social relatedness of MZ twinship is associated with a process similar to phenotypic matching. Phenotypic similarity offers an index of genetic similarity, although not a perfect one. Freedman (1979) has considered that correspondence between genotypic and phenotypic similarity suggests evolved mechanisms associated with attraction between individuals who perceive similarities between themselves. An important point is that there is no reason to propose a special mechanism for responding to, or recognizing, an identical twin; rather, increased altruism directed toward the twin would be an extension of the more general principle. The relative infrequency of MZ twin births worldwide (3.5/1000 maternities; Bulmer, 1970) has been referenced as evidence against the idea of twins being selected for, and as contrary to the idea of unusual altruism directed toward the twin (Barash, 1979). This issue may be resolved if we consider that MZ and DZ twins simply provide a convenient design for testing evolutionary-based hypotheses concerning genetic and social relatedness. Gleeson, Clark, and Dugatkin (1994) have derived models to predict where twinning might occur and the detection of twinning alleles should they exist. (These authors acknowledge the lack of evidence of a genetic influence on human MZ twinning.)

## Twin Studies of Cooperation

Twin research on the implications of genetic relatedness for cooperative and altruistic behavior was conducted at the University of Chicago, between 1978 and 1982, under the supervision of Dr. Freedman. In that study, MZ twin children showed greater cooperation during completion of a joint puzzle-solving task than DZ twin children. In addition, MZ co-twins were more altruistic on a differential productivity task and indicated closer social relations on a Twin Affinity Questionnaire, relative to DZ co-twins (Segal, 1984, 1988). Later research has been an elaboration of these themes through the use of genetically informative research designs and related classes of questions.

The finding that social–interactional differences are associated with relative genetic relatedness defines a domain in which the search for mechanisms underlying cooperative behavior can proceed. By applying appropriate experimental manipulations it may be possible to identify these mechanisms. This might involve organizing MZ twins according to degree of resemblance in physical, intellectual, or personality traits, and looking for associations between degree of similarity and social affiliation. Psychodynamic theories of behavior would predict greater social closeness between "look-alike" MZ twins than between "un–look-alike" MZ twins (Siemon, 1980). Such a prediction would be made on the basis of mutual identification or other psychological process. Evolutionary reasoning makes the same prediction if we consider that phenotypic similarity provides an approximate index of genetic similarity.

## Twin Studies of Bereavement

Studies of singleton twins (twins whose co-twins are deceased) offer another informative strategy for examining genetic influence on social relations. However, degree of genetic relatedness and its correlates have rarely been considered among the features of previous social relationships thought to affect level of grief. A twin study of bereavement, initiated in 1983 at the University of Minnesota, aims to examine differences in grief-related behaviors between MZ and DZ twins and differences in twins' response to losing a twin and losing other relatives. Additional objectives include the formulation of guidelines for assisting bereaved twins and their families. This study is now ongoing in the Twin Studies Center at California State University, Fullerton.

Hypotheses associated with bereavement are similar to those concerning cooperation. In fact, they provide an alternative approach to the same class of questions. This effort also recalls Chagnon and Bugos's (1979) assertion that "crisis or conflict" situations are an appropriate place to begin to track biologically relevant dimensions of kinship relations.

The bereaved twin sample now includes more than 500 twins, although publications and papers in press are based on the first 280 cases. (Sample sizes vary depending on when data analysis was conducted.) Twins are identified through support groups for bereaved twins in the United States, England, and Australia; attorneys associated with wrongful death cases involving twins; members of the media; professional colleagues; and personal referrals. Most recently, twins have been identified through the Australian National Medical Research Council Twin Registry. Analyses include only those twins whose age at loss was 15 years or older, to ensure recollection of the experience of loss. The sample includes an overrepresentation of MZ twins and females, approximately two thirds each. Mean age of the total sample is 46.05 years ($SD = 16.20$) and does not differ significantly between zygosity groups. Mean age at loss of the twin was 39.11 years ($SD = 16.55$), and mean number of years between the time of loss and data collection was 6.93 years ($SD = 8.97$). The most frequent reasons for death were illnesses (55%) and accidents (27%). Zygosity diagnosis (determination of twin type) is accomplished by administering a modified version of a standard physical resemblance questionnaire.

Participants complete a comprehensive Twin Loss Survey that they receive by mail. This survey includes a Grief Intensity Scale (adapted from Littlefield & Rushton, 1986), the Grief Experience Inventory (Sanders, Mauger, & Strong, 1985) and a Coping Scale (Littlefield, 1984). Additional questions concern the nature of the twin relationship, attitudes toward twinship, and current preoccupation with the deceased twin. Health history and social relationship timelines have recently been added. Several papers are available (see Segal & Blozis, 1996; Segal & Bouchard, 1993; Segal & Roy, 1995; Segal, Wilson, Bouchard, & Gitlin, 1995), so only a selective sampling of findings will be presented.

## Grief Intensity Scale

Grief intensity (as recalled 1 to 2 months following the loss of the twin) was rated on a 7-point scale (1 = no grief; 7 = total devastation, suicide point). Ratings were significantly higher for bereaved MZ than DZ twins [$F\,(1, 63) = 6.82$, $p < .01$], controlling for years since loss. Main effects for sex and the sex x zygosity interaction were nonsignificant (Segal & Bouchard, 1993). More recent analyses (Segal & Bouchard, 1994) confirm the significantly higher ratings by bereaved MZ than DZ twins [$F\,(1, 268) = 7.95$, $p < .01$], and also indicate significantly higher ratings by bereaved female than male twins [$F\,(1, 268) = 7.14$, $p < .01$].

A series of paired *t*-tests (with a more complete sample of 447 twins) compared grief intensity ratings for the deceased twin and other relatives. Findings from this analysis are presented in Figure 1. Significant group differences were indicated for all available kinship categories. (The single exception concerned the comparison of twin with spouse for which the grief intensity ratings did not differ; this finding is discussed later in the chapter. These data have several interesting features: (a) Once past immediate relatives for whom the coefficient of genetic relatedness is .50 (i.e.,

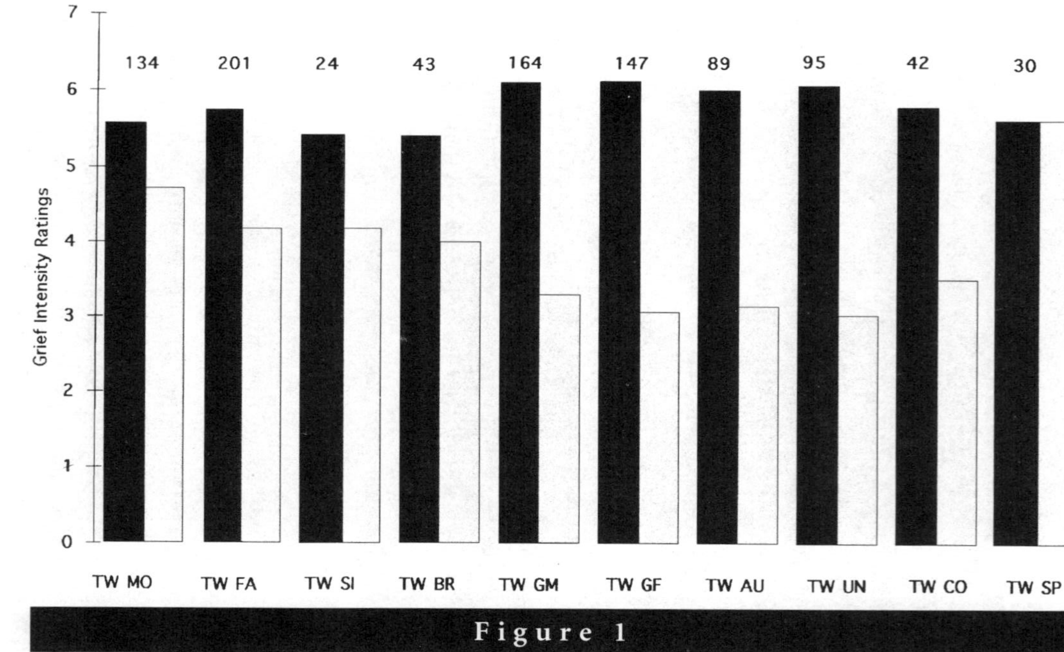


**Figure 1**

Grief intensity ratings for deceased twins and other deceased relatives.

NOTE: TW = twin; MO = mother; FA = father; SI = sister; BR = brother; GM = grandmother; GF = grandfather; AU = aunt; UN = uncle; CO = cousin; SP = spouse. Number of pairs in each comparison is indicated at the top of the bars. All differences were significant at $p < .001$.

parents, siblings and children), the level of grief declines rather dramatically. It is interesting to note that Burnstein, Crandall, and Kitayama (1994) observed this same trend in a study of altruism and decision making. They noted that from the point of view of inclusive fitness, the difference between a parent, sibling, or child, and an aunt, uncle, niece, or nephew (with whom the coefficient of genetic relatedness is .25), is more significant than the difference between any individual from the second set and a cousin (for whom the coefficient of genetic relatedness is .125). In the present study, the mean grief intensity rating for deceased cousins actually exceeded those of the second group, but only slightly. (b) There was no difference in mean grief intensity ratings for deceased twins and spouses, although only 30 cases were available. The bereavement literature generally indicates that spouse loss is one of the most devastating forms of loss and that adult sibling loss is less stressful (Sanders, 1979–1980; Weiss, 1993). Thus, the lack of difference between twin and spouse ratings underlines twinship as an especially significant relationship in general, and as an especially meaningful sibship in particular.

In this analysis, bereaved twins included both MZ and DZ twin survivors. When these data were analyzed separately for MZ twins, the difference in ratings for each comparison widened. Particularly interesting was the direction of the difference in the case of spousal loss. MZ twins ($n$ = 17) showed a slightly higher mean rating for the co-twin than the spouse, whereas the reverse was observed for DZ twins ($n$ = 13). Confirmation of this finding will strengthen bereavement theories that refer to correlates of genetic relatedness as contributors to individual differences in response. It should be noted that included among the aunts, uncles, and cousins were some nonbiological relatives (e.g., spouses of biological aunts and uncles); analyses of an exclusively biological sample yielded a similar pattern of findings. Adopted twins were excluded from this set of analyses with the exception of the spouse comparison.

Finally, too few twins had lost children to permit statistical analysis, thereby precluding this potentially informative comparison. Both MZ and DZ twins share half their genes with their children (as do all parents), but they differ in relatedness to their co-twin. (DZ twins share exactly half their genes with each child, but share half their genes, on average, with their co-twin.) It is, therefore, possible that the relative magnitude of DZ twins' grief intensity ratings for deceased children and deceased co-twins might vary as a function of their genetic relatedness and perceived similarity to each of these individuals. In the case of MZ twins, it is possible that grief intensity ratings for deceased co-twins would exceed those for deceased children (due to the greater genetic relatedness between MZ co-twins than between parents and children); however, age might be a moderating factor, with lower grief intensity ratings for deceased co-twins occurring at older ages. Age of the decedent at loss (if past adolescence) would be expected to negatively correlate with grief because loss of individuals within their reproductive period would reduce the potential inclusive fitness of close relatives (Crawford, Salter, & Jang, 1989). These researchers presented raters with hypothetical situations in which families had lost either two sons or two daughters in an automobile accident, and then asked them to judge the grief intensity of the parents. They reported a higher correlation between grief intensity and reproductive value than between grief intensity and age of the deceased individual.

## Other Measures

Most scale scores on the Grief Experience Inventory were significantly higher for surviving MZ than DZ twins, as anticipated (Segal et al., 1995). Analysis of the Coping Scale showed that after controlling for sex of survivor and age at loss, bereaved MZ twins experienced higher levels of coping difficulties and somatic symptoms than bereaved DZ twins. A path model depicting relationships among predictors (e.g., zygosity, sex, and reproductive status of the deceased), mediating variables (e.g., social closeness) and outcome measures (e.g., grief intensity, coping difficulties, and somatic symptoms) is being developed (Segal & Blozis, 1996). Predictions derive from evolutionary reasoning and a psychobiological theory of bereavement that views the preexisting relationship between survivor and deceased as a regulator of biological systems (Hofer, 1994).

Collectively, these findings are consistent with the view that genetic relatedness influences bereavement response. As in the case of cooperative behavior, organizing participants along dimensions of phenotypic resemblance might identify correlates of relatedness that can illuminate the findings. Additional research designs to test evolutionary-based hypotheses of bereavement include studies of MZ and DZ twins reared apart and studies using adoptive relatives, organized according to awareness, or lack of awareness, of rearing status.

## NOVEL TWIN STUDY DESIGNS

Other novel applications of twin research methods can inform behavioral–genetic, ethological, and evolutionary-based research in human development. This task would be enhanced by (a) more fully utilizing existing twin models, and (b) supplementing traditional twin models with other genetically informative research designs.

## NEW APPLICATIONS OF EXISTING TWIN METHODS

Some new applications of existing twin methods for examining social–genetic and evolutionary-based hypotheses will now be described. These studies, which are described later, are in varying stages of completion—some are published or in press, others are awaiting publication, and one is in the form of a proposal.

### MZ Half-Sibling Study

The MZ Half-Sibling Model includes MZ twins, their spouses, and their children. The offspring of MZ twins (although genetically first cousins and culturally reared as such) are genetically equivalent to half-siblings because they share a genetically identical parent. The unique relationships generated by the members of these families allow powerful tests of genetic and environmental influences on behavior. Gottesman and Bertelsen

(1989) compared the risk of psychopathology among children born to the members of MZ and DZ twin pairs discordant for schizophrenia. The children of MZ twins (whether affected or unaffected) were at elevated and equal risk for the disorder (16.8% and 17.4%, respectively), whereas the risk was elevated only for children born to affected DZ twins (17.4%), relative to their unaffected co-twins (2.1%). These findings demonstrate that the diathesis for schizophrenia may be genetically transmitted to offspring even in the absence of clinical expression in the parent generation. The MZ Half-Sibling design showed a similar pattern of findings for manic-depressive illness (Bertelsen, 1990).

However, the potential of MZ half-sibling families for examining evolutionary-based hypotheses has not been realized. One prediction is that greater altruism should be directed toward nieces and nephews by twin aunts and uncles in MZ half-sib families than in DZ twin families (Segal, 1993). MZ twin aunts may provide more care for nieces and nephews than DZ twin aunts, possibly associated with increased contact. However, to hold frequency of contact per se responsible for the quality of the social relationship would fail to consider the full complexity of causal influences. A more comprehensive interpretation would consider that the *higher proportion of genes* shared between MZ twin aunts and their nieces/nephews (50%), relative to that shared between DZ twin aunts and their nieces/nephews (25%, on average), might affect the social relationship, resulting in increased contact.

## Twin Children With Unfamiliar Partners: Genes, Environment, and Gender

Influences on cooperative behavior have been of considerable interest to developmental researchers. The twin study to be summarized applied a social–genetic perspective in an analysis of social interaction between unfamiliar partners (Segal, Connelly, & Topolski, 1996). Developmental social genetics is concerned with the proximal effects of the genotypes of individuals on social–interactional processes and outcomes. A major theme is that individual and joint behaviors may be differently affected by the genotypes of the interactants (Fuller & Hahn, 1976; Hahn, 1990). The critical role of early experience in the nature of later social behaviors is recognized.

Scott's (1977) well-known work on social behavior in dogs guided the hypotheses and design of this study. Using several dog breeds, Scott showed that early rearing with a genetically dissimilar partner was associated with relatively increased cooperation during later interactions with an unfamiliar partner, either from the same or different breed. In contrast, rearing with a genetically similar partner was associated with relatively reduced cooperation when interacting with an unfamiliar other. This study of dogs suggested parallels to the social situations of MZ and DZ twin pairs. Specifically, it was expected that pairs of unfamiliar MZ twins would display less cooperation than pairs of unfamiliar DZ twins. Cooperative behavior was also compared between unfamiliar male and female pairs. It was anticipated that female pairs would show greater cooperation than male pairs.

The sample included children from 14 MZ twin pairs (4 male and 10 female) and 16 same-sex DZ twin pairs (6 male and 10 female). Twins ranged in age between 8.0 to 11.7 years, with a mean age of 9.56 years ($SD$ = 1.08). Zygosity was assessed by blood-typing analyses and/or a physical resemblance questionnaire (see Segal & Russell, 1991, 1992). The children were organized into 30 unfamiliar partnerships by pairing each MZ and DZ co-twin with a child from a different MZ or DZ pair, as shown in Figure 2. Partners were matched for sex, age, and IQ. Each pair was videotaped during completion of two puzzles.

Puzzle completion sessions were evaluated on various dimensions of cooperation by a panel of six judges. Repeated measures analysis of variance indicated significantly higher ratings among female than male pairs on cooperation [$F$ (1, 13) = 6.54, $p < .025$], mutuality [$F$ (1, 13)= 4.80, $p < .05$], and accommodation [$F$ (1, 13) = 6.12, $p < .03$]. There were no significant puzzle or puzzle x gender effects for any of the dependent measures.

| Pair A: | | Pair B: | |
|---|---|---|---|
| A1 | A2 | B1 | B2 |
| A1B1* | | A2B2* | |
| A1B2 | | A2B1 | |

*Raters evaluated the 1st encounter only

**Figure 2**

Construction of unfamiliar twin partnerships.

Social–interactional differences between unfamiliar MZ and DZ dyads were *not* detected. It was suggested that twins in the age range and social classes represented may experience sufficient diversity in their social experiences, enabling cooperative interactions with unfamiliar partners during childhood. The suggestion that twins (especially MZ) may be socially disadvantaged as a result of similar appearance and treatment (Siemon, 1980) may apply only to a minority of cases. It is also conceivable that a more novel task than puzzle solving may have yielded the anticipated twin group differences between unfamiliar pairs.

## Twins as Couples: Ethological Analysis of Social Behavior

> It has been said that, in its haste to step into the twentieth century and to become a respectable science, Psychology skipped the preliminary descriptive stage that other natural sciences had gone through, and so was losing touch with the natural phenomena. (Tinbergen, 1963, p. 411)

Naturalistic observations of interactions within nonhuman social primate groups reveal that the frequency of spatial proximity and social exchange (including altruistic acts) are associated with degree of kinship

(Cheney, Seyfarth, & Smuts, 1986; Kummer, 1968; Kurland, 1977). Several such studies of human social behavior have also been reported. Chagnon (1979), in studies of Yanomamo villages, found that acts of assistance and defense were performed more frequently among individuals with high coefficients of relationship, relative to individuals with lower coefficients of relationship. When village residents reorganized themselves into smaller social units, these new villages were characterized by higher coefficients of relationship than the original village. Hames (1979) observed a linear relationship between the frequency of interaction among members of the Ye'kwana of Venezuela and their degree of genetic relationship. These studies are provocative because they direct attention to a generally neglected variable, *genetic relatedness*, as possibly underlying the quality and quantity of interaction within human social groups.

Reports of twins' social behaviors in unstructured settings ("twins in the wild") have, unfortunately, primarily consisted of case studies (Malmstrom & Silva, 1986) or unsystematic observations (Koch, 1966). Many psychological twin studies employing observational methods have shown insufficient appreciation for the relative genetic relatedness of co-twins as possibly influencing behavioral processes and outcomes (see, for example, Goldberg, Perrota, Minde, & Corter, 1986; Gottfried, Seay, & Leake, 1994; Mann, 1992; Paluszny & Gibson, 1974; Vandell, Owen, Wilson, & Henderson, 1988). Exceptions to the foregoing include twin studies of infant attachment and social behaviors (Finkel et al., 1993; Plomin & Rowe, 1979; Ricciuti, 1993), empathy (Zahn-Waxler, Robinson, & Emde (1992), and language development (Lytton, 1980).

The Nearest Neighbor Technique was developed for the study of social and spatial affinities of sex–age classes within troops of hamadryas baboons. It may, however, be appropriately used for behavioral research on other species (Kummer, 1968). The Nearest Neighbor Technique has been successfully adapted to analyses of play preferences among young school children (Omark, 1972; Taylor, 1979). This method also affords a viable tool for comparing these behaviors between MZ and DZ twin pairs in unstructured situations. According to Kummer, members of social species characteristically show "mobile concentrations," rather than even distributions within their habitats.

Evolutionary reasoning predicts that MZ co-twins should (a) be located at closer physical distances and (b) engage in more frequent social contacts, relative to DZ co-twins. Should these predictions be supported, they would both complement and corroborate data gathered from laboratory experiments (Segal, 1984), questionnaire studies (Rushton, Fulker, Neale, Nias, & Eysenck, 1986), and clinical interviews (Frank & Cohen, 1980; Siemon, 1980), which reveal greater affiliation and altruism within MZ twinships than DZ twinships. Most important, observations of "twins in the wild" offer a means for reconciling laboratory and real-life situations.

A pilot study conducted at the University of Chicago included eight MZ pairs and four DZ pairs (Segal, 1988). The mean age of this subsample (drawn from an initial sample of 105 twin pairs) was 8.26 years ($SD$ = 1.34). MZ twin pairs were additionally organized according to hand-concordance and hand-discordance (four pairs each). This procedure was done to examine the possibility that differences in hand preference, which have been associated with differences in cerebral organization in singleton populations (Springer & Deutsch, 1985; also see McManus & Bryden, 1993), might be associated with social–interactional characteristics of twin pairs. The behaviors of each twin were recorded simultaneously at 10-second intervals:

1. Nearest neighbor + interaction
2. Second nearest neighbor + interaction
3. Third nearest neighbor + interaction
4. Nearest neighbor, absence of interaction
5. Second nearest neighbor, absence of interaction
6. Third nearest neighbor, absence of interaction
7. Verbal interaction, absence of spatial proximity
8. Nonverbal interaction, absence of spatial proximity
9. Observation uncertain
10. Absence of spatial proximity and interaction

All observations were made on school playgrounds during recess periods, with the exception of one twin pair that was observed during a free play session in the classroom. The mean observation time was 20.77 minutes per pair.

Group differences in physical proximity and social interaction among MZ hand-concordant, MZ hand-discordant, and DZ pairs were significant for the proportion of observations recorded as social closeness item 1 (nearest neighbor + interaction). MZ hand-discordant twin pairs scored highest, followed by MZ hand-concordant twin pairs and DZ twin pairs. Twin group rankings for variables 1 + 2, and for 1 – 1 and 1 – 2 (simultaneous recording of 1 or 2 for each twin) followed the same pattern, with differences that approached, but did not achieve, statistical significance. MZ twin pairs exceeded DZ twin pairs on all measures, with the exception of the frequency of 0 and 4–4 events.

Results from this preliminary analysis are consistent with studies reporting closer social bonds between MZ twin pairs, relative to DZ twin pairs. The potential of ethological methods for capturing subtle aspects of social interaction between twins that may be overlooked in more restrictive settings was demonstrated. Most important, the correlates of degree of genetic relatedness appear to play a role in social preferences, and would be worth pursuing in future analyses. Organizing MZ twin pairs according to hand preference would allow further examination of associations between behavioral correlates of brain organization and social relations.

Two naturalistic studies of twin interaction, modeled after the one just discussed, have recently been completed (Lay, Christian, & Segal, 1996). The first compared social interaction and physical proximity using 13 MZ and 13 DZ twin pairs, 8 to 11 years old, observed across two occasions. MZ–DZ differences were similar to those found in the preliminary analysis. The second study compared gender differences and developmental trends in social interaction and physical proximity using 26 same-sex DZ and 17 opposite-sex DZ twin pairs from kindergarten/first grade and fourth/fifth grade. Same-sex twins displayed more frequent social interaction with one another than opposite-sex twins. However, contrary to expectation, gender (DZ same-sex males versus DZ same-sex females) and grade differences in social behavior were not found.

## Twins as Couples: Prisoner's Dilemma

A pilot study compared the behaviors of 14 MZ and 11 DZ adolescent twin pairs during a Prisoner's Dilemma game (Segal, 1991). Features of the Prisoner's Dilemma game derive from the situation of a prisoner confronting the choice of confessing to a crime without knowing if the collaborator will be forthcoming. When both players do not confess gain is maximized; otherwise, confession is the best strategy. Choice of strategy reflects the degree of trust that partners invest in each other (Jones & Gerhard, 1967). Game theorists have recognized parallels between the Prisoner's Dilemma and reciprocal altruism (Cosmides & Tooby, 1992; Trivers, 1985). Reciprocal altruism refers to the exchange of altruistic acts between individuals that may be separated in time. Genetic relatedness may influence altruistic behavior but is not a necessary requirement for its occurrence (Barash, 1982). Trivers (1985) has suggested that reciprocity is regulated by an emotional system that includes friendship, moralistic aggression, gratitude and sympathy, guilt and reparative altruism, and a sense of justice.

A significant multivariate effect of zygosity [$F$ (3, 19) = 3.38, $p < .04$] was demonstrated, whereas the effects of sex and the zygosity x sex interaction were nonsignificant. Univariate tests were significant for both cooperative [$F$ (1, 21) = 4.44, $p < .05$] and competitive events [$F$ (1, 21) = 6.05, $p < .02$]. As expected, the frequency of cooperative and competitive choices was significantly higher among MZ and DZ twin pairs, respectively. Age and gender were not correlated with any of the response combinations.

The Prisoner's Dilemma game was recently completed by additional twin pairs, yielding a sample of 59 MZ twin pairs and 37 DZ same-sex twin pairs (Segal & Hershberger, 1996). Zygosity was established by serological analysis or a standard physical resemblance questionnaire. In addition to testing for twin group differences in cooperation, competition, and exploitation, some further analyses are being applied. They include profile analysis to examine twin group differences in level (total number of events) and parallelism (score profile), and time–series analyses to assess relationships between responses across trials (both within individuals and between co-twins), and consistency in the patterning of responses over time.

## "Neo-Classic" Twin Method: Olfactory Recognition

A number of animal studies have demonstrated identification and recognition of conspecifics by olfactory cues (Schleidt, 1980). Organisms may possess unique "olfactory signatures" that stimulate olfactory receptors in kin who are sensitive to these cues (Beecher, 1982; Porter, Cernoch, & Balogh, 1985). The possibility that individuals may use olfactory cues to discriminate among relatives, as well as between relatives and nonrelatives, has been a recent focus of research interest. Hamilton's (1964) theory of kin selection (reviewed earlier) is partly responsible for this interest. A number of family studies demonstrating olfactory recognition of relatives are now available, as are several twin studies (see Segal & Topolski, 1995; Segal, Topolski, Wilson, Brown, & Araki, 1995).

A new series of studies has applied a twin research perspective to the study of olfactory perception and recognition. In one such study it was hypothesized that MZ co-twins would be more easily matched on the basis of olfactory cues, relative to DZ twins (Segal, 1995; Segal & Grimes-Hillman, 1995). Participants included 21 MZ twin pairs (10 male and 11 female) and 16 DZ same-sex twin pairs (8 male and 8 female). Mean age of the twins was 15.5 years ($SD = 3.83$) and ranged between 10.6 to 25.8 years. Twins were requested to wear t-shirts for three consecutive nights and to refrain from using perfume or other cosmetics during this period. Only Ivory soap was used for washing. Twins also completed a diet diary to determine if key dietary differences were associated with greater differences in body odor.

A panel of judges sniffed a target t-shirt and selected the "relative" from an array of three t-shirts. (The three shirts belonged to the co-twin and to two unrelated twins of similar age and the same sex.) Averaging across pairs yielded mean proportions of accuracy equal to .62 ($SD = .08$)

for MZ twins and .67 ($SD$ = .09) for DZ twins. Contrary to expectation, the proportion of correct identifications for MZ twins was not significantly greater than that of DZ twins. Older twins showed greater differences in their intake of spicy foods than younger twins, which might be associated with the lower frequency of correct identifications among older pairs. It was suggested that lack of relatedness and lack of familiarity of the judges with the twins may partly explain the nonsignificant findings. Most previous studies that have reported accuracy in the identification of individuals by olfactory cues from garments have used genetically related or familiar raters.

Additional studies modeled after the present one would be welcome. Porter has asserted that to "assess the influence of familiarization on the development of recognition of particular kin, one would ideally like to test individuals with the signatures of relatives with whom there has been no prior association" (1987, p. 194). Studies using reared apart MZ and DZ twins would be potentially informative. Spouses and children (who have resided with one twin but not the other) could be requested to distinguish between the odors of reared apart twins. Twins reared apart and together might be asked to identify a garment worn by the co-twin from an array of garments (Segal & Topolski, 1995). Such studies are able to separate the effects of genetic and environmental influences underlying kin recognition. As such, they provide another example of the utility of behavioral–genetic techniques for examining evolutionary-based questions and predictions.

## New Research Design: Unrelated Siblings of the Same Age

Unrelated individuals reared together from infancy who are the same age (UST-SA) are of special research interest. These siblings enter the family at nearly the same age and time and undergo developmental events in coordinated fashion. In short, these sibling pairs replicate the rearing circumstances of DZ twins. In addition, their situation is precisely the reverse of MZ and DZ twins reared apart: reared apart twins share genes but not environments, whereas UST-SAs share environments but not genes. Thus,

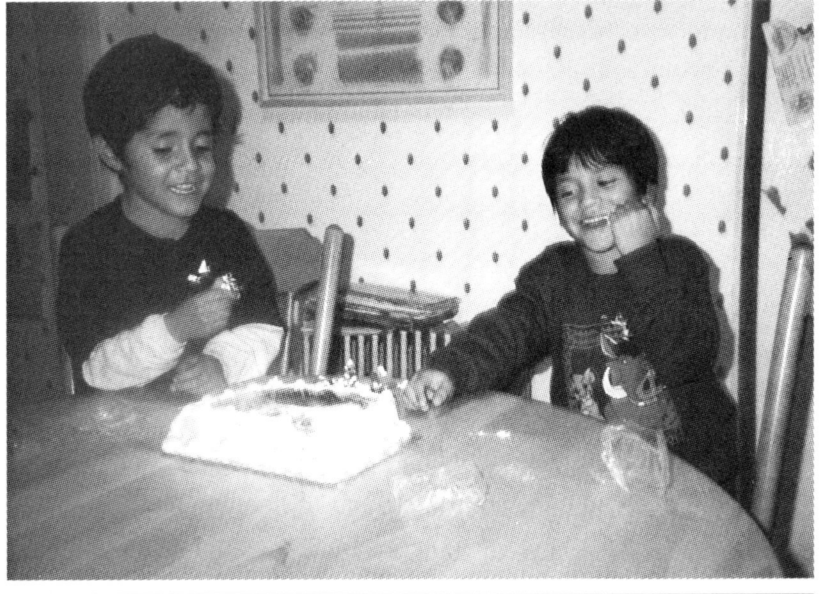

**Figure 3**

Pair of unrelated siblings reared together of the same age (UST-SA). (Courtesy of the family)

UST-SAs offer behavioral geneticists a novel research design for estimating the contribution of shared environmental factors to phenotypes of interest. They also provide evolutionary psychologists with a new method for clarifying the implications of biological relatedness and rearing status for social relatedness.

A study of IQ similarity in 21 pairs of UST-SAs has recently been completed (Segal, 1997). Unrelated individuals, age 4 years and older, who had been reared in the same home prior to 1 year of age, were invited to participate. Siblings differed in age by less than 9 months of age and attended the same school grade. Pairs in which one or both individuals had experienced adverse birth events that may have affected intellectual ability were excluded. The mean age of the 21 pairs was 9.36 years (*SD* = 6.65), and ranged between 4 to 26 years. A pair of UST-SAs is shown in Figure 3.

Tests included the age-appropriate Wechsler IQ test. The mean Full Scale IQ for the 21 pairs was 106.12 ($SD$ = 14.75) and ranged between 84 to 148. The Full Scale IQ intrapair difference was 15.38 ($SD$ = 11.45), and ranged between 0 to 42. In contrast, the average MZ and DZ intrapair differences are 6 and 10 points, respectively (Plomin & DeFries, 1980). The IQ intraclass correlation was $r_i$ = .17, considerably below values reported for MZ twins reared together ($r_i$ = .86), MZ twins reared apart ($r_i$ = .72), DZ twins reared together (.50–.60), and siblings reared together ($r_i$ = .47; see McGue, Bouchard, Iacono, & Lykken, 1993).

The very modest IQ correlation for UST-SAs shows that a shared rearing environment typical of the twin situation does not predict IQ similarity. It seems likely that each child selectively experienced the opportunities available in their family settings, illustrative of active gene–environment correlation. The arguments of critics who claim that twin resemblance is primarily a function of similar treatment, rather than genes, are clearly challenged. The present findings are considered preliminary in view of the small sample size. Data are, however, being collected on additional cases to see if these early findings remain stable. In addition to the IQ tests, several other forms are completed by parents and by siblings in some cases. Analysis of the Child Behavior Checklist (Achenbach, 1991) is under way for comparison with published data on MZ and DZ twins and adoptees.

The UST-SA design can also be used to study social relatedness, especially among biological–adoptive pairs, in which there are other near-in-age biological children in the family. It would be of theoretical interest to determine if affiliation proved stronger between biological pairs, relative to adoptive pairs, despite the greater difference in age and immediate social environments. These data are starting to be collected from some of the older pairs. In a previous study, greater feelings of social closeness and familiarity between reunited twins than between twins and their adoptive siblings were indicated (Segal, 1988). This pattern of findings challenges more traditional theories concerning the bases of human social relationships.

## CLOSING COMMENTS

Twin research is more than a century old, yet continues to grow and prosper. As Dr. Freedman indicated nearly 30 years ago and as demonstrated by the present series of studies, a twin research perspective can lend fresh insights into human developmental processes. Many new and exciting applications of the twin method have yet to be incorporated into behavioral–genetic, ethological, and evolutionary-based analyses. Such efforts can underline important connections among these three disciplines that have been overlooked for too long.

## REFERENCES

Achenbach, T. M. (1991). *Manual for the Child Behavior Check List/4-18 and 1991 Profile.* Burlington, VT: Author.

Barash, D. P. (1979). *The whisperings within: Evolution and the origins of human nature.* New York: Harper & Row Publishers.

Barash, D. P. (1982). *Sociobiology and behavior* (2nd ed.). New York: Elsevier.

Beecher, M. D. (1982). Signature systems and kin recognition. *American Zoologist, 22,* 477–490.

Bertelsen, A. (1990, August). *Twin offspring study in manic-depressive disorders.* Paper presented at the World Psychiatric Association Regional Symposium: Etiology of Mental Disorder, Oslo, Norway.

Bulmer, M. G. (1970). *The biology of twinning in man.* Oxford: Clarendon Press.

Burnstein, E., Crandall, C., & Kitayama, S. (1994). Some neo-Darwinian rules for altruism: Weighing cues for inclusive fitness as a function of the biological importance of the decision. *Journal of Personality and Social Psychology, 67,* 773–789.

Chagnon, N. A. (1979). Mate competition, favoring close kin and village fissioning among the Yanomamo Indians. In N. A. Chagnon & W. Irons (Eds.), *Evolutionary biology and human social behavior: An anthropological perspective* (pp. 86–132). North Scituate, MA: Duxbury Press.

Chagnon, N. A., & Bugos, P. E., Jr. (1979). Kin selection and conflict: An analysis of a Yanomamo ax fight. In N. A. Chagnon & W. Irons (Eds.), *Evolutionary biology and human social behavior* (pp. 213–238). North Scituate, MA: Duxbury Press.

Cheney, D., Seyfarth, R., & Smuts, B. (1986). Social relationships and social cognition in nonhuman primates. *Science, 234,* 1361–1366.

Cosmides, L., & Tooby, J. (1992). Cognitive adaptations for social exchange. In J. H. Barkow, L. Cosmides, & J. Tooby (Eds.), *The adapted mind: Evolutionary psychology and the evolution of culture* (pp. 163–228). New York: Oxford University Press.

Crawford, C. B., Salter, B. E., & Jang, K. L. (1989). Human grief: Is its intensity related to the reproductive value of the deceased? *Ethology and Sociobiology, 10,* 293–309.

Dawkins, R. (1982/1992). *The extended phenotype: The long reach of the gene.* Oxford: Oxford University Press.

Finkel, D., Wille, D., & Matheny, A. (1993). Preliminary results from a twin study of infant–caregiver attachment. *Behavior Genetics, 23,* 551.

Frank, R. A., & Cohen, D. J. (1980) Preadolescent development: Case studies in twins. *Yale Journal of Biology and Medicine, 53,* 471–483.

Freedman, D. G. (1979). *Human sociobiology: A holistic approach.* New York: Free Press.

Fuller, J. L., & Hahn, M. E. (1976). Issues in the genetics of social behavior. *Behavior Genetics, 6,* 391–406.

Gleeson, S. K., Clark, A. B., & Dugatkin, L. A. (1994). Monozygotic twinning: An evolutionary hypothesis. *Proceedings of the National Academy of Science, 91,* 11363–11367.

Goldberg, S., Perrota, M., Minde, K., & Corter, C. (1986). Maternal behavior and attachment in low-birthweight twins and singletons. *Child Development, 57,* 34–46.

Gottesman, I. I., & Bertelsen, A. (1989). Confirming unexpressed genotypes for schizophrenia. *Archives of General Psychiatry, 46,* 867–872.

Gottfried, N. W., Seay, B. M., & Leake, E. (1994). Attachment relationships in infant twins: The effect of co-twin presence during separation from mother. *Journal of Genetic Psychology, 155,* 273–281.

Hahn, M. E. (1990). Approaches to the study of genetic influence on developing social behaviors. In M. E. Hahn, J. K. Hewitt, N. D. Henderson, & R. H. Benno (Eds.), *Developmental behavior genetics: Neural, biometrical and evolutionary approaches* (pp. 60–80). New York: Oxford University Press.

Hames, R. (1979) Relatedness and interaction among the Ye'Kwana: A preliminary analysis. In N. A. Chagnon & W. Irons (Eds.), *Evolutionary biology and human social behavior: An anthropological perspective* (pp. 239–249). North Scituate, MA: Duxbury Press.

Hamilton, W. D. (1964). The genetical evolution of human behaviour. *Journal of Theoretical Biology, 7,* 1–52.

Hofer, M. A. (1994). Hidden regulators in attachment, separation, and loss. In N. A. Fox (Ed.), The development of emotion regulation: Biological and behavioral considerations [Monograph]. *Monographs of the Society for Research in Child Development, 59,* 192–207.

Hur, Y. M., McGue, M., & Iacono, W. G. (1995). Unequal rate of monozygotic and like-sex dizygotic twin births: Evidence from the Minnesota Twin Family Study. *Behavior Genetics, 25,* 337–340.

Jones, E. E., & Gerhard, H. B. (1967). *Foundations of social psychology.* New York: John Wiley & Sons.

Koch, H. (1966). *Twins and twin relations.* Chicago: University of Chicago Press.

Kummer, H. (1968). *Social organization of hamadryas baboons: A field study.* Chicago: University of Chicago Press.

Kurland, J. A. (1977). Kin selection in the Japanese monkey. In F. S. Szalay (Ed.), *Contributions to primatology, 12* (pp. 1–145). Basel, Switzerland: S. Karger.

Lay, C. M., Christian, D. L., & Segal, N. L. (1996). *Ethological approach to social relatedness: A twin study.* Manuscript in preparation.

Littlefield, C. H. (1984). *When a child dies: A sociobiological perspective.* Unpublished doctoral dissertation, York University, Toronto.

Littlefield, C. H., & Rushton, J. P. (1986). When a child dies: The sociobiology of bereavement. *Journal of Personality and Social Psychology, 51,* 797–802.

Luke, B., Bigger, H. R., Leurgans, S., & Sietsema, D. (1996). The cost of prematurity: A case-control study of twins vs. singletons. *American Journal of Public Health, 86,* 809–814.

Lytton, H. (1980). *Parent–child interaction: The socialization process observed in twin and singleton families.* New York: Plenum Press.

Malmstrom, P. M., & Silva, M. N. (1986). Twin talk: manifestations of twin status in the speech of toddlers. *Journal of Child Language, 13,* 293–304.

Mann, J. (1992). Nurturance or negligence: Maternal psychology and behavioral preference among preterm twins. In J. H. Barkow, L. Cosmides, & J. Tooby (Eds.), *The adapted mind: Evolutionary psychology and the evolution of culture* (pp. 367–390). New York: Oxford University Press.

Martin, A. (1996, February 8). Is society really ready for more multiples? *New York Times,* pp. B1, B6.

McGue, M., Bouchard, T. J., Jr., Iacono, W. G., & Lykken, D. T. (1993). Behavioral genetics of cognitive ability: A life-span perspective. In R. Plomin & G. E. McClearn (Eds.), *Nature, nurture and psychology* (pp. 59–76). Washington, DC: American Psychological Association.

McFadden, D. (1993). A masculinzing effect on the auditory systems of human females having male co-twins. *Proceedings of the National Academy of Sciences, USA, 90,* 11900–11904.

McManus, I. C., & Bryden, M. P. (1993). The neurobiology of handedness, language, and cerebral dominance: A model for the molecular genetics of behavior. In M. H. Johnson (Ed.), *Brain development and cognition: A reader* (pp. 679–702). Cambridge, MA: Basil Blackwell.

Miller, E. M. (1994). Prenatal sex hormone transfer: A reason to study opposite-sex twins. *Personality and Individual Differences, 17,* 511–529.

Neale, M. C., & Cardon, L. R. (1992). *Methodology for genetic studies of twins and families.* Dordrecht: Kluwer Academic.

Omark, D. R. (1972). *Peer group formation in young children.* Unpublished doctoral dissertation, University of Chicago, Chicago.

Paluszny, M., & Gibson, R. (1974). Twin interactions in a normal nursery school. *American Journal of Psychiatry, 131,* 293–296.

Plomin, R., & DeFries, J. C. (1980). Genetics and intelligence: Recent data. *Intelligence, 4,* 15–24.

Plomin, R., & Rowe, D. C. (1979). Genetic and environmental etiology of social behavior in infancy. *Developmental Psychology, 21,* 391–402.

Porter, R. H. (1987). Kin recognition: Functions and mediating mechanisms. In C. Crawford, M. Smith, & D. Krebs (Eds.), *Sociobiology and psychology: Ideas, issues and applications* (pp. 175–203). Hillsdale, NJ: Erlbaum.

Porter, R. H., Cernoch, J. M., & Balogh, R. D. (1985). Odor signatures and kin recognition. *Physiology and Behavior, 34,* 445–448.

Resnick, S. M., Gottesman, I. I., & McGue, M. (1993). Sensation seeking in opposite-sex twins: An effect of prenatal hormones? *Behavior Genetics, 23,* 323–329

Ricciuti, A. E. (1993). Child–mother attachment: A twin study. *Society for Research in Child Development Abstracts, 60,* 567.

Rushton, J. P., Fulker, D. W., Neale, M. C., Nias, D. K. B. & Eysenck, H. J. (1986).

Altruism and aggression: The heritability of individual differences. *Journal of Personality and Social Psychology, 50,* 1192–1198.

Sanders, C. M. (1979–1980). A comparison of adult bereavement in the death of a spouse, child, and parent. *Omega, 10,* 303–322.

Sanders, C. M., Mauger, P. A., & Strong, P. N., Jr. (1985). *A manual for the Grief Experience Inventory.* Charlotte, NC: The Center for the Study of Separation and Loss.

Schleidt, M. (1980). Personal odor and non-verbal communication. *Ethology and Sociobiology, 1,* 225–231.

Scott, J. P. (1977). Social genetics. *Behavior Genetics, 7,* 327–346.

Segal, N. L. (1984). Cooperation, competition, and altruism within twin sets: A reappraisal. *Ethology and Sociobiology, 5,* 163–177.

Segal, N. L. (1988). Cooperation, competition and altruism in human twinships: A sociobiological approach. In K. B. MacDonald (Ed.), *Sociobiological perspectives on human development* (pp. 168–206). New York: Springer-Verlag.

Segal, N. L. (1991, April). *Cooperation and competition in adolescent MZ and DZ twin pairs during a Prisoner's Dilemma game.* Paper presented at the biennial meeting of the Society for Research in Child Development, Seattle, WA.

Segal, N. L. (1993). Twin, sibling and adoption methods: Tests of evolutionary hypotheses. *American Psychologist, 48,* 943–956.

Segal, N. L. (1995). Twin research on olfactory characteristics. In A. N. Gilbert (Ed.), *Explorations in aroma-chology: Compendium of aroma-chology research 1982–1994* (pp. 25–28). New York: Olfactory Research Fund.

Segal, N. L. (1997). Same-age unrelated siblings: A unique test of within-family environmental influences on IQ similarity. *Journal of Educational Psychology, 89,* 381–390.

Segal, N. L., & Blozis, S. A. (1996). *Psychobiological and evolutionary perspectives on coping and health characteristics: A study of bereaved twins.* Manuscript submitted for publication.

Segal, N. L., & Bouchard, T. J., Jr. (1993). Grief intensity following the loss of a twin and other close relatives: Test of kinship–genetic hypotheses. *Human Biology, 65,* 87–105.

Segal, N. L., & Bouchard, T. J., Jr. (1994, August). *Grief intensity in bereaved monozygotic and dizygotic twins.* Paper presented at the annual convention of the American Psychological Association, Los Angeles, CA.

Segal, N. L., Connelly, S. L., & Topolski, T. D. (1996). Twin children with unfamiliar partners: Genotypic and gender influences on cooperation. *Journal of Child Psychology and Psychiatry, 37,* 731–735.

Segal, N. L., & Grimes-Hillman, M. (1995). Twin study of genetic relatedness and odor similarity. *Aroma-chology Review, 4,* 2, 10–12.

Segal, N. L., & Hershberger, S. L. (1996). *Cooperation and competition between twins: Findings from a Prisoner's Dilemma game.* Manuscript submitted for publication.

Segal, N. L., & Roy, A. (1995). Suicide attempts in twins whose co-twins' deaths were non-suicides. *Personality and Individual Differences, 19,* 937–940.

Segal, N. L., & Russell, J. (1991). IQ similarity in monozygotic and dizygotic twin children: Effects of the same versus separate examiners: A research note. *Journal of Child Psychology and Psychiatry, 32,* 703–708.

Segal, N. L., & Russell, J. M. (1992). Twins in the classroom: School policy issues and recommendations. *Journal of Educational and Psychological Consultation, 3,* 69–84.

Segal, N. L., & Topolski, T. D. (1995). The genetics of olfactory perception. In R. L. Doty (Ed.), *Handbook of clinical olfaction and gustation* (pp. 323–343). New York: Marcel Dekker.

Segal, N. L., Topolski, T. D., Wilson, S. M., Brown, K. W., & Araki, L. (1995). Twin analysis of odor identification and perception. *Physiology and Behavior, 57,* 605–609.

Segal, N. L., Wilson, S. M., Bouchard, T. J., Jr., & Gitlin, D. G. (1995). Comparative grief experiences of bereaved twins and other bereaved relatives. *Personality and Individual Differences, 18,* 511–524.

Siemon, M. (1980). The separation–individuation process in adult twins. *American Journal of Psychotherapy, 34,* 387–400.

Springer, S. P., & Deutsch, G. (1985). *Left brain, right brain* (Rev. ed.). New York: W. H. Freeman.

Taylor, B. (1979). The onset of children's preferences for same-sex play neighbors. In D. G. Freedman, *Human sociobiology: A holistic approach* (p. 191). New York: Free Press.

Tinbergen, N. (1963). On aims and methods of ethology. *Zeitschrift für Tierpsychologie, 20,* 410–433.

Trejo, V., Derom, C., Vlietinck, R., Ollier, W., Silman, A., Ebers, G., Derom, R., & Gregersen, P. K. (1994). X chromosome inactivation patterns correlate with fetal-placental anatomy in monozygotic twin pairs: Implications for immune relatedness and concordance for autoimmunity. *Molecular Medicine, 1*, 62–70.

Trivers, R. L. (1985). *Social evolution.* Menlo Park, CA: Benjamin/Cummings.

Vandell, D. L., Owen, M. T., Wilson, K. S., & Henderson, V. K. (1988). Social development in infant twins: Peer and mother–child relationships. *Child Development, 59*, 168–177.

Weiss, R. (1993). Loss and recovery. In M. S. Stroebe, W. Stroebe, & Hansson, R. O. (Eds.), *Handbook of bereavement: Theory, research, and intervention* (pp. 271–284). Cambridge: Cambridge University Press.

Zahn-Waxler, C., Robinson, J. L., & Emde, R. N. (1992). The development of empathy in twins. *Developmental Psychology, 28*, 1038–1047.

Zazzo, R. (1960). *Les jumeaux: Le couple et la personne.* Paris: Presse Universitaire de France.

# Section II Conclusion

Robert L. Trivers

I salute Irving Gottesman's courage and competence over these years in working in an area that is prone to so much misunderstanding, so much controversy, and so much strong feeling. He, particularly, has done yeoman-like work over the years on schizophrenia and other types of mental disorders and their possible genetic components, beginning with twin studies, but he has also examined developmental instability in schizophrenia (Gottesman, 1991; Torrey, Bowler, Taylor, & Gottesman, 1994). There are several books out, I am pleased to see back there [at the book exhibit], summarizing some of his recent work (e.g., Gottesman, 1991). He is far too modest to talk about this, but I think I am allowed to reveal something that I have learned on good authority, which is that next week's *Nature Genetics* (*11*:3, November 1, 1995) will have a series of papers on linking-relationships between particular chromosomes and schizophrenia. I am certainly looking forward to these papers.

The papers may well be the cosmic payoff for the years of work invested in this area because now one can combine the earlier work with modern, powerful techniques in genetics. The Human Genome Project, an international collaboration dedicated to identifying the location and function of all human genes, is yielding numerous findings, among them new linkage markers. Linkage markers are genes found on the same chromosome as a trait of interest (e.g., schizophrenia) and that enable scientists to track the transmission of that trait within families. It seems reasonable that in 5 or 10 years we will be able to describe specific DNA sequences in which the base pairs will be sequenced and, as a consequence, we will

The material presented here was transcribed from a videotape of the Festschrift, Saturday, October 28, 1995, and edited slightly.

know what product has been made by the gene. Once this is accomplished we may make considerably more progress toward elucidating the underlying etiology of mental disorders. And we can, of course, realize the hope that was implicit in genetic work all along—namely, that it will point to the appropriate environmental intervention. If you deny the genetics out of hand, which happens so often, you foreclose actually pinning down what is going on, if there is a genetic component—and, of course, there is a genetic component to everything.

I have felt for some time that genetics without biology is a bad idea. One of the problems that we deal with is that there are social scientists who regularly "fall off a horse" and discover genetics or, at least, they discover that things are heritable. Dick Herrnstein, whom I counted as a personal friend when I was at Harvard, was one such person. He devoted all of his young adult years to the old pigeon stimulus–response model in which genetics is completely irrelevant. And then he fell off his horse one day and learned about heritability, but he did not necessarily carry anything else from biology with him. The point is that biology is built up of a mass of information and interlocking concepts that help one to understand genetic information—concepts like natural selection that will help one think about how societal trends may interact with genes.

Another example is James Q. Wilson (also a Harvard professor, now at UCLA) who wrote a book called, *The Moral Sense* (1993). Again, the only thing he took from biology is that there are genes involved, therefore, there are genetic components to moral behavior. If only one could define moral behavior in the first place! When Wilson defines moral behavior he uses nothing from biology. For example, if we work up a theory of fairness, coming out of reciprocal altruism with a certain logic and with a whole series of wonderful findings from chimps (Axelrod & Hamilton, 1981; de Waal, 1991; Trivers, 1971), he does not want to deal with it. He is back in his other world, but he is adding heritability. He ends up with a completely bogus moral system in which he pulls words out of a hat and says, "Here is what morality is." Fairness I liked, but duty and self-control I did not really warm to as pillars of morality. Duty always sounds like, "Hans, you must do your duty!" It is a term used by others to manipulate your own behavior with regard to what they say you are supposed to do. And as for self-control, I know I am a gene or two short on that, so perhaps I am biased against this notion.

The other problem is not so much with the genetics as with the terms that are linked to this genetics. *Criminality, aggression, intelligence*—can we define them, and what do we actually mean by them? I am not pleased by a long tradition in the social sciences that says, "We don't really need to define them." You may remember the famous comment in the 1920s that said, "Intelligence is what the IQ test measures." Well, that is a nifty end run around a scientist's responsibility to define the term being measured and then show that the measurement measures what was defined. You cannot overlook the definitional aspect.

Regarding criminality, we know that that is completely socially defined. It is a matter of what laws have been passed that define something as *criminal.* Yet, in our minds we have a sense of somebody lurking around, acting in a criminal way, so we think that there is something in criminality other than just a socially defined variable. However, Dr. Gottesman quite correctly pointed to certain wicked features of our laws, especially as they relate to race. In this connection, I call attention to an excellent book called *Malign Neglect* by Michael Tonry (1994), which makes some of the points to which Dr. Gottesman was alluding. Irv talked especially about the crack cocaine–powder cocaine sentencing mismatch that criminalizes some juvenile Black males for what are relatively trivial quantities of this drug. But there is a larger story, and this is embedded in a larger pattern of which most of us are fairly unconscious: If one looks at the rate at which Black men commit major crimes (I am talking about murder, rape, aggravated assault, forcible entry into property, etc.), the relative rate at which Black men commit these crimes compared to White men (and it *is* a male game) has not changed in 20 years (1975 to 1995). *It has not changed* (Tonry, 1994). So, if the rate at which people are being incarcerated reflects our concern with these major crimes, there should not have been a change in the relative rate at which the races have been incarcerated. Black men are still committing those crimes at a per capita rate five to seven times as high as the White per capita rate per crime, but the point is that the relative numbers have not changed. However, beginning in 1980, exactly coincident with the Reagan–Bush years, there was an incredible increase in the general rate of incarceration, disproportionately falling on Black men, so that their per capita rate of incarceration has almost doubled during a period of time in which the White rate has hardly changed (Tonry, 1994). It is all happening, Tonry pointed out (and he has the statistics to prove it), because of the "war on drugs"—it all has to do with criminalizing the small quantities, the so-called "street dealer." So, of course, if one looked at this from a genetic standpoint and were ignorant of the social facts, then one would find all sorts of curious features, because criminality has expanded to include some people who would not be considered criminals a mere 10 years earlier. There is not going to be any parent–offspring correlation at all but there is a genetic one because, of course, gene frequencies differ between White and Black people, on average. And yet it has little or nothing directly to do with the behavioral difference between the groups, but it has a lot to do with how society—which, of course, is largely controlled by the dominant group—defines a crime. In summary, in this tricky area of behavioral genetics, we must be especially conscious of language, of how we are using our terms, defining them, and so on.

Many people of my generation cut our teeth on J. Paul Scott's old dog work. And I can remember as a teaching fellow at Harvard in the late 1960s and early 1970s being so pleased that I could "trot out" Dr. Scott's dogs, so to speak, to show some basic but important concepts (Scott, 1964). Of course, behavior has genetic components as one can demonstrate nicely in a species that one is permitted to breed. And, of course, the proper way to think about these genetic components is that they interact with the environment in various complicated ways to generate the phenotypic traits that we are actually talking about.

I enjoyed seeing the data on gender differences in the way in which size might affect aggressive interactions and, especially, the importance of size differences in the male–female relationship. There, remember, we saw the strongest effects of relative size in determining who was dominant. And it reminded me of data from humans on the murder rate in marriages of men killing women versus women killing men. Daly and Wilson, who have done so much valuable work on similar kinds of data, have reviewed this in recent papers (see Dobash, Dobash, Wilson, & Daly, 1992; Wilson & Daly, 1992). American women, looking cross-culturally, are the closest to achieving parity in this statistic, but what was even more striking is that Black American women are the only group around the world who are killing their spouses slightly more frequently than they are being killed by them (Wilson & Daly, 1992).

Incidentally, Daly and Wilson (Dobosh et al., 1992) point out an obvious fact that is worth bearing in mind when one is comparing statistics about men killing wives versus women killing husbands. The abuse is all still going, almost all of it, in one direction—men toward women. Most of the cases in which women kill men are after a long history of abuse of the woman by the man, although sometimes after a short history. However, these cases are rarely a culmination of a long history of abuse that finally ends in murder, as in the case of men killing women.

Dr. Scott mentioned that we are the sexiest species around, with the possible exception of the Bonobo. He noted that the most common marital arrangement in modern society is the pair, one male and one female, with polyandry occurring much less often. However, R. Robin Baker and Mark A. Bellis (1995) published a book called *Human Sperm Competition*, which deals in enormous detail with the situation of *sexual polyandry* (i.e., a woman having sexual relations with two different men within a sufficiently short period—e.g., a 5-day period), so that the sperm of the two men can principally be in conflict over access to her eggs. Further study of such phenomena will, undoubtedly, revise our current views of many aspects of human sexuality.

I was very pleased to hear Dr. Scott state the opinion that parental care is underemphasized in our culture. He also mentioned overemphasis on individualism and competitiveness and so on. I helped to popularize the term *parental investment* in biology, which tries to emphasize what a fundamental variable it is—and this includes male parental investment, too, when you can find it (Trivers, 1972).

Nancy Segal has done some very creative work combining twin research and evolutionary concepts. I remember casting around as a teacher for any examples of degree of relatedness predicting human behavior and people measuring it, and it was discouraging that one had only studies of ground squirrels. We can tell a lot more about kinship in ground squirrels in a biological sense than we can about our own species! Part of the problem is that we have an army of social scientists measuring the wrong variables, so that not enough of them are measuring the variables that would appear to be valid. And so I remember my pleasure when I came across Nancy Segal's (1984) comparison of the interactions between identical and fraternal (or sororal) twins—the degree of relatedness of 1 versus 1/2 to 1/4, because not all of these twins are full siblings.[1] At the time, it seemed that one problem in interpreting her evidence was that it was not clear that selection had worked very strongly on the phenomenon of being an identical twin. We know that the rate of identical twinning is only about 3 per 1000, and we know that this rate is invariant around the world (Bulmer, 1970). We also know that identical twins (see also Ball & Hill, 1996) have higher mortality statistics than fraternal twins and, as a consequence, it was likely that they were often selected against. So I did not want to interpret her data at that time, but it is now so pleasing to follow her argument that these data suggest an avenue into mechanisms that are involved in cooperative interactions and that these mechanisms may have been selected in kin interactions with lower degrees of relatedness. It may not have specifically been selected regarding the phenomenon of being an identical twin but, in any case, this opens up some more biology.

*Twins as couples* is a beautiful concept, and there are a lot of things that can be drawn out of it. For example, we know that sex hormone effects in utero for rodents can be very, very strong, and who is "sitting next door to you" in utero can have a potent effect on both males and

[1] Superfecundated twins result from the fertilization of ova during separate coital acts occurring in the same menstrual cycle (Campbell, 1988). Several cases of twins fathered by different males have been documented in the medical literature (see, for example, Verma, Luke, & Dhawan, 1992). The genetic relatedness of such twins would be 1/4. The frequency of this twinning event is unknown, but it is assumed to be infrequent.—Eds.

females (Clark, Karpink, & Galef, 1993). A female with two brothers "next door" becomes masculinized, and vice versa. In humans the literature is not nearly so dramatic, but there is a suggestive literature that there is some hormonal interaction presumably going on in twins, opposite-sex pairs compared to same-sex pairs, and that again is a fruitful line of research.

There is a case in cattle that shows that the germinal cells of a twin might migrate to its co-twin's genital ridge and the germinal cells of the co-twin actually might be a mixture of the germinal cells of each twin (see Gandelman, 1992, and references therein). There is a more recent intriguing paper on this phenomenon in a marine invertebrate, in which case neighbors sometimes fuse, at least part way. Sure enough, it has been discovered that after the fusion the germinal tissue starts heading over to colonize the nearby gonad of the other individual (Pancer, Gershon, & Rinkevich, 1995). Up to 29% of the offspring of one can actually come genetically from the other.

The MZ twin-family relatedness study is another clever application of this phenomenon of twins in a nonconventional way relating to degrees of relatedness. In utero conflict can, of course, go on and it might be fun someday to measure that. I remember this dramatically because my wife gave us twins the second time out (twin girls) and I can remember when she was pregnant she used to show me "twin fights," and they were very dramatic. These twins were born 8 pounds, 1 ounce and 7 pounds. You could see a twin fight break out—arms and legs kicking back and forth and, indeed, the more dominant twin had kicked the other one way up and during delivery she had to be "hauled out" after the first presented. They were interacting biosocially, not just hormonally, and this situation could presumably affect later interactions.

Unrelated "twins" reared together offers a new twist on adoption studies. Nancy Segal described an ongoing study in which she compares behavioral similarity of unrelated siblings of nearly the same age, reared together since infancy. This design is the virtual "opposite" of identical twins reared apart, and is an improvement over ordinary adoption designs in which siblings may differ in age and in age at placement in the home.

She is finding little intellectual similarity in these pairs, demonstrating that the shared family environment has a negligible impact on this behavior. This design also enables many exciting tests of the effects of being reared in a "twin-like" situation on social affiliation and related behaviors. It will help to refine our understanding of how genetics and social variables interact to produce outcomes. I was just pleased with every aspect of Nancy Segal's application of twin methodology to a series of different biological problems.

## REFERENCES

Axelrod, R., & Hamilton, W. D. (1981). The evolution of cooperation. *Science, 211,* 1390–1396.

Baker, R. R., & Bellis, M. A. (1995). *Human sperm competition: Copulation, masturbation and infidelity.* London: Chapman & Hall.

Ball, H. L., & Hill, C. M. (1996). Reevaluating "twin infanticide." *Current Anthropology, 37,* 856–863.

Bulmer, M. G. (1970). *The biology of twinning in man.* Oxford: Clarendon Press.

Campbell, D. M. (1988). Aetiology of twinning. In I. MacGillivray, D. M. Campbell, & B. Thompson (Eds.), *Twinning and twins* (pp. 27–36). Chichester, England: John Wiley & Sons.

Clark, M., Karpink, P., & Galef, B. (1993). Hormonally mediated inheritance of acquired characteristics in Mongolian gerbils. *Science, 364,* 712.

de Waal, F. (1991). The chimpanzee's sense of social regularity and its relation to the human sense of justice. *American Behavioral Scientist, 34,* 335–349.

Dobash, R. P., Dobash, R. E., Wilson, M., & Daly, M. (1992). The myth of sexual symmetry in marital violence. *Social Problems, 39,* 71–91.

Gandelman, R. (1992). *Psychobiology of behavioral development.* New York: Oxford University Press.

Gottesman, I. I. (1991). *Schizophrenia genesis: The origins of madness.* New York: W. H. Freeman.

*Nature Genetics.* (1995, November 1). Vol. 11(3).

Pancer, Z., Gershon, H., & Rinkevich, B. (1995). Coexistence and possible parasitism of somatic and germ cell lines in chimeras of the colonial urochordate *Botryllus schlosseri. Biological Bulletin, 189,* 106–112.

Scott, J. P. (1964). Genetics and the development of social behavior in dogs. *American Zoologist, 4,* 161–168.

Segal, N. L. (1984). Cooperation, competition and altruism within twin sets: A reappraisal. *Ethology and Sociobiology, 5,* 163–177.

Tonry, M. (1994). *Malign neglect: Race, crime, and punishment in America.* Oxford: Oxford University Press.

Torrey, E. F., Bowler, A. E., Taylor, E. H., & Gottesman, I. I. (1994). *Schizophrenia and manic-depressive disorder: The biological roots of mental illness as revealed by the landmark study of identical twins.* New York: Basic Books.

Trivers, R. L. (1971). The evolution of reciprocal altruism. *Quarterly Review of Biology, 46,* 35–57.

Trivers, R. L. (1972). Parental investment and sexual selection. In B. Campbell (Ed.), *Sexual selection and the descent of man 1871–1971* (pp. 136–179). Chicago: Aldine.

Verma, R. S., Luke, S., & Dhawan, P. (1992). Twins with different fathers. *Lancet, 339,* 63–74.

Wilson, J. Q. (1993). *The moral sense.* New York: Free Press.

Wilson, M. I., & Daly, M. (1992). Who kills whom in spouse killings? On the exceptional sex ratio of spousal homicides in the United States. *Criminology, 30,* 189–215.

SECTION III

# Biological Approaches to Developmental Issues: Rethinking the Data

SECTION III INTRODUCTION

# Biological Approaches to Developmental Issues: Rethinking the Data

Glenn E. Weisfeld

This section illustrates the point that biology offers numerous insights into developmental processes. Genes and environment interact in various complex ways that are currently being elucidated (Michel & Moore, 1995). Examples of these developmental interactions include the influence of (a) trophic factors on neuronal development, (b) maternal stress on prenatal hormones and then on behavioral sex differentiation, (c) early experience on the development of the brain's sensory systems, (d) maternal diet during pregnancy and lactation on food preferences, (e) breast versus bottle feeding on IQ, (f) maternal hormones (also transmitted through the milk) on bonding, and (g) tactile and vestibular stimulation of premature newborns on growth and susceptibility to apnea, respectively. A truly interactionist, biopsychological framework is necessary to account for the complexity of development.

The section begins with chapter 8, by Robert S. Marvin, on child–parent attachment. Marvin relies heavily on primatological observations to inform his analysis of human attachment. This is in keeping with Archer's (1992) contention that animal models are useful for human research in that they can highlight crucial developmental variables that may be obscured by the complexity of human behavior and can also reveal categories of behavior that have relevance for human studies.

Chapter 9, by Ritch C. Savin-Williams and Lisa M. Diamond, reviews several competing etiological theories of sexual orientation and shows how particular interpretations of sexual orientation research are associated with certain political positions. Chapter 10 is by Peter H. Wolff. As Dr. Freedman has done, Wolff describes ethnic differences in behavior using two examples: flushing in response to alcohol inhibition and dyslexia. Using these two examples, he makes a series of important points about the subtleties of development.

## REFERENCES

Archer, J. (1992). *Ethology and human development.* Savage, MD: Barnes & Noble Books.

Michel, G. F., & Moore, C. L. (1995). *Developmental psychobiology: An interdisciplinary science.* Cambridge, MA: MIT Press.

# 8

# Ethological and General Systems Perspectives on Child–Parent Attachment During the Toddler and Preschool Years

Robert S. Marvin

Throughout his career, Daniel Freedman expanded his thinking *coincidently* into evolutionary theory, systems theory, theories of cognitive development, studies of nonhuman primates, and anthropology. Characteristically, he focused his attention on the description of different levels of organization between the individual and his or her broader social and biological contexts. This led him to the process of identifying how those levels are developed and maintained via circular feedback loops between the "lower" and "higher" levels. The studies discussed in this chapter, which focus on toddlers' and preschoolers' attachment to their caregivers, intersect directly with Freedman's systemic approach, placing that approach within the study of developmental changes in the organization of attachment behavior. The chapter is based on the idea that developmental changes in any skill, system, or variable must be understood in the contexts of (a) other behaviors with which this behavior is co-organized, as well as the outcome or function of those patterns of behaviors; and (b) the family,

The author would like to thank Nancy L. Segal for her help and support in the completion of this chapter.

peer group, community, or other social context into which the child is moving at that point in his or her development.

In his 1993 paper with Jane Gorman, Dr. Freedman proposed a framework for the study of child–parent attachment in our species that, although occasionally proposed before, has still not taken hold to an extensive degree (Freedman & Gorman, 1993). Freedman and Gorman proposed that different levels of organization, within the individual and between the individual and his or her broader social and biological context, are developed and maintained via circular feedback loops between the lower and higher levels. Within this view, the causal relationships between lower and higher levels are, in fact, context dependent, with feedback from higher levels being necessary for actualization of the lower levels, as well as the other way around. As was characteristic of his early work on the differential effects of handling on various canine species, Freedman (1979) continued to emphasize the importance of viewing any biological phenomenon, whether it be phylogenetic, ontogenetic, or cultural, as a network of systemic relations and causal feedback loops (e.g., Freedman, 1979).

Combined with the work of Bowlby (e.g., 1969) and Ainsworth (e.g., 1967), this contextual, systemic framework leads to a paradigm shift (Kuhn, 1970) in the study of the attachment bond between children and their parents. This shift is inherent in the work of many ethologists and attachment researchers, but has received so little attention in the recent literature that it is now having very little influence on the field. The basic idea is that a child's development tends to occur in the form of "packages"—in the form of generally coincidental, coordinated changes across a number of behavioral systems. It is important to note that the changing behavioral systems are not only those in the child *but in the caregiver or attachment figure as well.* And the existence of these packages of changes is not without purpose or function. In fact, they change coincidentally for the very reason that they will be able to continue to serve one or more biological functions in a successful manner. In this chapter, I will review some of the early general systems theory/cybernetics work and early primate field work that anticipated this point of view and consider some of

Bowlby's and Ainsworth's work that more or less explicitly use it. I will then discuss some applications of this perspective to the cross-cultural study of attachment, to the study of attachment during the preschool years, and finally to the study of maladaptive, or disordered, attachments.

For the past 20 years, the study of individual differences has occupied so much of the focus in attachment research that exploration of the *ontogeny* of attachment has nearly been abandoned. Ainsworth's identification of three "primary" strategies of attachment (e.g., Ainsworth, Blehar, Waters, & Wall, 1978), Main and Solomon's (1990) discovery of a "disorganized" pattern of attachment, and Main and colleagues' research on adults' attachment strategies (e.g., George, Kaplan, & Main, 1985; Main, Kaplan, & Cassidy, 1985) have contributed enormously to our understanding of differential strategies within intimate relationships, as well as child and adult psychopathology. However, the history of biology demonstrates that despite some analogical similarities between immature and mature forms of an organism, any attempt to understand adaptive or maladaptive versions of the mature form without constant reference to structural transformations throughout ontogeny is doomed to failure (e.g., Bateson, 1976; Waddington, 1957). This will certainly be no less the case in the study of human attachment.

This contextual model is taken from a combination of the theoretical work on general systems by W. Ross Ashby, observational studies of primate development conducted mainly during the 1960s and 1970s, and from the work of John Bowlby. The model proposes that ontogenetic change takes place in a form we might think of as "organizational packages"—coherent and generally adaptive *groupings* of coinciding changes. These "packages" consist of coincidental changes in behavioral and internal working model skills and of changes in the form of interactions between the youngster and other conspecifics. I, therefore, argue, as does Dr. Freedman, that it is every bit as important to understand development in terms of its *context* as it is in terms of its reductionist, *causal* determinants. The basic model, which follows, is based on the notion that the organization of attachment–caregiving interactions at any point in development has the biological function of protecting the youngster from danger, while at the same time allowing it as much independence as possible within which to learn and develop.

## MODELS OF DEVELOPMENT

### General Systems Model

Ashby proposes, at a very abstract systemic level, that if a system is to survive there must be certain invariants among its constituent elements and certain invariants in its relationship with its environment (Ashby, 1952, 1956). In certain essential respects—which ones depending on the system—variety must be kept within certain limits, or the system will not survive. In human development the best known examples are, of course, our many physiological invariants. Again at this abstract level, Ashby anticipated one of the most central notions of Bowlby's theory of attachment: He proposed that if one system does not have the ability to control input from the environment in a manner that keeps these essential variables within the limits required for survival, then it must be coupled with another system that does have the necessary variety to control the variety of the first system. In other words, there must be a close coupling, or "bond," between the two systems that serves to protect the less "self-reliant" system. This is a formal statement of Bowlby's basic thesis regarding the biological function of child–parent attachment: It serves to protect the child from a wide range of dangers—from either internal changes or environmental inputs—that would push some essential variable(s) beyond the system's (i.e., the child's) limits of survival.

This coupling can have another, developmental, aspect. In many biological organisms, the protective coupling has a component that facilitates the youngster's tendency to explore and learn—in other words, to develop the skills necessary to protect itself through its autonomous integration in the larger group. Within this protective relationship, the developing organism thus becomes progressively less and less dependent on the bond with its parent (the system with more variety) to provide that protection. Eventually, the child contains the necessary variety within itself and within its coupling with its social network to control internal change and environmental input in ways that maintain its essential variables within the limits necessary for survival. This compound, and very complex, developmental pattern constitutes the crux of Ainsworth's concept of the child's use of its mother as a secure base for exploration (e.g., Ainsworth, 1967).

Placing these concepts in the contexts of both ontogeny and biological function, the following proposal can be made: At each point in development, the nature of the attachment–caregiving interactions between the youngster and its attachment figure(s) serves to compensate for, and to complement, the lack of motor, communication, and social skills on the youngster's part, such that the youngster is always protected while being afforded as much independence as possible within which to learn those skills. Within this framework, one important component of ontogeny is the youngster's developmental acquisition of more mature and self-reliant motor, communication, and social skills, *coincidental* with a complementary decrease and/or change in the parent–offspring interaction that serves to protect the youngster (cf. Trivers, 1972, on parental investment).

This proposal has at least three important and related corollaries:

1. The youngster's locomotor skills, communication skills, information processing skills, and more generally its "internal working model" of itself in relation to others in its group are all skills that will tend to fit together in a manner that makes adaptive sense. These skills will tend to be organized systemically into functional "packages" that can be fully understood only by studying them in the context of their organization with each other and in the context of the patterns of interactions the youngster has with its social and physical environment during that same period of development. This corollary also implies that complex organizations of the behavior of parents (and other conspecifics) will take the form of complementary "packages" that are adaptive, given the organization of the youngster's current skills and behavior.
2. Developmental change takes the form of generally coincidental changes within and across the many behavioral systems that consti-

tute the functional "packages" described previously. The change may enhance or diminish any *specific* behavior or behavior system. The change in the attachment figure's behavior is as much a part of the youngster's developmental change as is the change in its own behavior. The change will tend to have the outcome of "transferring" increased responsibility to the youngster while continuing to maintain those variables necessary for survival within their critical limits.

3. Individual, and cultural, differences in attachment–caregiving behavior will tend to consist of different organizations of the behavior of both the attachment figure and the youngster: again, organizations that are reciprocally adapted to one another (Freedman & Gorman, 1993). From this perspective, a maladaptive organization—or *psychopathology* at the level of the individual or dyad—can be seen as one in which behavioral systems in the youngster and/or the attachment figure fail to be organized with each other in a manner that protects the youngster while affording it the opportunity to explore.

## Primate Model of Development

As has been true also for much attachment research, the primate field studies of the 1960s and 1970s offer the most extensive illustrations of, and support for, these ideas. More recent studies of nonhuman primates have focused more closely on the *mechanisms* involved in subsets of these patterns and on interspecies similarities and differences (see Chism, 1991; Suomi, 1995). However, the basic patterns and information from which the patterns can be inferred were discovered during those early field studies.

There appears to be general consensus across the early field studies of many different nonhuman primate species that there are two major organizational periods during both infancy (Infancy-1 and Infancy-2), and the juvenile period (Juvenile-1 and Juvenile-2). In this chapter, I will be concerned primarily with the second period of infancy. Each period is defined in terms of specific organizations of the youngster's *locomotor, feeding, and communication* skills, and in the case of many species, the infant's fur color (natal coat), which appears to have the effect of making the youngster extremely attractive to more mature conspecifics and of eliciting gentle and often caregiving behavior. Equally important, each period is further defined in terms of the complementary organization of the mother's behavior and often of the behavior of other conspecifics. In turn, developmental change from one period to the next is defined in terms of complex patterns of changes in the youngster's behavioral systems, as well as of the mother's behavior. These changes are clearly understood as a progressive, adaptive shift in responsibility for protection of the youngster from the close tie to the mother to the youngster's self-reliant integration into the larger troop through mature motor and communication skills.

Surprisingly similar functional and developmental patterns have been described for baboons by Hall and DeVore (1965) and Altmann (1980); for gibbons by C. R. Carpenter (1964); for langurs by Jay (1965); for chimpanzees by Goodall (e.g., Lawick-Goodall, 1968); and for mountain gorillas by Schaller (1963).

### *Infancy-1 Period*

One of the most direct statements of this complex set of systemic relations among infant skills, maternal behavior, protection, and self-reliant functioning was made by Goodall in discussing the nature of maternal protection in chimpanzees. Goodall listed a number of ways in which the mother protects her offspring, ending with, "Finally, she protects (her infant) from social encounters with other individuals until it is able to react correctly to the various expressive calls and movements of the adult" (Lawick-Goodall, 1968, p. 235). Characteristics of the infant and of social interaction involving the infant are as follows. These characteristics are generally applicable to all the primate species listed earlier, as well as to our own species.

*Infant characteristics.*

- Locomotor skills poorly developed;
- Communication skills relatively undeveloped, other than signals used in the context of separation, distress, or playful interaction with the mother;
- Unable to respond to most communicative sounds and gestures made by adults.

*Characteristics of social interaction.*

- Continuously in very close proximity or physical contact with the mother;
- Suckles frequently;
- Mother protects from danger and denies or carefully monitors contact with other troop members;
- Infant does not actively participate in play with other young.

In discussing these mother–infant relationships in chimpanzees, Goodall (1965) stated that the Infant-l has very little communicative skill, other than such gestures as the "hoo" whimper, screaming, and laughing: signals that operate very specifically to gain and maintain physical proximity and contact with his mother and to elicit protection *by others* in general. Until about 10 months of age, the infant is unable to respond to the many ritualized sounds and gestures made by adults, and the mother must be able to retrieve him at a moment's notice. Before this time separation between mother and infant is, therefore, minimal or nonexistent.

This view, as systematic, sensible, and productive as it has been in studies of nonhuman primates, has had very little impact on the study of human development, at least within the mainstream of the developmental literature. In fact, however, during the same period as the early primate field studies, there were numerous studies of human infants and mothers across diverse cultural settings, suggesting that this set of characteristics does apply from birth to perhaps 10 to 15 months of age. Among others, this includes the descriptive work of Ainsworth in Uganda and Baltimore (e.g., Ainsworth, 1967; Ainsworth et al., 1978); Konner (1972) in the Kalahari Desert; Marvin, VanDevender, Iwanaga, LeVine, and LeVine (1977) in Nigeria; and Leiderman and Leiderman (1974) in East Africa. These studies suggest that, at least in most cultures, there is an initial early period in human development during which infants typically spend most of their waking time in close proximity or contact with a primary caregiver or her surrogate. During this period, the infant's expressive communication skills are very limited, and its receptive skills are nearly nonfunctional. Those skills that are present are those that function to elicit closer physical contact, suckling, or intimate face-to-face gaze and vocalization with the caregiver. Also during this period, caregivers tend to be especially careful in their protective monitoring of physical contact between the infant and others, and the infant is not capable of playing with other young children.

### *Infancy-2 Period*

Phyllis Jay (1965) was even more specific in discussing the relationship between the development of social skills while the infant still benefits from close maternal attention and protection:

> Threat gestures directed by a large juvenile to an adult are responded to with threat or aggressive behavior. Similarly, a submissive gesture may avert impending adult aggression. The juvenile's skill in displaying gestures, and its longer consistent sequences of gestures and vocalizations, contribute to effective communication of the juvenile's emotional state, whereas the infant intersperses recognizable social gestures with random, often play, behavior. (pp. 229–230)

Characteristics of the infant, and its social interaction, are as follows:

*Infant characteristics.*

- Completes milk dentition;
- Still suckles, but also eats solid foods;
- Locomotor skills not yet completely developed;
- Communication skills that are used across a distance in organizing protective contact attachment figure are well developed;
- Practicing those communication skills required for stable integration into larger troop, but these are not yet fully developed.

*Characteristics of social interaction.*

- Semi-independent of caregiver in locomotion;
- Frequent excursions from and back to attachment figure, but does not become widely separated from her;

- Except under conditions of immediate danger, infant assumes primary responsibility for gaining/maintaining physical proximity and contact to attachment figure;
- Attachment figure and infant keep close visual contact with one another and reunite quickly under conditions of danger or distress;
- Plays actively with other members of the troop, as the practice of communicative signals required for autonomous integration within the troop occurs.

In chimpanzees, Infancy-2, which lasts from about 6 months to about 4 years, is initiated by a change in the infant's natal coat (Lawick-Goodall, 1968). During this phase, there are increasingly lengthy excursions from the mother, but to a greater or lesser degree both parties keep constant watch on each other. Interaction with peers occupies more and more of the youngster's time, and it gradually develops those communicative signals that are necessary outside the context of its relationship with its mother. Gradually the responsibility for proximity with mother shifts to the infant itself. By the time it is 2 years old, the chimp has developed enough of the ritualized gestures and responses to others' gestures to enable it to hurry to its mother of its own accord when appropriate.

Although there is still much physical contact between mother and youngster during this phase, most contact is visual. As the Infancy-2 phase continues, the youngster spends more and more time off his mother, and by 3 years of age it has learned almost all the adult communicative patterns, and interacts with adults more cautiously. However, the mother continues to keep a constant watch on her offspring and continues to protect it from other chimps when necessary.

There is much less information available for the *human* parallel to the Infancy-2 period. However, the combined work of Ainsworth (1967), Anderson (1972), Blurton Jones (e.g., 1972, 1993), Konner (1972), Marvin (1977), Marvin and Greenberg (1982), Stewart and Marvin (1984), Marvin, VanDevender, Iwanaga, LeVine, & LeVine, (1977), McGrew (1972), and Mossler, Marvin, and Greenberg (1976) suggests that the basic primate model remains generally applicable to the toddler and preschool periods, from 12 to 18 months to 4 to 6 years of age.

### *Juvenile Period*

During the Juvenile period, the youngster is able to maintain its essential variables within the limits of survival through its own, more highly developed feeding, motor, and communication skills. The stable use of these skills allows it to use its integration within the larger social group as the coupling through which it controls variety. It is, therefore, during this period that the youngster no longer needs such an exclusive, protective tie with its mother.

*Juvenile characteristics.*

- Largely independent of mother for feeding;
- Locomotor skills highly developed;
- All receptive and expressive communication skills required for autonomous integration into the troop are developed.

*Characteristics of social interaction.*

- Travels with mother, but otherwise spends much time interacting with other troop members;
- Mother may have another offspring;
- Mother may occasionally protect, but the juvenile is primarily responsible for its own protection through effective communication with adults and other juveniles.

During the Juvenile period, lasting from about 3½ to 4 years to about 7 years, the young chimp has developed all the adult patterns of communication, and the mother protects it only occasionally. The juvenile is no longer dependent on the mother for food, transportation, and protection, and male juveniles are seen to separate from their mothers for days at a time. As puberty approaches, the young chimp accompanies its mother increasingly less often (however, female juveniles tend to remain with the mother more than do males). During most of this third phase it continues to *travel* with the mother. When they are not traveling it spends much time away from her and engages in peer interaction for long periods of time. Finally, during this stage older males begin to rebuff the juvenile, and although the mother still protects it occasionally (and does so even into adolescence), it must now abide almost entirely by the adult patterns of communication and social organization.

## STUDIES OF INFANCY-2 IN HUMANS

In humans, the transition from Infancy-1 to Infancy-2 is consistent with the transition to Bowlby and Ainsworth's Phase 3 in the development of attachment, that of "goal-corrected proximity seeking" (e.g., Bowlby, 1969). It is at this point that the infant has developed "object and person permanence" (Bell, 1970), as well as a coherent, internal working model of its attachment figure and itself, a set of plans it uses purposefully to organize proximity and contact with her, and the use of mother as a "secure base for exploration" (e.g., Ainsworth, 1967). It is regarding the early part of this period that so much research on human attachment has been conducted, using both the strange situation (e.g., Ainsworth et al., 1978) and home visit data (e.g., Bell & Ainsworth, 1972; Belsky & Isabella, 1988). The bulk of this research has focused on the course of, and mechanisms involved in, individual differences (e.g., Ainsworth et al., 1978; Cassidy & Marvin, 1992; Fonagy, Steele, & Steele, 1991; George, Kaplan, & Main, 1985; Main & Cassidy, 1988). Even these individual differences, however, are seen as variations on the general organizational theme of using the attachment figure as a secure base for exploration.

## SYSTEMIC VARIATIONS IN THE SECURE BASE PATTERN

Ainsworth's discovery of the secure base phenomenon was a pivotal contribution to the study of human attachment *and* of parent–infant interaction

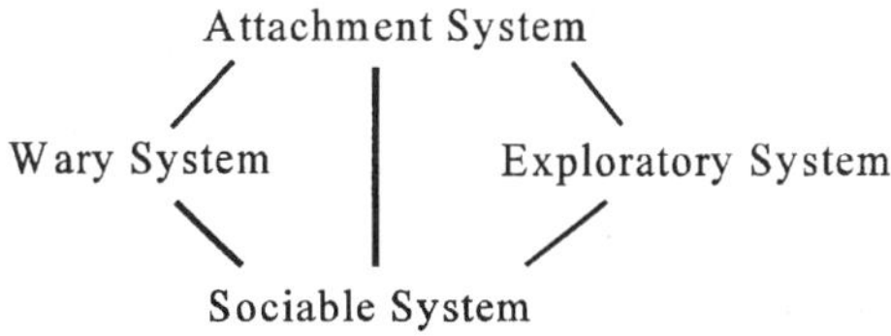


**Figure 1**

Organization Among Behavioral Systems

in numerous primate species (e.g.. Suomi, 1995). It has proven to be important not only because it is nearly universal among primates and many other species, but also because it is such a powerful example of the first corollary to Ashby's proposal outlined earlier. That is, the construct of a "secure base for exploration" refers to a number of behavioral systems that are patterned systemically into a functional organization and that can only be fully understood in the context of their organization with each other. In the case of this particular construct, the reference to systemic "wholeness" or nonsummativity is not vague and metaphoric: It refers *specifically* to the manner in which the behavioral systems involved serve as activating and terminating conditions for each other.

Ainsworth proposed that the infant's attachment behavior system, wary/fear behavior system, and exploratory behavior system operate together in a dynamic balance, or equilibrium, to form a complex secure base pattern (e.g., Ainsworth, 1967, Ainsworth et al., 1978; Ainsworth & Marvin, 1995; Bischoff, 1975). The three infant behavioral systems can be expanded to four to include the sociable behavior system (Figure 1). The distinction between the exploratory and the sociable systems is heuristic because the form of, and circumstances under which, the infant plays with or retreats from an unfamiliar adult are quite distinct from those under which it plays with or retreats from an unfamiliar toy. This distinction will become especially apparent later in this chapter.

When the infant's attachment or wary systems are minimally activated or inactive, its exploratory system can easily be activated to interact with its physical environment, or its sociable system can be activated to interact with other children or adults. Activation of the infant's wary/fear system by something novel or frightening serves to terminate the exploratory system and (under many circumstances) activate the attachment system. Retreat to an attachment figure as a "haven of safety" (Ainsworth, 1967) and termination of the attachment system will often, in turn, terminate the wary system and re-activate the exploratory or sociable system.

This dynamic equilibrium makes clear, adaptive "sense" and is proposed as one cybernetic process through which the Infant-2 competently assumes much of the responsibility for protective proximity and contact with its attachment figures. Note that during this period the organization of the child's behavioral systems is just as "sensibly" complemented by the caregiver's behavioral organization. The Infant-2 generally is allowed to assume the primary responsibility for protective proximity and contact as long as the caregiver does not assess the level of danger to be beyond the infant's ability to accurately assess the danger or to regain contact on its own.

One common strategy for assessing the validity of a construct such as the secure base is to see if the construct holds across species, breeding populations, or cultures. In the case of humans, the question might be, "Do infant–caregiver dyads in distinctly different cultures display the same pattern of behavior? However, there are at least two levels at which this question could be asked. First, at a more superficial, or "phenotypic," level the question would be, "Do infant–mother dyads in distinctly different cultures display the same specific behaviors in the same, observable organization?" Specifically, as they begin to locomote, do all infants tend to move away from their mothers to explore, return to them when startled or distressed, and then move off again when soothed—and focus primarily on one attachment figure in doing so?

A second, "genotypic" level is one that reflects the underlying cybernetic/control systems organization. Here the suggestion would be that infant–caregiver dyads in distinctly different cultures, in fact, display phenotypically *different* patterns of secure-base behavior in adapting to their specific physical–social ecologies. However, these distinct patterns actually reflect the same underlying cybernetic/control systems organization (cf. Freedman & Freedman, 1969; Freedman & Gorman, 1993).

## Hausa of Nigeria

Marvin et al. (1977) found exactly this relationship in their study of infant–caregiver attachment among the Hausa of Nigeria. In this subculture, the specific organization of the secure base differed significantly from that observed in most Western cultures, whereas the underlying rules for its operation, and the function it served, did not.

At the time the study was conducted, the Hausa were an agriculture-based, polygynous culture in which wives were generally secluded within family compounds where they tended individual gardens and cared for their families. The number of people living in a given compound averaged 10, with a maximum of 30. The living huts were made of baked clay, mud, or cornstalk. The floors were usually of dirt and mats. Huts contained open fires, holes in the ground, and utensils on the floors. There were many chickens and small mammals running loose with access to the huts. In contrast to most Western cultures, there was little or no attempt to organize the physical environment in a manner that would minimize the possibility of injury to infants and young children during the course of their exploration. Thus, relative to most Western infants, these Hausa infants were being raised in a relatively dangerous physical environment.

The interactions between 15 infants and their caregivers were sampled during three 1-hour visits to each infant's compound within a 4-week period. The oldest infant was 14 months of age, and all were capable of independent locomotion. Thus, the infants in this study were *early* in the Infancy-2 period.

The infants had a median of four principal caregivers, all of whom cared for the infant despite the fact that the biological mother was continuously physically available. In all cases the mother took virtually complete responsibility for feeding, bathing, and other physical routine caregiving activities. All other caregiving activities—for example, comforting, restriction from dangerous objects or activities, vocalizing, playing, and encouraging vocalizing and motor skills, were shared among the familiar adults and older children. Half of the biological mothers provided less than 50% of these other caregiving activities.

When not asleep, the Hausa infants were almost always in physical contact with a principal caregiver. They spent an average of 55 minutes of every hour in physical contact with a caregiver, whereas Ainsworth found that similar-aged infants in her Baltimore sample were in physical contact with their mothers for an average of 6 minutes each hour (M. D. S. Ainsworth, personal communication, 1994). This close proximity was maintained both by the infants (only two of whom were ever observed to locomote well beyond arm's reach to explore) and by the caregivers, who restricted the infants from breaking physical contact 45% of the time the infants attempted to do so.

Only two infants were ever observed to use their caregivers as a secure base for *locomoting off* to explore. However, all 15 were observed regularly to use their caregivers as secure bases for *visual* and *manipulatory* exploration. All infants would play when seated right next to a caregiver, but 13 of the 15 infants consistently ceased visual or manipulatory exploration and protested whenever the caregiver even momentarily moved away.

The Hausa caregivers were extremely responsive to infant signals, responding to essentially all of the more obvious ones within a matter of seconds. For example, 92% of all recorded cries ($n = 178$) were responded to by someone, and all but two of these were responded to within 30 seconds. This is in contrast to Ainsworth's Baltimore sample, in which only 62% of infant cries were responded to during the fourth quarter of the first year of life.

In a manner that "fits" this high responsiveness to signals and high restriction of locomotor exploration, these Hausa infants displayed many fewer active attachment behaviors (e.g., reaching, clinging, approaching, following) than do most Western infants of the same age. Only two of these locomotor infants were observed to follow a caregiver when she moved away, and only 11 were seen to approach a caregiver while she remained stationary in close proximity. It is surprising to note that only four of the infants were ever observed to cling to a caregiver. Instead, these

Hausa infants depended on "signal" attachment behaviors such as smiling, looking, crying, and calling as means for achieving and maintaining physical proximity and contact.

Thus, among the Hausa there is a highly complex, coherent and "sensible" fit among characteristics of the physical ecology, social ecology, patterns of caregiving, and infant characteristics. The high infant mortality rate from both illness and injury (LeVine, 1974) is consistent with a cultural adaptation of heightened caregiver monitoring and responsiveness to infant cues. The relatively dangerous physical environment, extremely high availability of caregivers, and restriction of infant exploration are all in equilibrium with one another; this would be adaptive at least until the infant's locomotor skill and ability to recognize danger are sophisticated enough to avoid the surrounding hazards. This suggestion is supported by less formal observations of the 18- to 24-month-old children in the same compounds: They were allowed to explore with very little restriction—and they did so.

These physical and social ecology variables are also in equilibrium with characteristics of the infants: (a) using attachment figures for visual and manipulatory, but not locomotor, exploration; (b) using predominantly signal rather than motor attachment behaviors; and (c) becoming attached to a relatively large number of caregivers. It is likely, in a causal sense, that each of these characteristics feeds back on the others and facilitates their continuing, stable organization. Although this equilibrated system is phenotypically quite distinct from the organization that has been identified in so many studies of Western families, at the level of systemic rules outlined by Ashby (1952, 1956), the two cultures appear to be operating according to the same set of *underlying* constraints and options. In both cases, the specific form of attachment–caregiving interactions between the infant and its attachment figures serve to compensate for the lack of motor, communication, and social skills on the infant's part, such that the youngster is always protected while being afforded as much independence as possible within which to learn those skills. Although clear differences emerge in the specific patterns of interaction, the patterns are organized systemically into coherent, equilibrated, and functional packages of physical and social ecology, and characteristics of both infant and caregiver, that are fully comprehensible only when placed in the larger context of their relations with one another.

## THE DEVELOPMENT OF COY EXPRESSIONS

The third corollary to Ashby's proposal states that developmental change consists of coincidental changes in the *organization* of the child's behavioral systems and of the behavior of its caregivers. Furthermore, these changes will tend to have the outcome of transferring increased responsibility to the child while still maintaining essential variables within the limits necessary for survival. Marvin and his colleagues (e.g., Greenberg & Marvin, 1982; Marvin, 1977; Mossler et al., 1976) have described how the decline in children's distress at separations from their mothers is organized developmentally with the acquisition of communication skills such as perspective-taking and the negotiation of plans regarding separations and reunions. These findings have illustrated how the child, toward the end of the Infancy-2 period and the transition to the Juvenile period, assumes additional autonomy in protecting itself within its interaction with its mother.

As in the case of the chimpanzee and other nonhuman primates, however, this developmental, organizational change is also taking place in the context of increased, autonomous integration into the larger group (relatively) independent of the primary caregivers. In order to maintain its essential variables within the limits of survival, the youngster must assume increased responsibility in protecting itself from potential harm (e.g., aggression) from adult conspecifics other than the caregiver. This is accomplished not only through verbal communication, but also through the predictable use of nonverbal communication such as coy expressions. Tracing the development of these expressions illustrates the developmental transfer of protection from the close bond with the mother to the child itself.

Coy expressions (Marvin, Marvin, & Abramovitch, 1973) take the form of expressions that (a) draw attention to the individual displaying the expression and either (b) mimic some of those characteristics of infants that make them particularly attractive to adults, such as the rounded belly or open mouth; or combines behavioral elements normally utilized in approaching and avoiding another person into a static, ritualized position—for example, turning the head away while maintaining eye contact. These expressions are seen as communicating an interest in interacting with the person toward whom the expression is displayed, while at the same time communicating a hesitancy and self-consciousness about doing so. Thus, the expression appears to reflect an ambivalent, approach–avoidance conflict. Finally, the "predictable outcome" of the expression is seen as eliciting gentle and playful feelings or behavior on the part of the other, and in the process diminishing potential aggression from that person.

Behaviorally, coy expressions consist of a complex combination of at least the following eight expressive elements:

- *Smile:* Open- or closed-mouth smile;
- *Head to Shoulder:* The child's head is lowered toward the shoulder or the shoulder is raised toward the head. Eye contact is usually maintained;
- *Open Mouth:* The lower jaw drops, with or without relaxed lips; the degree of openness varies;
- *Tongue Out:* The tongue protrudes, either to the side or downward; the mouth may be open or closed;
- *Belly Out:* With the shoulders kept in line with the feet, the stomach is protruded outward, almost invariably toward the other person;
- *Side Glance:* The head is turned away from the other person, while eye-contact is maintained;
- *Touch Face:* One or both hands are brought up to and manipulate the face—for example, scratching the nose, covering the mouth, putting a finger in the mouth, "primping" the hair;
- *Rolled Lower Lip:* The lower lip is stretched over and covers the lower teeth. The mouth may be closed or open.

Each of these elements is in the nonverbal repertoire of toddlers and young preschoolers; however, the predictable, complex combinations of elements usually perceived as coy expressions tend not to be exhibited until near the end of the preschool period. Adults tend not to perceive the earlier, simpler expressions as coy; but they perceive the more complex combinations as coy, find them exceedingly attractive, and experience them as eliciting gentle and protective feelings in themselves (Marvin & Mossler, 1976).

A number of studies have suggested that organizational changes that are consistent with a shift from the Infancy-2 to the Juvenile periods take place in children's attachment behavior between the third and fourth birthdays (e.g., Goldberg, Washington, & Janus, 1996; Marvin, 1977; Stewart & Marvin, 1984). Consistent with the proposal outlined in this chapter, one component of these developmental changes should be a coinciding shift from the unpredictable expression of *elements* of coy expressions to the predictable expression of complex *combinations* of elements.

In a study of 46 2- to 5-year-old children being introduced to an unfamiliar, friendly, adult, Marvin et al. (1973) videotaped the children's nonverbal expressions and identified the occurrence of each of the coy elements listed earlier. The complexity of each child's expression when the unfamiliar adult first entered the room was compared. As shown in Figure 2, there is a significant shift in the complexity of the expressions at the same age as other studies have suggested further, organizational changes in attachment behavior.

Other observations made during the course of the study are consistent with the proposed shift in responsibility for protection from the child–parent bond to the child itself. Specifically, the 2- and 3-year-olds, when they first saw the stranger, tended either to continue playing and ignore the stranger; or to retreat to mother, display one or two elements of a coy expression, and then engage with the stranger after using mother as a secure base for sociable interaction. The 4- and 5-year-olds, however, were much more likely to stand when the stranger entered, display a full coy expression toward her, and then engage her without retreating to the mother. Again, it is clear that a full understanding of these expressions is

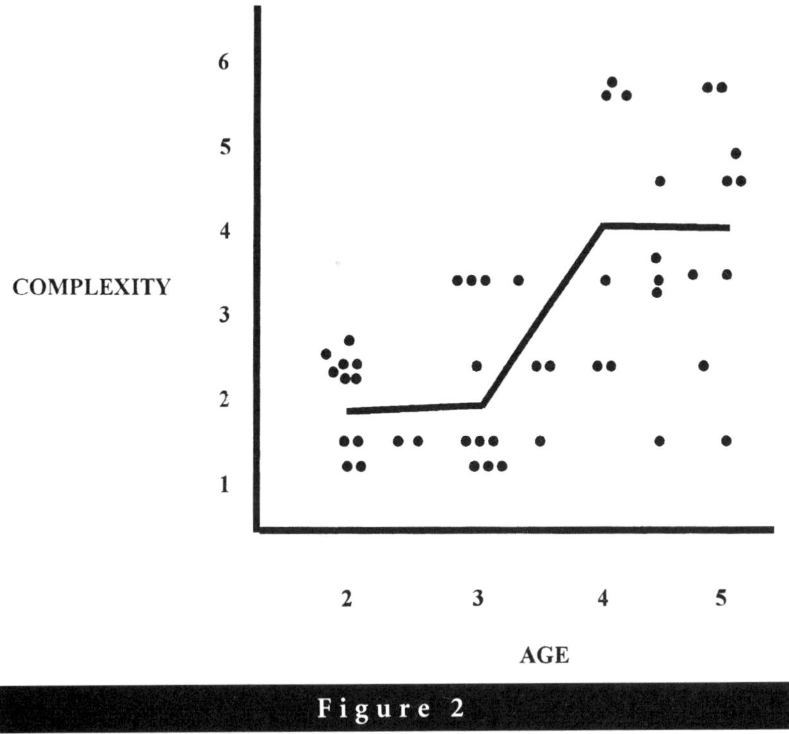


Figure 2

Complexity of Coy Expressions

possible only by viewing their development and use, in the context of both the changing relationship with the mother and of the changing patterns of interaction with unfamiliar conspecifics.

## DISORGANIZATION IN DEVELOPMENT

As mentioned in the introduction, one of the corollaries of Ashby's proposal, as applied to attachment behavior, is that maladaptive organization, or psychopathology, can be seen as a patterning of behavioral systems that fails to protect the youngster while affording it the opportunity to explore and develop more autonomous strategies for controlling variety. In a recent study of preschool Romanian children raised under horrifying, institutional conditions and then adopted into Canadian homes, Goldberg and

Marvin (1996) observed patterns of attachment behavior and of behavior toward a strange adult that appear to fit this definition of a disordered system.

The early literature on institutionalized children (e.g., Goldfarb, 1943) suggested that these children had difficulty forming stable attachments when placed in adoptive homes. They were also reported to exhibit "indiscriminately friendly behavior" toward strangers. This behavioral organization is consistent with a pattern of inadequate protection from a variety of dangers—a pattern for which the child itself is largely responsible.

The sample in this recent study consisted of 18 Romanian adoptees between the ages of 3 to 5 years, who had been living with their adoptive parents for at least 6 months, and a comparison sample of nonadopted children matched for age, gender, and attachment classification. The children were videotaped in the Strange Situation (Ainsworth et al., 1978), and their strategies of attachment toward their adoptive mothers were assessed using the preschool attachment classification system developed by Cassidy and Marvin (1992). Their reactions to a friendly stranger were classified using a system developed by Greenberg and Marvin (1982).

In this sample, half of the Romanian children displayed attachment patterns toward their adoptive mothers that were classified as "secure." They greeted their mothers happily on reunion, initiated pleasant interaction with them, and displayed no avoidant or ambivalent behavior. This is approximately the same percentage of secure children in low-risk samples. It is surprising that none of the Romanian children displayed "avoidant" attachment patterns, the most common insecure pattern! At first, these results seemed to contradict Goldfarb's (1943) work, as well as attachment theory and much primate work in general.

However, when these results are placed in the context of the children's reactions to the stranger, a different picture emerges. Many of the Romanian adoptees displayed indiscriminately friendly behavior toward the stranger: When she entered the room, they tended to greet her, approach her with no wariness whatsoever, and initiate playful interaction. Some of these children even displayed attachment behavior toward the stranger immediately on her entrance. From the perspective of ordered versus disordered *organizations* of behavior, however, the more important finding was that it was the adoptees classified as *secure* who tended to display this indiscriminate behavior toward the stranger. Romanian adoptees classified as insecurely attached to their Canadian mothers tended *not* to display this pattern. In the Canadian comparison sample, *no* children classified as secure exhibited this indiscriminately friendly pattern: All displayed some wariness and either retreated to their mothers as a haven of safety, displayed coy expressions toward the stranger, or ignored her and continued playing.

If replicated in a larger sample, these results would suggest that many of these adoptees have developed a strategy of behaving toward almost any adult in the same, friendly way. This organization of behavioral systems might, in fact, be adaptive in the short run: Based on their histories, these children might understandably have developed a strategy of making themselves available to be cared for by *any* adult conspecific. However, in the long run this would probably raise the risk of injury or maltreatment. And as an organization of behavioral systems within the child and between the child and both parents and other conspecifics, it is a variant that certainly does not exhibit the same adaptive "fit" as the various patterns found in a range of cultures.

## CONCLUSION

The studies reviewed in this chapter cover a wide range of traditional "disciplines": ethology, anthropology, and developmental psychology. These are disciplines that are often seen as operating from quite different, and usually conflicting, paradigms. However, it is very possible that the most important basis for these conflicts is the tendency, especially in developmental psychology, to skip the "descriptive" phase of the science, to rely too exclusively on the search for causal mechanisms and processes, and to avoid studying and modeling the chosen phenomenon within the many contexts in which it takes place. It is just these constricting tendencies on which Freedman's work has had, and should continue to have, a correcting effect.

The study of attachment has many roots in evolutionary theory, ethology, and anthropology and, therefore, perhaps suffers less from these limitations than the study of many other areas of child development. However, the field of attachment research is in danger of narrowing its focus so much in the direction of causal mechanisms involved in *differential* pathways of development that it risks both premature closure of its descriptive phase, as well as increasing isolation from other areas of social science research. To avoid this, it will be necessary to continue in-depth collaboration not only with cognitive science but with ethology, evolutionary biology, behavior genetics, and anthropology. Even more important, it will be necessary to maintain ties with the type of systems-level descriptions and causal analyses proposed by Ashby (1956) and Freedman and Gorman (1993).

## REFERENCES


Ainsworth, M. D. S. (1967). *Infancy in Uganda: Infant care and the growth of love.* Baltimore: Johns Hopkins University Press.

Ainsworth, M. D. S., Blehar, M. C., Waters, E., & Wall, S. (1978). *Patterns of attachment: A psychological study of the strange situation.* Hillsdale, NJ: Erlbaum.

Ainsworth, M. D. S., & Marvin, R. S. (1995). On the shaping of attachment theory and research. In E. Waters, B. E. Vaughn, G. Posada, & K. Kondo-Ikemura (Eds.), Caregiving, cultural, and cognitive perspectives on secure-base behavior and working models: New growing points of attachment theory and research. *Monographs of the Society for Research in Child Development, 244,* 60, 3–21. Chicago: University of Chicago Press.

Altmann, J. (1980). *Baboon mothers and infants.* Cambridge, MA: Harvard University Press.

Anderson, J. W. (1972). Attachment behaviour out of doors. In N. G. Blurton Jones (Ed.), *Ethological studies of child behavior* (pp. 199–215). Cambridge: Cambridge University Press.

Ashby, W. R. (1952). *Design for a brain.* New York: John Wiley.

Ashby, W. R. (1956). *An introduction to cybernetics.* New York: John Wiley.

Bateson, P. P. G. (1976). Rules and reciprocity in behavioural development. In

P. P. G. Bateson & R. A. Hinde (Eds.), *Growing points in ethology* (pp. 401–421). Cambridge: Cambridge University Press.

Bell, S. M. V. (1970). The development of the concept of the object as related to infant–mother attachment. *Child Development, 40,* 291–311.

Bell, S. M., & Ainsworth, M. D. S. (1972). Infant crying and maternal responsiveness. *Child Development, 43,* 1171–1190.

Belsky, J., & Isabella, R. (1988). Maternal, infant and social–contextual determinants of attachment security. In J. Belsky & T. Nezworski (Eds.), *Clinical implications of attachment* (pp. 41–94). Hillsdale, NJ: Erlbaum.

Bischoff, N. A. (1975). A systems approach toward the functional connections of attachment and fear. *Child Development, 46,* 801–817.

Blurton Jones, N. G. (1972). *Ethological studies of child behavior.* Cambridge: Cambridge University Press.

Blurton Jones, N. G. (1993). The lives of hunter–gatherer children: Effects of parental behavior and parental reproductive strategy. In M. E. Pereira & L. A. Fairbanks (Eds.), *Juvenile primates: Life history, development, and behavior* (pp. 309–326). New York: Oxford University Press.

Bowlby, J. (1969). *Attachment and loss. Vol. I. Attachment.* New York: Basic Books.

Carpenter, C. R. (1964). *Naturalistic behavior of non-human primates.* University Park: Pennsylvania State University Press.

Cassidy, J., & Marvin, R. S. (1992). *Attachment organization in preschool children: Procedures and coding manual.* Unpublished manual, University of Virginia.

Chism, J. (1991). Ontogeny of behavior in humans and nonhuman primates: The search for common ground. In J. D. Loy & C. B. Peters (Eds.), *Understanding behavior: What primate studies tell us about human behavior* (pp. 90–120). New York: Oxford University Press.

Fonagy, P., Steele, H., & Steele, M. (1991). Maternal representations of attachment during pregnancy predict the organization of mother–infant attachment at one year of age. *Child Development, 62,* 891–905.

Freedman, D. G. (1979). *Human sociobiology: A holistic approach.* New York: Free Press.

Freedman, D. G., & Freedman, N. (1969). Behavioral differences between Chinese–American and European–American newborns. *Nature, 244,* 1227.

Freedman, D. G., & Gorman, J. (1993). Attachment and the transmission of culture: An evolutionary perspective. *Journal of Social and Evolutionary Systems, 16,* 297–329.

George, C., Kaplan, N., & Main, M. (1985). *Adult attachment interview.* Unpublished manuscript, University of California, Berkeley.

Goldberg, S., & Marvin, R. (1996, April). *Child–parent attachment and indiscriminately friendly behavior toward strangers in Romanian orphans adopted into Canadian families.* Paper presented at the Biennial Meeting of the International Society for Infant Studies, Providence, RI.

Goldberg, S., Washington, J., & Janus, M. (1996). *Stability and change in attachment from infancy to preschool.* Unpublished manuscript, University of Toronto.

Goldfarb, W. (1943). Infant rearing and problem behavior. *American Journal of Orthopsychiatry, 13,* 249–265.

Goodall, J. (1965). Chimpanzees of the Gombe Stream Reserve. In I. DeVore (Ed.), *Primate behavior: Field studies of monkeys and apes.* New York: Holt, Rinehart & Winston.

Greenberg, M. T., & Marvin, R. S. (1982). Reactions of preschool children to an adult stranger: A behavioral systems approach. *Child Development, 53,* 481–490.

Hall, K. R. L., & DeVore, I. (1965). Baboon social behavior. In I. DeVore (Ed.), *Primate behavior: Field studies of monkeys and apes* (pp. 53–110). New York: Holt, Rinehart & Winston.

Jay, P. (1965). The common langur of North India. In I. DeVore (Ed.), *Primate behavior: Field studies of monkeys and apes* (pp. 197–247). New York: Holt, Rinehart & Winston.

Konner, M. (1972). Maternal care, infant behavior and development among the !Kung. In R. Lee & I. DeVore (Eds.), *Kalahari hunter gatherers: Studies of the !Kung San and their neighbors* (pp. 218–245). Cambridge, MA: Harvard University Press.

Kuhn, T. S. (1970). *The structure of scientific revolutions* (2nd ed.). Chicago: University of Chicago Press.

Lawick-Goodall, J. van. (1968). The behavior of free-living chimpanzees in the Gombe Stream Reserve. *Animal Behaviour Monographs, 1,* 164–311.

Leiderman, P. H., & Leiderman, G. F. (1974). Affective and cognitive consequences of polymatric infant care in the East African Highlands. *Minnesota Symposium on Child Psychology, 8,* 81–110.

LeVine, R. A. (1974). Parental goals: A cross-cultural view. *Teacher's College Record, 76,* 226–239

Main, M., & Cassidy, J. (1988). Categories of response to reunion with the parent at age six: Predictable from infant attachment classifications and stable over a one-month period. *Developmental Psychology, 24,* 415–426.

Main, M., Kaplan, N., & Cassidy, J. (1985). Security in infancy, childhood and adulthood: A move to the level of representation. In I. Bretherton & E. Waters (Eds.), Growing points of attachment theory and research. *Monographs of the Society for Research in Child Development, 50,* 66–104.

Main, M., & Solomon, J. (1990). Procedures for identifying infants as disorganized/disoriented during the Ainsworth strange situation. In M. T. Greenberg, D. Cicchetti, & E. M. Cummings (Eds.), *Attachment in the preschool years: Theory, research, and intervention* (pp. 121–160). Chicago: University of Chicago Press.

Marvin, R. S. (1977). An ethological–cognitive model for the attenuation of mother–child attachment behavior. In T. M. Alloway, L. Krames, & P. Pliner (Eds.), *Advances in the study of communication and affect. Vol. III: Attachment Behavior* (pp. 25–60). New York: Plenum Press.

Marvin, R. S., & Greenberg, M. T. (1982). Preschoolers' changing conceptions of their mothers: A social–cognitive study of mother–child attachment. In D. Forbes & M. T. Greenberg (Eds.), *New directors for child development: Children's planning strategies. No. 18* (pp. 47–60). San Francisco: Jossey-Bass.

Marvin, R. S., Marvin, C. N., & Abramovitch, L. I. (1973, March). *An ethological study of the development of coy behavior in young children.* Paper presented at the Biennial Meeting of the Society for Research in Child Development, Philadelphia, PA.

Marvin, R. S., & Mossler, D. G. (1976). A methodological paradigm for the description and analysis of non-verbal expressions: Coy expressions. *Representative Research in Social Psychology, 7,* 133–139.

Marvin, R. S., VanDevender, T. L., Iwanaga, M., LeVine, S., & LeVine, R. A. (1977). Infant-caregiver attachment among the Hausa of Nigeria. In H. M. McGurk (Ed.), *Ecological factors in human development* (pp. 247–260). Amsterdam: North Holland.

McGrew, W. C. (1972). *An ethological study of children's behavior.* New York: Academic Press.

Mossler, D. G., Marvin, R. S., & Greenberg, M. T. (1976). The early development of conceptual perspective taking in 2–6 year old children. *Developmental Psychology, 12,* 85–86.

Schaller, G. (1963). *The mountain gorilla: Ecology and behavior.* Chicago: University of Chicago Press.

Stewart, R. B., & Marvin, R. S. (1984). Sibling relations: The role of conceptual perspective taking in the ontogeny of sibling caregiving. *Child Development, 55,* 1322–1332.

Suomi, S. J. (1995). Influence of attachment theory on ethological studies of biobehavioral development in non-human primates. In S. Goldberg, R. Muir, & J. Kerr (Eds.), *Attachment theory: Social, developmental, and clinical perspectives* (pp. 185–201). Hillsdale, NJ: Analytic Press.

Trivers, R. L. (1972). Parental investment and sexual selection. In B. Campbell (Ed.), *Sexual selection and the descent of man.* Chicago: Aldine.

Waddington, C. H. (1957). *The strategy of the genes.* London: Allen & Unwin.

9

# Sexual Orientation as a Developmental Context for Lesbians, Gays, and Bisexuals: Biological Perspectives

Ritch C. Savin-Williams and Lisa M. Diamond

Throughout his scholarly life, Daniel G. Freedman has been at the center of a sometimes heated academic debate concerning the relative role that biology has in human development. At times he has enraged his opponents by refusing their attempts to frame the debate solely in terms of traditional scientific paradigms. Rather, Dr. Freedman has drawn on data from many disciplines, including philosophy, religion, anthropology, physics, and political science, to make his case.

In this chapter, we continue this tradition, discussing the politics of a biological perspective on one often neglected aspect of human development, sexual orientation. The modern essentialist versus social constructionist debate in many ways mimics the sociobiological versus cultural relativism debate that so consumed much of Dr. Freedman's life work. We review the former debate, drawing on data from disciplines as diverse as molecular biology and political science. Beliefs about the etiology of

See Savin-Williams and Diamond (in press) for elaboration of these ideas. We are deeply indebted to the editorial assistance of Kenneth M. Cohen.

same-sex attractions have shifted temporally, vary by gender and sexual orientation, and implicate a political ideology.

In class, Dr. Freedman was fond of challenging students to gather their own data "in the real world." We continue this tradition, presenting data regarding beliefs about the origins of same-sex attractions and the potential benefits and liabilities of biological research for the individual, his or her family and friends, politics, national priorities, religion, and science. Dr. Freedman never shied from academic controversy or grandiosity and we are not the ones to go against this precedent.

The assertion that sexual orientation is an important context for understanding developmental issues facing children and adolescents assumes that because of their sexuality gay, lesbian, and bisexual individuals have a substantially different life course than do heterosexual individuals. The counter argument is that development among sexual minorities requires no special attention because they are essentially similar to heterosexuals except in the objects of their sexual desires. Although many socially and biologically oriented scientists approach the question of similarities and differences between heterosexual and nonheterosexual individuals as a strictly empirical question, others politicize this debate in modern discussions concerning gays in the military, same-sex marriages, and sex education in the schools. Despite one's best intentions to maintain an academic level of inquiry, such loftiness does not obliterate the powerful political context shaping both the asking and the answering of questions regarding the significance of sexual orientation as a context for development.

The "similarity versus difference" issue has historical roots in a hotly contested political domain concerning strategies for gay, lesbian, and bisexual civil rights and social acceptance (see discussion in D'Emilio, 1983). This perspective is reflected in the social science literature of the late 1970s and early 1980s that explored the gay and lesbian "lifestyle" as a healthy mirror-image alternative to heterosexuality. D'Emilio (1983) referred to advocates of this position as *accommodationists.* This conservative, "fitting in" stance maintains, "If you treat us respectably then we will be normal, good citizens with civic responsibilities and appropriate behaviors" (Savin-Williams, 1990, p. 174). Gay, lesbian, and bisexual individuals should look, act, walk, and talk like heterosexuals; value marriage and family just like heterosexuals; have the same career aspirations; and hold the same mainstream values.

Recently, the sameness position has been labeled conservative and Republican, "saving a place at the table" in mainstream society for lesbians, gays, and bisexuals (see discussion in Bawer, 1993; Kirk & Madsen, 1989; Sullivan, 1995). Some argue that similarities to heterosexuals should be emphasized to dispel historical and contemporary myths portraying gay, lesbian, and bisexual people as psychologically damaged and dangerous individuals intent on winning "special rights" and inclined toward promiscuity, seduction, and child molestation. The recent public debate regarding gays in the military has been dominated by the sameness position. The argument for inclusion holds that lesbians and gays are neither less physically nor less mentally capable, trustworthy, nor sexually controllable than heterosexuals. "Queer" activists are condemned as doing more harm than good, providing the "wrong image at the wrong time, exemplifying what our friends in straight society fear most: confusing sex roles, presenting dykes and queens as members of the community, advocating the sexual rights of minors, and threatening the social and political system" (Savin-Williams, 1990, p. 174).

The uniqueness position argues that lesbians, bisexuals, and gays have *distinctive* life courses that must be understood in their own right and on their own terms. Advocates of this position maintain that regardless of the origins of sexual orientation, the very fact of engaging in sexual and affectional relationships with the same sex leads to experiences, self-concepts, and perspectives that are inherently and immutably different from those of heterosexuals. Some have attempted to re-appropriate the word "queer" to describe their deep sense of difference and uniqueness as an empowering and unifying strength, rather than as a stigma. These queer activists also advocate alignment with other oppressed groups, such as African Americans and women, for perceived common goals.

Champions of the uniqueness position argue that it does more harm than good to dispel false stereotypes of gay, lesbian, and bisexual individuals by projecting a similarly false image of these individuals as identical to heterosexuals in all respects save for the choice of sexual partners. They condemn this as acquiescence to the heterosexual norm, which they maintain is exactly what most heterosexuals who fear gays, bisexuals, and lesbians would prefer—for sexual minorities to become invisible.

In an important and reverberating critique of the "sameness" perspective, Kitzinger (1987) argued that "liberal humanistic" research on lesbians that emphasized their similarities to heterosexual women depoliticized lesbianism, masking the sociocultural context of heterosexism out of which their lives have historically been crafted. Although nineteenth-century psychologists constructed gay men and lesbians as deviant and dangerous, Kitzinger argued that twentieth-century liberal humanistic research reconstructed lesbianism as safe and harmless in order to neutralize the political threat that lesbian, gay, and bisexual individuals posed to the predominant heterosexual social order by their very existence.

The clash between these two positions can be seen in the argument within gay and lesbian communities that has taken place over same-sex marriage. One side is exemplified by Bob and Rod Jackson-Paris—one a gay supermodel and the other a Mr. Universe—who proudly proclaim their traditional marriage and life in the suburbs (Perry, 1990). Another perspective is presented by Brownworth who maintained that marriage is about ownership, slavery, and domination:

> Marriage is an unnatural state predicated on the dominance of one partner over another. . . . It is about the buying, selling and trading of a commodity—women—and by extension, children and property. . . . Our entire lesbian and gay civil rights movement is *supposed* to be about inclusivity, equality, egalitarianism. . . . Queers can do better than borrowing from the worst elements of straight culture when our own is so rich and full of real, not institutionalized, promise. (1996, pp. 93, 97–98)

These positions are infused with political ramifications, and charges of political correctness and incorrectness in print and the public arena have repeatedly surfaced. Speakers have been jeered at professional conferences and more than one professional gay or lesbian scientist has been isolated because of his or her views. Documenting these events, exploring the reasons for the political sensitivity, and fully examining the consequences of these realities are beyond the scope of this chapter.

Questions of sameness and difference also provoke controversy because of their close connections with, and implications for, theories of etiology. If sameness is maintained, then no particular need exists to address issues of etiology; it is a moot point. If difference is maintained, then the *derivation* of the dissimilarities between sexual minorities and heterosexuals becomes a source of debate, one that has indeed dominated academic theory and research.

## DEVELOPMENTAL THEORY AND ETIOLOGY

### Etiology Theories

Although it is not possible to give a comprehensive overview of contemporary and historical explanations of sexual orientation (see Ellis, 1996a, 1996b), it is worthwhile to briefly note several of the competing etiological theories of sexual orientation. Environmentally based theories that have little or no empirical support, or that have been empirically discredited, include psychoanalytic theories proposing a relationship between strong, dominant mothers and detached fathers and their gay sons (Bieber et al., 1962); explanations positing that individuals with negative heterosexual experiences are likely in response to turn to same-sex experiences (Gallup & Suarez, 1983); and social learning approaches that suggest that adolescents may incorrectly "imprint" on the same sex instead of the other sex during puberty (Storms, Stivers, Lambers, & Hill, 1981).

A more plausible socially based theory invokes labeling phenomena (Kagan, 1964). In these scenarios a child who engages in gender-atypical behavior is subsequently labeled "sissy," "dyke," or "fag" by peers. The child self-labels in this fashion, eventually leading to acquisition of a gay or lesbian identity. Although a pure labeling approach to sexual orientation is dubious, this does not rule out the possible facilitative role of labeling experiences in the formation of a sexual identity for children with gender-atypical characteristics and same-sex attractions.

The two major competing biological theories of sexual orientation invoke genetics and prenatal hormones. The former is supported by recent DNA (Hamer & Copeland, 1994) and twin studies (Bailey & Pillard, 1991; Bailey, Pillard, Neale, & Agyei, 1993). Twin studies have found varying levels of concordance for same-sex orientation in line with genetic relatedness; however, most research has failed to find evidence of perfect concordance for identical twins, indicating that nongenetic factors may play a significant role in mediating genetic effects (Baily, 1996). Prenatal hormone theory argues that nonnormative levels of certain hormones at specific times during fetal development "masculinize" the brains of women or "feminize" the brains of men, resulting in a same-sex orientation (Ellis, 1996a). Empirical support for this theory comes primarily from studies of rodents and other nonhuman animals.

One attempt to blend biological and environmental variables is Bem's "exotic becomes erotic" formulation.

> Biological variables, such as genes, prenatal hormones, and brain neuroanatomy, do not code for sexual orientation per se but for childhood temperaments that influence a child's preferences for sex-typical or sex-atypical activities and peers. These preferences lead children to feel different from opposite- or same-sex peers—to perceive them as dissimilar, unfamiliar, and exotic. This, in turn, produces heightened nonspecific autonomic arousal that subsequently gets eroticized to that same class of dissimilar peers: Exotic becomes erotic. (1996, p. 320)

Bem marshaled an impressive array of research studies to buttress his theory. Biological theorists are most likely to object to Bem's placement of the genetic component in terms of temperament, rather than sexual orientation itself.

## Two Positions: Essentialist and Social Constructionist

Assuming that lesbian, gay, and bisexual individuals have *unique* life courses, two theoretical stances have been articulated regarding their developmental trajectories. The debate concerns whether sexual attractions lead to developmental uniqueness or whether the uniqueness precedes the sexual attractions. The first has been attributed to essentialist positions that have strong biological underpinnings. According to essentialists, gays, lesbians, and bisexuals have a unique developmental trajectory because of the genetics, hormones, or neuroanatomical structures responsible for their *sexual orientation.* Essentialists are seldom purists in that many recognize the importance of environmental factors in determining sexual orientation. However, all posit an "it" that is an enduring characteristic of the individual and beyond the purview of "choice."

The second position has been articulated by social constructionists. Because their sexual attractions to same-sex individuals have been recognized by others, lesbians, bisexuals, and gays are treated differently and view themselves differently, ultimately leading to the incorporation of a socially constructed *sexual identity.* Their unique developmental trajectory follows, shaped in large part by historical and cultural conceptions of what it means to be attracted to same-sex individuals during that time and place. The origins of same-sex attractions for social constructionists ultimately become uninteresting, unimportant, and unworthy of serious academic discussion.

In the ongoing debate over etiology, issues are often simplified according to the following formula: If sexual orientation is biologically based, then certain essential differences between heterosexual and sexual minority individuals can be identified. Following this line of reasoning, a biological position would logically lead one to conclude that sexual orientation manifests itself in the cognitions, affects, and behaviors of gays, lesbians, and bisexuals. One consequence is that because lesbians are more likely to have a "male-type" brain and gay men to have a "female-type" brain, lesbians and gay men are likely to enter gender-atypical occupations. Lesbians should excel in mechanistic and spatial thinking and be more aggressive, unemotional, and harsh; gay men should excel in verbal abilities and be more passive, emotional, and sensitive. Thus, lesbians become athletes, mechanics, and military personnel; gay men become interior decorators, nurses, and florists.

The biological uniqueness position has been characterized by its opponents as reactionary and deterministic, with charges leveled that further investigations will lead researchers to attempt corrective gene therapy or neurosurgery for homosexuality. If sexual orientation is a matter of genetics, would not parents with a high probability of having a gay baby be discouraged from conceiving? Or, at the least, should they be told about the status of their fetus so that they can decide whether to abort?

Adherents to the religious right are, in this instance, in company with the radical left in their opposition to biological origin theory and research. For example, Jim Aist, a plant pathologist at Cornell University, is a self-proclaimed "expert" on the genetic basis of homosexuality, scientific methodology, and biblical studies. In a recent self-published and self-promoted handout to "homosexual" students, Aist wrote,

> Advocates of homosexuality claim that recent research has shown that homosexuality is innate, or inborn, and that, therefore, homosexual behavior should be valued and encouraged as a normal expression of human sexuality. Are these claims true, and should we really encourage homosexuality?
>
> A perusal of the original articles in which this recent information was published revealed an appalling lack of scientific rigor, and consequently, reliability, in most of them. Moreover, in none of these studies was it possible to draw an unequivocal conclusion that homosexuality is caused by biological factors.
>
> From a Biblical perspective, the answer to this question is "no", because the Bible clearly condemns homosexual behavior as sin. Any genetic influence toward such behavior would not, therefore, be ordained by God but would likely be a consequence of the fall of man (Romans 8:20-22). (Aist, 1994)

The religious right rejects biological theories because if homosexuality is innate then it must be viewed as natural and, consequently, "God given." They maintain instead that homosexuality is a choice to sin or an adaptation to an early seduction or to homosexual propaganda and that reparative therapy and hence redemption are possible (Aist, 1994).

On the other side of the debate, it usually follows that if sexual orientation is socially mediated, then any observed differences between heterosexual and sexual minority individuals must also be environmentally determined. For example, a social constructionist might argue that because culture stigmatizes same-sex dating and romance during the adolescent years, gay and lesbian youths are unable to connect intimacy and sexuality, leading to problematic developmental consequences such as substance abuse, prostitution, and suicide attempts. Dating those you do not love and loving those you cannot date may lead to such young adult problems as sexual promiscuity, asexual romances, fusion (enmeshed) romances, and short-lived relationships (Diamond, Savin-Williams, & Dube, in press; Savin-Williams, 1994, 1996).

The cultural uniqueness position has been labeled by accommodationists as radical and counterproductive to winning mainstream acceptance of homosexuality. Others fear that it promotes the view that sexuality is a matter of choice and, thus, individuals can choose when and how to be sexual. Following this perspective, antigay activists might maintain that if one can choose to be gay then one can simply choose to be heterosexual. Furthermore, if sexual orientation is a matter of choice, then if vulnerable children are taught about homosexuality in the classroom might they "choose" same-sex partners when they grow up?

The most defensible position to take in these matters is that different causes may operate for different individuals. The view that not all individuals have identical pathways in the development of their sexuality is not a new concept (Bailey, 1996; Garnets & Kimmel, 1993; Savin-Williams, in press). Two possibilities exist: diversity among and diversity within groups. As an example of diversity among groups, prenatal hormones may determine sexual orientation for those with gender-atypical behaviors and interests (Meyer-Bahlburg, 1993), whereas "feminine lesbians" and "masculine gays" may be affected by psychosocial factors (Bell, Weinberg, & Hammersmith, 1981). Diversity within groups implies not simply that some gays are born that way and others are made but that a unique blend of biological, psychosocial, and cultural factors is responsible for sexual orientation in different individuals (Richardson, 1987).

Regardless of whether the etiology of sexual orientation is singular or multiple, the vast diversity in individuals' experiences of their same-sex attractions and desires is undeniable. Knowing the precise origins of sexual orientation tells us little about the manifest and internalized aspects of same-sex sexuality in different cultural and historical circumstances and for different genders, ages, social classes, and ethnic groups.

## OPINIONS REGARDING ETIOLOGY: A STUDY OF COLLEGE STUDENTS

### Public Opinion

Public opinion during the past several decades has decidedly favored a social or environmental etiology for homosexuality (Ellis, 1996a). Although some shifting has occurred during the past decade (Table 1), less than one third of the American populace reports that they believe that homosexuality is inborn. Among gay men and women, however, biological origins out-distance other etiological explanations. This is truer of gay men than of lesbians. For example, in a study of 2500 male readers of the gay and lesbian newsmagazine, *The Advocate* (Lever, 1994), nine of ten gay and bisexual men reported experiencing their sexuality as "essential"

**Table 1**

**Beliefs About the Origins of Homosexuality**

Gallup Poll

| | Inborn | Develops | Preference | No Opinion | Other |
|---|---|---|---|---|---|
| 1983 | 16% | 25% | 37% | 22% | — |
| 1993 | 31% | 14% | 35% | 8% | 12% |

*The Advocate* (1994)

| | Biology | Choice | Social |
|---|---|---|---|
| Gay Men | 92% | 4% | 4% |
| Lesbians | 56% | 16% | 28% |

(Table 1). Only 4% believed that they chose to be gay or that environmental factors made them gay. Lesbians are more likely to grant a role for choice and circumstance in their sexual self-identification (Golden, 1996; Hencken, 1984)—four times as likely in Lever's (1995) *The Advocate* follow-up of 2550 lesbian and bisexual women.

One replicated finding is that heterosexual individuals who believe in a biological or genetic etiology for homosexuality are those most likely to have liberal attitudes toward sexual minorities (Ernulf, Innala, & Whitam, 1989; Piskur & Degelman, 1992; Whitley & Bernard, 1990). For example, a recent report of Midwest college students found that male students who believed that homosexuality was caused by learning, socialization, or some other aspect of the environment were less willing than those who believed in the innate etiology of homosexuality to date or marry the child (sexual orientation unspecified) of a lesbian (King & Black, 1995). This finding is contrary to the impression that those with a biological orientation to human characteristics tend to be most conservative in their politics and religion. Whether the "no-choice" belief in homosexuality preceded the liberal attitudes, or is the consequence of associating with and accepting sexual minorities, has not been determined.

## A Study

To investigate attitudes toward biological research on homosexuality and beliefs regarding the potential benefits and liabilities of such research, questionnaires (see Exhibit 1) were distributed to a potential pool of 174 students who took a Cornell University class, "Introduction to Sexual Minorities," during one of two semesters in 1995. Completed questionnaires were received from 143; the other students either were absent the day the questionnaire was introduced or declined to complete the questionnaire.

Nearly three quarters of respondents identified themselves as heterosexual. More than one half (53%) of the class were heterosexual women and 19% were heterosexual men. The others were sexual minority women (17%) and men (11%) who claimed to be bisexual, gay, lesbian, questioning, or "not heterosexual." The two classes were composed of approxi-

## Exhibit 1

### Questionnaire Given to Students

*Circle*

Sex: Female Male

Sex ID: Bisexual, Heterosexual,
Asexual, Lesbian, Gay,
Questioning, Other ________________

1. To what extent do biology and environment/life experiences account for homosexuality (give in percentage points so that total equals 100%)

   BIOLOGY ________ ENVIRONMENT ________

2. Do you approve of research that attempts to understand the biological origins of homosexuality?

   Yes ________ No ________ Mixed ________

   Why or Why Not?

3. What do you feel are the benefits and liabilities of research on biologic origins of homosexuality?

   Benefits:

   Liabilities:

**Table 2**

**Cornell Students' Explanations for Causes of Homosexuality**

| | |
|---|---|
| Biological | 66% |
| Biological/Social | 22% |
| Social | 12% |

| By Sexual Orientation | Biological | Biological/Social | Social |
|---|---|---|---|
| Heterosexuals | 72% | 17% | 12% |
| Sexual Minorities | 50% | 38% | 13% |

mately 60% Whites, 25% Asian Americans, 10% Latinos, and 5% African Americans. Participants were highly educated, primarily college sophomores and juniors.

## Biological Versus Social Origins

Two thirds of all respondents reported that they believed that homosexuality has primarily biological origins, and 88% responded that biology plays a causative role at least half of the time (Table 2). More heterosexuals than sexual minorities postulated a primary role for biology, but the two groups did not differ regarding the importance of environmental factors in causing sexual orientation.

These findings diverge considerably from public opinion polls. This likely reflects the far greater liberal attitudes of heterosexual students who enrolled in a course on sexual minorities and the large number of gay activists who took the class. During the first semester (spring 1995) a standardized homophobia scale (Hudson & Ricketts, 1980) was to be given at the beginning and conclusion of the course to assess the effects of taking the course on attitudes toward gay people. However, the initial questionnaire had such a high ceiling effect and a narrow band of attitudes, all on the positive side, that giving the scale twice would have been pointless. Thus, the students may well represent that subset of the population noted earlier who are accepting of, and believe in a biological origin of, homosexuality.

The gay students, however, were less likely than recent surveys (e.g., Lever, 1994, 1995) would indicate to attribute a sole biological cause to homosexuality. The queer politics that appeared to permeate many of the "out" gay students who took the course may account for this variation. The queer objection to biological research and theory was emotionally illustrated by a gifted poet and gay male student who took the course. After reading an overview of the biological theories on the origin of homosexuality he wrote in a course paper:

> I think they [the studies] were offensive and oppressive both in their content and in the fact that they were poor as scientific studies. . . . Such a study is blatantly based on homophobia and heterosexism. I do not need science telling me that I'm "normal" and, that it's okay to be me. I dealt with that disaster long ago. . . . It tells straight readers that Lesbians and Gays must have science's pat on the back to be okay. It tells straight readers that there is something wrong with "HOMOSEXUALS" that "THEY" can't help and that must be found out so that "THEY" can be validated. I don't want their pity. I'm not your bitch don't hand your shit on me.

In answer to the question of whether biological research should be conducted, only 8% of the students gave an explicit "no" answer. This percentage increased to 18% when only those who believed in a social origin were asked. Nearly half (48%) of all students reported that biological research should be conducted; 44% replied "yes and no." Again, those who believed in a social origin were less willing (29%) to respond "yes."

## Benefits of Biological Research

When asked to list the benefits and liabilities of biological research, most students gave multiple answers. The most common *benefit*, given by nearly half of the students, is to increase understanding, acceptance, and compassion. Two students expressed these sentiments:

> I believe that if a biological basis for homosexuality is found, many people will come to the realization that homosexuality is innate

> and thus "From God." This discovery would undermine the biggest conservative argument of homosexuality being UN-natural.
>
> It's good to question things and it is human nature to wonder "Why?" but it shouldn't be necessary in an ideal world. Being that the world is not ideal, a biological origin might shut up some opponents of homosexuality.

More than one quarter (28%) listed basic science, knowledge, and curiosity as sufficient reason to study the biological causes of homosexuality. This view was voiced by three students:

> I think that knowledge extends our understanding and acceptance of the world around us including ourselves and furthers our promotion/growth as a developing species and world society. I believe humans have an innate curiosity and quest for knowledge.
>
> We run the risk of misusing science no matter what we are studying. Humans always want to know why things are the way they are. We must ask why.
>
> What bad things could come of more research about anything?

The third most popular (17%) benefit noted was that biology validates homosexuality as a normal variant because it shows that one does not choose to be gay. One student wrote,

> I believe that our society has become very scientifically oriented (at least media-inflated science) and if a biological/genetic basis for homosexuality can be found then I believe that many people will open their minds and become less fearful of the idea of homosexuality. It will allow them to "blame" biology and hopefully they will stop "blaming" the people.

Finally, one in ten believed that a biological origin might help gay people feel better about themselves. For example, one student approved of research on the biological origins of homosexuality:

> As long as the intent is not to fix it. Since a lot of GLB's [gays, lesbians, and bisexuals] have always been that way having a biological reason *may* be nice. It would also calm the fears of the idiots who think gay persons are going to convert their children.

## Liabilities of Biological Research

In terms of *liabilities*, six in ten students expressed concern that biological research would result in eugenics, attempts to cure homosexuality, and the practice of aborting gay fetuses. One student expressed these apprehensions:

> I also worry about repercussions such as genetic engineering of GLB FETUSES, and possible aborting [of] such. Also I worry that the biological origin will be referred to as a MUTATION.

Nearly one quarter (23%) noted that biological research is irrelevant, reductionistic, a waste of money, or a detraction from other more important problems. Two students represented these views:

> Who cares? Let's just figure how to make everyone happy. This obsession with biology seems so superficial.

> Why must we always find an explanation for everything? If it isn't harmful to society in general, then I believe that we should simply accept it for what it is and move on. They should try to find an explanation for why people discriminate instead since this behavior is harmful to society.

Others opposed biological research because they believed it posits homosexuality as pathological, a disease, or deviant (15%) or it is inherently unethical or offensive to gays (7%). One young woman said that she felt that homosexuality is a natural feeling:

> Why does there have to be an explanation for it? It is not a disease. There are no biological explanations for heterosexuality (at least I am now aware of).

### Mixed Benefits and Liabilities

Many of the students expressed mixed feelings about the benefits and liabilities of biological research on homosexuality. Two students noted their reservations:

> I feel that if it's conducted in good science and purpose then it's fine. But if researchers are covertly looking for a cure then it's wrong. But on the other hand, once published, the results will be available to all. Maybe I am just paranoid.

> I generally approve of any research which attempts to find out more about human nature. However, I am skeptical about the political motivations behind the research on a biological basis of homosexuality. Why do we need this research?

Reflecting the times, one student warned of the need to save government money.

> People have the right to know why they are the way they are. Don't think it is necessary to spend government money on this, unless it can be shown that knowing the origins of homosexuality can somehow improve their situation.

## CONCLUSION

These students are clearly not representative of the general population, but their views may reflect the changing attitudes toward homosexuality that are prevalent in a younger generation of North Americans. Most were supportive of biological research and could see many benefits of such research. They had reservations similar to those expressed by many opponents of current biological research studies into various other aspects of human behavior. Genetic engineering, eugenics, labeling, and misuse of data frightened many of these students. Some felt that such research is essentially irrelevant, detracts from real problems such as homophobia, and implies that homosexuality is deviant.

Despite these reservations, the students were willing to endorse biological research because it promotes both basic and applied science. Biological research satisfies our natural curiosity, fulfills our need to discover the truth, and fosters compassion and understanding. Many felt that through biological research the public can be convinced that its homophobic attitudes need to be altered and that gay people would feel better about themselves because they would realize that they had done nothing wrong to become other than heterosexual.

Neither the sameness nor uniqueness position is defensible from a developmental perspective because, as we understand the empirical literature, lesbians, bisexuals, and gays are both similar to and different from heterosexuals within the general population. We find little political or scientific comfort in any approach that attempts to argue either case to the exclusion of the other. Some gay, lesbian, and bisexual individuals may indeed have sex-atypical brain anatomy and functions; in many other areas of physiological characteristics, however, sexual minorities are indistinguishable from heterosexuals. Some lesbian, bisexual, and gay adolescents face psychosocial stresses as a result of being a sexual minority in North American culture that are not experienced by their heterosexual peers. Undeniably, however, sexual minority adolescents face the same developmental tasks as do heterosexual adolescents: establishing a personal identity, negotiating relations with parents, and experimenting with new sexual desires.

The myth of *the* gay individual or *the* gay lifestyle dies hard. As scientists we, too, frequently fall into the trap of homogenizing sexual minorities. Researchers have unquestioningly pursued characteristics thought to distinguish "homosexual" from "heterosexual" samples, as if each category was a sacred, unvarying entity. Rare is the scientist who describes within-group variations or the diversity inherent among populations of gays, bisexuals, and lesbians. Research that treats all sexual minority individuals as if they were following an identical developmental pathway obscures important developmental processes.

From a developmental perspective, one should not become either an essentialist or a social constructionist. Much of the contemporary debate regarding the biological and social origins of sexual minority populations implicitly denies the infrastructure of developmental psychology: Behavior is a function of the interaction between the person and the environment. Those who dichotomize sexual orientation into pure biological or social causation fall into a dangerous quagmire. To deny any role for biology affirms an untenable scientific view of human development. Equally harsh and deterministic would be to deny the significance of the environment in shaping biological properties. In fact, it should be recognized that a phenomenon the etiology of which is based in social interaction or social structure is no more under the individual's control or a matter of choice than that which can be traced to a biological origin. It is impossible to study the significance of sexual orientation as a context for development without understanding *both* the physiology, neuroanatomy, and genetics of the individual *and* the meanings that same-sex attractions, desires, and behavior hold in our culture at this particular moment in time. When discussing sexual orientation as a context for child or adolescent development, notions of a "biology-free" or "culture-free" phenomenon do not exist.

We propose that adopting a position of diversity is the most scientifically justifiable resolution to these ongoing debates. The diversity exists in the multiple pathways or patterns that characterize the developmental processes of lesbian, bisexual, and gay individuals. The complex interplay of forces that shape development implies variations in the degree to which a particular individual is influenced by biological and social factors, a process that may be similar to or different from that of heterosexuals. For example, an individual may have "become" gay for primarily biological reasons, another for primarily social reasons, and a third for some balanced interplay between biological and social components. The task of developmental research on this topic is to discover characteristics of sexual minority individuals in general *and* to investigate intrapopulation similarities and differences. This approach promotes an understanding of diversity not only between populations of gays and heterosexuals, but also within bisexual, gay, and lesbian populations.

The college students who completed the biological/social origins questionnaire appreciated the complexity of these issues. They endorsed biological research, not solely because of its significance for etiological questions, but because it also promotes increased compassion for and acceptance of sexual minorities. They had their reservations, especially regarding the misuse of biological research by those who would eliminate or reduce the number of gays, lesbians, and bisexuals. Their liberal attitudes and acceptance of biological explanations for homosexuality support previous research that associate these two attitudes. If the public is becoming more accepting of the role that biology has for sexual attractions and desires, and if such attitudes are associated with increased acceptance and support of lesbians, bisexuals, and gays, then there is much to celebrate. Let us hope that these students are the harbingers of the future.

## REFERENCES

Aist, J. R. (1994). *Help for homosexuals.* Unpublished manuscript, Cornell University, Ithaca, NY.

Bailey, J. M. (1996). Gender identity. In R. C. Savin-Williams & K. M. Cohen (Eds.), *The lives of lesbians, gays, and bisexuals: Children to adults* (pp. 71–93). Fort Worth, TX: Harcourt Brace.

Bailey, J. M., & Pillard, R. C. (1991). A genetic study of male sexual orientation. *Archives of General Psychiatry, 48,* 1089–1096.

Bailey, J. M., Pillard, R. C., Neale, M. C., & Agyei, Y. (1993). Heritable factors influence sexual orientation in women. *Archives of General Psychiatry, 50,* 217–223.

Bawer, B. (1993). *A place at the table: The gay individual in American society.* New York: Poseidon Press.

Bell, A. P., Weinberg, M. S., & Hammersmith, S. K. (1981). *Sexual preference: Its development in men and women.* Bloomington: Indiana University Press.

Bem, D. J. (1996). Exotic becomes erotic: A developmental theory of sexual orientation. *Psychological Review, 103,* 320–335.

Bieber, I., Dian, H. J., Drellich, M. G., Dince, P. R., Grand, H. G., Gundlach, R. H., Kremer, M. W., Rifkin, A. H., Wilbur, C. B., & Bieber, T. B. (1962). *Homosexuality: A psychoanalytic study.* New York: Basic Books.

Brownworth, V. A. (1996). Tying the knot or the hangman's noose: The case against marriage. *Journal of Gay, Lesbian, and Bisexual Identity, 1,* 91–98.

D'Emilio, J. (1983). *Sexual politics, sexual communities: The making of a homosexual minority in the United States, 1940–1970.* Chicago: University of Chicago Press.

Diamond, L. M., Savin-Williams, R. C., & Dube, E. M. (in press). Intimate peer relations among lesbian, gay, and bisexual adolescents: Sex, dating, passionate friendships, and romance. In W. Furman, C. Feiring, & B. B. Brown (Eds.), *Contemporary perspectives on adolescent romantic relationships.* New York: Cambridge University Press.

Ellis, L. (1996a). The role of perinatal factors in determining sexual orientation. In R. C. Savin-Williams & K. M. Cohen (Eds.), *The lives of lesbians, gays, and bisexuals: Children to adults* (pp. 35–70). Fort Worth, TX: Harcourt Brace.

Ellis, L. (1996b). Theories of homosexuality. In R. C. Savin-Williams & K. M. Cohen (Eds.), *The lives of lesbians, gays, and bisexuals: Children to adults* (pp. 11–34). Fort Worth, TX: Harcourt Brace.

Ernulf, K. E., Innala, D. M., & Whitam, F. L. (1989). Biological explanation, psychological explanation, and tolerance of homosexuals: A cross-national analysis of beliefs and attitudes. *Psychological Reports, 65,* 1003–1010.

Gallup, G. G., Jr., & Suarez, S. D. (1983). Homosexuality as a by-product of selection for optimal heterosexual strategies. *Perspectives in Biology and Medicine, 26,* 315–319.

Garnets, L. D., & Kimmel, D. C. (1993). Lesbian and gay male dimensions in the psychological study of human diversity. In L. D. Garnets & D. C. Kimmel (Eds.), *Psychological perspectives on lesbian and gay males experiences* (pp. 1–51). New York: Columbia University Press.

Golden, C. (1996). What's in a name? Sexual self-identification among women. In R. C. Savin-Williams & K. M. Cohen (Eds.), *The lives of lesbians, gays, and bisexuals: Children to adults* (pp. 229–249). Fort Worth, TX: Harcourt Brace.

Hamer, D., & Copeland, P. (1994). *The science of desire: The search for the gay gene and the biology of behavior.* New York: Simon & Schuster.

Hencken, J. (1984). Conceptualizations of homosexual behavior which preclude homosexual self-labeling. *Journal of Homosexuality, 9,* 53–63.

Hudson, W. W., & Ricketts, W. A. (1980). A strategy for the measurement of homophobia. *Journal of Homosexuality, 5,* 356–371.

Kagan, J. (1964). Acquisition and significance of sex typing and sex role identity. In M. L. Hoffman & L. W. Hoffman (Eds.), *Review of child development research* (pp. 137–167). New York: Sage.

King, B. R., & Black, K. N. (1995, May). *Extent of relational stigmatization by heterosexuals of lesbians and their children.* Paper presented at the Midwestern Psychological Association.

Kirk, M., & Madsen, H. (1989). *After the ball: How America will conquer its fear and hatred of gays in the 90's.* New York: Doubleday.

Kitzinger, C. (1987). *The social construction of lesbianism.* London: Sage.

Lever, J. (1994, August 23). Sexual revelations. *The Advocate,* pp. 17–24.

Lever, J. (1995, August 22). Lesbian sex survey. *The Advocate,* pp. 21–30.

Meyer-Bahlburg, H. F. L. (1993). Psychobiological research on homosexuality. *Sexual and Gender Identity Disorders, 2,* 489–500.

Perry, D. (1990, March 13). Built to last. *The Advocate,* pp. 32-37.

Piskur, J., & Degelman, D. (1992). Effect of reading a summary of research about biological bases of homosexual orientation on attitudes toward homosexuals. *Psychological Reports, 71,* 1219–1225.

Richardson, D. (1987). Recent challenges to traditional assumptions about homosexuality: Some implications for practice. *Journal of Homosexuality, 13,* 1–12.

Savin-Williams, R. C. (1990). *Gay and lesbian youth: Expressions of identity.* New York: Hemisphere.

Savin-Williams, R. C. (1994). Verbal and physical abuse as stressors in the lives of lesbian, gay male, and bisexual youths: Associations with school problems, running away, substance abuse, prostitution, and suicide. *Journal of Consulting and Clinical Psychology, 62,* 261–269.

Savin-Williams, R. C. (1996). Dating and romantic relationships among gay, lesbian, and bisexual youths. *The lives of lesbians, gays, and bisexuals: Children to adults* (pp. 166–180). Fort Worth, TX: Harcourt Brace.

Savin-Williams, R. C. (in press). *. . . And then I became gay: Young men's stories.* New York: Routledge.

Savin-Williams, R. C., & Diamond, L. D. (in press). Sexual orientation as a developmental context for lesbian, gay, and bisexual children and adolescents. In W. K. Silverman & T. H. Ollendick (Eds.), *Developmental issues in the clinical treatment of children and adolescents.* Boston: Allyn & Bacon.

Storms, M. D., Stivers, M. L., Lambers, S. M., & Hill, C. A. (1981). Sexual scripts for women. *Sex Roles, 3,* 257–263.

Sullivan, A. (1995). *Virtually normal: An argument about homosexuality.* New York: Knopf.

Whitley, J., & Bernard, E. (1990). The relationship of heterosexuals' attribution for the cause of homosexuality to attitudes toward lesbians and gay men. *Personality and Social Psychology Bulletin, 16,* 369–377.

10

# What Can the Genotype Tell Us About Complex Human Conditions?

Peter H. Wolff

Although Daniel Freedman and I have never worked together, I have known of his pioneering studies in human ethology for many years; and we have had a number of profitable discussions about the relation of genetic variations and their expressions in the human phenotype. I benefited greatly from these discussions, especially when we disagreed (as we still may) because they encouraged me to reassess my own a priori assumptions. This chapter reflects some of our agreements and disagreements on issues of mutual interest.

In this chapter, two examples from earlier and current studies are summarized that examine the relation between genetic variations and their presumed behavioral consequences. Both examples raise procedural and theoretical issues that have been of central interest in Dr. Freedman's research programs: (a) Which among the almost infinite number of possible differences between individuals or groups are of potential theoretical interest for understanding human development and adaptation? (b) How

This report was prepared while the author was supported by a grant (HD-28085) from the National Institute for Child Health and Human Development.

should human groups be classified to capture such differences? (c) What relationships between biological (genetic) variables and their behavioral consequences can be inferred from current knowledge in the relevant disciplines, and how can such relationships be tested empirically in humans? (d) Are linear causal explanations in terms of natural selection acting on random mutations sufficient to account for the induction of novel properties in complex systems?

## ALCOHOL FLUSHING

### Population Differences

The first example concerns a single major gene variation with visible behavioral effects but debatable consequences for human interests. Folk psychology has long recognized that members of Japanese, Chinese, and some other Asian ethnic groups flush dramatically after drinking small amounts of ethyl alcohol, whereas most Caucasian individuals of European descent show no visible effect after drinking equivalent amounts. Physical anthropology traditionally classified ethnic groups who flush to alcohol as members of the Mongoloid Major Mating Population (MMMP) and has distinguished them from two, four, or many more distinct racial groups (Dobzhansky, 1962; Garn, 1971). Conspicuous traits such as skin pigmentation, facial features, and body build have traditionally served as the taxonomic basis for defining racial types. Although objective biochemical criteria have now largely replaced these traits, none of the classifications can claim to have found any general scientific acceptance (Cavalli-Sforza, Menozzi, & Piazza, 1994). For this discussion, I have adopted the less pejorative but equally ill-defined terms "populations" and "ethnic groups" as a basis for making comparisons between groups that were traditionally defined as races.

The anecdotal observation that members of some Asian ethnic groups flush predictably to small amounts of alcohol was examined objectively in representative groups of *native* Japanese, Taiwan Chinese, and European Caucasian adults and newborn infants, native Korean adults and *American born* Japanese and Chinese, North American Cree Indian and South American Cuna Indian adults. The sample characteristics, alcohol doses, and methods of recording and analysis have been described in detail elsewhere (Wolff, 1972, 1973, 1977). Changes of blood volume in the facial skin (optical density), pulse pressure (difference between systolic and diastolic blood pressure), and pulse rate were measured by transillumination or reflectance plethysmography of the earlobe and forehead respectively (see Figure 1; see also Shearn, Berkman, Hill, Abel, & Hinds, 1990).

Transillumination plethysmography was accomplished by passing the light from a small low-voltage tungsten bulb and Wratten Filter with a peak transmission at the isosbestic point for reduced hemoglobin and oxyhemoglobin through the earlobe and measuring changes of blood flow as a function of changes in optical density. Reflectance plethysmography was based on the same principle except that the light was reflected from blood in the forehead skin (MedaSonics Model PPG 13). Skin temperature was recorded from the forehead, cheek, and inner surface of the lower arm; visible flushing was recorded by direct observation and by infra-red photography, and all study participants were asked to report subjective symptoms throughout the trial.

In persons who flush visibly to alcohol, the response usually begins in the soft tissues around the eyes and then spreads to the whole face, neck, and upper trunk. Even when intense, the flush rarely spreads beyond this well-defined region. Table 1 indicates that 70% to 80% of Japanese, Taiwan Chinese, and Korean adults; Japanese and Chinese 3- to 4-day-old healthy infants; and a slightly smaller number of North and South American Indian adults flushed visibly after drinking small amounts of alcohol. (For logistic reasons it was not possible to test Korean and Native American infants.) The first measurable flush occurred within 3 minutes after participants began drinking; it usually reached its peak 12 to 17 minutes after participants had finished drinking and then lasted for another 30 to 45 minutes. The increase in optical density was associated with an increase in pulse pressure and usually with a 1- to 2-degree Celsius increase of facial temperature, although the forearm skin temperature did not change. Latency of the flushing response was tested in two Chinese

**ALCOHOL FLUSHING RESPONSE**

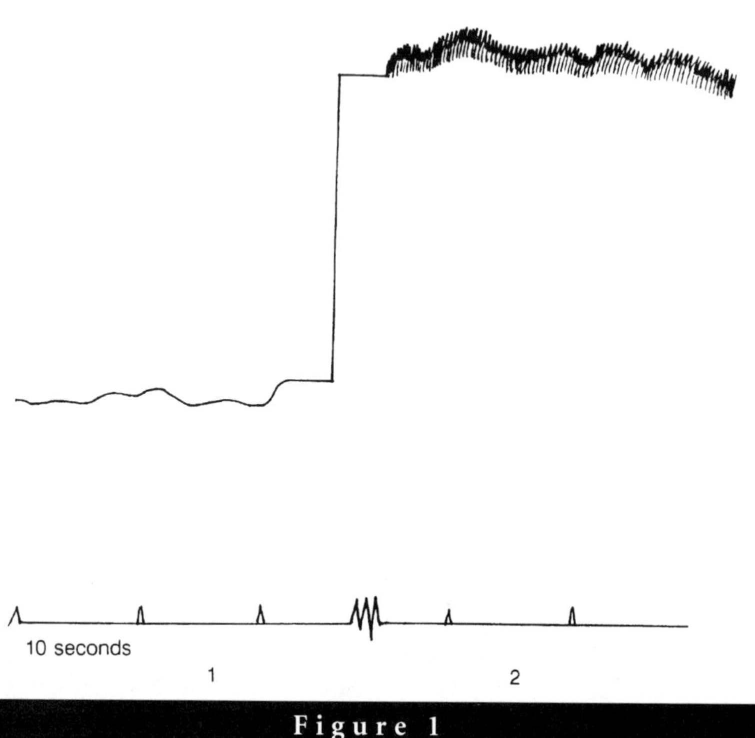


**Figure 1**

Increase of optical density and pulse pressure in earlobe after alcohol ingestion, in a Chinese adult male: (1) baseline recording; optical density begins to increase 80 sec after completion of drinking; (2) after 8 minutes, relative optical density has increased by 43 mm. Changes in pulse pressure are indicated by an increase in phasic excursions of the channel registering optical density. Ordinal: Optical density in mm, not scaled.

adults by administering 5% ethanol in 5% dextrose intravenously at 60 drops/min. Both participants began to flush measurably within 20 to 30 seconds after the start of the infusion.

There were no significant gender differences in the physiological response to alcohol, and no differences between *native* and *American born* Japanese, Taiwan Chinese, or Korean adults. Asians who drank frequently responded as often as, but less intensely than, Asians who rarely or never

**Table 1**

**Alcohol Flushing: Ethnic Group Comparisons**

| Group | Increase, Optical Density (mm) | Increase, Pulse Pressure (%) | Mean Change, Face Temperature, Degrees °C |
|---|---|---|---|
| Caucasian | | | |
| Adults ($n$ = 50) | 4 | 3 | +0.1 |
| Infants ($n$ = 20) | 1.7 | 0 | |
| Japanese | | | |
| Adults ($n$ = 38) | 36.8* | 257* | +1.8 |
| Infants ($n$ = 25) | 18.8* | | |
| Taiwan Chinese | | | |
| Adults ($n$ = 24) | 37.7* | 246* | +1.4* |
| Infants ($n$ = 10) | 14.6* | + | |
| Korean | | | |
| Adults ($n$ = 20) | 17.4* | 161* | +1.3* |
| American Indians | | | |
| South and North ($n$ = 30) | 20.1* | 98 | +1.2* |

NOTE: Difference between Caucasian and any other group * $p < .001$; + data not reliable.

drank. However, their response was still greater than that of Caucasians who either did or did not drink frequently.

Fewer than 10% of white Caucasian adults or infants showed any vasomotor response after drinking equivalent weight-adjusted amounts of alcohol. In the few Caucasians who flushed, the magnitude of the response was consistently less than that of Asian ethnic subgroups, even after they had consumed twice the usual amount of alcohol.

Other investigators have subsequently shown that other groups of Native Americans and Canadian Inuit also flush to alcohol (Goedde et al., 1986). However, Navaho, Lakota, and Pueblo Indians were found *not* to flush to alcohol (Crabb, Dipple, & Thomasson, 1993; Mendoza, Smith, Poland, Lin, & Strickland, 1991). The number of distinct American Indian groups studied to date is too small to test the possibility that the geographic

**Table 2**

**Alcohol Flushing: Hybrid Groups**

| Group | Increase, Optical Density (mm) | Increase, Pulse Pressure (%) | Mean Change, Face Temperature, Degrees °C |
|---|---|---|---|
| Caucasian Adults (*n* = 50) | 4 | 3 | +0.1 |
| American born; two Asian parents (*n* = 15) | 64* | 280* | +1.6* |
| American born; one Asian parent (*n* = 20) | 59* | 304* | +2.2* |
| American born; one Asian grandparent (*n* = 4) | 43* | 160* | +1.8* |

NOTE: Difference between Caucasian and other groups * $p < .001$.

distribution of flushing among Native Americans corresponds to the successive waves of migration from Asia across North and South America (Szathmary, 1985; Zegura, 1985). The number is, however, sufficient to caution against generalizing from limited samples in order to draw far-reaching typological conclusions about "Asians," "Amerindians," "Chinese," "Caucasians," or "Africans" (Cavalli-Sforza et al., 1994).

The likelihood that alcohol flushing is genetically transmitted was examined by comparing American-born adults with two Asian parents ("full Asians"), those with one Chinese, Japanese, or Korean parent and one Caucasian parent ("half-Asians"), and those with one Asian grandparent and three Caucasian grandparents ("one quarter Asian"). Hybrid individuals flushed with the same frequency and intensity as persons with two Asian parents (see Table 2). Three additional adults with one Asian *great-grandparent* and seven Caucasian great-grandparents ("one eighth Asians") also showed a significant flushing response. No formal pedigree or molecular genetic analyses were carried out, but the behavioral findings suggested that alcohol flushing is transmitted as a dominant trait.

The alcohol-flushing trait is generally assumed to be unique to ethnic groups of known Asian origin. Some investigators have, in fact, suggested that flushing may identify an inborn error of metabolism (Goedde et al., 1989). To date, however, only ethnic groups of Asian and European descent have been tested systematically. The same procedure was therefore used to test Basques from Southern France, Roma (Gypsies) living in Greece, Moroccan and Yemenite Jews living in Israel, and Eritreans from the highlands of East Africa as well as African Americans.

Basques and Roma were chosen because both groups probably are relatively closed mating populations by virtue of their unique languages (Cavalli-Sforza et al., 1994; Gronemeyer & Rakelmann, 1988; Heiberg, 1984; Mourant, 1954). At the same time they differ from one another in the sense that Basques have no known linguistic, cultural, or genetic links to Asian populations, whereas Roma are thought to have migrated from the Asian subcontinent of Northern India. Indeed, their language shows some striking similarities to classic Sanskrit and modern Hindi (Comrie, 1990; Gronemeyer & Rakelmann, 1988; Singhal, 1982). Eritreans and Moroccan and Yemenite Jews were chosen because of their relative geographic isolation; and African Americans, who make up a genetically heterogeneous group, were included as a contrast group to Eritreans. Caucasians of European descent again served as the comparison group.

To control for the possible confounding of measurements by differences in skin pigmentation, facial flushing was first tested in response to *nonspecific* vasodilator agents (oral nicotinic acid, amyl nitrate inhalation). All groups responded to these agents in nearly the same way, suggesting that skin pigmentation would not interfere with plethysmographic comparisons of alcohol flushing.

Table 3 indicates that Jews from Morocco responded with a slight increase of optical density, whereas those from Yemen (and those from Eastern Europe who have not been included) showed no response whatever. Eritreans and African Americans also showed no measurable flush, even after consuming twice the alcohol given to Asian subgroups, although two adults with an African American father and a Korean mother both flushed visibly to the standard amount of alcohol. By contrast Basques flushed to alcohol with the same frequency and intensity as Chinese and Japanese, whereas non-Basques living in the same region did not differ

**Table 3**

**Alcohol Flushing: Other Ethnic Groups**

| Ethnic Group | Increase, Optical Density (mm) | Mean Change, Pulse Pressure (%) | Mean Change, Face Temperature, Degrees °C |
|---|---|---|---|
| European Caucasian ($n$ = 30) | 3 | 3 | +0.1 |
| Basque ($n$ = 15) | 36.3** | 160** | +0.9* |
| Roma ($n$ = 12) | 32.9** | 187** | 0 |
| Moroccan Jews ($n$ = 10) | 12.6** | 7 | 0 |
| Yemenite Jews ($n$ = 10) | 0 | 0 | 0 |
| African American and Etritrean ($n$ = 14) | −1 | 0 | −0.9 |

NOTE: Differences relative to Caucasian sample $^{*}p < .01$, $^{**}p < .001$.

from other Caucasians of European descent. In a similar way, Roma flushed with about the same frequency and intensity as Asian subgroups, but contrary to expectations, indigenous northern Indians from Gujarathi province showed no flushing response to alcohol.

Several experiments were performed to explore the physiological basis of alcohol flushing by testing the effect of several pharmacologic agents known to affect vasomotor tonus on alcohol flushing. For example, atropine and its synthetic analog propanthelene bromide (Probanthine), are known to inhibit the action of acetylcholine on postganglionic cholinergic vasomotor nerves (Goodman & Gilman, 1985). When Probanthine was given to adult participants 1 hour before the alcohol challenge, Caucasians of European descent who did not flush to alcohol alone showed a dramatic increase of alcohol flushing (see Figure 2). Japanese and Chinese who flushed to alcohol alone also showed a slight, but significant, increase of flushing after premedication with Probanthine. By contrast, Eritreans and African Americans, who did not flush to alcohol alone, also did not respond with any measurable flush to the combination of Probanthine or

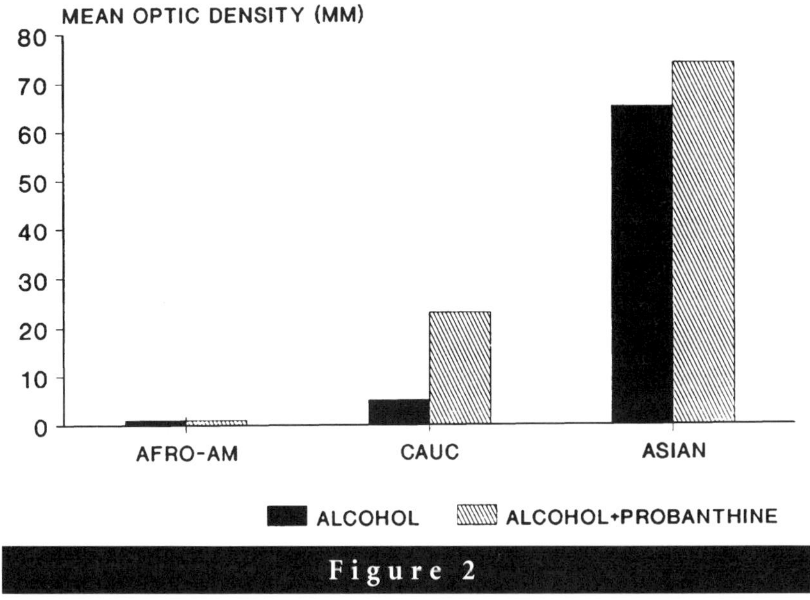


**Figure 2**

Combined effects of Probanthine and alcohol on the flushing response in subgroups of Asian, Caucasian, and African descent.

atropine and alcohol. The experiments were not extensive enough to clarify the mechanism of alcohol flushing, but they clearly indicated that the population differences in alcohol metabolism pertain not only to Caucasians of European descent and ethnic groups of Asian descent, but Caucasians of European descent and ethnic groups of African descent.

## The Genetics of Alcohol Flushing

The enzyme *alcohol dehydrogenase* (ADH) metabolizes ethyl alcohol to acetaldehyde, and the enzyme *acetaldehydase* (ALDH) oxidizes acetaldehyde further to acetic acid. Both enzymes are present in humans in at least two, and probably more, isozymes that differ in their relative rates of alcohol and acetaldehyde metabolism (Novoradovsky et al., 1995). For example, some alcohol dehydrogenase isozymes convert ethanol rapidly to acetaldehyde, whereas others do so much more slowly (Crabb et al., 1993; Goedde, Agarwal, & Harada, 1983; Yoshida, 1994). In the same way, some isozymes of acetaldehydase are metabolically inactive, whereas others metabolize acetaldehyde to acetic acid efficiently and at a rapid rate.

The relevance of such variations for this discussion derives from the fact that most Japanese and Chinese, and some groups of Native Americans and Canadian Inuit, have an inactive isozyme of acetaldehyde (Crabb et al., 1993; Goedde et al., 1986) that is transmitted vertically as a single dominant gene (Crabb, Edenberg, Bosron, & Li, 1989) whereas Caucasians of European descent as well as Navaho, Lakota, Pueblo, and probably some other Native American groups, have the *active* acetaldehydase isozyme (Crabb et al., 1989; Gill, Liu, & Deitrich, 1992; Tu & Israel, 1995).

However, 85% to 90% of Japanese and some groups of Native Americans and only 5% to 20% of Caucasians of European descent have the rapidly metabolizing variant of alcohol dehydrogenase (Crabb et al., 1993; Goedde et al., 1992; Stamatoyannopoulos, Chen, & Fukui, 1975). As a net consequence, some Asian ethnic groups convert alcohol to acetaldehyde rapidly but oxidize acetaldehyde slowly, so that their blood levels of acetaldehyde rise quickly and are maintained at a high level for relatively long periods. Elevated blood acetaldehyde levels acting directly on peripheral blood vessels may therefore be the main cause of alcohol flushing.

Some investigators have shown that opiate antagonists, such as nalmafene, effectively block the alcohol flush in ethnic groups who flush to alcohol alone (Braniuk, Morray, & Mabbee, 1987; Ho et al., 1988). Thus, alcohol flushing may be caused in part by central nervous system pathways, rather than exclusively determined by acetaldehyde acting on peripheral blood vessels (Miller et al., 1987). Moreover, the remarkably short latency in the onset of when blood levels of alcohol are still very low suggests that the flushing response may be mediated, at least in part, by the direct action of circulating alcohol on the central nervous system.

Asians who flush to alcohol frequently report unpleasant symptoms that are very similar to symptoms reported by chronic alcohol patients who drink while on Antabuse, which blocks the oxidation of acetaldehyde (Goodman & Gilman, 1985). A number of investigators have therefore advanced the hypothesis that populations who flush to alcohol and experience the associated aversive symptoms are protected against alcohol abuse and chronic alcoholism (Crabb et al., 1993; Goedde et. al, 1983; Tu & Israel, 1995; Yoshida, 1994). The hypothesis is attractively simple but hardly consistent with cross-national epidemiological comparisons on the prevalence of chronic alcoholism. For example, alcoholic beverages and alcoholism were probably unknown among Native American Indians before the arrival of European settlers in North America (O'Brien & Chafetz, 1991). Since then, the prevalence of chronic alcoholism in the population has steadily increased and is now the single most critical public health problem among many groups of Native Americans and Inuit—whether or not they flush to alcohol (Dozier, 1966; Indian Health Service, 1990; O'Brien & Chafetz, 1991; Robbins, 1994).

In a similar way, the incidence of chronic alcoholism in Japan has increased rapidly since the end of World War II; and by 1964, 15% of all admissions to psychiatric hospitals were for chronic alcoholism (Sargent, 1967); and the prevalence of chronic alcoholism among Thais (who flush to alcohol) increased dramatically after large numbers of foreign troops were billeted in Thailand during World War II (Chafetz, 1964).

Such evidence cannot be reconciled with the claim that genetic variations in alcohol metabolism protect Asian ethnic groups against chronic alcoholism (see also Chao, 1995; Cheung, 1993). On the contrary, the epidemiological evidence suggests that the destruction of traditional economic and cultural practices and values by historical catastrophes (e.g., the repeated displacement of Native Americans from their homelands; the total restructuring of Japanese society after World War II) may predispose any society to a rapid increase in alcohol abuse and chronic alcoholism, such effects being perhaps exaggerated by an intrinsic (genetic) sensitivity to alcohol.

## Blushing and Flushing

More than a century ago, Darwin (1872) reported that emotional blushing in response to shame is largely confined to the exposed skin surfaces of the face, ears, neck, and upper chest to which he referred as the *blush skin*. He further speculated that the vasomotor control of this "most peculiar and . . . most human of all emotional expressions" (p. 309) may have been specialized by natural selection but there has been relatively little progress in clarifying the functional basis of emotional blushing (Darwin, 1872; see also Leary, Britt, Cutlip, & Templeton, 1992; Shearn et al., 1990). The remarkable similarity in the anatomical distribution of flushing and blushing suggests that the two vasomotor responses may share common neural pathways, so that the physiological mechanisms of alcohol flushing may also serve as a point of departure for more focused investigations of blushing.

Physiological studies have demonstrated, for example, that (a) the blush skin is innervated by autonomic nerve endings that differ from those of other skin vessels or of the deeper blood vessels (Fox, Goldsmith, & Kidd, 1962; Whelan, 1967); (b) the blush skin is supplied with both central and peripheral sensory and neuromotor pathways (Braniuk et al., 1987; Ho et al., 1988; Malpas, Robinson, & Maling, 1990); and (c) pharmacologic agents affecting vasomotor tone frequently have very different effects on the blush skin than on other skin surfaces (Hertzman, 1950; Mellander, Andersson, Afzelius, & Hellsfranel, 1982; Wertheimer, Redisch, Hirschhorn, & Steele, 1955).

The correlation between flushing and blushing was tested by comparing the blushing tendencies of 20 young Americans with two Asian parents, 5 Americans with 1 Asian and 1 Caucasian parent, and 20 adults with 2 Caucasian parents. The sample was limited to males because of the continuing controversy of whether females do or do not blush more readily than males (Darwin, 1872; Leary et al., 1992; Shields, Mallory, & Simon, 1990). Blushing was provoked experimentally on the basis of the clinical observation that persons who blush spontaneously in social situations are said to also blush more readily when their attention is called to the trait (Leary et al., 1992). Each participant was asked whether he ever blushed, under what conditions he usually did so, and whether he felt embarrassed at that time; during the initial interview, the examiner stared at the participant's face in a somewhat provocative manner. Blushing was measured by the same methods of plethysmography as alcohol flushing. Nearly all American-born Asian subjects with one or two Asians parents (87%) blushed visibly to the experimental provocation, whereas only two Caucasians did [$X^2$ $(df = 1) = 14.4$, $p < .001$]. Emotional blushing was also significantly correlated with alcohol flushing, $X^2$ $(df = 1) = 11.2$, $p < .001$), but the finding is difficult to interpret because many more Asians than Caucasians in the sample flushed to alcohol.

The preliminary findings suggest that individuals who flush to alcohol are also predisposed to emotional blushing; and that the same central nervous system pathways may control the vascular response of flushing and blushing, even though the mechanisms are not the same. However, the onset of blushing was more rapid (< 10 sec) and the response lasted for a much shorter time (30 to 60 sec) than alcohol flushing, so that the underlying mechanisms may not be identical. Moreover, cross-national surveys indicate that the frequency of self-reported blushing is highest among English men, but they do not flush to alcohol (Edelman, 1987). Finally, the frequency and intensity of blushing depend critically on the person's initial psychological and physiological state (Leary et al., 1992; Shields et al., 1990); and at least by self-report, many individuals never blush when they feel ashamed or embarrassed.

From a very different perspective, population differences in alcohol flushing do, however, call attention to a class of intrinsic human differences that may have far more serious biological and social consequences. There is now ample evidence that ethnic groups differ extensively in their pharmacologic response to a broad spectrum of biologically active agents, including barbiturates, diphenhydramine (Benadryl), ephedrine, phenytoin (Dilantin), and isoniazid (an antituberculosis drug); natural foods such as lactose (Kretchmer, Hurwitz, Ransome-Kuti, Dungy, & Alikija, 1971); and in the distribution of endogenous enzymes that metabolize important drugs other than alcohol (see Kalow, 1982, and Price-Evans, 1993, for detailed reviews).

The clinical importance of such findings is illustrated by population differences in response to psychoactive drugs. Most of these drugs are manufactured in the United States, where the safety and efficacy of neuroleptics, tricyclic antidepressants, and benzodiazapines are carefully tested in clinical trials before the drugs are distributed commercially. Most of the clinical trials are performed either on Caucasians of European descent or more recently on mixed populations. However, scant attention is given to the possibility that ethnic groups may differ in drug sensitivity. Instead, the safety and efficacy criteria established for one homogeneous or heterogeneous population often become the "gold standard" for worldwide distribution. Yet, many Asian groups require substantially lower doses of psychoactive drugs to achieve the same therapeutic effect (Lin, Poland, Smith, Strickland, & Mendoza, 1991). These ethnic groups often experience serious toxic side effects, including irreversible tardive dyskinesia, when they are medicated by the gold standard (Gram, Brosen, Sindrup, Skjelbo, & Nielsen, 1992; Kalow, 1982; Price-Evans, 1993). Although less well studied, other ethnic groups may require higher doses to achieve the same therapeutic or protective effect and may experience serious adverse or even fatal consequences when treated according to some implicit or explicit standard established on a very different population (Chen & Poth, 1929; Strickland et al., 1991). In other words, what is good for some ethnic groups is not necessarily good for others.

Such group differences, of which I have listed only a few, confront the conscientious investigator with the ethical dilemma of whether or not, within what limits, and in what directions, to investigate the biological (genetic) basis of ethnic group or population differences. Any blanket proscription against clinical studies of population differences on the assumption that social equality depends on biological identity exposes the principle of social equality to the constant danger of being overturned every time a biological difference is discovered by chance. Moreover, as several of the examples illustrate, such proscriptions sometimes have serious medical consequences. In the case of behavioral variations with less obvious medical effects, the proscription may lead to the pejorative conclusion that groups or individuals who differ from what we assume to be true about our own group, must be abnormal or suffer from a pathological affliction.

Perhaps of greater social concern are the choices that lead to a relentless search for biological differences between so-called races in order to "explain" population or ethnic group differences in complex behavior or cultural practices. Such pursuits usually lead to false and untestable conclusions with far reaching and often harmful social consequences (Hubbard & Wald, 1993; Kitcher, 1985).

## FAMILIAL SUBTYPES OF DEVELOPMENTAL DYSLEXIA

Unlike population differences in drug metabolism, the group differences in complex human conditions that are of more direct interest for human behavior genetics, developmental psychobiology, and biological psychiatry either are genetically determined only in a trivial sense or have a polygenic etiology that cannot be studied by current methods of molecular genetics (Baron, Endicott, & Ott, 1990; Risch, 1990). Yet, current trends in biological psychiatry and in some other clinical neurosciences suggest that the same reductionist model is applied with increasing frequency and enthusiasm to discover the causes and natural history of complex human conditions. In the remarks to follow I will argue that entirely different models of development and behavioral organization will be required if we are to understand or explain the operational characteristics of complex human conditions.

As a concrete example, I will use our current studies on familial subtypes of developmental dyslexia: Dyslexia is an etiologically and clinically heterogeneous syndrome of "unexplained" reading failure that occurs in persons of normal intelligence who have been exposed to an adequate learning environment and who have intact visual, auditory, and peripheral speech mechanisms (Ellis, 1984). By definition, dyslexia is a developmentally mutable but species-specific condition. The initial diagnosis of dyslexia is usually based on "unexplained" reading failure, but this symptom is usually part of a broader syndrome that also includes linguistic, cognitive, perceptual, and motor deficits (Denckla, 1993). Some of the associated findings are probably coincidental; others may provide important clues about the underlying causes of dyslexia that still remain a topic of active controversy. However, there is no consensus on how dyslexia should be clinically defined. Therefore, it is also not possible to decide before the fact which of the associated findings might be of theoretical importance.

Current consensus holds that language deficits, and specifically impaired phonological processing, are the "core" deficit in developmental dyslexia (Ellis, 1984; Lovett, 1993; Pennington, 1995; Snowling, Stackhouse, & Rack, 1986; Vellutino, 1979). However, there is a growing body of evidence indicating that the orthographic characteristics of the language will codetermine not only national differences in the prevalence of the disorder but also the qualitative dimensions of profiles of language impairment (Caravolas, 1993; Ehri, 1993; Wimmer, 1993; Wolf, Pfeil, Lotz, & Biddle, 1994). Because English orthography is among the most difficult to master among all alphabetic languages, impaired phonological processing may not be the core deficit in languages with transparent orthographies. In other words, what may be true about English-speaking dyslexic students does not necessarily hold for Spanish- or Italian-speaking dyslexic students. Moreover, a growing body of evidence suggests that significantly reduced rates of word retrieval and information processing may identify an independent subtype of dyslexia even in English speakers (Bowers & Wolf, 1995; Wolf, 1986).

From a biological perspective, developmental dyslexia is known to aggregate in families (Hallgren, 1950); and familial subtypes of dyslexia are generally thought to have a genetic etiology (Finucci, Guthrie, Childs, Abbey, & Childs, 1976; Pennington, 1991). However, the exact mechanisms of genetic transmission remain controversial (Cardon et al., 1994; Decker & Bender, 1988; Lewitter, DeFries, & Elston, 1980; Pennington, 1995; Rabin, Wen, Hepburn, & Lubs, 1993; Smith, Kimberling, Pennington, & Lubs, 1983) and the phenotype that is vertically transmitted in dyslexia families remains essentially unknown.

Any systematic genetic analysis of familial dyslexia is therefore confronted by a clinical condition the phenotype of which is poorly defined and confounded by many phenocopies, the genetic etiology of which remains controversial, and the phenotypic expression of which depends critically on the cultural context and the structure of the language in which the condition is manifested.

## Familial Dyslexia Studies

Our familial dyslexia studies were based on the assumptions that (a) the behavioral phenotype is almost certainly not reading failure per se; (b) the various language deficits observed in dyslexia are surface manifestations of an underlying variation in behavioral coordination that transcends cultural and linguistic differences; and (c) the "core deficit" in dyslexia may reside in "physiologically plausible" dimensions of behavior (Hammond, 1982) that can be mapped on current knowledge of central nervous system function, as well as on component behavioral processes shared across languages.

The physiologically plausible dimension we chose for investigating behavioral phenotypes in familial dyslexia was *temporal resolution* in coordinated motor action. There is now converging evidence from many sources that temporal parameters of manual motor coordination are controlled by neural processes that overlap extensively with those for timing control in speech and language (Keele, Cohen, & Ivry, 1990; Kelso, 1995; Kimura & Archibald, 1974; Llinas, 1993; MacNeilage, 1987; Ojemann, 1984). At the same time, the motor system is well suited for the experimental decomposition of various temporal parameters (frequency, timing precision, serial ordering) without destroying the integrity of the complex behavior under investigation (Lashley, 1951; Sperry, 1952).

In cross-sectional studies (Wolff, 1993; Wolff, Michel, & Ovrut, 1990; Wolff, Michel, Ovrut, & Drake, 1990), we had demonstrated that half of all dyslexic students from 7 to 28 years of age have significant deficits of temporal resolution on tasks of bimanual coordination and motor speech repetition. Dyslexic students *with* motor coordination deficits came from families in which other members were also dyslexic, and most dyslexic students who were sporadic cases did not have motor coordination deficits.

In subsequent familial dyslexia studies, we therefore tested the hypothesis that motor coordination deficits identify a behavioral phenotype in familial subtypes of dyslexia and that this phenotype cosegregates with reading impairment in half of dyslexia families. Dyslexia families were ascertained through probands attending specialized schools for the remedial education of severely dyslexic students of normal intelligence. All families first completed questionnaires about the incidence of reading and spelling problems, school performance, reading habits, and the like among all first- and second-degree relatives of dyslexic probands. The questionnaire data (summarized in Wolff & Melngailis, 1994) served as the basis for selecting families in which (a) probands were sporadic cases; (b) the mother's side of the family was affected (reading-impaired); (c) the father's side of the family was affected; and (d) both parents were affected. All probands and relatives in those families were examined by a detailed protocol that included experimental measures of temporal resolution in motor coordination, experimental measures of language performance, and standardized psychometric tests.

An analysis of the questionnaire data indicated that:

1. Males outnumbered females by 4 : 1 among students attending the special schools, but after probands were excluded, the ratio of affected males to females among family members was 1.4 : 1, suggesting that the generally assumed intrinsic gender differences in dyslexia are greatly exaggerated by gender biases of ascertainment, diagnosis, and treatment.
2. Siblings with one affected parent were at greater risk for reading difficulties than siblings with no affected parents; siblings with an affected *father* were at greater risk than those with an affected *mother*; and siblings with *two* affected parents were at twice the risk for reading deficits when compared to those with one affected parent.
3. In families with two affected parents, the parents themselves also had more severe reading and spelling deficits than same-gender parents in families with one affected parent. In other words, more severely affected adults were more likely to marry dyslexic partners than mildly affected adults. Such *assortative mating* probably had an

independent effect on the risk for dyslexia among offspring (Wolff & Melngailis, 1994).

The same family members were examined for temporal information processing in motor action. They were asked to tap the two index fingers on touch-sensitive plates in various patterns of interlimb coordination at different rates specified by a metronome and to repeat two or three nonsense syllable strings at different prescribed rates. The results indicated that:

1. Half of all affected (reading-impaired) first-degree relatives from 7 to 56 years of age showed significant deficits of temporal information processing in bimanual coordination and motor speech repetition when compared with age-matched normal readers from the same families and biologically unrelated normal readers. The motor coordination deficits were most succinctly characterized by a "frequency-timing threshold": Regardless of reading status, family members and unrelated normal controls had no difficulty performing the motor tasks when the prescribed response frequency was set low enough. However, all research participants had difficulty performing the motor tasks when at high frequencies well below maximum possible tapping speed. The frequency threshold at which participants could no longer maintain any given pattern of motor coordination differed systematically as a function of age. However, within age groups the frequency measure that distinguished affected family members with motor coordination deficits from affected family members without motor deficits, nonaffected family members, and biologically unrelated normal readers was the frequency threshold at which timing precision in coordinated action deteriorated (Woolf, Melngailis, Obregon, & Bedrosian, 1995).

   In the perceptual domain, Lovegrove (1993) demonstrated that the visual contrast sensitivity function in response to high *temporal frequency* gratings is significantly reduced in 70% to 80% of dyslexic students, whereas group differences in the contrast sensitivity function in high *spatial frequency* low temporal frequency gratings are more variable. Likewise, Tallal and her colleagues (Tallal, Stark, & Mellits, 1985; Tallal et al., 1996) have reported that language- and reading-impaired children have difficulty discriminating pairs of nonlinguistic auditory stimuli when these are presented at short interresponse intervals but perform like normal children when interresponse intervals are stretched out.

2. Affected relatives *with* bimanual coordination and motor speech repetition deficits aggregated in families in which the probands also had significant motor coordination deficits; by contrast, affected relatives *without* motor coordination deficits aggregated in families where the probands did not have any motor deficits.
3. The risk for impaired motor coordination was twice as great, and the severity of motor impairment in motorically affected offspring was significantly greater, in affected offspring with two affected parents than in those with one affected parent.
4. Naming latencies on tasks of rapid automatized naming (RAN), or the speed of naming visually presented lexical items within one semantic domain, is probably the single most informative language screening measure for identifying dyslexic participants at almost any age (Denckla & Rudel, 1978). In our studies, naming latencies on the RAN task were significantly prolonged in half of the affected relatives, and these were again the affected relatives with significant motor coordination deficits (Wolff et al., 1995).

## Discussion

The example of alcohol flushing was introduced to illustrate a strategy for investigating genotype–phenotype relations in a relatively "simple" physiological trait that can be measured objectively, can be shown to correlate with a specific major gene variation, and can therefore be analyzed by the currently available procedures of molecular genetics (Novoradovsky et al., 1995; Thomasson, Beard, & Li, 1995). The second example, by contrast, was introduced to highlight the major conceptual and methodological difficulties that are inherent in any research program that proposes to investigate the genetic basis of complex human conditions at a microscopic level of analysis and to identify some of the more obvious reasons why reductionist models will probably not clarify the origins or functional properties of the behavioral phenotype.

Implicitly or explicitly, most current research programs on the genetics of dyslexia proceed on the implicit or explicit assumption that informed knowledge of the molecular genetic variation is essential for understanding the condition, for elucidating its causes, and for eventually making detailed long-term predictions. The assumption follows directly from the widely accepted premise that the human genome specifies the human organism; that random variations of the genome therefore also specify divergent pathways of biological and behavioral development; and that the behavioral features shared by biologically related groups represent contingently useful accidents of nature that are passed down through the progeny.

However, such "predetermined epigenetic" models of development (Gottlieb, 1983) do not indicate in what sense genes or the genome might be said to specify the organism. Nor do they clarify the processes by which qualitatively new modes of operation are induced during evolution or ontogenesis from antecedent conditions (including the genetic code) not containing such modes of operation. Yet, *that* is precisely the core problem to be resolved by all the developmental sciences.

Developmental models that start with the a priori assumption that the source of all order and of qualitatively new patterns of behavioral coordination can ultimately be reduced to natural selection acting on random mutations modified by contingent reinforcements of a predictable environment are confronted by conceptual and methodological difficulties that may be insurmountable. Such difficulties have long been suspected by biologists, but they have rarely been addressed explicitly.

To illustrate the point, I will assume that whatever their proximal or final causes, familial subtypes of developmental dyslexia are mediated by functional variations of central nervous system organization. The human brain contains at least $10^{10}$ neurones, each neurone probably makes $10^4$ connections with other neurones, and neuronal function is modulated by at least 50 neurotransmitters. Therefore, the adult brain must impose order on more than $10^{15}$ independent degrees of freedom, the number probably being several orders of magnitude larger in the developing nervous system. However, the human genome contains at most about $10^5$ structural genes, only a subset of which is committed to specifying brain organization. The ultimate question that confronts any linear causal perspective on genotype–phenotype relations in familial dyslexia is therefore how a subset of the $10^5$ structural units of the human genome can impose order on $10^{15}$ degrees of freedom in order to specify a nervous system that is adaptive, undergoes constant transformations during development, and can induce novel modes of function not anticipated by the genetic code.

Such computations have now led many biologists to the inescapable conclusion that the sources of order in living things cannot be entirely, or even to a large extent, specified by natural selection or by "chance caught on the wing" (Monod, 1971). Therefore, they have advanced the hypothesis that selection may itself be an expression of deeper natural laws.

Biology has also long recognized that complex organisms are neither hard-wired nor hard-programmed mechanisms, but inherently, fundamentally, and profoundly nonlinear systems. Under the appropriate initial conditions, their component subsystems will sometimes switch "spontaneously" from one marginally stable state to another, recombining in new patterns and inducing novel properties that have not been anticipated either in genetic "programs" or in the regularities of the physical and social environment (Gottlieb, 1983; Gould, 1977, 1993). What, then, might be the sources for such spontaneous pattern formation?

More recently, these intuitions have been formalized and made increasingly explicit, for example, in Thom's catastrophe theory, Prigogine's dissipative structure theory, Lorenz's chaotic dynamics, and Kelso's dynamical systems perspective to which I will here refer collectively as the emerging "science of complexity" (Kaufmann, 1993, 1995; Yates, 1987, 1993). This is not the proper occasion to attempt any detailed exposition of the new perspective. Nevertheless, a brief description of its basic concepts is in order to illustrate why the perspective may have direct relevance for the theoretical problems of emerging order that are under discussion.

It has long been known that simple physical systems such as snowflakes or drops of oil in water exhibit spontaneous pattern formation or self-organization, even though there is no organizer to prescribe the patterns. Recent advances in the biological and neural sciences have made it amply clear that the same capacity for spontaneous pattern formation is far more widespread than was once suspected; and that much of the order that emerges is not prescribed in a priori executive programs.

The theory of complexity that confronts such deeper questions explicitly assumes that, given a sufficient degree of compositional complexity, organisms made up of many interactive and dynamically unstable subsystems will maintain themselves in a marginally stable state for extended periods by the dissipation of energy. Minor fluctuations of the organism's internal dynamics, or minor perturbations in the surroundings, are usually "absorbed," so that the organism maintains itself in a conservative or self-equilibrating state.

However, under different initial conditions, the same perturbations will drive the ensemble into regions of critical instability followed by spontaneous "self-organization" and induce novel properties and modes of operation. Yet, there is no *self* to do the self-organizing. Instead, the order emerges "for free" according to principles of spontaneous pattern formation that can be defined operationally by mathematical tools of nonlinear dynamics (e.g., in terms of "attractors," "Poincaré maps," and the like). The genetic "code" may set the boundaries on the kinds of transformations that can occur, but it neither specifies what novel patterns of behavior will emerge nor the processes that induce the novelties.

Evolutionary changes and development are therefore assumed to proceed in a circular rather than linear causal chain: Living systems as a whole are transformed by interactions among their subsystems; and local dynamic interactions are continually modified by the novel behavior of the organism that emerges. With the introduction of concepts of spontaneous pattern formation, self-organization, and the like, the perspective attempts to dispense with the ghost in the machine—in other words, extrinsic executive agencies that specify how systems will function and in what direction they will develop, without retreating to positions of vitalism, preformed epigenesis or, for that matter, creationism.

Experiments carried out in many apparently unrelated domains in the context of the emerging science of complexity converge on the conclusion that much of the order in developing systems, although entirely determined, arises without specific regard for any genes, networks of interacting genes, proteins, cells, or organs. Thus, the origins of order can often be understood and explained without detailed knowledge about the component parts making up the system (Kaufmann, 1993, 1995; Yates, 1993). Such experiments also suggest that it may be impossible to predict long-term outcomes from exhaustive knowledge of the organism's initial conditions—not because we do not know enough, but because the fundamental nonlinearity of operations in living things makes it *inherently* impossible to make detailed long-term predictions (Kaufmann, 1993, 1995; Yates, 1993).

From such considerations follows the specific conclusion that it may also be inherently impossible to predict long-term outcomes in complex human conditions such as familial dyslexia on the basis of even the most refined knowledge of the organism's genome. Empirical correlations between genetic variations and behavioral phenotypes can serve as healthy antidotes to radical environmentalist explanations for clinical and developmental abnormalities, but they tell us nothing about the nature of the condition itself or about the process by which behavioral phenotypes emerge from genetic variations.

## CONCLUSIONS

The examples discussed in this chapter imply two very different, although perhaps complementary, strategies for investigating the origin of human differences in which a genetic etiology is suspected. The currently preferred strategy takes its cues from Darwin's extraordinarily successful model of natural selection, searches for preprogrammed random variations, correlates these with loosely defined clinical phenotypes, and then examines the shared features among genetically related family or group members (e.g., genders, races, ethnic groups), treating them as contingent accidents passed down through the progeny as fixed causal units. Within limits, this strategy was successful in identifying the biological (genetic) basis of alcohol flushing, although it largely failed to clarify the larger social consequences of the genetic variation.

As I suggested earlier, however, most of the human behavioral variations that have been investigated by, and are of interest to, behavior genetics, evolutionary psychology, and biological psychiatry involve complex conditions that cannot be analyzed in terms of either simple or complex linear genotype–phenotype correlations. In the preceding section I gave some of the reasons why empirical research on such conditions may require very different assumptions about genotype–phenotype relations and about brain-behavior relations, why one might have to assume a circular causation in complex systems, and why one might have to assume a qualitatively different research strategy. Such a strategy examines the organizational properties of the behavioral phenotype under consideration, rather than trying to reduce it to the system's biochemical or genetic constituents; and it sets as its task a formal analysis of the processes that make possible the induction of novel structures and functions from antecedent conditions not containing such properties. Further, it assumes that neither linear correlations between variations of metabolic pathways and their phenotypic expression in complex behavior, nor the statistical demonstration of quantitative or qualitative behavioral differences between genders, so-called races, or any other convenient classification of human groups, will shed much light on the processes by which such variations of complex behavior emerge. Instead, such studies are likely to lead to facile generalizations by analogy and to socially harmful conclusions about the origins and implications of human differences.

Depending on the scientific question of interest, each strategy may have both advantages and disadvantages. Thus, neither can claim any ultimate theoretical or moral superiority.

## REFERENCES

Baron, M., Endicott, J., & Ott, J. (1990). Genetic linkage in mental illness. Limitations and prospects. *British Journal of Psychiatry, 157,* 645–655.

Bowers, P. G., & Wolf, M. (1995). Theoretical links among naming speed, precise timing mechanisms and orthographic skill in dyslexia. *Reading and Writing, 5,* 69–85.

Braniuk, J. W., Morray, R. B., & Mabbee, W. G. (1987). Naloxone, ethanol and the chlorpropamide alcohol flush. *Alcoholism: Clinical and Experimental Research, 11,* 1518–1520.

Caravolas, M. (1993). Language-specific influences of phonology and orthography on emergent literacy. In J. Altabirra (Ed.), *Cognition and culture: A cross-cultural approach to psychology* (pp. 117–205). Amsterdam: North Holland/Elsevier.

Cardon, L. R., Smith, S. D., Folker, D. W., Kimberling, W. J., Pennington, B. F., & De Fries, J. C. (1994). Quantitative trait locus for reading disability on chromosome 6. *Science, 266,* 276–279.

Cavalli-Sforza, L. L., Menozzi, P., & Piazza, A. (1994). *The history and geography of human genes.* Princeton, NJ: Princeton University Press.

Chafetz, M. E. (1964). Consumption of alcohol in the Far and Middle East. *New England Journal of Medicine, 271,* 297–301.

Chao, H. M. (1995). Alcohol and the mystique of flushing. *Alcoholism: Clinical and Experimental Research, 19,* 104–109.

Chen, K. K., & Poth, E. J. (1929). Racial differences as illustrated by mydriatic action of cocaine, enphthalmine and ephedrine. *Journal of Pharmacology and Experimental Therapeutics, 36,* 429.

Cheung, G. W. (1993). Beyond liver & culture: A review of theories and research in drinking among Chinese in North America. *International Journal of the Addictions, 28,* 1497–1513.

Comrie, B. (1990). Introduction. In B. Comrie (Ed.), *The world's major languages* (pp. 1–29). New York: Oxford University Press.

Crabb, D. W., Dipple, K. M., & Thomasson, H. R. (1993). Alcohol sensitivity, alcohol metabolism, risk of alcoholism, and the role of alcohol and aldehyde dehydrogenase genotypes. *Journal of Laboratory and Clinical Medicine, 122,* 234–240.

Crabb, D. W., Edenberg, H. J., Bosron, W. F., & Li, T. K. (1989). Genotypes of aldehyde dehydrogenase deficiency and alcohol sensitivity: The inactive ALDH2.2 allele is dominant. *Journal of Clinical Investigation, 83,* 314–316.

Darwin, C. (1872). *The expression of emotion in animals and man.* London: Murray.

Decker, S. N., & Bender, B. G. (1988). Converging evidence for multiple genetic forms of reading disability. *Brain and Language, 33,* 197–215.

Denckla, M. B. (1993). A neurologist's overview of developmental dyslexia. *Annals of New York Academy of Sciences, 682,* 23–26.

Denckla, M. B., & Rudel, R. G. (1978). Anomalies of motor development in hyperactive boys. *Annals of Neurology, 3,* 231–233.

Dobzhansky, T. (1962). *Mankind evolving.* New Haven, CT: Yale University Press.

Dozier, E. P. (1966). Problem drinking among American Indians. *Quarterly Journal of Studies in Alcoholism, 27,* 72–87.

Edelman, R. (1987). *The psychology of embarrassment.* New York: Wiley.

Ehri, L. C. (1993). How English orthography influences phonological knowledge as children learn to read and spell. In R. J. Scholes (Ed.), *Literacy and language analysis* (pp. 21–44). Hillsdale, NJ: Erlbaum.

Ellis, A. W. (1984). *Reading, writing and dyslexia: A cognitive analysis.* Hillsdale, NJ: Erlbaum.

Finucci, J. M., Guthrie, J. T., Childs, A. L., Abbey, H., & Childs, B. (1976). The genetics of specific reading disability. *Annals of Human Genetics, 40,* 1–23.

Fox, R. H., Goldsmith, R., & Kidd, D. J. (1962). Cutaneous vasomotor control in human head, neck and upper chest. *Journal of Physiology, 161,* 298–311.

Garn, S. M. (1971). *Human races.* Springfield, IL: Thomas.

Gill, K. Liu, Y., & Deitrich, R. A. (1992). The relationship between ALDH-2 genotype, alcohol metabolism, and the flushing response in American Indians and Orientals. *Alcohol, Alcoholism, 27* (Suppl. 1), 42.

Goedde, H. W., Agarwal, D. P., Fritze, G., Meier-Tackmann, D., Singh, S., Beckmann, G., Bhatra, K., Chen, L. Z., Fang, B., Lisker, R., Park, Y. K., Rothhammer, F., Saha, N., Segal, B., Srivasta, L. M., & Czeizel, A. (1992). Distribution of ADH2 and ALDH2 genotypes in different populations. *Human Genetics, 88,* 344–346.

Goedde, H. W., Agarwal, D. P., Harada S. (1983). Pharmacogenetics of alcohol sensitivity. *Pharmacology and biochemistry of behavior, 18* (Suppl. 1), 161–166.

Goedde, H. W., Agarwal, D. P., Harada, S., Rothhammer, F., Whittaker, J. O., & Lisker, R. (1986). Aldehyde dehydrogenase polymorphism in North American, South American and Mexican Indian populations. *American Journal of Human Genetics, 38,* 395–399.

Goedde, H. W., Sing, S., Agarwal, D. P., Fritze, G., Stapel, K., & Paik, G. K. (1989). Genotyping of mitochondrial aldehyde dehydrogenase in blood samples using allele-specific oligonucleotides: Comparison with phenotyping in hair roots. *Human Genetics, 81*, 305–307.

Goodman, L. S., & Gilman, A. (1985). *The pharmacological basis of therapeutics* (7th ed.). New York: MacMillan.

Gottlieb, G. (1983). The psychobiological approach to developmental issues. In P. H. Mussen (Ed.), *Handbook of child psychology, Vol. II.* Fourth Edition (pp. 1–26). New York: Wiley.

Gould, S. J. (1977). *Ontogeny and phylogeny.* Cambridge, MA: Harvard University Press.

Gould, S. J. (1993). Evolution of organisms. In C. A. R. Boyd & D. Noble (Eds.), *The logic of life* (pp. 15–42). Oxford: Oxford University Press.

Gram, L. F., Brosen, K., Sindrup, S., Skjelbo, E., & Nielsen, K. K. (1992). Pharmacogenetics in psychopharmacology: Basic principles. *Clinical Neuropharmacology, 15* (Suppl. 1), Part A: 76A–77A.

Gronemeyer, R., & Rakelmann, G. A. (1988). *Die Zigeuner.* Cologne, Germany: DuMont.

Hallgren, B. (1950). Specific dyslexia ("congenital word blindness"): A clinical and genetic study. *Acta Psychiatrica et Neurologica Scandinavia* (Suppl. 65), 2–289.

Hammond, G. R. (1982). Hemispheric differences in temporal resolution. *Brain and Cognition, 1*, 95–118.

Heiberg, M. (1984). *The making of the Basque nation.* Cambridge: Cambridge University Press.

Hertzman, A. B. (1950). Vasomotor regulation of the cutaneous circulation. *Physiological Reviews, 39*, 280–306.

Ho, S. B., DeMaster, E. G., Shaffer, R. B., Levine, A. S., Mosley, G. O., Go, V. L. W., & Allen, J. I. (1988). Opiate antagonist nalfene inhibits ethanol induced flush in Asians: A preliminary study. *Alcoholism: Clinical and Experimental Research, 12*, 705–712.

Hubbard, R., & Wald, E. (1993). *Exploding the gene myth.* Boston: Beacon Press.

Indian Health Service. (1990). *Trends in Indian health.* Washington, DC: U.S. Department of Health and Human Services.

Kalow, W. (1982). Ethnic differences in drug metabolism. *Clinical Pharmacokinetics, 7*, 373–400.

Kaufmann, S. A. (1993). *The origin of order.* New York: Oxford University Press.

Kaufmann, S. A. (1995). *In step with the universe.* New York: Oxford University Press.

Keele, S. W., Cohen, A., & Ivry, R. I. (1990). Motor programs: Concepts and issues. In M. Jeannerod (Ed.), *Attention and performance* (Vol. XIII, pp. 84–113). Hillsdale, NJ: Erlbaum.

Kelso, J. A. S. (1995). *Dynamic patterns.* Cambridge, MA: MIT Press.

Kimura, D., & Archibald, Y. (1974). Motor function of the left hemisphere. *Brain, 97,* 337–350.

Kitcher, P. (1985). *Vaulting ambition.* Cambridge, MA: MIT Press.

Kretchmer, N., Hurwitz, R., Ransome-Kuti, O., Dungy, C., & Alikija, W. (1971). Internal absorption of lactose in Nigerian ethnic groups. *Lancet,* August 21, 392–395.

Lashley, K. S. (1951). The problem of serial order in behavior. In L. A. Jeffries (Ed.), *Cerebral mechanisms in behavior* (pp. 112–136). New York: Wiley.

Leary, M. R., Britt, T. W., Cutlip, W. D. & Templeton, J. L. (1992). Social blushing. *Psychological Bulletin, 112,* 446–460.

Lewitter, F. I., DeFries, J. C., & Elston, R.C. (1980). Genetic models of reading disabilities. *Behavior Genetics, 10,* 9–30.

Lin, K.-M., Poland, R. E., Smith, M. W., Strickland, T. L., & Mendoza, R. (1991). Pharmacokinetic and other related factors affecting psychotropic responses in Asians. *Psychopharmacology Bulletin, 27,* 427–439.

Llinas, R. (1993). Is dyslexia a dyschronia? *Annals of the New York Academy of Sciences, 682,* 48–56.

Lovegrove, W. (1993). Weakness in the transient visual system: A causal factor in dyslexia. *Annals of the New York Academy of Sciences, 682,* 57–69.

Lovett, M. (1993). Developmental dyslexia. In F. Boller & J. Garfman (Eds.), I. Rapin & S. Segalowitz (Sec. Eds.), *Handbook of neuropsychology* (Vol. 7, pp. 163–185). Amsterdam: Elsevier.

MacNeilage, P. F. (1987). The evolution of hemispheric specialization for manual function and language. In S. P. Wise (Ed.), *Higher brain functions* (pp. 285–309). New York: Wiley.

Malpas, C. P., Robinson, B. J., & Maling, T. J. B. (1990). Mechanism of ethanol-induced vasodilation. *Journal of Applied Physiology, 68,* 731–734.

Mellander, S., Andersson, P. O., Afzelius, L. E., & Hellsfranel, P. (1982). Neural beta-adrenergic dilation of the facial veins in man. A possible mechanism in emotional blushing. *Acta Physiologica Scandinavia, 114,* 393–399.

Mendoza, R., Smith, M. W., Poland, R. E., Lin, K.-M., & Strickland, T. L. (1991).

Ethnic psychopharmacology: The Hispanic and native American perspective. *Psychopharmacology Bulletin, 27,* 449–461.

Miller, N. S., Goodwin, D. W., Fowler, C., Jones, F. C., Pardo, M. P., Anand, M. M., Gabrielli, W. F., & Hall, T. B. (1987). Histamine receptor antagonism of intolerance to alcohol in the Oriental population. *Journal of Nervous and Mental Disease, 175,* 661–667.

Monod, J. (1971). *Chance and necessity.* New York: Knopf.

Mourant, A. E. (1954). *The distribution of human blood groups.* Oxford: Blackwell.

Novoradovsky, A., Tsai, S. J., Goldfarb, L., Peterson, R., Long, J. C., & Goldman, D. (1995). Mitochondrial aldehyde dehydrogenase polymorphisms in Asian and American Indian populations: Detection of new ALDH2 alleles. *Alcoholism: Clinical and Experimental Research, 19,* 1105–1110.

O'Brien, R., & Chafetz, M. (1991). *The encyclopedia of alcoholism.* New York: Facts on File.

Ojemann, G. (1984). Common cortical and thalamic mechanisms for language and motor function. *American Journal of Physiology, 246,* R901–R903.

Pennington, B. F. (1991). Annotation: The genetics of dyslexia. *Journal of Child Psychology and Psychiatry, 31,* 193–201.

Pennington, B. F. (1995). Genetics of learning disabilities. *Journal of Child Neurology, 10* (Suppl. 1), S69–S77.

Price-Evans, D. E. (1993). *Genetic factors in drug therapy: Clinical and molecular pharmacogenetics.* Cambridge: Cambridge University Press.

Rabin, M., Wen, X. L., Hepburn, M., & Lubs, H. A. (1993). Suggestive linkage of developmental dyslexia to chromosome 1p34-p36. *Lancet, 342,* 178.

Risch, N. (1990). Genetic linkage and complex diseases, with special reference to psychiatric disorders. *Genetic Epidemiology, 7,* 3–16.

Robbins, M. L. (1994). Native American perspective. In J. U. Gordon (Ed.), *Managing multiculturalism in substance abuse services* (pp. 148–176). Thousand Oaks, CA: Sage.

Sargent, M. J. (1967). Changes in Japanese drinking patterns. *Quarterly Journal of Studies in Alcoholism, 28,* 709–722.

Shearn, D., Hill, B. E., Abel, A., & Hinds, L. (1990). Facial coloration and temperature responses in blushing. *Psychophysiology, 27,* 687–693.

Shields, S. A., Mallory, M. E., Simon, A. (1990). The experience and symptoms of blushing as a function of age and reported frequency of blushing. *Journal of Nonverbal Behavior, 14,* 171–187.

Singhal, D. P. (1982). *Gypsies: Indians in exile.* Meerut, India: Folklore Institute.

Smith, S. D., Kimberling, W. J., Pennington, B. F., & Lubs, H. A. (1983). Specific reading disability: Identification of an inherited form through linkage analysis. *Science, 219,* 1345–1347.

Snowling, M., Stackhouse, J., & Rack, J. (1986). Phonological dyslexia and dysgraphia—A developmental analysis. *Cognitive Neuropsychology, 3,* 309–339.

Sperry, R. W. (1952). Neurology and the mind/brain problem. *American Scientist, 40,* 291–312.

Stamatoyannopoulos, G., Chen, S. H., & Fukui, M. (1975). Liver alcohol dehydrogenase in Japanese: High population frequency of atypical form and its possible role in alcohol sensitivity. *American Journal of Human Genetics, 27,* 789–796.

Strickland, T. L., Ranganath, V., Lin, K.-M., Poland, R. E., Mendoza, R., & Smith, M. W. (1991). Psychopharmacologic considerations in the treatment of black American populations. *Psychopharmacology Bulletin, 27,* 441–448.

Szathmary, E. (1985). Peopling of North America: Clues from genetic studies. In R. Kirk & E. Szathmary (Eds.), *Out of Asia* (pp. 79–104). Canberra, Australia: Journal of Pacific History.

Tallal, P., Miller, S. L., Bedi, G., Byma, G., Wang, X., Nagarajan, S. S., Schreiner, C., Jenkins, W. M., & Merzenich, M. M. (1996). Language comprehension in language-learning impaired children with acoustically modified speech. *Science, 271,* 81–84.

Tallal, P., Stark, R., & Mellits, D. (1985). The relationship between auditory temporal analysis and receptive language development. *Neuropsychology, 23,* 527–534.

Thomasson, H. R., Beard, J. D., & Li, T.-K. (1995). ADH2 gene polymorphisms are determinants of alcohol pharmacokinetics. *Alcoholism: Clinical and Experimental Research, 19,* 1494–1499.

Tu, C. C., & Israel, Y. (1995). Alcohol consumption by Orientals in North America is predicated largely by a single gene. *Behavior Genetics, 25,* 59–65.

Vellutino, F. R. (1979). *Dyslexia: Theory and research.* Cambridge, MA: MIT Press.

Wertheimer, L., Redisch, W., Hirschhorn, K., & Steele, J. M. (1955). Patterns of surface temperature response to various agents. *Circulation, 11,* 110–114.

Whelan, R. F. (1967). *Control of peripheral circulation in man.* Springfield, IL: Thomas.

Wimmer, H. (1993). Characteristics of developmental dyslexia in a regular writing system. *Applied Psycholinguistics, 14,* 1–33.

Wolf, M. (1986). Rapid alternating stimulus naming in the developmental dyslexias. *Brain and Language, 27*, 360–379.

Wolf, M., Pfeil, C., Lotz, R., & Biddle, K. (1994). Towards a more universal understanding of the developmental dyslexias: The contribution of orthographic factors. In V. Berninger (Ed.), *The varieties of orthographic knowledge I: Theoretical and developmental issues* (pp. 137–171). Dordrecht, Netherlands: Kluwer.

Wolff, P. H. (1972). Ethnic differences in alcohol sensitivity. *Science, 175*, 449–450.

Wolff, P. H. (1973). Vasomotor sensitivity to alcohol in diverse Mongoloid populations. *American Journal of Human Genetics, 25*, 193–199.

Wolff, P. H. (1977). Biological variations and cultural diversity. In P. H. Leiderman, S. R. Tulkin, & A. Rosenfeld (Eds.), *Culture and infancy: Variations in the human experience* (pp. 357–381). New York: Academic Press.

Wolff, P. H. (1993). Impaired temporal resolution in developmental dyslexia. *Annals of New York Academy of Sciences, 682*, 87–103.

Wolff, P. H., & Melngailis, I. (1994). Family patterns of developmental dyslexia: Clinical findings. *American Journal of Medical Genetics, 54*, 122–131.

Wolff, P. H., Melngailis, I., Obregon, M., & Bedrosian, M. (1995). Family patterns of developmental dyslexia: Behavioral phenotypes. *American Journal of Medical Genetics, 60*, 494–505.

Wolff, P. H., Michel, G. F., & Ovrut, M. (1990). The timing of syllable repetitions in developmental dyslexia. *Journal of Speech and Hearing Research, 33*, 281–289.

Wolff, P. H., Michel, G. F., Ovrut, M., & Drake, C. (1990). Rate and timing precision of motor coordination in developmental dyslexia. *Developmental Psychology, 26*, 349–359.

Yates, E. F. (1987). *Self organizing systems: The emergence of order.* New York: Plenum Press.

Yates, E. F. (1993). Self organizing systems. In C. A. R. Boyd & D. Noble (Eds.), *The logic of life* (pp. 189–218). Oxford: Oxford University Press.

Yoshida, A. (1994). Genetic polymorphisms of alcohol metabolizing enzymes related to alcohol sensitivity and alcoholic disease. *Alcohol and Alcoholism, 29*, 693–696.

Zegura, S. (1985). The initial peopling of the Americas. An overview. In R. Kirk & E. Szathmary (Eds.), *Out of Asia: Peopling the Americas and the Pacific* (pp. 1–18). Canberra, Australia: Journal of Pacific History.

# Section III Conclusion

Glenn E. Weisfeld

In his wide-ranging chapter, Marvin points out that attachment involves a functional, changing process of interaction between caregiver and infant. This process is adaptive for the infant in multiple ways; in particular, the infant remains protected from harm while becoming increasingly self-reliant motorically, perceptually, and socially. Thus, adaptive needs presumably are balanced as development proceeds. Along with this progression, the infant becomes increasingly more responsible than the caregiver for maintaining proximity between them. Marvin also suggests various proximate mechanisms for some of these developmental changes. He notes the disappearance of the simian natal coat, a feature that seems to enhance the infant's appeal. This change in coat color presumably weakens the mother's tie to her infant, allowing for greater exploratory activity by the latter.

Another proximate mechanism is the attainment of the cognitive concept of object permanence, which, Marvin contends, promotes the process of attachment. In this context it may be useful to cite the research of A. Diamond (1985) on the neural basis of object permanence. She related the development of an object-retrieval task in rhesus monkeys (in effect, Piaget's object permanence task) to maturation of the dorsolateral prefrontal cortex. Both the behavior and this brain region develop between 2 and 4 months of age. Lesion studies demonstrated that this brain area is essential for performing the retrieval task. In a similar way, this brain area matures during the second half of the first year of life in humans—just the time when the capacity for object permanence appears. It is not surprising that the capacity for object permanence seems to be species-wide in humans (Konner, 1991).

Marvin then applies this normative, primate model of development of the attachment process to his own observational research on various human populations. He interprets cultural variability within an adaptive context, and, in the Romanian example, recognizes the role of experience in modifying behavior. This work illustrates the value of observational research for studying infant behavior. It also highlights the importance of nonverbal emotional expressions—for example, coy behavior and other infantile attachment signals. It is clear from this example alone that there are probably many human emotional expressions besides the six universal facial expressions documented by Ekman and Friesen (1971); see also Eibl-Eibesfeldt (1989). In sum, this chapter is an interdisciplinary tour de force, bringing together diverse theoretical perspectives and data into a functionalist framework. It recognizes that development is social, dynamic, adaptive, complex, and compounded of various evolved and experiential factors.

Savin-Williams and Diamond's chapter also has many virtues. What I find especially admirable and instructive is its fidelity to the principles of science. Savin-Williams and Diamond proceed logically from science to ideology, rather than allowing their particular ideological positions, whatever these may be, to dictate scientific conclusions. In so doing, they show both a faith in the power of scientific research to illumine social and political issues and their confidence that they can live with whatever political conclusions seem consistent with the scientific evidence about human nature. This indicates a true idealism in that they are willing to sacrifice their personal political preconceptions to the greater good of societal enlightenment.

Wolff's chapter epitomizes his work in general by making a number of telling points about development. Using the alcohol flushing response as an example, he demonstrates that ethnic groups sometimes differ in their biochemistry; these differences may help explain the common underlying metabolic process, constituting as they do naturalistic variants; these differences may carry therapeutic implications; ethnic differences in behavior, in this case alcohol consumption, are not necessarily a result of biochemical differences but may reflect sociological factors; and, last but not least, revealing ethnic differences may lead to invidious ethnic comparisons. This section of the chapter also offers a comparison between blushing and alcohol flushing, thus showing how physiological analysis can aid in behavioral classification.

Wolff's other example concerns dyslexia. He demonstrates that documentation of ethnic variability in dyslexia was useful in showing that reading difficulty does not constitute the basic deficit; this symptom is less prominent in non-English readers, English orthography being extraordinarily complex. Also, one might add, an evolutionary perspective would make it clear that reading cannot be a fundamental behavior, because it could not have occurred before the comparatively recent invention of writing. Along these lines, Wolff points out, a hypothesized deficit must be physiologically (in this case, neurologically) plausible. He goes on to demonstrate that a basic deficit that underlies a clinical condition can sometimes be identified by examining pedigrees: If the suspected deficit runs strongly in families and the condition itself is highly heritable, then that deficit may be pathognomonic. Two other points are also of interest: The risk for severe dyslexia has been shown to be raised to an extra degree by having two affected parents because those who marry other dyslexics tend to be *severely* affected. The other point is that preconceptions about the sex difference in a disease can perpetuate misinformation about sex ratios. Males outnumbered females 4 : 1 for dyslexia at a special school, but the sex difference among the probands' family members (excluding the probands themselves) was only 1.4 : 1.

The developmental complexities revealed by these chapters confirm the claim by Tinbergen (1963) that function, phylogeny, development, and proximate causation are interrelated. All must be studied, as the authors of this section recognize. In addition, physiology, anatomy, and behavior are functionally related, just as the biological and cultural programs for behavior are usually complementary. These broad principles are consistent with Dr. Freedman's holistic outlook.

## REFERENCES

Diamond, A. (1985). Development of the ability to use recall to guide action, as indicated by infants' performance on AB. *Child Development, 56*, 868–883.

Eibl-Eibesfeldt, I. (1989). *Human ethology.* Hawthorne, NY: Aldine de Gruyter.

Ekman, P., & Friesen, W. (1971). Constants across cultures in the face and emotion. *Journal of Personality and Social Psychology, 17*, 124–129.

Konner, M. J. (1991). Universals of brain development in relation to brain myelination. In K. R. Gibson & A. C. Petersen (Eds.), *Brain maturation and cognitive development* (pp. 181–223). Hawthorne, NY: Aldine de Gruyter.

Tinbergen, N. (1963). On the aims and methods of ethology. *Zeitschrift für Tierpsychologie, 20*, 410–433.

SECTION IV

# Naturalistic Studies of Behavior: How Does a Cross-Cultural Approach Inform Ongoing Research?

# Naturalistic Studies of Behavior: How Does a Cross-Cultural Approach Inform Ongoing Research?

Carol C. Weisfeld

A holistic approach to the study of human behavior assumes that biology and culture function together, each constraining and enabling the other. It is a way of thinking about human activity, and, to a great extent, it influences the direction a researcher takes. A holistic view demands that the researcher gather data across cultural groups, in search of cultural differences, to be sure, but also in search of universals. Such universals may point to function and to selective pressures operating in the course of evolution. The question of function, then, becomes central to one's work as one searches for behavioral patterns that have promoted human survival in different cultural contexts. The four chapters in this section illustrate how a cross-cultural approach can inform human developmental research.

In each chapter the contributors have used an ethological approach to study the behaviors of interest, in the cultures of interest. Ethological methods are ideal for forcing one to set one's own cultural expectations aside. Such methods increase the likelihood that one will come away with a more objective perception of the dynamics of another culture (or indeed another gender, or another species). Each chapter in this section represents a cultural exploration through which some functional aspect of human behavior comes into focus.

Beginning with Tinbergen's notion of multiple levels of causation, Dr. Nicholas G. Blurton Jones and his collaborators, Kristen Hawkes and James F. O'Conell, analyze gathering behavior in Hadza children in chapter 11. Their work represents a search for the function of a behavior that sets Hadza culture apart from the cultures of other, neighboring hunter–gatherers. In chapter 12, Dr. Paul Ekman, who has studied human facial expression in many cultural groups, wrestles with a similar functional question. He urges readers to think of emotional expression as part of a neural network involving senders and receivers, rather than as a simple effect of something going on physiologically within the sender alone.

Dr. Robert LeVine, representing a biocultural perspective within anthropology, contrasts child-rearing practices in four countries in chapter 13. These practices, he maintains, reflect underlying values in different cultural groups. Specifically, he addresses the question of whether these values are embedded in personality differences and whether these variations are influenced by genetic population differences. Again, thinking about behavior in a holistic way fashions the questions the researcher must address.

In a chapter that might have a secondary title having to do with "moral tales from the field," I discuss hard lessons learned from cross-cultural research. Chapter 14 lists ways in which cross-cultural experience can teach the observer to abandon old ways of thinking and to assume new ways of thinking about human behavior. Finally, Professor Wolfgang Schleidt, representing the European ethological tradition, concludes this section with his view of past accomplishments and future challenges for those who utilize naturalistic methods to study behavior across cultures.

11

# Why Do Hadza Children Forage?

Nicholas G. Blurton Jones, Kristen Hawkes, and James F. O'Connell

Daniel Freedman's research, on interactions between inheritance and environment in dogs, on infant behavior as adaptations to promote the infant's survival, and on individual differences among newborns and the probable effects of these on their interactions with adults, encouraged the first author to persist in exploring a variety of biological approaches to studying human behavior. By "biological approaches" we refer not just to explanations by "wet lab" physiology, nor by identification of influential genes (both currently much more exciting fields than one could judge from the average textbook), but to quantitative naturalistic observation (Blurton Jones, 1972; Borgerhoff-Mulder & Caro, 1985), to the identification of the four major questions as causation, development, adaptation and origins (Tinbergen, 1963), and to behavioral ecology, a theoretical paradigm that has developed around the study of adaptation (Krebs &

We wish to thank the Tanzania Commission on Science and Technology for permission to conduct research in Tanzania. We thank several hundred individual Hadza for their patience and good spirits, and our field assistants Gudo Mahiya and the late Sokolo Mpanda for their expertise and collegiality. We thank David Bygott and Jeannette Hanby for providing a home away from home and vital logistic facilities, Professor C. L. Kamuzora of the University of Dar es Salaam, and numerous citizens of Mbulu district for help and friendship. The research was funded by the National Science Foundation, the Swan Fund, B. Bancroft, the University of Utah, and the University of California Los Angeles.

Davies, 1987). More specifically, Dr. Freedman's work encouraged us to think about the child's own agenda. In this chapter we present some analyses provoked by the idea that this agenda centers around the child's survival and future reproduction. These issues might be easier to investigate in the hunting and gathering economy in which our species evolved. Although it seems to have a gained a footing in anthropology, the adaptationist paradigm is seldom employed in psychology, yet it addresses many of the same aspects of behavior as interest psychologists.

Children of the Hadza hunter-gatherers of northern Tanzania forage successfully, and extensively, even children aged 5 to 10 often acquire half their "recommended daily allowance" of calories by their own efforts. For many, such an observation shows the importance of learning subsistence activities and the value placed by society on learning such economic activity. But here we wish to offer a more child-centered approach, which traces its ancestry to research in biology on life history and behavioral ecology. We will ask what Hadza children might gain from foraging and how foraging might enhance their fitness.[1]

Life history theory implies that prereproductive life is primarily waiting time—time spent growing to the optimal size to begin reproduction (Charnov, 1993; Roff, 1992; Stearns, 1992; Stearns & Koella, 1986). We are probably wrong to think that childhood evolved in order for more learning to occur. Although it may be worth filling some of the waiting time with activities of future value, including learning, we are certainly wrong to ignore other selection pressures that may have acted on the immature organism (Bowlby, 1969; Freedman, 1974). If we tried to ac-

[1] Excellent introductory readings in behavioral ecology are Krebs and Davies (1987, 1991), and for the application to humans, Smith and Winterhalder (1992).

Usage of "fitness" ranges from something close to the core concept "the rate of spread of a gene through a population" to the almost metaphorical, but defensible usage in behavioral ecology, as the ultimate economic good (an economic good is something people strive for, "goods"—stuff, not moral quality), the only outcome about which one need not ask, "why would organisms pursue that outcome?" Natural selection has favored individuals that respond to circumstances with behavior that leaves the greatest number of descendants (plus descendants of close kin, inclusive fitness; Hamilton, 1964). This optimal behavior will vary with the circumstances (environment and behavior of other individuals), which determine the payoff from each possible behavior. Behavioral ecologists aim to predict behavior from circumstances (given the assumption that behavior maximizes fitness). Sometimes behavior is already known; then predictions can be made and tested about the economic payoffs given by circumstances. We should be able also to predict and account for the way behavior varies with circumstances.

count for Hadza children's foraging solely by the value of foraging as a learning experience, we would be forced to argue that among the !Kung hunter-gatherers of northwestern Botswana, where children forage very little, subsistence was easier to learn. Because !Kung and Hadza subsistence techniques are extremely similar (using a digging stick, pounding things with rocks, shooting with bow and poison arrows), and in each, hunting and gathering provided the main bulk of their food at the time of observation, this position would be hard to support.

Elsewhere we have addressed the question of why !Kung children do not forage, and looking mainly from the viewpoint of mother's reproductive interests, pointed to two issues: (a) the costs of foraging unaccompanied by adults seem to be greater in the !Kung environment, and the food rewards are much lower; (b) even in the company of adults, because of the processing costs of the main plant foods, !Kung children contribute more to their mother's assumed goal of maximizing the rate at which food is made available to her and her children ("team returns") if they are left home than if they are taken along on a gathering trip (Blurton Jones, Hawkes, & Draper, 1994a, 1994b; Hawkes, O'Connell, & Blurton Jones, 1995). These accounts assume that more food is usually worth getting. Here we ask, "what for?" What do Hadza children get from spending time acquiring food? What would we expect Hadza children to do with their time while they wait to be big enough for it to pay to begin reproducing?

We consider six possibilities, the first two derived from the nonecologist's "common sense": (a) their mothers bear more children than they can support so the children must work to make up the shortfall; (b) they learn subsistence skills. Then from the evolutionary ecologist's "common sense" we suggest: (c) that although mother allocates food optimally between number of births and providing for each child, her optimum will not be identical to each child's optimal level of nutrition (Trivers, 1974), so children forage to increase their own food intake and gain fitness, for instance because better nourished children survive infectious diseases more successfully, or because larger adults reproduce more successfully (see Hill & Hurtado, 1996); (d) that they gain inclusive fitness by helping mother and aunts raise more siblings and cousins (like helpers at the nest among birds, Brown, 1987; Emlen, 1995; Turke, 1988; see Krebs & Davies, 1987, pp. 243–256, for an introduction to inclusive fitness and kin selection); (e) that they gain from kin by virtue of later help they receive from these kin. Close kin contribute inclusive fitness, even if the siblings or cousins never meet again after childhood. Here we suggest that kin also may be valuable in a different, simpler manner, if there are ways in which they might be likely to provide important help later in life, and are more likely to do so than are non-kin. (f) that they enhance their attractiveness as future spouses by accumulating reputations as hard-working foragers. Of course, all may be important outcomes and we may not be able to exclude any of them. But we may be able to show that variation in payoff from one or more of these is associated with predictable variation in behavior, or that one of them has no payoff, or that it has a payoff but cannot account for an observation. Let us see what observations and analyses were provoked and with what results.

Some prefatory remarks are urgently needed for a psychological audience: (a) Hadza children have fun while they forage; (b) Our initial intention is to say nothing about motivation, conscious or unconscious; (c) We are not assuming a very tightly canalized form of genetic influence, much less than current genetic and neurodevelopmental evidence suggests is often actually the case! Nor are we trying to write about developmental processes; we will discuss later the difference between our work and studies of gender role identification, and of socialization as illustrated by LeVine in chapter 13.

We are writing about foraging, and many readers will think of this as "work." Within our paradigm everything an organism does may be important, so we find ourselves unable to distinguish work from other activities in a meaningful way. But the reader needs to know that Hadza children (much like adults) engage in foraging with a spirit of adventure, joy, fun, and achievement. Their foraging is interrupted by chat, joking and gentle teasing, resting, grooming, singing, and rushing about, all accompanied with smiles and laughter. Their foraging seldom appears to be a response to instructions from adults, and even if adults leave them with instructions, they have no way to know whether the children followed them. Children often leave camp to forage long after the women have gone, and men are often out of sight at "the men's place," and the food that children get is usually all eaten up by the time the women return.

In this chapter we are writing about outcomes of behavior, and the effects of these on evolutionary fitness. Our assumption is that the behavior of organisms is often efficient (and so are the mechanisms by which behavior is acquired) in the sense that the organism responds to a range of circumstances in such a way as to produce the behavior that most enhances fitness under those circumstances. Thus behavior will vary with circumstances in ways that are predictable—if we can work out which of two alternative ways of behaving would most enhance fitness in a particular set of circumstances then we can predict which behavior we expect to see. In principle we should then be able, as in animal behavioral ecology, to develop a predictive study of variation in behavior with circumstances, with no assumptions about motivation or proximate mechanisms—other than that they tend to be efficient. The idea is quite well established in biology, stemming from Tinbergen (1963) and Lorenz's elaboration of what they claimed were the four main "why?" questions in biology: (a) What made the individual do that now? (physiology, causation, motivation) (b) By what process did this individual grow up to react that way? (development, learning, embryology of the brain). (c) Why are mechanisms of causation and development like those maintained (survival value, behavioral ecology)? (d) Why did this species solve its survival problems in that particular way (origin, phylogeny, evolutionary history)?

The classical statement of the behavioral ecology paradigm is that we measure costs and benefits of different possible activities, compute optimal behavior, then test whether this is the behavior found in nature. But because usually we know more about what children do than we know about what they get from it, field studies are likely to need predictions from behavior to costs and benefits, rather than vice versa. Some of the predicted costs and benefits may be possible to assess, as we attempt to illustrate in this chapter. Bock (1995) has conducted a detailed study of the trade-offs between immediate material returns and hypothetical longer term returns from learning in the activities of children in rural

Botswana. His research takes this approach much further than we have, and his publications should be eagerly awaited.

## THE HADZA

The eastern Hadza are a group of 700 to 800 people who occupy a 2500 $km^2$ area in the Eastern Rift Valley, south and east of Lake Eyasi, in northern Tanzania. The climate of this region is warm and dry. Annual average rainfall is in the 300 mm to 600 mm range, most of it falling in the 6- to 7-month wet season (November to May) (Schultz, 1971). Vegetation is primarily mixed savanna woodland; medium to large animals are locally abundant. Ethnographic data on the eastern Hadza is most available in the publications of James Woodburn (e.g., 1964, 1968a, 1968b, 1972, 1979, 1988).

The language, Hadzane, has been studied by Woodburn and others and more recently by Sands and colleagues (Sands, 1995; Sands, Maddieson, & Ladefoged, 1993). Linguists agree only that its connection to any other African language family is very remote indeed. Hadza must have remained culturally distinct from their neighbors (who currently represent the Bantu, Nilotic, and Cushitic language families) for many hundreds of years. At the beginning of this century, it appears that only the Hadza occupied this country (Baumann, 1894; Obst, 1912). They apparently lived entirely by hunting and gathering. Local incursions by non-Hadza pastoral and agricultural groups are recorded as early as the 1920s and have continued to the present (McDowell, 1981; Woodburn, 1988). Archaeological evidence suggests that farmers and pastoralists have been present for several centuries, and hunter-gatherers appear to have been present far longer (Mehlman, 1988). During the past 50 years, various segments of the Hadza population have been subjected to a series of government- and mission-sponsored settlement schemes designed to encourage them to abandon the foraging life in favor of farming (McDowell, 1981; Ndagala, 1988). None of these schemes has been successful, and in every case most of the Hadza involved returned to the bush, usually within a few months. In each instance some Hadza avoided settlement and continued to live as full-time hunter-gatherers.

A summary of the daily cycle gives some feel for life in a Hadza bush camp. Between 7 A.M. and 9 A.M. people arise, wait for the cold to wear off; women sharpen and harden their digging sticks (sometimes helped by their children) and assemble to prepare to go out to forage. Men leave for an early morning "walk about" (hunt) and move to "the men's place" on the edge or just outside camp where those in camp spend the day. Small children face the question of whether their mothers will take them or leave them in the care of an older brother; young teenage girls decide whether to go with the women or stay home; teenage boys decide whether to go as "guards" for the women or stay home, often to leave for the bush later with a few friends. During our observations, between 9 A.M. and 11 A.M., the children in camp usually did some foraging. Between 11 A.M. and 1 P.M. they might forage more, or eat and play. The temperature reaches its daily high by 1 P.M. Between 1 P.M. and 3 P.M., everyone who is in camp tends to be resting in the shade. Between 3 P.M. and 5 P.M., the women come home, and children interrupt whatever they are doing to get a share of the food the women brought. Between 5 P.M. and 7 P.M. the temperature has fallen to pleasant levels and most people are at home. Children play vigorous games, forage some more, and if there are several teenage girls in camp singing and dancing will begin and last until 9:30 or 10 at night. In the late dry season men will be organizing and preparing themselves for a cold night in a hunting blind at a nearby water hole or game trail. By 7 P.M. all but the men who left for the night are in their houses and around the fire. People eat an evening meal and then visit and chat in each other's houses and fireplaces. On moonless nights an epeme dance (a sacred ceremony) may be held, in which all participate. Silence, but for coughs, the occasional crying child, once in a while a noisy domestic dispute, closely investigating hyenas, and distant comforting lions, lasts from late evening until the next morning.

## PROCEDURES

Data reported came from several different procedures—censuses (Blurton Jones, Smith, O'Connell, Hawkes, & Kamuzora, 1992), interviews with women about their reproductive history and other topics, and observations during which behavior was recorded and food weighed. Interviews were conducted with an interpreter (Kiswahili to Hadzane). The behavior and food observations were made on different field visits from the censuses and interviews; the two kinds of data collection cannot be combined because census and interview are disruptive and require the researcher to move camp constantly. The interpreter and field assistant for all the censuses and interviews was Gudo Mahiya, a Hadza with secondary school education and a mild manner, fluent in Kiswahili, and of course a native-speaking Hadza. We collected data on children's behavior in five ways, each to be discussed in turn.

*Child excursions.* We followed a group of children as they left camp to go gathering, stayed with them until they returned to camp, and weighed the food they acquired. We continued observation to record time spent processing the food, which allowed us the opportunity to calculate weight of food collected per hour of foraging and processing (including breaks to talk or play). Laboratory analyses of calorie value of the main food (Galvin, Hawkes, Maga, O'Connell, & Blurton Jones, 1991) allowed us to convert the figures to return rates (kilocalories acquired per hour of effort, the most widely used measure of rate at which energy is acquired in foraging studies; Stephens & Krebs, 1986). Some of the results are shown in Figures 1 through 3. Age was estimated from a regression of relative age rank on known birth years (see Blurton Jones et al., 1992).

*Women's foraging trips.* On some of the days we followed the main group of women as they left camp in the morning and stayed with them and any children who accompanied them until they returned to camp 4 to 7 hours later. On these days we could not obtain a record of the amount of food brought home by children who had not accompanied the women.

*One-hour focal follows.* We followed individual children on a set schedule for 1 hour each. Because there is a clear daily schedule to life in a Hadza bush camp, in 1986 and 1989 we divided the day into six 2-hour chunks (7–9, 9–11, 11–1, 1–3, 3–5, 5–7) and observed each child once in five of six different time periods. These follows seldom included an

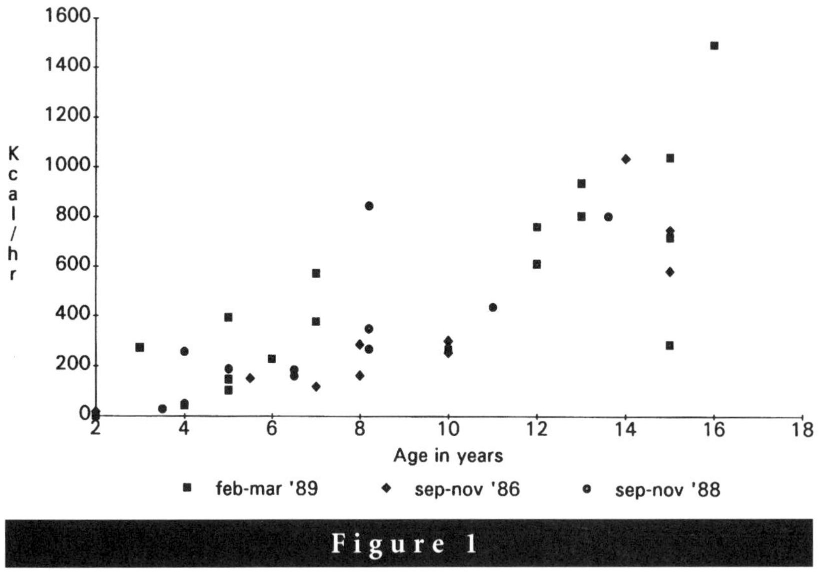


**Figure 1**

Returns (kcal acquired per hour searching and digging) for Makalita roots by age of forager.

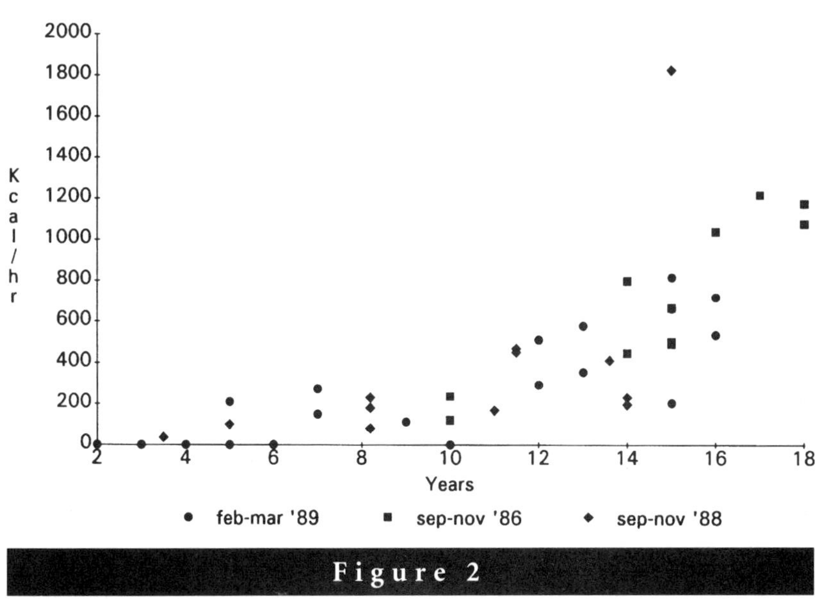


**Figure 2**

Returns (kcal acquired per hour searching and digging) for //ekwa roots by age of forager.

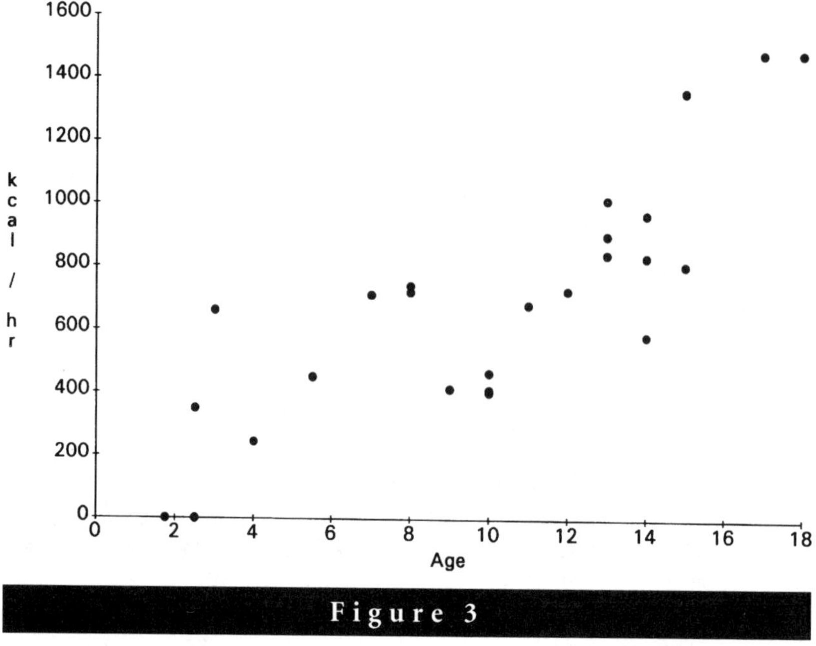


**Figure 3**

Returns (kcal acquired per hour collecting and processing) for Baobab fruit by age of forager.

entire foraging trip so they form a different sample of the children's time from the excursions. They did, however, sometimes include a child arriving in camp with food, and food brought in by the focal child was weighed and recorded. Food brought in by any other child that came to our attention, or that was brought to our attention by a child, was weighed, at cost of a momentary interruption of the 1-hour follow.

*"Ad Lib" food weighings.* We weighed food arriving in camp at any time during the daylight hours when we were also in camp.

*"Ad Lib" departure and arrival notes.* At any time, including during follows, when we noticed individuals leave camp or return we noted name and time. Of course if the observer was out of camp, such occurrences could not be observed.

These records give us estimates of the minimum amount of food each child brought home and time spent foraging each day that the observer stayed all day in camp. Occasionally a child may have brought home more but did not call us to weigh it, or escaped our attention, or we were out of camp following children for a while (on as many as three excursions near camp, usually not more than one). We did not attempt to prorate the data for the amount of time we spent out of camp on such a day. If there were systematic differences between genders and ages in their effort to conceal food from us, or in their tendency to return home with food when we were out of camp, these data could be misleading. We think there were no such biases. It was rather easy to see who was coming and going, and children of all ages seemed proud to show us what they had collected. Too few occasions were missed to seriously distort the data.

Data from three field seasons of observation are used here for analysis of foraging efficiency and amount of food acquired by children; 37 children aged 2 to 18 years in late dry season 1986; 20 children aged 3.5 to 17 in late dry season 1988 (Hawkes et al., 1995, tables 2, 3, and 4); 20 children aged 2 to 16 in wet season 1989. Sixty-one different individual children were observed: 13 were observed first in 1986, then a second time in 1989. Two first observed in 1986 were again observed in 1988, and another in 1988 and 1989. The figures, thus, show mixed longitudinal data. The longitudinal data show changes with age that parallel the patterns suggested by the mixed longitudinal data.

## RESULTS

Figures 1 through 3 show that calorie returns for each main resource increase with age, reaching adult values late in the teenage years. In Figure 4 returns for Makalita roots (*Eminia antennulifera,* a common quarry for young children perhaps because the roots are not far below the surface) are plotted against each child's body weight. There were no significant differences in return rate (efficiency) by gender, either among younger children (aged 5 to 10) or among teenagers.

Figure 5 shows the amount of food brought home and recorded for each child (averaged from 3 to 30 days of observation per child) of various ages. Children under about 10 eat most of their roots and Baobab fruit

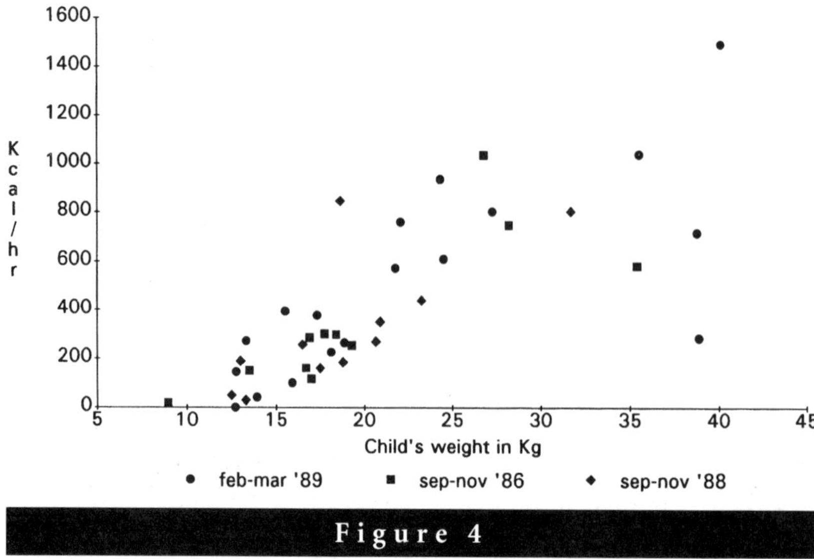


**Figure 4**

Returns (kcal acquired per hour searching and digging) for Makalita roots by body weight of forager.

back in camp. (*Adansonia digitata,* the large pod-like fruit, falls to the ground where it is easily gathered, though it can also be brought down by throwing sticks. The outer shell is cracked by stepping on it, or by smashing it with a stick, revealing a white sweet and sour refreshing pith that contains the seeds that are difficult to open but contribute significantly to the great nutritional value of this food.) Berries are eaten out of camp and at home. Baobab take lengthy processing, which is done at home by people of all ages. In the bush the odd bit of pith from Baobab fruit is sucked as a refresher. In camp the pods are emptied onto a rock and pounded with a hand-sized pebble. Children crush the seeds and pith mixed with water, eating as they work, and spitting out seed shells to hammer off more of the kernel. Adult women pound the fruit dry, winnowing off the seed shells, to combine the pith and kernels in a fine powder for later consumption. Because most of the data reported here are for roots and Baobab, we need not add food eaten in the bush when trying to arrive at a daily food intake for under 10-year-olds. This is not so for older children. When they accompany women into the bush they eat quite a lot before returning

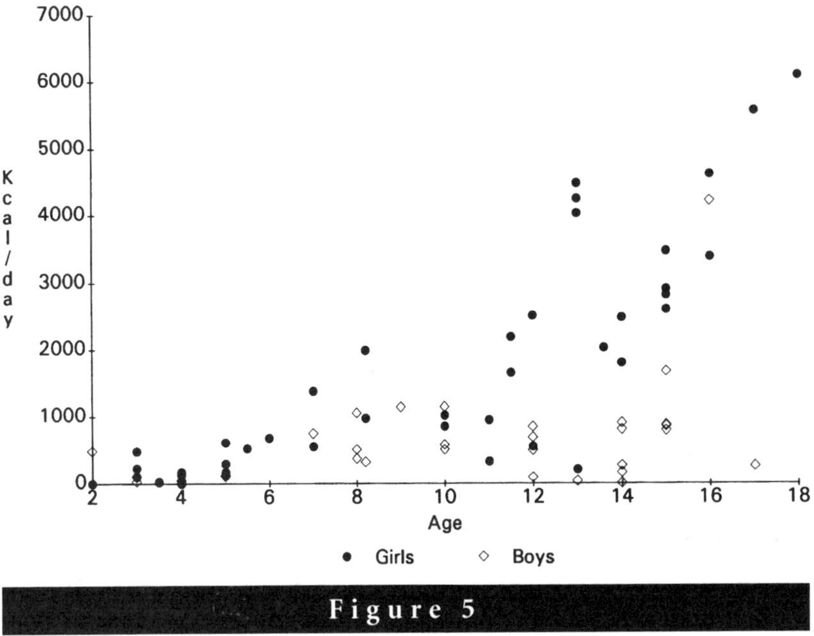


**Figure 5**

Calorie value of food brought back to camp by age of forager (combining data from 1986, 1988, 1989).

to camp. Women often stop and cook roots after a morning's dig, and during berry excursions everyone eats on the job. Thus, for the older children the recorded amounts brought home are well below the amount the child has acquired. Some of the teenagers are bringing home much more than their calorie RDA (recommended daily allowance, adjusted for size and age as in Blurton Jones & Sibly, 1978; recent revisions of RDA will not significantly alter these patterns) and have already eaten more in the bush. Children under 10 bring home at least half of their calorie recommended daily allowance. Above this age boys and girls sharply diverge; girls tend to bring home much more than their daily requirement, and boys apparently tend to fall further and further behind their requirement.

We find no significant difference between food brought home by boys and girls aged 10 or younger ($t$-test, $t$ = -0.742, $N$ = 42, $p$ = .463, and there is no significant contribution of gender ($p$ = .210) after age is entered

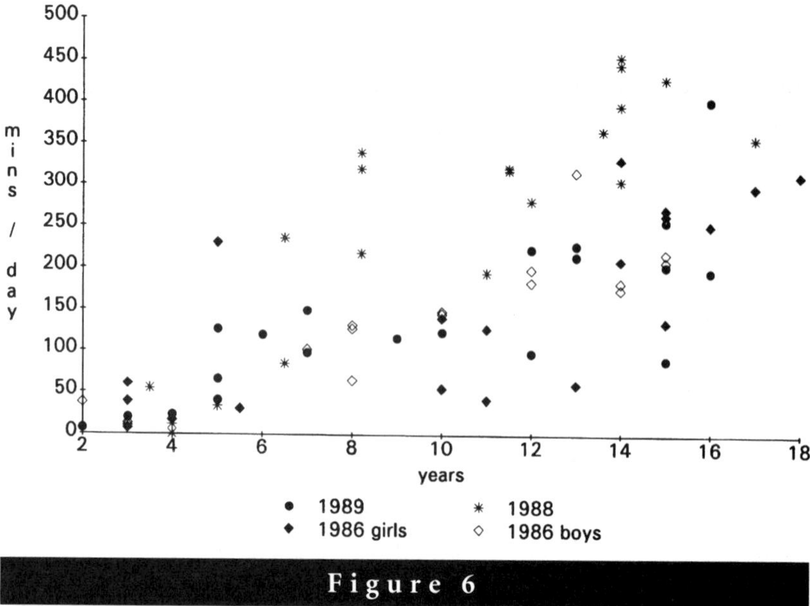


**Figure 6**

Time spent foraging by children plotted against age of child.

first in a regression). Among the group of children who are older than 10, the difference is significant ($t$-test, $t = 5.679$, $N = 35$, $p < .001$); there is also a significant contribution of gender ($p < .001$) after age is entered first in a regression.

Figure 6 shows our best estimate of the average amount of time a day the children spent foraging. There is great variability and a tendency to increase with age. Durations range from less than an hour a day among the under 5-year-olds to 7.5 hours a day among teenagers. Several of the highest values come from the 1988 berry season. Actual durations of trips to the berry groves were greater than shown (577 minutes, or 9+ hours), children did not go to the berry grove every day, and the product of average trip duration × fraction of days visiting berry groves is illustrated. As when children accompany women to dig //ekwa roots, the duration seems to be set by the adult women; children seldom return home unaccompanied from these lengthier trips. Hawkes et al. (1995) argued that children accompany women when the "team returns"—in other words, calories acquired by mother plus calories acquired by child divided by time elapsed (time spent on the excursion, not mother's time plus child's time), are greater than team returns obtained by foraging separately.

## ANALYSIS

Why do Hadza children forage so much? What do they get out of the food they collect? After all, !Kung children manage to survive and grow up without contributing so conspicuously to their own food intake. Why should Hadza children let their mothers off the hook? As outlined in the introduction, we consider first two "common-sense" suggestions, followed by four that derive more closely from behavioral ecology theory. We propose and test predictions that should follow if behavior functions to increase the proposed benefits. All these benefits might accrue, but we should seek evidence about them.

### 1. Hadza Children Are Forced to Forage Because Their Mothers Give Birth to More Babies Than They Can Support

"Common sense" might argue that fertility is the prime mover: Hadza women are more fertile than !Kung women (Blurton Jones et al., 1992), so the children have to make up the shortfall. If children were responding directly to hunger resulting from mother's excess birth rate we should see a correlation between time spent foraging and family size, even when we control for age. We do not ($r = -0.088$, $n = 52$ child-seasons). Regressions that predict time spent foraging from family size, controlling for child age (older children forage for longer), show no significant contribution from family size, either for the whole sample or when the sample is limited to children under 12, presumably the most vulnerable and thus most likely to show such an effect ($p = .189$). Among the 12 and older children there is also no indication of an effect of family size ( $r = .091$ $p = .672$, $n = 24$). The data do not fit with the view that children forage to fill a shortfall that results from their mothers' high fertility. In our 1989 paper we suggested that the higher Hadza fertility results from the children's ability to feed themselves, consonant with the adaptationist expectation that mothers should trade-off fitness and number of offspring (e.g., Smith & Fretwell 1974).

## 2. Hadza Children Forage to Learn Adult Subsistence

Field workers have a long tradition of reporting children's work and subsistence activity as illustrating the importance of learning their subsistence practices. But do they actually learn all this time? Does it really take 18 years to learn to dig roots, pick berries, and crush Baobab pods? Presumably it takes some amount of time, but after a while more practice may produce negligible improvements in efficiency—in other words, perhaps there are diminishing returns to time spent learning these particular tasks.

Return rates (kcal obtained per minute of pursuit and processing) increase with child's age for each food we measured. One might be inclined to interpret the increase as a measure of the amount the children have learned. But curves of foraging return rates against body weight are identical to those against age (see Figs. 1 and 4). Perhaps strength, or simply weight, entirely accounts for the increase in return rate. Weight and age are both correlated with return rates for Baobab fruit ($r = .767$ and .808), Makalita roots ($r = .785$ and 755), and //ekwa roots ($r = .680$ and .636). The effect of weight can account for the effect of age and vice versa (age does not correlate significantly with residuals of weight × return rate).

A more forceful argument comes from the gender differences observed among teenagers. The return rates of teenage boys when they do pursue roots or Baobab are as high as those of girls and for berries a shade higher. But because boys older than about 12 bring less home, unless they can eat much more than girls can eat, they must be spending less time pursuing roots and Baobab, even though they are spending as much time foraging as girls. They spend most of their time out of camp trying to shoot at birds and animals and looking for honey. Thus, they get less "practice" at digging roots and processing Baobab than girls. But girls do not gain any efficiency from all this excess "practice." Clearly, even if children may learn a bit about digging and pounding when small, continued benefits of learning cannot account for the amount of foraging that they do.

### 3. Hadza Children Forage to Enhance Their Own Survival and Growth

The combination of child fitness and number that is optimal for mother's fitness may be at a level of offspring fitness slightly lower than each offspring would favor. So children who can add to their food intake might grow slightly faster and survive slightly better than those who cannot. Hawkes, O'Connell, and Blurton Jones (1997a), using a dataset from 1985 to 1986, show that at certain seasons, after controlling for age, children who spend more time foraging gain more weight. Here we add a less direct argument. If children forage to enhance their growth and survival they should forage as efficiently as they can. All organisms require energy to survive, grow, and reproduce. Time spent acquiring food is costly, in terms of exposure to risks and in terms of the opportunity costs of other fitness-enhancing ways to spend the time. Do Hadza children conform with predictions about behavior of efficient foragers (Stephens & Krebs, 1986)?

Hadza plant foods are patchily distributed, and the diet breadth model should not apply. Patch theories imply that individuals should exploit the most rewarding patch until it is depleted to a level at which alternative patches become attractive. All we can report currently is that the under 10-year-old Hadza children in the 1986 and 1989 field seasons spent most of their time in pursuit of the most rewarding food—Baobab—but that contrary to simple patch theory they also spent time pursuing roots. Their mothers also alternated between these resources, independently of the children as far as we can see. In 1988 children aged 5 and up spent most of their foraging time pursuing berries, much more rewarding than the alternatives observed that season.

If Hadza children were not behaving as efficient foragers we might count this as evidence against the idea that they were aiding their own growth and survival. But even if they are efficient, the resources they gather

**Table 1**

**Children's Gifts of Food to Kin Versus Unrelated Children**

| 1989 data | To cousin or sibling | To unrelated child |
|---|---|---|
| Follows with gift to | 23 | 11 |
| Follows with no gift to | 47 | 59 |

NOTE: $p < .05$.

may mainly give them a fitness benefit by outcomes other than their own growth or survival, such as the number and fitness of their siblings.

We have indications of inefficiency in older Hadza children's foraging. Some teenage girls bring home much more than they could possibly eat (Fig. 5). They would lose little personal survival if they acquired a little less food. Among the children older than 10, boys do not target the foods that give them the highest return rates—they target the least rewarding, honey and birds. This suggests that teenage boys are *not* foraging to enhance their own survival and growth.

## 4. Hadza Children Forage to Gain Inclusive Fitness by Increasing the Number and Survival of Close Kin

If Hadza children's foraging benefits them by increasing the number of siblings and cousins a mother and her sisters raise, then we should expect to observe Hadza children giving food to close kin more than to distant kin or unrelated children. Our 1-hour focal follows provided useful data to examine this question. We recorded transfers of food, from the focal child to others and identified the others. We have shown that number of transfers is closely correlated with amount of food transferred: People who receive small pieces less often receive anything from the same source. Table 1 shows number of hour follows with a transfer from focal child to a cousin or sibling or to a less closely related child. Tabulating food received from others shows a similar pattern ($p < .01$), as shown in Table 2. There is a clear tendency for transfers to be biased toward relatives. This bias

**Table 2**

**Children Receiving Gifts of Food From Kin Versus Unrelated Children**

| (1989 data) Receive | From cousin or sibling | From unrelated child |
|---|---|---|
| Follows with gift from | 40 | 13 |
| Follows with no gift from | 30 | 57 |

NOTE: $p < .01$.

could arise from children spending more time near close relatives when food is around, but this is not material to our argument. Every child is free to go where she or he pleases, almost all their time is spent out of doors, and during daylight they are seldom inside a house. Even inside a Hadza house they are usually visible to other children.

If children's food acquisition and distribution functions to increase the number and fitness of close kin, gifts of food are likely to be most effective if directed to younger children. The effect of a certain amount on the survival of the younger child should be greater than its effect on an older child. The loss of food given away will be less on an older child than it would be on a younger one. Thus, transfers should mostly be from older to younger. There was, in fact, a strong bias toward giving to younger kin ($p <. 001$).

The data are compatible with an inclusive fitness gain from children's foraging among the under 10-year-olds. But there is a complication. Boys and girls gain the same amount of fitness from the existence of close relatives. So they should bring home the same amount of food to share with their younger siblings and cousins. Figure 5 shows that they do not. Teenage boys bring home much less than teenage girls. The gender difference appears after age 10.

If children forage partly to feed younger kin, then we might expect children with more young kin to forage more. A complication arises from the value of a child as a babysitter as well as as a forager, and this is not easy to investigate because babysitting can be done at home in camp and while out in the bush with mother. We find no influence of number of young kin (siblings and cousins under 5 years old) on the amount of food girls bring home ($p = .873$), controlling for the girl's age. Among the boys there is a borderline significant effect of number of young kin ($p = .056$, after controlling for age). Boys with more kin bring back more food. Perhaps for boys, there is a trade-off between whatever they get from chasing birds and honey on the one hand and the fitness benefit of helping to feed younger siblings on the other hand. When the presence of younger siblings increases the payoff from provisioning them, boys bring home more food.

The 1986 field season offered two anecdotes in support of a trade-off between care of kin and hunting. Jumapili, a boy aged about 12, got a large thorn in his foot that none of us could extract. He became quite lame for a week or so. He didn't leave camp with the women or older boys during this time: Hunting and climbing trees for honey would have been painful and unrewarding. Instead he spent much of his time, according to our observations, with his 2-year-old cousin, his closest younger kin (he had no younger siblings). When he recovered the use of his foot he was out in the bush with other boys or guarding the women on their foraging trips. Another boy, Juma, about 15, was an orphan who lived with his grandmother and spent time with his uncle, an age mate, the youngest in their household and his best buddy. They spent a part of most days out in the bush collecting honey and shooting at anything that moved, occasionally killing a small bird. But toward the end of the author's stay Juma's 3-year-old half-brother came to stay. Juma spent all of each day collecting and processing Baobab fruit and feeding it to his little brother. He gave up whatever boys get from rushing about in the bush to tend his orphaned little brother.

## 5. Hadza Children Forage to Increase the Number of Close Kin for the Help These Kin Return Later in Life

How do we explain why teenage girls bring home more food than boys? For a while, the answer seemed to be that girls gained more from siblings later in life than boys gained. When analyzing our 1985 census data we found that, controlling for age, women with more live siblings had more live children (coefficient $b = 0.174$, $p = .038$). There seemed to be a payback from siblings that benefited the woman's reproductive success. The phenomenon might indicate merely that fertility is heritable, but the observation concerns live siblings, not siblings ever born, and the importance of large sibships in Hadza residence patterns biased us to pursue the payback possibility. Perhaps teenage girls bring home more food than boys because they are going to reap the added benefit of help from their grown-up siblings.

Our explanation supposes that there is no such later payback to men from adult siblings. But when we eventually looked back at the census data, we found an even stronger correlation for men. Men with more live siblings had more live children, again after controlling for the man's age (coefficient $b = 0.559$, $p = .007$). As might be expected, the adult siblings seem to effect reproductive success by different routes. Women with more siblings produce live children faster. Men with more siblings have more wives (sequentially). Each wife raises surviving children at the same rate as wives of men with fewer live siblings. In a population with such high mortality people should quite strongly discount the future and we may doubt that such remote payback would be worth a response. The slight difference in when the payback comes to men and to women (especially when offset against the stronger correlation found among the men) is unlikely to give a significant difference in payoff received by boys and by girls. So we conclude that boys could gain as much payback as girls by provisioning their younger siblings. Why do they often forgo this benefit? What other advantage do they pursue?

## 6. Hadza Children Forage to Begin to Gain Reputations

Several studies have shown that individuals with high reputations have high reproductive success (Chagnon, 1979; Irons, 1979; Turke & Betzig, 1985). Omark and Edelman (1975) and others have shown that quite young children form opinions about the abilities of others. A reputation may be hard to change in a society in which the people you grow up with include most of the people you will live among for the rest of your life and who are nearly all linked by kinship or marriage, and where gossip exists (other primates cannot gossip—transmit a bias about an absent individual—although like people, nonhuman primates may be able to transmit a bias about an individual when the individual is there to be identified). In that case it may be important to make an early start on gaining a reputation. Perhaps the activities of Hadza teenagers are those that enhance their reputations as hard-working foragers. Just how hard it is to change a reputation may depend on details such as the rate of change of the audience, the relative weight the audience gives to gossip and to personal observation (this weighting would presumably have itself been subject to natural selection). Our search of the "gossip" literature failed to unearth any serious attempt at modeling these phenomena.

Because of our interest in men's reproductive strategies and the role of hunting in these (Hawkes, 1990, 1991; Hawkes, O'Connell, & Blurton Jones, 1991), we had asked women to name two or three men that were eager and successful hunters, two or three that were experts at making arrow heads, and two or three that were experts at trade and dealing with outsiders. We chose these as criteria that Woodburn had mentioned as Hadza qualifications for getting and staying married, and that seemed from our field experience to be clearly important aspects of men's activity. Some men were never named, some only once, some more than once, and a few many times. Because women wander less than men and primarily know the people in their natal region, we divided the number of nominations by the number of women interviewed in the region where a man currently lived. The resulting nomination rates were then correlated with measures suggested by our research questions.

First we looked to see whether these "reputations" reflected objective reality. The nominations as a good hunter correlated positively with observed hunting success in the two seasons of data in which we recorded hunting success (for the 1985–1986 field season of Hawkes and O'Connell, $r = .731$, $N = 13$ men, $p < .05$; and for the late 1986 field season of Blurton Jones, 1986, $r = .682$, $N = 12$, $p < .05$).

Do reputations correlate with men's reproductive success? The superior growth rate of good hunters' children suggested they might (Hawkes,

1993: $r = .913$, $p < .05$), also true of the data from Blurton Jones' 1986 field season ($r = .772$, $p < .05$). From interviews conducted in 1992 we calculated reproductive success of the wives. Because older women were extremely hard to interview and gave accounts greatly at variance with previous records of their children, we interviewed only women in or approaching the child-bearing years (about 18 to 45). A count of number of children would be meaningless, almost completely dependent on the woman's age. Thus, we calculated a figure that represents the extent to which a woman is producing children above or below the expected rate for her age. Because age-specific fertility is not constant but follows an inverted U shape we used the residuals of number of children born (and number of children still alive) regressed on woman's age plus age squared (see also Hill & Hurtado, 1996). Hadza husbands' nomination rate was correlated with residuals of total surviving children reported by the 48 women, and with surviving children born since 1985 when we began collecting data ($r = .299$, $p < .039$; $r = .285$, $p = .05$). Men with more nominations tended to have wives who produced live children faster. This may not be due to the successful hunters providing more food for their wife and children. Meat is shared almost evenly between all the households in camp. Successful hunters tend to have wives who are more efficient foragers than other women (Hawkes et al., 1997a).

We looked for a fitness correlate of reputation in one more way. Many older Hadza men have young wives, usually married after deserting an older wife by whom he had fathered children. We had seen that the correlation of reproductive success with number of live siblings observed in the 1985 census data was a result of men with more siblings having had more wives. We took the 34 men aged 40 to 65 from the two regions in which women were interviewed about men's reputations; the ages were chosen to include men whose first wife might have reached the end of her child-bearing years and yet were still active and physically robust. We found that the men with higher reputations (nominated versus not nominated) were more likely to have a wife less than 45 years old than the men with lower reputations (Fisher's exact test, $p = .045$). Thus, a reputation may help a Hadza man raise a second family in the second part of his adult life. The effect on a man's reproductive success from a second family is very large indeed.

So there are three kinds of evidence that gaining a reputation as a successful hunter, arrow maker, or trader brings reproductive advantages. Is this why teenage boys give up productive labor for running about the bush with their bows pursuing the lowest return foodstuffs—honey and birds? Teenage boys target the least economically rewarding resources. Are they trying to make a headstart on their reputation?

We have no direct evidence with which to pursue this suggestion. We were encouraged to incorporate the questions in the interviews of women after asking a group of boys to name good hunters. They had strong opinions, mostly about young men who were just a few years older than themselves. But the youngest newly married women had the weakest opinions. Several could only name their father as an expert. This suggests that young women may not be using reputation to choose a husband. But perhaps their older relatives are expressing approval or disapproval based on such reputations.

We have not asked men to nominate expert hunters, but suspect that they would give rapid and confident responses like the teenage boys. Are reputations with other men important, and are teenage boys actually better understood as competing with each other than as seeking reputations among women? There could be several reasons for competing for reputations with other boys. They may gain the kind of future tolerance that Hawkes (1990 and elsewhere) has suggested may accrue to generous and successful hunters, and others may seek to stay in the same camp as the known determined hunter. If boys are competing for reputations among the girls that concern features that make them eligible spouses, they are in competition with other boys over these features, and the most efficient mechanism might entail paying more attention to how they match up to other boys than to what the girls think of them.

Girls may be just as interested in building reputations as good foragers. We have little evidence beyond the anecdotal. Adult women claim that all women are experts, only naming a few older women as much more productive and able than the majority. But women who were more efficient foragers had husbands who were more successful hunters (Hawkes et al., 1997b). If girls gain from a reputation as a good forager, they can promote this by the same behavior as they employ to help feed their younger siblings. This might account for the massive amounts of food brought home by teenage girls, and the lack of correlation with number of younger siblings, in contrast to the boys among whom reputation and siblings are promoted by different, incompatible activities (trying to hunt, foraging for plant foods). This is a richly complex topic we have scarcely begun to explore.

## DISCUSSION

### Summary and Conclusions

We showed that the amount that Hadza children forage cannot be explained by its effect on subsistence techniques (learning), because it has no such effect. Although teenage girls forage more than teenage boys, they achieve no higher return rates from all their extra practice. The fine motor skills of accurate archery might be more difficult to learn or maintain, but boys are accurate shots before their teenage years, and if learning to shoot is so important they should not spend so much time pursuing plant foods. Foraging returns (Kcal/min) increased with age, as might be expected if they were being learned, but the return rates could be predicted as well from body weight as from age. Return rates may increase with age merely because strength increases with age.

As would be expected if children receive fitness benefits from foraging, children aged 5 to 10 behaved as efficient foragers. They spent most time on the patchy food types that yield the highest returns. But boys over 10 concentrated on food resources that yielded very low returns: collecting honey and hunting. We showed that food brought home is given to younger close kin, and that both genders gain as adults from having more live kin, women by raising more children, men by acquiring more wives. Thus, children's help to their younger kin may increase the helper's fitness in two ways—first as inclusive fitness; second as a result of help received from those kin in later life. Controlling for age, boys with more young close kin (siblings or cousins) brought home more food. There was no significant effect of younger kin among the girls.

We suggested that teenage boys might spend time trying to hunt because it begins to establish their reputation as hard working hunters. This would require that reputations exist, reflect actual hunting success, and relate to reproductive success, and that boys' activity enhances their reputations. We confirmed the first three but have collected no data with which to test the fourth. There is some evidence that variation in behavior of teenage boys can be accounted for by a trade-off between gains from reputation against gains from helping raise siblings. We reported two "case histories" that illustrated this. Two more boys stood out for the high amount of food that they brought home. Both were the oldest of large sibships. Both were sometimes given the task of holding and entertaining the youngest while the mother left camp. Both had access to an axe and owned a bow and arrows and used them. But both brought in more plant foods than other boys. Teenage boys, by pursuing honey and birds, forego the benefits of a greater number of calories brought home. Perhaps for these two individuals, the greater benefit in kin that could accrue from the extra calories rendered the potential loss in reputation worth sacrificing.

## Problems

Several methodological problems that need to receive attention in behavioral ecology are evident in this work. One is especially prominent. When there are several likely fitness-enhancing outcomes of an activity, we should try to resist two temptations: (a) the easy answer—all must have an influence, so we don't need to investigate; (b) to claim any one of them as the sole "aim" of the behavior. Thus, children gain from the food they gather by eating it, and by giving some to kin, and some of the benefit from kin accrues from later help as well as from inclusive fitness. No one of these is the "real" explanation of why children forage; advantages of each type apparently accrue. We might have been able to exclude some of these benefits. For instance, children might have been found to eat everything themselves and bring home no "surplus" at any age. Adult kin may have turned out to give no advantage beyond inclusive fitness. Reputations could have turned out to have no correlation with observed hunting effectiveness or any measure of reproductive success. Reciprocation from adult kin turned out not to be able to account for gender differences in teenage foraging because advantages of adult kin accrue equally to men and to women. Seeking reputations could account for the difference, so long as boys and girls differ either in their concern with gaining a reputation or in the behavior that gives them a good reputation.

Rather than seek the "real" explanation we might do better to attend to explaining variation. Teenage boys gain benefits from hunting honey and birds but also from bringing home food for siblings. When the gains from care of kin are greater (when the gains reach a higher level before diminishing to a rate at which it pays to switch to another activity), we should expect more plant food collection, and this is how some of the boys behaved. We might sometime look for similar trade-offs in the behavior of early teenage girls: Can we explain some of the variation in how much they go to the bush digging roots with the women (which gives them a lower return rate than if they foraged near home) by the presence of babies to be entertained while their mother or sister digs?

## Why Not Interpret Hadza Children's Foraging in the Light of Gender Role Psychology?

By now the psychologist reader will be bursting to protest, "Of course teenage boys don't want to maximize the food they bring home, they want to look like men." Quite possibly true. And Hadza girls are probably happy to act like women. Why have we not discussed the observed gender differences and the economic irrationality of Hadza teenage boys in terms of gender roles and gender identity? These terms have not figured in behavioral ecological thinking because our aim is to seek indications of consequences for reproductive success, and concepts from psychology seem more relevant to the proximate mechanisms or developmental processes. Even if we had a good record of what Hadza children of each age said were the tasks, attributes, and qualities of males and females, we would want to know what they got out of believing these things and what they got out of taking such joy in fulfilling them, and we would be very curious about why their ideas change with age or fail to coincide closely with observed behavior. We are confident that Hadza boys as young as 7 would tell you that men hunt and women dig, but they proudly show you the roots they have excavated! Our questions could be seen as asking whether mechanisms of gender identity and gender-role acquisition work efficiently to promote fitness. Thus, we might try to test whether these mechanisms shape behavior more efficiently than another form of learning. Perhaps we will learn a little more about the mechanisms if we understand the tasks they were built to accomplish.

What do we feel like saying about teenage psychology? "There are reasons why boys are so 'irresponsible.' " "No wonder the teenage ego is so fragile if life-shaping reputations are at stake so early." "For boys, running about in the woods trying to hunt and find honey is more fun than digging and picking and taking stuff home to mom, and we have some indications about why that emotional value evolved." If reputations need to be worked on so early, and have such far-reaching results, we may see a reason behind the fragility of the teenage ego. This may lead us to examine it as a more important feature of that life phase and less as an inconvenient pathology. Making an early start on a reputation may be of much less direct value to a teenager in the mobile suburbs than in Hadza society, and the proximate mechanisms with which evolution equipped us may or may not be able to adjust accordingly. In the less mobile inner-city neighborhood, for example, an early start on a reputation may be nearly as important as in Hadza society. It may also help if we understand more about the arenas in which teenage boys and girls may be expected to build reputations and the degree to which these arenas are adjustable. What does it take to make being a "nerd" more valued than being a "jock"? Steinberg's (Steinberg, Dornbusch, & Brown, 1992) emphasis on the role of peer support in enhancing the academic careers of American teenagers comes quickly to mind—perhaps the arena in which the majority of teenagers strive for reputations should be expected to usually overwhelm parental exhortation?

## Why Not Interpret Hadza Children's Foraging in the Light of Existing Psychological and Anthropological Theories of Socialization?

Why have we not written about socialization in this account? Mainly because we have no knowledge of how it comes about that Hadza children grow up to behave the way they do, we have been looking to see whether they behave in ways that might enhance their fitness and whether expecting them to behave this way enables us to predict behavior. Thus, we are assuming "socialization" is part of a developmental process, perhaps contributing to fitness (but we must account for the different fitness interests of parents and children). The idea of socialization is used to address questions such as, "Do children forage because adults encourage them?" often with the implication that this is all we need to know! In reality Hadza adults may have no influence whatever on whether children forage; they are absent from camp when the children leave, and return after the children have eaten all the food they collected. Children could deceive the adults any way they chose! In interviews about whether children can forage in their current location, women give no indication that children are encouraged or discouraged. In contrast, !Kung adults told us that they try to influence children *not* to forage, and we went on to gather some evidence to show that their efforts may enhance fitness of parent and child. Even if Hadza adults did encourage children to forage, we should still ask why adults do this and why children comply or refuse.

Our account of Hadza children foraging begins from a view almost diametrically opposite to the view from which LeVine writes about parents and children in chapter 13. There he makes the argument that by and large parents get the children they want, a usefully focused question among the unstructured claims of traditional socialization literature. My approach has come from a different direction: Children try to be the children they want. LeVine treats children as passive recipients, we treat them as active strategizers. But there is an excellent reason why it is going to be difficult to tell whether either or both of us is correct: We would expect a good deal of overlap between the interests of parents and children, especially if parent–offspring conflict is expected to be lower in larger families (Clutton-Brock, 1991; Lazarus & Inglis, 1986), and LeVine and the authors all work in high fertility societies!

If it is true that teenagers gain from a good reputation, then much will also depend on in whose eyes their reputation stands. If the parental generation has any influence on mate choice, then the teenager who strives to gain a good reputation needs to attend to the values or gossip of adults as well attending to peers and to an "objective" criterion shown to directly assess value as a mate. If adults had no influence on mate choice, or little perception of contemporary fitness criteria, or had fitness interests less consonant with those of their children, it might pay the children to pay less heed to adults.

## Generalizations

Can we expand or organize the idea of children's fitness agendas any further? The benefits of foraging that we have discussed can be set in three larger groupings, which may lead us to pay attention to wider aspects of children's behavior. Children can enhance their fitness by promoting their own survival (not necessarily by foraging like Hadza children, but perhaps by staying out of danger, or by trying to extract more resources from mother), by increasing their inclusive fitness through the number and fitness of their close kin, and attempting to influence their future reproductive success (for instance by learning adult skills, or perhaps by enhancing their reputations, or by building alliances).

Trade-offs between major goals such as survival and investment in future reproduction might be rewarding to think about. When returns to effort directed at survival are high, and survival is enhanced by time consuming activity (as among Hadza children but not among !Kung children), then investment in future reproduction may take second place. Where the child can do little to affect its own survival prospects (gains little from efforts in that direction), it may as well expend any effort that it can toward future reproduction, so long as this does not cost it too much in survival. Future reproductive success may be influenced by subsistence skills but also by choice of mate and social relationships. Into this background of real-life trade-offs, a few societies in the past 2000 years have introduced schooling. Where schooling has been directly linked to high material rewards (e.g., salaried government employment in Mandarin China and postindependence Africa), it has received enthusiastic support from parents and children. In other places and times the enthusiasm of children has been less than overwhelming and always less than educators would like. We too easily forget that under many circumstances, staying alive, finding a spouse, and building a network may be much more important.

Our work on Hadza children illustrates that remembering that selection acts on the young as well as the mature (if less strongly on the old!) enables us to make a variety of testable predictions that we have not seen made by proponents of other paradigms. Because questions of adaptive outcome are different from questions of proximate cause and individual development, the adaptationist approach to childhood can be pursued without premature attempts to match it with psychology's mainstream. We can continue our parallel play, and we will see where it leads.

## CONCLUSION

We accounted for much of the variation in how Hadza children spend their time without having to fall back on the difficult-to-test interpretation of their behavior as "in order to learn." We did this by predicting aspects of behavior from the assumption that children would have been selected to make trade-offs between current survival, promotion of kin, and future reproductive prospects. We suggested that the teenagers may be beginning to build reputations as hard-working foragers. Evidence that reputations make a difference to men's reproductive success was also provided. This implies that teenagers might care about what others think of them, and that what others think of them might have a real influence on their futures. We are, thus, encouraged to think of teenagers' interest in their images, and gender roles as something more important than an irritating frailty.

The assumption that children are not simply unformed objects on a developmental assembly line but that they have been directly subject to natural selection and may pursue their own agenda (ideas provoked by Dr. Freedman's work on infant adaptations) is able to generate many testable predictions. Some tests of these notions were presented in this chapter. Many questions about reputations are generated by our approach, but they remain unanswered.

## REFERENCES

Baumann, O. (1894). *Durch massailand zur nilquelle.* [Through Masailand to the source of the Nile]. Berlin: Reimer. (Reprinted as *Through Masailand to the source of the Nile*, 1968, New York: Johnson Reprint)

Blurton Jones, N. G. (1972). (Ed.). *Ethological studies of child behavior.* London: Cambridge University Press.

Blurton Jones, N. G., Hawkes, K., & Draper, P. (1994a). Differences between Hadza and !Kung children's work: Original affluence or practical reason? In E. S. Burch & L. Ellana (Eds.), *Key issues in hunter gatherer research* (pp. 189–215). Oxford: Berg.

Blurton Jones, N. G., Hawkes, K., & Draper, P. (1994b). Foraging returns of !Kung adults and children: Why didn't !Kung children forage? *Journal of Anthropological Research, 50,* 217–248.

Blurton Jones, N. G., & Sibly, R. M. (1978). Testing adaptiveness of culturally determined behaviour: Do bushman women maximise their reproductive success by spacing births widely and foraging seldom? In N. G. Blurton Jones & V. Reynolds (Eds.), *Human Behaviour and Adaptation: Society for Study of Human Biology Symposium No 18* (pp. 135–158). London: Taylor & Francis.

Blurton Jones, N. G., Smith, L. C., O'Connell, J. F., Hawkes, K., & Kamuzora, C. L. (1992). Demography of the Hadza, an increasing and high density population of savanna foragers. *American Journal of Physical Anthropology, 89,* 159–181.

Bock, J. A. (1995). *The determinants of variation in children's activities in a Southern African community.* Unpublished doctoral dissertation, University of New Mexico, Albuquerque.

Borgerhoff-Mulder, M., & Caro, T. (1985). The use of quantitative observation techniques in anthropology. *Current Anthropology, 26,* 232–262.

Bowlby, J. (1969). Attachment. *Attachment and Loss* (Vol. 1). London: Hogarth Press.

Brown, J. L. (1987). *Helping and communal breeding in birds: Ecology and evolution.* Princeton, NJ: Princeton University Press.

Chagnon, N. A. (1979). Is reproductive success equal in egalitarian societies? In N. A. Chagnon & W. Irons (Eds.), *Evolutionary biology and human social behavior* (pp. 374–401). North Scituate, MA: Duxbury.

Charnov, E. L. (1993). *Life history invariants.* Oxford: Oxford University Press.

Clutton-Brock, T. H. (1991). *The evolution of parental care.* Princeton, NJ: Princeton University Press.

Emlen, S. T. (1995). An evolutionary theory of the family. *Proceedings of the National Academy of Sciences, USA, 92,* 8092–8099.

Freedman, D. G. (1974). *Human infancy: An evolutionary perspective.* Hillsdale, NJ: Erlbaum.

Galvin, K. A., Hawkes, K., Maga, J. A., O'Connell, J. F., & Blurton Jones, N. (1991). *The composition of some wild plant foods used by East African hunter-gatherers.* Manuscript in preparation.

Hamilton, W. D. (1964). The genetical evolution of social behaviour I, II. *Journal of Theoretical Biology, 7,* 1–52.

Hawkes, K. (1990). Why do men hunt? Benefits for risky choices. In E. Cashdan (Ed.), *Risk and uncertainty in tribal and peasant economies* (pp. 145–166). Boulder, CO: Westview Press.

Hawkes, K. (1991). Showing off: Tests of an hypothesis about men's foraging goals. *Ethology and Sociobiology, 12,* 29–54.

Hawkes, K., O'Connell, J. F., & Blurton Jones, N. G. (1991). Hunting income patterns among the Hadza: Big game, common goods, foraging goals and the evolution of the human diet. *Philosophical Transactions of the Royal Society of London B, 334,* 243–251.

Hawkes, K., O'Connell, J. F., & Blurton Jones, N. G. (1995). Hadza children's foraging: Juvenile dependency, social arrangements, and mobility among hunter-gatherers. *Current Anthropology, 36,* 688–700.

Hawkes, K., O'Connell, J. F., & Blurton Jones, N. G. (1997). *Why do Hadza men hunt?* Manuscript in preparation.

Hawkes, K., O'Connell, J. F., & Blurton Jones, N. G. (in press). Hadza women's time allocation, offspring provisioning, and the evolution of long post-menopausal lifespan. *Current Anthropology.*

Hill, K., & Hurtado, A. M. (1996). *Ache life history: The ecology and demography of a foraging people.* New York: Aldine de Gruyter.

Irons, W. (1979). Cultural and biological success. In N. A. Chagnon & W. Irons (Eds.), *Evolutionary Biology and Human Social Behavior* (pp. 257–272). North Scituate, MA: Duxbury.

Krebs, J. R., & Davies, N. B. (1987). *An introduction to behavioral ecology* (2nd ed.). Oxford: Blackwell Scientific Publications.

Krebs, J. R., & Davies, N. B. (1991). *Behavioral ecology: An evolutionary approach* (3rd ed.). London: Blackwell Scientific Publications.

Lazarus, J., & Inglis, I. R. (1986). Shared and unshared parental investment, parent-offspring conflict and brood size. *Animal Behavior, 34,* 1791–1804.

McDowell, W. (1981). *A brief history of the Mangola Hadza.* Unpublished manuscript prepared for The Rift Valley Project, Ministry of Information and Culture, Dar es Salaam, Tanzania.

Mehlman, M. (1988). *Later quaternary archaeological sequences in northern Tanzania.* Unpublished doctoral dissertation, University of Illinois, Champaign-Urbana.

Ndagala, D. (1988). Free or doomed? Images of the Hadzabe hunters and gatherers of Tanzania. In T. Ingold, D. Riches, & J. Woodburn (Eds.), *Hunters and Gatherers* (pp. 65–72). Oxford: Berg.

Obst, E. (1912). Von Mkalama ins Land der Wakindiga [From Mkalama to the land of the Wakindiga]. *Mitteilungen der Geographischen Gesellschaft in Hamburg, 26,* 3–45.

Omark, D. R., & Edelman, M. S. (1975). A comparison of status hierarchies in young children: An ethological approach. *Social Science Information, 14,* 87–107.

Roff, D. A. (1992). *The evolution of life histories: Theory and analysis.* New York: Chapman & Hall.

Sands, B. (1995). *Evaluating claims of distant linguistic relationships: The case of Khoisan.* Unpublished doctoral dissertation, University of California, Los Angeles.

Sands, B., Maddieson, I., & Ladefoged, P. (1993). The phonetic structures of Hadza. *UCLA Working Papers in Phonetics, 84,* 67–88.

Schultz, J. (1971). *Agrarlandschaftliche Veränderungen in Tanzania (Mbulu/Hanag Districts).* Hamburg: Weltform.

Smith, C. C., & Fretwell, S. D. (1974). The optimal balance between size and number of offspring. *The American Naturalist, 108,* 499–506.

Smith, E. A., & Winterhalder, B. (1992). (Eds.). *Evolutionary ecology and human behavior.* New York: Aldine de Gruyter.

Stearns, S. C. (1992). *The evolution of life histories.* Oxford: Oxford University Press.

Stearns, S. C., & Koella, J. (1986). The evolution of phenotypic plasticity in life history traits: Predictions for norms of reaction for age- and size-at-maturity. *Evolution, 40,* 893–913.

Stephens, D. W., & Krebs, J. R. (1986). *Foraging theory.* Princeton, NJ: Princeton University Press.

Steinberg, L., Dornbusch, S. M., & Brown, B. B. (1992). Ethnic differences in adolescent achievement: An ecological perspective. *American Psychologist, 47,* 723–729.

Tinbergen, N. (1963). On aims and methods of ethology. *Zeitschrift für tierpsychologie, 20,* 410–433.

Trivers, R. L. (1974). Parent-offspring conflict. *American Zoologist, 14,* 249–264.

Turke, P. W. (1988). Helpers at the nest: Childcare networks on Ifaluk. In L. Betzig, M. Borgerhoff-Mulder, & P. Turke (Eds.), *Human reproductive behavior: A Darwinian perspective* (pp. 173–188). Cambridge: Cambridge University Press.

Turke, P. W., & Betzig, L. L. (1985). Those who can do: Wealth, status, and reproductive success on Ifaluk. *Ethology and Sociobiology, 6,* 79–87.

Woodburn, J. C. (1964). *The social organization of the Hadza of North Tanzanyika.* Unpublished doctoral dissertation, Cambridge University.

Woodburn, J. C. (1968a). An introduction to Hadza ecology. In R. B. Lee & I. DeVore (Eds.), *Man the hunter* (pp. 49–55). Chicago: Aldine.

Woodburn, J. C. (1968b). Stability and flexibility in Hadza residential groupings. In R. B. Lee & I. DeVore (Eds.), *Man the hunter* (pp. 103–110). Chicago: Aldine.

Woodburn, J. C. (1972). Ecology, nomadic movement and the composition of the local group among hunters and gatherers: An East African example and its implications. In P. J. Ucko, R. Tringham, & G. W. Dimbleby (Eds.), *Man, settlement and urbanism* (pp. 193–205). London: Duckworth.

Woodburn, J. C. (1979). Minimal politics: The political organization of the Hadza of north Tanzania. In W. Snack & P. Cohen (Eds.), *Politics and leadership: A comparative perspective* (pp. 244–266). Oxford: Clarendon Press.

Woodburn, J. C. (1988). African hunter-gatherer social organisation: Is it best understood as a product of encapsulation? In T. Ingold, D. Riches, & J. Woodburn (Eds.), *Hunters and gatherers* (Vol. 1, pp. 31–64). Oxford: Berg.

12

# Expression or Communication About Emotion

Paul Ekman

Daniel Freedman was working on his first research grant in 1961 at Langley Porter Neuropsychiatric Institute when I arrived there as a postdoctoral fellow to initiate my research on facial expression and gesture. His interest in behavior genetics, and more broadly in the biological basis of behavior, was at that time quite out of vogue and not at all compatible with my own approach, which strictly emphasized social learning. Over the years the evidence from my cross-cultural research and from Dr. Freedman's cross-cultural studies converged, requiring an evolutionary perspective and recognition that emotional expressions are biosocial phenomena.

The two questions this chapter addresses presume that the reader accepts the evidence that there are universals in facial expressions of emotion. Granting that, the question still can be asked about what it is that we know when we observe a facial expression of emotion. Is it an emotion term, such as the person is *angry, afraid, disgusted, sad, happy,*

My research is supported by a Research Scientist Award from the National Institute of Mental Health (MH06092).

and so forth? Or is it some other kind of message about what is happening inside the person or what the person is likely to do? Should we consider these as messages sent to us, a form of communication, or are they involuntary expressions of an internal state? First I will describe what information can be provided by a facial expression of emotion and then whether it is better to conceptualize these as communication rather than expression.

## WHAT INFORMATION IS PROVIDED BY FACIAL EXPRESSIONS?

Consider the expression shown by the woman looking directly out in Figure 1. I took this photograph in 1967 when I was working in the highlands of what is now called Papua New Guinea. Consider the diverse information that someone who observes this expression, totally out of context, just as it appears on the page, might obtain.

- Someone insulted/offended/provoked her.
- She is planning to attack that person.
- She is remembering the last time someone insulted her.
- She is feeling very tense.
- She is boiling.
- She is about to hit someone.
- She wants the person who provoked her to stop what he/she is doing.
- She is angry.

Compare this to the information that can be obtained from the expression shown by another person from Papua New Guinea in Figure 2.

- Someone or something revolted him.
- He is thinking about how to get rid of it.
- He is remembering the last time he was revolted.
- He is feeling nauseous.
- He feels like he's on a roller-coaster.

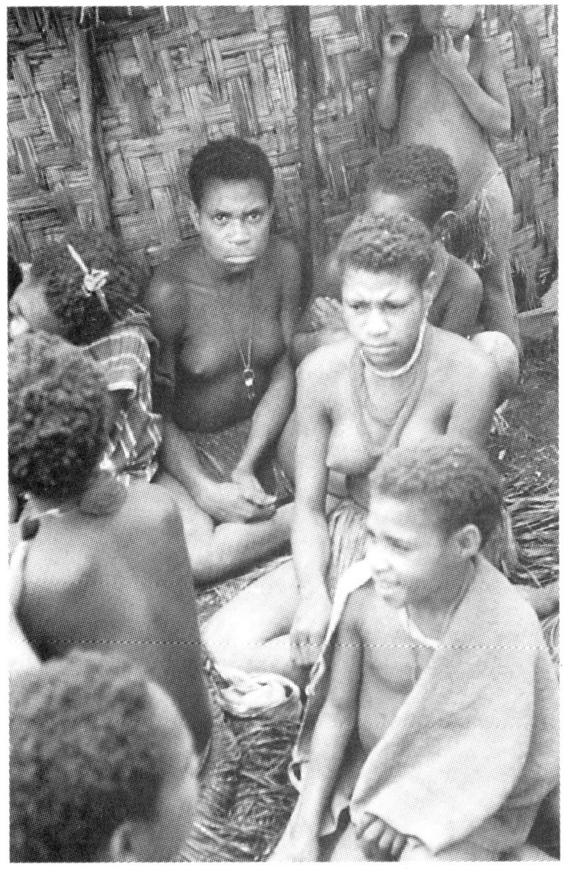

**Figure 1**

Woman in New Guinea Highlands, 1967. Copyright Paul Ekman, 1980. Ekman, P. (1980). *Face of Man: Universal Expression in a New Guinea Village.* New York: Garland. Used by permission.

- He is going to leave.
- He wants the person who revolted him to stop what he/she is doing.
- He is disgusted.

Each expression provides very different information, yet they both provide information about the same seven kinds or *domains* of information.

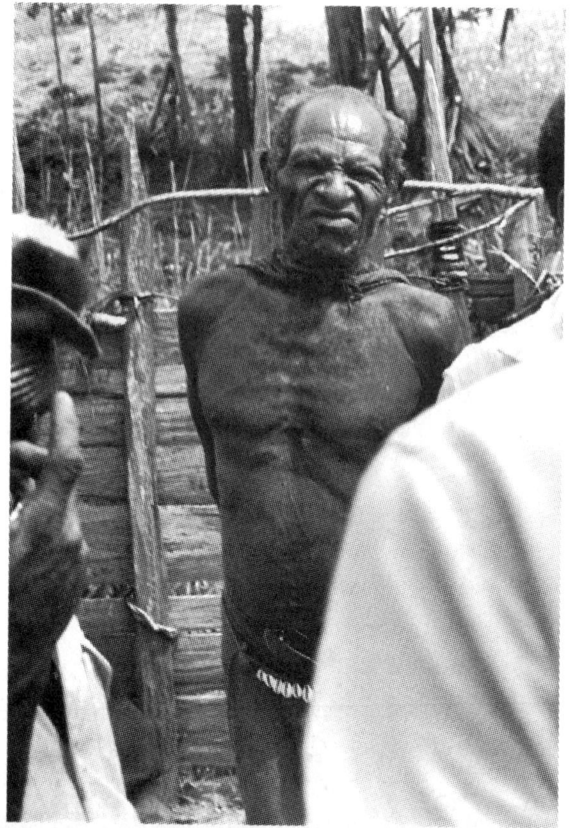

**Figure 2**

Man in New Guinea Highlands, 1967. Copyright Paul Ekman, 1980. Ekman, P. (1980). *Face of Man: Universal Expression in a New Guinea Village.* New York: Garland. Used by permission.

1. The antecedents, the events that brought about the expression;
2. The person's thoughts: plans, expectations, memories;
3. The internal physical state of the person showing the expression;
4. A metaphor;
5. What the expresser is likely to do next;
6. What the expresser wants the perceiver to do;
7. An emotion word.

Note that Hinde (1985a) made some of these distinctions in his discussion of expression, as has Smith (1985).

We do not know which information domains those actually engaged in a conversation derive from each other's expressions. It could be only one information domain or all of them. Which it is may depend on who those people are, how well they know each other, what they are talking about, their social class, and their culture. In other words, we do not know the answer, and there is no certain way to find out.

The people involved in the conversations could not tell us. Even if we interrupted an individual and asked her what she thought when she saw a particular expression on the other's face, we would not find out. For she could only tell us what she thinks happened. Although that is interesting to know, it is likely to be a retrospective construction, not what actually happens when the expression first registers. The initial translation of an expression into some meaning (any one of the information domains listed) is likely to be so immediate that we are not aware of the process we go through. Darwin noted this in saying, "It has often struck me as a curious fact that so many shades of expression are instantly recognized without any conscious process of analysis on our parts" (1872/1955, p. 359).

There are exceptions, of course, when we ponder the meaning or significance of an expression. This happens when an expression is unusual or its occurrence at a particular moment in time is incongruous with everything else that is happening. Then the persons trying to figure out the meaning of the expression are quite aware of their thought processes, but these may not be the thought processes that are typically involved when expressions are translated into meaning immediately.

Although we cannot find out what people actually do, we can find out what they *can* do. We can determine if each of the domains of information listed earlier *can* be derived from an expression. We know that if we show people a facial expression of emotion they will agree in their choice of which emotion word (anger, fear, etc.) fits the expression. But what if we ask them to choose which plan a person is making, which event preceded the expression, which sensations might be felt, and so forth? A preliterate people that Friesen and I studied in Papua New Guinea (Ekman, 1972) and another such group that Karl Heider (unpublished, described in Ekman, 1973) studied in West Iran had no trouble identifying the events associated with particular facial expressions. Rosenberg and Ekman (1995) also found that Americans show similar agreement. To my knowledge no one has yet determined whether each of the other information domains I listed can be derived from facial expressions. That work could be done, and I expect it would find that agreement is good for each domain of information. Facial expression can provide, I believe, each of these different types of information, but that is not a demonstrated fact within or across cultures.

I think we use emotion words—*anger, fear, disgust, sadness,* and so forth—as a shorthand, an abbreviated way to refer to the various events and processes that make up the phenomenon of emotion. Each word refers to a different set of these organized, integrated processes. When someone says or thinks—that woman is angry or that man is disgusted—we do not know which of these events or processes they are considering or if they are actually considering any of them. It is much more convenient, if less precise, to use the single emotion term than to list, as I have in these examples, the various information domains that term encompasses. But remember, as my examples show, I know very different sets of information for *anger* than for *disgust.*

I expect that most people who use emotion words use them in this short-hand fashion, but we do not know if people in all cultures do so. If we were to show people a videotape of an expression and ask them to tell us about the person, I expect they would use these emotion words more often than they would describe an antecedent event or what the person is about to do next, or any of the other information domains I have listed. Perhaps the tendency to use emotion terms (*anger, fear,* etc.) rather than antecedent events, sensations, consequent acts, is related to education, with more educated people more likely to use the emotion terms. Also, in research it is easier to write a single word than many words, and this may bias people to use them.

When an expression is seen out of context, alone without the usual accompaniments of speech, body movement, posture, and knowledge of what is transpiring, the expression does convey information, but not as much information as when it is seen in context. When the observer has no ongoing relationship with the person who shows the expression, no past experience, no current knowledge or intended future, then the information provided by the expression cannot be as precise. The reader cannot know, for example, what is revolting the man in Figure 2, not even whether it is someone's social action or a taste of food he just had.

In actual life we never see a facial expression of emotion totally out of social context, unless we glance at a magazine. Even when we see an expression on the face of a stranger who walks by on the street, we have contextual information—the person's dress, gait, what we know about the types of people who at that time of day are in that location, and so on. To remove an expression from its social context and then ask us what it means is to put us into a unique situation, deprived of all the other sources of information that we use to amplify, make more precise, and confirm the information we get from an emotional expression. Yet, standing alone, facial expressions of emotion do have meaning and provide information about each of the domains I listed. Whether the information is accurate or not is a different matter. My research (Ekman, 1985) has shown that most people can quite successfully lie with their facial expressions, but careful measurement can usually unmask such attempts.

Before moving on let me describe the specific situations in which the expressions shown in Figures 1 and 2 occurred. I did not know that in this culture a single man endangers himself and a single woman by paying obvious attention to her in public. I did just that and photographed the reaction she showed in Figure 1. No one then knew what a camera was. I moved away, and others who saw what happened probably excused my behavior, knowing I was a well-meaning but uncivilized person. The man in Figure 2 was watching me eat some of the canned food I had brought with me. His reaction to my food was similar to my reaction to some of the food he would often eat.

# WHAT SHOULD WE CALL THESE EXPRESSIONS?

Now let us consider whether we should call these expressions or communications. In an article titled, "Was the 'Expression of the Emotions' a misleading phrase?", the ethologist Robert Hinde said, "The phrase carries the implication that the behavior Darwin studied involved simply the expression of an internal state" (1985b, p. 985). Margaret Mead described her very similar dissatisfaction with the term *expression* in the introduction she wrote to a now out of print edition of Darwin's expression book: "When we substitute the word *communication* for Darwin's word *expression*, each of his questions, asked with such vigor and acumen . . . can be asked anew" (1955, p. vi). I also was uncomfortable with this term. In my first book *Emotion in the Human Face* (co-authored with Friesen and Ellsworth), I wrote, "I have avoided the phrase *facial expressions* because it implies that some inner state is being manifested or shown externally" (1972, p. 3).

There seems little doubt that what we were all objecting to —the idea that expressions make manifest an internal state—is precisely what Darwin meant by using that term in his book *The Expression of Emotion in Man and Animals.* He wrote about "expressions of our feelings by certain movements" (1872/1955, p. 14), that actions that "regularly accompany a state of mind are at once recognized as expressive" (p. 349). Facial movements, he said, "reveal the state of mind" (p. 356).

I have come to think that there is nothing wrong per se with the word *expression*, for these facial movements are outward manifestations of changes that have occurred and are occurring internally in the brain. Information about some antecedent event has been processed and evaluated, setting off the cascade of events that make up emotion: Memories are being retrieved, expectations formed, plans made, actions may be about to occur, and sensations may be felt. All of this does happen internally, in the brain. Expression is part of those changes and a sign that those changes are happening.

Although some have argued that the use of the term *expression* might imply that the focus is only on internal states, ignoring the impact of expressions on others who perceive them, that is not necessarily so. Facial expressions do communicate information, but we have to be careful, because the word *communication* may seem to imply that expressions are made intentionally to send a message. Although people can make facial movements deliberately to send a message, facial expressions of emotion are not so made. Darwin noted that emotional expressions are involuntary but he noted that "such movements may be voluntarily and consciously employed as a means of communication. Even infants, if carefully attended to, find out at a very early age that their screaming brings relief, and they soon voluntarily practice it" (1872/1955, p. 355). Darwin was not comfortable with making this distinction, however. A page later he wrote, "In the course of the foregoing remarks and throughout this volume, I have often felt much difficulty about the proper application of the terms, will, consciousness and intention" (p. 356).

Although Darwin correctly recognized the importance of distinguishing facial movements made deliberately to communicate from involuntary emotional expressions, it is understandable that he found this distinction difficult. So too do most ethologists today. Most of those who currently study animal communication simply do not consider whether the animals make a signal intentionally to communicate or not. No doubt it is often difficult to know which is which when dealing with animals that you cannot ask and that do not speak when they also show expressions.

## VOLUNTARY VERSUS INVOLUNTARY

Just because it is difficult does not mean we should not consider it. Such thinking would return us to the worst days of behaviorism when many psychologists would not consider that people think because there was no way to observe thoughts directly! The question of what generates emotional expressions—are they intentionally made to send a message or unintentional signs of what is happening?—is fundamental to our understanding of expression and of emotion. Although it has become fashionable (Hinde, 1985a; Zivin, 1985) to avoid dichotomies such as voluntary–involuntary, or intentional–unintentional, nature may not avoid them. Clearly there are actions that are totally involuntary, such as the startle reflex, and actions that are totally voluntary, such as my decision to use the word *decision* in writing this sentence.

I propose that all facial expressions of emotion are involuntary; they are never voluntarily or deliberately made. Note, I say all *facial expression of emotion*, not all facial movements; facial expressions of emotion are a subset of facial movements, as I will explain shortly.

When an emotion occurs, impulses are always sent to the facial muscles. There is no choice about that. We can choose to try to interfere with the appearance of that expression, we may be able to interrupt the action of the facial muscles or dampen them so that nothing is visible, but we cannot choose to prevent the impulses from being sent to the facial nerve. We can also choose to make a set of facial movements that resemble a facial expression of emotion, but it will differ detectably from an emotional expression.

My claim that all facial expressions of emotion are involuntary is controversial. Many would argue that they are voluntary or that it does not matter if they are voluntary or involuntary, intentionally made to communicate or not. Perhaps it is because part of my own research focuses on lies (Ekman, 1985/1992) that I find it so important to make this distinction. Sometimes the liar's emotional expressions betray the lie, despite the liar's intention to mislead. That is because that expression is involuntary. And lies sometimes succeed because the liar *has* managed to fabricate something that closely resembles an emotional expression and it is believed. The liar has managed voluntarily to produce something that looks as if it is an involuntary expression.

It is not just when dealing with humans and more specifically with their lies that it is necessary to consider whether expressions are involuntary or not. A central argument today about the nature of signaling among all animals is whether their signals are reliable or serve to manipulate and exploit those who see them.

## FOUR MISTAKEN BELIEFS ABOUT FACIAL EXPRESSIONS

There are four reasons why so many of those who study human and animal communication believe it is *not* important to consider intentionality and the issue of whether expressions are involuntary. It is a result, I think, of four mistaken beliefs, which I will explain: (a) if I get a message someone must have intentionally sent it; (b) if expression is ever absent when emotion is present then expression must be deliberate; (c) if some facial movements are voluntary, and all facial expressions are facial movements, then facial expressions of emotion must be voluntary; and (d) everything that happens, including expressions, when people converse is done to send messages.

### Mistake 1

We are informed by many actions a person performs that are not intended to send a message to us. Suppose we see someone fall over dead from a heart attack. The last look on that person's face as they feel acute pain, the death rattle, the slump to the ground—these ghastly actions and sounds provide us with very important messages. We are informed by them, but that does not mean the person made that expression, slumped to the ground, and groaned to send us the message "I am dead." These signs are not made to send a message to us, even though we get the message.

Consider a less extreme example. If someone burps, we are informed about their gastrointestinal activity, and perhaps also about their manners. In Western cultures "polite" adults do not burp to send a message "my stomach is upset" or "I ate too fast" or "I really enjoyed that morsel." That does not mean that burping cannot be so performed. Children often burp intentionally, but that does not mean it is *always* done intentionally. And in some cultures burps are required comments on how satisfactory the meal was. Incidentally, I expect that a student of burps would be able to detect the difference between those that are performed to send a message and those that escape the person's attempt to inhibit them.

Facial expressions of emotion are highly *informative*, but they are not intended by the person making them to be so. They may have been shaped and preserved by evolution because they are informative, but that refers to their origin, not to how and why they occur in our current lives. Other types of facial movements that I will describe shortly are not simply informative; they are intended by the expresser to communicate a message to the receiver.

## Mistake 2

Having dismissed then the first false belief—if I get a message someone must have intentionally sent it—let us consider the next one: If expression is ever absent when emotion is present then expression must be deliberate. That logic presumes that facial expressions of emotion are either like reflexes or like words. They are neither. If facial expressions of emotion were reflexes, such as the startle, it would be nearly impossible to interfere with them and totally suppress their appearance. That is not so for facial expressions of emotion. It is possible for most people to inhibit, through deliberate choice of the moment or overlearned habit, their involuntary facial expressions of emotion. Not always, not everyone, but sometimes. It is well known that the facial nucleus, the staging point for impulses that travel to the muscles to produce the contractions that we see as a visible change in facial appearance, receives impulses from many different parts of the brain.

We all know that we can voluntarily make many (but not all) facial movements. My own research (Ekman, Roper, & Hager, 1980) identified which are the easiest and hardest to make and how early in life it is possible to voluntarily perform them. We also know that we can, to some extent, inhibit facial expressions of emotion; but there is no parallel research that documents just how well this can be done for every emotional expression, at varying levels of intensity, at different ages. Although my work on this (Ekman, O'Sullivan, Friesen, & Scherer, 1991) is much more limited we did find that individuals differ in their ability to inhibit involuntary facial movement.

The fact that an emotional expression can be inhibited does not mean that when an expression does occur, when it is not inhibited, it is made deliberately to send a message. For most people inhibition is not easy when an emotion begins abruptly and is strong. That is because the involuntary impulses to make the expression travel quickly to the facial nucleus to produce large contractions of the muscles when an emotion is intense. Some people will be able, some of the time, to block or dampen those impulses. If measurements were made, I believe evidence would be found of the impulses to make the expression and the impulses that attempt to squelch it.

Individuals differ not only in how easily they can inhibit expressions, but also in whether they typically do so or not. Thus we know that some people are "poker faced" and others nearly always reveal exactly how they feel even when they do not want to. There are not only these individual differences, but cultural groups differ also in when they call for the management of facial expressions. It is worth digressing a bit to explain these cultural differences in the management of expression, because the failure to recognize these differences has led to much miscommunication between members of different cultures. For example, Americans act more friendly than they really are; Japanese smile even when they disagree or do not like what is occurring; and so forth.

Ekman and Friesen (1969) coined the phrase *display rules* to designate attempts to manage involuntary expressions of emotion that include attenuating, amplifying, inhibiting, or covering the involuntary expression with the sign of another emotion. Display rules specify not only what type of management is required, but when, in what social situation. For example, when the winner is announced in a beauty contest and the final contestants stand on stage, all those who find out that they have lost follow the display rule of inhibiting any sign of disappointment or anger. Instead they mask those feelings with a smiling sign of happiness about the winner's success. The only one who cries when the announcement is made is the winner. She is the only one who no longer has to follow the display rule that the loser does not cry. The distress she was anticipating if she lost emerges.

Display rules are learned, should vary across cultures, and may differ among distinct social groups within a culture. Our study of display rules (Ekman, 1972) found that Japanese more than Americans attempted to conceal negative emotional expressions in the presence of an authority figure, using a masking smile. In this very same study we found no difference in the facial expressions of Japanese and Americans when they watched unpleasant and pleasant films when they were alone. We had predicted that when we brought a scientist into the room to watch the films with them, they would show different facial activity. In response to a respected person, Japanese would follow the display rule to mask negative emotion with a polite smile. No one has yet delineated all of the display rules within any culture, although there has been considerable research about how and when young children learn display rules (Saarni, 1979). It is worth noting two studies in progress that further support this logic regarding display rules. Kupperbusch (1996) repeated part of our Japanese–American display rule study, but whereas we had studied males in both cultures, she is studying just females in the United States. When watching unpleasant films, there was a decrease in their negative facial expressions when an authority figure was present. Tsai (1996) in her doctoral dissertation examined couples in which both members were Chinese–American and couples in which both were Caucasian–American, when they attempted to resolve a conflict. Only the Chinese–American couples showed less autonomic nervous system activity when an authority figure was present.

A display rule may be such an overlearned habit that it operates automatically without the person considering what to do or even being aware of managing the expression. Or the display rule may have been performed so rarely that it is not an automatic habit but an ideal to follow. In the latter case the person will be more likely to be aware of trying to manage the expression when it operates and could readily choose not to do so.

It is not certain how often people in any culture show facial expressions that are not managed by display rules. I expect that some display rules are so well established that some people may follow them even when they are alone. And some people when alone may imagine the reactions of others, and then follow the appropriate display rule, as if the others were present. And finally, there may be display rules that specify the management of expression not just with others but when alone.

The fact that expressions may often be managed by display rules, and that sometimes this management is voluntary, does not mean that the facial expressions of emotion that are being managed are also voluntary. If they were voluntary there would be no need to manage them. It is precisely because facial expressions of emotion are involuntary that we learn to manage these expressions, sometimes succeeding in totally inhibiting their visible appearance. The capability to inhibit an expression of emotion or modify it does not contradict my claim that the impulse for the expression is itself involuntary.

### Mistake 3

We have now dealt with two of the mistaken beliefs about facial expressions of emotion that have led many scientists to ignore the question of whether signals are intended to send a message and whether emotional expressions in particular are involuntary or voluntary. First, we disposed of the belief that if you get a message someone must have intentionally sent it. We can be highly informed by actions that were not made for the purpose of informing us. Then we examined the idea that if an expression is ever absent when emotion is present, then expression must be deliberate. The fact that we can sometimes choose to inhibit or otherwise manage our emotional expressions does not mean that the emotional expressions are also voluntary actions that we can choose to make or not. Now let us consider the third mistaken belief: If some facial movements are voluntary, then emotional expressions must be voluntary.

There is no question that there are many voluntary facial movements, and shortly I will describe some of them. But that does not mean that facial expressions of emotion are also voluntary. The facial muscles are not dedicated just to the display of emotional expressions, they are deployed for many different kinds of actions. It is a mistake to not recognize that the face is a multisignal system—to not grasp that there are a number of voluntary, intentional facial signals, in addition to the involuntary emotional expressions. The tricky part is that some of these voluntary facial movements are intended to resemble an emotional expression.

Facial movements occur to accomplish various activities such as kissing, eating, speaking, spitting, and so forth. Facial movements may also be deployed to symbolically communicate in the same way that hand gestures can send a message. The wink is such an example. These facial movements—the symbolic gestures or what Friesen and I have called *emblems* (Ekman & Friesen, 1969) are as deliberate as the choice of a word and as easy to *not* make as it is to choose not to speak or not say a particular word.

Another related set of facial movements is what I have called *conversational signals* (Ekman, 1979). Here a facial movement is used much as the hands can be to illustrate speech as it is spoken. Facial movements, typically the eyebrows, accent, underline, or provide syntax for the speech as it is spoken. Although these conversational signals may be deliberately made, they often occur involuntarily, just as a momentary increase in the loudness of the voice to emphasize a word, or rising intonation contour at the end of a sentence to mark a question, occurs without deliberate choice.

The fact that these conversational signals are usually involuntary may seem confusing, for so are facial expressions of emotion. But conversational signals and facial expressions of emotion differ in three ways. Most important, the conversational signals are part of the structure of the conversation, part of the flow of talk, and governed by the rules that govern the production of speech. Although facial expressions of emotion often occur during conversation, their location in the speech flow is related not to the structure of talk but to the semantics, revealing an emotional reaction to what is being said or not being said.

The second way to distinguish conversational signals from facial expressions of emotion is by the scope of the facial movements deployed. Conversational signals are almost without exception limited to a single facial movement in one region of the face—most often an eyebrow raise or lower, sometimes a raised upper eyelid or tightened lower eyelid, or pressed lips. The facial expressions of emotion usually involve activity across the face, although attempts to manage an expression may result in a more limited display. A third difference is that conversational signals typically utilize easy-to-make facial movements, whereas some of the movements involved in facial expressions of emotion are hard to perform deliberately.

There are two other types of facial movement that are most often confused with facial expressions of emotion. *False expressions* are intended to be so confused, resembling as closely as is possible the expression they resemble. The person who makes a false expression intends to create the impression in the perceiver that an emotion is actually being felt when it is not. My research, and the research of many other investigators, has found it possible to distinguish false from true expressions of enjoyment (Ekman, 1992a). I believe it would be possible also to distinguish false from emotional expressions for the other emotions. The signs that distinguish facial expressions of enjoyment from false facial expressions of enjoyment are subtle. They are detectable by careful, precise measurement. They can be spotted as they occur by those who know what to look for, but most people miss those signs and are misled by false expressions (Ekman, Friesen, & O'Sullivan, 1988).

The other type of facial movement that resembles a facial expression of emotion is intended not to be confused with it. These are what I have called *referential expressions* (Ekman, 1979). These typically occur during conversation, when the speaker refers to an emotion not being felt now but that was felt in the past or might be felt in the future. Take, for example, a person who says he had been afraid of what he would learn from a biopsy report and was so relieved when it turned out to be negative. When the word *afraid* is said, the person stretches back his lips horizontally, referring facially to fear.

Such referential expressions are transformations of emotional expressions, typically changing the time course and the scope of the expression. In my example, just the mouth movement not the changes in the eye and brow area is used to refer to fear not felt now, and it would be likely to be made very quickly, much more quickly then the actual expression of emotion would be. Time is often stretched out in mock referential expressions, in which the reference is not just to emotion not felt now but adds a humorous note as well to a reference to not feeling the emotion.

An example is holding a smile much too long on the face to state that enjoyment was not felt.

Referential expressions must differ from the true emotional expression for two reasons. If they resemble the actual expression of emotion the perceiver might be confused and think the expresser feels that emotion now. And if the full expressions were to be made, there is a possibility that the person will begin to reexperience the emotion. My research (Ekman, 1992a) has shown that assembling on one's face all of the movements found universally for an emotional expression often produces distinctive changes in both the autonomic nervous system and the central nervous system, changes that occur when the emotion is brought about by more usual means.

Referential expressions may be either voluntary, chosen deliberately at the moment with awareness of the choice, or involuntary, occurring by habit, or much like the words spoken, emitted without awareness of the processes by which the words are chosen. In this way they differ also from facial expressions of emotion, which I propose can never be voluntary. They also differ from facial expressions of emotion, as I described, in terms of the scope of facial movement, which is more limited, and the duration, which is shorter or longer than the usual expression of emotion.

The psychologist–psychoanalyst Rainer Krause (1995, personal communication) in response to a lecture I gave about these distinctions suggested another type of facial movements that resemble but are not emotional expressions, which he has often observed in psychotherapy sessions. The patient in giving an account of another person's actions and emotions enacts that person's emotions. These *emotional role-playing* actions may be referential, referring to the emotions the other person was manifesting. Or, the person who is giving the account may actually not simply put on a facade, but in his or her actions may "become" for a few moments that other person. When that happens I expect the person would not show referential expressions but actual emotional expressions. The person is then not talking about the other person's emotions, but actually experiencing the other person's emotions as they depict that person.

## Mistake 4

The last mistaken belief that may have led to the failure to recognize the involuntary nature of facial expressions of emotion is based on the belief that because expressions often occur when people talk to each other they must simply be another kind of signaling language. Because people choose to converse, and at least some of what they say is deliberately chosen, the logic of this mistaken belief presumes that emotional expressions must also be chosen to send a message to the receiver. The mistake is not to recognize that emotional expressions are involuntary reactions to what is transpiring in the conversation.

The most extreme version of this mistaken view was forwarded by Kraut and Johnston (1979) and later resurrected by Fridlund (1991). Both sets of research noted that some facial expressions of emotion occur more often when people are with others than when they are alone or not being observed by another person. Inexplicably they then argued that these emotional expressions cannot be emotional, for if they were they would occur only when people are alone, not just when they are with others. These expressions do not have anything to do with emotions, these psychologists maintain, they instead should be considered as signals of what the person is going to do next.

There are two fatal flaws in such reasoning. First, the investigators fail to recognize that some emotional expressions do occur when people are alone. And display rules that prohibit the expression of some emotions in some social contexts may result in some emotional expressions being shown more often when alone than with another person. Even more serious is their failure to understand what emotion is about, a failure to understand when emotions occur and what they accomplish.

Emotional expressions will often occur during interaction with another person, for our emotions are most often aroused by the actions of others. I believe

> the primary function of emotion is to mobilize the organism to deal quickly with important interpersonal encounters, prepared to do so

> in part, at least, by what types of activity have been adaptive in the past. The past refers in part to what has been adaptive in the past history of our species, and the past refers also to what has been adaptive in our own life history. (Ekman, 1992b)

Given such a view of emotion, there is every reason to expect conversations or more broadly social interactions will be the chief occasion when emotions are aroused and emotional expressions will be manifest. Of course we can and do have emotions when we are neither in the presence of others nor imagining that we are. Emotions occur, for example, in response to nature (thunder, a sunset, a tornado), to other animals (a dog's attack or attachment behavior), to the loss of physical support, auto-erotic activity, and so forth.

Facial expressions of emotion not only occur in response to the actions of others, but they commonly occur in response to what others say or while we are saying something to others. They are not governed, however, by the process of speech itself, by syntax rules for example, but as I noted earlier they occur in response to the meaning of what is said. The contrast between language and emotional expressions is an important one.

Johnson-Laird (1990), introducing a book on communication, wrote,

> All human groups speak a language, and all human languages have a grammar and a lexicon. The lexicon always has words for dealing with space, time and number, words to represent the true and false, and words for communicating logical relations . . . the power of language derives from three principal factors: First the lexicon provides speakers with a large repertoire of individual symbols (words). Second, the grammar enables these symbols to be combined into an unlimited number of distinct symbolic messages (sentences). Third, these messages are not under the immediate control of the local environment. They can be intentionally used to refer to other states of affairs including those that are remote, hypothetical, or imaginary. (pp. 6–7)

In a similar vein George Gaylord Simpson wrote in 1967

> Language is . . . the most diagnostic trait of man; all normal men have language; no other now living organisms do. . . . In any animal societies . . . there must be some kind of communication in the very broadest sense. One animal must receive some kind of information about another animal. That information may be conveyed by specific signals. . . . They reflect the individual's physical, or more frequently, emotional state. They do not, as true language does, name discuss, abstract or symbolize. They are . . . emotion signals not discourse. (p. 32)

Facial expressions of emotion unlike language cannot be performed voluntarily. Expressions of emotion have a much more limited set of referents than language. There is no syntax or grammar, and they are compelled in a sense that speech is not.

## RARE OR FREQUENT OCCURRENCE

The last matter to consider, although briefly, is whether or not the universal facial expressions of emotion are common in social life or rarely seen. It has become fashionable of late to argue that even if there are universal expressions, they are not seen often (Cornelius, 1995; Russell, 1995). It is foolish to generalize about social life as if it is made of one cloth. Facial expressions of emotion are frequently seen in highly emotional situations, such as when disturbed couples attempt to resolve conflicts (Gottman, J., personal communication, 1995). Of course in some highly charged emotional situations, people will be highly motivated to conceal their emotions, and some may succeed. And some people will always attempt to conceal their emotions, in any situation. Emotional expressions are infrequent when emotions are not experienced. Unfortunately most of the experiments psychologists have designed to study emotion have been quite arid, not likely to elicit robust emotional reactions, with rarely any verification that emotion has occurred other than self reports that are vulnerable to demand characteristics. We should not draw any conclusions about the absence of emotional expressions in such studies, other than about the inadequacy of the experimenter's ingenuity.

## CONCLUSION

I have suggested that seven different classes of information may be conveyed by a facial expression of emotion: antecedents; thoughts; internal state; a metaphor; what the expresser is likely to do next; what the expresser wants the perceiver to do; or an emotion word. I have also argued that facial expressions of emotion are involuntary, although we can voluntarily try to interfere or disguise these expressions. Emotional expressions do communicate information to conspecifics, and that is important in understanding their evolution, they are not deliberately made in order to communicate. I have challenged the views of those who say we should not call these *expressions* but *communicative signals,* those who argue that they are unrelated to internal state. Instead I have shown these are two sides of the same coin, and that the failure to recognize this is based on four misunderstandings about the nature of expression.

## REFERENCES

Cornelius, R. R. (1995). *The science of emotion: Research and tradition in the psychology of emotions.* Upper Saddle River, NJ: Prentice Hall.

Darwin, C. (1955). *The expression of the emotions in man and animals.* New York: Philosophical Library. (Originally published 1872)

Ekman, P. (1972). Universals and cultural differences in facial expressions of emotion. In J. Cole (Ed.), *Nebraska symposium on motivation, 1971* (pp. 207–283). Lincoln: University of Nebraska Press.

Ekman, P. (1973). Cross-cultural studies of facial expressions. In P. Ekman (Ed.), *Darwin and facial expressions: A century of research in review* (pp. 169–222). New York: Academic Press.

Ekman, P. (1979). About brows: Emotional and conversational signals. In M. von Cranach, K. Foppa, W. Lepenies, & D. Ploog, (Eds.), *Human ethology* (pp. 169–248). Cambridge: Cambridge University Press.

Ekman, P. (1985). *Telling lies: Clues to deceit in the marketplace, marriage, and politics.* New York: W. W. Norton. Second edition, 1992.

Ekman, P. (1992a). Facial expression of emotion: New findings, new questions. *Psychological Science, 3,* 34–38.

Ekman, P. (1992b). An argument for basic emotions. *Cognition and Emotion, 6,* 169–200.

Ekman, P., & Friesen, W. V. (1969). The repertoire of nonverbal behavior: Categories, origins, usage, and coding. *Semiotica, 1,* 49–98.

Ekman, P., Friesen, W. V., & Ellsworth, P. (1972). *Emotion in the human face: Guidelines for research and an integration of findings.* New York: Pergamon Press.

Ekman, P., Friesen, W. V., & O'Sullivan, M. (1988). Smiles when lying. *Journal of Personality and Social Psychology, 54,* 414–420.

Ekman, P., O'Sullivan, M., Friesen, W. V., & Scherer, K. R. (1991). Face, voice and body in detecting deception. *Journal of Nonverbal Behavior, 15,* 125–135.

Ekman, P., Roper, G., & Hager, J. C. (1980). Deliberate facial movement. *Child Development, 51,* 886–891.

Fridlund, A. J. (1991). Sociality of solitary smiling: Potentiation by a implicit audience. *Journal of Personality and Social Psychology, 60,* 229–240.

Hinde, R. A. (1985a). Expression and negotiation. In G. Zivin (Ed.), *The development of expressive behavior: Biology–environment interactions* (pp. 103–116). Orlando, FL: Academic Press.

Hinde, R. A. (1985b). Was "the expression of the emotions" a misleading phrase? *Animal behavior, 33,* 985–992.

Johnson-Laird, P. N. (1990). Introduction: What is communication. In D. H. Mellor (Ed.), *Ways of communicating* (pp. 1–13). Cambridge: Cambridge University Press.

Kraut, R. E., & Johnston, R. E. (1979). Social and emotional messages of smiling: An ethological approach. *Journal of Personality and Social Psychology, 37,* 1539–1553.

Kupperbusch, C. (1996). *Cultural difference and display rules in nonverbal expression of emotion.* Master's Thesis in progress, San Francisco State University.

Mead, M. (1955). Preface. In C. Darwin, *The expression of the emotions in man and animals* (pp. vi). New York: Philosophical Library.

Rosenberg, E. L., & Ekman, P. (1995). Conceptual and methodological issues in the judgment of facial expression of emotion. *Motivation and Emotion, 19,* 111–138.

Russell, J. A. (1995). Facial expressions of emotion: What lies beyond minimal universality? *Psychological Bulletin, 118*, 379–391.

Saarni, C. (1979). Children's understanding of display rules for expressive behavior. *Developmental Psychology, 15*, 424–329.

Simpson, G. G. (1967). *The meaning of evolution* (Rev. edition). New Haven, CT: Yale University Press.

Smith, W. J. (1985). Consistency and change in communication. In G. Zivin (Ed.), *The development of expressive behavior: Biology-environment interactions* (pp. 51–76). Orlando, FL: Academic Press.

Tsai, J. L. (1996). *Cultural and contextual influences on the emotional responding of Chinese American and European American couples during conflict.* Doctoral dissertation, University of California, Berkeley.

Zivin, G. (1985). Separating the issues in the study of expressive development: A framing chapter. In G. Zivin (Ed.), *The development of expressive behavior: Biology–environment interactions* (pp. 3–26). Orlando, FL: Academic Press.

13

# Mother–Infant Interaction in Cross-Cultural Perspective

Robert A. LeVine

Daniel Freedman's interest in behavioral differences among human populations brought him into a productive argument with anthropologists of child development, including me: Like us, he assumed diversity at the population level rather than uniformity of behavioral development in the human species. However, he also challenged our automatic environmentalist interpretation of that diversity, forcing us to think about how to prove it, rather than presume it. Dr. Freedman's proposal to make infancy the arena for this debate played an important role in stimulating the growth of cross-cultural research on infancy in the early 1970s. By examining the infant's first postpartum interactions with its environment and continuing observations during the first year and beyond, it became possible to describe the emergence of social behavior patterns with a realistic knowledge of their starting points, as well as the environmental conditions that facilitated them. This chapter emphasizes the impact of the cultural environment on mother–infant interaction, but it owes to Dr. Freedman its focus on the infant's experience of the social world.

I begin by reviewing some of the basic tenets of cross-cultural research with infants. Then, I explore the cultural contexts of parental behavior and early environments among the Gusii infants and their families in Kenya and among middle-class American mothers and their infants in suburban Boston. Cultural goals and precocity in child development are compared among study results from Japanese, German, Gusii, and American populations. Finally, I present an agenda for future research.

Dr. Freedman and I were faculty colleagues in Human Development for his first 10 years at the University of Chicago, and for much of that time we had adjacent offices. I was the only anthropologist in Human Development (until Rick Shweder arrived in 1973) and Dr. Freedman was the only biologically oriented psychologist. We both taught most of the doctoral students who came through HD, and there were two students—Jerry Barkow and Bob Marvin—who worked closely with both of us. It was through Dr. Freedman that I first met Mary Ainsworth and Berry Brazelton during the late 1960s.

I learned a great deal from Dr. Freedman in those days; he was involved with such "oddities" as infant studies and human ethology, which we now recognize as frontiers of the human sciences. I had to learn about these oddities in order to argue with him and to keep up with our students like Jerry and Bob. Dr. Freedman was always good to argue with, and in fact it was his public debate with Bill Caudill over infant behavior in Japan and the United States (Caudill & Frost, 1972) that convinced me to undertake infant research in Africa. Caudill and Weinstein (1969) had shown, in one of the earliest cross-cultural studies using naturalistic observations of infant behavior, that Japanese babies at 3 to 4 months were less active than a comparison group of American middle-class babies, and they had interpreted it in terms of culturally influenced maternal behavior. Dr. Freedman challenged them by proposing the alternative possibility that Japanese infants were temperamentally less active at birth, and Caudill accepted the challenge and conducted comparable observations of California infants who were of entirely Japanese ancestry but had American-born mothers. They turned out to be more similar to the Americans than to the Japanese of the original comparison, favoring an explanation based on cultural environment rather than heredity. Because the studies were crude and did not involve neonatal assessment, however, they were hardly

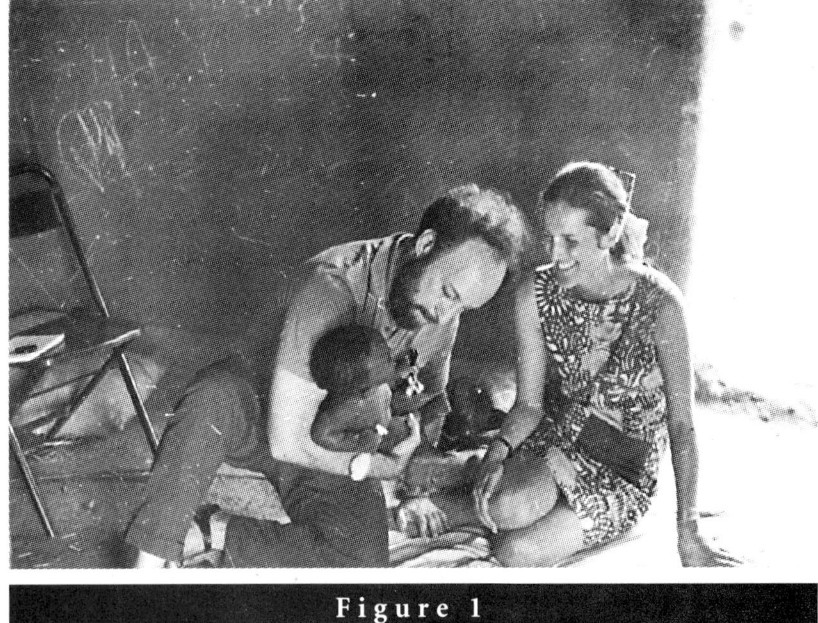

**Figure 1**

Daniel Freedman and Sarah LeVine with a Hausa baby in Zaria. Used by permission of author.

conclusive, and it was apparent not only that more research was needed on this issue but also that the investigation of culture and human development should begin at birth. Thus when I initiated a program of child development research in northwestern Nigeria in 1969, I persuaded Dr. Freedman to visit and advise us on neonatal assessment and attachment observations. Figure 1 shows Dr. Freedman with my wife and collaborator Sarah LeVine and a Hausa baby in Zaria.

## INFANT CARE PRACTICES AMONG HUMANS

We know much more about human infant care now than we did 25 years ago. I shall state some basic points on which I believe Dr. Freedman (Freedman & Gorman, 1993) and I, as well as other cross-cultural researchers, agree.

1. There is great diversity in infant care practices across human populations. The population-level comparison of distributions of parental behavior and developmental patterns, and their relationships with environmental parameters (as in population genetics, epidemiology, and demography), must form part of a biocultural perspective on parental care and offspring development in the human species.
2. The cultural variations in infant care practices are not simply reducible to an evaluative dimension of healthy versus pathological or adaptive versus maladaptive but indicate alternative normal pathways for parental behavior and the behavioral development of young children.
3. Social and behavioral conditions that vary at the population level and affect child care include maternal fertility and sibship size, the allocation of child care among members of the domestic group (e.g., the involvement of older siblings and fathers), the time–energy budgets of mothers and their forms and frequencies of interaction with offspring at different ages, and the child's socially significant behavior (e.g., crying, proximity-seeking, compliance, and speech) as it emerges over the first 2 years of a child's life.
4. Parental behavior in a particular population is organized by the culturally formulated goals for child development that parents share and that guide their behavior toward their offspring. These include nonbehavioral goals such as survival and health as well as behavioral goals related to the moral values and institutionalized careers of their culture. Parental care practices and the specific lines of offspring development they promote are goal corrected—in other words, responsive to the perception that a child's development is moving toward or away from the culturally formulated goals.

These points may seem obvious to some, but they run counter to the universalist positions concerning mother–infant relationships articulated by Trevarthen (1988), Papousek and Papousek (1987), and Bowlby (1969, 1988). Trevarthen (1988) has insisted on the universality of "innate intersubjectivity" between mother and infant, although his own videotaped data show significant contrasts between Yoruba and Scottish mothers in their responsiveness to infants. Papousek and Papousek (1987) offered the concept of "intuitive parenting," patterns of parental response to infants that require no learning and are common to all humans. Bowlby (1969, 1988) and Ainsworth (e.g., Ainsworth, Blehar, Waters, & Wall, 1978) take account of variability in the mother–infant relationship but give it a clinical flavor with their concepts of sensitive versus insensitive maternal care and secure versus insecure attachment. They posit a relatively narrow range for adaptive patterns of care and attachment, outside of which the child may be at risk for psychopathology. Despite Ainsworth's (1967, 1977) early observations in Uganda, there is no place in the Bowlby–Ainsworth model for variability across populations in cultural standards of "normal," "adaptive," or "optimal" attachment relationships.[1] The assumption is that the criteria for normal development were set through natural selection millions of years ago and should not vary widely at the population level within the human species. In a similar way, Bowlby conceptualized the child's proximity-seeking as "goal-corrected" according to a genetically transmitted template but did not perceive that parental practices are goal-corrected in accordance with a culturally formulated agenda. These universalist positions are accepted by many psychologists as representing the biological reality of human development.

There is no denying that parental care and offspring development in humans are heavily influenced by our mammalian heritage, our primate legacy, our species-typical systems of reproduction and ontogeny, the gene frequencies in our breeding populations, our individual genetic constitutions, and environmental factors varying across and within populations. To treat universalist and relativist accounts of the mother–infant relationship as if they were necessarily opposed jeopardizes credibility and stands against the sophisticated position Freedman and Gorman articulated in their 1993 paper. The glass is both half full and half empty, and by emphasizing one truth at the expense of the other we can create a false and fruitless debate (see Blurton Jones, 1972).

The problem confronted in this chapter is that developmental psychol-

[1] A 1995 interview with Mary D. S. Ainsworth, conducted by Robert S. Marvin, explores her recent views on attachment theory with reference to universality and cross-cultural differences, assessment methods, individual differences, and other issues (*see* Ainsworth & Marvin, 1995).—Eds.

ogists usually leave out the population-level perspective and evidence of cross-cultural variations in their consideration of human parental care and offspring development. The following sections provide an illustration of what it might mean to take cross-cultural evidence seriously in a science of early child development.

## THE CULTURAL SHAPE OF PARENTAL BEHAVIOR AND EARLY ENVIRONMENTS

My research group has been doing field work among the Gusii people, agropastoralists of southwestern Kenya, since 1955 (LeVine & LeVine, 1966), initially as part of the Six Cultures Study of Socialization (Whiting, 1963; Whiting & Edwards, 1988; Whiting & Whiting, 1975). During 1974 to 1976, we assembled an interdisciplinary team of investigators to conduct a 17-month longitudinal study of 28 Gusii infants and their families in one area, and then collected comparable data on mother–infant interaction, at home and in the laboratory, among several samples of about 20 middle-class American mothers in suburban Boston, Massachusetts (LeVine et al., 1994). (We shall refer to these samples as if they were representative of the Gusii and American middle-class populations, noting here the provisional character of such a claim.) The conditions of parenthood and infant care among the Gusii that contrast with those of Boston include domestically organized agricultural production, high fertility (an average of ten children per married woman), a tradition of polygynous marriage, and a reliance on children (often older siblings) to take care of infants while mothers work in the fields. Gusii infants are breast-fed for an average of 16 months, sleep with their mothers at night, and are carried on the backs of their mothers and child caregivers in the daytime. But Gusii infant care as a system can only be understood in terms of the cultural model followed by mothers who shape the proximal environments of their offspring over the first 2 years of life.

A cultural model, meaning an ethnographic reconstruction of the premises on which the parents of a given population base their child care practices, can be seen as having three parts: a moral direction, a pragmatic

**Table 1**

**Maternal Attention in Early Child Care: Quantity and Quality**

| | Gusii: Pediatric model | American: Pedagogical model |
|---|---|---|
| Goal | Protection | Active engagement, social exchange |
| Means | Soothing | Simulation, protoconversation |
| Temporal distribution over first 30 months | Decreasing | Increasing |
| Cultural script for selective responsiveness | Respond to distress | Respond to babble |
| | Modulate excitement | Elicit excitement |
| | Commands | Questions, praise |

NOTE: From *Child care and culture: Lessons from Africa* (p. 249), by R. A. LeVine, S. Dixon, S. LeVine, A. Richman, P. H. Leiderman, C. H. Keefer, & T. B. Brazelton, 1994, New York: Cambridge University Press. Copyright 1994 by Cambridge University Press. Reprinted with permission.

design, and a set of conventional scripts for action. The moral direction refers to their normative assumptions about what is best for an infant and what the goals are to which mothers and other caregivers should be devoted. The pragmatic design means their general (adaptive) strategy for attaining these goals, specific behavioral devices used, and the schedule for their deployment over infancy and early childhood. The conventional scripts for action are socially expected sequences of caregiving behavior in specific situations, such as responding to the infant's states and communicative signals, that are considered not only normal but natural and necessary.

The differences between Gusii and American White middle-class mothers in the kinds and amount of attention they give their infants over the first 30 months of life are summarized schematically as cultural models in Table 1. The first column breaks the model down into goals (i.e., moral direction), means and temporal distribution (pragmatic design), and script for responding to infant signals (the conventional script for action). The Gusii model is called *pediatric* because it is based on maternal concerns with the survival, health, and physical growth of their infants, and the American model *pedagogical* because it is more concerned with the behavioral development of the infant and its preparation for educational interactions. These titles are interpretations of the divergent moral directions of the two models; they represent different ways of construing the problems of infant care and how maternal attention should be allocated toward their solution in two different settings.

The evidence supporting this comparison, including detailed and systematic observations, is provided in a monograph reporting the results (LeVine et al., 1994). It demonstrates that mothers in the two cultures have different practices reflecting contrasting agendas for infant development, that each agenda has a logic (it makes sense as means toward culturally formulated ends) and an ethic (mothers believe their own practices to be in the best interests of their children), and that maternal behavior in accordance with culture-specific models results in a distinctive pattern of social and communicative interaction over the course of infancy and early childhood. Thus a microscopic examination of infant social environments in two different populations reveals a greater divergence of early interactions than universalist models would predict, and it suggests that they constitute alternative pathways for behavioral development consistent with health and growth under varying conditions. The question of what impact they have on the short-term and long-range psychosocial development of the child is taken up in the following section.

## CULTURAL GOALS AND PRECOCITY IN CHILD DEVELOPMENT

The Gusii–American comparison implies that, as the mothers of a particular population follow the culture-specific agenda of a local model of infant care, they selectively facilitate the development of certain potentials and capacities of the child rather than others. Cultural images of maturity entail and elaborate particular goals for a child's development, providing

**Table 2**

**Culturally Formulated Goals and "Precocious" Child Behavior**

| Population | Culturally Formulated Goals | "Precocious" Child Behavior |
|---|---|---|
| Japanese | • Sensitivity to others' feelings (*omoiyari*)<br>• Indirect discourse | • Indirect speech strategies at 5 years |
| German | • Self-reliance (*selbständigkeit*)<br>• Social distance between parent and child | • Self-comforting during caregiver absence (1–12 months)<br>• Type A (anxious avoidant) at 12 months |
| American Middle-Class | • Self-confidence, social engagement | • Talkative, assertive at 2–5 years |
| Gusii of Kenya | • Respect (*ogosika*)<br>• Obedient–responsible (*okoigweera*) | • Quiet, easily calmed in first year<br>• Compliant years 1–5<br>• Responsible babysitter 6+ |

parents with standards for guiding the behavioral development of the child.

Table 2 portrays a preliminary comparison of results from Japanese and German studies with findings from the Gusii and American research. In each case goals for behavioral development formulated in a cultural model are hypothesized to promote the early ("precocious" by the standards of *other* cultures) emergence of a particular behavior that has been selectively facilitated in infancy and early childhood. Starting at the bottom, the Gusii want children who are respectful, obedient, and responsible, in childhood as well as later, and their implementation of the pediatric model outlined on Table 1 promotes these virtues in their early stages: Babies who cry infrequently and are easily quieted during the first year, who respond obediently to maternal commands as they acquire language comprehension skill, and who are able to be responsible babysitters for their infant siblings at the age of 6, and sometimes younger. (We also posit a respect–obedience model that takes over as the child's survival is ensured.) Their expectations for exciting social interaction are low, compared with American children, and their ability to fit into the family hierarchy as workers is precocious by American standards (LeVine et al., 1994).

American middle-class parents want their offspring to become mature adults who are self-confident and socially engaged, and they set about promoting those virtues during infancy, as the pedagogical model suggests. They involve the infant in social interactions designed not only to be cognitively stimulating and emotionally exciting but also to promote sociability and self-esteem, using reciprocal vocalization, verbal interaction, and frequent questioning and praise as primary methods. The results are children who are talkative and verbally assertive in the preschool years, precociously so by the standards of other cultures. (Among the Gusii, to call a young child talkative, *omokwani*, is pejorative, implying a lack of respect.)

In Germany, self-reliance (*selbständigkeit*) is an explicit goal of mature development, but it is interpreted as involving a greater social distance between child and mother than among contemporary American middle-class parents, who nonetheless value "independence" as a developmental goal (Harkness, Super, & Keefer, 1992; LeVine & Norman, 1997). German mothers promote this virtue during infancy by leaving the baby alone in bed on awakening in the morning and at other times when the mother goes out of the house; they also push away a baby who gets "too close" and refuse to indulge one who cries for companionship, a behavior they consider indicative of being spoiled, *verwöhnt* (Grossmann & Grossman, 1981, 1991; Grossmann, Grossmann, Spangler, Suess, & Unzner, 1985; LeVine & Norman, 1997). It is noteworthy that these maternal behaviors are considered morally unacceptable among contemporary middle-class Americans, and certain behaviors—like leaving a baby unattended when the mother goes out shopping—constitute criminal neglect in most states—if not all—of the United States.

What is the result? The Grossmanns report that in their Bielefeld sample (Grossmann et al., 1985), the 10-month-old infants initiated pickup by their mothers less often and took less notice of their comings and goings than in Ainsworth's Baltimore study. Furthermore, 49% of the Bielefeld babies at 12 months, compared with 26% of the Baltimore infants, were classified as anxious-avoidant (A) in the Strange Situation, meaning they avoided their mother in the reunion episodes of the situation (Grossmann et al., 1985). A similar result has been found in East Berlin (Ahnert, Meischner, Zeibe, & Schmidt, in press), but in American studies the proportion of A babies is usually one quarter or less. The Grossmanns also reported that infants classified as B-3 in the Strange Situation, considered "optimal" by U.S. researchers, would be thought spoiled and immature in Germany. There is, in other words, a fair amount of evidence to support the conclusion that German infants are precociously capable of self-comforting as opposed to seeking comfort from their mothers, at home and in the Strange Situation, in accordance with their parents' concept of mature behavior.

Finally, a central goal of behavioral development for Japanese parents is *omoiyari*, translatable as empathy or interpersonal sensitivity, which includes the ability to avoid face-to-face confrontations by the strategic use of indirect speech locutions—for example, criticizing someone by expressing dissatisfaction in a grossly understated way or by attributing it to an impersonal observer or by verbally disguising the target of the criticism. Clancy (1986) has shown how Japanese mothers help their 2-year-old children learn that mother's faintly and sweetly expressed wishes have the force of imperatives. Kelly's (1989) observations of 5- to 7-year-old Japanese children interacting with their peers revealed that some of these children spontaneously used indirect speech strategies in attempting to control those whose misbehavior (e.g., monopolizing toys) was blocking them in some way. In other words, by the age of 5 some Japanese children have acquired the mature, culturally approved, way of avoiding interpersonal confrontations through the use of indirect speech, and they do so with their peers. Here again is precocity by outside standards that has been promoted by the mother in selectively facilitating the child's development toward culturally formulated goals.

These are examples, supported by varying types of evidence ranging from ethnographic observations to laboratory-based assessments, of how cultural goals can drive early behavioral development, selecting for precocious facilitation those behaviors that represent the highest priorities for parents of that culture. Far from being conclusive, the evidence calls for further comparative research on early development in diverse cultures.

## AN AGENDA FOR FUTURE RESEARCH

The examples of Table 2 point to an agenda for future research organized around several questions:

1. If the precocious behavior illustrated by the cases of Table 2 is linked to cultural and social factors, as argued previously, to what extent is its development also facilitated by population-specific temperamental factors that might have a genetic basis?[2]
2. Do the cross-cultural variations in precocity indicate early progress toward cultural goals of behavioral development that provides momentum advantageous in the next stage of cultural acquisition? Assuming that parental conceptions of desirable interpersonal relations are selectively guiding the child's acquisition of interactive dispositions during the first 2 to 3 years, is there subsequent environmental support for continued progress along the same lines? To what extent does the precocious learning constitute a head start for the child of a particular culture? Pursuit of these questions will illuminate the role of early learning in the child's acquisition of culture.
3. Does precocious behavior indicate internalization of *cultural* norms for feeling and thinking as *personal* preferences and aversions, indi-

[2] Recent research demonstrating population-specific differences in selected infant behaviors is available. Kagan, Arcus, & Snidman (1993) observed differences in motor activity and emotional expression among Caucasian American, Irish, and Chinese infants. Other research demonstrating behavioral differences between Caucasian and Asian infants, specifically ease of arousal, is summarized in that chapter. Kagan et al. note that although these data are consistent with genetic influence on individual differences in temperament, environmental factors substantially contribute to the modulation and malleability of the temperamental profile.—Eds.

cating a psychological impact that goes beyond overt behavior? This question involves the distinction between a child's learning to conform to social rules—for example, of respect (Gusii), verbal interaction (U.S. middle-class), social distance (Germany), and face-to-face accommodation (Japan)—and acquiring a psychological disposition—for example, an internal working model of interpersonal relations—that becomes part of the self or of intrapsychic representations and regulations (Bretherton, 1987; Stern, 1985).

4. Does the cultural shaping of child behavior through social interaction during the preschool years, birth to 6 years, influence the subsequent development of motivation, capacities, conflicts, and identities (Whiting & Edwards, 1988)?

The research needed to answer these questions is not high on the agenda of funding agencies, and there are too few cross-cultural investigators doing too few studies of early childhood with excessively small samples. But the evidence is being slowly accumulated, partly by Dr. Freedman's former students and colleagues, in populations all over the world. When the evidence is in, we will have a much more refined understanding of population variations in the early environments of the human species and what they indicate concerning developmental flexibility in social development during infancy and early childhood. This knowledge will provide an empirical basis for the biocultural science of human development toward which Dr. Freedman has been working all these years.

Dr. Freedman and his students have helped those of us in child development research to see that parental care and the development of offspring are diversified across populations in the human species. Research throughout the past 25 years has revealed cross-cultural variations in patterns of infant care. More specifically, it has described the population-specific goals of parents in different cultures, indicating that they seek to promote and facilitate different behaviors in their infants according to local cultural models of the life span. This body of research has also revealed that infants and young children of different cultures manifest precocity in behaviors that their parents consider to be related to cultural goals, as illustrated in this chapter. However, these findings are fragmentary and should be viewed as leads for future research. Among the unanswered questions are the extent to which early precocity is maintained into later parts of the life span and whether cultural variation in parental ideals and practices is influenced by population differences in infant temperament that might reflect genetic variation.

## REFERENCES

Ahnert, L., Meischner, T., Zeibe, M., & Schmidt, A. (in press). Socialization concepts of Russian and German mothers in infant caretaking. In P. M. Crittenden (Ed.), *The organization of attachment relationships: Maturation, culture and context.* New York: Cambridge University Press.

Ainsworth, M. D. S. (1967). *Infancy in Uganda.* Baltimore: Johns Hopkins University Press.

Ainsworth, M. D. S. (1977). Infant development and mother-infant interaction among Ganda and American families. In P. H. Leiderman, S. R. Tulkin, & A. Rosenfeld (Eds.), *Culture and Infancy* (pp. 49–68). New York: Academic Press.

Ainsworth, M. D. S., Blehar, M., Waters, E., & Wall, S. (1978). *Patterns of attachment: A psychological study of the strange situation.* Hillsdale, NJ: Erlbaum.

Ainsworth, M. D. S., & Marvin, R. S. (1995). On the shaping of attachment theory and research: An interview with Mary D. S. Ainsworth (Fall, 1994). In E. Waters, B. E. Vaughn, G. Posada, & Kondo-Ikemura, K. (Eds.), *Caregiving, cultural, and cognitive perspectives on secure-base behavior and working models: New growing points of attachment theory and research.* Monographs of the Society for Research in Child Development, Serial No. 244, Vol. 60, Nos. 2-3 (pp. 1–21). Chicago: University of Chicago Press.

Blurton Jones, N. (1972). Characteristics of ethological studies of human behavior. In N. G. Blurton Jones (Ed.), *Ethological studies of child behavior* (pp. 3–33). Cambridge: Cambridge University Press.

Bowlby, J. (1969). *Attachment and loss I: Attachment.* New York: Basic Books.

Bowlby, J. (1988). *A secure base.* New York: Basic Books.

Bretherton, I. (1987). New perspectives on attachment relations: Security, communication, and internal working models. In J. Osofsky (Ed.), *Handbook of infant development* (2nd ed., pp. 1061–1100). New York: John Wiley.

Caudill, W., & Frost, L. (1972). A comparison of maternal care and infant behavior in Japanese–American, American and Japanese families. In U. Bronfenbrenner & M. A. Mahoney (Eds.), *Influences on human development* (pp. 329–342). Hinsdale, IL: Dryden.

Caudill, W., & Weinstein, H. (1969). Maternal care and infant behavior in Japan and America. *Psychiatry, 32,* 12–43.

Clancy, P. (1986). The acquisition of communicative style in Japanese. In B. Schieffelin & E. Ochs (Eds.), *Language socialization across cultures* (pp. 213–250). New York: Cambridge University Press.

Freedman, D., & Gorman, J. (1993). Attachment and the transmission of culture—An evolutionary perspective. *Journal of Social and Evolutionary Systems, 16,* 297–329.

Grossmann, K., Grossmann, K. E., Spangler, G., Suess, G., & Unzner, L. (1985). Maternal sensitivity and newborns' orientation responses as related to quality of attachment in northern Germany. In I. Bretherton & E. Waters (Eds.), Growing points of attachment theory and research (pp. 233–256). *Monographs of the Society for Research in Child Development, 50* (1–2, Serial No. 209).

Grossman, K., & Grossman, K. E. (1991). Newborn behavior, the quality of early parenting and later toddler–parent relationships in a group of German infants. In J. K. Nugent, B. M. Lester, & T. B. Brazelton (Eds.), *The cultural context of infancy* (Vol. 2, pp. 3–38). Norwood, NJ: Ablex.

Grossmann, K. E., & Grossman, K. (1981). Parent–infant attachment relationships in Bielefeld. In K. Immelman, G. Barlow, L. Petrovich, & M. Main (Eds.), *Behavioral development: The Bielefeld interdisciplinary project* (pp. 694–699). New York: Cambridge University Press.

Harkness, S., Super, C., & Keefer, C. H. (1992). Learning to be an American parent: How cultural models gain directive force. In R. D'Andrade & C. Strauss (Eds.), *Human motives and cultural models* (pp. 163–178). New York: Cambridge University Press.

Kagan, J., Arcus, D., & Snidman, N. (1993). The idea of temperament: Where do we go from here? In R. Plomin & G. E. McClearn (Eds.), *Nature, nurture and psychology* (pp. 197–210). Washington, DC: American Psychological Association.

Kelly, V. (1989). *Peer culture and interactions among Japanese children.* Unpublished doctoral dissertation, Harvard Graduate School of Education, Cambridge, MA.

LeVine, R. A., Dixon, S., LeVine, S., Richman, A., Leiderman, P. H., Keefer, C. H.,

& Brazelton, T. B. (1994). *Child care and culture: Lessons from Africa.* New York: Cambridge University Press.

LeVine, R. A., & LeVine, B. B. (1966). *Nyansongo: A Gusii community in Kenya.* New York: John Wiley.

LeVine, R. A., & Norman, K. (1997). The infant's acquisition of culture: Early attachment re-examined from an anthropological viewpoint. In H. Mathews & C. Moore (Eds.), *Proceedings of 1995 Conference of Society for Psychological Anthropology.* New York: Cambridge University Press.

Papousek, H., & Papousek, M. (1987). Intuitive parenting: A dialectic counterpart to the infant's integrative competence. In J. D. Osofsky (Ed.), *Handbook of infant development* (2nd ed., pp. 669–720). New York: Wiley.

Stern, D. (1985). *The interpersonal world of the infant.* New York: Basic Books.

Trevarthen, C. (1988). Universal cooperative motives: How infants begin to know the language and the culture of their parents. In G. Jahoda & I. M. Lewis (Eds.), *Acquiring culture* (pp. 37–91). London: Croom Helm.

Whiting, B. B. (Ed.). (1963). *Six cultures: Studies of child rearing.* New York: John Wiley.

Whiting, B. B., & Edwards, C. P. (1988). *Children of different worlds.* Cambridge, MA: Harvard University Press.

Whiting, B. B., & Whiting, J. W. M. (1975). *Children of six cultures.* Cambridge, MA: Harvard University Press.

14

# Marriage in Cross-Cultural Perspective

Carol C. Weisfeld

Throughout the 1970s, Daniel G. Freedman and his graduate students at the University of Chicago studied dominance relations from an ethological perspective, following the work of Chance and Jolly (1970) and Kummer (1968). Dr. Freedman's students (e.g., Omark, Omark, & Edelman, 1975; G. Weisfeld, 1978; G. Weisfeld, Muczenski, Weisfeld, & Omark, 1987) successfully adapted the dominance model to describe the structure of children's school groups. Because the initial studies were most appropriate in describing boys' social structures, Freedman encouraged his students to observe girls in natural settings, to discover structures operating in female groups in schools (Parker, 1976), and summer camps (Savin-Williams, 1977, 1987).

The next logical extension was to examine boy–girl relations in natural settings, and it was Dr. Freedman who insisted that this had to be done in multiple cultural contexts, given the variation in cultural views regarding male–female relationships (Weisfeld, Weisfeld, & Callaghan, 1982). Freedman's basic assumptions, then, regarding naturalistic and cross-cultural methodologies underlie the work referred to in this chapter, which describes lessons learned from studying males and females who are married to each other.

Dr. Freedman's approach, sometimes called a holistic approach to the study of behavior, is summarized eloquently:

> In our work, we envision a circular feedback system among levels of organization (often representing academic disciplines), with causal effects going in both directions, from any level of organization. . . . We are convinced that apparent causal relationships between lower and higher levels, as between DNA and gene action, or Mendelian genes and behavior, are in fact context dependent, and feedback from higher levels is necessary for the actualization of lower level events. All of this strongly suggests that circular causation, or feedback, best describes the nature of relationships between levels and that circular rather than linear thinking best reflects natural processes. . . . Thus, in considering levels of organization, we should be aware that lower levels are, in a great many cases, as affected by upper levels as the other way around. . . . Biological reductionism, in other words, has deep problems when confronting the real world. (Freedman & Gorman, 1993, pp. 298–299)

Glenn Weisfeld and I have carried Dr. Freedman's assumptions regarding context dependency forward in our continuing study of male–female relations, and we have discovered an additional benefit: Cross-cultural research exposes errors. All good research, to be sure, exposes errors, but cross-cultural research does so with a thoroughness not seen in other approaches. This chapter covers six different classes of errors that cross-cultural research exposes. Examples from our own research on marriage will be presented as illustrative of such errors.

To begin, it is important to introduce the collaborative project from which examples will be drawn. An international study of marital satisfaction was undertaken in England, at the University of London Goldsmiths' College. It was there that Drs. Robin J. H. Russell and Pamela A. Wells developed the Marriage and Relationship Questionnaire, since published in short form in Great Britain as the MARQ (Russell & Wells, 1993). Their original questionnaire was a multipurpose marriage survey containing 179 questions on variables potentially related to marital satisfaction. It is organized into two matching books, one for the husband and one for the wife (the short-form MARQ is also appropriate for each partner in a nontraditional relationship). The Russell and Wells questionnaires have been designed to serve a number of theoretical viewpoints, including a sociobiological approach. This latter viewpoint assumes that evolution has had an impact on the behavior of all species, including Homo sapiens. Sociobiology applies biological principles, in particular, to social behaviors. For example, mate selection is viewed as a key element in enhancing one's biological fitness through successful reproduction. Thus, sociobiologists expect that natural selection will have played a role in producing behaviors that men and women ordinarily display toward each other. Those behaviors may, in many cases, be understood to be functional, to be operating at a not-very-conscious level, and to be resistant to cultural pressure for change. The MARQ contains questions related to variables of interest to sociobiologists and to researchers who take a more traditional psychological or sociological approach. Questions cover such domains as personality and physical characteristics, values, resources, genetic relatedness to others in the household, interactions with the spouse and children, and so on. Buried within the questionnaire are scales that measure happiness or problems in a variety of spheres, such as life circumstances and the quality of the romantic relationship.

My husband, Dr. Glenn Weisfeld (see chapter 17), and I became associated with Russell and Wells in 1987, when we were on sabbatical in London. We collaborated with them in analyses of their data on married British men and women. The British sample now numbers more than 1200 couples. We were subsequently joined by Dr. Olçay Imamoğlu, who chairs the psychology department at Middle East Technical University in Ankara, Turkey. Professor Imamoglu and her students have gathered data on approximately 400 couples, mostly Moslem families, in Turkey. The other members of this international research group are Drs. Qi Dong and Jiliang Shen, psychology professors at Beijing Normal University in China. They and their students have gathered data on approximately 300 couples in Beijing. Finally, we continue to gather data on American couples, mostly from Detroit, Michigan; at the time this book goes to press, this sample numbered approximately 400 couples.

The original goal was to discover factors contributing to marital satisfaction in these different cultural groups. In the course of our efforts, a great deal of new and unexpected information has been revealed, largely owing to the tendency for cross-cultural research to expose errors. Each class of error will be described separately, with an example from our experience.

## ERROR #1: YOU'RE USING THE WRONG THEORY

There are times when one is tempted to give up on a theory entirely. One should first reexamine the way the theory is being applied, to see if it needs modification in order to explain the complexity of the behaviors that one observes. For example, when we first began analyzing our data on British couples, we began with a fairly straightforward concept from sociobiology, the concept of hypergyny, or the tendency for females to marry upward in social status. The human data show a widespread tendency for females to prefer males who are older, wealthier, or higher in social status (Daly & Wilson, 1983; Dickemann, 1975). Therefore, we hypothesized that those marriages in which the husband had more family wealth or more family income than his wife did would be happier marriages. We also hypothesized that this higher status for the husband would grant him more decision-making power in the marriage than his wife. In short, we predicted that happier marriages would be those in which the husband made more of the important decisions than his spouse did. Our measure of marital happiness was based on the husband's and wife's responses to such items as, "Do you regret having married your spouse?" and, "Have you thought of divorce?" We compared their scores on these measures to their scores on the question, "Who usually makes most of the important decisions?"

None of our predictions was supported in exactly the way we had

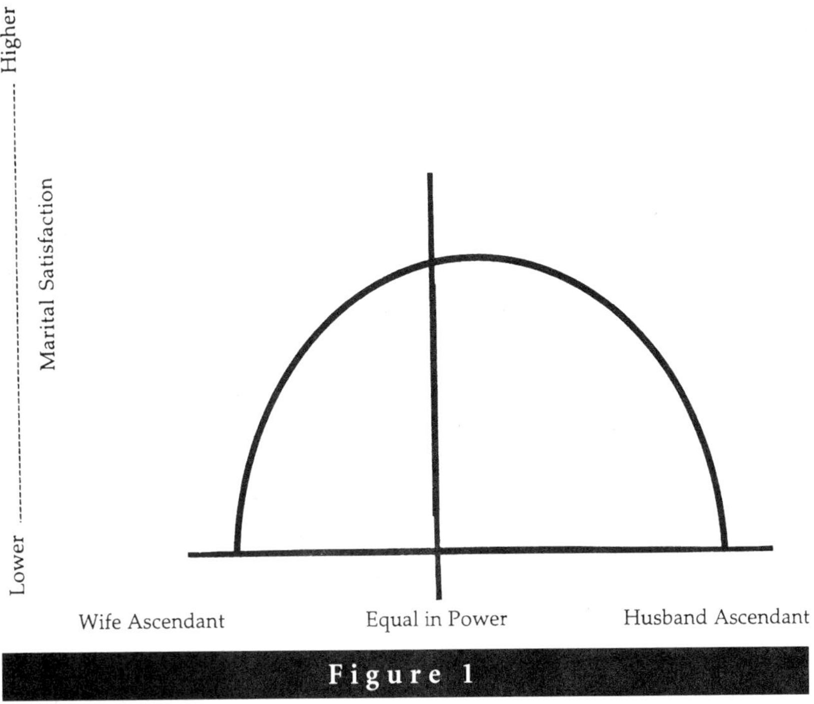


**Figure 1**

Marital satisfaction is associated with a slight degree of perceived husband ascendancy in decision making. Based on Weisfeld, Russell, Weisfeld, & Wells (1992).

expected. In these British families, the husband's control of wealth or income did not predict greater marital satisfaction. The pattern for decision making, however, proved to be quite interesting. A regression analysis revealed a curvilinear relationship shown in Figure 1. As the curve indicates, satisfaction in the marriage decreases if *either* spouse is too dominant in decision making. The arrangement in which the wife is ascendant over her husband is particularly damaging to marital satisfaction. Furthermore, contrary to popular belief (at least in the United States), perfect egalitarianism is not the optimal arrangement. The happiest couples in our British sample were those in which the husband was moderately ascendant over his wife; that is, they were couples who agreed that the husband made important decisions somewhat more often than the wife. Most interesting was the finding that this slight ascendancy on the part of the husband was more important to the wife than it was to the husband. Going back to our theory, we concluded that we were probably looking at a compromise between hypergyny (the tendency for women to marry upward in status) and homogamy (positive associative mating, or the tendency for like to be attracted to like). A similar pattern for intelligence was discovered, with the happiest marriages being those in which the couple identified the husband as slightly more intelligent than the wife. An interesting twist appeared with regard to attractiveness, with more satisfied couples reporting that the wife was slightly more physically appealing than the husband (Weisfeld, Russell, Weisfeld, & Wells, 1992).

In summary, the application of sociobiological theory itself was not completely wrong, but we had been applying it too simplistically. As often happens, the real-life situation is a compromise among opposing forces creating circular feedback, as Freedman and Gorman (1993) described.

## ERROR #2: YOU'RE NOT LOOKING AT ENOUGH LEVELS

In the United States, one of our graduate students, Norma Schell, had decided to examine the Detroit couples and their decision-making patterns as part of her dissertation research. She discovered that, for these Americans also, there was a tendency for more satisfied couples to have a somewhat greater male contribution to decision making. She and I undertook an ethological study in which couples were filmed making an actual decision—deciding which gift they would accept from us as a reward for having participated in the study. The films were analyzed in order to measure visual dominance in dyadic interaction, or the ratio of looking while speaking to looking while listening. Visual dominance, as defined by Noller (1984), is a measure of power, with the dominant person looking while speaking but being less inclined to look while the other person speaks. Analyses showed that more satisfied couples in this American sample had visually dominant husbands (Schell & Weisfeld, 1995). Schell and I were pleased with these findings, believing we had a consistent picture of marital relations. However, as we watched the films again and again, we realized that these husbands were not actually making the decisions about the gift. In almost every film, the person who actually got what was wanted and verbalized the decision to the experimenter was the wife. As Schell put it, the husband appeared to be the one in charge, and the two of them agreed in the questionnaire measure that he made more of the decisions. In real life, however, at least in this case, the wife seems to be the one who decided and who got her way. We speculate that it may be functional to project a public image of the husband's high status, regardless of the home dynamics. This lesson has led us to a deeper, ongoing consideration of multiple levels of reality and multiple levels of perception in the marriage relationship.

## ERROR #3: YOU'RE ASKING THE WRONG QUESTION

It was necessary to translate the questionnaire into Chinese in order to gather data from Beijing. When our colleagues arranged for the first translation, they returned the questionnaire minus one question. That question read, "Do you find sexual fulfillment outside your marriage?" At that point we felt we could probably talk frankly about this. So, when we inquired, our colleagues' response was that there is no need to ask that question. Our next query: Why not? The answer was that marital infidelity does not happen in China. Glenn and I suspected that infidelity might be one of those phenomena that are not supposed to happen and, therefore, cannot be researched in China. We were candid with our colleagues, and they in turn were candid with us. They suggested that it probably would not do much good to ask the question, but they decided to leave it in. The point is that they themselves decided to retain this question, and we will all find out whether or not it does any good to ask it in the People's Republic.

Again, our Chinese colleagues were surprised that we would hypothesize that, everywhere, marital satisfaction would decrease with the arrival of children. They were aware that American data suggested that outcome. They made it clear to us, though, that when married people know that they can have only one child, that child becomes the focus of immense satisfaction. At this time, it does indeed look as if modern Chinese families might show a unique pattern in this regard. We are aware that Dr. Freedman wishes to continue to do research on Chinese family interactions and personality development as affected by the one-child policy. This is an issue of great theoretical and applied importance, and it deserves a great deal of attention.

## ERROR #4: YOU'RE NOT ASKING THE RIGHT QUESTION

Professor Olçay Imamoğlu is a progressive-thinking Turkish woman. She brings to her work a firm grounding in psychology and a commitment to feminist goals within the context of a Moslem country. She came to England with a real enthusiasm for using the Russell and Wells questionnaire. One of her first inquiries, however, was whether or not she could add about 20 additional questions as she translated the questionnaire into Turkish. The first of these additional questions was, "Is yours an arranged marriage?" She explained that in Turkey marriage customs are changing very rapidly. Her marriage was arranged, for example. She added that she very much approved of the arrangement in her case. Both of her children, however, who were young adults, would be marrying someone of their own choosing.

Dr. Imamoglu anticipated that "love matches" would be more satisfying than arranged matches. This is in contrast to what popular wisdom has held, namely, that arranged matches "start out cold and turn hot" and that love matches "start out hot and turn cold." What Professor Imamoglu eventually demonstrated in her Turkish couples is that love matches are, indeed, more satisfying. Arranged marriages never reach the level of "hotness" maintained in love matches, even after the so-called honeymoon period is over. We believe that this is one of the first research efforts in which this point has been demonstrated by questioning both the husband and the wife (see Imamoğlu, 1994).

## ERROR #5: YOU'RE NOT LISTENING TO YOUR DATA

Back in the United States again, data collection on American couples continued, for the most part in the metro Detroit area, by means of a convenience sample. The vast majority of couples were White and middle-class. There had been some difficulty recruiting volunteers from other racial and socioeconomic segments of society, and so our research assistants focused on obtaining a broader sample. To date, approximately 70 Black couples have participated in the marriage study in the Detroit area. When the data were analyzed by race (Black and White couples), some troubling findings emerged—less satisfaction and more problems among the Black couples, as compared to the White couples. It turned out, however, that distinctions based on social class had not been included in these initial analyses. That is, the information was available to separate the White couples into White middle-class and White lower-class, and the same for the Black couples. The next step was the obvious one: We needed to analyze the data using those variables. When that analysis was complete, an unexpected picture emerged.

The reanalyzed data showed that White middle-class couples are in a world apart, where relationships are very satisfying and problems are few. Black couples show relationships that are not quite so satisfying, and problems that are somewhat more serious. Most important, social class makes almost no difference for Black couples. Black married couples in the United States, at least in the present sample, seem to be in a type of medium range with respect to marital satisfaction, regardless of socioeconomic standing. Apparently other, noneconomic forces are having an impact on the quality of their relationships. See Figure 2 for the general pattern of results.

The next surprise that emerged from the data was the pattern seen in

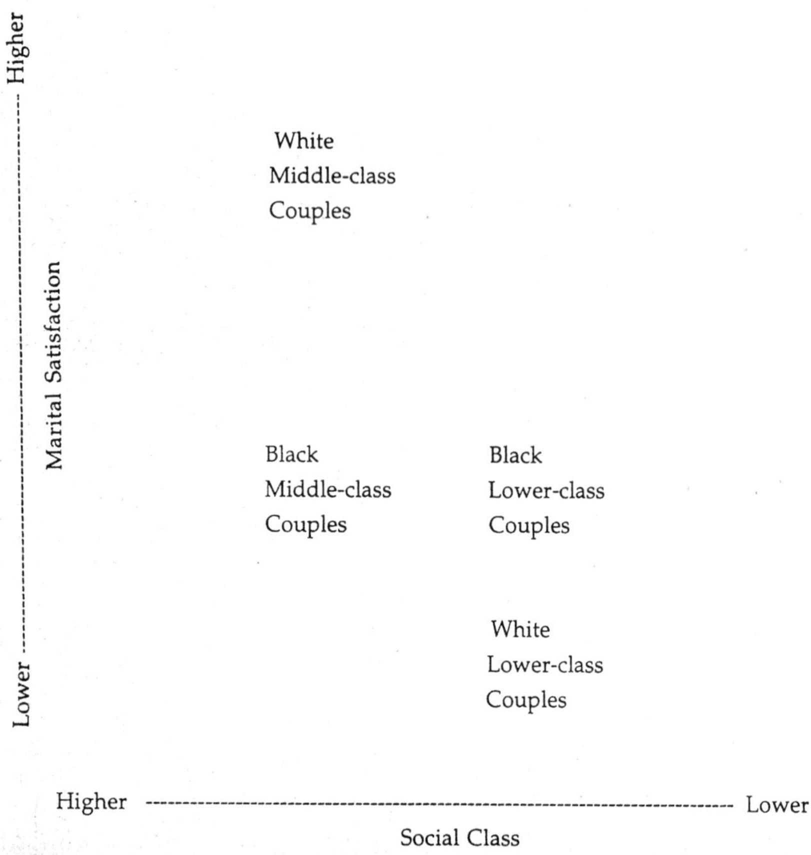

Lower ---------- Higher
Marital Satisfaction

White
Middle-class
Couples

Black
Middle-class
Couples

Black
Lower-class
Couples

White
Lower-class
Couples

Higher ---------- Lower
Social Class

**Figure 2**

Relationship between social class and marital satisfaction is stronger for White American couples than for Black American couples. Based on Weisfeld, Russell, Wells, and Weisfeld (1997).

White lower-class couples. Their relationships are characterized by a marked unhappiness with each other as partners, and their worries about their financial well-being and life circumstances throw a pall over the quality of family life (Weisfeld, Russell, Wells, & Weisfeld, 1997). In terms of future research efforts and applications that address the needs of families, it appears that researchers may want to focus some attention on White lower-class couples.

## ERROR #6: YOU'RE MISSING THE POINT ENTIRELY

Drs. Russell and Wells have been our collaborators on the class and race comparison for the U.S. couples, and the team completed a comparison of couples in the United States and Great Britain, as well. When the data came out of the computer at Goldsmiths' in London, there were very few apparent differences between our two cultures on either side of the Atlantic. One significant difference between British and American couples was detected, and that was in the area of values. American couples are *more traditional* than British couples. "Of course you're more traditional," the British members of the team explained. "You took all our Puritans, and they're still having their effects on you."

This did not make sense to the American members of the team. After all, the divorce rate in the United States is nearly twice the divorce rate for those liberal, progressive couples in the United Kingdom (Goode, 1993). The second significant difference between the two cultural groups was then examined. British husbands feel more in love with their wives than American husbands do. Specifically, British husbands feel more passion, more closeness. Again the British investigators were amused at our puzzlement. "Doesn't it occur to you," they asked, "that love may make a stronger marriage than religious obligation does?" That, after all, would be consistent with what the Turkish team found, that love is a key to satisfaction in marriage. Indeed, it looks as if marriages may be happier if they start out as love matches, and they may last longer if they continue to be love matches.

In summary, one could say that many errors have been made along the way. The key is to pay attention to them and apply the lessons to future efforts. The whole process calls to mind a discussion that took place at a workshop on cross-cultural awareness in 1994, in Detroit. The speaker was Bruce Henman, who is a Native American and a social and spiritual leader for the Chippewa community in Michigan. He gave this lesson at the workshop:

> This is an old Indian saying. Think about your own head. You have two eyes, two ears, and only one mouth. That means that you are supposed to spend twice as much time looking and listening as you do talking. That is how you will understand things. (Henman, 1994)

Indeed, putting oneself in the situation in which one must deal with information from many cultures requires more looking, more listening, and more rethinking than any of these researchers had ever realized would be the case. Nonetheless, Dr. Freedman's assumptions concerning the holistic, circular nature of behavioral influences have served us well. Ethological and cross-cultural methods, moreover, have played a key role in enabling us to recognize errors and recover from them.

## REFERENCES

Chance, M. R. A., & Jolly, C. J. (1970). *Social groups of monkeys, apes and men.* New York: E. P. Dutton.

Daly, M., & Wilson, M. (1983). *Sex, evolution, and behavior.* Boston: Willard Grant Press.

Dickemann, M. (1975). The ecology of mating systems in hypergynous dowry societies. *Social Science Information, 18,* 163–195.

Freedman, D. G., & Gorman, J. (1993). Attachment and the transmission of culture—An evolutionary perspective. *Journal of Social and Evolutionary Systems, 16,* 297–329.

Goode, W. J. (1993). *World changes in divorce patterns.* New Haven, CT: Yale University Press.

Henman, B. (1994, April). *Native American Views.* Paper presented at the meeting Wrestling with Cultural Competence, Detroit, Michigan.

Kummer, H. (1968). Social organization of hamadryas baboons. Chicago: University of Chicago Press.

Imamoğlu, O. (1994). A model of gender relations in the Turkish family. *Journal of Economics and Administrative Studies,* 1–14.

Noller, P. (1984). *Nonverbal communication and marital interaction.* Oxford: Pergamon Press.

Omark, D. R., Omark, M., & Edelman, M. (1975). Formation of dominance hierarchies in young children: Action and perception. In T. Williams (Ed.), *Psychological Anthropology.* The Hague: Mouton.

Parker, R. (1976). *Social hierarchies in same-sex peer groups.* Unpublished PhD dissertation, University of Chicago.

Russell, R. J. H., & Wells, P. A. (1993). *Marriage and Relationship Questionnaire.* Sevenoaks, Kent, England: Hodder & Stoughton.

Savin-Williams, R. C. (1977). *Dominance–submission behaviors and hierarchies in young adolescents at a summer camp.* Unpublished PhD dissertation, University of Chicago.

Savin-Williams, R. C. (1987). *Adolescence: An ethological perspective.* New York: Springer.

Schell, N. J., & Weisfeld, C. C. (1995, August). *Marital power dynamics: A Darwinian perspective.* Paper presented at the meeting of the European Sociobiological Society, Cambridge, England.

Weisfeld, G. E. (1978). *A longitudinal study of dominance in boys.* Unpublished PhD dissertation, University of Chicago.

Weisfeld, C. C., Russell, R. J. H., Wells, P. A., & Weisfeld, G. E. (1997). *A comparison of British and American marriages, with emphasis on American class and race comparisons.* Manuscript submitted for publication.

Weisfeld, G. E., Muczenski, D., Weisfeld, C. C., & Omark, D. (1987). Stability of boys' social success over an eleven-year period. In J. A. Meacham (Ed.), *Interpersonal relations: Family, peers, friends.* Basel, Switzerland: Karger Press.

Weisfeld, G. E., Russell, R. J. H., Weisfeld, C. C., & Wells, P. A. (1992). Correlates of satisfaction in British marriages. *Ethology and Sociobiology, 13,* 125–145.

Weisfeld, C. C., Weisfeld, G. E., & Callaghan, J. W. (1982). Female inhibition in mixed-sex competition in young adolescents. *Ethology and Sociobiology, 3,* 29–42.

# Section IV Conclusion

Wolfgang M. Schleidt

What are cross-cultural naturalistic studies of behavior? Naturalistic studies of behavior do not involve testing sophisticated hypotheses under uniform laboratory conditions. Instead, behavior is observed in its natural setting and viewed within a Darwinian framework of adaptation, survival value, fitness, and kinship. The naturalistic approach forces the investigator to disregard fancy theories and sophisticated hypotheses, at least in the initial phase of the project, but offers the reward of insights that usually remain hidden behind the blinders of a more focused analysis of a question, in which only two alternative answers are admitted: yes or no.

What is meant by cross-cultural studies is somewhat ambiguous, however, because this has to do with not only people of different cultures but of different natures, as well. Culture and nature are closely intertwined in any one individual, as well as in all levels of human society: Humans are, by their nature, cultural beings.[1] Part of Western culture is to value an inquisitive mind that constantly probes the limits of what we can know. Therefore, the human mind cannot be stopped from trying to unravel the intertwining of culture and nature, from exploring their interaction. Thus, ultimately, *cross-cultural* is also synonymous with *cross-natural*.

## CROSS-NATURAL HUMAN CULTURE AND CROSS-CULTURAL HUMAN NATURE

Culture is the result of an evolutionary process, in perfect analogy to organismic speciation. Within the past million years the evolution of

[1] *Der Mensch ist von Natur ein Kulturwesen* (Gehlen 1960/1988).

Homo sapiens occurred in a great variety of environments with very different selection pressures acting on local population and geographical isolation. Genetic and cultural drift in isolated populations resulted in considerable diversity in gross anatomy, physiology, and general appearance. Migration, followed by fusion of different populations within new boundaries, led to new and unique combinations. Culture, especially in the form of verbal language, resulted in cultural, as well as biological, isolation among neighboring populations, which Erikson (1966) has called "cultural pseudo-speciation." In recent millennia religious and political beliefs now raise invisible boundaries within geographically homogeneous areas, isolating groups and resulting in hatred and bloodshed unrivaled by any other creature. Civil war became the most advanced form of human collective insanity. Our "culture" is killing us, not our "nature."

A very instructive example of a long history of alternating episodes of local isolation and migration is the Hungarian ethnic identity and its relation to other cultures, languages, and biological populations of Eurasia. The roots of the Hungarian language have been traced back to nomadic tribes originating between China and Mongolia. These tribes are assumed to have moved west about 2000 years ago and settled in the Ural region. About 1000 years ago, some of these tribes moved on and settled in three more or less distinct groups in Europe as Lapps, Finns, and Hungarians. They absorbed different amounts of native populations and later immigrants into their population.

Based on an analysis of gene frequencies (biological traits that ride along with culture), it has been stated that, compared to the populations of Central Europe (sampled in Czechoslovakia, Germany, Poland, Serbia-Bosnia, and Switzerland), "Lapps are slightly more than 50% European, Hungarians are 87% European, and Finns are 90% European" (Guglielmino, Piazza, Menozzi, & Cavalli-Sforza, 1990, p. 63). Figure 1 not only illustrates the over-all geometry of such estimates from a slightly different angle but shows a very striking feature of the Hungarian sample drawn in Budapest, the nation's capital; it fits right in the middle of the European cluster. In a similar way, as I observed myself, a random sample drawn

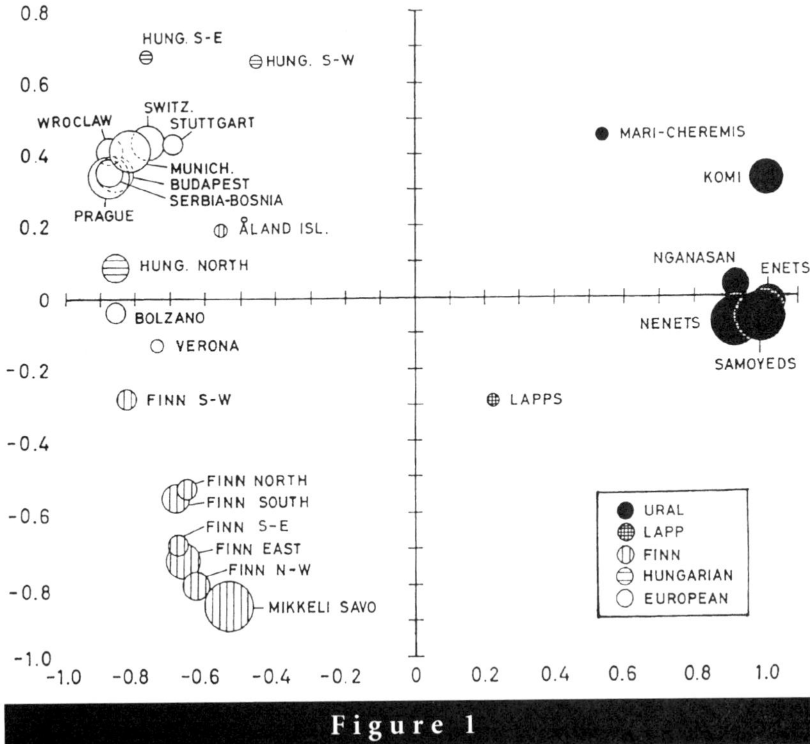


**Figure 1**

Plot of five ethnic groups according to the two first principal coordinates. The circular area is inversely proportional to the error in the representation of each point (population) on the plane. Thus, the two-Euclidian distance between any pair of points is reliable only when associated to the areas indicated by large circles. Note that the sample drawn in Budapest fits well within the "European" cluster, whereas samples from provincial areas of Hungary are scattered around the European cluster, and all these are strikingly separate from the clusters of Finns, Lapps, and Uralic populations. Figure from Guglielmino et al. (1990). Copyright © 1990. Reprinted by permission of Wiley-Liss, Inc., a subsidiary of John Wiley & Sons, Inc.

from the neonates of Vienna's university hospital maternity ward has a very different ethnic composition, as compared to a sample drawn from the maternity ward of a hospital in an outer district of Vienna, and different again from that in a district hospital of rural Austria. I have also visited maternity wards in Washington, DC, on various occasions over the past

30 years, and it appears to me that cultural diversity in this area may be within the same order of magnitude.

## NATURALISTIC, CROSS-CULTURAL STUDIES OF BEHAVIOR

Blurton Jones's study of foraging Hadza children in their natural environment strikes me as an outstanding example of naturalistic and cross-cultural research. It is clearly naturalistic because the investigator, trained in the natural science of bird watching for most of his scientific career, has directed his naturalistic curiosity toward the behavior of children within their natural setting. This study is clearly cross-cultural, because the investigator has spent many hours observing and analyzing the behavior of children of his own Western culture in their natural environment (e.g., a nursery). He has also observed the behavior of children of !Kung, Bushmen living in Botswana whose hunter-gatherer lifestyle and dependence on subsistence techniques are very similar to those of the Hadza in Tanzania. The chapter is a search for answers to the central question: Why do Hadza children forage and children in Bushman culture and in Western culture do not? This is an excellent example of the new level of sophistication that can be reached by probing beyond the traditional limits of psychological theories of hunger, reward, or learning.

By examining the behavior of children in the much wider framework of biological variables such as kinship, individual and inclusive fitness, time spent, calories gained, costs and benefits, trade-offs, and the like, we can shake off the restraint imposed by academic specialization. Thus, we can acquire a more realistic picture of childhood and adolescence, not only in the culture of the Hadza hunter–gatherers, but in our own culture as well.

LeVine's cross-cultural perspective of mother–infant interaction is strikingly different from that of Blurton Jones. I, therefore, want to use it to probe the very limits of the naturalistic, cross-cultural approach. Here, at the onset of the study, a complex set of interaction variables is cast into two clearly different models, sharply contrasting the two cultures of primary concern: the "pediatric" Gusii model (Third World starving mother to be saved by the World Bank) and the "pedagogical" Bostonian[2] model (middle-class housewife in search of a piano teacher she can afford). The stage is set for the alternatives "survive or learn," which is confirmed by somewhat selective observations and with insufficient concern for the complex interactions among the various variables and their consequences. For example, in Table 1 we find two different "cultural scripts for selective responsiveness": Gusiis respond to distress, whereas Bostonians respond to babble. However, these behaviors are best seen in the wider context of the typical Gusii baby being in bodily contact with a caregiver and the typical Bostonian baby spending the majority of time isolated within a sterile, but artificially enriched, environment. As such, to a Gusii mother the faintest baby cry becomes a matter of concern, whereas a Bostonian mother is glad when her baby does not cry; her baby's babbling is, by sheer contrast, music to her ears. Is it possible that the Gusii baby's babbling attracts more attention from the father or little sister guardian than from the mother, whereas the Bostonian baby's babbling cannot reach the ears of the siblings or father because they are pursuing projects and goals outside the home? The point to emphasize is that a cross-cultural approach to baby babbling may reveal rich, truthful patterns of behavior only when based on observations made within the complex "natural" context.

Ekman's work on facial movements and emotions contains outstanding examples of the naturalistic and cross-cultural approach—his study of expressions of universal emotions in Papua New Guinea (Ekman, 1980). In this chapter both the naturalistic and cross-cultural serve more specifically as a frame of reference, lifting the problem out of the academic confines of data sets gleaned from students attending college courses in psychology, the common stand-in for "Middle Class America" (i.e., USA[3]). I feel that the strength of this chapter lies in its broad scope and in its applicability to humans of all ages and cultures. Even though Ekman is

[2] LeVine calls it the "American" model, but because Gusii are inhabitants of Kenya and Bostonians inhabitants of the United States, only "Bostonian" is a fair alternative to Gusii.

[3] Many people erroneously believe that "America" is acceptable as synonym or abbreviation for "United States."

dealing with human "universals," both on the level of facial expressions and on the level of the underlying emotions, he is aware that he has to expect diversity. The cross-cultural study of "display rules" is an excellent example: Japanese use smiling to actively mask negative emotions and in this way prevent unintentional information leakage, whereas in our Western culture we assume a poker face.

C. Weisfeld's chapter on marital satisfaction is a superbly conceived, highly educational presentation of cross-cultural research as a method for avoiding the pitfalls that are so common in studies of human development. The strength of her case rests on broad cultural diversity, close cooperation with native colleagues while developing the questionnaires and collecting the data, and remarkable sample sizes (Britain, $N = 1200$ couples; China, $N = 200$; Turkey, $N = 450$; USA, $N = 400$). She not only exposes six different types of common errors in such studies, but also highlights certain fringe benefits resulting from the need to agree with colleagues of a different culture: not only to speak, but to think in a common language.

## WHAT HAVE WE GAINED?

Let me repeat the specific question, raised at the beginning: How does a cross-cultural approach to naturalistic studies of behavior inform ongoing research? My answer is that by accepting feedback from "nature" and applying it to our 'hypotheses concerning nature,' we are led to a very efficient iterative approach toward understanding the complexity of human behavior. Simply moving a set of laboratory studies into a less restricted environment, or into a foreign country, is unlikely to provide new insights; the results are likely to be very different, of course, but their interpretation would be difficult or impossible. The time-proven method is to start with fine-grained investigations of limited scope, alternating between laboratory and field. In this way the salient variables can be located, specific questions asked, and data sets collected and used to analyze those specific variables, preferably one at a time. In the 1960s, when the "deprivation experiment" came into use in ethological investigations concerning the effects of varying experience on behavioral development, these methods were discussed at great length and have remained ready for use (e.g., Lorenz, 1965).

What is so special about the "naturalistic" study? It is a bottom-up approach, starting with basics and the addition of new variables, as needed. The inherently broad scope of observation keeps hypotheses in close contact with data, "down to earth," and makes it less tempting to "drift off" into highly sophisticated hypotheses that require unrealistic assumptions (e.g., "all things being equal"; they rarely are). In the bottom-up approach, the most salient variables acting on the system are evident and, therefore, logical flaws in deductive reasoning are more easily detected. Thus, mid-course corrections of procedures become possible during an ongoing investigation, and the accumulation of uninformative data can be prevented, thus ensuring efficient utilization of resources.[4]

When I use the phrase "accepting feedback," I think of scientific inquiry as an alternation between inductive and deductive reasoning. The transformation of individual observations into scientific data forces us to critically examine our procedures and classification schemata. Unforeseen events, difficulties, and sources of error enable refinement of hypotheses. In fact, any "source of error," instead of being viewed as a hinderance of due progress, can be investigated and evaluated; I know of splendid scientific careers that started with an inquiry into a nasty source of error.[5]

The iterative approach toward understanding nature by "trial and success" is most likely the oldest and most reliable method, as long as it is not restricted by magical thinking, religious strife, or political power struggles. At its best, it is playful exploration, curiosity finding a challenge, a match in nature. Within ethology this iterative approach had been advocated, especially by Konrad Lorenz. He even formalized it in his basic design for teaching ethology in a (hypothetical) four-volume textbook.[6]

---

[4] Instead of abusing the sample size *N* as an indicator of prestige, due consideration can be given to ethical issues surrounding the use of human and animal research participants.

[5] Jürgen Aschoff's research on circadian rhythms (e.g., Aschoff, 1981) started as an attempt to pinpoint the causes of what were at that time unexplained daily fluctuations in human body temperature.

[6] Only volume one (Lorenz 1977; the 1948 version was published posthumously in 1992) and volume three (Lorenz, 1981) were published. However, starting at the University of Vienna in 1948, he lectured in this mode for many years in a cycle running through four successive semesters.

In the introduction to his first volume (Lorenz, 1992) he called it "writing in a circle" *(im Kreise schreiben).* He started with a first draft as the basis for a four-semester cycle of teaching ethology: (a) Laying the epistemological foundations for the investigation of organismic behavior; (b) looking at different animal species, from protozoa to mammals; (c) summarizing the general principles of organismic behavior; (d) looking at the biological bases of human behavior. A new cycle begins again at (a), as an improved version of (a), because in (b), (c), and (d), numerous problems arose, requiring modification not only of the original draft of (a) but of the others as well. In this way the content and sophistication of Lorenz's lectures improved with each repetition. He was not writing and teaching in a circle but rather in a rising spiral. Science evolves, like biological systems, not by destruction and replacement, but by improvement. The individual death of a falsified hypothesis is part of the scientific growth process, providing more space for those that resist falsification. Nothing succeeds like success!

A cross-cultural approach to the study of human behavior potentiates the time-proven comparative method, developed first within comparative morphology and sharpened by biostatistics, comparative psychology,[7] comparative physiology, and ethology. It is centered on a vantage point that allows us to detect differences in both cultural and biological variables and gives greater depth to our view of behavioral similarity and diversity. Even though it may be futile to trace a particular behavioral trait to one or to the other source, we can learn from either one. In particular, we learn to be very cautious in drawing our samples and in interpreting our results. For example, when considering Robert LeVine's comparison of mother–infant interactions, based on samples drawn from populations in Japan, Germany, and "Middle-Class America," or Carol Weisfeld's perspective on marriage, with samples drawn from populations in Great Britain, Turkey, China, and the United States, we must be aware that homogeneity within some convenient cultural variables (e.g., language, nationality,

[7]This is based on a comparison of a variety of animal species, not just on the use of rats and pigeons as substitutes.

place of birth, or residence) does not guarantee cultural or biological homogeneity. Remember my example of Uralic genes in Europe; in fact, language (one of the most powerful cultural variables) can span a wide diversity, not only of subcultures but also of biological subpopulations. Language can unite and divide populations, but not only in the commonly assumed sense that a nation is united by "a common language" and separated from its enemies as those speaking a different tongue: Austrians and Germans were said to be "divided by their common language."[8] Small differences in the use of a language can become striking markers of ethnic identity, subcultures, or subregions. Speaking the same dialect may serve as a group bond.

The cross-cultural approach is no panacea for coming up with global statements about humanity or for finding the ideal, average, or normal human being. It is more likely to expose human complexity and diversity. Given the diversity of factors under consideration, the cross-cultural approach provides more and deeper insights by allowing the concurrent study of different systems that subserve similar, as well as different, functions. In the ideal cross-cultural study, which involves study participants of different ethnic origins as well as investigators of these cultures, the different views add depth to any one culture, as if seen with more than one eye.

## REFERENCES

Aschoff, J. (1981). A survey on biological rhythms. In J. Aschoff (Ed.), *Handbook of behavioral neurobiology* (Vol. 4, pp. 3–10). London: Plenum Press.

Ekman, P. (1980). *The faces of man.* New York: Garland STPM Press.

Erikson, E. H. (1966). Ontogeny of ritualization in man. *Philosophical Transactions of the Royal Society London, B251,* 337–349.

Gehlen, A. (1960). *Der Mensch, seine Natur, und seine Stellung in der Welt* [Man: His nature and place in the world]. Berlin: Junger & Durrhaupt.

Guglielmino, C. R., Piazza, A., Menozzi, P., & Cavalli-Sforza, L. L. (1990). Uralic genes in Europe. *American Journal of Physical Anthropology, 83,* 57–68.

[8] The language is German; this saying is attributed to the Viennese writer Karl Kraus.

Lorenz, K. (1965). *Evolution and modification of behavior.* Chicago: Chicago University Press.

Lorenz, K. Z. (1977). *Behind the mirror—A search for a natural history of human knowledge.* New York: Harcourt Brace Jovanovich.

Lorenz, K. Z. (1981). *The foundations of ethology.* New York: Springer.

Lorenz, K. Z. (1992). *Die Naturwissenschaft vom Menschen: Eine Einführung in die vergleichende Verhaltensforschung; Das "Russische Manuskript" (1944–1948).* Munich: Piper.

SECTION V

# Evolutionary Analyses: New Issues and Continuing Controversies

SECTION V INTRODUCTION

# Evolutionary Analyses: New Issues and Continuing Controversies

Glenn E. Weisfeld

The work of the sociobiologists, especially Hamilton (1964), opened the way to a more accurate and fruitful view of biological fitness than prevailed when evolutionists were still in thrall of the notion of group selection. Modern adaptationist approaches to the study of human behavior have captured the public's imagination and led to an increase in the number of behavioral scientists utilizing Darwinian theory.

The first chapter in this section is by Robert L. Trivers, one of the most important and versatile theorists in sociobiology. His papers on reciprocal altruism (Trivers, 1971), sexual selection and parental investment (Trivers, 1972), variations in the sex ratio (Trivers & Willard, 1973), and parent–offspring conflict (Trivers, 1974) have all led to entire lines of productive research. That someone could turn out these four works in successive years is marvelous. Each of these seminal contributions began with some basic biological phenomenon—altruism between nonkin and even allospecifics, the size disparity of egg and sperm, the sex difference in mortality rates, and the partial incongruity of genes between parent and offspring.

In chapter 15, Trivers again begins with a fundamental biological phenomenon: genomic imprinting. He traces its behavioral implications in such a way as to generate what will doubtless prove to be a series of novel and testable hypotheses about human behavior.

Jerry H. Barkow has written one widely cited book (Barkow, 1989) and co-edited another (Barkow, Cosmides, & Tooby, 1992). Like Trivers—and as one of Dr. Freedman's students—Barkow has found his inspiration in interdisciplinary analysis. Having done extensive field work in Nigeria, he has combined anthropology with evolutionary psychology. He is perhaps best known for his work on prestige striving, which he has argued is universal and hence probably has an evolved basis (e.g., Barkow, 1975, 1980). Barkow may have focused on this basic emotion because of his training in the ethological tradition; an ethogram is essentially a catalog of the basic motivated behaviors of a species.

In chapter 16 he turns his attention to the emotions in general. He shows how evolutionary thinking about human evolution and behavior can offer useful implications for understanding and assessing happiness and the particular emotions it comprises. He argues that evolutionary theory and research can provide insights about human nature, thus leading to more realistic models of our needs, capacities, and limitations than have been available to philosophers, social scientists, and social reformers previously. Again in the Freedman tradition, he makes bold to suggest that the sexes, as well as age groups, differ in their basic emotional needs.

I wrote chapter 17, the last in this section. I have pursued many of the same topics as Barkow over the years, such as the family under Islam. Both of us have also been interested in humor, myself as a theorist and Barkow as a practitioner. My chapter focuses on the emotion of pride and shame, which Barkow refers to as *prestige striving.* Both of us agree that this emotion evolved from dominance behavior in other primates and that a comparative, evolutionary analysis offers fruitful insights into its properties.

## REFERENCES

Barkow, J. H. (1975). Social prestige and culture: A biosocial interpretation. *Contemporary Anthropology, 16,* 553–572.

Barkow, J. H. (1980). Prestige and self-esteem: A biosocial interpretation. In D. R. Omark, F. F. Strayer, & D. G. Freedman (Eds.), *Dominance relations: An etholog-*

*ical view of human conflict and social interaction* (pp. 318–332). New York: Garland.

Barkow, J. H. (1989). *Darwin, sex and status: Biological approaches to mind and culture.* Toronto: University of Toronto Press.

Barkow, J. H., Cosmides, L., & Tooby, J. (1992). *The adapted mind: Evolutionary psychology and the generation of culture.* New York: Oxford University Press.

Hamilton, W. D. (1964). The genetical evolution of social behaviour (Parts I & II). *Journal of Theoretical Biology, 7,* 1–52.

Trivers, R. L. (1971). The evolution of reciprocal altruism. *Quarterly Review of Biology, 46,* 35–57.

Trivers, R. L. (1972). Parental investment and sexual selection. In B. Campbell (Ed.), *Sexual selection and the descent of man, 1871–1971* (pp. 136–179). Chicago: Aldine de Gruyter.

Trivers, R. L. (1974). Parent-offspring conflict. *American Zoologist, 14,* 249–264.

Trivers, R. L., & Willard, D. E. (1973). Natural selection of parental ability to vary the sex ratio of offspring. *Science, 179,* 90–91.

15

# Genetic Basis of Intrapsychic Conflict

Robert L. Trivers

*The connection between Bob Trivers and Dan Freedman dates back to the mid-1970s, coincident with the publication of Edward O. Wilson's book,* Sociobiology: The New Synthesis *(1975).*[1] *This new discipline, which examines the biological bases of social behavior with reference to evolutionary concepts and principles, sparked considerable controversy. Its challenges to traditional beliefs about the origins of human social behavior excited those who believed that psychological analyses needed a bioevolutionary component. In response to the promptings of colleagues, Freedman arranged to meet Trivers during a visit to Harvard University. He "learned much about sociobiology from Trivers" during their first short session together. The two currently share an interest in the nature and origins of internal conflict.*

*This chapter examines the novel concept that internal psychological conflict may have a genetic basis. This idea is explored with reference to the*

---

Some of the material presented here was transcribed from a videotape of the Festschrift, held at the University of Chicago, Sunday, October 29, 1995, and edited slightly.

[1] The introduction to this chapter was written by the editors of this volume.

*recently discovered phenomenon of genomic imprinting—in other words, the differential expression of certain genes in offspring dependent on whether inheritance of these genes is maternal or paternal. Genomic imprinting is viewed as* the *major advance in understanding kinship since Hamilton's (1964a, 1964b) theory of kin selection, and it leads to a series of predictions regarding internal psychological conflict that may affect interactions with relatives.*

## GENETIC SOURCES OF CONFLICT

There are probably many sources for internal conflict in humans, including some that are classically mapped on to parent–offspring interactions in which at least one parent is represented by a strong internal "voice." Recently, there has been compelling evidence of a novel source of inner conflict that is genetic. This is initially very surprising because humans consist of genetically identical somatic cells working for the gonads, and there is no conflict expected between them. The liver and the kidney, for example, are not in conflict over how many resources to remove from the bloodstream, because they are all genetically identical, nonreproductive, and working for the gonads. As evolutionary researchers have understood from Hamilton's (1964a, 1964b) kinship theory, however, they are also working with reference to other individuals, such as close relatives, attempting to confer benefits and avoid conferring costs.

The nutshell of the present argument is that within an individual *genetic elements do not all enjoy the same degree of relatedness to a close relative.* In the case of two full brothers, the Y chromosome "sees" the pair as being identically related. The autosomes only "see" them as half related, so there is a possibility for conflict, over evolutionary time and within a single individual, between these genetic elements. Over evolutionary time it is possible to imagine a mutant on the Y chromosome that says, in effect, "Treat brothers as if they are identical twins, but neglect sisters." (Sisters and brothers have no overlap of self-interest because sisters lack the Y chromosome.) Mitochondrial DNA says, "Value only sisters because only sisters pass on mitochondrial DNA." Two full brothers share identical mitochondrial DNA, but neither reproduces it, because mitochondrial DNA is only transmitted from mother to progeny.

A Y mutant such as described above could appear and should start to spread if located on the appropriate genetic element. However, if it did, it would immediately set up a selection pressure on the much larger array of autosomal genes to counteract this spread—in other words, to "turn off" the Y chromosome mutant. This process is conflict over evolutionary time, but could be resolved in an individual's psyche or physiology, as well. This is because there are competing elements generated by these different genes that may compete for control of the individual.

Until recently, the outline of the preceding argument was understood, but imagined to be unimportant because the genetic elements referred to are minority elements in the extreme. The Y chromosome is approximately 1% of the genome by amount of DNA, but it is mostly inert. It has very few functioning genes per unit length compared to the autosomes or to the X chromosome. Thus, individuals have considerably less than 1% of the genes available on "that side of the fight" versus all of the autosomes "united against it." Mitochondrial DNA is one tenth of 1% of total DNA, so it is also a minority element.

In the past 5 years, it has been exciting to understand that autosomes do not act in unison. Instead, paternal genes (genes inherited from the father) are in some circumstances in conflict with maternal genes (genes inherited from the mother). There is the same kind of evolutionary conflict based on differing self-interest and the same possibility for internal conflict, and that is the focus of the following discussion.

## GENOMIC IMPRINTING

The phenomenon that has been discovered is called *genomic imprinting* (see Barlow, 1995). Genomic imprinting leads to exact degrees of relatedness through each parent instead of probabilistic degrees of relatedness. (This concept is addressed again later.) These exact degrees of relatedness mean that genes can act according to parent of origin, "on behalf of father" or "on behalf of mother." This leads to quite disparate degrees of relatedness—in other words, the difference between 1/2 and 0, as will be demonstrated. Furthermore, there is now abundant evidence that there are forms of internal physiological conflict within single individuals, which map on to these two opposing genetic elements. Remember that these are not minority elements, but rather half of the autosomes versus the other half of the autosomes. In a female, this process also includes her X chromosomes, so that the paternal X and maternal X chromosomes are in some expected disagreement. In principle, all of a female's genome, leaving aside the mitochondrial DNA, are involved in an antagonistic interaction by parent of origin.

What is the phenomenon? Genomic imprinting refers to what is also sometimes called *parent-specific gene expression.* A classic assumption of Mendelian genetics, which is true for the vast majority of genes, is that a gene in an individual is active in the same way regardless of which parent contributed it. In other words, the gene is the same stretch of DNA with no information "left over" from the transmission. Thus, if one is a heterozygote for eye color (brown being dominant and blue being recessive), the individual will have a brown phenotype regardless of which parent contributed the genes. Genomic imprinting refers to a small minority of known genes that have the property of being expressed in an individual only if inherited from a particular parent. Thus, there are paternally active genes, genes that are active in a person only if donated by the father. A mother could donate the identical set of DNA at that locus; however, it is inactivated, or *imprinted.* (Imprinting refers to the negative state, but because the present intent is to model the active state it is easier to use the language of paternally active and maternally active genes.)

There are, in turn, genes active in an individual only if donated by the mother. Think back to the eye color locus to see how it works. If the gene is paternally active and one received the brown allele from the father, the phenotype would be brown (blue is the recessive trait). However, if an individual received the blue allele from the father, the brown eye allele from the mother is inactivated and the blue phenotype is expressed. In other words, the phenotype is different even though the genotype is identical.

## IMPLICATIONS OF GENOMIC IMPRINTING FOR KINSHIP THEORY

It was the brilliance and beauty of David Haig, an Australian evolutionary biologist who received his PhD in the 1980s, to recognize that *genomic imprinting has very striking implications for measuring degrees of relatedness* (Haig, 1992, 1993; Haig & Trivers, 1995). This observation escaped the notice of geneticists who resisted learning about kinship theory. It is instructive to review this process with reference to interactions between hypothetical half-brothers.

If individuals have a common mother, then the old-fashioned way of measuring degrees of relatedness (e.g., as taught in *Social Evolution,* Trivers, 1985) comes from the work of Hamilton (1964a, 1964b). Specifically, a nonimprinted gene in one son (half-sibling 1) has a 50 : 50 chance that it came from the mother and a 50 : 50 chance that it came from the father. This is what is meant by a probabilistic degree of relatedness—in other words, no additional information is available. If the gene is in the mother, she passed it to her other son (half-sibling 2) 50% of the time ($1/2 \times 1/2 = 1/4$). Imagine, instead, that this is a paternally active gene; the active state of an allele is now being modeled so the effects of the gene when inactive can be disregarded for the moment. The following argument can be made: The gene is active in half-sibling 1 and it is a paternally active gene. Therefore, it is known that it came from the father *and,* therefore, is not present in half-sibling 2. The two half-siblings have different fathers so the degree of relatedness for the paternally active genes is 0. In contrast, if the gene were maternally active it would be active in half-sibling 1 and so would have come from the mother. There is a 1/2 chance the mother passed the gene to half-sibling 2; hence, $r = 1/2$, so the old-fashioned degree of relatedness of 1/4 for a half-sibling can be seen as an average of the degree of relatedness of 1/2 through the mother and 0 through the father.

The difference between 1/2 and 0 is considerable. Cancer researchers or molecular biologists attempt to explain imprinting in terms of cancer, as a device to prevent asexual reproduction, and various other inappropriate events (Haig & Trivers, 1995). They think that cancer is a big selection pressure. However, it is known that cancer is a relatively weak selection pressure, but the difference between 1/2 and 0 starting at the beginning of life is considerable. An example, using mice, illustrates how this process works. It is known that mouse siblings in utero are a mixture of half- and full siblings; typically, a mother mates with at least two different males per litter. (In the interest of simplicity, every offspring and every future offspring are designated as half-siblings.) In the case of half-siblings 1 and 2, in utero, if the gene is not imprinted, it says they are related by 1/4, on average, so the relationship is valued by 1/4. However, if it is paternally active it says, "We are not related, nor am I [half-sibling 1] related to any of my mother's future progeny, they mean nothing to me, genetically speaking." Therefore, paternally active genes are expected to be associated with greater parental investment from mother, faster growth in utero, larger size at birth, increased aggressivity in interactions with siblings, and other similar characteristics. Maternal genes are expected to be exactly the opposite.

There are three organisms in which genomic imprinting has been studied in some depth: mice, humans, and corn. Mice and humans map almost exactly on to each other. The rule for mice (which is statistically significant in different cases) is this: Paternally active genes or paternally active gene regions (areas in which the gene has not yet been located but in which a paternally active gene is known to be present) are associated with more rapid fetal growth rates, larger size at birth, greater suckling motion, and other comparable features. Maternally active genes tend to have the opposite effect.

Moreover, a parallel fact comes from flowering plants such as corn, and the structure of interest here is the endosperm, which is a triploid structure. The point is slightly more complicated to argue, but the logic is essentially the same. There are little ovules that are pollinated by pollen that are coming partly from at least two other plants. Therefore, there is a mixture of half- and full siblings on each cob that is especially important for paternally active genes. Paternally active genes, or gene regions, are associated with large, fat kernels of corn stuffed with resources. In contrast, maternally active genes are associated with kernels that tend to be shriveled and small, or devoid of certain nutrients.

The foregoing provides the basic theory and it extends to all kinship interactions, not just the early mother–offspring interactions on which Haig concentrated (Haig & Trivers, 1995). Most of the genes described are early acting genes, but the selection process applies to any kin interaction. For example, it is a fact that in ground squirrels, females often give warning calls. Females also tend to be half-sisters much of the time, and female kinship is important in nature. This means that the maternal genes of a female are going to make for closer relations to these other females, while the paternal genes are going to make for more distant relations. Maternal genes might be expected to lead to cries of, "Squawk! Squawk!" when a predator approaches, whereas paternal genes might be expected to lead to a little burst of internal fright. "Keep quiet!" They might say, "Remember yourself and get to your burrows!"—which is what a paternal gene is closer to representing under these circumstances.

## PHYSIOLOGICAL AND PSYCHOLOGICAL CONFLICTS

There are exact examples of internal physiological conflicts. The following is a model for what psychological conflicts might look like.

*Igf2* and *Igf2r* are the most amazing pair of genes in terms of this story (Haig & Graham, 1991). They are found in both humans and mice. In mice, *Igf2* (insulin-like growth factor-2) increases rates of mitosis, increases rates of cell division, increases growth rates, and increases body size at birth by 40%. It is paternally active. To put it differently, if a disrupted form of the paternal allele is inherited so that neither is operating in the offspring, the maternal one having been silenced by imprinting, the result is a dwarf that is 40% smaller but is otherwise perfectly proportioned (see Haig & Trivers, 1995).

*Igf2r* is insulin-like growth factor 2 receptor. However, it is not a receptor in the conventional biochemical sense of being the receptor through which *Igf2's* effects are activated. Its function is to take certain chemicals into the lysosome and degrade them. It evolved in mammals, after the evolutionary divergence from the lineage leading to chickens, a secondary binding site for *Igf2*. Its effect is to remove *Igf2* from the bloodstream and to degrade it. It reduces body size by 25% to 30%, and it reduces circulating levels of *Igf2* by a factor of 2.7 (Lan et al., 1994). In other words, the result is exactly what would be expected if internal conflict is a reality—a kind of inefficient system that nearly ends up back at the center point. (It actually has a slight upward bias, itself an interesting fact.) However, it is almost a wash, and these are strong counter-posing selection pressures.

Examples of possible psychological conflicts are important to explore. I will begin with a theoretical possibility of internal conflict concerning inbreeding. I will then review interesting evidence suggesting that the body is relatively *more maternal* in some sections and relatively *more paternal* in other sections—in other words, that it has relatively more paternally (or maternally) active genes expressing themselves in different tissues, hence the tissues themselves may be in conflict, including physiological conflict (especially in the brain).

Imagine you are contemplating a sexual encounter with your first cousin and guiding your thoughts with reference to evolutionary logic. The inbreeding increases the degree of relatedness to any resulting child, which gives a genetic benefit, but it also increases the homozygosity of the child, which imposes a cost (inbreeding depression). But you are inevitably related to your cousin on one side of your genome and not the other (absent parental inbreeding). If your cousin is your mother's brother's child, then your *maternal* genes are closely related (usually $r = 1/4$), whereas your paternal genes are unrelated ($r = 0$). Hence, both sets of genes suffer the cost of inbreeding depression, but only the maternal genes enjoy an increase in relatedness.

Given the foregoing, the maternal side of the self may be saying, "You know kissing cousins are cute, especially when there is a resemblance on the mother's side," whereas a moralistic tone might be generated by the paternal genes: "But what about the defects generated?!" It is in this manner that internal psychological conflict associated with these degrees of relatedness can be envisioned.

Another informative example involves chimeric mice. Chimeric mice are a mixture of normal mice cells, fertilized in the normal way, with cells introduced very early in development such that they form a coherent developing fetus for almost a full term. The relative propagation rates of the different cell types can be studied. There is an introduction of gynogenetic cells—in other words, asexually reproduced via mitosis from a female. Such cells only have a double set of maternally active genes and no paternally active genes. Alternatively, something called androgenetic cells are introduced. These have a double dosage of genes inherited from the male, but none from the female, so they have two sets of paternally active genes and no maternally active genes. A set of these very recent experiments show that different parts of the body end up with relatively paternally active cells or maternally active cells that can be intuitively linked to the underlying logic of imprinting (Fundele & Surani, 1994).

A skeleton tends to have more paternally active cells and genes. It is the skeleton that has to first enlarge and elongate if the body is to increase in size. This is one function paternally active genes tend to "want" to perform, at least early in development. The neocortex and most of the brain are maternally active; only the hypothalamus is paternally active. There are just evolutionary guesses as to what is taking place, but one possibility is that those same kinship decisions discussed earlier (e.g., "Do I give a warning call, whom do I nurse, how much do I let her into my territory, is that my aunt or my half-aunt, or my first cousin or my second cousin?") are mostly maternal decisions, so the cognitive processes undergirding them in the neocortex might be expected to be maternal. The hypothalamus regulates growth, but it also regulates appetite; thus, the more egocentric, "numero uno" factor may operate here. In an internal argument, the neocortex might be saying metaphorically, "Family is nice, family is important, I like family," whereas the hypothalamus might answer, "Me first!" or "I'm hungry!"

## THE X CHROMOSOME

Paternally active and maternally active X chromosomes in women are especially interesting. In a woman's body, as in a female mouse body, a given X chromosome is turned off in any given cell. Tissues tend to have both kinds of cells so that women have both X chromosomes active in the tissue. However, there are whole stretches of cells (as is known with respect to coat color in calico cats) that have only one or the other X chromosome expressing itself. It has now been shown in mice that there are bands of brain cells that are relatively maternally active, then paternally active, then maternally active, not unlike streaks or bands going across the cortex (Tan et al., 1995). Are they sometimes in conflict, as expected, over appropriate behavior?

## SUMMARY AND SOME FURTHER THOUGHTS

The foregoing certainly suggests the possibility of internal conflicts directed by different sets of cells—for example, alternating bands of brain cells. The X chromosomes have especially interesting properties in regard to genomic imprinting, but further discussion of this particular phenomenon is beyond the scope of the present chapter. In summary, a critical point is that the most important advance in understanding kinship since Hamilton's work is genomic imprinting. This is because genomic imprinting changes how all the fundamental degrees of relatedness are assessed. It changes how one measures the degree of relatedness to the parent. It is an inevitable consequence of this twist on kinship theory that there should be, and almost certainly is, internal conflict run by the gene expressing itself physiologically. It seems certain that this process will eventually be demonstrated psychologically as well.

The mechanism of genomic imprinting is still poorly understood. Methylation of DNA is involved in some way, but cause and effect are uncertain. There are, presumably, genes involved in imprinting other loci; some tentative evidence has been put forward regarding mice.

A final point is that, in this work, two people who have the same genome are *not* compared. The same genes can be inherited from each parent, but apparently something epigenetic, either a protein bound to DNA or a difference in methylation status (hypermethylated or hypomethylated) is involved. Some factor has to be passed down, and it is not the DNA genetic structure itself. It will be important to watch for new developments over the next several years that will enhance understanding of this intriguing process.

## REFERENCES

Barlow, D. P. (1995). Genetic imprinting in mammals. *Science, 270,* 1610–1613.

Fundele, R. H., & Surani, M. A. (1994). Experimental embryological analysis of genetic imprinting in mouse development. *Developmental Genetics, 15,* 515–522.

Haig, D. (1992). Genomic imprinting and the theory of parent–offspring conflict. *Developmental Biology, 3,* 153–160.

Haig, D. (1993). Genetic conflicts in human pregnancy. *Quarterly Review of Biology, 68,* 495–532.

Haig, D., & Graham, G. (1991). Genomic imprinting and the strange case of the insulin-like growth factor II receptor. *Cell, 64,* 1045–1048.

Haig, D., & Trivers, R. (1995). The evolution of parental imprinting: A review of hypotheses. In R. Ohlsson, K. Hall, & M. Ritzen (Eds.), *Genomic imprinting: Causes and consequences* (pp. 17–28). Cambridge: Cambridge University Press.

Hamilton, W. D. (1964a). The genetical evolution of social behaviour. I. *Journal of Theoretical Biology, 7,* 1–16.

Hamilton, W. D. (1964b). The genetical evolution of social behaviour. II. *Journal of Theoretical Biology, 7,* 17–52.

Lan, M., Stewart, C. E., Lin, Z., Bhatt, M., Rotwein, P., & Stewart, C. L. (1994). Loss of the imprinted *Igf2*/cation-independent mannose 6-phosphate receptor results in fetal overgrowth and perinatal lethality. *Genes and Development, 8,* 2953–2963.

Tan, S.-S., Faulkner-Jones, B., Breen, S., Walsh, M., Bertram, J., & Reese, B. (1995). Cell dispersion patterns in different cortical regions studied with an X-inactivated transgenic marker. *Development, 121,* 1029–1039.

Trivers, R. L. (1985). *Social evolution.* Menlo Park, CA: Benjamin/Cummings.

Wilson, E. O. (1975). *Sociobiology: The new synthesis.* Cambridge, MA: Harvard University Press.

16

# Happiness in Evolutionary Perspective

Jerome H. Barkow

One of the things I learned from Daniel Freedman is that new theoretical perspectives require reexamination of the familiar. In this chapter, the familiar concept to be reexamined is human happiness and the new (to many) theoretical perspective that of evolutionary biology, an approach long espoused by Dr. Freedman. I begin by looking briefly at how philosophers have viewed happiness, before moving on to contrast the public-health idea of happiness favored by social scientists with the individual-level focus of clinical psychologists and psychiatrists. My major concern, however, is what, if anything, evolutionary psychology tells us about the subject. Oddly enough, evolution joins with Medieval Roman Catholicism in a discussion of how, although the "seven deadly sins" definitely do not lead to happiness, in earlier hominid environments they

This paper is based on a talk given in Chicago on October 29, 1995, on the occasion of the Festschrift for Daniel G. Freedman. The author wishes to thank the Reverend Seth Indulgence for his aid during that presentation and during the writing of this paper. Thanks are due, as well, to Dr. Nancy Segal, the chief organizer of that conference, and to her co-organizers, Carol and Glenn Weisfeld. I am also grateful to Nancy Segal and Carol and Glenn Weisfeld in their capacity as editors of this volume. They provided helpful (and rapid-response!) editing of an earlier draft of this paper. Remaining errors remain my own responsibility, of course.

may have yielded adaptative advantage. I conclude the chapter by exploring how evolution could have left our species with so profound a capacity for the ultimate lack of happiness—extreme pain.

Of course, no single chapter can begin to do justice to the topic for, if one may equate the quest for happiness with the alleviation of distress then there is no subject, not even sex, that has received so much attention in so many literatures. Happiness is of course an English-language folk term rather than technical term. It can refer to an episodic or even fleeting mood—a "moment of happiness"— or to an enduring disposition. Psychiatrist Randolph Nesse, for example, clearly had the latter in mind when he wrote,

> The happy person is energetic, optimistic, assertive, socially outgoing, eager to start new projects, and makes substantial investments in people and projects with confidence that they will pay off. The sad person is lethargic, pessimistic, submissive, socially withdrawn, excessively realistic about personal abilities, and has little initiative for new relationships and projects. (1989, p. 273)

In contrast, English-language folktales traditionally conclude not with "they were *happy* ever after" but with the more realistic "they lived *happily* ever after," the adverbial rather than adjectival form of the term, suggesting that not every one of their moments was indeed *happy.*

## PHILOSOPHICAL DISCUSSIONS OF HAPPINESS

Philosophical discussions of happiness (often closely linked to, but distinct from, considerations of "the good life") compare in complexity to psychiatric discourse about the subject in much the same way as psychiatric discourse compares to folktales. For example, in the context of a discussion of medical ethics and quality of life (that is, that which makes a life worth living), Brock (1993) summarized three approaches to the good life: the hedonist, preference satisfaction, and ideal theories. He went on to explain that

> What is common to hedonistic theories . . . is that they take the ultimate good for persons to be the undergoing of certain kinds of conscious experience. The particular kinds of conscious experience are variously characterized as pleasure, happiness, or the satisfaction of enjoyments that typically accompanies the successful pursuit of our desires. (1993, p. 96)

Preference satisfaction theories involve people getting what they want, regardless of the extent this accomplishment renders them particularly happy; such theories "take a good life to consist in the satisfaction of people's desires or preferences." If you wanted to travel to Boston and do so, Brock argued, you have also traveled (from this perspective) toward the good life. Finally, those who define the good life in terms of an ideal theory argue that "it consists of realization of specific, explicitly normative ideals" (Brock, 1993, p. 97). Brock's example is the ideal of the individual being a "self-determined, autonomous agent" (p. 97). Note that, as with preference satisfaction, realizing this ideal is not affected by whether its realization does or does not make the person happier in life: If personal autonomy is an aspect of one's ideal theory of the good life then achieving it (or not) counts as an indicator regardless of whether the individual ever desired to be autonomous and regardless of whether he or she is made more happy or less happy by his or her personal autonomy.

Even if one limits discussion of happiness and its synonyms to the social–behavioral sciences, the relevant literature remains vast because, in so many cases, the ultimate research goal boils down not so much to that of increasing human knowledge but rather to that of enhancing human happiness. To simplify, let us begin with a heuristic dichotomy, that between researchers who focus on the individual *qua* individual, and those who concern themselves with entire populations.[1] A psychotherapist would be in the former category, a government economic advisor in the latter. With some overlap, we are distinguishing between the psychological/psychiatric fields and the social sciences.

[1] Some, such as family therapists, straddle these two categories.

## The Collectivity Versus the Individual

Social scientists, by definition, focus on the collectivity, population, culture, or society. They take what might be termed a public health approach to happiness, implicitly assuming that the necessary, if not necessarily sufficient, conditions for that state involve eliminating or at least minimizing social iniquities and inequities. For example, they seek not so much to make children happy as to understand and ultimately to abolish the social conditions believed to lead to child poverty and child abuse. In a similar way, they focus on collective phenomena such as racial, religious, and gender discrimination; ethnic conflict; ageism; our tendency to see the disability rather than the *person* with the disability ("ableism"); and so forth. Mass education is often treated as the remedy for such problems. Social scientists influenced by Marxist (and Marxian) thought tend to see gross inequalities in the control of resources and other forms of power as the root cause of collective misery and often see the redistribution of power and wealth as the *sine qua non* for widespread well-being. In contrast, some thinkers in the ecology or Green movement see human happiness as requiring a rethinking of our species' relationship with "nature" or the environment (e.g., the various contributors to *Turtle Talk* [Plant and Plant, 1990]).[2]

If social scientists take a public health approach to happiness, psychologists, social workers, and psychiatrists take a more clinical stance. Rather than seeking to alter society, they attempt to help the individual adapt to that society. The means to adaptation are vast, ranging from counseling and the provision of emotional support to psychoanalysis, behavior modification, cognitive therapy, and drug therapy. The last is particularly popular among psychiatrists, who have been known to advocate mood-altering drugs not only for the ill but also for many of the merely unhappy (e.g., Kramer, 1994).

---

[2] Bookchin (1990), who couples the two approaches in a sophisticated manner, sees ecological problems as stemming from social problems that, in the end, are caused by the tendency for human beings to seek to dominate; when we cease striving to dominate one another, argued Bookchin, we will cease seeking to dominate "nature."

There are often tensions between advocates of individual-level versus system-wide remedies for unhappiness. Many social reformers, for example, privately dismiss individual therapy as an elitist "band-aid" solution, unfeasible for the masses and generally provided only to the most economically privileged portion of the population. The social reformers are often enough criticized in turn, though perhaps more by advocates of competing schemes of social reform than by the individual-level practitioners.

## The Assessment of Happiness

Unlike philosophers and theologians, social and behavioral scientists often seek to *measure* happiness, requiring that they operationally define this ordinarily definition-defying folk term. In general, however, the relevant literatures, although often using the word "happiness," tend to subsume this state under the equally uncertain but less connotationally burdened phrase, "quality of life" (e.g., the title of Nussbaum & Sen, 1993). Quality of life measures have two practical uses. At the collective level, economists, sociologists, and policy makers often find it necessary to compare the relative well-being or quality of life of different communities and even of different countries. At the level of the individual, health care providers, patients, and the families of patients must often determine quality of life in assessing treatment and care options. At both levels, quality of life is assessed in the manner of a syndrome but with specific indicators taking the place of symptoms.

## Medical Quality of Life Assessment

The theoretical and practical problems involved in assessing treatment options constitute perhaps the major focus of the field of medical ethics. In practice, as Brock has told us, "the common view is now that health care decision-making should be a process of shared decision-making between patient (or the patient's surrogate in the case of an incompetent patient) and physician" (Brock, 1993, p. 102). Actual decisions must weigh both "objective" and "subjective" judgements concerning what is a "good life," and include consideration of the worth of the patient's life to the patient.

Brock explains that good clinical measures of quality of life reflect all three of the philosophical approaches previously discussed (the hedonist, preference satisfaction, and ideal theories). He goes on to provide three different examples of medical quality of life assessment instruments that include such items as degree of physical mobility and extent of aid required, social support, activity level, extent of self-reliance, and emotional state (Brock, 1993, pp. 118–122).

## Social Science Quality of Life Assessment

Social science approaches to the measurement of quality of life are as diverse as are those of the health professions. Because in the past there has been heavy criticism of exclusively economic measures of well-being, such as per capita income or Gross National Product, more inclusive scales have been developed (Erikson, 1993). For example, the Swedish "Level of Living" surveys, originally developed in 1968, use nine indicators, including contacts with health personnel and ability to walk 100 meters (to assess level of health and access to health care), work situation, income and wealth, level of education, marital status and social contacts with others, number of persons per room, exposure to violence and thefts, leisure, and political participation (Erikson, 1993). Note that the factors of personal ability–talent and local climate–weather are excluded, although a case for their inclusion could certainly be made (Erikson, 1993). In similar fashion, no account is taken of personal satisfaction with one's life. Scales of life satisfaction do exist but in this case are not included on the grounds that what is here being ascertained pertains to objective welfare rather than to subjective satisfaction (Erikson, 1993). The Level of Living surveys permit the "objective" comparison of populations with one another and over time. Allardt (1993) presented, as an alternative to that of the Swedish study, the approach pioneered in the 1972 Scandinavian welfare study. This comparative study included many of the indicators of the Swedish efforts but added to these some "subjective" factors such as measures of satisfaction with living conditions, social relations, and feelings of personal growth versus alienation (Erikson, 1993). Environmental indicators, such as level of mercury in fish and degree and nature of air pollution, were also added.

## AN EVOLUTIONARY PERSPECTIVE

Quality of life assessments, whether medical–individual or socioeconomic, are brave and necessary attempts to quantify that which would initially appear to be essentially unquantifiable. There are strong elements of the arbitrary and of the culture-bound in such scales. For example, is ignorance bliss? Annas did not think so when she wrote that, "It cannot, of course, be right that the happiest women should turn out to be those whose horizons are so limited that they cannot even conceive of alternatives" (1993, p. 282). Would an assessment protocol developed under the aegis of the late Ayatollah Khomeini of Iran be particularly similar to those developed in Europe or North America? Does each gender require its own set of measures (Annas, 1993)? Most important for present purposes, what connection do quality of life measurements bear to our shared ideas of human happiness? Can an evolutionary approach illuminate such imponderables? In similar fashion, can an evolutionary perspective aid the social reformer's mission of alleviating human suffering? Can it at least explain the only limited success of such endeavors?

The particular evolutionary approach to be taken here is that associated with evolutionary psychology (Barkow, Cosmides, & Tooby 1992; Buss 1990, 1991, 1994; Symons 1979). This perspective presents the human mind as not merely highly complex but as consisting of various "mental organs," each of which evolved to solve a specific adaptive problem (e.g., what decision rules to use to select a mate likely to enhance our genetic fitness, how to determine if an individual is likely to reciprocate our aid at a later time, which habitat would be the most fitness-enhancing, etc.). Although no doubt domain–general processes exist, the emphasis is on specializations. In the course of human evolution, our ancestors faced a range of problems of adaptation, and these problems constituted the selection pressures that ultimately shaped our brains. An important exercise, therefore, involves identifying the evolutionarily relevant features of our earlier environment, the environment to which we are presumably adapted. Assuming that we have been sedentary cultivators for only the past 10,000 or so years and have existed far longer as a species, the difficult question of precisely what constitutes the human environment of evolutionary adaptedness (EEA) arises (Barkow, 1989; Foley & Lee, 1989; Megarry, 1995; Teltser, 1995; Tooby & DeVore, 1987).

Unfortunately, it is simplistic to speak of a single EEA. Natural selection is an ongoing process and the environments to which human beings were adapting in the past no doubt were perpetually altering and continue to do so. Moreover, there is no reason to believe that our reliance on that body of socially transmitted information loosely termed "culture" is a new phenomenon in our species' history or that the great cultural diversity typical of our species is anything but ancient (Barkow, 1989). Fortunately, evolutionary theory, paleoanthropology, and the somewhat circular process of reasoning backward combine to permit us to generate numerous hypotheses about the EEA, and therefore, about human psychology. Such psychological hypotheses require empirical evaluation to precisely the same extent as do hypotheses from any other source. Thinking about the EEA, however, has proven to be an exceptionally fertile source of hypotheses. Moreover, the results, rather than remaining isolated intellectual paradigmatic islands each with its own assumptions and jargon, take their place as a coherent continuation of biology. To be specific, reference is made to the application to our own species of the same evolutionary biology that has been so successful in accounting for and predicting the behavior of all other species to which it has been applied. Unlike other paradigms (e.g., that of Skinnerian behaviorism), the results very often seem to be so intuitively plausible and compatible with much of Western folk psychology that one might almost refer to evolutionary psychology as "Granny's psychology" (Barkow, 1994). Evolutionary psychology has dealt with the nature of human cognition, aesthetic preference in landscape, sexuality and gender differences, weaning conflict and sibling rivalry, violence and aggression, jealousy, ethnocentrism, social class and prestige-striving, friendship and reciprocity, gossip, nepotism, and a host of other topics.[3] Thus far, however, these topics have not included that of human happiness.

## DOES EVOLUTIONARY PSYCHOLOGY TELL US ANYTHING ABOUT HAPPINESS?

Evolution is not about maximizing the happiness of gazelles or zebras, bacteria or fungi, rats or human beings. Evolution is about relative gene frequencies: Genes that increase the probability of their carriers surviving and reproducing increase their frequency in the gene pool. The behavioral and morphological traits to which these genes give rise are referred to as *adaptations.* From this perspective, that rush of gratitude we tend to feel when someone aids us, and the pleasure of returning that favor (especially when we can do so with little inconvenience to ourselves) is there because mutual aid would, in the EEA, have increased the probability of survival and reproduction. The emotions underlying such *reciprocal altruism* would have made such behavior more likely; and the genes underlying these emotions would therefore have increased in frequency in the gene pool (Arnhart, 1995; Cosmides, 1989; Cosmides & Tooby, 1992; Trivers, 1971). Because offspring carry one half of the genes of each of their parents, these "genes for altruism" and the reciprocal altruism adaptation they underlie became more widespread in the population, in the EEA, and today have become part of our evolved psychology—of Granny's psychology, if one wishes. As Nesse put it, "Mood is a motivator" (1989, p. 273). Our feelings of attraction, pleasure, gratitude, anger, jealousy, and tenderness all serve to organize our behavior in ways that, at least in the EEA, would presumably have tended to increase our genetic fitness, our genetic representation in future generations.

Our happy moods and feelings fit this perspective well. We find the chemical indicators of what would have been nutritious foods in the EEA to be pleasurable—that is, the tastes of salt and sugar and of fat and of

[3] For an introduction to evolutionary psychology, see Barkow (1989); Barkow, Cosmides, and Tooby (1992); Buss (1990, 1991, 1994); or many of the articles appearing in any issue of the journals *Evolution and Human Behavior* (formerly *Ethology and Sociobiology*) or *Human Nature.*

animal protein. We avoid the unpleasant—the bitter or strongly sour—that are the tastes of many plant toxins and of putrefaction. We experience joy at being reunited with good friends and relatives, anger at having a rival surpass us, distrust of strangers but trust of the familiar, and so forth. In each case, it is not difficult to believe that these emotions are adaptations in that, in the EEA, they would have tended to enhance the genetic fitness of the ancestors from whom we derive these traits. From this perspective, would enduring happiness have been selected for? The answer is, unfortunately, no.

If emotions were selected to organize behavior in adaptive ways, then, given the necessity for a range of frequently changing behaviors, no constant affective state, not even happiness, could have been adaptive for more than a brief period. Perpetual orgasm would have led to a quick demise at the hands of predators, rivals, or simply as a result of dehydration. Perpetual heightened vigilance would likely have interfered with relationships of reciprocal altruism, with food collection, and perhaps even with mating. Perpetual happiness would have led to highly maladaptive, disorganized behavior—the same reaction to a threat as to a friend or mate, the same reaction to a poison as to a food, the same reaction to a barren landscape as to one replete with indicators of food and drink (e.g., trees, flowers, streams, or lakes). Alfred E. Neuman, the endlessly smiling, mindlessly happy "What, me worry?" icon of *Mad Magazine* would never have survived in the EEA. After all, if our emotions evolved to organize our behavior in an adaptive manner they must change continually, tracking changes in our social and physical situation.[4]

## Happiness and Sin

Can we not in a sense subvert evolution by seizing on one of the positive emotions and designing our lives in order to maximize it? Religion, folk wisdom, common experience (and, of course, Granny) all agree that this is a path to misery rather than to perpetual joy. Let us take the seven

[4] See Pugh (1977) for a thoughtful, and largely compatible, discussion of human emotions.

deadly sins of Medieval Catholicism—sins that might better be renamed "the seven pleasures"—and briefly conjecture as to why each would (in small and situationally appropriate quantities) have likely been adaptive in the EEA (and may still be, today), and why as perpetual or dominant states they would likely have been maladaptive.

*Pride:* Feelings of pride would presumably have been adaptive when associated with self-esteem and with a sense of group membership (that is, pride in the group). Overbearing pride, however, is by definition arrogance, the verbal and nonverbal communication to others that one is so much their superior that ordinary norms of social interaction do not apply. This assumption of superiority, even when not contested, rubs the noses of those around one in their relative inferiority and thereby risks alienating them; the arrogant may therefore find that they have forfeited their relationships of reciprocal altruism. Excessive pride would, therefore, have been maladaptive.

*Avarice:* To seek and to accumulate that which is scarce and valuable as food, as shelter, or as a tool or tool-material would have had apparent adaptiveness. To do so excessively would have risked provoking the envy (see below) of others, not only inviting aggression but perhaps also forfeiting reciprocal altruism.

*Lust:* EEA hominids who never experienced lust were presumably a great deal less likely than others to become our ancestors. Perpetually lustful individuals, however, would have incurred the sexual jealousy and anger of others, risking violent retaliation and the forfeiting of reciprocal altruism. Excessive lust would also have been likely to interfere with other activities, such as those involved in finding food and shelter.

*Anger:* Anger in situations in which it would have led to defense of limited resources—mates, offspring, and other relatives; access to food and shelter—would have clearly been adaptive. To be angry, however, involves a risk of invoking anger in others and, thus, not only rupturing relationships but also becoming involved in physical violence. Thus, the perpetually angry would have been likely to experience difficulty in forming friendships and sexual relationships and to have been exposed to frequent and dangerous violence. Perpetual anger, in the EEA and probably today, is maladaptive.

*Gluttony.* Given that the availability of food sources during the EEA would presumably have varied at the very least by season, eating heavily when food was in abundance and storing extra calories for periods of scarcity would have been highly adaptive as a hedge against starvation (Scrimshaw & Dietz, 1995); but seeking to monopolize food would once again have risked rupturing adaptive social relationships. (Extant nomadic hunter–gatherers are very rarely obese, and it does not seem likely that obesity to the point at which it endangers health, common today, would have been common during most of the EEA. To reason in a circular fashion, the fact that, unlike the health of the whale and the seal, human health is in fact damaged by excess adiposity, suggests that no strong selection pressure existed during the EEA for health under conditions of what physicians so undiplomatically term "morbid obesity." It is nevertheless possible that, in some populations even today, some degree of obesity continues to be insurance against possible future famine.)

*Envy:* Envy is the goad to ambition. In the EEA, a feeling that urged one to equal or surpass others in skills involved in resource acquisition would clearly have been adaptive. Envy may also have been adaptive, at times, when it incited direct challenge of others, or even theft. In general, however, human beings interpret chronic and strong envy as evidence of lack of skill, standing, and resources, and as an indication that one would not make a trustworthy partner in reciprocal exchanges. Excessive envy is today, therefore, and probably was in the EEA, one more way of damaging one's social relationships.

*Sloth:* If we equate sloth with the tendency to rest and to husband one's energy, then it is clear how it would have often been adaptive in the EEA. Rest, however, by reasonable definition is that which comes at the expense of other activities, such as seeking resources and reciprocating the altruism of others. Overindulgence in rest—sloth—would therefore have been maladaptive in the EEA (and perhaps remains so, today).

The Roman Catholic seven "deadly sins" are typical of the Judaeo–

Christian–Islamic tradition, labeling desire (especially strong desire) as *sin*, to be fought against. Eastern religions have comparable teachings—but for them desire is not sin, it is the very root of *un*happiness (Miller, 1995). Religion and folk wisdom therefore appear to echo evolutionary psychology in the belief that a focus on pleasure or desire cannot lead to enduring contentment and happiness.

## Evolution and Pain

If evolutionary psychology is correct in viewing emotions and moods as evolved organizers of behavior, and happiness as situational and episodic rather than indwelling and chronic, then what of unhappiness and misery? Should they, too, not have been selected to be situational and episodic? If so, then why, from an evolutionary perspective, are we capable of (to be dramatic) dying in slow agony from an infected wound or even of being tortured to death?

The last question is, perhaps, the least difficult to approach from an evolutionary perspective: Once an organism has been so damaged that it will not survive in its EEA, its internal state is almost, but not quite, evolutionarily irrelevant. That is, its internal state cannot affect the relative frequencies in the gene pool of the genes it carries unless that state is reflected in behavior that alters the chances of survival and reproduction of one or more of the kin of the dying individual. These kin, by definition, share a proportion of the genes of that individual, so that at least in theory its actions could affect in some way the frequency of the genes it itself carries. A highly imaginative person might invent a scenario in which the last movements and vocalizations of the dying individual both reflected its internal state and in some way affected the behavior of its kin, thereby indirectly affecting gene frequencies. However, it seems rather unlikely that, as a general rule, during the EEA the internal state of the dying would have had much to do with subsequent evolution. Dying in agony—or simply the unhappiness of the dying—would appear, therefore, to have had little or nothing to do with evolution and adaptation. The state of mind and the suffering of the dying are indeed extremely important topics in their own right, but they are (perhaps fortunately) largely irrelevant to the present discussion of happiness and its absence.

What, then, of the unhappiness of the living? Evolutionary psychology predicts that unhappiness, like happiness, should be episodic and situational. Here again, folk wisdom, with its adages of life having its "ups and downs," and religion with its counsel of patience, suggests that the prediction is accurate and unhappiness is indeed episodic. There are, however, people who somehow seem to be unhappy regardless of what befalls them, people who appear to be permanently depressed. From an evolutionary perspective, the ancestors who presumably carried their genes should have been disadvantaged and selected out. Here we come up against one of the most intellectually unsatisfying (though perhaps entirely valid) aspects of evolutionary psychology: It is always possible to explain away exceptions. Let us label a state of impervious happiness as "morbid euphoria," and perpetual unhappiness as "clinical depression."[5] How can they exist?

Two answers to this evolutionary conundrum present themselves. The first invokes the concept of pleiotropy, the principle that a gene may have many effects and may have been selected for one of these effects in spite of another. Individuals with fixed emotional or mood states could be experiencing "side effects" of genes actually selected because they have entirely different, and adaptive, additional or alternative consequences. As stated previously, this is a legitimate, but quite unsatisfying, way of accounting for the maladaptive. The second answer to the conundrum of emotional illness has more face validity: No organism is a perfect biological machine—bones break, arteries become occluded, infections occur. Enduring, situationally resistant moods and emotions may be just what the psychiatrists and clinical psychologists usually consider them to be—

[5]Some may prefer the term "mania" to "morbid happiness." Happiness, however, tends to connote a degree of contentment not necessarily associated with the manic state.

pathology, illness representing malfunction, mood disorders requiring therapy.

## CONCLUSIONS

What light has an evolutionary perspective shed on the question of human happiness? Granny may not be impressed. There are those who yearn to find in biology some sort of "natural" guide to morality, ethics, and perhaps the meaning of life. Such seekers might have hoped, too, that by examining our evolutionary psychology we could have come across a royal road to happiness. The actual results are far more modest: We can conclude only that we should expect human happiness to be episodic and most often situational; that the goal of a perfect and event-impervious happiness is illusory; and that fulfilling desire does not lead to happiness. We may indeed succeed in living happily, but we will never be continuously happy.

The implications for those who seek to assess quality of life, whether for individuals or for populations, are equally modest. Assessment of quality of life remains a process primarily involving culture and values, with one important exception: Although these assessments already include some measure of social support or involvement, evolutionary psychology suggests that the importance of the social may be greatly underestimated by current methods. If the preceding analysis has any validity, then our human emotional structure could only have evolved in the context of an EEA involving societies with a very high degree of interdependence and with powerful selection pressures for the maintenance of strong social bonds (cf. Dunbar & Spoors, 1995). This conclusion is not surprising. The ethnographic record attests that, everywhere, human beings live amid a complex web of social relationships. In a similar way, the young field of psychoneuroimmunology attests to the extreme importance of social factors to human well-being (Kaplan, 1991), while the literature on social support clearly shows that "social connectedness" is associated with health and a sense of contentment (Berkman, 1985; House, Landis, & Umberson,

1988). Even a relationship with a pet greatly bolsters health and happiness (Siegel, 1993). Both social scientists and health care professionals might, therefore, consider increasing the weight of social involvement in their quality of life protocols.[6]

It was noted earlier that social scientists often play the role of social reformers, designing their research to reveal the prevalence and preconditions of social problems and attempting to alleviate what they perceive as inequality and oppression. Does an evolutionary analysis of happiness assist them? Here, the answer is probably "no," but there are no grounds for despair: What may well be needed to improve the effectiveness of social reformers is not a focus on happiness per se but on our complex evolutionary psychology and its implications.

Such a focus might aid in two ways. (a) It was suggested earlier that social reform fails often enough. Indeed, there are always those individuals who maintain that conditions following any particular social reform or revolution have become worse than they were prior to the (allegedly) corrective social change. No doubt they are at times correct. Typically, those who were the "good guys" when they had no power may become the "bad guys" when they get it. As Bertrand Russell long ago pointed out, many of us suffer from the romantic myth of "the superior virtue of the oppressed" (1950, pp. 58–64) and experience a sense of betrayal when it turns out that oppression does not generate moral superiority or when optimistically conceived efforts at social reform are selfishly subverted by the newly empowered. Evolutionary psychology may increase the effectiveness of efforts at deliberate social change and reform by presenting a

[6] This chapter has not discussed the substantial evolutionary psychology literature on gender and sex. Had it done so, it would have concluded that the answer to Annas's (1993) question about whether each gender needs its own measures of quality of life would definitely be in the affirmative. The reader interested in theory and data pertaining to gender differences in evolutionary perspective may wish to consult some of the following: Buss (1994); Ellis and Symons (1990); Fisher (1989, 1992); Gowaty (1992); Hrdy (1983); Kimura (1992); Masters (1989); Small (1992); Symons (1979); Townsend (1995); Townsend, Kline, and Wasserman (1995); van der Dennen (1992).

In similar fashion, this chapter has not dealt with whether different age groups need different measures of quality of life—that is, different conceptions of happiness. Here, again, the answer would likely be in the affirmative, from the perspective of evolution. Interested readers may consult, for example, Draper and Belsky (l990); Lerner and Voneye (1992); or MacDonald (1988).

more realistic picture of human nature than has been provided by other disciplines. There is a considerable literature in evolutionary psychology dealing with deceit, self-deception, ethnocentrism, and our tendency to systematically distort information and memory in predictable ways (see Barkow, 1989; Krebs, Dennis, Denton, & Higgins, 1988; Lockard & Paulhus, 1988). Familiarity with this literature might well help reformers to improve their effectiveness.

(b) Evolutionary psychology may also aid the social reformer when it is applied to the deliberate analysis of specific social problems. Much insightful work has already appeared dealing, for example, with homicide (Daly & Wilson, 1988), rape (Bixler, 1992; Campbell, 1993; Ellis, 1989a; Thornhill & Thornhill, 1992), sexual harassment (Radwan, 1995; Studd & Gattiker, 1991), child abuse (Gelles, 1991), psychopathy (Mealey, 1995), war (Low, 1993), crime in general (Ellis, 1989b), and other serious social problems.

Finally, let us end with some optimism: Evolutionary psychology teaches that ceaseless contentment and happiness are not so much impossible as pathological, but evolutionary psychology may also suggest ways to at least improve the ratio of happy to unhappy sequences. Rohner (1975), in an important holocultural study (cross-cultural survey) of child rejection, found that both across individuals and across cultures, parental rejection of children has profound and negative effects. Rejected children and the adults they become are likely to be hostile, insecure, dependent, and low in self-esteem. However, Rohner found *no* parental rejection of children among hunter–gatherers[7]. On the contrary, he found parental warmth and indulgence. Our ancestors in the EEA were indeed gatherer–

[7] Some argue that the term *hunter–gatherer* is sexist because it places the usual male occupation, hunting, first, relegating "gathering," the usual female occupation in such societies, to second place. Of course, in some societies both women and men gather, and in some women also hunt. Thus, *gatherer–hunter* is as valid a term as is *hunter–gatherer* and I therefore will use these terms interchangeably and alternately. However, "forager" is not (to me) an acceptable synonym because it seems to slight the degree of planning and foreknowledge involved in both gathering and in hunting (knowledge and planning at least as great, if not greater, than that involved in cultivation and in pastoralism). It should also be noted that Rohner does not distinguish between sedentary and mobile hunter–gatherers. His generalizations about parental warmth seem most clearly to apply to mobile gatherer–hunters. [See Kelly (1995) for discussion of the complexities of the hunter–gatherer category.]

hunters, but contemporary hunter–gatherers are not the ancestors of anyone save their own descendants. Nevertheless, even contemporary gatherer–hunters must be much closer in their ways of life to our ancestors than are cultivators and pastoralists. It thus seems reasonable to suggest that parental rejection was rare in the EEA, and human children are adapted to an environment that includes parental warmth. What else may we learn from reconstruction of the EEA?

This brief chapter is not the place in which to attempt an answer to this question. As our knowledge of the fossil record, of paleoarchaeology, and of experimental evolutionary psychology increases, however, we may expect to learn much more about the EEA. No one can seriously propose that we return to a hunter–gatherer way of life, but it may be possible to modify the way we live to better resemble, in terms of key parameters, the EEA. Parental warmth and nonrejection of children would be, following Rohner, one such parameter. A strong system of social relationships that provide much social support when needed would be another. As we learn more about the EEA, we should also learn more about how to shape our societies and cultures to ensure, if not an impossibly enduring happiness, at least the alleviation of much of human misery.

## REFERENCES

Allardt, E. (1993). Having, loving, being: An alternative to the Swedish model of welfare research. In M. C. Nussbaum & A. Sen (Eds.), *The quality of life* (pp. 88–94). Oxford: Oxford University Press.

Annas, J. (1993). Women and the quality of life: Two norms or one? In M. C. Nussbaum & A. Sen (Eds.), *The quality of life* (pp. 279–296). Oxford: Oxford University Press.

Arnhart, L. (1995). The new Darwinian naturalism. *American Political Science Review, 89,* 389–400.

Barkow, J. H. (1989). *Darwin, sex, and status: Biological approaches to mind and culture.* Toronto: University of Toronto Press.

Barkow, J. H. (1994). Evolutionary psychological anthropology. In P. K. Bock (Ed.), *Handbook of psychological anthropology* (pp. 121–138). Westport, CT: Greenwood.

Barkow, J. H., Cosmides, L., & Tooby, J. (Eds.). (1992). *The adapted mind. Evolutionary psychology and the generation of culture.* New York: Oxford University Press.

Berkman, L. F. (1985). The relationship of social networks and social support to morbidity and mortality. In S. Cohen & S. L. Syme (Eds.), *Social support and health* (pp. 241–262). Orlando, FL: Academic Press.

Bixler, R. H. (1992). Men: A genetically invariant predisposition to rape? *Behavioral and Brain Sciences, 15,* 381.

Bookchin, M. (1990). *Remaking society: Pathways to a Green future.* Boston: South End Press.

Brock, D. (1993). Quality of life measures in health care and medical ethics. In M. C. Nussbaum & A. Sen (Eds.), *The quality of life* (pp. 95–132). Oxford: Oxford University Press.

Buss, D. M. (1990). Evolutionary social psychology: Prospects and pitfalls. *Motivation and Emotion, 14,* 265–286.

Buss, D. M. (1991). Evolutionary personality psychology. *Annual Review of Psychology, 42,* 459–491.

Buss, D. (1994). *The evolution of desire.* New York: Basic Books.

Campbell, A. (1993). *Men, women and aggression.* New York: Basic Books.

Cosmides, L. (1989). The logic of social exchange: Has natural selection shaped how humans reason? Studies with the Wason selection task. *Cognition, 31,* 186–276.

Cosmides, L., & Tooby, J. (1992). Cognitive adaptations for social exchange. In J. H. Barkow, L. Cosmides, & J. Tooby (Eds.), *The adapted mind: Evolutionary psychology and the generation of culture* (pp. 163–228). New York: Oxford University Press.

Daly, M., & Wilson, M. I. (1988). *Homicide.* Aldine de Gruyter: New York.

Dunbar, R. I. M., & Spoors, M. (1995). Social networks, support cliques, and kinship. *Human Nature, 6,* 273–290.

Ellis, B. J., & Symons, D. (1990). Sex differences in sexual fantasy: An evolutionary psychological approach. *Journal of Sex Research, 27,* 527.

Ellis, L. (1989a). *Theories of rape: Inquiries into the causes of sexual aggression.* New York: Hemisphere.

Ellis, L. (1989b). Evolutionary and neurochemical causes of sex differences in victimizing behavior: Toward a unified theory of criminal behavior and social stratification. *Social Science Information, 28,* 605–637.

Erickson, R. (1993). Descriptions of inequality: The Swedish approach to welfare research. In M. C. Nussbaum & A. Sen (Eds.), *The quality of life* (pp. 67–83). Oxford: Oxford University Press.

Fisher, H. E. (1989). Evolution of human serial pairbonding. *American Journal of Physical Anthropology, 78,* 331.

Fisher, H. E. (1992). *The anatomy of love: The natural history of monogamy.* New York: Norton.

Foley, R. A., & Lee, P. C. (1989). Finite social space, evolutionary pathways, and reconstructing hominid behavior. *Science, 243,* 901–906.

Gelles, R. J. (1991). Physical violence, child abuse, and child homicide: A continuum of violence or distinct behaviour? *Human Nature, 2,* 59–72.

Gowaty, P. A. (1992). Evolutionary biology and feminism. *Human Nature, 3,* 217–249.

House, J. S., Landis, K. R., & Umberson, D. (1988). Social relationships and health. *Science, 241,* 540–545.

Hrdy, S. B. (1983). Behavioral biology and the double standard. In S. K. Wasser (Ed.), *Social behaviour of female vertebrates* (pp. 3–17). New York: Academic Press.

Kaplan, H. B. (1991). Social psychology of the immune system: A conceptual framework and review of the literature. *Social Science and Medicine, 33,* 909–924.

Kelly, R. (1995). *The foraging spectrum: Diversity in hunter–gatherer lifeways.* Washington, DC: Smithsonian Institution Press.

Kimura, D. (1992). Sex differences in the brain. *Scientific American, 267,* 153–159.

Kramer, P. D. (1994). *Listening to Prozac.* New York: Penguin.

Krebs, D., Dennis, D., Denton, K., & Higgins, N. C. (1988). On the evolution of self-knowledge and self-deception. In K. B. MacDonald (Ed.), *Sociobiological perspectives on human development* (pp. 103–139). New York: Springer-Verlag.

Lerner, R. M., & Voneye, A. (1992). Sociobiology and human development: Arguments and evidence. *Human Development, 35,* 12–33.

Lockard, J. S., & Paulhus, D. S. (Eds.). (1988). *Self-deception: An adaptive mechanism.* Englewood-Cliffs, NJ: Prentice-Hall.

Low, B. S. (1993). An evolutionary perspective on war. In W. Zimmerman & H. K. Jacobson (Eds.), *Behavior, culture, and conflict in world politics* (pp. 13–56). Ann Arbor: University of Michigan Press.

MacDonald, K. (Ed.). (1988). *Sociobiology and human development.* New York: Garland.

Masters, R. D. (1989). Gender and political cognition: Integrating evolutionary biology and political science response. *Politics and the Life Sciences, 8,* 31–40.

Mealey, L. (1995). The sociobiology of sociopathy: An integrated evolutionary model. *Behavioral and Brain Sciences, 18,* 523–599.

Megarry, T. (1995). *Society in prehistory: The origins of human culture.* London: Macmillan.

Miller, T. (1995). *How to want what you have: Discovering the magic and grandeur of ordinary existence.* New York: Henry Holt.

Nesse, R. M. (1989). Evolutionary explanations of emotions. *Human Nature, 1,* 261–289.

Nussbaum, M. C., & Sen, A. (Eds.). (1993). *The quality of life.* Oxford: Oxford University Press.

Plant, C., & Plant, J. (1990). *Turtle talk: Voices for a sustainable future.* Philadelphia: New Society.

Pugh, G. E. (1977). *Biological bases of human values.* New York: Basic Books.

Radwan, J. (1995). On oestrous advertisement, spite and sexual harassment. *Animal Behaviour, 49,* 1399–1400.

Rohner, R. P. (1975). *They love me, they love me not.* New Haven, CT: HRAF Press.

Russell, B. (1950). *Unpopular essays.* New York: Simon & Schuster.

Scrimshaw, N. S., & Dietz, W. H. (1995). Advantages and disadvantages of obesity. In I. de Garine & N. J. Pollock (Eds.), *Social aspects of obesity* (pp. 147–162). Amsterdam: Gordon & Breach.

Siegel, J. M. (1993). Companion animals: In sickness and in health. *Journal of Social Issues, 49,* 157–167.

Small, M. F. (1992). The evolution of female sexuality and mate selection in humans. *Human Nature, 3,* 133–156.

Studd, M. V., & Gattiker, U. E. (1991). The evolutionary psychology of sexual harassment in organizations. *Ethology and Sociobiology, 12,* 249–290.

Symons, D. (1979). *The evolution of human sexuality.* New York: Oxford University Press.

Teltser, P. (Ed.). (1995). *Evolutionary archaeology.* Tucson: University of Arizona Press.

Thornhill, R., & Thornhill, N. W. (1992). The evolutionary psychology of men's coercive sexuality. *Behavioral and Brain Sciences, 15,* 363–421.

Tooby, J., & DeVore, I. (1987). The reconstruction of hominid behavioral evolution through strategic modeling. In W. G. Kinzey (Ed.), *The evolution of human behavior: Primate models* (pp. 183–237). Albany: State University of New York Press.

Townsend, J. M. (1995). Sex without emotional involvement: An evolutionary interpretation of sex differences. *Archives of Sexual Behavior, 24,* 173–206.

Townsend, J. M., Kline, J., & Wasserman, T. H. (1995). Low-investment copulation: Sex differences in motivations and emotional reactions. *Ethology and Sociobiology, 16,* 25–52.

Trivers, R. L. (1971). The evolution of reciprocal altruism. *Quarterly Review of Biology, 46,* 35–37.

van der Dennen, J. M. G. (Ed.). (1992). *The nature of the sexes: The sociobiology of sex differences and the "battle of the sexes."* Groningen: Origin Press.

17

# Discrete Emotions Theory With Specific Reference to Pride and Shame

Glenn E. Weisfeld

Can evolutionary principles be useful in identifying the basic human emotions? In this chapter I try to make this case, using as the main example the neglected emotions of pride and shame. Thus the purpose here is twofold: to specify (but not to originate) ethological principles that may be useful in identifying and analyzing emotions, and to apply these principles to the analysis of pride and shame. More recent research on this emotion will be stressed, including my own on a possibly universal value evoking pride and shame.

I was led to both the general goal of applying ethology to the study of emotions and the specific one of analyzing pride and shame by Daniel Freedman's work. The first publication I read on human ethology, and one of the first in the field, was Dr. Freedman's (1967) chapter in Etkin's *Social Behavior From Fish to Man*. Its evolutionary, functional perspective on human behavior struck me as the homing ground for my peregrinations in the psychological literature. In the dominance hierarchy section of that chapter, Dr. Freedman referred explicitly to the emotion of shame. Several years later, when I went to the University of Chicago to study under him, I found that his students were applying the dominance hierarchy model to the study of children's peer interactions. This dovetailed neatly with my longstanding interest in pride and shame, which I felt was a basic but neglected human emotion.

I had become interested in the emotions in high school, when my friend Jeffrey Meldman and I pondered serious ethical matters and concluded that, if we wished to help promote human happiness, we needed to know more about the forms that happiness and unhappiness take. This literally and figuratively sophomoric interest in the emotions, fortuitously for me, is also of central importance to ethologists, who mainly study observable motivated behaviors. So I am somewhat embarrassed to confess that I have been interested in the emotions since high school, and perhaps have not made much progress since then. I still believe, however, that constructing a list of the basic emotions is a central task of psychology. What principles, then, may be useful in specifying the basic emotions?

## CONSTRUCTING A LIST OF THE BASIC EMOTIONS: SOME PRINCIPLES

### Principle 1: Emotions Are the Basic Behaviors

One evolutionary principle that may point the way to a list of the basic emotions is that *it is, in fact, important to describe the basic behaviors of a species, and these basic behaviors constitute the animal's motives, or emotions.* That is, the ethogram of a species comprises its feeding, mating, aggressive behaviors, and so forth—its motives. An ethogram is an inventory of the behaviors that the species in question is observed to exhibit in its natural habitat. Compiling an ethogram is the first step in describing the naturalistic behavior of a species. It seems logical that describing the human ethogram—the set of basic human motives—would provide the same sort of framework for organizing the study of human behavior (e.g., Eibl-Eibesfeldt, 1989; Pugh, 1977).

This descriptive phase, it is often lamented, was largely bypassed by psychology (Charlesworth, 1992). In short, psychology has not utilized the basic emotions as a framework for studying human behavior. Perhaps as a result, the corpus of psychological knowledge is weakly organized and integrated. One might even say facetiously that the chapters in introductory psychology textbooks systematically describe the behavior of psychologists—developmental psychologists, social psychologists, biopsychologists, and so forth—as much as they do aspects of human behavior. To the extent that psychology is integrated, the emphasis is on general behavioral capacities, especially learning and cognition, rather than on specific, observable behavioral tendencies—in other words, motivated behaviors, or emotions, as it is in ethology (e.g., Crawford, 1987).

Among psychologists who do study emotion and motivation, there is little agreement on the identity of the basic emotions. Psychologists, especially those who do not take a comparative viewpoint, have proposed a wide variety of lists of emotions based mainly on semantic distinctions—which of course are subject to the cultural relativism of language (see Shweder, 1994). For example, psychologists have labored to distinguish fear from anxiety; liking from loving; and effectance motivation from competence motivation, intrinsic motivation, and mastery motivation.

In contrast, evolutionists have shown quite a bit of agreement on their lists, from McDougall (1923) to Pugh (1977). This general agreement presumably is a result of common adherence to certain principles of behavior, all stemming from Darwinian theory. One emotion that evolutionists seem to recognize but few others do is pride and shame (e.g, Barkow, 1989; Pugh, 1977). Thus, pride–shame constitutes a test case for demonstrating the utility of evolutionary analysis for identifying a neglected but very important human emotion.[1]

### Principle 2: Human Emotions Are Species-Wide

*Basic human emotions, like animal motives, should be defined as species-wide.* Thus, cross-cultural research is necessary in order to identify the

[1] Most modern ethologists consider pride and shame to be the positive and negative ranges of a single emotion, as shall I. Consistent with this, one cannot simultaneously feel proud and ashamed of one's merit on the same criterion of performance. Thus, pride corresponds with high self-esteem and shame with low self-esteem. Further, the expressions of pride and shame are antithetical and hence mutually exclusive. McDougall (1923), however, recognized two distinctive "instinctive impulses": self-assertion and submission.

basic emotions. To take our main example, pride and shame are reported universally (Edelmann, 1990; Sueda & Wiseman, 1992). In every culture, children compete for social standing from about age 2 or 3 years onward, at which time the expressions of pride and shame also emerge (Lewis, Sullivan, Stanger, & Weiss, 1989; Mascolo & Fischer, 1995). Yet many books on motivation do not recognize pride and shame as basic and universal; in fact, some textbooks do not mention them at all (e.g., Carlson & Hatfield, 1992). This attitude may be a vestige of the secondary conditioning interpretation of evaluative reinforcement, convincingly refuted by Hill (1968).

Atkinson's (1958) and McClelland's (1958) theories refer to achievement motivation, but this is usually construed as limited to competitive laboratory and scholastic tasks and entrepreneurial occupations—certainly a very culture-bound and artificial conception of the scope of pride and shame. Furthermore, the terminology of "achievement motivation," resolved into "hope of success" and "fear of failure," seems vague and derivative. "Hope of success" seems really to mean self-confidence and receptiveness to competitive challenges, and "fear of failure" low self-confidence and avoidance of competition (see Weisfeld, 1980). Thus, these terms actually refer to the anticipation of future outcomes and affects and not to current experience.

Some scholars (e.g., Lewis, 1993) distinguish between shame and guilt, evidently on the grounds that there are "shame" cultures and "guilt" cultures. But very few data actually address the question of shame versus guilt cultures (Barrett, 1995). This distinction is probably merely semantic, with some situations (especially privately experienced feelings of having transgressed social norms) said to trigger guilt, and other situations (especially, publicly observed failures) shame or embarrassment. The distinction among shame, guilt, and embarrassment is vague and variable, suggesting that no fundamentally different aspects of behavior are being tapped. Lewis stated, "Many events are capable of eliciting any one of them" (Lewis, 1993, p. 566), and reports that some authors distinguish among these emotions merely on the basis of intensity. It seems more parsimonious to recognize the similarities rather than the dubious and superficial differences among guilt, shame, embarrassment, and failure. These experiences all seem to entail the same affect and expressions, such as blushing (Lewis, 1993). Given their many similarities, they are unlikely to have separate phylogenetic origins. For example, the expressions accompanying these experiences are similar, except that guilt (if defined as occurring in private) is seldom accompanied by any emotional expression. Blushing, like other emotional expressions, seldom occurs in private (Leary & Meadows, 1991). Theorists such as Lewis (1993) seem to favor developing ever more complex models of human emotions rather than striving for parsimony and appreciating the power and heuristic value of animal models.

### Principle 3: Rudiments of Human Emotions Exist in Other Species

Emotions, being complex and multi-faceted, took a long time to evolve; therefore it is unlikely that a given human emotion has no antecedents in other primates. *There are probably at least rudiments of each human emotion in other species.* As Panksepp put it, "I see no credible alternative to the proposition that all mammals probably experience essentially similar types of basic emotional and motivational feeling states" (1994b, p. 399). Ekman wrote, "Emotions are likely to be observable in other primates. It is possible that there might be some emotions unique to humans, but no convincing evidence exists that is so" (1994, p. 16). For example, pride and shame in humans probably evolved from dominance behavior in other species. Many parallels in status striving between humans and animals have been noted by human ethologists, as will be described.

### Principle 4: Affect Is Primary

Emotions have several facets—elicitors, visceral changes, expressions, overt behaviors—but are best identified by their affects. Self-reported affects may seem to be a weak basis for identifying fundamental behaviors. But, as Fonberg (1986, p. 302) has written, the perception of affects is as objective as the perception of visual or acoustic stimuli. In fact, *there are some compelling reasons for regarding affects as primary in identifying emotions* (cf. Zajonc, 1984). Panksepp (1994b) observed that there seems to be one affect for each basic emotion or motive—hunger and feeding, drowsiness and sleep, fear and flight, and so on. In other words, there is one-to-one correspondence between affects and adaptive motivated behaviors.

This cannot be said for emotional expressions that accompany some (but not all) motives, despite Ekman's assertion that "If there is no distinctive universal facial expression associated with a given state, which functions as a signal, I propose that we not call that state an emotion" (1994, p. 330). For example, some affects have no distinct expression (e.g., hunger in adults[2], love, music appreciation), and even infants often seem to experience affects without any accompanying expression (Camras, 1994). Also, some expressions, such as those for happiness and sadness, lack specificity. And if facial expressions are the sine qua non of emotion, does this mean that few animals besides the primates, in which alone facial expression is well developed, experience emotion?

The other facets of emotion likewise have their limitations as indicators of basic emotions. A distinct pattern of *visceral changes* does not characterize fatigue or interest, for example. And there is little specificity for the *stimulus conditions* that elicit an affect or for the *overt behavior* that follows; these can be variable and multitudinous in a flexibly behaving primate such as humans. For example, an omnivorous primate might react with hunger to a wide range of foods and then might obtain and consume them by means of a great variety of movements. And the same movement might serve multiple motives—for example, a female primate that presents might be engaging in either appeasement or sexual behavior. Thus, affects seem to be the single most reliable indicator of the emotion being experienced. Focusing on affects leads us to recognize pride–shame as a distinct emotion.

## Principle 5: Emotions Are Not Acquired Through Learning

If emotions are species-wide, they cannot be acquired through learning. In other words, *there are no learned motives* (see Panksepp, 1994a). We

[2] Babies have a hunger cry. This example reveals a weakness of using emotional expressions as the hallmark of an emotion. Is hunger an emotion in infants but not in adults?

do learn when to experience a given affect (for example, the acquisition of fear of speeding autos), and how to fulfill an emotional need (get back on the sidewalk). But basic affective capacities, such as fear or sexual motivation, are not acquired through modeling, practice, or instruction. Even pride–shame is not a learned motive, despite its being "social." Nevertheless, the means of fulfilling this emotion—our values—depend greatly on learning. We learn how to gain approval in our particular cultural circumstances. Yet the same is true of fulfilling the hunger motive: We learn what to eat. All emotions are influenced by genes and experience and by internal and external factors. They all have an evolved basis.

### Principle 6: Emotions Have Functions

Emotions, being evolved entities, have identifiable functions. *Each emotion serves to enhance fitness.* This may seem trivial, but psychologists seldom discuss the adaptive advantage of a given emotion for the individual, let alone its phylogeny (e.g., Lewis, 1993). Pride and shame prompt the individual to seek higher social status, which usually carries with it various prerogatives that enhance fitness.

### Principle 7: Cognition Subserves Behavior

*Rationality evolved to serve preexisting motivational needs.* If reasoning capacity did not serve biological imperatives, it would not have evolved. "Valueless" thought would waste the organism's effort. Thus, higher cognitive powers did not eclipse emotional control (see Panksepp, 1994a). Abstract thought is perhaps "higher" only in the sense that it is exclusively telencephalic, whereas the limbic system pervades the telencephalon, diencephalon, and mesencephalon.[3] Although cortical inhibition of subcortical processes can occur, so can the reverse, as when a child faints from holding his breath and then reflexively resumes breathing. Thus, the neocortex

[3]These three terms refer to the anteriormost of the five divisions of the vertebrate brain. In mammalian evolution, the first division, the telencephalon, came to expand greatly; it includes the cerebrum.

did not take over from the archecortex and paleocortex. In hominid evolution, the limbic system increased greatly in size even while the neocortex was expanding (Ervin & Martin, 1986, p. 147). In addition, as Izard (1977) has argued, we are always in the throes of an emotion (at least when awake or dreaming). Even when we think we are behaving "purely rationally," we are in actuality planning to fulfill some emotional desire. We are anticipating, or experiencing vicariously, a future emotional state. As we do so, we show signs of being emotional. In rehearsing these scenarios, we experience the anticipated affect and its characteristic visceral changes and emotional expression, albeit in attenuated form (Heath, 1986, p. 20).

We are especially apt to use foresight with regard to pride and shame (see Damascio, 1994), because so much of what we do is subject to the approval of others. We anticipate pride and shame at every turn and shape our behavior accordingly. This is rational, but it is also emotional. Sociopaths, no matter how intelligent, do not do this; they are relatively impervious to social evaluation. Incidentally, the connection between foresight and pride–shame is suggested by their both being mediated principally by prefrontal cortical structures; see Damascio (1994) and Panksepp (1994b).

## Principle 8: Emotions Are Fundamentally Subcortical

Features of emotion that are later to evolve cannot underlie more primitive features. Motivated behavior, present in all animals and mediated by the subcortex, predated the great expansion of the neocortex in mammalian evolution. Thus, *higher neocortical cognitive processes cannot underlie the development of basic emotional capacities.* Furthermore, the reward and punishment centers of the brain—those areas whose electrical stimulation is sought out or avoided by laboratory animals—are located within the hypothalamus and limbic system, not the neocortex (Buck, 1988).

Not surprisingly to evolutionists, the notion that the cognitive capacity for self-recognition underlies the development of pride and shame has recently been refuted. Schneider-Rosen and Cicchetti (1991) defined self-recognition in toddlers as touching a red spot on their noses reflected in a mirror. There was no relation between the participants' self-recognition and their experiencing shame, measured as averted gaze after failure.

However, it may be that abstract cognitive processes are necessary for a particular affective capacity to advance to a new realm of behavior. For example, competing for "toughness" in children emerges at about 2 years of age (Edelman & Omark, 1976). This behavior precedes accurate judgment of the ranks of other members of the dominance hierarchy, an ability that matures at about 6 years and seemingly rests on attainment of the cognitive capacity of transitivity. In a similar way, taking pride in succeeding at a solitary task precedes exhibiting pride in winning a race or other social competition (Heckhausen, 1984; Stipek, 1995). Consistent with this observation, Heckhausen (1984) established that engaging in competition against others required a mental age of 3 1/2 years. But it is unlikely that an emotional behavior emerges *in the first place* solely because of the maturation of a general cognitive ability. Developmentally and phylogenetically, emotions are more primordial than cognitions (Zajonc, 1984). Confirming the primacy of affect, Stipek (1995) observed that even 2-year-olds reacted to success with smiles and expansive posture and with boasting ("I did it!"). Children who failed reacted with averted gaze and closed postures. Frowning after failure, however, did not emerge until about 4 years of age, so this behavior may be subject to cultural display rules.

Another example of the importance of phylogenetic sequence is that of facial expression and affects. One rather recent, mainly higher primate, trait is facial expression. Facial expressions cannot be basic to affects, which seem to be experienced even by fish, which have reward and punishment areas in their brains (Rolls, 1975). Therefore, the notion that affect depends mainly on emotional expression (the facial feedback hypothesis) is highly improbable, and in fact has been reported only inconsistently (Buck, 1988). Moreover, it is unlikely that the brain keeps itself in ignorance about its affective state until it sends information to the face and viscera and then gets it back.

## Principle 9: Other Facets Are Useful for Identifying Basic Emotions

*Despite the primacy of affect (Principle 3), other facets are also useful for identifying the basic emotions.* For example, the existence of universal emotional expressions can be revealing, despite the limitations referred to under Principle 4. Indeed, there may be emotions whose universal expressions have not yet been recognized. Some of these expressions may be vocal. Given the importance that Ekman places on universal expressions (1994), it is perplexing that he limits himself to a small number of facial expressions. Why would the apparently universal prevalence of laughter, crying, tremulous voice, and sexual vocalizations not constitute evidence of universal emotional states, especially because some of them are accompanied by facial movement patterns? Also, what about the facial expression of drowsiness (drooping eyelids and yawning) or bodily expressions such as shivering? It would seem that emotional expression, although not the sine qua non of emotion, may have additional lessons to offer in analyzing the basic emotions.

What about the expression of pride and shame? As Darwin (1872) described them, pride and shame have distinct, stereotypic expressions with a consistent developmental onset, suggesting hard-wired, evolved behavior. Proud, successful people carry themselves expansively and conspicuously. Their gaze is direct (especially while speaking) and their manner is relaxed. An ashamed or unsuccessful individual exhibits an antithetical demeanor and may blush. These emotional expressions have been described in children (Geppert & Gartmann, 1983; Heckhausen, 1984; Stipek, 1995) and in adults (Izard & Dougherty, 1980; Tomkins, 1963). Researchers may have failed to recognize pride–shame as fundamental because it lacks a unique facial expression (Izard & Malatesta, 1987)—aside from blushing, which requires color recording equipment. However, there are also fairly specific expressions of approval and disapproval that elicit pride and shame in the receiver—for example, attention, smiling, anger, ridicule, and contempt. This observation, as Pugh argued (1977, pp. 285, 352), further supports the idea of an evolved basis for pride and shame, because nonverbal signals and responsiveness to them tend to evolve together.

### Principle 10: Each Basic Human Emotion Has Features With Homologues in Other Species

If all human emotions possess at least rudiments in other species (Principle 3), then *we can expect to find homologies between each basic human emotion and some motive in other species.* These homologies support the notion that the human emotion in question evolved from the animal emotion and therefore is basic. The next section will describe some of the homologies between pride–shame in humans and dominance–submission in other animals, especially primates. The object is to present evidence for the evolved basis of pride–shame and to use the dominance model to analyze this emotion further. Not coincidentally, much of the research pertaining to this topic has been conducted by Daniel Freedman's students (see Omark, Strayer, & Freedman, 1980). This line of research seems to have begun with Maslow's (1937) observations of dominance behavior in monkeys in Madison's Vilas Park Zoo.

## HOMOLOGIES BETWEEN PRIDE–SHAME AND DOMINANCE–SUBMISSION

One of the homologies between pride–shame in humans and dominance–submission in simians pertains to emotional expression. Dominance and submission expressions assume similar form in humans and other animals, except for blushing (Weisfeld & Linkey, 1985). This rather obvious homology has even reached the attention of popular writers (Maclay & Knipe, 1972), not to mention the pervasiveness of colloquial comparisons such as "proud as a peacock." Despite these and other homologies, few psychol-

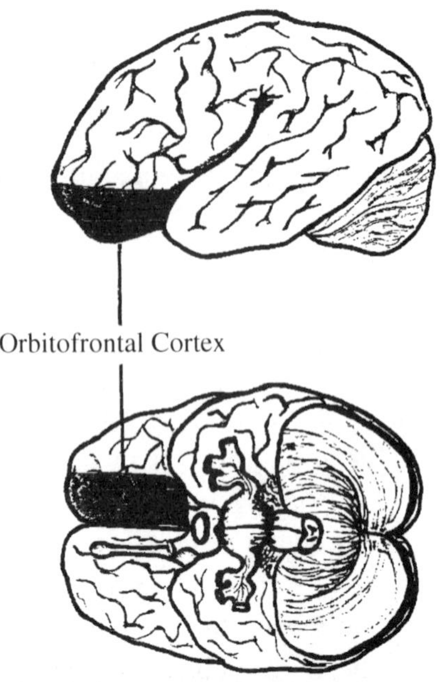


Figure 1

The Human Orbitofrontal Cortex.
*Source.* Drawing by Miriam Weisfeld.

ogists who have studied pride and shame have utilized the dominance hierarchy model proposed by Darwin (1872) and elaborated by McDougall (1923) and, later, by human ethologists (e.g., Barkow, 1989; Mazur, 1983; Omark, Omark, & Edelman, 1975; Pugh, 1977; Rajecki & Flanery, 1981; Savin-Williams, 1977; Weisfeld, 1980). Two recent works devoted exclusively to this emotion manage to avoid mentioning other species entirely (Lewis, 1993; Tangney & Fischer, 1995).

Neurological research has elucidated other such homologies. Pride–shame seems to involve the orbitofrontal cortex (see Figure 1). People with orbitofrontal lesions are described as showing diminished concern with their social standing and social mores, reduced capacity for shame and embarrassment, or lowered self-esteem (Ervin & Martin, 1986), and even sociopathy (Schore, 1994). Patients often lose their concern with conscientiously performing their job or even observing the most basic social courtesies (reviewed by Weisfeld & Linkey, 1985). These personality, or motivational, changes can be succinctly characterized as reflecting an impairment of the emotion of pride and shame. In a similar way, posterior orbitofrontal lesions in simians can lower aggressiveness and dominance rank (Fuster, 1980) or cause inappropriate reactions to the ranks of their cagemates. Analogously, the famous frontal lobe patient Phineas Gage was described as manifesting little deference for his fellows (Damascio, 1994). Many early neurological interpretations of this deficit invoked cognitive terms—in other words, impairment of the ability to foresee the consequences of one's actions. However, most accounts now refer to emotional or personality changes—reduced sensitivity to others' reactions to one's behavior. The motivational nature of the orbitofrontal cortex is indicated by its limbic cytoarchitecture and connections (Kandel, Schwartz, & Jersell, 1995) and by the fact that the posterior orbitofrontal cortex is a reward center in monkeys and humans (Passingham, 1993; Rolls, 1975). In addition, an epileptic focus in the orbitofrontal cortex in humans can release affective symptoms (Ervin & Martin, 1986).[4]

Recent research on the neurotransmitter serotonin has revealed additional parallels between pride–shame and dominance–submission. Men who are group leaders tend to have high serotonin levels, as do dominant male vervet monkeys; being submitted to elevates a monkey's serotonin level (Raleigh & McGuire, 1994). Male vervets with low serotonin levels tend to be highly aggressive, and men with low levels are at risk of committing homicide. Monkeys with low serotonin levels also often misinterpret benign social signals (such as play invitation) as threatening. In a similar way, highly aggressive boys typically interpret innocuous actions as hostile, as though they are expecting mistreatment (Dodge, 1980). Consistent with the notion of a link between dominance behavior and the orbitofrontal

[4] It is important not to oversimplify the functions of the orbitofrontal cortex. For example, this area seems to contain association areas for taste and for olfaction (Fuster, 1995). Single neuronal units reflect satiety to specific flavors of food, indicating their sensitivity to motivational need. Furthermore, sensory integration seems to occur in this structure for taste, olfaction, and vision, in that some cells respond to stimuli of more than one modality, especially if the stimuli have been associated by discrimination training.

cortex, dominant monkeys possess numerous serotonin-2 receptors in this and related limbic structures (Damascio, 1994).[5]

There is also a hormonal parallel. Testosterone levels rise in men who have won various tests of skill (Mazur, 1983), just as they do in male rhesus monkeys that have risen in rank (Rose, Bernstein, & Gordon, 1972). In neither case is it necessary that the male win a physical contest. However, in the human research, the victory had to reflect skill and not luck. Testosterone seems to enhance persistence in both sexes (Henry, 1986), which is presumably adaptive if one is experiencing success, as well as to stimulate spermatogenesis, which would be adaptive for a high-ranking male.

Additional parallels exist between the dominance system in simians and competitive social relations in humans (see Weisfeld, 1980). In both cases, success raises aspirations, and failure lowers them. Then, too, challenges are usually directed at others of similar or unknown ability. Furthermore, dominant simians and successful people tend to welcome challenges, seek out others, persist at tasks, exercise leadership, discipline subordinates, and command attention. In many studies, dominant animals have greater reproductive success than subordinates (Ellis, 1995). The same may be true of men, too, if attracting, gaining, and retaining mates are taken as proxies for reproductive success (Weisfeld, Russell, Weisfeld, & Wells, 1992). In a more direct test, university men with the lowest dominance scores were the most likely to be virgins (Komarovsky, 1976).

Further similarities between animal dominance hierarchies and human competition concern the consequences of a violation of equity. A subordinate may usurp a dominant animal's prerogative, or a dominant animal may continue to attack a loser that has submitted. Such violations of social norms must be punished, so the victim often reacts with rage—a vigorous attack. In a similar way, equity in human relationships is en-

[5] John Price and others (e.g., Sloman & Price, 1987) have advanced the related notion that clinical depression can be interpreted as a manifestation of sustained subordinate behavior. Consistent with the model presented here, in unipolar depression there have been reports of elevated rates of glucose metabolism in the orbitofrontal cortex (Baxter et al., 1985; Biver et al., 1994).

forced by anger, which is triggered by violations of social norms (Weisfeld, 1972). It is interesting to note that some monkeys, apes, and humans with orbitofrontal lesions exhibit a reduced capacity for anger when mistreated (Damascio, 1994, pp. 45, 57, 74). This may relate to the fact that monkeys with orbitofrontal lesions sometimes do not alter their behavior when it is no longer being rewarded (Rolls, 1975).

Trivers (1971) described the punitive role of moralistic anger in reciprocal altruism and how this and other emotions enforce equitable exchanges. It may be possible to understand the evolution of these emotions underlying reciprocal altruism in terms of the dominance hierarchy. Trivers explained that guilt can preempt a punitive attack by appeasing the moralistic aggressor. But guilt, or shame, probably evolved from submissive behavior. In both guilt and submission, the individual relinquishes prerogatives and shows similar nonverbal expressions. Trivers also discussed the emotion of gratitude. The human recipient of a favor feels gratitude. But perhaps gratitude is affectively identical to shame, or guilt, and likewise evolved from submission. This may be the same unpleasant feeling of lowered status, and it likewise leads to yielding of resources and expressions of obeisance. Also, the emotion of pride (not discussed by Trivers) may play a role in reciprocal altruism (Weisfeld, 1980). Pride, being a pleasant feeling, may provide a psychological incentive for social success or approved behavior, such as altruism. Pride also carries an expectation of reward, so that the altruist, like a dominant animal, expects and accepts resources. That is to say, pride complements gratitude in motivating the transfer of resources from recipient to altruist.

Thus, human cooperation is not simply a bartering of goods and services; social status, or dominance, is affected by most every transaction. We are highly sensitive to considerations of equity or status, because they can affect future tangible outcomes. Participants in a study often declined a favor if they foresaw no opportunity for repayment, apparently because of the burden of gratitude, or lowered status (Greenberg & Shapiro, 1971). In a similar way, if we receive undeserved or excessive praise or attention, we may blush with embarrassment (A. H. Buss, 1980). Thus, blushing may function as a submission signal, as an acknowledgement of favors received and of one's obligation to reciprocate (Castelfranchi & Poggi, 1990).

In humans, reciprocal altruism is complicated by the capacity for language. We use words to express our intention to restore equity when circumstances permit. Threats, thanks, apologies, and boasting symbolize the behaviors that are prompted by anger, gratitude, guilt, and pride. But these words can be viewed as an extension of the dominance system (Weisfeld, 1980). This is shown by the fact that compensation for faux pas can occur even without verbal exchanges. In the following examples, nonverbal expressions and actions suffice to restore equity: Preschoolers who broke a rigged toy either tried to repair it—make compensation—or else averted their gaze guiltily, as though acknowledging their obligation to make restitution, but seldom did both (Barrett, 1995). In a similar way, embarrassed adults whose blushing was observed by the experimenter acted less ingratiatingly (cf. "gratitude") than participants who believed their blushing had not been observed (Landel & Leary, 1992). And adult participants who observed an accomplice either make reparation for disrupting a store display or appear embarrassed rated him more favorably than if he simply walked away (Semin & Manstead, 1982).

## PREPOTENT VALUES

Another parallel between pride–shame and dominance–submission concerns the criteria of social success. In young children across cultures, as Omark et al. (1975) found, dominance seems to depend mainly on toughness, or fighting ability, as it does in many animals. Thus, fighting ability may be a prepotent value in children, just as there are prepotent elicitors of fear, interest, and disgust. In fact, another principle concerning human emotions may be that all of them can be elicited by both prepotent and learned stimuli (cf. Panksepp, 1986). It would make adaptive sense to be motivated by both phylogenetically ancient and recently experienced stimuli.

Several investigators have proposed the existence of some other evolved human values. Izard (1977) suggested that nakedness may be inherently shameful to people because holding this value would lead to seeking privacy for sexual relations. Darwin (1872) thought that when other people pay attention to our appearance, especially our faces, we can become embarrassed. Pugh (1977) suggested that certain traits, such as attractiveness, physical grace, courage, competence, and generosity, may be inherently admirable or praiseworthy.

Pugh (1977) also suggested that being smiled at by a potential mate may be inherently gratifying. In addition, sexual failure or jealousy may be deflating; male vervet monkeys that observed another male copulating experienced a fall in serotonin (McGuire, 1994). Pugh (1977) also proposed that solving a complex problem may trigger pride, in addition to a feeling of intellectual satisfaction. Further, the psychological tendencies to react with anger when wronged and with guilt when wronging another may be cases of evolved values (Pugh, 1977); the reciprocity norm is universal.

Multiple and culturally variable criteria of social success operate in humans. This variability has been taken to indicate that these values are relative (Fürer-Haimendorf, 1967), but perhaps they are not completely so. To study these values in adolescent boys, we gathered questionnaire data in London, Detroit, and Beijing (Boardway & Weisfeld, 1994; Dong, Weisfeld, Boardway, & Shen, 1996). As expected, the criteria of social success among peers varied somewhat across the three countries. Chinese adolescents whose classmates regarded them as leaders and as socially dominant tended to be good students. These high-ranking individuals were also perceived as exhibiting dominance displays (erect posture, direct gaze, relaxation, and commanding attention). In the United States, dominant boys were good athletes. In England, both these criteria operated and shaped the pattern of nonverbal dominance displays in boys, as shown in Table 1.

However, some values seemed to operate in all three countries. High-ranking adolescent boys were predicted to be economically successful;

**Table 1**

**Correlation of Various Attributes With Personality Measures and Nonverbal Expressions of Social Dominance in Three Countries**

| | United States | | China | | England | |
|---|---|---|---|---|---|---|
| DETERMINANTS | MEAS | EXPRES | MEAS | EXPRES | MEAS | EXPRES |
| Athletic | .51* | .48* | .32 | .28 | .58** | .52** |
| Intelligence | .24 | .36 | .80** | .61** | .57** | .53** |
| Fairness | — | — | — | — | −.04 | .05 |
| Attractiveness | .50*+ | .48*+ | .52** | .66** | .48** | .40** |
| Alert in crisis | .42* | .45* | .76** | .67** | .52** | .53** |
| Father potential | .44* | .40* | .36 | .19 | .17* | .22** |
| Earning potential | .61* | .48* | .69** | .71** | .48** | .51** |
| Dress fashion | — | — | .31+ | .57**+ | .68** | .43** |
| Complimenting | .35 | .31 | .33 | .28 | — | — |
| Masculinity | — | — | .65** | .62** | — | — |
| Humorousness | — | — | .45** | .53** | — | — |
| Well-groomed | — | — | .36+ | .57**+ | .25** | .29** |

NOTE: Correlations for United States and Chinese samples are for ratings *of* boys only for comparability with the British sample. Except where noted, ratings *by* girls and boys were collapsed for the U.S. and Chinese samples. Social status measures (MEAS) and expressions (EXPRES) are composites of those items best representing the construct in a particular sample.
**Significance at $p < .001$
* Significance at $p < .01$
+ Ratings by girls only
*Source:* Data from Boardway and Weisfeld (1994).

compare this finding with D. M. Buss's (1994) research on the widespread appeal of wealthy men as husbands. High-ranking boys in all three countries were also physically attractive, even in the Chinese school, where dating was nonexistent and little effort and expense were devoted to dress.

This was more than just sexual attraction, in that adolescents who were valued by the opposite sex were also valued by their own sex. Why should this be? It may be adaptive to seek out, imitate, and defer to certain same-sex companions—for example, to males who exhibited skill at hunting or warfare (Barkow, 1989) or to females knowledgeable about food

**Table 2**

**Means for Ethnic Groups in Nonverbal Expressions of Dominance, English Sample**

| Ethnicity | *N* | Mean | *SD* |
|---|---|---|---|
| White | 41 | 6.1 | 0.9 |
| African | 26 | 5.5 | 0.9 |
| Asian (Indian) | 23 | 6.3 | 1.0 |
| Turkish | 2 | 7.5 | 1.2 |
| Caribbean | 46 | 5.6 | 0.7 |

NOTE: The EXPRESSIONS is a composite of the Paid attention by others and Erect posture items, which best represented that construct. A lower score reflects a higher mean rating on that attribute. Created from data in Boardway and Weisfeld (1994).

gathering or infant care. High-ranking individuals tend to be imitated and to receive higher social evaluations (Weisfeld, Omark, & Cronin, 1980).

Thus, attractiveness and other traits may be prepotent human values. Research on these prepotent elicitors of various emotions is what many sociobiologists are doing (e.g., Chisholm, 1996). But this research involves particular emotions and hence fits within an ethological framework.

Some additional findings from this research may be of interest. Some differences in dominance displays were found among the ethnic groups comprising the English sample. Africans and Caribbeans exhibited significantly more displays than Whites and East Indians, as shown in Table 2.

We also measured overrating of self on the various traits. As Omark (1980) suggested, overrating may reflect the salience of the trait for the individual. Consistent with this view, English boys overrated themselves on desirability to girls, Chinese boys on achievement motivation, and Chinese girls on concern for others.

## CONCLUSION

It would seem to be important to study all of the human emotions, including pride–shame and the esthetic emotions (although in a sense all emotions are esthetic). If we can develop an ethogram of the basic human emotions, we will have identified the building blocks of human behavior. Another, unique advantage of an ethological approach to the emotions is that it allows identification of their biological functions. Knowing the functions of an emotion and its facets may reveal how and why it varies across ages, sexes, populations, and individuals. And so the emotions model may provide a framework broad enough to accommodate all of Dr. Freedman's diverse research.

## REFERENCES

Atkinson, J. W. (1958). *Motives in fantasy, action, and society.* New York: Van Nostrand Reinhold.

Barkow, J. H. (1989). *Darwin, sex and status: Biological approaches to mind and culture.* University of Toronto Press.

Barrett, K. C. (1995). A functionalist approach to shame and guilt. In J. P. Tangney & K. W. Fischer (Eds.), *Self-conscious emotions: The psychology of shame, guilt, embarrassment, and pride* (pp. 25–63). New York: Guilford Press.

Baxter, L. R., Phelps, M. E., Mazziotta, J. C., Schwartz, J. M., Gerner, R. J., Selin, C. E., & Sumida, R. M. (1985). Cerebral metabolic rates for glucose in mood disorders. *Archives of General Psychiatry, 42,* 441–447.

Biver, F., Goldman, S., Delvenne, V., Luxen, A., DeMaertelaer, V., Hubain, P., Mendlewicz, J., & Lotstra, F. (1994). Frontal and parietal metabolic disturbances in unipolar depression. *Biological Psychiatry, 36,* 381–388.

Boardway, R. H., & Weisfeld, G. (1994, August). *Social dominance among English adolescent boys.* Poster presented at the International Society for Human Ethology Congress, Toronto, Canada.

Buck, R. (1988). *Human motivation and emotion* (2nd ed.). New York: Wiley.

Buss, A. H. (1980). *Self-consciousness and social anxiety.* San Francisco: W. H. Freeman.

Buss, D. M. (1994). *The evolution of desire.* New York: Basic Books.

Camras, L. A. (1994). Two aspects of emotional development: Expression and elicitation. In P. Ekman & J. Davidson (Eds.), *The nature of emotion: Fundamental questions* (pp. 396–399). New York: Oxford University Press.

Carlson, J. G., & Hatfield, E. (1992). *Psychology of emotion.* Orlando, FL: Holt, Rinehart & Winston.

Castelfranchi, C., & Poggi, I. (1990). Blushing as a discourse: Was Darwin wrong? In W. R. Crozier (Ed.), *Shyness and embarrassment: Perspectives from social psychology* (pp. 230–254). New York: Cambridge University Press.

Charlesworth, W. R. (1992). Darwin and developmental psychology: Past and present. *Developmental Psychology, 28,* 5–16.

Chisholm, J. S. (1996, June). *Attachment and time preference: Algorithms for the contingent development of reproductive strategies.* Paper presented at the convention of the Human Behavior and Evolution Society, Evanston, IL.

Crawford, C. (1987). Sociobiology: Of what value to psychology? In C. Crawford, M. Smith, & D. Krebs (Eds.), *Sociobiology and psychology: Ideas, issues and applications* (pp. 3–29). Hillsdale, NJ: Erlbaum.

Damascio, A. R. (1994). *Descartes' error: Emotion, reason, and the human brain.* New York: Grosset/Putnam.

Darwin, C. (1872/1965). *The expression of the emotions in man and animals.* (Reprinted) Chicago: University of Chicago Press.

Dodge, K. A. (1980). Social cognition and children's aggressive behavior. *Child Development, 51,* 162–170.

Dong, Q., Weisfeld, G., Boardway, R., & Shen, J. (1996). Correlates of social status among Chinese adolescents. *Journal of Cross-cultural Psychology, 27,* 476–493.

Edelman, M. S., & Omark, D. R. (1976). An ethological approach to the study of cognitive development. In C. Smock (Ed.), *Symposium on early growth.* Athens, GA: Mathemagnetic Activities Program.

Edelmann, R. J. (1990). Embarrassment and blushing: A component–process model, some initial descriptive data and cross–cultural data. In W. R. Corzier (Ed.), *Shyness and embarrassment: Perspectives from social psychology* (pp. 205–229). Cambridge: Cambridge University Press.

Eibl-Eibesfeldt, I. (1989). *Human ethology.* Hawthorne, NY: Aldine de Gruyter.

Ekman, P. (1994). All emotions are basic. In P. Ekman & R. J. Davidson (Eds.), *The nature of emotion: Fundamental questions* (pp. 15–19). Oxford: Oxford University Press.

Ellis, L. (1995). Dominance and reproductive success among nonhuman animals: A cross-species comparison. *Ethology and Sociobiology, 16,* 257–333.

Ervin, F. R., & Martin, J. (1986). Neurophysiological bases of the primary emotions. In R. Plutchik & H. Kellerman (Eds.), *Emotion: Theory, research, and experience* (pp. 145–170). New York: Academic Press.

Fonberg, E. (1986). Amygdala, emotions, motivation, and depressive states. In R. Plutchik & H. Kellerman (Eds.), *Emotion: Theory, research, and experience. Vol. 3: Biological foundations of emotion* (pp. 301–331). New York: Academic Press.

Freedman, D. G. (1967). A biological view of man's social behavior. In W. Etkin, *Social behavior from fish to man* (pp. 152–188). Chicago: University of Chicago Press.

Fürer–Haimendorf, C. von (1967). *Morals and merit.* London: Weidenfeld & Nicolson.

Fuster, J. M. (1980). *The prefrontal cortex: Anatomy, physiology, and neuropsychology of the frontal lobe.* New York: Raven Press.

Fuster, J. M. (1995). *Memory in the cerebral cortex.* Cambridge, MA: MIT Press.

Geppert, U., & Gartmann, D. (1983, August). *The emergence of self-evaluative emotions as consequences of achievement actions.* Paper presented at the biennial meeting of the International Society for the Study of Behavioral Development, Munich, Germany.

Greenberg, M. S., & Shapiro, S. P. 1971). Indebtedness: An adverse aspect of asking and receiving help. *Sociometry, 34,* 290–301.

Heath, R. G. (1986). The neural substrate of emotion. In R. Plutchik & H. Kellerman (Eds.), *Emotion: Theory, research, and experience* (pp. 3–35). New York: Academic Press.

Heckhausen, H. (1984). Emergent achievement behavior: Some early developments. In J. Nicholls (Ed.), *Advances in motivation and achievement: The development of achievement motivation* (Vol. 3, pp. 1–32). Greenwich, CT: JAI Press.

Henry, J. P. (1986). Neuroendocrine patterns of emotional response. In R. Plutchik & H. Kellerman (Eds.), *Emotion: Theory, research, and experience* (pp. 37–60). New York: Academic Press.

Hill, W. F. (1968). Sources of evaluative reinforcement. *Psychological Bulletin, 69,* 132–146.

Izard, C. E. (1977). *Human emotions.* New York: Plenum Press.

Izard, C., & Dougherty, L. (1980). *A system for identifying affect expressions by holistic judgments (AFFEX).* Newark: University of Delaware, Instructional Resources Center.

Izard, C., & Malatesta, C. (1987). Perspectives on emotional development: I. Differential emotions theory of early emotional development. In J. Osofsky (Ed.), *Handbook of infant development* (2nd ed., pp. 494–553). New York: Wiley.

Kandel, E. R., Schwartz, J. H., & Jersell, T. M. (Eds.) (1995). *Essentials of neural science and behavior.* Norwalk, CT: Appleton & Lange.

Komarovsky, M. (1976). *Dilemmas of masculinity: A study of college youth.* New York: Norton.

Landel, J., & Leary, M. R. (1992, March). *Social blushing as a face-saving display.* Paper presented at the meeting of the Southeastern Psychological Association, Knoxville, TN.

Leary, M. R., & Meadows, S. (1991). Predictors, elicitors, and concomitants of social blushing. *Journal of Personality & Social Psychology, 60,* 254–262.

Lewis, M. (1993). Self-conscious emotions: Embarrassment, pride, shame, and guilt. In M. Lewis & J. M. Haviland (Eds.), *Handbook of emotions* (pp. 563–573). New York: Guilford Press.

Lewis, M., Sullivan, M., Stanger, C., & Weiss, M. (1989). Self development and self-conscious emotions. *Child Development, 60,* 140–156.

Maclay, G., & Knipe, H. (1972). *The dominant man.* New York: Delacorte Press.

Mascolo, M. F., & Fischer, K. W. (1995). Developmental transformations in appraisals for pride, shame, and guilt. In J. P. Tangney & K. W. Fischer (Eds.), *Self-conscious emotions: The psychology of shame, guilt, embarrasment, and pride* (pp. 64–113). New York: Guilford Press.

Maslow, A. H. (1937). Dominance-feeling, behavior, and status. *Psychological Review, 44,* 404–429.

Mazur, A. (1983). Hormones, aggression, and dominance in humans. In B. B. Svare (Ed.), *Hormones and aggressive behavior* (pp. 563–576). New York: Plenum Press.

McClelland, D. C. (1958). Methods of measuring human motivation. In J. W. Atkinson (Ed.), *Motives in fantasy, action, and society* (pp. 7–42). New York: Van Nostrand Reinhold.

McDougall, W. (1923). *Outline of psychology.* New York: Scribner's.

McGuire, M. T. (1994, August). *Environmental contingencies and physiological change.* Invited address presented at the conference of the International Society for Human Ethology, Toronto, Canada.

Omark, D. R. (1980). The Umwelt and cognitive development. In D. R. Omark, F. F. Strayer, & D. G. Freedman (Eds.), *Dominance relations: An ethological view of human conflict and social interaction* (pp. 231–258). New York: Garland Press.

Omark, D. R., Omark, M., & Edelman, M. S. (1975). Formation of dominance hierarchies in young children: Action and perception. In T. Williams (Ed.), *Psychological anthropology* (Vol. 14, pp. 87–107). The Hague: Mouton.

Omark, D. R., Strayer, F. F., & Freedman, D. G. (1980). *Dominance relations: An ethological view of human conflict and social interaction.* New York: Garland Press.

Panksepp, J. (1986). The anatomy of emotions. In R. Plutchik & H. Kellerman (Eds.), *Emotion: Theory, research, and experience* (pp. 91–124). New York: Academic Press.

Panksepp, J. (1994a). The basics of basic emotion. In P. Ekman & R. J. Davidson (Eds.), *The nature of emotion: Fundamental questions* (pp. 20–24). Oxford: Oxford University Press.

Panksepp, J. (1994b). Evolution constructed the potential for subjective experience within the neurodynamics of the neomammalian brain. In P. Ekman & R. J. Davidson (Eds.), *The nature of emotion: Fundamental questions* (pp. 396–399). Oxford: Oxford University Press.

Passingham, R. (1993). *The frontal lobes and voluntary action.* Oxford: Oxford University Press.

Pugh, G. E. (1977). *The biological origin of human values.* New York: Basic Books.

Rajecki, D. W., & Flanery, R. C. (1981). Social conflict and dominance in children: A case for a primate homology. In M. E. Lamb & A. Brown (Eds.), *Advances in developmental psychology* (Vol. I, pp. 87–129). Hillsdale, NJ: Erlbaum.

Raleigh, M. J., & McGuire, M. T. (1994). Serotonin, aggression, and violence in vervet monkeys. In R. D. Masters & M. T. McGuire (Eds.), *The neurotransmitter revolution* (pp. 129–144). Carbondale: Southern Illinois University Press.

Rolls, E. T. (1975). *The brain and reward.* New York: Pergamon Press.

Rose, R. M., Bernstein, I. S., & Gordon, T. P. (1972). Plasma testosterone levels in rhesus: Influences of sexual and social stimuli. *Science, 178,* 643–645.

Savin-Williams, R. C. (1977). Dominance in a human adolescent group. *Animal Behaviour, 25,* 400–406.

Schneider-Rosen, K., & Cicchetti, D. (1991). Early self-knowledge and emotional development: Visual self-recognition and affective reactions to mirror self-images in maltreated and non-maltreated toddlers. *Developmental Psychology, 27,* 471–478.

Schore, A. N. (1994). *Affect regulation and the origins of self.* Hillsdale, NJ: Erlbaum.

Semin, G. R., & Manstead, A. S. R. (1982). The social implications of embarrassment displays and restitution behavior. *European Journal of Social Psychology, 12,* 367–377.

Shweder, R. A. (1994). "You're not sick, you're just in love": Emotion as an interpretive system. In P. Ekman & R. J. Davidson (Eds.), *The nature of emotion: Fundamental questions* (pp. 32–44). New York: Oxford University Press.

Sloman, L., & Price, J. S. (1987). Losing behavior (yielding subroutine) and human depression: Proximate and selective mechanisms. *Ethology and Sociobiology, 8,* 99s–109s.

Stipek, D. (1995). The development of pride and shame in toddlers. In J. P. Tangney & K. W. Fischer (Eds.), *Self-conscious emotions: The psychology of shame, guilt, embarrassment, and pride* (pp. 237–252). New York: Guilford Press.

Sueda, K., & Wiseman, R. L. (1992). Embarrassment remediation in Japan and the United States. *International Journal of Intercultural Relations, 16,* 159–173.

Tangney, J. P., & Fischer, K. W. (1995). *The self–conscious emotions: The psychology of shame, guilt, embarrassment, and pride.* New York: Guilford Press.

Tomkins, S. (1963). *Affect, imagery, consciousness: The negative affects* (Vol. 2). New York: Springer.

Trivers, R. L. (1971). The evolution of reciprocal altruism. *Quarterly Review of Biology, 46,* 35–57.

Weisfeld, G. E. (1972). Violations of social norms as inducers of aggression. *International Journal of Group Tensions, 2,* 53–70.

Weisfeld, G. E. (1980). Social dominance and human motivation. In D. R. Omark, F. F. Strayer, & D. G. Freedman (Eds.), *Dominance relations: An ethological view of human conflict and social interaction* (pp. 273–286). New York: Garland Press.

Weisfeld, G. E., & Linkey, H. E. (1985). Dominance displays as indicators of a social success motive. In J. Dovidio & S. Ellyson (Eds.), *Power, dominance, and nonverbal behavior* (pp. 109–128). New York: Springer.

Weisfeld, G. E., Omark, D. R., & Cronin, C. L. (1980). A longitudinal and cross-sectional study of dominance in boys. In D. R. Omark, F. F. Strayer, & D. G. Freedman (Eds.), *Dominance relations: An ethological view of human conflict and social interaction* (pp. 205–216). New York: Garland Press.

Weisfeld, G. E., Russell, R. J. H., Weisfeld, C. C., & Wells, P. A. (1992). Correlates of satisfaction in British marriages. *Ethology & Sociobiology, 13,* 125–145.

Zajonc, R. B. (1984). On primacy of affect. In K. R. Scherer & P. Ekman (Eds.), *Approaches to emotion* (pp. 259–270). Hillsdale, NJ: Erlbaum.

# Section V Conclusion

Roger J. R. Levesque

Sometimes it is difficult to breathe life into old theories, especially controversial ones. Yet Trivers, Barkow, and Weisfeld have done just that. They propose that our understanding of human emotions and psychological functioning can be deepened if we consider important research and theoretical contributions from evolutionary perspectives.

Trivers discusses a simple, yet incredible, advance in genetic research: Some genes seem to be differentially active in offspring, depending on which parent contributed them. Trivers presents several possible implications of the finding that organisms may have different gene regions that are more "maternal" or "paternal." For example, he proposes that most of the brain is maternally active, whereas the hypothalamus and most of the skeleton tend to be paternally active. Given that paternal and maternal genes may have different evolutionary agendas, it is possible that physiological conflict exists. By extension, it is also possible that differential maternal and paternal activations may contribute to intrapsychic conflict. For example, the costs and gains that would be derived from inbreeding, based on differentially activated maternally and paternally contributed genes, could conceivably lead to psychological conflict.

Trivers's proposals certainly encourage a rethinking of the role of genetics and parental contributions to human nature. Although the mechanisms guiding the parent-specific gene expressions remain poorly understood and speculative, their implications are worth considering. Because some internal conflict regulated by gene expression clearly operates at physiological levels, there is no reason to doubt that it would have psycho-

Nancy L. Segal and Glenn E. Weisfeld's comments on earlier drafts of this essay were greatly appreciated.

logical effects as well. For example, it is not difficult to make a link from understanding how conflict surrounding inbreeding might lead to jealousy and other psychological conflicts. However, it would be important to remind ourselves that genes do not code directly for any behavior, feeling, or thought. Although Trivers properly highlights the crucial importance of genetic influences, genetic contributions cannot be divorced from ecological and cultural influences. In this regard, Trivers's analysis begins what is likely to become a very fruitful line of exciting research and innovative thinking: His discussion promises to contribute to our understanding of exactly how genes and evolution recursively affect social, ecological, and cultural influences. Clearly, new work in genetics provides the opportunity to rethink established theories concerning, for example, the bases of social relatedness and affiliation and to reexamine phenomena that have heretofore not benefited from genetically derived and evolutionary analyses.

Weisfeld's work epitomizes the utility of rethinking phenomena from evolutionary perspectives. He proposes that psychologists concerned with basic human emotions have missed important opportunities to pursue more sophisticated approaches to the study of emotions. He optimistically asserts that evolutionary theory could serve as a metatheory to identify basic human emotions, the motives that underlie human behavior. Weisfeld supports his proposal by a remarkably thorough analysis of a basic emotion: pride–shame. His approach skillfully emphasizes the role of social and biological forces as he examines the important qualities necessary for the construction of an ethogram of human emotions, which includes human universality, cross-species homologies, presence at birth, and adaptiveness.

Although Weisfeld explores the now familiar topic of human emotions, his analysis is actually quite bold. He does not take the substantial literature on the psychology of emotions on its own terms. For example, he does not integrate psychological data through the use of evolutionary principles. Instead, he does the reverse: He uses evolutionary principles to guide his exploration. By doing so, he moves beyond basic psychology; he uses examples from other species and other cultures. Quite surprisingly, he chooses an emotion many others would find to be highly culturally influenced: pride–shame is known to be a self-reflexive or moral emotion. Indeed, this emotion is so apparently culturally determined that it has been asserted that some cultures have been primarily identified by its variants (e.g., shame and guilt cultures; see Piers & Singer, 1971). Yet, Weisfeld's analysis appropriately reveals that, on closer scrutiny, there are more than simply social and cultural forces at work.

Although a fine analysis of basic emotions and their evolutionary ties, Weisfeld's approach does not address how and why more complex emotions may (or may not) vary from culture to culture; nor does he address the possible important contribution culture may play in the expression of different emotions. Admittedly, that is not central to his analysis. However, although breaking down complex emotions into more basic emotions is a useful way to describe which ones may be universal and why they might be so, this effort does not necessarily assist those concerned with the expression and experience of complex emotions.

Barkow seemingly picks up where Weisfeld leaves off. He adeptly provides an examination of one of the most complex, multifaceted and multidetermined emotions: happiness. Like Weisfeld, Barkow reexamines an immensely researched concept from the perspective of evolutionary psychology. His analysis is insightful and instructive.

Barkow's analysis of different approaches to happiness leads him to appropriately observe the tendency among theorists to focus on either individual or societal aspects of happiness. The end result of these limited approaches is that they focus either on adapting individuals to societies or on adapting societies to individuals. These foci have important repercussions, particularly in terms of designing interventions. The former approach intervenes at individual levels and focuses on inner subjectivity, whereas the latter focuses on objective notions of human welfare and seeks to abolish social conditions leading to distress (e.g., poverty, child abuse, racism, and discrimination) and looks to methods for alleviating distress (e.g., education, redistribution of resources). Barkow properly emphasizes that these approaches essentially miss the big picture. He correctly asserts that a proper analysis of happiness would include both individual and social factors and, in that regard, that evolutionary theory provides a more comprehensive framework for analyzing the multiple facets of human happiness than other current approaches.

In his analysis of the potential contribution of evolutionary theory to human happiness, Barkow importantly notes that evolutionary theory is actually not about maximizing happiness. Evolutionary principles relate to relative gene frequencies: Genes that increase the probability of their carriers' surviving and reproducing increase the frequency of their representation in the gene pool. Feelings that organize our behaviors in ways that would have tended to increase our genetic fitness, the genetic representation in future generations, would have been adaptive and would have evolved along with behavioral and morphological traits. He appropriately proposes that any strong emotion experienced in perpetual or dominant states would likely have been maladaptive. Not surprisingly, he thus concludes that happiness is necessarily illusory.

Viewed in this light, the contributions of evolutionary biology are indeed quite modest. Yet, evolutionary principles are *not* insignificant. As Barkow finds, evolutionary theory may never assist reformers to move people toward constant happiness; yet that does not mean that evolutionary theory is not useful. Happiness is not necessarily perpetual, and even people who are often miserable by other people's standards may perceive themselves as generally happy. Evolutionary theory at least suggests paths that may lead us toward momentary happiness. For example, evolutionary principles suggest that an important way to achieve at least minimal levels of happiness is through involvement in social support systems and social networks. This, undoubtedly, constitutes one of evolutionary theory's most useful insights. Clearly, encouraging sociality and cooperation is a critical step toward alleviating the plight of many. Indeed, the need to foster sociality was the major thrust that made the culturally (and biologically) constituted "sins" that Barkow examines as deadly as they are.

Culture and the forces of evolution aim to encourage cooperation and sociality, or at least to balance individual urges that would be counterproductive to both individual and group fulfillment. If those insights were taken seriously, the impact on individuals and society would be substantial. Specifically, the insights offered by evolutionary theory could be harnessed to provide solutions to pressing human issues, such as the alleviation of poverty and various forms of violence. At the very least, they could illuminate the forces that obfuscate positive societal development. Nurturance, cooperation, and concern for collective welfare, undoubtedly, are as much a part of human nature as are, for example, competitive lusts and impulses for power, control, and dominance.

Although Trivers, Weisfeld, and Barkow reason from different perspectives and emphasize different levels of thinking related to genetics, evolution, psychology, and culture, they all end up enlightening longstanding psychological concerns, controversies, and enigmas. Their contributions are truly profound. The three authors essentially challenge basic social assumptions of humanness. Each even-handedly demonstrates how we are connected to others, particularly our parents and even other species, and how such connections must be taken seriously if we are to avoid more missed opportunities and to embrace more realistic hopes of society's ability to move us *all* toward optimal development.

## REFERENCE

Piers, G., & Singer, M. B. (1971). *Shame and guilt.* New York: Norton.

SECTION VI

# Film Retrospective: The Method and the Medium

# Film Retrospective: The Method and the Medium

Daniel G. Freedman

The following are meant to be elucidating comments about the six films I have authored or co-authored, plus some general remarks about the use of film and video in the social and behavioral sciences. Whatever success I have had as an instructor has been a result in large part to my devotion to actual behavior and, thus, to filmed phenomena. Among my current colleagues who are similarly disposed, the names of Napoleon Chagnon and Tim Asch are the most prominent. But I must also acknowledge the inspiration of Charles Koford's (1966) remarkably clear film, *Rhesus Monkeys of Cayo Santiago Island,* which was an inspiration for my own work on gender differences in young children. I have also greatly enjoyed showing classes the early films made by Konrad Lorenz in which he demonstrated imprinting in Greylag Geese, and those of Lorenz's mentor, Oscar Heinroth, demonstrating the cuckoo's instinctive parasitization of a songbird's nest.

There are, of course, a great many wonderful "nature" films, and in some cases these films will have to document animals that have either become extinct or whose environments have been radically altered. It is a rich world out there, and one can only be astounded that American psychology only recently discovered that even the rat is far more interesting than the learning theory it was meant to elucidate.

## *CONSTITUTIONAL AND ENVIRONMENTAL INTERACTIONS IN REARING FOUR BREEDS OF DOGS* (1962)

My intention in this film was to document a study in which I was the principal investigator (Freedman, 1958). Inasmuch as I was a central element in the study—I was rearing puppies in two consistently opposed ways (highly disciplinary vs. affectionately playful) over a 5-week period—I felt that the methodology might be dismissable as outrageously subjective unless I could document what I was doing.

The study was meant to emulate two contrasting forms of child rearing described by David M. Levy (1943) in his book, *Maternal Overprotection.* Both modalities, Levy hypothesized, might produce psychopathy, which can be defined as the inability to inhibit one's impulses or to delay reward. One mode, very highly permissive rearing, entailed allowing (or even encouraging) the child to tyrannize its parents by never punishing him—so that the child might internalize a sense of easy dominance over parents and others normally in control. The second hypothesized modality, deprivation of love, was to so overuse discipline or maltreatment of the child as to obviate affectional bonds. In either case, Levy proposed, identification with the parental role (Superego) would be greatly weakened.

Inasmuch as a considerable amount of this behavior could be transferred to handler–dog interactions, the puppy study developed via a series of pilot studies (reported in Freedman, 1967). Camcorders were not available in the 1950s, or we would surely have documented those very interesting pilot studies in which (a) a puppy was raised in a boys' dormitory, receiving no punishment for any transgression (including its eliminative behavior) from 3 to 8 weeks of age; (b) a littermate was raised without any social interplay—in isolation; and (c) a third littermate was given to a middle-class family, with two children, who agreed to paper train it and play with it. After the 8 weeks, all puppies were tested with a version of the "incorporation of punishment" test, initially developed by John Whiting, the Harvard experimental psychologist/social anthropologist. The results were most promising, and led to the larger study documented by the film.

I have never tired of watching this film, although I have seen it hundreds of times. The footage is so rich that I seem to come up with something new each time I watch, nor has the film become dated for current students. In that respect it is indeed deserving of the term "classic study." The advantage of having filmed this study is quite obvious. I knew at the time that the behavior exhibited was too rich for my descriptive capacities and that a film was required for that reason—and for the methodological one mentioned previously.

## *DEVELOPMENT OF THE SMILE AND FEAR OF STRANGERS, WITH AN INQUIRY INTO THE INHERITANCE OF BEHAVIOR* (1963)

This film documented what I considered to be a theoretically important aspect of the broader-based study of infant identical and fraternal twins we were conducting through the auspices of the California Department of Mental Health. The overall study was intended to explicate the role of genetics in early developmental events, but because of the drama of the two phenomena, the smile and the fear of strangers, these behaviors became the specific focus of the film.

Watching development in the first year is akin to embryological development, because so much happens in so short a time and, in addition, one can film it without the special gadgets required to film a fetus. The parallel was not lost to Spitz who spoke of behavioral "organizers" in the first natal year as a continuation of comparable physiological prenatal events. As a student of Spitz's collaborator, Katherine Wolf (Spitz & Wolf,

1946), it was not surprising that the development of the smile in the first 4 months, and the fear of strangers in the last part of the first year (Spitz's social organizers) became the focus of this, my first film with humans.

Other than Spitz (1959), no major psychological theorist considered "smiling" to be an important developmental issue. Freud never wrote of it per se, and Piaget (1952), who was primarily concerned with cognition, did not look at smiling with any care, considering it but an epiphenomenon of "surprise." Schneirla (1959), exemplifying Marxist theory as applied to human development, wrote that smiling was a learned response, shaped from early grimaces by the social rewards (and intentions) of doting parents! Spitz himself had to do some acrobatics to unite these two phenomena (smiling and fear of strangers) with psychoanalytic theory, and it remained for the psychoanalytic revisionism of John Bowlby (1969/1982) to produce a more reasonable theoretical accounting. My favorite treatment of the "meaning" of infant smiling, however, remains that of Kurt Goldstein (Goldstein, 1957).[1]

As part of the study's methodology, we filmed each twin separately, once a month, from 1 through 12 months of age (with considerable follow-up footage through 4 to 5 years). These films enabled us to conduct an important substudy: I showed the first-year films of "half of each twinship" to a group of four child psychologists, and their task was to fill out the Bayley Infant Behavior Profile on each child. Comparable footage on the "other half of the twinship" was shown to a second group of child psychologists, who underwent the same procedure as the first. Using this method, we were able to eliminate bias in ratings, and the fact that identicals were rated on average more alike provided reasonably firm evidence for the role of heredity in early development (Freedman & Keller, 1963).

In the summer of 1963, when I was relatively young and groping for an identity among the major players in human infancy research, I showed

[1] I have traversed much the same ground in somewhat greater detail in the introduction to my book, *Human Infancy* (1974).

the "smile and fear of strangers" film at a meeting, called the "Determinants of Infant Behavior III," held at the CIBA Foundation in London, and chaired by John Bowlby. The discussion following the presentation and film (Foss, 1965) was remarkably hostile to a genetically weighted view of development, and I give myself credit for having (apparently) maintained my "cool" under the onslaught. Actually, I have always relished being tagged politically incorrect; but, as in classical Oedipal conflict, I have also wanted to be admired for taking such "original" positions. Thus I was enormously pleased when the venerable Harriet Rheingold commented privately that she wished she had made that film. I believe the reason for her remark was that the film contained phenomena with which we were all familiar—but that no one had heretofore put together in quite this way.

Again, this film has held up well over time. The allusion in the summary to the evolutionary function of both the smile and fear of strangers is still newsworthy, and evolutionary theory (in conjunction with Goldstein's phenomenology) remains the best context for an intellectual appreciation of these two remarkable phenomena. A final word: A certain amount of biological nonsense is put to rest by this study, namely that "if a behavioral trait has important evolutionary function, it will show little or no genetic variation." That is patently not the case with the smile and fear of strangers!

## *SEX DIFFERENCES IN CHILDREN'S PLAY* (1973)

This film was made during a very productive phase in which many graduate students were working with me: At the doctoral level and working in the general arena of sex differences were Marilyn DeBoer, Dickson McLean, Richard Savin-Williams, Carol Cronin, Glenn Weisfeld, Don Omark, Murray Edelman, and Richard Parker (this film was part of Parker's doctoral work). There were also a large number of master's-level studies and term papers, as reported in the appendix to my book, *Human Sociobiology* (Freedman, 1979).

The film itself was shot entirely on the playground of the University Laboratory Schools located alongside Judd Hall, where the Committee on Human Development was housed. Richard Parker, who did all the filming, was a shy, near drop-out, and the opportunity to work with film was clearly regenerative for him. He was a sensitive observer, and the filming followed many months of hanging out on the playground. Don Omark, who was himself working with many of the same children, was of great help to Richard. (Don appears in one memorable scene seated on the ground, clipboard in hand, with a 7-year-old girl draped over his shoulder as he tries to remain a neutral observer.)

The dodgeball sequences in the film eventually became the basis for Carol Cronin Weisfeld's doctoral research (Weisfeld, 1980). The film's observations have recently been greatly corroborated by Thorne's work (1993), wherein her naturalistic observations match my own to a remarkable degree. My only disagreement was in the interpretation of the observations, with my emphasis on the sociobiological, hers on differential learning and the social experiences of boys and girls. In my review of her work, I asked if it is not time for Western social scientists to adopt the Eastern idea of yin/yang and, by doing so, recognize the comparable simultaneity of culture and biology (Freedman, 1994).

Some of the commentary in this film has been dubbed sexist, and one offended student asked that her name be omitted from the acknowledgments at the film's end. This was a period of heightened feminine awareness and I had felt a little tweaking was in order, so I commented on the repetitiousness and rhythmicity in girls' play, as contrasted with boys' social competitiveness and inventiveness. This is what Parker observed and filmed, and I believe it is true to life. The battle of the sexes is an old and venerable one, and no final word seems possible, or even desirable. The tension between the genders is God given and essential, and I do believe this film documents some of that.

# *CROSS-CULTURAL DIFFERENCES IN NEWBORN BEHAVIOR* (1974)

This little film distills a major study of behavioral differences at birth among some seven ethnic groups (Freedman, 1974) and, although it focuses on Navajo versus Caucasian American contrasts, there are short forays into Japan, Kenya, and Aboriginal Australia. It is another example of the radical streak in me, for I knew that these demonstrations of newborn differences were politically incorrect, and as mentioned previously, it has been an important theme in my life that I live on the edge of acceptability (a trait, incidentally, that brought Bob Trivers and me together). Even as I had tweaked feminism, this was a tweaking of the social science establishment—for example, Margaret Mead and her intellectual antecedents (Boas)—all those who (apparently) believed in the blank slate *(tabula rasa)* at birth.

The publication that preceded this film, "Behavioral Differences Between Chinese-American and European-American Newborns" (Freedman & Freedman, 1969), was initially submitted to *Science*, but rejected on a split review. I wrote the editor that this was a better and more important study than either of the two I had previously published in *Science* so he gave it to another set of reviewers—and again there was a split decision. I then submitted the same manuscript to *Nature*, the editor of which reported that he, too, had received a split verdict, but that he had chosen to publish it. Remarkably, it has since been widely reprinted and cited, but with nary a questioning editorial, dissenting study, or even a replication. Many self-deceptions are at a near-conscious level, and the findings of this study, so self-evidently true, simply forced the relinquishment of something we did not believe anyway.

I should mention that I owe special thanks to T. Berry Brazelton for working with me on the development of the newborn examination used in those studies, now generally known as the Brazelton Test. We experienced some narcissistic authorship difficulties at one point, but we have since put that behind us. Getting older and detaching from one's own ego can be a delightful process. I might add that I know scientists beset by the reverse process, excessive pride and obsessive defense of one's priority and accomplishments, and this is a very nasty way to end one's days.

Finally, I must note that in the version of this film that I have shown to my classes, I have appended comparative footage of a Caucasian and a Navajo mother simply asked to "get the attention of your 3-month-old." These are segments from Jack Callaghan's (1977) master's thesis, and at least one former student, now teaching at a university, has expressed disappointment that these addenda are not part of the PCR (Pennsylvania Psychological Cinema Register)[2] rental. These segments are, indeed, striking examples of differential enculturation, well underway at 3 months of age. Joined, as they are, with the genetic implications of group differences among newborns, they nicely make the point of biological and cultural simultaneity.

## *NAVAJO CHILDHOOD* (1982)

This film, made with Jack Callaghan, was a warm, loving experience for both of us. It was also something of an adventure, for we traveled to the reservation without any commitments or assurances that we could do a sound film about growing up Navajo. One thing led to another, and we befriended the Lee family, traders to the Navajo at Keams Canyon, Arizona. They suggested we hang around the trading post and get to know the Navajo by helping out at the store, which Jack and I gladly did. We soon focused on Irene Yazzie, a particularly pleasant and intelligent woman who, as head of a local extended family, was just the person we were looking for. Irene, for her part, saw in us an opportunity to tell the Navajo side of a long-standing boundary dispute with the Hopis.

Three male grandchildren, who were not yet school-age, were living on Irene's compound and were, therefore, available for daily observation and filming. Jack and I set up our tent on Irene's land and began our work. For approximately 2 months, we filmed the daily trek with the sheep

[2]This is now called Pennsylvania State University Audio-Visual Services.—Eds.

(the sheep were taken out for the entire day, an equestrian job divided between Irene's husband, David, and a grown daughter—occasionally accompanied by one of the boys and always by the dogs); the occasional slaughter of an animal for a ceremony; and several interviews with Irene, including one inside her hogan and one as she was weaving at her outdoor loom. Our focus, however, was on the three children in their daily play and meditation (they often sat in trees and chanted). Jack and I felt wonderful about this shoot, and we both felt we were doing exactly what we wanted to be doing. When Mihaly Csikszentmihalyi (1991) talks of being in a state of "flow," this filming experience invariably comes to mind.

The resulting 2000-foot color film, however much Jack and I loved doing it, was never accepted for distribution, and so it lies dormant as an electro-print, which I show on occasion to filmmakers and anthropologists.

## *THE CHILDREN OF EDWARD RIVER* (1984)

The Edward River film was another labor of love and adventure. My 19-year-old niece, Julie Singer, and I set off for Australia with the intention of replicating the Navajo film experience with an Aboriginal population. We arrived in Canberra, where I had been invited by Derek Freeman to be a guest at the Department of Anthropology at the Australian National University, and we made that our initial embarkation point. Because we were loaded with film equipment, the university loaned us a four-wheel-drive vehicle, and we set off for Queensland, eventually tying in with Australia's Flying Doctors, who operated out of Cooktown. They advised us to film at Edward River on the Gulf of Carpenteria, assuring us it was as pristine an Aboriginal setting as we were likely to find. For example, just a few years before, the doctors had been prevented from landing there because the natives were brandishing spears at the airstrip, angry over reduced alcohol rations.

The doctors generously deposited us at Edward River on their next flight, and the Queensland administrator allowed us to stay in the dentist's quarters, which were only used 1 day a month. As many anthropologists have found, people in forsaken places are often generous to visitors, perhaps largely because life there is often tedious and boring. Furthermore, hot climates may add to the ennui of the Europeans, who then find a new face enervating.

Our first night at Edward River was a "beer night," and I taped the sounds floating in from the beer canteen, several hundred feet away. I thought of going over, but I was simply too frightened to do it. There was some lovely a cappella singing at first, but then it became boisterous and chaotic, with some particularly loud, quarrelsome voices. The expressions of anger were strange and harrowing—sounds we had not heard before—and Julie and I knew that we were having an "adventure." Some time later, we actually filmed a spear-to-spear confrontation (largely bluff, but scary) taking place just outside our quarters, something I was careful not to be seen doing. It felt as though I was peeking back through the years, into the frightening "wild times" that Mickey Rivers, my Edward River informant, said had characterized his own childhood earlier in the century. His memories were of random spearings and, indeed, we found that children's nightmares at Edward River in the 1980s still involved fear of unpredictable adult aggression.

All in all, the finest thing about this film, as I have said elsewhere, is the love with which the Aboriginal children were filmed. If the person behind the lens feels it, it somehow ends up touching the viewer. However, despite my own positive review, we have as yet found no distributor for this film either. The main problem was that, although it was nicely edited by my good friend, Sharon Couzin, former chair of the film department at the Art Institute of Chicago, the sound could not be synchronized with the visuals because our Eclaire camera had been somewhat off-speed. Sharon had to substitute background sounds and a loop of a cawing crow so that the film does not have the "presence" created by synchronized sound. It was first shown at the 1991 meetings of the Central States Anthropology Society in Cincinnati, and a video is available from the author.

Incidentally, the same Eclaire camera created something of a disaster for Jack Callaghan and me when we filmed an out-of-sync interview with Don Talayesva, the Hopi Sun Chief (Simmons, 1942) in his final days at a nursing home in Phoenix. I believe, however, that with present technology both footages might be resynchronized.

## *THE CROSS-CULTURAL VIDEO STUDY OF MOTHERS AND THEIR TWO-YEAR-OLDS* (IN PROGRESS)

For more than a decade my students and I have been gathering videotapes of mothers and their toddlers (2-year-olds) in a variety of cultural settings. As described elsewhere, we have subjected these tapes to Q-sorting in order to retain some of the richness of interaction, while obtaining comparative statistics between cultures. Selections from these 150 or so tapes form the cornerstone of my course in cross-cultural childhood, but as yet no visual or written publications have appeared. I am (slowly) assembling the space and equipment in my new abode in New Mexico for such work, but it must compete with my even stronger need to meditate and get my psychic estate in order. As my gerontological colleagues in the Committee on Human Development have long been aware, the priorities of a 69-year-old are not those of someone in his 40s.

## REFERENCES

Bowlby, J. (1969/1982). *Attachment and Loss. Volume 1: Attachment.* New York: Basic Books.

Callaghan, J. W. (1977). *Anglo, Hopi and Navajo mothers and their face-to-face interactions with their infants.* Unpublished master's thesis, University of Chicago.

Csikszentimihalyi, M. (1991). *Flow: The psychology of optical experience.* New York: Harper Collins.

Foss, B. M. (1965). Hereditary control of early social behavior. *Determinants of infant behavior III.* London: Methuen.

Freedman, D. G. (1958). Constitutional and environmental interactions in four breeds of dog. *Science, 127,* 585–586.

Freedman, D. G. (1967). The origins of social behavior. *Science Journal, 3,* 69–73.

Freedman, D. G. (1974). *Human infancy: An evolutionary perspective.* Hillsdale, NJ: Erlbaum.

Freedman, D. G. (1979). *Human sociobiology: A holistic approach.* New York: Free Press.

Freedman, D. G. (1994). Book review. [Review of the book *Gender play: Girls and boys in school] American Journal of Education, 102,* 259–260.

Freedman, D. G., & Freedman, N. C. (1969). Behavioral differences between Chinese-American and European-American newborns. *Nature, 224,* 1227.

Freedman, D. G., & Keller, B. (1963). Inheritance of behavior in infants. *Science, 140,* 196–198.

Goldstein, K. (1957). The smiling of the infant and the problem of understanding the "other." *Journal of Psychology, 44,* 175–191.

Heinroth, O. (no date). *Triebhandlungen des nestjungen KUCKUCKS* [Film]. Available from Institut für den Wissenschaftlichen Film. Göttingen, Germany. C385.

Koford, C. (1966). *Rhesus monkeys of Santiago Island, Puerto Rico* [Film]. (Available from the Pennsylvania State University Audio-Visual Services, University Park, PA, PCR-30958)

Levy, D. M. (1943). *Maternal overprotection.* New York: Columbia University Press.

Lorenz, K. Z. (no date). *Ethologie der Graugans* [Film]. Available from Institut für den Wissenschaftlichen Film. Göttingen, Germany. C560.

Piaget, J. (1952). *The origins of intelligence in children.* New York: Norton.

Schneirla, T. C. (1959). An evolutionary and developmental theory of biphasic processes underlying approach and withdrawal. In M. R. Jones (Ed.), *Nebraska Symposium on Motivation* (pp. 1–42). Lincoln: University of Nebraska Press.

Simmons, L. W. (Ed.). (1942). *Sun Chief: The autobiography of a Hopi Indian.* New Haven, CT: Yale University Press.

Spitz, R. A. (1959). *A genetic field theory of ego formation.* New York: International Universities Press.

Spitz, R. A., & Wolf, K. M. (1946). The smiling response: A contribution to the ontogenesis of social relations. *Genetic Psychology Monographs, 34,* 57–125.

Thorne, B. (1993). *Gender play: Girls and boys in school.* New Brunswick, CT: Rutgers University Press.

Weisfeld, C. C. (1980). *Boys and girls in competition: The context and communication of female inhibition.* Unpublished doctoral dissertation, University of Chicago.

Dr. Freedman at Jackson Memorial Laboratories, Bar Harbor, Maine (1955–1957), conducting a study on the effects of different disciplinary practices on four dog breeds. The indulgent rearing style is displayed here.

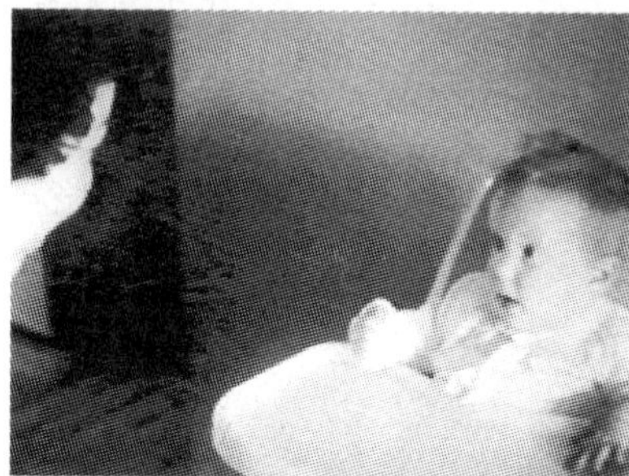

Lori B and Lisa B, identical twins, at 7 months, 0 days, illustrating subtle but consistent differences with mother. (From the film, *Development of the Smile and Fear of Strangers, With an Inquiry Into Inheritance of Behavior.*)

Hausa sib-care, Nigeria, 1969.

Hausa extended family, Nigeria, 1969.

Dr. Freedman with a young Nigerian boy during a visit with Jerry Barkow, Nigeria, 1969.

Preschool girls playing "paper, scissors, stone." Kyoto, 1971.

School recess, Navajo boys at play. Crown Point, New Mexico, 1973.

Taken during filming of *Navajo Childhood*, project with Jack Callaghan. Skunk Springs, 1974.

**18**

# Film Commentary: *Constitutional and Environmental Interactions in Rearing Four Breeds of Dogs*

John Paul Scott

One of the major problems of observational studies of behavior is the difficulty of making an objective record of ongoing activity. Furthermore, given the nature of adaptive behavior, which is variable, one can never exactly repeat an observation. One solution to this problem is to prepare a motion picture of the behavior, which provides a sample that can be repeated over and over again. In addition, this procedure produces a record that is ideal for presenting the research to scientific audiences. Contemporary social scientists frequently use magnetic videotape—now an inexpensive and practical technology—to record their studies. However, this was a novel methodology in the 1950s, when Daniel Freedman first recorded some of his research using 16mm color film. This chapter (as does chapter 19 for another film) discusses and evaluates the topic and methodology of one of Dr. Freedman's earliest filmed studies, *Constitutional and Environmental Interactions in Rearing Four Dog Breeds,* which documented gene–environment interactions in dog behaviors. This film, part of Dr. Freedman's PhD dissertation, was created at the Jackson Laboratories in Bar Harbor, Maine, where I was then chair of the Division of Behavioral Studies.

## EXPERIMENTAL DESIGN AND METHODOLOGY

Dr. Freedman's dissertation tested the effects of permissive versus forced disciplinary training of puppies of four different breeds: two litters each of Shetland sheepdogs, basenjis, wire-haired fox terriers, and beagles. Following weaning at 3 weeks of age, each litter of four was divided into two matched pairs. Thereafter, one pair was indulged and the second pair was disciplined, twice daily during two 15-minute periods, from the third to the eighth week of age. Indulged puppies were encouraged in any activity they initiated and were never punished. Disciplined pups, by contrast, were restrained in the experimenters' laps and were later taught a variety of commands, including following on a leash.

When the pups were 8 weeks old, a revised punishment test was initiated in which eating meat from a bowl was punished with a swat on the rump and a shout of "No!" The experimenter left the room after 3 minutes and then observed through a one-way glass, recording the time that elapsed before the puppy ate again.

Dr. Freedman did most of the filming himself, although he was assisted by various staff members, in particular Seymour Levine, now a professor of psychobiology at Stanford University. Most of the experimental portions of the study were filmed using a one-way mirror so as not to interfere with the puppies' behavior, although several scenes were filmed outdoors. The equipment was a Bolex 16mm camera, and a tripod was used whenever possible. Capturing the behavior of the puppies in this way was not difficult, especially because animals are oblivious to the sight and sound of a camera. In contrast, young children are harder to film because they may be sensitive to the presence of a camera, a factor that might affect their responding in a given situation.

## KEY FINDINGS

The film clearly conveys the varying behavioral responses of the four different breeds. The beagles and the wire-haired terriers—both sets of which were highly attracted to the experimenter—showed behavioral differences resulting from the mode of rearing. However, the basenjis and the Shetland sheep dogs—both timid and inhibited breeds—did not. Although the differential treatment had clear-cut effects on the behavioral outcomes, it also had an unexpected effect—namely, that the puppies became attached to the human handlers in any case. The combination of indulgent treatment and strong constitutional attraction enhanced the effectiveness of the later punishment.

## DISCUSSION

Film and videotape provide a marvelous medium for recording, preserving, and analyzing behaviors expressed in experimental and naturalistic settings. Dan's film is now a classic that many students of psychology have enjoyed and have learned from during the past 25 years. It has held up well over the many years since it was made because it conveys the concept of gene–environment interaction so simply and beautifully.

It is unfortunate that so few psychologists have chosen to document their findings in film or videotape. As Paul Ekman has commented in chapter 12 of this volume, it seems that many researchers are so caught up in the process of measuring behavior that they have lost appreciation for the phenomenon itself. Anyone who has had the opportunity to observe a bird in flight, a dog in search of food, or a child at play knows that some actions and events may be enormously informative about the nature of that organism in that situation. When the behavior is captured on film it can be examined repeatedly, possibly generating new insights and directions. Sharing the film with colleagues and students is a sure way to share the enthusiasm as well.

19

# Film Commentary: *Development of the Smile and Fear of Strangers, With an Inquiry Into Inheritance of Behavior* and *Cross-Cultural Differences in Newborn Behavior*

Lewis P. Lipsitt

When I once again viewed Daniel Freedman's two films, *Development of the Smile and Fear of Strangers, With an Inquiry Into Inheritance of Behavior* (1963) and *Cross-Cultural Differences in Newborn Behavior* (1974) in 1996,[1] having not seen them for 20 years, I was struck, as one can be with history that one has lived through and has been intimately attached to, with how preciously innovative and courageously provocative some of our colleagues in the field of child development have been.

At the time these films were made, many of us who were studying infants were well aware of the behavioral repertoire of the newborn. In fact, in our laboratories we delighted in showing off the remarkable capacities of the baby, even in the first day or two of life.

There was the stepping reflex, in which we could see the rudiments of walking behavior just by holding the baby upright above a mattress and lowering its legs to the "deck." The newborn would simulate walking, one

[1] The films are available from Penn State Audio-Visual Services, University Division of Media and Learning Resources, The Pennsylvania State University, University Park, PA 16802.

step after the other. And we would talk of how this was perhaps the predecessor action of real walking behavior, a reflexively "compelled" or "obligatory" behavior, as Myrtle McGraw (1943) called it, which would eventually be replaced by "voluntary" or learned walking behavior as cortical tissues matured. We would also cite Zelazo, Zelazo, and Kolb (1972) to the effect that if this "involuntary" behavior were sufficiently practiced in the course of the first year of life, "trained babies" would eventually walk earlier than infants who did not receive such repetitive experience.

Other responses that delighted our students and other visitors were the rooting reflex, the grasp reflex, the Babinski, the Moro, and even the swimming reflex when we had an opportunity to demonstrate it. Seeing babies "doing" these things somehow made them more "human," more like grown-ups, somehow precocious, and certainly very cute. Looking at babies watching your face, moving their heads and eyes from side to side to follow your own movements somehow gave them an air of sociability of which most people do not initially suspect the newborn to be capable.

When our visitors saw the baby take the nipple in its mouth and deftly wrap its lips around it and begin to suck, that was their stereotypic baby, and they could understand that. Babies in their view were creatures made up largely of a gastro-intestinal system with a pleasure-seeker at one end and a discharge system at the other. Crying behavior was just part of that system; when the baby craves feeding, crying will begin.

Even the arousal response of the newborn to annoying stimulation other than hunger—like loud noises, a heel prick, or a pinch—seemed to astound our visitors. Most of them had heard that babies do not really feel pain, and most of them would give that as the reason, as they understood it, that unanesthetized circumcision would be allowed. (I was reluctant to tell the uninitiated that sometimes unanesthetized open-chest surgery was done with newborns.)

An especially poignant part of the response repertoire of the newborn is the respiratory occlusion reflex. It does not require actual blockage of respiration to elicit the response; the mere "threat" of occlusion, such as a gauze pad placed lightly over the baby's nostrils and mouth, will produce a reaction that can be graded from little or no response to a very pronounced, "angry" response. This response is part of Brazelton's Neonatal Behavior Assessment Scale (Brazelton, 1973), and has been administered as part of Frances Graham's neonate test (1956) as well as the Graham-Rosenblith (Rosenblith, 1961) modification of it.

Absence or marked diminution of the respiratory defensive behavior has been documented in infants at risk for crib death. Lipsitt (1976, 1979) and Burns and Lipsitt (1991) have described the response as one of those initially in the behavioral repertoire of newborns and lasting in various strengths to around 2 to 4 or 5 months of age, the period of jeopardy for crib death. At this time, it becomes displaced or elaborated, like so many of the reflexes the developmental course of which McGraw documented (1943), by a mature, cortically mediated enhancement of the rudimentary, reflexive response. At this point the response system is said to be "learned" or "voluntary."

## *DEVELOPMENT OF THE SMILE AND FEAR OF STRANGERS IN THE FIRST YEARS OF LIFE*

This has been a long, but necessary prelude to a major point about Dr. Freedman's observations and his films, which, because he does the narration himself, provide excellent insight into his creative, ethological orientation. The treatment he gives in these films is evolutionary and behavioral, with a heavy emphasis on the congenitality of the responses just described. Although one gathers from the term "cross-cultural" in the title of one of the films that the films might promote an experientialist's bias, the impact of the film, coupled with the narration, is in support of inherited, racial factors. The 1963 film on the development of the smile and fear of strangers in the first year of life is, in fact, based on a Freedman article appearing in *Science* in 1963 on the "Inheritance of Behavior in Infants."

In this film, Dr. Freedman shows the developmental sequencing of the smile, including its transition from a fairly automatic, nonsocial (but nonetheless engaging) upward slip of the facial musculature and squinting of eyes, to the eventually-to-be-acquired responsive smile. Along with this, we see the subsequent development of the fear of strangers going hand in hand, as it were, with the gradual increase in social reciprocity. As the smile intensifies and becomes increasingly responsive to familiar figures in the infant's life, so does the onset and progression of stranger-apprehension become increasingly apparent. Dr. Freedman's careful observational skills and his well-known capacity for drawing parallels, for making appropriate developmental distinctions, and for seeing the evolutionary utility (and beauty) in these response propensities make these films appealingly instructive.

Of special interest to Dr. Freedman, and then to his audience, are his observations, coupled with the catches on camera, of concordances of development in identical twins and discordances of development in fraternal twins. He allows that there is no perfect law here; from the data published in the 1963 *Science* article on which the film is based, however, the statistical findings corroborate that identicals are more likely to have common or similar developmental trajectories with respect to smiling and stranger-fear than are fraternal twins. The excerpted film clips are reasonably convincing.

There is a piece on blind infants in this film. Dr. Freedman shows that the early smiles in blind infants are fleeting ones. Vision, he says, is required for a prolonged social smile. It becomes apparent from the pictures and from Dr. Freedman's discussion that babies' behavioral patterns are like many other behavior patterns found throughout the life span. There is a generality that is relevant for understanding the difference between sighted and blind infants in smiling behavior: The natural conditions of life that *instigate* behavior are not necessarily the conditions that *perpetuate* that behavior. The smile is perhaps instigated subcortically, producing early and fleeting smiles in blind infants. But if there are no reciprocating smiles in the child's environment, the early manifested smile has little or no opportunity to be rewarded, and thus perpetuated. I am not sure that Dr. Freedman would accommodate his understanding to this particular generality, but it is tempting nonetheless to make that observation based on his films. I confess to being an interactionist.

That deaf infants, as Dr. Freedman pointed out, do not have this insufficiency of smiling behavior and development, relative to infants with no sensory deficit, would seem to substantiate this explanation. One wishes that this might have been said in the narration but, of course, the film is dated 1963 when reinforcement paradigms for understanding behavioral transitions and developmental progressions in infants were not immensely popular.

Dr. Freedman has a way of getting in his biological orientation to gender–behavior differences. At one point in this film he asserts (just in passing, as a woman handling a baby is followed by a man handling perhaps the same baby) that there is a natural "male discomfort with babies." I do not think there were any data on this: It was merely an anecdote, perhaps a clinical observation; some would say it was a gratuitous comment. But students "learn" as much from such off-handed remarks of experts as they do from bulk data. It would not be worth mentioning, except to make the point that our field has had a history in which some not very pleasant pseudo-generalizations have been made on the basis of race, gender, or other identifying characteristics. And as often as not, those generalities had to be reversed once the reliable, quantitative data arrived.

## *CROSS-CULTURAL DIFFERENCES IN NEWBORN BEHAVIOR*

The second film, on cross-cultural differences in newborn behavior, appeared in 1974, and is as much a classic period piece as the first. A group of infants 48 hours of age and younger, with mean age of 30 hours, was examined and observed using a fairly quantitative approach to the study of differences among genetic–cultural groups on a variety of response domains. A common scale ranking intensity of response was used to score infants on, for example, the "automatic walk." The walk, as discussed previously, can be seen in some newborns, strongly in some and weakly in others, when the baby is held upright above a flat surface and his or her feet are lowered to that surface. It is a rather remarkable sight when a strong, alert baby begins to lift one leg at a time, dropping the first as the second comes up. If the examiner moves the baby forward as the child does this, it looks like the child is "walking with support." No newborn, of course, ever supports his or her own weight in the process.

In his examination and demonstration of this "walking" behavior, found routinely in healthy Caucasian babies, Freedman found that even healthy full-term Navajo infants were seriously deficient in manifesting the behavior. The film demonstrates vividly that the Navajo infants had limp responses and seemed to simply squat to the mattress when placed in the usual position for eliciting this response. But there is the rub: If a behavior common to one race or culture is not readily elicited in another, should the latter be regarded as developmentally or behaviorally abnormal? Without longitudinal developmental data, we cannot be sure of assertions of this sort. Predictive validity is the nub of the issue.

Especially striking in the film is the demonstration of individual differences in the "defensive reaction" to a cloth or gauze placed lightly over the nostrils and mouth of the newborn. Testing for this response has been incorporated into several infant assessment procedures under the assumption that infants who have only weak responses to this threat to respiratory occlusion are somehow at risk. In fact, the peril associated with a deficient respiratory defense response has been linked to SIDS by Lipsitt (1976, 1979), who described a neurobehavioral process (involving failure of transition from subcortical to full cortical functioning and inadequate learning experience) which could account for some of the deaths. Anderson-Huntington and Rosenblith (1976), moreover, provided data relevant to the proposition that newborns lacking vigor of responsivity are more likely to succumb later to crib death. This is especially important in connection with Freedman's demonstrations. According to U.S. Public Health Service epidemiological data, American Indians have some of the highest rates of crib death relative to other racial or ethnic groups in the United States.

The Navajo children seen in this film seemed, also, to have very weak responses to momentary loss of body support, as when dropped an inch or so. Thus it appears that weak defensive behaviors of several sorts may be indigenous to the Indian population studied by Dr. Freedman.

The racial–cultural differences with which Dr. Freedman concerned himself decades ago may be of immense importance, both for understanding basic developmental processes and for purposes of detecting individuals at birth who may be at risk for handicaps at critical developmental junctures later in life. Unfortunately, comparative studies of the sort that Dr. Freedman pioneered seem to have become less interesting to today's developmentalists. One hopes that the fashion pendulum will prompt us eventually to examine, once again and more closely, the fascinating behaviors documented in these films. It is important that we do so in order to understand the nature of the newborn and to divine the significance of infantile behaviors for life-span human development. Dr. Freedman will be honored best when his pioneering, creative style is emulated with enhanced technologies and is carried into the future.

## REFERENCES

Anderson-Huntington, R. B., & Rosenblith, J. F. (1976). Central nervous system damage as a possible component of unexpected deaths in infancy. *Developmental Medicine and Clinical Neurology, 18,* 480–492.

Brazelton, T. B. (1973). Neonatal behavioral assessment scale. *Clinics in developmental medicine* (No. 50). London: Spastics International Medical Publications in association with William Heinemann Medical Ltd.

Burns, B., & Lipsitt, L. P. (1991). Constitutional and environmental risk factors in Sudden Infant Death Syndrome (SIDS). *Journal of Applied Developmental Psychology, 12,* 159–184.

Freedman, D. G. (1963). *Development of the smile and fear of strangers, with an inquiry into inheritance of behavior* [Film]. (Available from Pennsylvania State University Audio-Visual Services, University Park, PA, No. 22696)

Graham, F. K. (1956). Behavioral differences between normal and traumatized newborns: I. The test procedures. *Psychological Monographs, 70,* Whole No. 427.

Lipsitt, L. P. (1976). Developmental psychobiology comes of age: A discussion. In L. P. Lipsitt (Ed.), *Developmental psychobiology: The significance of infancy.* Hillsdale, NJ: Erlbaum.

Lipsitt, L. P. (1979). Critical conditions in infancy. *American Psychologist, 34,* 973–980.

McGraw, M. B. (1943). *The neuromuscular maturation of the human infant.* New York: Hafner.

Rosenblith, J. F. (1961). The modified Graham behavior test for neonates: Test–retest reliability, normative data and hypotheses for future work. *Biologica Neonatorum, 3,* 174–192.

Zelazo, P. R., Zelazo, N., & Kolb, S. (1972). "Walking" in the newborn. *Science, 176,* 314–315.

SECTION VII

# Behavior Genetics, Human Ethology, Evolutionary Psychology, and Culture: Looking to the Future

# Behavior Genetics, Human Ethology, Evolutionary Psychology, and Culture: Looking to the Future

Nancy L. Segal

The chapters in this section include novel conceptualizations and interpretations of existing material with reference to behavioral–genetic, ethological, cultural, and evolutionary psychological perspectives, as well as original analyses and conclusions drawn from new data sets.

Drs. Susan L. Trumbetta and Irving I. Gottesman (behavioral genetics), Dr. Wolfgang M. Schleidt (human ethology), and Dr. Roger J. R. Levesque (evolutionary psychology) examine various issues in mating behavior and family violence with reference to their special areas of expertise. Trumbetta and Gottesman use twin data to explore genetic influences on marital status. They offer a creative reconceptualization of pair-bonding that is likely to encourage rethinking of current theoretical and applied work in this area. Schleidt traces some key developments in the history of ethological investigation. He uses these events as a backdrop to the important thesis that human behavior, specifically variations in mating systems, must be studied with the concepts of global diversity and local adaptation in mind. Levesque brings a unique background in psychology and law to an evolutionary-based analysis of a current human problem, family violence. He shows that evolutionary insights may help to identify and rectify ecological instabilities and uncertainties associated with family conflict and child maltreatment.

Salient themes and controversies posed by these three chapters are identified and discussed by Dr. Freedman in the conclusion to this section. It is likely that the issues posed here (and elsewhere in this volume) will stimulate further dialogue and debate among readers.

20

# Pair-Bonding Deconstructed by Twin Studies of Marital Status: What Is Normative?

Susan L. Trumbetta and Irving I. Gottesman

In this chapter we will challenge received wisdom about the causal chains preceding the observations that not everyone gets married, and that, of those who do, about half will eventually divorce, domains that attract quite a bit of attention from a wide spectrum of scientists.

Quite a furor was raised when Plomin, Corley, DeFries, and Fulker (1990) proclaimed that there were appreciable genetic contributors to the individual differences detectable in the time children spent watching television (Plomin et al., 1990; Plomin, Corley, Defries, & Fulker, 1992; Prescott, Johnson, & McArdle, 1991). Everyone knows there are no "genes for TV-watching," because television did not exist in the evolutionary history of our species. A similar outcry was heard when McGue and Lykken (1992), also using the twin method, reported that another complex behavior—divorce—was under appreciable genetic influence. Once again the logic for the protest is the observation that, at least in terms of legal status, neither marriage nor divorce were part of our biological heritage. How, then, to overcome such resistance to empirical facts but (a) to replicate and confirm the veridicality of such facts, and (b) to empathize with the concerns expressed and to lay out the logic of gene-to-behavior pathways for complex outcomes, with an emphasis on probable mediators of the end products?

Like television viewing, divorce is "heritable, but not inherited" (Plomin et al., 1990, p. 371), and it is more accurately understood as a manifest index of complex latent processes (such as a capacity for interpersonal problem solving) rather than as a simple Mendelian phenotype (like PKU or Huntington's disease). Unlike television viewing, however, which had no functional equivalent before the twentieth century, marriage has long had a functional equivalent of cohabitation for family formation and child rearing. Marriage or its functional equivalent have existed in all human societies throughout recorded history. Insofar as marriage resembles pair-bonding patterns found in other species, it provides an index of behavioral patterns related to the formation and maintenance of stable heterosexual partnerships, presumably of adaptive significance in evolution for procreation and the optimal nurturance of offspring. Divorce and its functional equivalents diverge from these normative pair-bonding patterns.

To the extent that genes may "cause" divorce, their influence is more distal than proximal: Molecular geneticists will never find "genes for divorce" but may discover genes associated with aspects of brain functioning that, in turn, mediate one's preferences and capacities to form stable heterosexual relationships that, in turn, influence one's likelihood of marriage and divorce. Genetic influences on marital status are complex, indirect, and probabilistic, with a sequence of multidimensional processes mediating between genotype and this particular social outcome.

## HETEROGENEITY OF PHENOTYPE

Further complicating any phenotypic study of divorce is its heterogeneity. Potential causes of divorce are numerous, and the process of marital dissolution can follow many paths to disparate outcomes. Given the dyadic architecture of divorce as well as its diverse patterns of cause, course, and outcome, it is somewhat surprising that divorce has shown patterns of heritability ranging from .26 (Lovett, 1992; Turkheimer, Lovett, Robinette,

& Gottesman, 1992) to .59 (Jockin, McGue, & Lykken, 1996). This suggests that, regardless of their heterogeneity, divorced persons have shown sufficient communalities as a group and sufficient differences from continuously married persons for the construct of divorce to be considered as an index of a latent phenotype or endophenotype (Gottesman & Shields, 1972). Table 1 presents findings from twin studies of divorce using the World War II Veteran Twin Registry and the Minnesota Twin Study.

One pathway by which genes appear to influence divorce risk is through heritable personality characteristics. Personality traits associated with divorce were recently examined using the Minnesota sample, and negative emotionality (related to neuroticism) showed positive correlations with divorce in men and women. A significant negative association was found between constraint and divorce in both sexes, with a significant negative association between impulse control and divorce in men only. Overall, 30% to 40% of divorce heritability could be attributed to genetic factors affecting personality variation for one spouse, suggesting that observed heritability for divorce is mediated, in part, through heritable personality traits (Jockin et al., 1996).

## NEVER MARRYING

If marriage indicates preferences and aptitudes for the formation of stable heterosexual relationships, then divorce does not represent the only departure from marriage: Never marrying also diverges from normative patterns of pair-bonding. Like divorced persons, those who never marry show considerable heterogeneity of traits and behaviors. Still, as with divorce, there may be enough communalities among the never-married to suggest a distinct phenotypic construct that shows consistent patterns of genetic influence.

If divorced and never-married status are similar enough in expression to be conjectured as variations of a single endophenotype, then they will show patterns of co-heritability. That is, among twin pairs discordant for ever marrying, never-married probands' identical co-twins will show higher rates of divorce than will their fraternal co-twins; and among twins

**Table 1**

**Twin Studies of Divorce: NAS-NRC World War II Veteran Twin Registry and Minnesota Twin Study**

| Index case | Target case | Number of pairs | Overall target divorce risk | Target risk if index is not divorced | Target risk if index is divorced | Odds Ratio ± S.E. | Tetrachoric correlation |
|---|---|---|---|---|---|---|---|
| **Results of Trumbetta (1996)** | | | | | | | |
| World War II Veteran Twin Registry | | | | | | | |
| 1972 respondents (divorced/separated or remarried or ever-married twins) | | | | | | | |
| MZ twin | MZ co-twin | 2093 | .089 | .080 | .187 | 2.347 ± .206 | .270 |
| DZ twin | DZ co-twin | 2195 | .083 | .082 | .098 | 1.199 ± .261 | .052 |
| 1985 respondents (divorced once, multiple marriages, separated of ever-married twins) | | | | | | | |
| MZ twin | MZ co-twin | 1270 | .158 | .146 | .219 | 1.500 ± .191 | .156 |
| DZ twin | DZ co-twin | 1123 | .154 | .152 | .168 | 1.106 ± .223 | .036 |
| **Results of McGue and Lykken (1992)** | | | | | | | |
| All males in Minnesota sample | | | | | | | |
| MZ twin | MZ co-twin | 275 | .171 | .118 | .426 | 5.51 ± .35 | .531 |
| DZ twin | DZ co-twin | 288 | .217 | .193 | .304 | 1.83 ± .33 | .205 |
| All twins over 40 (male and female combined) in Minnesota sample | | | | | | | |
| MZ twin | MZ co-twin | 267 | .217 | .139 | .500 | 6.21 ± .23 | .582 |
| DZ twin | DZ co-twin | 357 | .213 | .203 | .250 | 1.31 ± .21 | .091 |

discordant for divorce, divorced probands' identical co-twins will show higher rates of never marrying than will their fraternal co-twins. In such a case, a more general, dimensional construct of nonmarried status, such as a "failure to marry successfully," may be more informative than those of either divorce or lifetime singleness alone. Of course, because persons of never-married and divorced statuses differ in their marital histories; and as psychiatric epidemiology has demonstrated differences in relative rates of never marrying and divorce across diagnostic groups, bachelorhood and divorce must also be considered as separate phenomena. Indeed, given the complexity and heterogeneity of traits and behaviors associated with never marrying and divorce, each marital status may, under various conditions, serve as one index of multiple endophenotypes. Any apparent heritability of nonmarried status may be a function of the association between marital status and several, more directly heritable conditions.

In a study using the National Academy of Sciences–National Research Council (NAS-NRC) World War II Veteran Twin Registry, evidence for an association between divorce and never marrying was mixed: Although there was no direct evidence of co-inheritance, there was evidence that divorce and never marrying may express varying degrees of a continuum of pair-bondedness (Trumbetta, 1996; Trumbetta, Gottesman, & Turkheimer, 1995). Although proportionally more co-twins of ever-divorced than continuously married twins were never-married, the difference was not significant (chi-square = 1.57, 1 *df*, $p = .210$). Even when only the never-married or the continuously married were considered as index twins, rates of divorce in their co-twins did not differ significantly (chi-square = 3.22, 1 *df*, $p = .073$), although the direction of difference was consistent with the hypothesis of coheritability: 16.5% of co-twins of the never married were divorced compared to 13.5% of the co-twins of the continuously married. Although monozygotic pairs showed a slightly larger difference in rate of co-twin divorce between never married (16.1%) and ever-married, nondivorced twins (13.1%) than did dizygotic pairs (15.6% and 13.6%), this difference also failed to reach statistical significance.

Structural equation models of genetic and environmental contributors to variance in phenotypes defined as divorce, never-marrying, frequency of marital status changes, and a continuum of pair-bondedness revealed heritability ($h^2$) highest for ever- versus never-married [$h^2$ = .45, 95% confidence interval (c.i.) = .15 to .71], followed by pair-bondedness ($h^2$ = .42, c.i. = .33 to .49), frequency of marital status changes ($h^2$ = .28, c.i. = .06 to .37), and finally, ever-divorced versus continuously married ($h^2$ = .21, c.i. = .09 to .28). These findings suggest that endophenotypes for marital status may be more evident in the distinction between ever and never marrying than between divorce and nondivorce, once married, with a likelihood that marital status endophenotypes represent continuous distributions of complex traits.

Given the greatest heritability for marital status when defined in terms of ever or never marrying, it is likely that any heritable personality traits that diminish the likelihood of marriage may mediate some of the genetic influence on never marrying. Likely candidates include such personality traits as social introversion on the MMPI (Minnesota Multiphasic Personality Inventory) and alienation and social closeness on Tellegen's (1978) Multidimensional Personality Questionnaire (MPQ). Using the standard design of MZ (monozygotic) and DZ (dizygotic) adolescent twins reared together, Gottesman (1963, 1965) reported heritabilities of 0.71 and 0.33 in two different samples for MMPI social-introversion; by using a stronger design of identical twins and fraternal twins reared apart, DiLalla, Carey, Gottesman, and Bouchard (1996) reported a heritability for this scale of 0.34. The latter sample also provided estimates of heritability for MPQ alienation of 0.45 and one of 0.47 for social closeness. Such information may provide grist for the mills of both geneticists and evolutionary psychologists. With enough chaff removed and enough grains of salt added, we may jointly cook up something to interest a wider audience.

## REFERENCES

DiLalla, D. L., Carey, G., Gottesman, I. I., & Bouchard, T. J. (1996). Heritability of personality indicators of psychopathology via MMPI in twins reared apart. *Journal of Abnormal Psychology, 105,* 491–499.

Gottesman, I. I. (1963). Heritability of personality: A demonstration. *Psychological Monographs, 77*(Whole No. 572), 1–21.

Gottesman, I. I. (1965). Personality and natural selection. In S. G. Vandenberg (Ed.), *Methods and goals in human behavior genetics* (pp. 63–80.) New York: Academic Press.

Gottesman, I. I., & Shields, J. (1972). *Schizophrenia and genetics: A twin study vantage point.* New York: Academic Press. (2nd printing, 1978)

Jockin, V., McGue, M., & Lykken, D. T. (1996). Personality and divorce: A genetic analysis. *Journal of Personality and Social Psychology, 71,* 288–299.

Lovett, G. (1992). *The heritability of divorce: An analysis of two twin samples.* Unpublished master's thesis. University of Virginia, Charlottesville.

McGue, M., & Lykken, D. T. (1992). Genetic influence on the risk of divorce. *Psychological Science, 3,* 368–373.

Plomin, R., Corley, R., DeFries, J. C., & Fulker, D. W. (1990). Individual differences in television viewing in early childhood: Nature as well as nurture. *Psychological Science, 1,* 371–377.

Plomin, R., Corley, R., DeFries, J. C., & Fulker, D. W. (1992). Children's television viewing: Response to Prescott et al. *Psychological Science, 3,* 75–76.

Prescott, C. A., Johnson, R. C., & McArdle, J. J. (1991). Genetic contributions to television viewing. *Psychological Science, 2,* 430–431.

Tellegen, A. (1978). *Manual for the Multidimensional Personality Questionnaire.* Unpublished manuscript, University of Minnesota, Minneapolis.

Trumbetta, S. L. (1996). *A twin study of marital status.* Unpublished doctoral dissertation, University of Virginia, Charlottesville.

Trumbetta, S. L., Gottesman, I. I., & Turkheimer, E. N. (1995). There are no genes for divorce: There is genetic variance in stable, heterosexual pair-bonding [Abstract]. *Behavior Genetics, 25,* 291.

Turkheimer, E., Lovett, G., Robinette, C. D., & Gottesman, I. I. (1992). The heritability of divorce: New data and theoretical implications. *Behavior Genetics, 22,* 757.

# 21

# An Ethological Perspective on Normal Behavior Especially as It Relates to Mating Systems

Wolfgang M. Schleidt

"Normal" behavior falls within a wide range of behavioral diversity; mating diversity comprises a complex system of widely divergent behaviors. Both of these topics, which are closely related, can be illuminated when examined from an ethological perspective. In this chapter, I treat these as core concepts, from which other topics (e.g., conduct disorders, modes of therapy, and other corrective measures) may be developed. I begin by reflecting on the evolution of the ethological perspective. Then, I explore the diversity inherent in "normal" behavior. Cross-cultural examples illustrate the complexity of normality: koro goiter and cretinism. Finally, I explore the diversity of mating systems, including inclusive fitness and the ethological bases of celibacy.

## ETHOLOGICAL PERSPECTIVE

Ethology, the comparative study of behavior, is easy to define: it is the discipline which applies to the behavior of animals and humans all those questions asked and those methodologies used as a matter

> of course in all other branches of biology since Charles Darwin's time. (Lorenz, 1981, p. 1)

Or, more succinctly, "Human ethology can be defined as the biology of human behavior" (Eibl-Eibesfeldt, 1989, p. 4). Among the questions asked, four major problems stand in the foreground: causation, survival value, evolution, and ontogeny (Tinbergen, 1963, p. 411). As for the methods, the time-proven skills of comparative anatomy and comparative physiology (i.e., description, comparison, and due consideration of holistic, dynamic processes) within the individual organism are applied and modified for behavioral research (for detailed presentation of the basic issues see Eibl-Eibesfeldt, 1989; Gould, 1982; Hinde, 1982; and Lorenz, 1981).

When ethology evolved into a distinct field of biology, starting at the turn of this century and catching public attention just prior to the outbreak of World War II (e.g., Lorenz, 1935, 1937a, 1973b; Tinbergen, 1942), its pioneers fought an uphill battle, caught between "behaviorists who contended that all human behavior can be explained as a bundle of learned responses" and "anthropologists who are idealists and vitalists" (Lorenz, 1970, p. xx). In the early 1950s, idealism acquired a new face: epigenetics. In the 1970s, population geneticists (under the guise of sociobiology), as well as ecologists (behavioral ecologists), attempted what we now call in economics a "hostile takeover" of ethology. However, they defeated themselves by sporting claims that grew too extreme to be useful. Some vicious infighting occurred (see, for example, the analysis of battles between E. O. Wilson and R. C. Lewontin by Segerstrålle, 1990). In addition, Hamilton's (1964) explanation of the hypersociality of social insects was questioned, such as when the surprisingly low degree of relatedness in honey bees was reported by Moritz in 1993.[1] I feel that ethology is now a well-established discipline of biology and has a great future, especially as the necessary methods for the analysis of complex behavioral systems become increasingly available.

[1] There have been various challenges to Hamilton's reasoning and interpretations, but the core of his theory has been upheld (Wilson, 1994). Also see the preface to the collected papers of W. D. Hamilton for his brief discussion of this point (Hamilton, 1995).—Eds.

Let me close this introductory section with an episode from the history of science, because I trust we can learn from the history of physics and extrapolate into the future of ethology: David Hilbert, the famous mathematician, used to bemoan the poor physicists because he thought physics was much too complicated for them (Hund, 1969). However, Hilbert pitied the physicists and went on to develop new methods of mathematics and geometry that greatly enhanced the skills of physicists. In the same way, I feel that new forms of mathematical methods, derived from disciplines such as cybernetics, robotics, artificial intelligence, and artificial perception, will advance ethologists' skills in the study and understanding of complex behavioral and social systems (Schleidt, 1984).

## "NORMAL" BEHAVIOR: ACCEPT THE DIVERSITY OF NORMAL BEHAVIOR AND LEARN TO LIVE WITH COMPLEXITY

Ethology, in its early days, borrowed its descriptive, comparative method from comparative anatomy, paleontology, and taxonomy and its experimental skills from comparative physiology. It also adopted a modest amount of theorizing from these sibling disciplines, modest in comparison with contemporary philosophy, psychology, sociology, and other social sciences. Even though ethology endorsed the evolutionary stance of Darwinism (as did anatomy and paleontology but not philosophy and psychology), ethology became "stuck" in the same way as its sibling disciplines on pre-Darwinian concepts of "type" and functional blueprints of organismic design *(Baupläne).*

In the early years of genetics, the emphasis on Mendelian ratios of discrete traits gave "soft biology" the aura of hard mathematical "laws" for the first time. The geneticists' concepts of discrete traits agreed well with the ethological concept of fixed action patterns (explained in depth in Schleidt, 1964a), and the assumption that nature must have found a way to make them as precise and as stable as possible. Population genetics, dealing with arrays of alleles and traits on which natural selection can act, drew little attention from ethologists at that time. Soon it was realized, however, that stereotypy is not an absolute premium for instinctive movements but a compromise of a variety of selection pressures for and against stereotyped behavior (Finley, Ireton, Schleidt, & Thompson, 1983; Schleidt, 1974). Today ethology has available concepts and methods necessary for the analysis of patterns in the behavioral domain and for patterns in the organism's environment, concepts and methods that are consistent with current methods of basic science (Schleidt, 1985; Schleidt & Crawley, 1980).

Another important change has occurred in the recent history of the "Lorenz–Tinbergen school of ethology": Although the Lorenz group focused on fixed action patterns, the lowest level of behavioral complexity (Schleidt, 1964b), Tinbergen's seminal book, *The Study of Instinct* (1951), with its emphasis on hierarchical organization, encouraged students to solve problems from the top down (e.g., Baerends & Drent, 1970). In recent years, however, the gap between top and bottom is closing, not only in ethology (e.g., McFarland, 1971), but in applied fields as well (e.g., Minsky, 1985). As a consequence, the ethological approach can provide new insights into human behavior, from the lowest level of a Fixed Action Pattern to the delicate balance between human behavior and its fragile environment.

## DEFINING NORMALITY AMID GLOBAL DIVERSITY: KORO, GOITER, AND CRETINISM

We have finally begun to recognize the complexity of the underlying behavioral spectra and the importance of kin selection, cooperation, and competition within groups. We no longer struggle with a definition of normal behavior patterns that act for "the good of the species" (e.g., spare the life of a conspecific), in contrast to deviant behavior that works to the detriment of the species (e.g., badly wounding or even killing an allospecific). We can now define the "normality" of a "discrete chunk" of a behavioral pattern on statistical grounds, by the core area of an *n*-dimensional feature space of its most salient features (e.g., Schleidt, 1982). We realize, of course, that this core area can be defined only in respect to the population from which the data sample was drawn. As a consequence, we can see now that what is within the normal range of one population can be highly abnormal for another.

As a human example, let me briefly review the case of "koro" (genital retraction disorder). Occasional outbreaks of this condition occur in East Asia, offering a textbook case in cross-cultural psychiatry. Central to this syndrome is a strange behavior, observed mostly in relatively young men, described as a sudden retraction of the penis, accompanied by acute anxiety that can lead to the death of the victim (see Cohen, Tennenbaum, Teitelbaum, & Durst, 1995). Ethologically, koro may be viewed as the very opposite of penile erection, not in the context of mating but in its ancient role of a male–male threat display (Schleidt, 1994, 1995), which may culminate in rape of the defeated male. Thus, koro can be explained as a special case of a specific signal of submissive behavior rather than as a psychiatric "disorder."

Another case of human behavioral diversity of tragic proportion has been revealed recently in the context of a World Health Organization program to eliminate goiter and cretinism. This example is especially instructive because it highlights the many factors influencing certain phenotypes with specific behavioral changes: For example, highly educated medical administrators assume that levels of activity, fertility, and food requirements are "caused" by nothing more than a lack of iodine. It is reasoned that if sufficient quantities of iodine are provided to these poor people, they will be cured and happy. Biological systems are more complex, however. First, we must understand that goiter and cretinism in the specific areas of New Guinea and Zaire under consideration are not a product of "primitive, uncivilized culture," but rather a recent consequence of colonial interference; before colonial supremacy was imposed in these areas neither goiter nor cretinism had been observed. Apparently, the natives used to prepare a condiment from the ashes of special plants that contain, among other important trace elements, a sufficient amount of iodine. Only when colonial authorities and trade substituted cheap, "clean," pure NaCl, without iodine, for the old salty condiment did the health problems begin. In addition, fertility was diminished, lethargy spread, and the need for food was reduced considerably. Thus, these victims of colonial trade had gained the unique chance to exploit a new niche: They settled and lived reasonably "well" in areas in which previously human populations were unable to grow enough food to meet basic needs. These areas—we are talking here specifically of limy soils, leached by tropical rain in the north of Zaire—support only a rather meager growth of plants and animals. The people have now adjusted to this hostile environment, and found a new equilibrium with nature, but at the cost of goiter and an extremely high rate of cretinism (as high as 13% of live births). Now we "help" those poor people: A single injection of 10 ml poppy seed oil with iodine provides enough iodine for 6 years (Geelhoed, 1995).

The results are spectacular. Recently, I have heard the first progress report, 5 years after the program was started (G. Geelhoed, personal communication): Goiter was reduced and the birth of new cretins was eliminated; everybody feels great; women are pregnant or nursing; men are working from dawn to dusk, having cleared all the forest and turned any square foot of soil into a garden. In spite of all this effort, however, they cannot produce enough food, because their metabolic rate has doubled and the population is ever increasing. They long for more food, greater yield, artificial fertilizer. Teenagers, no longer able to make a living there, leave these remote villages for the big city slums. We play gracious god and set the most destructive, senseless acts.

The lesson is clear: We can no longer hope for simple solutions to complex problems. We must learn to see human behavior in both its global diversity and its local adaptations. We must take time and make an effort to gain insight into complex systems before we define something as a "disorder" and before we implement corrective measures that may create only more disorder.

## MATING SYSTEMS: LEARN TO LIVE WITH THE COMPLEXITY OF MATING SYSTEMS AND ACCEPT THE DIVERSITY OF BEHAVIOR

Do I need to point out that I simply reversed the subtitle of a preceding section? The major obstacle for a scientific analysis of mating systems is our individual bias in favor of a specific, basically religious, theological concept of both: reproduction and the marital bond between males and females. What makes our task difficult is that different religions have different biases, and in Western culture these biases are fed by various and often contradictory beliefs based on the Old Testament, New Testament, Talmud, Koran, and the teachings of Martin Luther, Karl Marx, Calvin Coolidge, and others. Monogamy is the law, in eternal splendor like the rock of Gibraltar, blessed by the various religious establishments and intertwined with a variety of practicalities, like two human beings of different gender sharing a room in a hotel, filing income taxes, or writing a will to dispose of earthly possessions in an orderly way.

In recent years, sociobiologists have claimed mating systems as their domain (see, for example, Thornhill & Thornhill, 1987) and, as a consequence, the contribution of ethology to this topic has been widely ignored. Therefore, I will return to ethology and to its roots in comparative morphology and examine the anatomical side of human sexual dimorphism, its development, and its ethnic diversity. Human development shares with all higher animals the feature of starting individual existence in a nonreproductive infantile state. Like nonhuman primates, humans develop considerable sexual dimorphism in size and general appearance. In addition, females have developed menopause, a nonreproductive phase allowing females to guide their last infant through a most crucial phase of childhood. These striking facts strongly suggest that in the human species, females and males are likely to pursue quite different strategies in their pursuit of inclusive fitness. Furthermore, a rule of thumb is that in sex dimorphic species, in which the males are bigger and more robust than the females, polygynous mating systems are most common. In contrast, reduced sexual dimorphism is indicative of monogamy. In fact, some monogamous bird species are so sexually monomorphic in appearance and behavior that—without exploratory surgery—only the female gender can be diagnosed reliably in the individual case, namely by observing the laying of an egg. In view of the universal sexual dimorphism in our own species, the range and diversity of human mating systems are heavily biased toward polygyny. What makes humans unique, compared to other primates, is the striking geographic, ethnic, and cultural diversity with respect to morphological and behavioral differences between infants and adults, and especially of sexual dimorphism. I have collected a considerable body of data on morphological markers of infantile state and infantile gender (mostly on pigmentation, e.g., Mongolian spots, linea nigra, blondism). However, in the interest of brevity, I will discuss two features of sexual dimorphism in adults that are rarely considered: (a) the diameter of the femur head, the ball at the upper end of the thigh bone that fits into a socket on the pelvis, as a general indicator of robustness; and (b) the length of the pubic bone that defines the ventral part of the pelvic girdle, as a measure of femininity.

Human females have wider pelvises to facilitate birth, whereas human males have very narrow pelves and broad shoulders, for bodily strength, protection of mates, and other functions. In all human populations for which I was able to obtain data, males are, on average, significantly more robust than females, ranging from males being 5.6% more robust than females in Andaman Islanders,[2] to 16% in Kerma (from a cemetery in the Nile valley, Sudan, 4000 BP). European White and United States Black populations center around 14% on this scale; from the available material of Neanderthal remains I calculated an amazing 19%. However, the sexual dimorphism in the pelvic girdle is even more spectacular than in robustness. Without adjusting for robustness, the pubic bone of Andaman Islanders females is 13.8% longer than that of their males, whereas for European Whites and United States Blacks the difference is between 6.7% and no difference. In Pygmies, however, pubic bones of the females are 1.8% shorter than those of males. Based on material from the large Bronze Age cemetery Franzhausen I[3] (Austria, 4000 BP) the difference is 6.5%, whereas for the Neanderthal it is 12.5% shorter! Over all, the diversity in form and degree of human sexual dimorphism—means of discrete populations ranging over more than 25% in pelvic length—is most remarkable. Considering the central role of the human pelvis not only in upright gait but in several other important behaviors (e.g., bending over to gather objects off the ground, mating, giving birth), we must expect an

[2] All population estimates, with the exception of Franzhausen, are based on data from Rosenberg, 1988.

[3] Based on data from Berner, 1988.

even greater diversity in the behavioral domain. Very little is known about the ontogeny of pelvic sexual dimorphism. Not only does the anatomy of the pelvis set constraints on behavior, but behavior shapes the form of the pelvis. As a consequence, the varying degrees of sexual dimorphism become manifest only after the organism has reached its final body size.

There are several other important human features to address. One is related to the two components of an organism's inclusive fitness: direct and indirect fitness—in other words, the individual's direct gain of genetic immortality through her or his own reproductive success (number of children) and the indirect gain from the reproductive success of kin (e.g., the number of children born to next of kin; Hamilton, 1964). Under certain circumstances, an individual has a higher chance of maximizing personal fitness by supporting next of kin and abstaining from reproduction; this may provide biological bases for some human traits believed to be associated with advances in culture and civilization—for example, homosexuality, celibacy, and self-sacrifice in martyrdom. The diversity of ways in which humans pursue their indirect fitness is amazing and possibly unique.

The other cluster of features is related to the many forms of human bonding (Freedman & Gorman 1993), of which the pair bond is only one of many alternatives. Recall Lorenz's 1935 and 1937b concepts of specific "companions," or the various discrete forms of bonds: e.g., the attachment of an infant to its parent, the bond between siblings, the bond of a mature individual to peers and mates, and the bond of a parent to an infant. Each of these ties constitutes a specific category of social relatedness with distinct features. Animals and humans have different needs for bonding at different ages and developmental stages, as Erikson (1950) has so instructively shown. Further analysis reveals an intricate interaction between the companions and the varying needs within each developmental stage (between the conceptual frameworks of Lorenz and Erikson; Schleidt, 1992), which sheds new light on the biological bases of bonding and communication in human mating systems (Schleidt, 1973).

Given the striking sexual dimorphism in humans resulting in a primary bias toward polygyny, but also considering the striking diversity in human sexual dimorphism, pursuit of fitness, bonding, and communication, it would be unlikely to find support for one "typical" human mating system. We should accept the presence of a wide variety of mating systems that coexist in various combinations, taking the form of polygyny, monogamy, celibacy, polyandry, promiscuity, male and female homosexuality, and other practices.

There is already considerable literature on various forms of human mating systems. Therefore, I wish to highlight some facets of the ethological basis of celibacy, a topic rarely discussed (i.e., not even mentioned in the index of the standard source of human ethology: Eibl-Eibesfeldt, 1989), as an example of a "non-mating" system. Celibacy may be appropriate for those who have no desire for sexual activity or who are impotent. According to the *DSM-III-R*, "studies in Europe and the United States indicate that in the young adult population, approximately 8% of the males have male erectile disorder. It has been estimated that approximately 20% of the total population have hypoactive sexual desire disorder, 30% of the male population have premature ejaculation and that approximately 30% of the female population have inhibited female orgasm" (American Psychiatric Association, 1987, p. 292). A brief flashback to the previous topic, "normal behavior": The label "disorder" is hardly justified when a substantial fraction of a population (8%, 20%, 30%) expresses a certain phenotype. The editors of the *DSM-IV* tried to correct this absurdity, but failed: They simply dropped the percentages and left the stigma of "sexual disorder" (American Psychiatric Association, 1994). Nevertheless, the high frequency of the absence of personal sexual desire can explain why it is easy for some individuals to preach celibacy and so difficult for others to practice it.

## CONCLUSION

As a closing statement in defense of the ethological perspective in human behavior, I cannot envision a more fruitful approach within the framework of the natural sciences than that of an integrative biology. It would be absurd to believe that any one single concept, such as learning, environment, instinct, culture, or fitness could do justice to the complexity of the living system of women and men.

## REFERENCES

American Psychiatric Association. (1987). *Diagnostic and statistical manual of mental disorders* (3rd ed. rev). Washington, DC: Author.

American Psychiatric Association. (1994). *Diagnostic and statistical manual of mental disorders* (4th ed.). Washington, DC: Author.

Baerends, G. P., & Drent, R. H. (1970). The herring gull's egg. *Behavior, 17* (Suppl.).

Berner, M. (1988). *Das frübronzezeitliche Gräberfeld von Franzhausen I. Demographische und metrische Analyse.* Doctoral dissertation, Universität Wien, Formal- und Naturwissenschaftliche Fakultät.

Cohen, S. Tennenbaum, S. Y., Teitelbaum, A., & Durst, R. (1995). The koro (genital retraction) syndrome and its association with infertility: A case report. *Journal of Urology, 153,* 427–428.

Eibl-Eibesfeldt, I. (1989). *Human ethology.* New York: Aldine de Gruyter.

Erikson, E. H. (1950). *Childhood and society.* (2nd ed., rev. 1963). New York: Norton.

Finley, J. Ireton, D., Schleidt, W. M., & Thompson, T. A. (1983). A new look at the features of mallard courtship displays. *Animal Behaviour, 31,* 348–354.

Freedman, D. G., & Gorman, J. (1993). Attachment and the transmission of culture—An evolutionary perspective. *Journal of Social and Evolutionary Systems, 16,* 297–329.

Geelhoed, G. W. (1995). *Metabolic maladaptation: Anthropologic consequences of medical intervention in correcting endemic hypothyroidism.* Unpublished master's thesis, George Washington University, Washington, DC.

Gould, J. L. (1982). *Ethology: The mechanisms and evolution of behavior.* New York/London: Norton.

Hamilton, W. D. (1964). The genetical evolution of social behavior. *Journal of Theoretical Biology, 7,* 1–16.

Hamilton, W. D. (1995). *Narrow roads of gene land. Vol. 1: Evolution of social behaviour.* Oxford: W. H. Freeman.

Hinde, R. A. (1982). *Ethology: Its nature and relations with other sciences.* Oxford: Oxford University Press.

Hund, F. (1969). *Grundbegriffe der physik.* Mannheim: Bibliographisches Institut.

Lorenz, K. Z. (1935). Der Kumpan in der Umwelt des Vogels. *Journal für Ornithologie, 83,* 137–215, 289–413.

Lorenz, K. Z. (1937a). Über die Bildung des Instinktbegriffes. *Die Naturwissenschaften, 25,* 298–300; 324–331. (Engl. transl. in Lorenz 1970).

Lorenz, K. Z. (1937b). The companion in the bird's world. *Auk, 54,* 245–273.

Lorenz, K. Z. (1970). *Studies in animal and human behaviour. I and II.* Cambridge, MA: Harvard University Press.

Lorenz, K. Z. (1981). *The foundations of ethology.* New York: Springer.

McFarland, D. J. (1971). *Feedback mechanisms in animal behaviour.* London: Academic Press.

Minsky, M. (1985). *The society of mind.* New York: Simon & Schuster.

Moritz, R. F. A. (1993). Intracolonial relationship in the honey bee colony (*Apis mellifera*): Molecular evidence and behavioral consequences. *Verhandlungen der Deutschen Zoologischen Gesellschaft, 86,* 151–158.

Rosenberg, K. R. (1988). The functional significance of Neandertal pubic length. *Current Anthropology, 29*(4), 595–617.

Schleidt, W. M. (1964a). Über die Spontaneitat von Erbkoordinationen. *Zeitschrift für Tierpsychologie, 21,* 235–236.

Schleidt, W. M. (1964b). Über das Wirkungsgefüge von Balzbewegungen des Truthahnes. *Die Naturwissenschaften, 51,* 445–446.

Schleidt, W. M. (1973). Tonic communication: Continual effects of discrete signs. *Journal of Theoretical Biology, 42,* 359–386.

Schleidt, W. M. (1974). How "fixed" is the fixed action pattern? *Zeitschrift für Tierpsychologie, 36,* 184–211.

Schleidt, W. M. (1982). Stereotyped feature variables are essential constituents of behavior patterns. *Behaviour, 79,* 230–238.

Schleidt, W. M. (1984). Wie der Computer "miau" auf deutsch Übersetzt. In F. Kreuzer (Ed.), *Nichts ist schon dagewesen* (pp. 137–155). Munich: Piper.

Schleidt, W. M. (1985). Learning and the description of the environment. In T. D. Johnston & A. T. Pietrewicz (Eds.), *Issues in the ecology of learning* (pp. 305–325). Hillsdale, NJ: Erlbaum.

Schleidt, W. M. (1992). Biological bases of age specific behaviour—The companions in man's world. *Evolution and Cognition, 1,* 147–159.

Schleidt, W. M. (1994). The nudity taboo—Uncommon sense in human communication? *Human Ethology Newsletter, 9,* 5–6.

Schleidt, W. M. (1995). Re: The koro (genital retraction) syndrome and its association with infertility (Letter to the Editor). *Journal of Urology, 153,* 1483–1484.

Schleidt, W. M., & Crawley, J. N. (1980). Patterns in the behavior of organisms. *Journal of Social and Biological Structures, 3,* 1–15.

Segerstrålle, U. (1990). The sociobiology of conflict and the conflict about sociobiology. In J. van der Dennen & V. Falger (Eds.), *Sociobiology and conflict: Evolutionary perspectives on competition, cooperation, violence and warfare* (pp. 273–284). London: Chapman & Hall.

Thornhill, N. W., & Thornhill, R. (1987). Evolutionary theory and rules of mating and marriage pertaining to relatives. In C. Crawford, M. Smith, & D. Krebs (Eds.), *Sociobiology and psychology: Ideas, issues and applications* (pp. 373–400). Hillsdale, NJ: Erlbaum.

Tinbergen, N. (1942). An objective study of the innate behaviour of animals. *Bibliotheca biotheretica, 1,* 39–98.

Tinbergen, N. (1951). *The study of instinct.* Oxford: Oxford University Press.

Tinbergen, N. (1963). On aims and methods of ethology. *Zeitschrift für Tierpsychologie, 20,* 410–433.

Wilson, E. O. (1994). *Naturalist.* New York: Warren Books.

22

# Evolving Beyond Evolutionary Psychology: A Look at Family Violence

Roger J. R. Levesque

This chapter explores a simple thesis: Evolutionary psychology has been so useful in clarifying *what is* that it seemingly has forgotten *what ought to be.* Indeed, evolutionary psychology can even assist in achieving what *can be.* To broaden the scope of evolutionary psychology and to explore its potential and practical utility, in this chapter I will examine evolutionary psychology's ability to inform the study of one of the most intractable social problems: family violence. A central theme is that evolutionary psychology provides us with an observational tool that helps mark indicators of violence. By alerting us to these indicators, it can guide intervention efforts and identify opportunities for necessary reforms.

## INDICATORS OF FAMILY VIOLENCE

Evolutionary psychology hypothesizes that family violence is an adaptation to ecological instability (Burgess & Draper, 1989). This argument rests on

Nancy L. Segal and Glenn E. Weisfeld's supportive reviews of this chapter were greatly appreciated. Likewise, I would like to give a deeply heartfelt thanks to Daniel Freedman, a remarkable human being whose unstinting personal and professional support never ceases to amaze me.

the proposition that human groups have been exposed to, and have adapted to, various ecological changes, such as famine, drought, war, or their opposites—such as food abundance, adequate rainfall, and peace. However, as the argument goes, humans have learned to approach these different situations differently. Some of these situations, especially those marked by rapid changes and instability, have been associated with spousal violence and child maltreatment. For example, researchers have shown how modern markers of ecological instability, such as underemployment, anxiety, alcohol abuse, and financial pressures, are common predictors of spousal violence, as well as child maltreatment (Korbin, 1995; Linsky, Bachman, & Straus, 1995).

In addition to the concept of ecological uncertainty and instability, the notion of paternal uncertainty delineated by evolutionary psychology continues to shed light on child maltreatment and family violence. Recall that the valuable resource of parental investment must be discriminately allocated in order to enhance parental fitness. That is, paternal ties make it adaptive for a male to make an extended parental investment: It simply does not make evolutionary sense to invest in children not possessing one's genes. Thus, without genetic ties, the risk of maltreatment, neglect, and even infanticide increases. More specifically, research clearly demonstrates that step-children disproportionately suffer from maltreatment, including gross mortality, physical assault, sexual abuse, neglect, and injuries (see Daly & Wilson, 1991).

It is interesting to note that paternal uncertainty also has been linked to violence against women. The link is not just seen in the obvious relationships between violence and jealousy or possessiveness, which have received robust support from research: Cross-culturally, male sexual jealousy is the most common trigger for wife battering (Counts, Brown, & Campbell, 1992). Paternal uncertainty is also seen in its contribution to the existence of patriarchal norms and values (see, e.g., Smuts, 1994). For example, societies are often organized in ways that reduce threats to the certainty of paternity—the prime example being the tenacity of the modern ideal of "traditional marriages." [To be sure, matrilineal societies exist and do exhibit less violence (for a classic comparative study, see Van Velzen &

Van Wetering, 1960); but these exceptions are noteworthy simply because they are so exceptional.] Patriarchal arrangements foster violence between intimates by, for example, supporting men's control of wealth and men's wielding of power over women. The result is that, again from the perspective of modern times, women who are most likely to be the victims of family violence are those who have less power by virtue of not being in the labor market, who are excluded from decision making in the family, and who have less education (e.g. Tift, 1993).

A third concept that has helped to clarify the incidence of family violence is the evolutionary-based notion of parental investment as it relates to parent–child conflict resulting from parents' evolutionary interest to control their children and their children's interest in controlling their own evolutionary destiny (Trivers, 1974). Although adolescent–parent relationships are not necessarily marked by conflict, those that are tend to result from issues relating to parental control and child liberation. In fact, considerable evidence indicates that too much parental control (or its alternative, not enough control) leads to children's maladaptive behaviors (see Baumrind, 1991). Thus, in addition to helping us to understand child maltreatment and relationship violence, evolutionary theory helps us to comprehend parent–child conflict, especially when children reach adolescence and begin the process of courtship and separation from families.

Parental investment theory has also helped to explain more subtle forms of maltreatment. The willingness of parents to support their children is a good example (Levesque, 1994a). For example, men's willingness to financially support children is related to paternal certainty—fathers who have had their paternity determined and who have strong bonds with their children are more likely to pay child support (Levesque, 1994a). It also has been noted how society generally tends *not* to want to support other people's children, as revealed by alarming rates of child poverty (Levesque, 1994a). Likewise, it has been shown that laws tend to hold parents responsible for their own biological children, as seen in child support reform efforts (Levesque, 1993). These laws can be seen as evidence of evolutionary forces at work. The focus on genetic ties is rather strong, even to the extent that nonbiological parents are generally exempt from supporting their step-children on divorcing the biological parent (Levesque, 1994a).

## EFFECTIVE GUIDE FOR INTERVENTION

Insights from evolutionary psychology relating to family violence underscore the enormous effort that will be needed if we are ever to control such behavior. Evolutionary forces foster conflict between family members—between parents, as well as between parent and child (e.g., Haig, 1993). Given these forces, there undoubtedly needs to be an attempt to realign powers within families. If put into practice, this concept would have quite radical repercussions. Specifically, this would imply more than encouraging equality between adult partners; it would also mean ensuring equality between parent and child, which is in opposition to current societal norms and legal rules. Partners are neither likely to be, nor to feel, equal; partners' relative contributions to household income and domestic labor continue to be uneven (Levesque, 1994a). Children essentially have no rights within families (Levesque, 1994b, 1994c); current laws that simply protect them from maltreatment are certainly a step in the right direction, but the legal threshold for acting in children's interests remains remarkably low.

In addition to realigning family dynamics, the evolutionary-based insight that ecological instability contributes to family violence suggests that ecological uncertainties must be addressed. This is also a radical approach from a crime-fighting perspective. The currently popular tendency at policy-making levels is to view crime as stemming largely from individual pathology, rather than as behavior arising from a sociocultural context; for example, James Q. Wilson laments that *individuals* simply have lost their "moral sense" (Wilson, 1993). Clearly, the approaches that blame and aim to punish individuals improperly set up dichotomies that divorce individuals from their social contexts. Antisocial behaviors undoubtedly have individual roots that are genetic, but those roots also have environmental underpinnings (see chapter 5, this volume). Evolutionary psychology suggests, then, that a much broader approach is required. For example, juvenile justice must be approached from a community-based perspective (see Levesque, 1996a; Levesque & Tomkins, 1995), which addresses youth's abilities to deal with ecological instabilities. Likewise, manifestations of precarious ecologies—such as neighborhoods characterized by poverty, deteriorated housing, and high population turnovers—must be addressed in order to alleviate community levels of uncertainty, both to deal with violent behavior (Levesque, 1996a, 1996b) and prevent maltreatment (Levesque, 1994d, 1995a), especially, sexual maltreatment (Levesque, 1995b, 1995c).

## HARNESSING EVOLUTIONARY INSIGHTS

Taking evolutionary psychology seriously means that the development of family support systems is needed if we are ever to deal effectively with family violence. We must encourage social networking, open up families to community influence, and adopt a community-based approach. Unfortunately, current laws tend to take the opposite approach: There is a major focus on preserving family privacy and preventing intrusion into the family domain; there is little concern for building supportive networks; and there is little concern for addressing community-level factors (Levesque, 1996c). What evolutionary psychology suggests, then, is that we need to take a radically different approach to family policy if we are ever to control family violence. Just as important, it reminds us to proceed cautiously; for example, worldwide changes in women's economic self-sufficiency have contributed to a rise in divorce rates (Goode, 1993), the repercussions of which have yet to be fully determined. A rethinking of prevailing child custody rules is also clearly warranted (Levesque, 1994a), as is the need to reconsider the place of children and youth in society (Levesque, in press).

In addition to suggesting a new approach to family policy, outcomes from evolutionary analyses suggest a need to re-orient evolutionary psychology itself. Despite offering a truly groundbreaking and comprehensive approach to the study of the human condition, evolutionary psychology seemingly remains trapped by its own success: It remains satisfied by simply documenting the status quo. It can be argued that we would benefit more from imagining and realizing what ought to be. Instead of falling prey to misguided notions that a biological predisposition necessarily leads to violent behavior, it would be more beneficial to harness evolutionary insights so as to initiate appropriate reforms.

## REFERENCES

Baumrind, D. (1991). The influence of parenting style on adolescent competence and substance use. *Journal of Early Adolescence, 11,* 56–95.

Burgess, R. L., & Draper, P. (1989). The explanation of family violence: The role of biological, behavioral, and cultural selection, *Crime and Justice: A Review of Research, 11,* 59–116.

Counts, D. A., Brown, J. K., & Campbell, J. C. (Eds.) (1992). *Sanction and sanctuary: Cultural perspectives on the beating of wives.* Boulder, CO: Westview Press.

Daly, M., & Wilson, M. (1991). A reply to Gelles: Stepchildren are disproportionately abused, and diverse forms of violence can share causal factors, *Human Nature, 2,* 419–426.

Goode, W. J. (1993). *World changes in divorce patterns.* New Haven, CT: Yale University Press.

Haig, D. (1993). Maternal-fetal conflict in human pregnancy, *Quarterly Review of Biology, 68,* 495–532.

Korbin, J. E. (1995). Social networks and family violence in cross-cultural perspective. In Gary B. Melton (Ed.), *The individual, the family, and social good: Personal fulfillment in times of change* (pp. 107–134). Lincoln: University of Nebraska Press.

Levesque, R. J. R. (1993). The role of unwed fathers in welfare law: Failing legislative initiatives and surrendering judicial responsibility, *Law and Inequality, 12,* 93–126.

Levesque, R. J. R. (1994a). Targeting "deadbeat" dads: The problem with the direction of welfare reform, *Hamline Journal of Public Law and Policy, 15,* 1–53.

Levesque, R. J. R. (1994b). The internationalization of children's human rights: Too radical for American adolescents? *Connecticut Journal of International Law, 9,* 237–293.

Levesque, R. J. R. (1994c). International children's rights grow up: Implications for American jurisprudence and domestic policy, *California Western International Law Journal, 24,* 193–240.

Levesque, R. J. R. (1994d). The sexual use, abuse and exploitation of children:

Challenges in implementing children's human rights, *Brooklyn Law Review, 60,* 959–998.

Levesque, R. J. R. (1995a). The failures of foster care reform: Revolutionalizing the most radical blueprint, *Maryland Journal of Contemporary Legal Issues, 6,* 1–35.

Levesque, R. J. R. (1995b). Prosecuting sex crimes against children: Time for "outrageous" proposals? *Law & Psychology Review, 19,* 59–91.

Levsque, R. J. R. (1995c). Combatting child sexual maltreatment: Advances and obstacles in international progress. *Law & Policy, 17,* 44–469.

Levesque, R. J. R. (1996a). Is there still a place for violent youth in juvenile justice?, *Aggressive and Violent Behavior, 1,* 69–79.

Levesque, R. J. R. (1996b). Future visions of juvenile justice: Lessons from international and comparative law, *Creighton Law Review, 29,* 801–823.

Levesque, R. J. R. (1996c). International children's rights: Can they make a difference in American family policy? *American Psychologist, 51,* 1251–1256.

Levesque, R. J. R. (in press). *Adolescent jurisprudence.* Chicago: American Bar Association.

Levesque, R. J. R., & Tomkins, A. J. (1995). Revisioning juvenile justice: Implications of the new child protection movement, *Journal of Urban and Contemporary Law, 48,* 87–116.

Linsky, A. S., Bachman, R., & Straus, M. A. (1995). *Stress, culture, & aggression.* New Haven, CT: Yale University Press.

Smuts, B. (1994). The evolutionary origins of patriarchy, *Human Nature, 6,* 1–32.

Tift, L. L. (1993). *Battering of women: The failure of intervention and case for prevention,* Boulder, CO: Westview.

Trivers, R. L. (1974). Parent-offspring conflict. *American Zoologist, 14,* 249–264.

Van Velzen, H. U. E. T., & Van Wetering, W. (1960). Residence, power groups and intra-societal aggression: An enquiry into the conditions leading to peacefulness within non-stratified societies, *International Archives of Ethnography, 49,* 169–200.

Wilson, J. Q. (1993). *The moral sense.* New York: Free Press.

# Section VII Conclusion

Daniel G. Freedman

## TRUMBETTA AND GOTTESMAN

Trumbetta and Gottesman (chapter 20) present evidence that even such obviously societal events as divorce or never marrying contain hereditary components. My initial associations to the very interesting chapter drew me back to the meetings on behavior genetics organized by Steven Vandenberg in the 1960s (Vandenberg, 1965, 1968). It became clear to me then that the larger the twin population, the greater the number of heritable traits, including traits that, on the face of them, could not be directly inherited. For example, "wanting to be a lawyer" and "bleaching one's hair" were both significantly heritable in the National Merit Scholarship studies of Nichols (1966), in which the *N* was 850 pairs. This led me to hypothesize that, given an infinite number of twins, an infinite number of behaviors could prove heritable (Freedman, 1974). This hypothesis, of course, fits with Hebb's (1953) position that the only solution he had found for the heredity–environment problem was that "all behavior is 100% inherited and 100% acquired," a quote I have repeated over the years. My discussion of nonduality in chapter 3 attempts to take this issue a little further.

My second set of thoughts on this deceptively simple chapter is concerned with so-called environmental (actually biosocial) effects on divorce and nonmarriage. For one thing, there are biosocial aspects of gender differences in personality that would affect rates of divorce. For example, serial monogamy appears most often as a male pattern (a form of polygyny), and it has often been cited as a dominant male's response to a monogamous culture (e.g., Freedman, 1979). In this case, divorce and a stronger than average tendency to philandering may make up the biosocial correlation we are seeking.

I should like also to raise the issue of one's early familial experiences, memories and interpretations of the parental marriage, and the unconscious lodging within the self of an "internal working model" based on these early associations. Attachment theory predicts (and postdicts) that these early experiences are crucially determinative of one's adult attachments and, by implication, one's marital history (e.g., Goldberg, Muir, & Kerr, 1995). Although I know of no statistical studies, the clinical evidence that the parental marriage forms a model for one's attitudes and feelings about marriage is very strong, and we need only note that this in no way contradicts the finding that divorce is heritable; it merely suggests that the two domains be joined in an intelligent way—and that, in fact, they comprise a single biosocial domain. In this regard, Bowlby clearly regarded attachment itself as in the biosocial domain—because he used animal behavior as a model—but then he erringly contrasted genetical with social inheritance, making an illogical claim for the salience of internal working models over genes (Bowlby, 1973, p. 323).

Although it is convenient to blame Descartes for this repeated clumsiness over dualities that are not actually dualities, he merely formalized what was in the air. Although his contemporary, Blaise Pascal (1640/1941), already saw the logical flaws in his bi-partite thinking, it remained for Eastern thinking to penetrate our Western ways and to make us aware that our customary dualities are intrinsically problematic—and that we are infatuated with seeking solutions to insoluble problems. Thus, in the field of "behavior genetics," we pride ourselves as not being "either–or" thinkers, opting instead for the "interaction" of heredity and environment. The statistical problems around interaction, however, have proved daunting, and satisfactory solutions are always just around the corner. As noted in chapter 3, I do believe a radically new mathematics—possibly based in chaos theory—may better model the essential unity of heredity and environment. When that occurs, science and the humanities will have at last found a common ground.

## SCHLEIDT

In chapter 21, Wolfgang Schleidt, as is his custom, raises many interesting issues. The cybernetic complexity surrounding human attempts to engineer social change is truly daunting, and Schleidt (and people of his and my age) tend to be wary of what a young and energetic Roger Levesque sees as a requirement—the initiation of social programs to better the lot of the suffering among us. (Bateson, too, as I have noted, was deeply suspicious of social engineering and, as a corollary, he also despised politics and politicians.)

Schleidt presents some fascinating original data on human gender dimorphism and wonders at the diversity within our species relative to other primates. One reason for this diversity is "lineal fissioning" (Neel & Ward, 1970). As discussed in chapter 3, lineal fissioning creates an evolutionary pace in humans some 100 times faster than in other mammals, largely because we can trace our ancestry and because we have developed means of genetically isolating ourselves from even our own second cousins. Thus, it is not a total mystery that we find such uncharacteristic diversity in the hominid primate.

Schleidt has very enlightening things to say about where ethology failed and where it is still a vital force. I should like to add to that discussion, however briefly, by contrasting two aspects of Lorenz's thinking, his holistic versus his mechanistic sides. With regard to the former, no one has more clearly stated the advantages of naturalistic observation than Lorenz. In his article on Gestalt perception (Lorenz, 1959/1971), he charmingly reports on a trip to the zoo with his young daughter, where she proves to be a natural taxonomist by correctly noting the relationships among various species. (Schleidt once tested my own Gestalt perception by presenting me with a Rubik cube and encouraging me to "go Gestalt." I failed miserably, which at the time pleased Schleidt, who was in an analytic phase. I recovered and attributed the failure to the misapplication of an otherwise healthy intuition.)

I have also been fond of Lorenz's open encouragement of "affectionate regard" for the creatures one is studying, asserting that one sees them more clearly that way. As noted elsewhere, this encouragement has greatly affected my own work. (As a playful aside, I can here try to even things with Schleidt, for the previous incident, by noting that his longtime creature of study has been the pea-brained turkey, a species that rarely summons up our deepest affection. . . . However, to be fair, he was using them to analyze specific hypotheses, and the work was more like that of von Holst and Saint-Paul (1960) who had implanted electrodes in the hypothalamus of chickens and were thereby able to stimulate normal appearing innate releasing mechanisms. I must also note that in Lorenz's *The Foundations of Ethology* (1981), there are no fewer than six references to the work of Wolfgang Schleidt, who was clearly one of Lorenz's favorite pupils.)

With regard to the mechanistic side of Lorenz's theorizing, Schleidt deals nicely with the new view of stereotyped behavior and fixed action patterns, noting how population genetics has served to modify the previous reliance on such discrete behaviors as proof of innateness. Certainly, the increase in ethological studies of mammals, in contrast to the original tendency to study only fish and birds, has also encouraged the shift away from Lorenz's view that innate and acquired elements are intercalated as links in a chain. Mammals simply mess up the picture by seamlessly uniting the innate and acquired and rendering such analyses moot (discussed further in chapter 3).

Finally, in expanding on his theme of complexity in human behavior, Schleidt brings up, all too briefly, the issue of human celibacy. I am personally interested because in Advaitist Hinduism, and in some forms of Buddhism, the achievement of enlightenment and celibacy are a singular process. Is it possible that nonduality, which is akin to or possibly the same as enlightenment, can be more readily experienced by the celibate? In psychoanalytic terms, does a diffused libido, as opposed to libidinal attachment to a specific "object," facilitate the experience of nonduality? If, as I propose at the end of chapter 3, scientists steeped in nonduality will indeed tend to be more centered and creative, perhaps institutes of higher learning will again become places in which celibacy is encouraged. After all, there is a certain cyclicity in history, and we are perhaps leaving a severely secular period for one of greater spirituality.

## LEVESQUE

In chapter 22, Roger Levesque, some might say, suffers from "oughtism." Why can he not stop pricking our collective consciences, insisting we reconsider our roles as citizens, that we arise out of our habitual comforts and act on the compassion we feel for the "lesser" among us? I could intellectualize, as is my wont, and point out that voices like his have been heard throughout history, and that indeed most of us have such a voice in our own heads—our consciences. Despite this, suffering has always been part of life, and probably will always be, and our only choice is to become habituated to it: In one way or another, we have all learned to live with beggars, the homeless, bagwomen, alcoholics, thieves, dishonesty, drugs, suicide, insanity, and so forth.

But consider that the Buddha enjoined his followers to know no rest until the least among them no longer suffered— that is, he enjoined them to have infinite compassion. To my mind, one such fully compassionate soul in our midst ripples into all hearts round him or her, and thereby energizes the loving parts of others. What Levesque is asking for, putting evolutionary psychology to the task of easing human suffering, will depend on compassionate individuals who also happen to be scientists, and all our lives would benefit enormously from just a few such persons.

This, of course, can get very complex, as when Arthur Jensen (1969) sincerely thought he was doing African Americans a good turn by pointing out that, on average, they required schooling with concrete rather than abstract subject matter, because, he claimed, that is where their strengths lie. We all know the results of that exercise in do-goodism.

However, I have experienced at least one scientist whose compassion seemed total: my mentor, Kurt Goldstein. Maslow, who loved Goldstein as much as I, gave me to understand that, as a relatively young scientist in Berlin, Goldstein had been highly competitive and a taskmaster with those in his laboratory. He was, in fact, a grand illustration of Erik Erikson's schema of life's stages. Thus, in his later generative years, when I knew him, he was able to let his natural compassion flourish, and everyone around him was affected by his grace and love. Further, the sort of work he did (working with the brain-injured) as well as the theory he advanced (self-actualization and holism) are clearly reflective of an optimistic and loving soul.

Although Roger Levesque has addressed the field of evolutionary psychology in general, and implored it, as a field, to make meaningful recommendations for curing our communities, my take is clearly at the level of individual scientists and on the paths that their own self-actualization takes them. I can only agree with Levesque's idealism and his call, and I end with the hope that appropriately compassionate souls are, even now, emerging among us.

## REFERENCES

Bowlby, J. (1973). *Attachment and loss. Volume 2: Separation.* New York: Basic Books.

Freedman, D. G. (1974). *Human infancy: An evolutionary perspective.* Hillsdale, NJ: Erlbaum.

Freedman, D. G. (1979). *Human sociobiology: A holistic approach.* New York: Free Press.

Goldberg, S, Muir, R., & Kerr, J. (Eds.). (1995). *Attachment theory.* Hillsdale, NJ: Analytic Press.

Hebb, D. O. (1953). Heredity and environment in mammalian behaviour. *British Journal of Animal Behaviour, 1,* 43–47.

Jensen, A. R. (1969). How much can we boost IQ and scholastic achievement? *Harvard Educational Review, 39,* 1–123.

Lorenz, K. Z. (1959/1971). Gestalt perception as a source of scientific knowledge. In *Studies in animal behavior* (Vol. 2, pp. 281–322). Cambridge, MA: Harvard University Press.

Lorenz, K. Z. (1981). *The foundations of ethology.* New York: Springer.

Neel, J. V., & Ward, J. H. (1970). Village and tribal genetic distances among American Indians and the possible implications for human evolution. *Proceedings of the American Academy of Sciences, 65,* 323–330.

Nichols, R. C. (1966). The resemblance of twins in personality and interests. *Research Reports (National Merit Scholarship Corporations) 2,* 1–23.

Pascal, B. (1670/1941). *Pensées.* New York: Random House.

Vandenberg, S. G. (Ed.). (1965). *Methods and goals in human behavior genetics.* New York: Academic Press.

Vandenberg, S. G. (Ed.). (1968). *Progress in human behavior genetics.* Baltimore: Johns Hopkins University Press.

von Holst, E., & Saint-Paul, U. (1960). Vom Wirkungsgefüge der Triebe. *Naturwissenschaften, 28,* 273–280. Cited in I. Eibl-Eibesfeldt (1989), *Human ethology.* New York: Aldine de Gruyter.

SECTION VIII

# Final Overview: Uniting Psychology and Biology

SECTION VIII

# Final Overview: Uniting Psychology and Biology

Glenn E. Weisfeld, Carol C. Weisfeld, and Nancy L. Segal

A glance at the chapters in this book provides more than a hint of Daniel G. Freedman's remarkable intellectual versatility. He conducted classic behavioral genetic research on dogs and extended this to humans. Additional work in this tradition is represented in the chapters by Bailey, Gottesman, Scott, and Segal. Dr. Freedman was a pioneer in recognizing and examining the many biological and experiential factors that affect development, an approach exemplified in the chapters by Marvin, Savin-Williams, and Wolff. Dr. Freedman also conducted, and continues to conduct, cross-cultural research, and he arranged for many of his students to continue this work. His biocultural perspective is still unusual in the behavioral sciences. This viewpoint is represented in the chapters by Blurton Jones, Ekman, LeVine, and C. C. Weisfeld. Dr. Freedman's findings from studies of infant behavior, many of which are summarized in his book *Human Infancy* (1974), are preserved in his films, commented on in this volume. He produced some of the earliest publications on evolved aspects of human behavior, including *Human Sociobiology* (1979), and in 1972 he helped found what became the International Society for

Human Ethology. This evolutionary perspective is the basis for the chapters by Trivers, Barkow, and G. Weisfeld.

Despite his wide range of interests—or perhaps because of it—Dr. Freedman's research constitutes variations on a single theme: an interactionist, holistic view of human behavior. This means that genetic, as well as environmental, influences must be considered. Beyond this, as Tinbergen (1963) stressed, complete understanding of a basic, species-wide human behavior requires describing it on four levels: not just its proximate, or immediate, causation, but also its developmental course, phylogenesis, and adaptive value. Studying all four facets of various behaviors, as Dr. Freedman has done, requires command of several distinct but related disciplines, including developmental psychology, behavioral genetics, biopsychology, anthropology, ethology, and sociobiology.

But mere recognition of Dr. Freedman's scholarship and originality alone misses the main point: His sort of research and that of the other contributors to this volume are important because they point the way toward integration of the various subdisciplines of psychology with each other, with biology, and with the other natural sciences.

Psychology is far from being a mature, internally coherent discipline. Unlike the natural sciences, it is an array of largely unrelated and even contradictory minitheories of various aspects of behavior. There is no unifying theory as exists for physics, chemistry, and biology, no theory that describes global human behavior. Lacking a unifying theory, psychology is cast adrift from the natural sciences that are conceptually integrated with each other and whose terms are often more precise than those of psychology.

What advantages would be gained by integrating psychology with biology? Interdisciplinary integration allows for cross-fertilization—the application of models and data from one field to another. Powerful, parsimonious, overarching models that embrace multiple disciplines are then sometimes possible. For example, principles of genetics, ethology, developmental psychobiology, cross-cultural psychology, and sociobiology are fruitfully applied to human behavior in the chapters of this book. More specifically, animal models, such as dominance hierarchization, play, and parent–infant bonding, have emerged from ethology to illuminate human social behavior. Many psychological explanations of behavior, by contrast, have never been tested in non-Western cultures. Biology also provides a critical test for psychological explanations; those that contradict accepted principles of biology must be reconsidered, such as the catharsis theory of aggression. Darwinism can also explain the adaptive value and hence normality of putatively pathological phenomena such as family conflict, sexual jealousy, anger, and guilt. A comprehensive model of normal human behavior would provide a framework for identifying and understanding pathological phenomena. In addition, research methods developed in one discipline can be adopted by another. For example, behavioral genetic methods and naturalistic observation, pioneered by biologists, could be used more extensively by psychologists. Naturalistic observation anchors the study of behavior to observable actions that can be readily compared across species and cultures.

What is the proper place of psychology in the hierarchy of the natural sciences? To evolutionists, psychology belongs atop biology, which in turn surmounts chemistry, which is based on physics. Behavior is a property of biological organisms, so the study of behavior logically connects it to the biological domain. Behavioral phenomena are products of the nervous system and, as such, follow the same principles as do other bodily systems. Psychology has often been so defined (e.g., Drever, 1952; Michel & Moore, 1995), but its potential link to biology has seldom been pursued in practice.

In order to unite psychology with biology, a good start might be made by acknowledging the connection between human social behavior and the social behavior of other species. We freely draw comparisons between human and animal sensory phenomena and perception and learning. But universal social behaviors are seldom considered to be homologous to the same phenomena in other primates. Psychology cannot be integrated with biology unless we overcome that dualism, the last bastion of the mind–body dichotomy. Integration will require acceptance not just of physiological parallels between human and animal brains but also of functional parallels, of the adaptive significance of various human social behaviors. The central theory of biology is Darwinism, not physiology. It is necessary, but not sufficient, to integrate psychological theories with biopsychological data.

If the application of evolutionary theory to our own species' behavior—to social behavior as well as other types—were to occur, what would it look like? First, there would be emphasis on species-wide behaviors, not on variability. No natural science dwells on diversity; all try to generalize, to establish laws that describe the main phenomena of interest. Psychology skipped over this descriptive stage in its history (Archer, 1992); the deficiency needs to be corrected. One may object that there are few human universals, but this is not true even of social behaviors. Numerous social motives exist everywhere, such as sexual behavior; general sociality; specific social affinities including nepotism, pair bonding, parent–offspring bonding, and friendship; prestige striving (pride and shame); and angry aggression. Furthermore, within each of these broad categories there exist some universals, including criteria of mate choice and of physical attractiveness, particular emotional expressions, antecedents of sexual jealousy, and factors affecting the intensity of parental feelings. These universals are central to any systematic description of human behavior, but they are remarked on by psychology, if at all, as peripheral and isolated findings. Instead, variation in human behavior as a function of learning and culture is constantly stressed, albeit with emphasis on research on contemporary Western society.

Once these universals, these building blocks of human behavior, were recognized, the causes of their variability could be addressed. Much interindividual variation is a result of genetic differences (see chapters by Bailey, Gottesman, Scott, and Segal in this volume). Individual differences in behavioral traits, in fact, are as much a result of genes as are individual differences in morphological traits (Plomin, 1990). Moreover, the influence of genes on most behaviors does not subside as children get older; rather, genes have as much influence in adolescence and adulthood as they had in infancy and childhood—and sometimes more, depending on the behavior of interest. These basic facts need to be conveyed to students, but they are often ignored in the current Zeitgeist of environmental determinism. Along with this, the complex nature of behavioral development needs to be explained in terms of various types of gene–environment interaction (Marvin, Savin-Williams & Diamond, and Wolff chapters, this volume; Michel & Moore, 1995). To paraphrase Plomin, it is time for work that "explores the hyphen in the phrase *nature–nurture*" (Plomin, 1994, p. xiii). Simplistic or vague developmental theories that are not grounded in biology need to be reevaluated.

Perhaps most important, functional analyses of universal human behaviors and developmental events are needed. The great, unique contribution of biology to psychology is the Darwinian perspective, Tinbergen's "why" question of function (Weisfeld, 1982). Why do particular bodily and behavioral changes occur at puberty, why are men generally larger than women, why does weaning occur when it does, why do various behavioral sex differences exist everywhere, why is the family universal, why are identical twins so cooperative? Applying a functional perspective requires knowledge of not just animal behavior but also prehistoric hominid society, because natural selection occurs so slowly that modern humans are still adapted to the forager life of the Pleistocene. Psychology needs to broaden its focus from the supposed utility of various actual or idealized behaviors for "adjusting to" modern Western society, to the true adaptive value of universal or widespread behaviors that are more representative of our hominid heritage. See, for example, transcultural descriptions of the human family (Stephens, 1963; van den Berghe, 1980). Even more fundamentally, psychology needs to admit that most of its explanations of social behavioral phenomena are limited to modern U.S. culture. In order to discover truly universal principles of social behavior and their respective functions, psychology needs to undertake a serious program of systematic cross-cultural research.

Functional analyses can shed light on complicated questions at both micro and macro levels of analysis. Examples of functional responses to mechanistic questions are provided in the chapters by Trivers, Barkow, and G. Weisfeld in this volume. As another illustration of functional analysis, incest avoidance is found not just in humans but in many other species, for the same adaptive reason: prevention of inbreeding depression effects. It turns out that physical closeness early in life, such as occurs between nuclear family members, fosters sexual aversion in children as well as in juvenile simians. On a more macro level, functional explanations can make sense of cultural phenomena. Cultural influences, like other factors in development, generally cooperate with genetic factors, as Dr. Freedman's research on infant behavior illustrated. Specifically, he has suggested that culture may reflect the unique, genetically influenced temperament of a relatively homogeneous population. Culture is not the rival of biology but rather its close partner in serving the interests of the organism. The chapters by Blurton Jones, Ekman, and C. C. Weisfeld in this book offer additional examples of this perspective.

Many psychologists, particularly those committed to a behaviorist and cognitive view of human behavior, may disagree with us about the usefulness of a closer working relationship between biology and psychology. Ethologists and their allies have often pondered the question of why the social sciences resist Darwinism (e.g., Charlesworth, 1986; Crawford, 1989). Trivers (1996) has suggested that widespread ignorance of biology is a factor. Nonetheless, it is already clear that several subspecialties within psychology, particularly clinical psychology, forensic psychology, and the psychology of women, have benefited from incorporating a more holistic and functional view of human behavior. These specific areas can provide many examples of concepts that have been clarified by combining biological and psychological knowledge and methods, such as the following.

Various clinical fields are beginning to accept biological analyses of pathological conditions. Clinical psychologists, over the course of time, have offered many causal explanations for obsessive–compulsive disorders such as excessive handwashing—for example, inadequate ego development as a cause had come out of a psychoanalytic view. Animal behavior specialists pointed out the functional nature of normal handwashing and compared it to species-specific behaviors regulated by the basal ganglia and associated structures in the brains of other mammalian species. Serotonin is one key neurotransmitter in this area of the brain; normal serotonin levels inhibit excessive species-specific self-cleaning and guarding behaviors, and abnormally low amounts of serotonin will allow abnormally high behavior frequencies to surface (Rapoport, 1989). Nowadays patients diagnosed with obsessive–compulsive disorder are most effectively treated with a combination of serotonin-related drugs and psychotherapy. Addressing the abnormality on multiple levels appears to offer the best hope for providing relief to patients (Wise & Rapoport, 1988). Similar functional insights may have important treatment implications for eating disorders such as anorexia nervosa (Surbey, 1987). The journal *Ethology and Sociobiology* devoted a special issue to "Mental Disorders in an Evolutionary Context" in 1994, and it is replete with articles describing many such connections to functional behaviors. *The Across-Species Comparison and Psychiatry Newsletter* is exclusively devoted to this perspective. In addition, the new field of Darwinian medicine (Nesse & Williams, 1994), with its adaptationist analysis of normal phenomena such as fever (Kluger, 1986) and morning sickness (Profet, 1992), offers important clinical implications for medicine.

In a similar way, Daly and Wilson (1988) provided crucial insights into the causes of murder in their volume *Homicide.* Their carefully compiled descriptive data filled a void for forensic psychologists, pointing to the power of male sexual jealousy and the dangers experienced by some children who are not cared for by their natural parents. The best use of their insights, which derived from sociobiological principles, may well be in prevention efforts targeted at families at risk.

Another specialty that is by necessity interdisciplinary, the study of the psychology of women, benefits enormously from a serious integration with knowledge of biology. As Watts (1984) pointed out, science is an essential foundation for formulating ideas about societal change. We have already seen some very thoughtful and powerful applications in articles on parenthood by Alice Rossi (1977) and by Draper and Harpending (1988). As additional examples, new insights into the complex patterns of male–female communication are coming out of work by J. M. Gottman

(1994); and a better understanding of female responses to stress is the product of Frankenhaeuser's work on hormones and competition (Frankenhaeuser et al., 1978). Hoyenga and Hoyenga's book on sex differences (1993) is a fine example of integrating information from biology and social psychology in describing male and female behaviors. In reviewing literature on gender stereotypes themselves, Lueptow, Garovich, and Lueptow concluded that "valid social psychological explanations for gendered personality traits cannot rest upon sociocultural models alone but must include interaction of this unchanging genetic underlay with changeable social structures and processes" (1995, p. 509).

These, in brief, are some of the potential advantages to psychology of an integration with biology and the other natural sciences. Unfortunately, mainstream social science often actively resists biological modeling of human behavior. A prominent developmental psychologist recently wrote, "I do not believe there is any evidence for a gene or any combination of genes affecting intellectual ability" (Horowitz, 1996, p. 227). This statement is irreconcilable with established findings in behavioral genetics. As we approach the completion of the Human Genome Project, expected by the year 2003, according to Francis Collins (quoted in Beardsley, 1996), it becomes crucial that we psychologists prepare ourselves to speak the gene-inclusive language that will be spoken by scientists. Just as we had no choice but to become computer-literate, we will soon need to be gene-literate.

Many of us have been laboring for many years in lonely isolation in the Darwinian fields—save for conspicuous champions such as Dr. Freedman. We have been heartened by the new spate of popular yet scholarly accounts of recent developments in sociobiology and ethology. Books by Sulloway (1996), Wright (1994), Buss (1994), and Eibl-Eibesfeldt (1989) have brought these concepts to widespread popular attention, as have feature articles in major newspapers and magazines. Psychology students are coming to us more frequently with a specific interest in the evolutionary perspective. Our hope is that their enthusiasm and natural curiosity about adaptationist questions will inspire our academic colleagues to inform themselves of these ideas too. Only then can we proceed to unify the study of behavior and reconcile it with the great ideas in biology that are revolutionizing science.

## REFERENCES

Archer, J. (1992). *Ethology and human development.* Savage, MD: Barnes & Noble Books.

Beardsley, T. (1996). Vital data. *Scientific American, 274,* 100–105.

Buss, D. M. (1994). *The evolution of desire.* New York: Basic Books.

Charlesworth, W. R. (1986). Darwin and developmental psychology: 100 years later. *Human Development, 29,* 1–35.

Crawford, C. (1989). Sociobiology: Of what value to psychology? In C. Crawford, M. Smith, & D. Krebs (Eds.), *Sociobiology and psychology: Ideas, issues and applications.* (pp. 3–30). Hillsdale, NJ: Erlbaum.

Daly, M., & Wilson, M. (1988). *Homicide.* New York: Aldine de Gruyter.

Draper, P., & Harpending, H. (1988). A sociobiological perspective on the development of human reproductive strategies. In K. B. MacDonald (Ed.), *Sociobiological perspectives on human development* (pp. 340–372). New York: Springer-Verlag.

Drever, J. (1952). *Dictionary of psychology.* Baltimore: Penguin.

Eibl-Eibesfeldt, I. (1989). *Human ethology.* New York: Aldine de Gruyter.

Frankenhaeuser, M., Von Wright, M., Collins, A., Von Wright, J., Sedvall, G., & Swahn, C. (1978). Sex differences in psychoneuroendocrine reactions to examination stress. *Psychosomatic Medicine, 40,* 334–343.

Freedman, D. G. (1974). *Human infancy: An evolutionary perspective.* New York: Wiley.

Freedman, D. G. (1979). *Human sociobiology: A holistic approach.* New York: Free Press.

Gottman, J. M. (1994). *What predicts divorce?* Hillsdale, NJ: Erlbaum.

Horowitz, F. D. (1996). Letter to *Science News, 150,* 227.

Hoyenga, K. B., & Hoyenga, K. T. (1993). *Gender-related differences.* Boston: Allyn and Bacon.

Kluger, M. J. (1986). Is fever beneficial? *Yale Journal of Biology and Medicine, 59,* 89–95.

Lueptow, L. B., Garovich, L., & Lueptow, M. B. (1995). The persistence of gender stereotypes in the face of changing sex roles: Evidence contrary to the sociocultural model. *Ethology and Sociobiology, 16,* 509–530.

Michel, G. F., & Moore, C. L. (1995). *Developmental psychobiology: An interdisciplinary science.* Cambridge, MA: MIT Press.

Nesse, R. M., & Williams, G. C. (1994). *Why we get sick: The new science of Darwinian medicine.* New York: Times Books.

Plomin, R. (1990). *Nature and nurture: An introduction to human behavioral genetics.* Pacific Grove, CA.: Brooks-Cole.

Plomin, R. (1994). *Genetics and experience.* Thousand Oaks, CA: Sage.

Profet, M. (1992). Pregnancy sickness as adaptation: A deterrent to maternal ingestion of teratogens. In J. H. Barkow, L. Cosmides, & J. Tooby (Eds.), *The adapted mind* (pp. 327–365). New York: Oxford University Press.

Rapoport, J. L. (1989). The biology of obsessions and compulsions. *Scientific American, 260,* 82–89.

Rossi, A. S. (1977, Spring). A biosocial perspective on parenting. *Daedalus, 106,* 1–31.

Stephens, W. N. (1963). *The family in cross-cultural perspective.* New York: Holt, Rinehart & Winston.

Sulloway, F. (1996). *Born to rebel.* New York: Pantheon Books.

Surbey, M. K. (1987). Anorexia nervosa, amenorrhea and adaptation. *Ethology and Sociobiology, 8,* 47S–61S.

Tinbergen, N. (1963). On the aims and methods of ethology. *Zeitschrift für Tierpsychologie, 20,* 410–433.

Trivers, R. (1996). Interviewed by F. Roes. *Human Ethology Bulletin, 11,* 1–3.

van den Berghe, P. L. (1980). The human family: A sociobiological look. In J. S. Lockard (Ed.), *The evolution of human social behavior* (pp. 67–85). New York: Elsevier.

Watts, M. (1984). *Biopolitics and gender.* New York: Haworth.

Weisfeld, G. E. (1982). The nature-nurture issue and the integrating concept of function. In G. B. Wolman (Ed.), *Handbook of developmental psychology* (pp. 208–229). Englewood Cliffs, NJ: Prentice-Hall.

Wise, S. P., & Rapoport, J. L. (1988). Obsessive-compulsive disorder: Is it a basal ganglia dysfunction? *Psychopharmacology Bulletin, 24,* 380–384.

Wright, R. (1994). *The moral animal.* New York: Pantheon Books.

APPENDIX

# Publications and Films by Daniel G. Freedman

## BOOKS AND EDITED VOLUMES

Freedman, D. G. (1974). *Human infancy: An evolutionary perspective.* Hillsdale, NJ: Erlbaum.

Freedman, D. G. (1979). *Human sociobiology: A holistic approach.* New York: Free Press.

Omark, D. G., Strayer, F. F., & Freedman, D. G. (Eds.). (1980). *Dominance relations: An ethological view of human conflict and social interaction.* New York: Garland Press.

## ARTICLES AND CHAPTERS

Freedman, D. G. (1958). Constitutional and environmental interactions in rearing of four breeds of dogs. *Science, 127,* 585–586.

*Reprinted in:*

- Dennenberg, V. H. (Ed.). (1971). *Biobehavioral basis of developments.* Sunderland, MA: Sinauer Associates.

---

Appendix compiled in part by Nancy L. Segal.

- Rosenblith, J., & Allensmith, W. (Eds.). (1962, 1966, 1972). *The causes of behavior.* Boston: Allyn & Bacon.
- Russell, R. W. (Ed.). (1963). *Frontiers in psychology.* Chicago: Scott Foresman.

Freedman, D. G. (1960). The flight response and critical periods in social development. In *Memoires du XIX Congrès Internationale de Sociologie* (Vol II, pp. 39–53).

Freedman, D. G., King, J. A., & Elliot, O. (1961). Critical period in the social development of dogs. *Science, 133,* 1016–1017.

Freedman, D. G. (1961). The infant's fear of strangers and flight response. *Journal of Child Psychology and Psychiatry, 4,* 242–248.

Freedman, D. G., Mallardi, A., & Mallardi, A. C. (1961). Studio sul primo manifestarsi della plaura delltestraneo nel bambino: Osservazioni comparative tra soggetti allevati in famiglia e soggetti allevati in comunita chiusa. *Atti de VI Congresso Nazionale della S.I.A.M.E.* (pp. 254–256).

Freedman, D. G., Ostwald, P., & Kurtz, J. (1962). The cries of infant twins. *Folia Phonetrica, 14,* 37–50.

*Reprinted in:*

- *Proceedings of the Second International Congress of Human Genetics 1963: Vol. I* (pp. 322–329). Rome: Instituto Gregor Mendel.

Freedman, D. G. (1963). The differentiation of identical and fraternal twins on the basis of filmed behavior. *Proceedings of the Second International Congress of Human Genetics* (Vol. I, pp. 259–262). Rome: Instituto G. Mendel.

Freedman, D. G., & Keller, B. (1963). Inheritance of behavior in infants. *Science, 140,* 196–198.

*Reprinted in:*

- Brackbill, Y., & Thompson, G. G. (Eds.). (1967). *Behavior in infancy and early childhood* (pp. 392–397). New York: Free Press.

- Hutt, S. J., & Hutt, C. (Eds.). (1973). *Early human development* (pp. 8–12). Oxford: Oxford University Press.
- *Supplement, Folia Psychiatrica et Neurologica Japonica.* (December, 1963).

Freedman, D. G. (1964). Smiling in blind infants and the issue of innate versus acquired. *Journal of Child Psychology and Psychiatry, 5,* 171–184.

Freedman, D. G. (1964). Family and mental health problems in a deaf population. *Eugenics Ouarterly, 2,* 177–179.

Freedman, D. G. (1965). Some effects of early rearing on later obedience in dogs. *Nordisk Verterinaermedicin, 17,* 111–117.

Freedman, D. G. (1965). Hereditary control of early social behavior. In B. M. Foss (Ed.), *Determinants of infant behavior: Vol. III* (pp. 149–159). London: Methuen.

Freedman, D. G. (1965). An ethological approach to the genetical study of human behavior. In S. G. Vandenberg (Ed.), *Methods and goals in human behavior genetics* (pp. 141–161). New York: Academic Press.

Freedman, D. G. (1967). Personality development in infancy: A biological approach. In Y. Brackbill (Ed.), *Infancy and childhood* (pp. 469–502). New York: Free Press.

*Reprinted in*:

- Washburn, S. L., & Jay, P. (Eds.). (1968). *Perspectives on human evolution: Vol. I* (pp. 258–287). New York: Holt, Reinhart & Winston.

Freedman, D. G. (1967). A biological view of man's social behavior. In W. Etkin, *Social behavior from fish to man* (pp. 152–188). Chicago: University of Chicago Press.

Freedman, D. G. (1967). The origins of social behavior. *Science Journal, 3,* 69–73.

*Reprinted in*:

- Bronfenbrenner, U., & Mahoney, M. (Eds.). (1972). *Influences on human development* (pp. 43–47). Hinsdale, NJ: Dryden Press.

Freedman, D. G. (1968). An evolutionary framework for behavioral research. In S. G. Vandenberg (Ed.). *Progress in human behavior genetics* (pp. 1–6). Baltimore: Johns Hopkins University Press.

Freedman, D. G. (1968). The ethological study of man. In A. S. Parkes (Ed.), *Genetic and environmental influences on behavior* (pp. 37–62). London: Oliver & Boyd.

Freedman, D. G. (1969). The survival value of beards. *Psychology Today, 3*, 36–39.

*Reprinted in*:

- *Readings in Psychology Today*. (1972). (2nd ed.). Del Mar, CA: CRM Books.

Freedman, D. G., & Freedman, N. C. (1969). Behavioral differences between Chinese-American and European-American newborns. *Nature, 224*, 1227.

*Reprinted in*:

- Bresler, J. B. (Ed.). (1973). *Genetics and society*. Reading, MA: Addison-Wesley.
- Stone, L. J. (Ed.). (1972). *The competent infant: A handbook of readings*. New York: Basic Books.

Freedman, D. G. (1971). The impact of behavior genetics and ethology. In H. Rie (Ed.), *Perspectives in child psychopathology* (pp. 219–266). Chicago: Aldine.

Freedman, D. G. (1971). Behavioral assessment in infancy. In G. B. A. Stoelinga & J. J. Van der Werfften Bosch (Eds.), *Normal and abnormal development of brain and behavior* (pp. 92–99). Leiden: Leiden University Press.

Freedman, D. G. (1971). Genetic influences on development of behavior. In G. B. A. Stoelinga & J. J. Van der Werfften Bosch (Eds.), *Normal and abnormal development of brain and behavior* (pp. 208–229). Leiden: Leiden University Press.

Brazelton, T. B., & Freedman, D. G. (1971). The Cambridge neonatal scales. In G. B. A. Stoelinga & J. J. Van der Werfften Bosch (Eds.), *Normal and abnormal development of brain and behavior* (pp. 104–132). Leiden: Leiden University Press.

Freedman, D. G. (1971). An evolutionary approach to research on the life cycle. *Human Development, 14,* 87–99.

Freedman, D. G. (1972). Genetic variations on the hominid theme: Individual, sex and ethnic differences. In F. J. Monks, W. W. Hartup, & J. De Wit (Eds.), *Determinants of behavioral development* (pp. 121–157). New York: Academic Press.

Freedman, D. G., & Omark, D. (1973). Ethology, genetics and education. In F. A. J. Ianni & E. Storey (Eds.), *Cultural relevance and educational issues: Readings in anthropology and education* (pp. 250–283). Boston: Little, Brown.

Freedman, D. G. (1975). The development of social hierarchies. In L. Levi (Ed.), *Society, stress and disease: Vol. II: Childhood and adolescence* (pp. 36–42). New York: Oxford University Press.

Freedman, D. G. (1975). Comment [Comment on the paper *Prestige and culture: A biosocial interpretation*]. *Current Anthropology, 16,* 564–565.

Freedman, D. G. (1976). Infancy, culture and biology. In L. P. Lipsitt (Ed.), *Developmental psychobiology: The significance of infancy* (pp. 35–54). Hillsdale, NJ: Erlbaum.

Savin-Williams, R. C., & Freedman, D. G. (1977). Bio-social approach to human development. In S. Chevalier Skolnikoff & F. Poirier (Eds.), *Primate biosocial development: Biological, social and ecological determinants* (pp. 563–601). New York: Garland.

Freedman, D. G. (1979). Ethnic differences in babies. *Human Nature, 2,* 36–43.

*Reprinted in:*

- Fitzgerald, H. E. (Ed.). (1980 and 1981). *Human Development (1980–*

*1981) and Human Development (1981–1982)*. Guilford, CT: Dushkin Press.

- Goldstein, E. C. (Ed.). (1980). *Ethnic groups*. Boca Raton, FL: Social Issues Resources Series.
- Gardner, J. K. (Ed.). (1982). *Readings in developmental psychology* (2nd ed.). Boston: Little, Brown.

Freedman, D. G., & DeBoer, M. (1979). Biological and cultural differences in child development. *Annual Review of Anthropology, 8,* 579–600.

Freedman, D. G. (1979). Riduzionismo e olismo in sociobiologia. In M. Cesa-Bianchi & M. Poli Franco Angelo (Eds.), *Atti del IV Congresso Biennale della ISSBD* (pp. 32–36). Milan: International Society for the Study of Behavioural Development.

Freedman, D. G. (1980). Sexual dimorphism and the status hierarchy. In D. R. Omark, F. F. Strayer, & D. G. Freedman (Eds.), *Dominance relations: An ethological view of human conflict and social interaction* (pp. 261–271). New York: Garland Press.

Freedman, D. G. (1980). Cross-cultural notes on status hierarchies. In D. R. Omark, F. F. Strayer, & D. G. Freedman (Eds.), *Dominance relations: An ethological view of human conflict and social interaction* (pp. 333–339). New York: Garland Press.

Freedman, D. G. (1980). The social and the biological: A necessary unity. *Zygon, 15,* 117–132.

Fajardo, B., & Freedman, D. G. (1981). Maternal rhythmicity in three American cultures. In T. M. Field, A. M. Sostek, P. Vietze, & P. H. Leiderman (Eds.), *Culture and early interactions* (pp. 133–148). Hillsdale, NJ: Erlbaum.

Freedman, D. G. (1983). Ethology and development. In J. McV. Hunt & N. Endler (Eds.), *Personality and Behavior Disorders: Vol. 1* (2nd ed., pp. 651–672). New York: Wiley.

Weisfeld, C. C., Weisfeld, G. E., Warren, R. A., & Freedman, D. G. (1983). The spelling bee: A naturalistic study of female inhibition in mixed-sex competition. *Adolescence, 18,* 695–708.

Freedman, D. G. (1984). Asking the right questions. *Behavioral and Brain Sciences, 7,* 153.

Freedman, D. G. (1984). Village fissioning, human diversity and ethnocentrism. *Political Psychology, 5,* 629–634.

Freedman, D. G. (1986). The biology of behavior, with inquiries into the inheritance of temperament, stone age art, and the peopling of Australia. *Variability and Behavioral Evolution, 259,* 237–261. (Academia Nazionale dei Lincei, Rome)

Freedman, D. G. (1989). The theory of logical typing: Context and paradox. *Continuing the Conversation, 19,* 3–4.

*Reprinted in:*

- Plooij, F. X. (Ed.). (1989). *Human Ethology Newsletter, 5,* 4–6.

Freedman, D. G. (1992). The many levels of attachment. *Behavioral and Brain Sciences, 15,* 515.

Freedman, D. G., & Gorman, J. (1993). Attachment and the transmission of culture—An evolutionary perspective. *Journal of Social and Evolutionary Systems, 16,* 297–329.

Messinger, D., & Freedman, D. G. (1992). Autonomy and interdependence in Japanese and American mother-toddler dyads. *Early Development and Parenting, 1,* 33–66.

Freedman, D. G. (1995). Ethological studies of subjectivity: The internal working model. *ASCAP (Across Species Comparison of Psychopathology) Newsletter, 8,* 3–11.

## REVIEWS

Freedman, D. G. (1980). An essay review of three books. Book review. [Review of the books *The sociobiology debate; Beast and man;* and *Sociobiology and human nature*]. *Social Biology, 27,* 81–83.

Freedman, D. G. (1982). Book review. [Review of the book *Human nature and history: A response to sociobiology*]. *Human Ecology, 10,* 163–166.

Freedman, D. G. (1982). Book review. [Review of the book *Foundations of ethology*]. *Ethology and Sociobiology, 3,* 151.

Freedman, D. G. (1983). Culture versus pre-culture? [Review of the book *Inbreeding avoidance*]. *Behavioral and Brain Sciences, 6,* 105.

Freedman, D. G. (1985). Temperament and mother's blood pressure. [Review of the book *Navajo infancy*]. *Contemporary Psychology, 30,* 7–8.

Freedman, D. G. (1987). Book review. [Review of the book *Sociobiology and the human dimension*]. *Ethology and Sociobiology, 6,* 121–122.

Freedman, D. G. (1994). Book review. [Review of the book *Gender play: Girls and boys in school]. American Journal of Education, 102,* 259–260.

## FILMS

Freedman, D. G. (1962). *Constitutional and environmental interactions in rearing four breeds of dogs* [Film]. (Available from Pennsylvania State University Audio-Visual Services, University Park, PA, PCR-22691: black & white; No. 22692: color)

Freedman, D. G. (1963). *Development of the smile and fear of strangers, with an inquiry into inheritance of behavior* [Film]. (Available from Pennsylvania State University Audio-Visual Services, University Park, PA, No. 22696)

Freedman, D. G., & R. Parker (1971). *Sex differences in children's play* [Film]. (Available from Pennsylvania State University Audio-Visual Services, University Park, PA, No. 33032)

Freedman, D. G. (1974). *Cross-cultural differences in newborn behavior* [Film]. (Available from Pennsylvania State University Audio-Visual Services, University Park, PA, No. 22605)

Freedman, D. G. (1982). *Navajo childhood* [Film]. (Available from Daniel G. Freedman & John W. Callaghan, Las Vegas, NM, as an electroprint)

Freedman, D. G. (1984). *The children of Edward River* [Film]. (Available from the Australian Institute for Aboriginal Studies, Canberra, New South Wales, Australia; also Daniel G. Freedman, Las Vegas, NM, on videocassette)

# Name Index

*Numbers in italics refer to listings in the reference sections; numbers followed by an "n" indicate listings in a note.*

# Subject Index

# About the Editors

**Nancy L. Segal** is a professor of psychology and director of the Twin Studies Center at California State University, Fullerton. She received a BA in psychology and English literature from Boston University in 1973, an MA in social sciences from the University of Chicago in 1974, and a PhD in behavioral sciences from the University of Chicago in 1982. She was a participant in the National Institute of Mental Health Summer Training Institute for Behavioral Genetics at the University of Colorado, Boulder, in 1975, and a recipient of a Lady Davis Fellowship at the Hebrew University, Jerusalem, in 1976. From 1982 to 1985 she was a postdoctoral fellow at the University of Minnesota, Department of Psychology, before becoming assistant director of the Minnesota Center for Twin Adoption Research, where she held a National Science Foundation Career Advancement Award (1988 to 1991). Dr. Segal is a fellow in both the American Psychological Association and the American Psychological Society and has been inducted into the Collegium of Distinguished Alumni at Boston University. She is the author of numerous scientific papers on twins and twin relationships and the contributing research editor for *Twins Magazine*. She is completing a book on twin studies, *Friendship Extraordinaire,* to be published in 1998 by Dutton.

**Glenn E. Weisfeld** is an associate professor of psychology at Wayne State University and edits the *Human Ethology Bulletin,* published by the International Society for Human Ethology. He majored in zoology at the University of Wisconsin, and received his doctorate in Human Development at the University of Chicago under Daniel G. Freedman. His dissertation research concerned the stability, nonverbal displays, and criteria of dominance rank in U.S. boys. Subsequent research on dominance was conducted on children and adolescents using Chinese, English, Hopi, and African American research participants. Dr. Weisfeld has conducted observational research on erectness of posture as a dominance display and on patterns of social evaluation between volleyball teammates. He has published several theoretical papers on human adolescence, and his *Evolutionary Principles of Human Adolescence* will be published by Westview Press in 1998. He has also written on the adaptive value of humor, the sociobiological basis of the traditional Arab family, puberty rites, the nature–nurture issue, street gang violence, adolescent pregnancy, drug abuse, child abuse, marital satisfaction, and the emotion of pride/shame.

**Carol C. Weisfeld** is a professor of psychology at the University of Detroit Mercy. She received a BA in English from St. Xavier College, and then taught elementary school for 5 years in Chicago, an experience that generated her interest in the interplay of biological and cultural influences on human development. The opportunity to study with Daniel G. Freedman at the University of Chicago led to her earning the MA and PhD degrees in the Committee on Human Development, with a dissertation that focused on boy–girl relations in competitive games in two cultures. For the past 18 years she has taught undergraduate and graduate courses on life-span development, sex differences and sex roles, and cross-cultural socialization. She also teaches a class on parenting at a center for Detroit families at risk. Her current research interests include determinants of marital satisfaction in different cultural settings and ethological analyses of male–female interactions.